BRITTANY

R Mattes/MICHELIN

Executive Editorial Director	David Brabis
Chief Editor	Cynthia Clayton Ochterbeck

THE GREEN GUIDE BRITTANY

Editor	Gwen Cannon
Contributing Writers	Grace Coston, Paul Shawcross
Production Coordinators	Allison M. Simpson, Anna Wilson
Cartography	Alain Baldet, Michele Cana, Peter Wrenn
Photo Editor	Lydia Strong, Cecile Koroleff
Proofreader	Gaven R. Watkins
Layout & Design	Nicole Jordan
Cover Design	Ute Weber

Contact Us:

The Green Guide
Michelin Maps and Guides
One Parkway South
Greenville, SC 29615
USA
☏ 1-800-423-0485
www.michelintravel.com
michelin.guides@us.michelin.com

Michelin Maps and Guides
Hannay House
39 Clarendon Road
Watford, Herts WD17 1JA
UK
☏ (01923) 205 240
www.ViaMichelin.com
travelpubsales@uk.michelin.com

Special Sales:

For information regarding bulk sales,
customized editions and premium sales,
please contact our Customer Service
Departments:
USA   1-800-423-0485
UK   (01923) 205 240
Canada 1-800-361-8236

Note to the reader

One Team …
A Commitment to Quality

There's just one reason our team is dedicated to producing quality travel publications—you, our reader. We want you to get the maximum benefit from your trip—and from your money. In today's multiple-choice world of travel, the options are many, perhaps overwhelming.

In our guidebooks, we try to minimize the guesswork involved with travel. We scout out the attractions, prioritize them with star ratings, and describe what you'll discover when you visit them.

To help you orient yourself, we provide colorful and detailed, but easy-to-follow maps. Floor plans of some of the cathedrals and museums help you plan your tour.

Throughout the guides, we offer practical information, touring tips and suggestions for finding the best views, good places for a break and the most interesting shops.

Lodging and dining are always a big part of travel, so we compile a selection of hotels and restaurants that we think convey the feel of the destination, and organize them by geographic area and price. We also highlight shopping, recreational and entertainment venues, especially the popular spots.

If you're short on time, driving tours are included so you can hit the highlights and quickly absorb the best of the region.

For those who love to experience a destination on foot, we add walking tours, often with a map. And we list other companies who offer boat, bus or guided walking tours of the area, some with culinary, historical or other themes.

In short, we test and retest, check and recheck to make sure that our guidebooks are truly just that: a personalized guide to help you make the most of your visit. After all, we want you to enjoy traveling as much as we do.

The Michelin Green Guide Team

PLANNING YOUR TRIP

INTRODUCTION TO BRITTANY

SYMBOLS

- 🙂 **Tips to help improve your experience**
- 🙂 **Details to consider**
- 🎭 **Entry Fees**
- 👣 **Walking tours**
- ⚷ **Closed to the public**
- 🕐 **Hours of operation**
- 🕐 **Periods of closure**

CONTENTS

DISCOVERING BRITTANY

HOW TO USE THIS GUIDE

Orientation

To help you grasp the "lay of the land" quickly and easily, so you'll feel confident and comfortable finding your way around the region, we offer the following tools in this guide:

- Detailed table of contents for an overview of what you'll find in the guide, and how it is organized.
- Map of Brittany at the front of the guide, with the principal sights highlighted for easy reference.
- Detailed maps for major cities and villages, including driving tour maps and larger-scale maps for walking tours.
- Map of Brittany's Regional Driving Tours, each one numbered and color coded.
- Principal sights ordered alphabetically.

Practicalities

At the front of the guide, you'll see a section called "Planning Your Trip" that contains information about planning your trip, the best time to go, different ways of getting to the region and getting around, basic facts and tips for making the most of your visit. You'll find driving and themed tours, and suggestions for outdoor fun. There's also a calendar of popular annual events in Brittany. Information on shopping, sightseeing, kids' activities and sports and recreational opportunities is also included.

LODGINGS

We've made a selection of hotels and arranged them within the cities, categorized by price to fit all budgets (see the Legend at the back of the guide for an explanation of the price categories). For the most part, we selected accommodations based on their unique regional quality, their Breton feel, as it were. So, unless the individual hotel or bed & breakfast embodies local ambience, it's rare that we include chain properties, which typically have their own imprint. If you want a more comprehensive selection of accommodations, see the red-cover *Michelin Guide France*.

RESTAURANTS

We thought you'd like to know the popular eating spots in Brittany. So we selected restaurants that capture the Breton experience—those that have a unique regional flavor and local atmosphere. We're not rating the quality of the food per se. As we did with the hotels, we selected restaurants for many towns and villages, categorized by price to appeal to all wallets. If you want a more comprehensive selection of dining recommendations in the region, see the red-cover *Michelin Guide France*.

Attractions

Principal Sights are arranged alphabetically. Within each Principal Sight, attractions for each town, village, or geographical area are divided into local Sights or Walking Tours, nearby Excursions to sights outside the town, or detailed Driving Tours—suggested itineraries for seeing several attractions around a major town. Contact information, admission charges and hours of operation are given for the majority of attractions. Unless otherwise noted, admission prices shown are for a single adult only. Discounts for seniors, students, teachers, etc. may be available; be sure to ask. If no admission charge is shown, entrance to the attraction is free.

If you're pressed for time, we recommend you visit the three- and two-star sights first: the stars are your guide.

STAR RATINGS

Michelin has used stars as a rating tool for more than 100 years:

★★★	Highly recommended
★★	Recommended
★	Interesting

SYMBOLS IN THE TEXT

Besides the stars, other symbols in the text indicate tourist information 🛈; wheelchair access ♿; on-site eating facilities ✕; camping facilities ⛺; on-site parking 🅿; sights of interest to children Kids; and beaches ⚓.

See the box appearing on the Contents page for other symbols used in the text.

See the Maps explanation below for symbols appearing on the maps.

Throughout the guide you will find peach-coloured text boxes or sidebars containing anecdotal or background information. Green-coloured boxes contain information to help you save time or money.

Maps

All maps in this guide are oriented north, unless otherwise indicated by a directional arrow. See the map Legend at the back of the guide for an explanation of other map symbols. A complete list of the maps found in the guide appears at the back of this book.

Addresses, phone numbers, opening hours and prices published in this guide are accurate at press time. We welcome corrections and suggestions that may assist us in preparing the next edition. Please send your comments to:

Michelin Maps and Guides
Hannay House
39 Clarendon Road
Watford, Herts WD17 1JA
UK
travelpubsales@uk.michelin.com
www.michelin.co.uk

Michelin Maps and Guides
Editorial Department
P.O. Box 19001
Greenville, SC   29602-9001
USA
michelin.guides@us.michelin.com
www.michelintravel.com

Principal sights

MANCHE

Phare de l'Île Vierge

l'Aber-Wrac'h

Trémazan

Route touristique

ROCHERS, CÔTE SAUVAGE

Pointe de Pern

ABERS

Pont de l'Iroise

OCÉANOPOLIS

Île d'Ouessant

Île Molène

Kerloas

BREST

le Conquet

D 789

Presqu'île de Plougastel

Pointe de St-Mathieu

Pointe des Espagnols

Camaret-s-Mer

POINTE DE PENHIR

× Crozon

PARC

NATUREL

Pointe de Dinan

Morgat ⚓

PRESQU'ÎLE DE CROZON

Cap de la Chèvre

Pointe de Leydé

Pointe de Brézellec

Réserve du Cap Sizun

Pointe du Van

Île de Sein

POINTE DU RAZ

St-Tugen

Pont-Croix

Audierne

Plozévet

N.-D. de Tronoën

Phare d'Eckmühl

Penmarch

OCÉAN

ATLANTIQUE

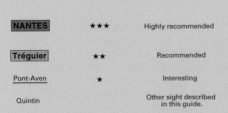

NANTES	★★★	Highly recommended
Tréguier	★★	Recommended
Pont-Aven	★	Interesting
Quintin		Other sight described in this guide.

Seaside resorts ⚓ are classified according to the quality and range of facilities offered.

Itinerary described in this guide: look up one of the sites in the index at the back of the guide to find the page where the tour is described.

0   20 km

MANCHE

CHERBOURG-OCTEVILLE · CAEN

Îles Chausey

Granville

LE MONT ST-MICHEL

ST-MALO

DINARD

Pointe du Grouin

Paramé · Cancale

St-Servan-s-Mer

St-Lunaire

Grand Aquarium-St-Malo

CÔTE D'ÉMERAUDE

Fort la Latte

CAP FRÉHEL

St-Cast-le-Guildo

Sables-d'Or-les-Pins

Erquy

St-Jacut-de-la-Mer

St-Briac-s-Mer

Mont Dol

Dol-de-Bretagne

Vallée de la Rance

Dinan

la Bourbansais

Tremblay

le Rocher-Portail

Combourg

Bécherel

les Iffs

Montmuran

Parc floral de Haute-Bretagne

Fougères

ILLE-ET-VILAINE

Champeaux

RENNES

Vitré

Écomusée du pays de Rennes

Laval · LE MANS

la Roche-aux-Fées

la Guerche-de-Bretagne

MAYENNE

Châteaubriant

MAINE-ET-

Blain

LOIRE-ATLANTIQUE

NANTES

le Val-André

St-Quay-Portrieux

Binic

Pointe du Roselier

Lamballe

Château de la Hunaudaye

St-Brieuc

Moncontour

Quintin

CÔTES-D'ARMOR

St-Méen-le-Grand

St-Léry

Tréhorenteuc

Forêt de Paimpont

École de St-Cyr-Coëtquidan

Ploërmel

Josselin

Guéhenno

Malestroit

Rochefort-en-Terre

la Gacilly

Manoir de l'Automobile à Lohéac

Redon

la Roche-Bernard

Forêt du Gâvre

Vallée de la Vilaine

Phare du Paon

Île de Bréhat

Pointe de l'Arcouest

Port-Blanc · St-Gonéry

Pointe de Bilfot

Paimpol

Pointe de Minard

Abbaye de Beauport

la Roche-Jagu

Pontrieux

Kermaria-an-Iskuit

Côte du Goëlo

Tréguier

Perros-Guirec

Ploumanach

Trégastel-Plage

Côte de Granit rose

Trébeurden

Île Milliau

Pleumeur-Bodou

Côte des Bruyères

Lannion

la Roche-Derrien

Pleubian

Kerfons

St-Michel-en-Grève

Tonquédec

Cairn de Barnenez

Rosanbo

Belle-Isle-en-Terre

Bourbriac

Plourac'h

Callac

Bulat-Pestivien

Guingamp

Île de Batz

Jardin exotique

Roscoff

Primel-Trégastel

Locquirec

St-Jean-du-Doigt

Carantec

Brignogan-Plages

Goulven · Kérouzéré

St-Pol-de-Léon

Baie de Morlaix

Morlaix

la Roche-Maurice

Bodilis

Korjoan

le Folgoët

Lampaul-Guimiliau

anderneau

la Martyre

St-Thégonnec

Plougonven

Guimiliau

ENCLOS PAROISSIAUX

Pencran

Commana

D'ARMORIQUE

Roc Trévezel

Plougastel-Daoulas

Sizun

Daoulas

Pén-ar-Hoat

Mgne St-Michel

Huelgoat

Gorges du Corong

andévennec

Forêt du Cranou

St-Herbot

Quimerch

RÉGIONAL

MONTS D'ARRÉE

N 164

Pleyben

Carhaix-Plouguer

Gorges de Toul Goulic

MÉNEZ HOM

Roche du Feu

FINISTÈRE

MONTAGNES NOIRES

Roc de Toullaëron

N.D.-du-Crann

Rostrenen

Gorges du Daoulas

Forêt de Quénécan

Lac de Guerlédan

Mur-de-Bretagne

Loudéac

Locronan

Mgne de Locronan

la Trinité-Langonnet

Parc et château de Trévarez

Douarnenez

Quilinen

Site du Stangala

Ste-Barbe

Ste-Fiacre

CORNOUAILLE

QUIMPER

Bords de l'Odet

le Faouët

Kernascléden

Pontivy

Forêt de Pont Calleck

Vallée du Blavet

Fouesnant-les-Glénan

Concarneau

Bois d'Amour

Roches du Diable

Site de Castennec

Poul Fetan

Reg-Meil

Pont-Aven

Quimperlé

Baud

Guéhenno

Kerguéhennec

Bénodet

Pointe du Cabellou

Moëlan-s-Mer

le Pouldu

Pont-Scorff

Hennebont

MORBIHAN

Forteresse de Largoët

Port-Manech

Merlevenez

Îles de Glénan

Lorient

Port-Louis

Ste-Anne-d'Auray

Larmor-Plage

Auray

Vannes

Port-Lay

Rivière d'Étel

Île de Groix

Trou de l'Enfer

Mégalithes

Cairn de Gavrinis

la Trinité-sur-Mer

Carnac

Locmariaquer

Golfe du Morbihan

Parc de Branféré

Pointe des Poulains

Sauzon

Stêr-Vraz et Stêr-Ouen

Port-Donnant

CÔTE SAUVAGE

Aiguilles de Port-Coton

Port-Goulphar

BELLE-ÎLE

Presqu'île de Quiberon

Pointe du Percho

Côte Sauvage

Port-Navalo

Quiberon

Carnac-Plage

Île aux Moines

Tumulus de Tumiac

Suscinio

Presqu'île de Rhuys

Île de Houat

Île de Hœdic

Pointe du Scal

Pointe du Bile

Pointe du Castelli

Kerhinet

GRANDE BRIÈRE

PARC NATUREL RÉGIONAL DE BRIÈRE

Île de Fédrun

la Turballe

Guérande

Presqu'île de Guérande

le Croisic

St-Nazaire

Batz-s-Mer

le Pouliguen

Pont routier St-Nazaire-St-Brévin

Pornichet

Pornic

LA BAULE

la Baule-les-Pins

LOIRE

ET-

ANGERS

MAINE-

POITIERS

GLOSSARY

Abbaye	abbey
Cap	cape
Cairn	tumulus
Château	castle
Côte	coast
Corniche	Cornice road
Enclos paroissiaux	parish close
Forêt	forest
Forteresse	fortress
Golfe	gulf
Île	island
Lac	lake
Parc zoologique	wildlife park, zoo
Presqu'île	peninsula
Réserve	nature reserve
Réservoir	reservoir
Roches	rocks
Vallée	valley

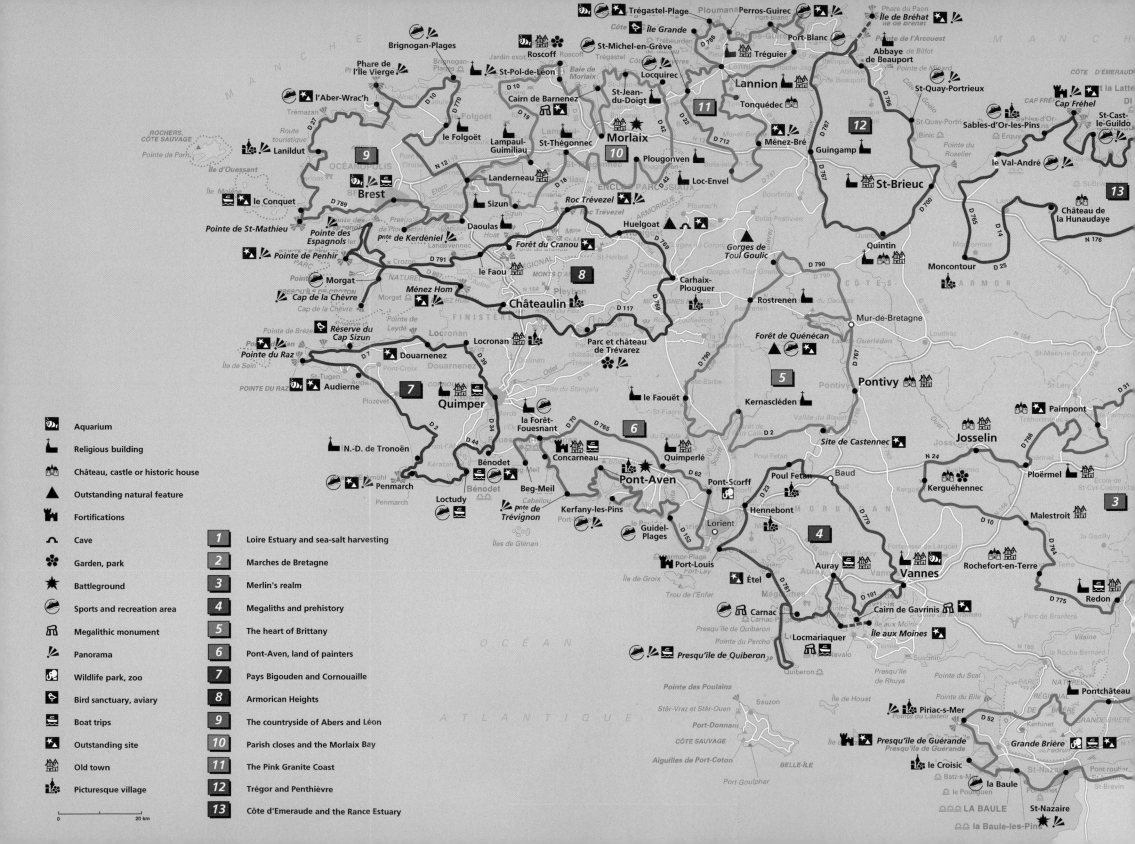

Légende (map legend):

- Aquarium
- Religious building
- Château, castle or historic house
- Outstanding natural feature
- Fortifications
- Cave
- Garden, park
- Battleground
- Sports and recreation area
- Megalithic monument
- Panorama
- Wildlife park, zoo
- Bird sanctuary, aviary
- Boat trips
- Outstanding site
- Old town
- Picturesque village

1 Loire Estuary and sea-salt harvesting
2 Marches de Bretagne
3 Merlin's realm
4 Megaliths and prehistory
5 The heart of Brittany
6 Pont-Aven, land of painters
7 Pays Bigouden and Cornouaille
8 Armorican Heights
9 The countryside of Abers and Léon
10 Parish closes and the Morlaix Bay
11 The Pink Granite Coast
12 Trégor and Penthièvre
13 Côte d'Emeraude and the Rance Estuary

0   20 km

Driving tours

For descriptions of these tours, turn
to the Planning Your Trip section following.

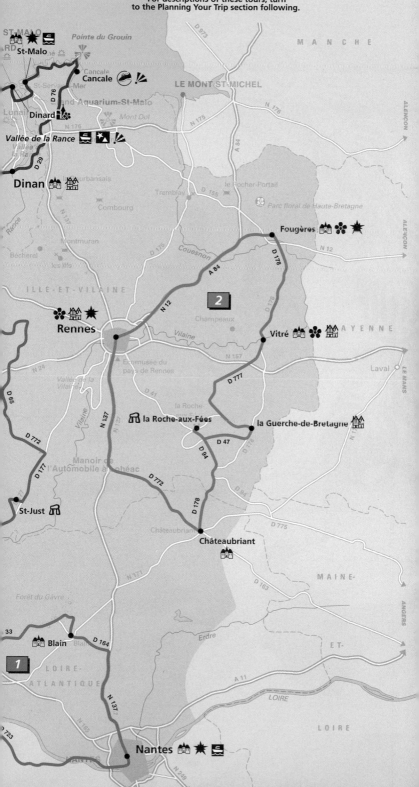

Faïence de Quimper

S. Sauvignier/MICHELIN

WHEN AND WHERE TO GO

Driving Tours

🚗 *See the Driving Tours map on p 12.*

1 The Loire estuary
240km/149mi starting from Nantes
The loire-Atlantique *département* benefits from healthy, dynamic economic activity: tourism centered on La Baule which boasts one of the finest beaches in Europe; shipbuilding focused on St-Nazaire where luxurious cruising liners are built; and the sea-salt industry concentrated around the medieval town of Guérande.

2 Brittany's border country
220km/137mi starting from Rennes
Old stones, old houses, old castles and legends of this region which, for many centuries, have preserved the secrets of the Kingdom of France... All this may belong to the past but it is by no means forgotten! Strolling along the lively streets of Rennes, one gets the impression that this modern capital has passed its forward-looking dynamism on to the towns, villages and historic sites of the area.

3 "Merlin" country
250km/155mi starting from Josselin
Experience the magic of Merlin the magician along this drive . First, the venerable and stately Château de Josselin overlooking the River Oust; next, a feast of international contemporary art at the heart of the formal grounds of the 18C Kerguéhennec castle; and then, a succession of old, carefully restored towns livened up by summer events. All this could be Merlin's doing! For the magician and his sweetheart fairy are not far away; their memory pervades the vast Paimpont Forest, known as *Brocéliande* in Arthurian legend.

4 Megaliths and prehistory
190km/118mi starting from Vannes
Natural beauty and splendid vestiges of earlier civilisations are the main attractions of this drive. The megalith civilisation, known for its standing stones, flourished among magnificent scenery around the Golfe du Morbihan. Towns like Vannes, Auray, Port-Louis and Hennebont are definitely worth the trip.

5 At the heart of the Brittany
225km/140mi starting from Pontivy
Bretons have maintained strong religious inclinations throughout the region's history. Rostrenen, Le Faouët and Kernascléden boast some of the most beautiful religious monuments to be found in inland Brittany (Argoat) where mystery is never very far...as illustrated by the legends of Guerlédan lake, Toul Goulic Gorge and Castennec. The heart of Brittany is a heart of granite; the stone bares its many subtle colours to the light, both in its natural state and in man-made creations.

6 Pont-Aven, land of painters
180km/112mi starting from Pont-Aven
Pont-Aven and the surrounding countryside enjoy a "special" light which performed a kind of miracle by attracting world-famous painters such as Paul Gauguin and Émile Bernard who immortalised the area. However, you don't have to be a painter to appreciate Pont-Aven and bask in the unique Breton light.

7 Pays Bigouden and Cornouaille
170km/106mi starting from Quimper
As its name suggests, Finistère feels like land's end. This feeling becomes overwhelming as one drives west from Quimper or Locronan towards the ocean's edge where the rocks, the waves , the sky and the sea all seem to mingle. Admire the vastness of the Pointe du Raz, the noble robustness of Notre-Dame-de-Tronoën and the Penmarsh reefs, all bathed in maritime air.

8 Amorican Heights
250km/155mi starting from Châteaulin
Visitors who like vast panoramas
will enjoy the Breton "mountains"...
or rather these hills culminating at
384m/1.260ft. From Roc Trévézel to
the Pointe de Penhir, from the Ménez-
Hom to the Pointe des Espagnols,
the road rises only slightly but the
vastness and the colours of the
landscapes are unique. Leave your car
in the parking areas dotted across the
heath and listen to the wind, playing
in syncopation with the raging sea.

9 The countryside of Abers and Léon
250km/155mi starting from Brest
This drive is a must for nature lovers:
cliffs, sand dunes, estuaries, peat
bogs and rivers form the landscape
of this still-unspoilt part of North
Finistère. There is an infinite variety of
colours from the dark grey slates and
Kersanton granite of the Brest area
to the golden sands and lichens of
Brignogan and Lanildut. It seems that,
in spite of repeated efforts, man has
failed to destroy the wild beauty of
this region which remains a sanctuary
for thousands of migrating birds.

10 Parish closes and Morlaix Bay
325km/202mi starting from Morlaix
Corbelled houses in Morlaix, churches
in St-Pol-de-Léon and Roscoff, parish
closes in Lampaul-Guimiliau and St-
Thégonnec, the bridge in Landerneau,
religious treasure in St-Jean-du-Doigt,
passage graves in Barnenez and all
found along this route. For good
measure, you will also discover Morlaix
Bay and the rocky Locquirec peninsula
whose natural beauty and attractive
beaches will appeal to visitors fond of
bathing and gathering shellfish.

11 The Pink Granite Coast
180km/112mi starting from Lannion
In a beautiful mineral transformation, granite worn smooth by erosion
takes on pink or reddish-beige hues
depending on the place and intensity
of the sun's rays. This phenomenon is
perhaps best enjoyed at the region's
resorts (St-Michel-en-Grève, Port-
Blanc, Perros-Guirec and Trégastel).
The inland areas offer different but
equally enchanting features such as
the Château de Tonquédec and the
Menez-Bré summit.

12 Trégor and Penthièvre country
160km/100mi starting from St-Brieuc
With the advent of rail travel in the
19C, the bay of St-Brieuc became the
birthplace of seaside tourism. However, the Côtes-du-Nord *département*
was later neglected by holiday-makers, perhaps because of the uninspir-
ing name. This was changed in 1990 to
Côtes-d'Armour, a name which does
more justice to this part of the Breton
coast facing the lovely island of Bréhat
with its remarkably mild climate.

13 TCôte d'Emeraude and the Rance Estuary
270km/168mi starting from Dinan
Whatever the weather, the sea
remains a beautiful emerald colour.
The very name of some of the sights
along this itinerary appeals to the
imagination: the Rance estuary, Cancale, St-Malo, Cap Fréhel, Les Sables-
d'Or...but there are also less renowned
yet enchanting places such as Dinan,
St-Cast, Le Val-André, Montcontour
and the Château de la Hunaudaye with
its cloak-and-dagger atmosphere.

Themed Tours

HISTORICAL ROUTES

Having been created in 1975 by the
organisations Demeure Historique and
Caisse Nationale des Monuments Historiques et des Sites (CNMHS), these
now 80 historical routes cover France.
They explore architectural, archeological, botanical or geological heritage
within a historical context: the Dukes
of Brittany, the Painters of Cornouaille.
These routes are signposted.
Five historical routes run through
Brittany: Châteaubriand, the regions
of Léon and Tréguier, the Painters of
Cornouaille, the Dukes of Brittany and
the Breton Marches.

ARTISTIC AND HISTORICAL CENTRES

Breton towns designated by the CNMHS as *"Villes d'Art et d'Histoire"* (Towns of Art and History) have been regrouped as a special unit in Brittany since 1984. Similarly, smaller towns of particular local character – *"Petites Cités de Caractère"* – have been administered as a regional association since 1977. These towns regularly hold medieval pageants, *son et lumière* (sound and light) shows, and traditional and modern festivals in their historic town centres. Tours accompanied by CNMHS approved guides are also available. Visitors can obtain relevant literature from tourist offices, rest places alongside main roads and motorways, or from the site's town hall *(mairie)*.

Ten Breton towns have been designated as *"Villes d'Art et d'Histoire"*:

Auray ☎ 02 97 24 09 75
Mail: infos@auray-tourisme.com
www.auray-tourisme.com

Concarneau ☎ 02 98 97 01 44
Mail: contact@tourismeconcarneau.fr
www.tourismeconcarneau.fr

Dinan ☎ 02 96 87 69 76
Mail: infos@dinan-tourisme.com
www.dinan-tourisme.com

Fougères ☎ 02 99 94 12 20
Mail: infos@ot-fougeres.fr
www.ot-fougeres.fr

Nantes ☎ 02 40 20 60 00
Mail: office@nantes-tourism.com
www.nantes-tourisme.com

Quimper ☎ 02 98 53 04 05
Mail: contact@quimper-tourisme.com
www.quimper-tourisme.com

Rennes ☎ 02 99 67 11 11
E-mail: infos@tourisme-rennes.com
www.tourisme-rennes.com

St-Malo ☎ 02 25 13 52 00
Mail: info@saint-malo-tourisme.com
www.saint-malo-tourisme.com

Vannes ☎ 02 97 47 24 34
Mail: info@tourisme-vannes.com
www.tourisme-vannes.com

Vitré ☎ 02 99 75 04 46
Mail: info@ot-vitre.fr www.ot-vitre.fr

There are 20 *"Petites Cités de Caractère"*: Bécherel, Châteaugiron, Châtelaudren, Combourg, Le Faou, Guerlesquin, Josselin, Jugon-les-Lacs, Léhon, Lizio, Locronan, Malestroit, Moncontour, Pont-Croix, Pontrieux, Quintin, La Roche-Bernard, Rochefort-en-Terre, Roscoff and Tréguier.
For details on the above, contact the *Associations régionales des Villes d'Art et d'Histoire et des Petites Cités de Caractère de Bretagne* 1 rue Raoul Ponchon - 35069 Rennes Cedex.
☎ 02 99 84 00 80 - Fax : 02 99 28 44 40, Mail : citesdart@tourismebretagne.com, www.brittanytourism.com

LIGHTHOUSES AND BEACONS

The Breton coast has the highest concentration of lighthouses and beacons on the entire French coast. A route running along the north Finistère coast leads past some of the most important lighthouses in Europe. For details contact Les Pays de Brest, BP 24, 29266 Brest Cedex, ☎ 02 98 44 24 96, www.bretagne.com.

SITES REMARQUABLES DU GOUT

French authorities have created a quality label for "remarkable gastronomic sites", places where the unique quality of local produce deserves special mention. In Brittany, these places include: Cancale, the salt marshes of Guérande, La Guilvinec, the salt marshes and the farming plain of Noirmoutier, and Riec-sur-Belon.

When to Go

Brittany has a reputation for rainy weather and heavy fog which rolls in from the sea, but it is rarely very cold. The climate is mild, thanks to the surrounding ocean waters and the tides, which keep the clouds moving and allow the sun to shine through regularly. The flora is a unique blend of Mediterranean and northern species. In summer, the weather is generally pleasant, usually not too hot.

Weather Forecast

For any outdoor activity, on sea or land, it is useful to have reliable weather forecasts. The French weather reporting service, Météo-France, can be consulted by telephone: ☏ 08 92 68 02 followed by the number of the département in question. For example, to obtain the forecast for the Morbihan, you would dial 08 92 68 02 56. (0.45 € per min) For holiday weather conditions, for example at sea, on the beach, in towns dial 3250 (0.34 € per min) or simply go to www.meteofrance.com.

BEAUFORT NUMBER	WIND NAME	WIND SPEED		CONDITIONS	
		knots	mph	Land	Sea
0	calm	1	1	smoke rises vertically	sea like a mirror
1	light air	1-3	1-3	smoke curves slightly upward	small ripples
2	slight breeze	4-6	4-7	leaves rustle	small wavelets
3	gentle breeze	7-10	8-12	leaves move constantly	large wavelets, some white horses
4	moderate breeze	11-16	13-18	dust and sand rise	small waves lengthening, frequent white horses
5	fresh breeze	17-21	19-24	shrubs sway	moderate waves, many white horses and some spray
6	strong breeze	22-27	25-31	electric cables hum	large waves, white foam crests and spray
7	moderate gale	28-33	32-38	trees sway, walking is difficult	white foam blown in streaks
8	fresh gale	34-40	39-46	walking into the wind impossible	fairly high waves, spindrift, foam blown in marked streaks
9	strong gale	41-47	47-54	damage to buildings	high waves, spray affects visibility
10	whole gale	48-55	55-63	trees uprooted	heavy rolling sea with very high waves and dense spray
11	storm	56-63	64-72	extensive damage	huge waves, sea covered with spindrift
12	hurricane	>64	>73	very rare inland	air and sea filled with foam and spray, visibility almost nil

KNOW BEFORE YOU GO

Useful Web Sites

www.ambafrance-us.org
The French Embassy's Web site provides basic information (geography, demographics, history), a news digest and business-related information. It offers special pages for children, and pages devoted to culture, language study and travel, and you can reach other selected French sites (regions, cities, ministries) with a hypertext link.

www.franceguide.com
The French Government Tourist Office - *Maison de France* - site is packed with practical information and tips for travelling to France. The home page has a number of links for more specific guidance, such as information tailored to your country of origin (such as for example British, Irish, American and Canadian travellers).

www.fr-holidaystore.co.uk
The Travel Centre in London is on-line with this service, providing information on all of the regions of France, including updated special travel offers and details on available accommodation.

www.visiteurope.com
The European Travel Commission provides useful information on travelling to and around 34 European countries, and includes links to some commercial booking services (ie vehicle hire), rail schedules, weather reports and more.

www.FranceKeys.com
This site has plenty of practical information for visiting France. It covers all the regions, with links to tourist offices and related sites. Very useful for planning the details of your tour in France.

French Tourist Offices

For information, brochures, maps and assistance in planning a trip to France travellers should apply to the official French Tourist Office in their own country:

AUSTRALIA – NEW ZEALAND

Sydney
Level 13, 25 Bligh Street, NSW 2000 Sydney
☎ +61 (0)2 92 31 52 44
Fax: + 61 (0)2 9221 8682
info.au@franceguide.com

CANADA

Montreal
1981 Ave. McGill College, Suite 490 Montreal PQ H3A 2W9
☎ +1 (514) 288 20 26;
Fax: +1 (514) 845 48 68.
canada@franceguide.com

EIRE

Dublin
☎ 1560 235 235; Fax (1) 874 73 24 (0.95 $ per min)
info.ie@franceguide.com

UNITED KINGDOM

London
178 Piccadilly, London W1J 9AL
☎ 09068 244 123 (60p/min at all times); Fax :(020) 7493 6594
info.uk@franceguide.com

UNITED STATES

East Coast   **New York**
444 Madison Avenue, 16th Floor, NY 10022
☎ +1 212 838 7800
Fax : +1 212 838 7855
info.us@franceguide.com

Midwest **Chicago**
205 North Michigan Avenue,
Suite 3770 Chicago, IL 60611
☏ +1 312 751 7800
Fax: +1 312 337 6339
info.chicago@franceguide.com

West Coast **Los Angeles**
9454 Wilshire Boulevard, Suite 715
Beverly Hills, CA 90212.
☏ +1 310 271 6665
Fax: +1 310 276 2835
info.losangeles@franceguide.com

Local and Regional Tourist Offices

Visitors may also contact local tourist offices for more precise information and to receive brochures and maps. The addresses, telephone numbers and web sites of local tourist offices are listed after the symbol 🛈 at the beginning of most of the Principal Sights described in this book. Below is the address for the regional tourist office and the departmental tourist offices for Brittany.

COMITÉ RÉGIONAL DE TOURISME

Bretagne
1 rue Raoul-Ponchon,
35069 Rennes Cedex.
☏ 02 99 36 15 15
Fax: 02 99 28 44 40
www.tourismebretagne.com

COMITÉ DÉPARTEMENTAL DE TOURISME

Ille-et-Villaine
4 rue Jean-Jaurès, BP 6046,
35060 Rennes Cedex 3.
☏ 02 99 78 47 47
Fax: 02 99 78 33 24
www.bretagne35.com

Loire-Atlantique
11, rue du Chàteau de l´Eraudière,
CS40698 44306 Nantes Cedex 3
☏ 0 2 51 72 95 33
www.loire-atlantique-tourisme.com

Côtes-d'Armor:
7 rue St-Benoît, BP 4620, 22406
Saint-Brieuc Cedex 2.
☏ 02 96 62 72 01
Fax: 02 96 33 59 10
www.cotesdarmor.com

Finistère:
11 rue Théodore-Le-Hars,
BP1419 29104 Quimper Cedex.
☏ 02 98 76 20 70
Fax: 02 98 52 19 19
www.finisteretourisme.com

Morbihan:
PIBS, allée Nicolas-Leblanc,
BP 408, 56010 Vannes Cedex
☏ 0 825 13 56 56
Fax: 02 97 42 71 02
www.morbihan.com

International Visitors

EMBASSIES AND CONSULATES

Australia **Embassy**
4, rue Jean-Rey, 75015 Paris
☏ 01 40 59 33 00; Fax 01 40 59 33 10

Canada **Embassy**
35, avenue Montaigne, 75008 Paris
☏ 01 44 43 29 00; Fax 01 44 43 29 99

Eire **Consulate**
4, rue Rude, 75016 Paris
☏ 01 44 17 67 00; Fax 01 44 17 67 60

New Zealand **Embassy**
7 ter, rue Léonard-de-Vinci, 75016 Paris
☏ 01 45 00 24 11; Fax 01 45 01 26 39.

UK **Embassy**
35, rue du Faubourg-St-Honoré, 75008
Paris
☏ 01 44 51 31 00; Fax 01 44 51 31 27

UK **Consulate**
16, rue d'Anjou, 75008 Paris
☏ 01 44 51 31 01 (visas)

USA **Embassy**
2, avenue Gabriel, 75008 Paris
☏ 01 43 12 22 22; Fax 01 42 66 97 83

USA **Consulate**
2 , rue St-Florentin, 75001 Paris
☏ 01 43 12 22 22.

DOCUMENTS

Passport

Nationals of countries within the European Union entering France need only a national identity card (or in the case of the British, a passport or a Visitor's Passport). Nationals of other countries must be in possession of a valid national **passport**. In case of loss or theft, report to the embassy or consulate and the local police.

Visa

No **entry visa** is required for Canadian US, Australian or New Zealand citizens for a stay of less than three months. Citizens of non-EU countries should check with the French Consulate (visa issued same day; delay if request submitted by mail) or visit www.diplomatie.gouv.fr/venir/visas/index.html

US citizens should obtain the booklet *Safe Trip Abroad*, which provides useful information on visa requirements, customs regulations, medical care etc for international travellers. Published by the Government Printing Office, it can be ordered by phone – ☎ 1-866- 512-1800 (toll free) – or consulted on-line at www.access.gpo.gov.

CUSTOMS

Apply to the Customs Office (UK) for a leaflet on customs regulations and the full range of "duty free" allowances; available from HMRC, National Advice Service, Written Enquiries Section, Southend on Sea, Alexander House, Victoria Avenue, Southend, Essex, SS99 1BD, ☎ 0845 010 9000 (☎ +44 208 929 0152 outside UK). The US Customs Service offers a downloadable publication *Know before you go* for US citizens odtainable from www.customs.ustreas.gov.

There are no customs formalities for holidaymakers bringing their caravans into France for a stay of less than six months but a touring caravan registration document should be carried. No customs document is necessary for pleasure boats and outboard motors for a stay of less than six months but

the registration certificate should be kept on board.

Americans can bring home, tax-free, up to US$800 worth of goods; Canadians up to CND$750; Australians up to AUS$900 and New Zealanders up to NZ$700. Persons living in a Member State of the European Union are not restricted in regard to purchasing goods for private use, but the recommended allowances for alcoholic beverages and tobacco are as follows:

Duty-Free Allowances	
Spirits (whisky, gin, vodka etc)	10 litres
Fortified wines (vermouth, port etc)	20 litres
Wine (not more than 60 sparkling)	90 litres
Beer	110 litres
Cigarettes	3200
Cigarillos	400
Cigars	200
Smoking tobacco	1kg

Accessibility

The sights described in this guide which are easily accessible to people of reduced mobility are indicated in the *Admission times and charges* section by the symbol &.

Useful information on transportation, holidaymaking and sports associations for the disabled is available from the Comité National Français de Liaison pour la Réadaptation des Handicapés (CNRH), 236 bis, rue de Tolbiac, 75013 Paris. Call their international information number ☎ 01 53 80 66 66, or write to request a catalogue of publications. On TGV and Corail trains operated by SNCF there are special wheelchair slots in 1st class carriages available for holders of 2nd class tickets. On Eurostar and Thalys special rates are available for accompanying adults. All airports are equipped to receive physically disabled passengers.

Web-surfers can find information for slow walkers, mature travellers and others with special needs at www.

access-able.com and www.handitel.
org. For information on museum
access for the disabled contact:
Direction, *Les Musées de France, Service
Accueil des Publics Spécifiques,* 6 rue
des Pyramides, 75041 Paris Cedex 1,

☎ +33 (0)1 40 15 73 00. Michelin publishes **The Michelin Guide France**
and the **Michelin Camping Caravaning France** which indicate hotels and
camp sites with facilities suitable for
physically handicapped people.

GETTING THERE

By Air

The various national and other
independent airlines operate services
to **Paris** (Charles de Gaulle-Roissy
airport 27km/14mi north, and Orly
airport 16km/10mi south). There are
also package tour flights with a rail
or coach link-up as well as fly-drive
schemes. Information, brochures and
timetables are available from the
airlines and from travel agents.
Direct flights are available from the UK
to Nantes (Air France), Rennes (flybe),
Dinard (Ryannair) Lorient (AerArran)
and Brest (flybe). Check carefully however - it can sometimes be cheaper to
fly via Paris.

By Sea

There are numerous **cross-Channel
services** from the United Kingdom
and Ireland and also the rail Shuttle through the Channel Tunnel. For
details apply to travel agencies or to:

Condor Ferries
The Quay, Weymouth, Dorset DT4
8DX ☎ 08702 435140
www.condorferries.co.uk

P &O
Channel House, Channel View
Road, Dover CT17 9JT.
☎ 08705 980 333
www.poferries.com

Speedferries
209 East Camber Office Building
Eastern Docks, Dover, Kent
CT16 1JA ☎ 08702 200570
www.speedferries.com

Brittany Ferries
Millbray Docks, Plymouth,
Devon, PL1 3EW; ☎ 08705 360 360
www.brittanyferries.co.uk

Portsmouth Commercial Port
George Byng Way, Portsmouth,
Hampshire PO2 8SP
☎ 023 9229 7391
www.portsmouth-port.co.uk

By Rail

Eurostar runs via the Channel Tunnel
between **London** (Waterloo) and **Paris**
(Gare du Nord) in 3hrs (bookings and
information ☎08705 186 186 (or go to
www.eurostar.com). From Paris-Gare
Montparnasse, the TGV Atlantique
(high-speed rail service) serves Nantes,
St-Nazaire and La Baule, Rennes, Lorient and Quimper as well as Rennes,
St-Brieuc and Brest. **Eurailpass and
Eurail Selectpass** travel passes which
may be purchased in the US. Contact
your travel agent or: **Rail Europe** 44
South Broadway, White Plains, NY
10601, ☎ 1-888-382-RAIL or 1-888-
382-7245 (www.raileurope.com) in
the USA and in the UK, 178 Piccadilly
London W1V OBA, ☎ 08708 371 371
(www.raileurope.co.uk). Information
on schedules can also be obtained
from **SNCF** at www.sncf.fr.
Tickets bought in France must be vali-
dated *(composter)* by using the orange
automatic date-stamping machines at
the platform entrance (failure to do so
may result in a fine).
The French railway company SNCF
operates a telephone information,
reservation and prepayment service in
English from 7am to 10pm (French time).
In France call ☎ 08 92 35 35 39 or from
outside France ☎+33 8 92 35 35 39.

GETTING AROUND

By Coach/Bus

Regular coach services are operated
from London to Paris:
Eurolines (National Express),
Ensign Court, 4 Vicarage Road,
Edgbaston, Birmingham, B15 3ES
☎ 08705 808080
www.nationalexpress.com/eurolines

Driving in France

The area covered in this guide is
easily reached by main motorways
and national routes. **Michelin map
726** indicates the main itineraries as
well as alternate routes for avoiding
heavy traffic during busy holiday
periods, and gives estimated travel
times. **Michelin map 723** is a
detailed atlas of French motorways,
indicating tolls, rest areas and services
along the route; it includes a table
for calculating distances and times.
Michelin Local maps 308, 309 and 316
cover the areas included in this guide.
There is a listing of Michelin maps and
plans at the back of the guide. The
latest Michelin route-planning service
is available on the Internet, **www.
ViaMichelin.com**. Travellers can
calculate a precise route using such
options as shortest route, quickest
route or Michelin-recommended route
and gain access to tourist information
(hotels, restaurants, attractions). The
service is available on a pay-per-route
basis or by subscription.

Documents

DRIVING LICENCE

Travellers from other European Union
countries and North America can
drive in France with a valid national
or home-state driving licence. An
international driving licence is useful
because the information on it appears
in nine languages (keep in mind that
traffic officers are empowered to
fine motorists). A permit is available

(US$10) from the National Auto Club,
Touring Department, 1151 E. Hillsdale
Blvd. Foster City, CA 94404 ☎ 1 800
622 2136 www.nationalautoclub.com
or contact your local branch of the
American Automobile Association.

REGISTRATION PAPERS

For the vehicle it is necessary to have
the registration papers (logbook) and a
nationality plate of the approved size.

INSURANCE

Certain motoring organisations (AAA,
AA, RAC and The Caravan Club) offer
accident insurance and breakdown
service schemes for members. Check
with your current insurance company
in regard to coverage while abroad. If
you plan to hire a car using your credit
card, check with the company, which
may provide liability insurance automatically (and thus save you having to
pay the cost for optimum coverage).

Highway Code

The minimum driving age is 18. Traffic
drives on the right. All passengers
must wear seat belts. Children under
the age of 10 must travel in the back
seat of the vehicle. Full or dipped
headlights must be switched on in
poor visibility and at night; dipped
headlights should be used at all times
outside built up areas. Use side-lights
only when the vehicle is stationary.
In the case of a **breakdown,** at least
one red warning triangle or hazard
warning lights are obligatory and
reflective safety jackets are recommended. In the absence of stop
signs at intersections, cars must
yield to the right. Traffic on main
roads outside built-up areas (priority
indicated by a yellow diamond sign)
and on **roundabouts** has right of way.
Vehicles must stop when the lights
turn red at road junctions and may

filter to the right only when indicated by an amber arrow.

The regulations on **drinking and driving** (limited to 0.50g/l) and **speeding** are strictly enforced – usually by an on-the-spot fine and/or confiscation of the vehicle.

SPEED LIMITS

Although liable to modification, these are as follows:

◆ toll motorways *(autoroutes)* 130kph/80mph (110kph/68mph when raining);

◆ dual carriageways and motorways without tolls 110kph/68mph (100kph/62mph when raining);

◆ other roads 90kph/56mph (80kph/50mph when raining) and in towns 50kph/31mph;

◆ outside lane on motorways during daylight, on level ground and with good visibility – minimum speed limit of 80kph/50mph.

PARKING REGULATIONS

In town there are zones where parking is either or subject to a fee; tickets should be obtained from the ticket machines (*horodateurs* – small change necessary) and displayed inside the windscreen on the driver's side; failure to display may result in a fine, or towing and impoundment. In some towns you may find blue parking zones (zone bleue) marked by a blue line on the pavement or road and a blue signpost with a P and a small square underneath. In this case you have to display a cardboard disc with various times indicated on it. This will enable you to stay for 1hr 30min (2hr 30min over lunch time) free. Discs are available in supermarkets or petrol stations (ask for a disque de stationnement); they are sometimes given away free.

TOLLS

In France, most motorway sections are subject to a toll *(péage)*. You can pay in cash or with a credit card (Visa, Mastercard).

Car Rental

There are car rental agencies at airports, railway stations and in all large towns throughout France. European cars have manual transmission; automatic cars are available in larger cities only if an advance reservation is made. Drivers must be over 21; between ages 21 and 25, drivers are required to pay an extra daily fee; some companies allow drivers under 23 only if the reservation has been made through a travel agent. It is relatively expensive to hire a car in France; Americans in particular will notice the difference and should make arrangements before leaving, take advantage of fly-drive offers, or seek advice from a travel agent, specifying requirements.

Rental Cars – Central Reservation in France	
Avis:	☎ 08 20 05 05 05 www.avis.fr
Europcar:	☎ 08 25 35 83 58 www.europcar.fr
Budget France:	☎ 01 44 77 88 01 www.budget.fr
Hertz France:	☎ 01 39 38 38 38 www.hertz.fr
SIXT-Eurorent:	☎ 08 20 00 74 98 www.sixt.fr
National-CITER:	☎ 08 25 16 12 20 www.citer.fr
Ada	☎ 08 25 16 91 69 www.ada.fr

Motorhomes

◆ **Worldwide Motorhome Rentals** offers fully equipped camper vans for rent. You can view them on the company's web page, ☎ 888-519-8969 US Toll Free, ☎ 530-389-8316 outside the US, Fax: 530-389-5490, Mail: reserve@mhrww.com, www.mhrww.com

◆ **Overseas Motorhome Tours Inc** organises escorted tours and individual rental of recreational vehicles, ☎ 888-519-8969 US, ☎ 1-310-543-2590 outside the US, Mail: omtusa@earthlink.net, www.omtinc.com

Petrol/Gasoline

French service stations dispense: *sans plomb 98* (super unleaded 98), sans plomb 95 (super unleaded 95), diesel/gazole (diesel) and GPL (LPG). Petrol is considerably more expensive in France than in the USA. Prices are listed on signboards on the motorways although it is usually cheaper to fill up after leaving the motorway. Check the hypermarkets on the outskirts of town for typically lower prices.

WHERE TO STAY AND EAT

Where to Stay

FINDING A PLACE TO STAY

Hotels and Restaurants are described in the Address Books within the Discovering the Sights section. Please refer to the accompanying map for a selection of recommended places for overnight stops. The Map Legend that appears on the inside cover flap of the Guide explains the symbols and abbreviations used. For example, hotels in the budget category, i.e. iess than 40€ are represented by ⊖, between 40€ and 65€ by ⊖⊖, between 65€ and 100€ by ⊖⊖⊜ and above 100€ by ⊖⊖⊜⊜. For an even greater selection, use the *Michelin Guide France* with its well known star-rating system and hundreds of establishments throughout France. The **Michelin Charming Places to Stay** guide contains a selection of 1,000 hotels and guesthouses at reasonable prices. Be sure to book ahead, especially during the high season, as Brittany is a very popular holiday destination.

For further information, **Loisirs Accueil** (280 boulevard St-Germain, 75007 Paris, ☎ 01 44 11 10 44, www.loisirsaccueilfrance.com) is a booking service that has offices in most French *départements*. Contact the tourist offices listed above for further information or go to www.resinfrance.com for internet booking.

A guide to good-value, family-run hotels, **Logis et Auberges de France** (www.logis-de-france.fr), is available from the French Tourist Office, as are lists of other kinds of accommodation such as hotel-châteaux, bed and breakfasts etc. **Relais et Châteaux** provides information on booking in luxury hotels with character:

◆ within France: ☎ 0 823 32 32 32
◆ within the UK:
    ☎ 00 800 2000 00 22
◆ within the US: ☎ 1 800 735 2478
◆ or go to: www.relaischateaux.com

ECONOMY CHAIN HOTELS

If you need a place to stop en route, these can be useful, as they are inexpensive (under 50€ for a double room) and generally located near the main road. While breakfast is available, there may not be a restaurant; rooms are small, with a television and bathroom. Central reservation details:

Akena
☎ 01 69 84 85 17
www.hotels-akena.com

B&B
☎ 08 92 78 29 29
(0.34€ per minute, from France)
www.hotel-bb.com

Etap Hôtel
☎ 0 892 688 900 (0.34€ per minute, from France)
www.etaphotel.com

Mister Bed
☎ 01 46 14 38 00
www.misterbed.fr

Villages Hôtel
☎ 03 80 60 92 70
www.villages-hotel.com

All the above hotels, except Mister Bed, have on-line resevation services. The hotels listed below are slightly more expensive (below 65€), and offer a few more amenities and services. Central reservation numbers:

- **Campanile**
  ☎ 0825 003 003
  (0.15€ per minute, from France)
  www.envergure.fr/campanileen.html
- **Kyriad**
  ☎ 0825 003 003
  (0.15€ per minute, from France)
  www.envergure.fr/kyriaden.html
- **Ibis**
  ☎ 0 892 686 686
  (0.34€ per minute, from France)
  www.ibishotel.com

All the above hotels have on-line reservation services.

RURAL ACCOMMODATION

The **Maison des Gîtes de France** is an information service on self-catering accommodation in the regions of France. *Gîtes* usually take the form of a cottage or apartment decorated in the local style where visitors can make themselves at home.

For a list of Gîtes in France and how to book, contact the Gîtes de France office in Paris: 59 rue St-Lazare, 75009 Paris Cedex 09, ☎ 01 49 70 75 75, or their representative, in the UK, **Brittany Ferries** (address above). The web site is quite complete and has an excellent English version (www.gites-de-france.fr).

Try contacting the local tourist offices as they also publish lists of available properties.

Gîtes de France publishes a booklet on bed and breakfast accommodation *(chambres d'hôtes)* entitled *Chambre et tables d'Hôte*. These include a room and breakfast at a reasonable price. You can also contact:
www.bed-breakfast-france.com which has a good selection of accommodation throughout the region.

There are two main youth hostel (auberge de jeunesse) associations in France:

- **Ligue Française pour les Auberges de Jeunesse**,
  67, rue Vergniaud Bat.
  K 75013 PARIS
  ☎ 01 44 16 78 78,
  Fax 01 44 16 78 80
  info@auberges-de-jeunesse.com
  www.auberges-de-jeunesse.com
- **Fédération Unie des Auberges de Jeunesse**,
  27 rue Pajol, 75018 Paris.
  ☎ 01 44 89 87 27,
  Fax 01 44 89 87 10
  fuaj@fuaj.org, www.Fuaj.org

Holders of an International Youth Hostel Federation card should contact the IYHF in their own country for information and membership applications (US ☎ +1 (301) 4951240 or www.hiusa.org; England and Wales ☎ +44 (1629) 592700 or www.yha.org.uk ; Scotland ☎+44 (1786) 891400 or www.syha.org.uk; Canada ☎ +1 613-273 7884 or www.hihostels.ca ; Australia ☎ +61 2 9565 1669 or www.yha.com.au; Main website: www.hihostels.com.

CAMPING

There are numerous officially graded sites with varying standards of facilities throughout Brittany; the **Michelin Guide Camping Caravaning France** lists a selection of the best camp sites. An International Camping Carnet for caravans is useful but not compulsory; it can be obtained from the motoring organisations or the Camping and Caravanning Club (Greenfield House, Westwood Way, Coventry CV4 8JH, ☎ 0845 130 7701 (www.campingand-caravanningclub.co.uk) or The Caravan Club (www.caravanclub.co.uk).

The **Fédération Française des Stations Vertes de Vacances,** BP 71698, 21016 Dijon Cedex, ☎03 80 54 10 49, (www.stationsvertes.com) lists accommodation, leisure facilities and natural attractions in rural locations on the website.

Where to Eat

The key on the cover flap explains the symbols and abbreviations used in these sections. Use the red-cover **Michelin Guide France**, with its famously reliable star-rating system and hundreds of establishments all over France, for an even greater choice. If you would like to experience a meal in a highly rated restaurant from The Michelin Guide, be sure to

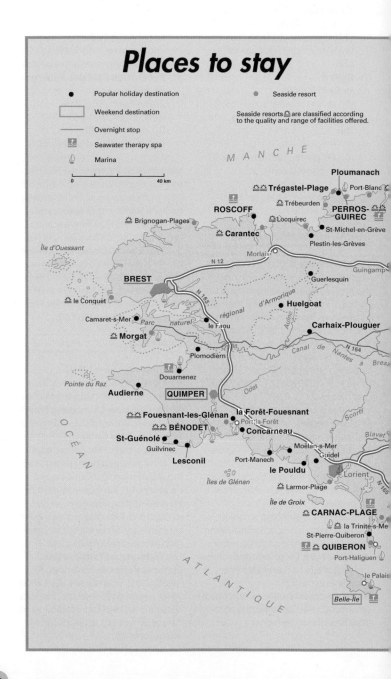

book ahead! In the countryside, restaurants usually serve lunch between noon and 2pm and the evening meal between 7.30 and 10pm. It is not always easy to find something in-between those two meal times as the "non-stop" restaurant is still a rarity in small towns in the provinces. However, a hungry traveller can usually get a sandwich in a café, and ordinary hot dishes may be available in a *brasserie*.

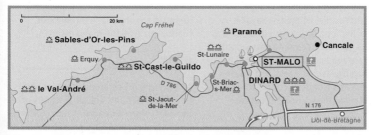

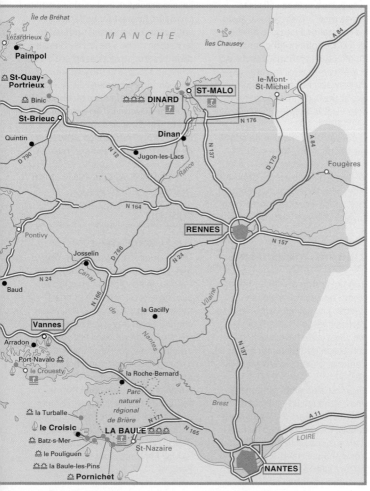

WHAT TO DO AND SEE

Outdoor Fun

CANOEING AND KAYAKING (RIVER AND SEA)

A canoe is propelled by a single-bladed paddle, whereas a kayak is propelled by a double-bladed paddle; sea kayaks are becoming very popular and are available for sale or for hire in the main seaside resorts. Sea-kayaking offers a wonderful opportunity to discover the magnificent Breton coastline.

"**Points Canoë nature**", "**Points Kayak de mer**" - These labels, given by the Fédération Française de canoë-kayak (FFCK), point out the centres which offer quality tourist activities. Their methods of teaching are labelled "École française de canoë-kayak". Inquire at the Fédération to get a list of these establishments.

The **Fédération française de canoë-kayak** - 87 quai de la Marne, BP 58, 94344, Joinville-le-Pont, ☎ 01 45 77 08 50 - www.ffcanoe.ass.fr - publishes, together with the IGN, a map entitled "France, canoë-kayak et sports d'eau vive, which shows all suitable waterways.

SAILING AND WINDSURFING

The rugged Breton coastline shelters numerous bays which make an ideal setting for sailing enthusiasts to practise their sport. Many of the Breton yacht clubs have a sailing school attached to them, for example the centre at Glénan. (www.glenans. asso.fr)
Windsurfing is possible from many beaches, although it is subject to certain rules; contact the yacht clubs for details. Windsurfers can be hired at all the major beaches, as can boats, with or without a crew, in season. For further information, contact the

Fédération Française de Voile, 17, rue Henri Bocquillon 75015 Paris, ☎ 01 40 60 37 00 (www.ffvoile.org), or **France Stations Nautiques,** 17, rue Henri Bocquillon 75 015 Paris, ☎ 01 44 05 96 55 (www.france-nautisme.com). Regattas are organised throughout the season in all the major resorts.

DIVING

This activity is becoming increasingly popular in Brittany. The clear waters of the inlets along Brittany's south coast (Port-Manech, Port-Goulphar to Belle-Ile) are rich in fish and marine plantlife, providing interest for underwater anglers and admirers of underwater landscapes alike. The Îles de Glénan diving centre attracts deep-sea divers, who can practise in the swimming pool during the winter.
Further information can be obtained from the **Comité interrégional Bretagne-Pays de Loire de la Fédération Française d'Études et de Sports Sous-Marins** 39 rue de la Villeneuve, 56100 Lorient, ☎ 02 97 37 51 51. Mail: cibpl.ffessm@wanadoo.fr (www.ffessm-cibpl.asso.fr).

FISHING

Freshwater Fishing
Obey national and local laws. You may have to become a member (for the year in progress) of an affiliated angling association in the departement of your choice, pay the annual angling tax or buy a day card. If you wish to fish on private land you must obtain permission from the landowner. Special two-week holiday fishing permits are also available.
A leaflet with a map and information called *Pêche en France* (Fishing in France) is available from Conseil Supérieur de la Pêche, Immeuble"le Péricentre" 16 Avenue Louisan, Bobet, 943132 Fontenay-sous-Bois, CEDEX Paris, ☎ 01 45 14 36 00 Fax: 01 45

14 36 60 (www.csp.environnement. gouv.fr).

Deep-Sea Fishing

From Mont-St-Michel Bay to the River Loire estuary, Breton coastal waters offer infinite possibilities to amateur deep-sea fishermen. Contact the local marine authorities, Service des Affaires Maritimes, (www.chasse-sous-marine.com) to find out about regulations governing fishing from boats or underwater. Fishing from the shore is not subject to any formal regulations, apart from the use of nets, which requires permission from the marine authorities. Different areas may however have particular coastal rules; it is advisable to find out what these are from the appropriate local authority.

RAMBLING

A number of long-distance footpaths **(sentiers de Grande Randonnée – GR)** cover the region described in this guide. Walking holidays and rambles are organised by L'Office deTourisme de la Baie de Saint-Brieuc, 7 rue Saint-Gouéno - BP 4435 22044, St-Brieuc, ☎ 0 825 00 22 22 (www.baiedesaint-brieuc.com) and France Randonnée, 9 rue des Portes-Mordelaises, 35200 Rennes, ☎ 02 99 67 42 21; Fax 02 99 67 42 23. (www.france-randonnee.fr) Argoat is criss-crossed by the GR footpaths 34, 37, 38, 341 and 380, which offer a range of pleasant rambles to walkers of all abilities.
The Topo-Guides, published by the **Fédération Française de la Randonnée Pédestre,** (www.ffrandonnee.fr) give detailed maps of the paths and offer valuable information to ramblers. You can find these and other guides and maps to local short-distance footpaths in local Tourist Information Centres and sports shops.

CYCLING

For information contact the **Fédération Française de Cyclotourisme,** 12 rue Louis Bertrand - 94207 IVRY SUR SEINE cedex, ☎ 01.56.20.88.88,

fax : 01.56.20.88.99 Mail : info@ffct. org (www.ffct.org) which will give you the details of its local representatives. Tourist Information Centres have lists of places to hire bicycles which includes some main railway stations.

RIDING

The possibilities for riding holidays in Brittany are numerous and open to riders of all abilities. For details, contact the following organisations:

Confédération nationale des usagers des loisirs équestres
(FREF) – 16 rue des Apennins, 75017 Paris. ☎ 01 56 09 01 93.

Formules Bretagne
Brittany Best Breaks.
☎0800 085 77 39
www.brittany-best-breaks.com

Comité Régional pour le Tourisme Equestre en Bretagne(CRTEB)
5 bis rue Waldeck Rousseau, BP307 56103 Lorient Cedex
☎ 02 97 84 44 03
cheval@equibreizh.com
www.equibreizh.com
www.ville-plerin.fr/aceca

Comités départementaux de tourisme équestre:

CDTE des Côtes-d'Armor – Association des cavaliers d'extérieur des Côtes-d'Armor (ACECA), 39 rue de la Mer, 22 190 Plérin-sur-Mer ☎ 02.96.73.12.38/ 02 96 74 68 05 aceca@tiscali.fr www.ville-plerin.fr/aceca)
CDTE du Finistère – 27 rue Laënnec - 29 710 PLONEIS ☎02 98 91 02 02 Mail: cdte29@tele2.fr www.equi29.com
CDTE de l'Ille-et-Vilaine – La Ferme de Chénedet 35 133 LANDEAN ☎ 02.99.97.35.46
CDTE de la Loire-Atlantique –3 rue Bossuet 44000 Nantes ☎ 02 40 48 12 27
CDTE du Morbihan – Bougerel 56450 Noyalo . ☎ 02 97 43 15 57

GOLF

Brittany boasts an important number of golf courses often located in very picturesque surroundings. The Comité régional du tourisme de Bretagne publishes a brochure listing some 30 golf clubs throughout the region's four *départements*.

The **Fédération française de golf**, 68 r. Anatole-France, 92309 Levellois-perret Cedex, ☎ 01 41 49 77 00; www.ffgolf.org

The **Ligue de golf de Bretagne**, Immeuble Calipso, 130 r.Eugène Pottier, 35000 Rennes; ☎ 02 99 31 68 80

WRESTLING

The gouren - have you heard of gouren? This traditional Breton wrestling competition, of Celtic origin, has its own federation. Its values are fair play and loyalty. This sport practised within a club offers exciting competitive matches (indoors in winter, but also outdoors in summer, during traditional festivals). Information: Ti ar Gouren, Maisonde la lutte et des sports bretons, Berrien (29), ☎ 02 98 99 03 80 or Comité national de gouren. Landerneau, ☎ 02 98 95 40 48

VOIE VERTE

Whether you are keen on roller-skating, cycling or walking, the *Voie Verte* from Mauron to Questembert, in the Morbihan area, is the perfect playing field. The old railway line has been renovated for the enjoyment of families and the disabled as well. This 53km/33mi itinerary, west of Paimpont forest, passes near Loyat, Malestroit, Molac, Monterlot, Ploërmel, Le Roc-St-André, St-Marcel. You can join it in several places. Information at the Tourist offices of Tréhorenteur (☎ 02 97 93 05 12), Ploërmel (☎ 02 97 74 02 70), Malestroit (☎ 02 97 75 14 57) and Questembert (☎ 02 97 26 56 00)

BOATING

The Channel and Atlantic coasts lend themselves particularly well to exploration by boat, be it under sail or motor-powered. The main marinas are indicated on the Places to stay map at the beginning of the guide; criteria dictating their selection include number of berths available and range of facilites offered (fuel, fresh water and electricity on the quayside, toilets and washing facilities, elevators or cranes for loading, repair workshops, security guards).

Activities for Children

Brittany has many attractive features besides beaches, calvaries and castles...A great variety of sights and leisure activities appeal to young visitors (aquariums, zoos, boat trips and unusual activities); in the *Sights* section, they are labelled with the symbol Kids .

Towns designated by the Ministry of Culture as "**Villes d'Art et d'Histoire**" organise discovery tours and cultural-heritage workshops for children. Fun books and specially designed tools are provided and the activities on offer are supervised by various professionals such as architects, stone masons, story-tellers, actors. This scheme, called "**L'été des 6-12 ans**" (summer activities for 6-12-year-olds) operates during school holidays.

Spas

A seaside setting (with the attendant healthy sea air, and seaweed) is well known as an excellent natural restorative for those suffering from fatigue or stress. *Thalassotherapy* (medical sea treatment, from the Greek *thalassa,* or sea) involves various techniques which maximise the beneficial effects of a seaside climate: *algotherapie* (seaweed and sea mud baths), *hydrotherapie* (spray-jets, sea-water showers or baths), *kinesitherapie* (massages, gymnastics), saunas, and sea-water spray treatments. The average length of a treatment at one of these thalasso-therapy centres is around 7-10 days. Brittany's major sea-water therapy centres are at La Baule, Belle-Ile-en-Mer, Carnac, Le Crouesty, Dinard, Perros-Guirec, Quiberon, Roscoff and St-Malo. For information and bookings, contact Brittany Tourism, 1, rue Raoul Ponchon 35069 RENNES CEDEX ☎ 0 800 085 77 39 (www.brittany-best-breaks.com)

Calendar of Events

PARDONS

PALM SUNDAY

Callac — Stations of the Cross Second Sunday in May ☎02 96 45 50 19

Quintin — Pardon of Notre-Dame-de-Délivrance, ☎ 02 96 74 92 17

ASCENSION DAY

St-Herbot — Pardon of St Herbot Third Sunday in May

Tréguier — Pardon of St-Yves, ☎ 02 96 92 95 11 (3rd Sunday in May)

Bubry — 230 fold 35 (1) Pardon of St-Yves ☎ 02.97.51.74.83

WHIT SATURDAY AND SUNDAY

Moncontour — Pardon of St-Mathurin, ☎ 02 96 73 49 57
St-Gildas Island — Blessing of the horses

SUNDAY AFTER WHIT SUNDAY

Rumengol Le Faou — Pardon of the Trinity

TRINITY SUNDAY AND EVE

Notre-Dame-du-Crann — Pardon, ☎ 02 98 93 84 78 (Chapel)

SATURDAY EVENING AND SUNDAY BEFORE THE FEAST OF ST JOHN THE BAPTIST (24 JUNE)

St-Tugen — Pardon, ☎ 02 98 74 80 28

LAST SUNDAY IN JUNE

St-Jean-du-Doigt — Pardon of St John the Baptist, ☎02 98 79 92 92
Plouguerneau — Pardon of St Peter and St Paul, ☎ 02 98 04 70 93
Le Faouët — Summer Pardon of St Barbara, ☎ 0 2 97 23 15 27

FIRST SUNDAY IN JULY (AND PRECEDING FRIDAY AND SATURDAY)

Guingamp — Pardon of Notre-Dame-de-Bon-Secours, ☎ 02 96 43 73 59
Montautour — Pardon Notre-Dame du Roc

SECOND SUNDAY IN JULY

Locronan — Petite Troménie (the Grande Troménie takes place every 6 years; the next one will be on the second and third Sundays of July 2007), ☎ 02 98 91 70 14

THIRD SUNDAY IN JULY

Carantec — St-Carantec Pardon, ☎ 02 98 67 00 43

25 AND 26 JULY (FEAST OF ST ANNE)

Ste-Anne-d'Auray — Grand Pardon of St Anne, ☎ 02 97 57 68 80

26 JULY (FEAST OF ST ANNE) AND FOLLOWING SUNDAY

Fouesnant — Grand and Petit Pardons of St Anne, ☎ 02 98 56 00 93

FOURTH WEEKEND IN JULY

Le Vieux Marché Côte d'Armor — Islamic-Christian pilgrimage to the Chapelle des Sept-Saints, ☎ 02 96 38 91 73

FOURTH SUNDAY IN JULY

Le Releg — Pardon of St Anne – Breton mass (11am) – Festival of Celtic Music (3.30pm)
Bubry 230 fold 35 (1) — Pardon of Ste-Hélène, ☎ 02 97 51 70 38

FIRST SUNDAY IN AUGUST

Persquen 230 fold 21 (1) — Pardon of Notre-Dame-de-Pénéty ☎ 02 97 39 35 30

15 AUGUST (FEAST OF THE ASSUMPTION) AND EVE OF 14TH

Perros-Guirec — Pardon of Notre-Dame-de-Clarté ☎ 2 96 23 21 64
Quelven — Pardon of Notre-Dame ☎ 02 97 25 04 10
Loudeac —Pardon de Querrien ☎ 02 96 28 01 32
Rumengol — Pardon of Notre-Dame-de-Rumengol
Porcaro — Pardon of the "Madone des Motards" (Our Lady of Bikers) ☎ 02.97.22.04.78 (http://madonedesmotards.ifrance.com)
Bécherel — Haute-Bretagne Troménie ☎ 02 99 66 75 23
Pont-Croix — Pardon of Notre-Dame-de-Roscudon(www.pont-croix.info)

SUNDAY AFTER 15 AUGUST

Rochefort-en-Terre — Pardon of Notre-Dame-de-la-Tronchaye ☎ 02 97 43 33 57
Carantec — Pardon of Notre-Dame-de-Callot, ☎ 02 98 67 00 43
Ploërdut — Pardon of Notre-Dame-de-Crénenan, ☎ 02 97 39 44 43

LAST SUNDAY IN AUGUST (AND EVE, AND FOLLOWING TUESDAY)

Plonévez-Porzay— Ste-Anne-la-Palud Grand Pardon, ☎ 02 98 26 17 18
Le Faouët — Pardon of St-Fiacre
La Baule —La Baule Pardon ☎ 02 40 24 56 29 www.pardon-de-la-baule.com.

FIRST SUNDAY IN SEPTEMBER

Camaret — Pardon of Notre-Dame-de-Rocamadour – Blessing of the sea ☎ 02 98 27 90 48
Le Folgoët — Grand Pardon of Notre-Dame, (8 septembre) ☎ 02 98 83 00 61
Lamballe — Pardon of Notre-Dame-de-la-Grande-Puissance
Pouldreuzic — Pardon of Notre-Dame-de-Penhors, ☎ 02 98 51 55 91

SECOND SUNDAY IN SEPTEMBER

Carnac — Pardon of St-Cornély, ☎ 02 97 52 08 08

8 SEPTEMBER

Josselin — Pardon of Notre-Dame-du-Roncier, ☎ 02.97.22.36.43

THIRD SUNDAY IN SEPTEMBER

Notre-Dame-de-Tronoën — Pardon, ☎ 02 98 82 03 16
Pontivy — Pardon of Notre-Dame-de-la-Joie ☎ 02 97 25 04 10

LAST SUNDAY IN SEPTEMBER

Hennebont — Pardon of Notre-Dame-du-Vœu, ☎ 02 97 36 24 52
Plouguerneau — Pardon of St-Michel ☎ 02 98 44 24 96

SUNDAY NEAREST 29 SEPTEMBER

Mont-St-Michel — Feast of the Archangel St Michael ☎ 02 33 60 14 30
Gourin — Bellringers' Pardon

2ND WEEKEND IN OCTOBER-

Vannes — Pardon de la Chapelle de Hamon
Fougères — Pardon de Notre-Dame des Marais ☎ 2 99 94 12 20

FIRST SUNDAY IN DECEMBER

Le Faouët — Winter Pardon of St Barbara ☎ 02 97 23 23 23

FESTIVALS AND SPORTING EVENTS

LAST WEEKEND OF JANUARY

Nantes — La Folle Journée music festival, ☎ 0 892 464 044 (0.34 €/mn) www.nantes-tourisme.com

APRIL

La Trinité-sur-Mer — Spi Ouest-France sailing event (mid April) www.spi-ouestfrance.com

Nantes — Carnival, ☎ 0 892 464 044 (0.34 €/mn)

Châteauneuf-du-Faou — Printemps de Châteauneuf-du-Faou music and dance festival ☎ 02.98.21.97.57 www.printemps-de-chateauneuf.org

MAY

Mont St-Michel — SpringFolk Festival ☎ 02 33 60 14 30

La Baule — International horse jumping competition ☎02 40 60 02 80 www.labaule-cheval.com

St-Malo — Étonnants Voyageurs (Astonishing Explorers), ☎ 02 99 31 05 74 www.etonnants-voyageurs.com

JULY

Vitré — Festival du Bocage (Rural festiva (first 2 weeks of July) ☎ 02 99 75 02 25 www.paysdevitre.org

Rennes — "Les tombées de la nuit" (Breton art festival- early July), ☎ 02 99 32 56 56 www.lestdnuit.com

Carhaix-Plouger — Vieilles Charrues Music Festival (third week of July), ☎ 082089 00 66 (local call); www.vieillescharrues.asso.fr

Dinan — Celtic Harp Festival (3rd week of July) ☎ 02 96 87 36 69 www.harpe-celtique.com

Polignac — Festival of Classical Music and Jazz (from mid July) ☎ 02 97 65 06 13 (from 1st July) http://festivalpolignac.com

Quimper — Cornouaille festival (week before 4th Sunday in July) ☎ 02 98 55 53 53 www.festival-cornouaille.com

Vannes — Jazz Festival, last week of July) ☎ 02 97 01 62 44 www.vannes-bretagne-sud.com/fr/jazzavannes

Dinan — Fête des remparts (every other year - next one 2008, third weekend). www.dinan-tourisme.com

FIRST FORTNIGHT OF AUGUST (INCLUDING 15 AUGUST)

Paimpol — Festival of Sea Chanties (Every two years, first weekend of August in 2007), ☎ 02 96 20 83 16 www.paimpol-goelo.com

Erquy — Festival of the Sea, (1st Sunday) ☎ 02 96 72 30 12 www.erquy-tourisme.com

Pont-Aven — Fête des Fleurs d'Ajonc (Gorse Festival, 1st Sunday), ☎ 02 98 06 04 70 www.pontaven.com

Lorient — Interceltic Festival, ☎ 02 97 21 24 29 www.festival-interceltique.com

St.Malo — La Route du Rock Festival ☎ 02 99 54 01 11 www.laroutedurock.com

Crozon — Festival du Bout du Monde Music Festival ☎ 02 98 27 00 32 www.festivalduboutdumonde.com

Dinard — International horse jumping event, ☎ 02 99 46 19 67 Mail: cso.maroille35@wanadoo.fr

Guingamp — Festivals of Breton Dance and of St-Loup, ☎ 02 96 43 73 89 www.dansebretonne.com

Perros-Guirec — Hydrangea Festival ☎ 02 96 23 21 15

Plomodiern — Ménez-Hom Folklore Festival, ☎ 02 98 8127 37 www.tourisme-porzay.com

Ile de Fédrun — Festival of the Brière Region – Boat Race ☎ 02 40 66 85 01 www.ot-lecroisic.com

Guérande — Celtic Festival, ☎ 02 40 24 96 71 www.ot-guerande.fr

Vannes — Grand Festival of Arvor,
☎ 02 97 47 24 34
www.fetes-arvor.org

MID TO LATE AUGUST

Roscoff — Fête de l'oignon rosé
☎02 98 61 12 13
www.roscoff-tourisme.com
Carnac — Menhir Festival
☎02 97 52 13 52
Concarneau — Festival of the Blue
Nets, ☎ 02 98 97 09 09
http://filetsbleus.free.fr
Moncontour —Medieval Festival
☎ 02 96 73 49 57 (every 2 years,
next 2007)
www.moncontour-medievale.com
Questember — Market Hall Festival
☎ 2 97 26 11 38
questembert.mairie@libertysurf.fr

SEPTEMBER

Moncontour — Festival Rue dell Arte
☎ 02 96 73 49 57
www.pays-moncontour.com
Rennes — Gallo (Local dialect)
Festival ☎ 02 99 38 97 65
bertaeyn.galeizz@wanadoo.fr

Loudec —Horse Festival (2nd weekend in Sept) ☎ 02 96 28 63 31
www.centrebretagne.com

OCTOBER

Rennes — Ebruitez-vous Arts Festival
☎ 02 99 38 97 73
info@rhizome.asso.fr
Dinard — British Film Festival,
☎ 02 99 88 19 04
www.festivaldufilm-dinard.com
St-Malo — Quai des Bulles (Comic-
Strip Festival), ☎ 02 99 40 39 63
Redon — "La Teillouse" chestnut
festival, ☎ 02 99 71 06 04.
www.tourisme-pays-redon.com/
fete/bogue_d_or.htm
Lanvellec — Baroque Music Festival
(last 2 full weeks of Oct)
☎ 02 96 35 14 14
festival.Lanvellec@wanadoo.fr
Nantes — Celtomania Festival (all
Oct) ☎ 0 2 51 84 16 07
www.celtomania.com

NOVEMBER

Nantes —3 Continents film Festival
(last week Nov.) ☎ 02 40 69 74 14
www.3continents.com

BASIC INFORMATION

Shopping

WHAT TO TAKE HOME

Oysters from Cancale, charcuterie
such as rillettes or boudin noir, globe
artichokes, chestnuts, cider, Muscadet
and Gros Plant wine, Breton mead
(hydromel), Breton butter biscuits.
Local crafts such as carved wood, lace,
Quimper pottery.
Travellers from America should note
that they are not allowed to take food
and plant products home, so this rules
out unpasteurized French cheeses and
fruit, for example.
Americans are allowed to take home,
tax-free, up to US$800 worth of goods,
Canadians up to CND$700, Australians

up to AUS$900 and New Zealanders
up to NZ$700.

MAIN MARKETS

Market day is an important event in
the life of local communities, and provides visitors also with an opportunity
to meet people, exchange news and
views, and find out a bit about the
region and local produce from those
who live and work there.

Sunday
Brest (St-Louis), Cameret-sur-Mer,
Cancale, Carnac, Etables-sur-Mer, La
Forêt-Fouesnant, Piérin, Plougneau,
Plouhinec, Rhuys

Monday

Auray, Bénodet, Châtelaudren, Combourg, Concarneau, Dinard, Douarnez, Guerlesquin, Pontivy, Pontrieux, Redon, Vitré

Tuesday

Brest, Le Croisic, Guilvanec Landerneau, Locmariaquer, Loctudy, Pont Aven, Quintin, St-Brieuc, St-Pol-de-Léon, La Trinité-sur-Mer

Wednesday

Carnac, Châteaubriant, Châteauneuf-du-Faou, Guérande, Lorient, Morlaix, Nantes, Quimper, Roscoff, Tréguier, Vannes

Thursday

Châteaugiron, Dinard, Le Croisic, Dinan, Hennebont, Lannion, Malestroit, Pont l'Abbé, Pont-Croix, La Roche-Bernard, Sarzeau

Friday

Arradon, Concarneau, Fouesnant, Guingamp, Jugon-les-Lacs, Landerneau, Paimpol, Perros-Guerec, Quimper, Quimperlé, St-Malo

Saturday

Bécherel, Le Bono, Le Croisic, Dol-de-Bretagne, Fougères, Guérande, Guingamp, Josselin, Landerneau, Locmariaquer, Lorient, Morlaix, Nantes, Pontivy, Port-Louis, Quiberon, Quimper, Redon, Rennes, Vannes, Vitré

For markets on slightly more unusual themes, try: the Book Market at Bécherel on the first Sunday of every month; the Flea Market (Marché aux Puces) at Dinan every Wednesday from the 3rd week in June to the 3rd week in September, otherwise the first Wednesday of the month ☎ 02 96 85 10 20; one of the largest cattle markets in Europe, the Aumaillerie Market at Fougères, opens every Friday morning at 5.00am.

FRESH FISH AUCTIONS

The fresh fish auctions which take place on the return of the fishing fleets are certainly lively and colourful affairs. They are generally held every day of the week 30min after the boats come in, and they last for about 2hr. The major ones are to be found at Audierne, Concarneau, Douarnenez, Erquy, Le Guilvinec, Loctudy and Lorient.

DISCOUNTS

Significant discounts are available for senior citizens, students, youth under 25, teachers and groups for public transportation, museums and monuments and for some leisure activities such as movies (at certain times of day). Bring student or senior cards with you, and bring along some extra passport-size photos for discount travel cards. The **International Student travel Confederation** (www.isic.org), global administrator of the International Student and Teacher Identity Cards, is an association of student travel organisations around the world. ISTC members collectively negotiate benefits with airlines, governments, and providers of other goods and services for the student and teacher community, both in their own country and around the world. The non-profit association sells international ID cards for students, youth under age 25 and teachers (who may get discounts on museum entrances, for example). The ISTC is also active in a network of international education and work exchange programmes. The corporation rate headquarters address is Herengracht 479, 1017 BS Amsterdam, The Netherlands; ☎ 31 20 421 28 00; Fax 31 20 421 28 10.

Business Hours

Department stores and chain stores are open Monday to Saturday, 9am to 6.30pm or 7.30pm. Smaller, more specialised shops may close during the lunch hour. Food stores (grocers, wine merchants and bakeries) are open from 7am to 6.30pm or 7.30pm. Some open on Sunday mornings. Many food stores close between noon and 2pm and on Mondays. Hypermarkets are usually open until 9pm or 10pm.

Notes and coins

The euro banknotes were designed by Robert Kalinan, an Austrian artist. His designs were inspired by the theme "Ages and styles of European Architecture". Windows and gateways feature on the front of the banknotes, bridges feature on the reverse, symbolising the European spirit of openness and co-operation.
The images are stylised representations of the typical architectural style of each period, rather than specific structures.

Classical

Baroque and Rococo

Romanesque

19C iron and glass

Gothic

Renaissance

20C modern

Euro coins have one face common to all 12 countries in the European single currency area or "Eurozone" (currently Austria, Belgium, Finland, France, Germany, Greece, Ireland, Italy, Luxembourg, The Netherlands, Portugal and Spain) and a reverse side specific to each country, created by their own national artists.

Euro banknotes look the same throughout the Eurozone. All Euro banknotes and coins can be used anywhere in this area.

Banks are usually open from 9am to noon and 2pm to 4pm and are closed on Mondays or Saturdays (except on market days); some branches open for limited transactions on Saturdays. Banks close early on the day before a bank holiday.

Post offices open Mondays to Fridays, 8am to 7pm, Saturdays, 8am to noon. Smaller branch post offices often close at lunchtime between noon and 2pm and in the afternoon at 4pm.

Electricity

The electric current is 220 volts. Circular two pin plugs are the rule – an electrical adaptor may be necessary. US appliances (hairdryers, shavers) will not work without one. Adapters are on sale in electrical stores and also at international airports.

Mail

Postage via air mail to:
- ✉ UK: letter (20g) 0.60€ (from 01.10.2006)
- ✉ North America: letter (20g) 0.90€
- ✉ Australia & NZ letter (20g) 0.90€

Stamps are also available from newsagents and *bureaux de tabac*.
Stamp collectors should ask for *timbres de collection* in any post office.

Money

CURRENCY

There are no restrictions on the amount of currency visitors can take into France, however, the amount of cash you may take out of France is subject to a limit, so visitors carrying a lot of cash should complete a currency declaration form on arrival.

BANKS

A passport is necessary as identification when cashing cheques in banks. Commission charges vary and hotels usually charge more than banks for cashing cheques for non-residents.

Most banks have cash dispensers (ATM) which accept international credit or debit cards and are easily recognised by the logo showing a hand holding a card. American Express cards can be used only in dispensers operated by the Crédit Lyonnais Bank or by American Express.

Credit cards
American Express, Visa (Carte Bleue), Mastercard/Eurocard and Diners Club are widely accepted in shops, hotels and restaurants and petrol stations. In the case of a lost or stolen credit card, ring one of the following 24-hour numbers:

American Express ☎ 01 47 77 72 00
Visa ☎ 08 36 69 08 80
Mastercard/Eurocard ☎ 01 45 67 84 84
Diners Club ☎ 01 49 06 17 50

Such loss or theft must also be reported to the local police who will issue a certificate to show to the credit card company.

PRICES AND TIPPING

Since a service charge is automatically included in the prices of meals and accommodation in France, it is not necessary to tip in restaurants and hotels. However if the service in a restaurant is especially good or if you have enjoyed a fine meal, an extra tip (this is the *pourboire*, rather than the *service*) is a well-appreciated gesture. Usually 1.5 to 3.5 euros is enough, but if the bill is big (a large party or a luxury restaurant), it is not uncommon to leave 7 to 8 euros or more.
Restaurants usually charge for meals in two ways: a menu that is a fixed-price menu with 2 or 3 courses, sometimes a small pitcher of wine, all for a stated price, or à la carte, the more expensive way, with each course ordered separately.
Cafés have very different prices, depending on where they are located. The price of a drink or a coffee is

Conversion tables

Weights and measures

1 kilogram (kg)	2.2 pounds (lb)	2.2 pounds
1 metric ton (tn)	1.1 tons	1.1 tons

to convert kilograms to pounds, multiply by 2.2

1 litre (l)	2.1 pints (pt)	1.8 pints
1 litre	0.3 gallon (gal)	0.2 gallon

to convert litres to gallons, multiply by 0.26 (US) or 0.22 (UK)

1 hectare (ha)	2.5 acres	2.5 acres
1 square kilometre (km^2)	0.4 square miles (sq mi)	0.4 square miles

to convert hectares to acres, multiply by 2.4

1centimetre (cm)	0.4 inches (in)	0.4 inches
1 metre (m)	3.3 feet (ft) - 39.4 inches - 1.1 yards (yd)	
1 kilometre (km)	0.6 miles (mi)	0.6 miles

to convert metres to feet, multiply by 3.28, kilometres to miles, multiply by 0.6

Clothing

Women							Men
	35	4	2½	40	7½	7	
	36	5	3½	41	8½	8	
	37	6	4½	42	9½	9	
Shoes	38	7	5½	43	10½	10	Shoes
	39	8	6½	44	11½	11	
	40	9	7½	45	12½	12	
	41	10	8½	46	13½	13	
	36	4	8	46	36	36	
	38	6	10	48	38	38	
Dresses &	40	8	12	50	40	40	Suits
Suits	42	12	14	52	42	42	
	44	14	16	54	44	44	
	46	16	18	56	46	48	
	36	08	30	37	14½	14,5	
	38	10	32	38	15	15	
Blouses &	40	12	14	39	15½	15½	Shirts
sweaters	42	14	36	40	15¾	15¾	
	44	16	38	41	16	16	
	46	18	40	42	16½	16½	

Sizes often vary depending on the designer. These equivalents are given for guidance only.

Speed

kph	10	30	50	70	80	90	100	110	120	130
mph	6	19	31	43	50	56	62	68	75	81

Temperature

Celsius	(°C)	0°	5°	10°	15°	20°	25°	30°	40°	60°	80°	100°

cheaper if you stand at the counter (*comptoir*) than if you sit down (*salle*) and sometimes it is even more expensive if you sit outdoors (*terrasse*).

Public holidays

Museums and other monuments may be closed or may vary their hours of admission on the following public holidays:

1 January	New Year's Day (*Jour de l'An*)
	Easter Day and Easter Monday (*Pâques*)
1 May	May Day (*Fête du Travail*)
8 May	VE Day (*Fête de la Libération*)
Thurs 40 days after Easter	Ascension Day (*Ascension*)
7th Sun-Mon after Easter	Whit Sunday and Monday (*Pentecôte*)
14 July	France's National Day (*Fête nationale*)
15 August	Assumption (*Assomption*)
1 November	All Saint's Day (*Toussaint*)
11 November	Armistice Day (*Fête de la Victoire*)
25 December	Christmas Day (*Noël*)

National museums and art galleries are closed on Tuesdays; municipal museums are generally closed on Mondays. In addition to the usual school holidays at Christmas and in the spring and summer, there are long mid-term breaks (10 days to a fortnight) in February and early November.

Telephone

PUBLIC TELEPHONES

Most public phones in France use prepaid phone cards (*télecartes*), rather than coins. Some telephone booths accept credit cards (Visa, Mastercard/Eurocard: minimum monthly charge 20F). *Télécartes* (50 or 120 units) can be bought in post offices, branches of France Télécom, *bureaux de tabac* (cafés that sell cigarettes) and newsagents and can be used to make calls in France and abroad. Calls can be received at phone boxes where the blue bell sign is shown; the phone will not ring, so keep your eye on the little message screen.

MICHELIN

Emergency numbers
Police: 17
SAMU (*Paramedics*): 15
Fire (*Pompiers*): 18

NATIONAL CALLS

French telephone numbers have 10 digits.
- Paris and Paris region numbers begin with 01;
- 02 in northwest France;
- 03 in northeast France;
- 04 in southeast France and Corsica;
- 05 in southwest France.

INTERNATIONAL CALLS

To call France from abroad, dial the country code (33) + 9-digit number (omit the initial 0). When calling abroad

To use your personal calling card	
AT&T	☎ 0-800 99 00 11
Sprint	☎ 0-800 99 00 87
MCI	☎ 0-800 99 00 19
Canada Direct	☎ 0-800 99 00 16

from France dial 00, then dial the country code followed by the area code and number of your correspondent.

International dialling codes
(00 + code):

International Information,
US/Canada: 00 33 12 11

International operator:
00 33 12 + country code

Local directory assistance: 12

International Dialling Codes (00 + code)			
Australia	☎ 61	New Zealand	☎ 64
Canada	☎ 1	United Kingdom	☎ 44
Eire	☎ 353	United States	☎ 1

CELLULAR PHONES

Cellular phones in France have numbers which begin with 06. Two-watt (lighter, shorter reach) and eight-watt models are on the market, using the Orange (France Télécom), SFR or Bouygues networks. Mobicartes are pay-as-you-go phone cards for mobile units. Cell phone rentals (delivery or airport pickup provided);

- **A.L.T. Rent A Phone** — ☎ 01 48 00 06 06; E-mail: altloc@jve.fr
- **Rent a Cell Express** — ☎ 01 53 93 78 00; Fax 01 53 93 78 09
- **Ellinas Phone Rental** — ☎ 01 47 20 70 00

Time

France is 1hr ahead of Greenwich Mean Time (GMT). France goes on daylight-saving time from the last Sunday in March to the last Sunday in October.
Some parts of Australia (north and west) are not observing daylight saving time (DST) at the moment.
In France "am" and "pm" are not used, but the 24-hour clock is widely applied.

When it is noon in France, it is
3am in Los Angeles
6am in New York
11am in Dublin
11am in London
7pm in Perth (6pm in summer)
9pm in Sydney (8pm in summer)
11pm in Auckland (10pm in summer)

For the best little places, follow the leader.

Looking for the latest news on today's best hotels and restaurants? Pick up the Michelin Guide and look for the Bib Gourmand and Bib Hotel symbols. With 45,000 addresses in Europe, in every category and price range, the perfect place to dine or stay is never far away.

Pleyben Calvary

S. Sauvignier/MICHELIN

NATURE

The relief of Brittany is the result of an evolutionary process which has taken place over millions of years. Crafted by the forces of the sea and crafted by the forces of the sea, the rugged coastline symboliezes the mystical beauty of the region, while the dynamic between land and sea has come to define its people and their culture.

The Sea

THE ARMOR

The name Armor (or more rarely Arvor) means "country near the sea." It was given to the coastal region by the Gauls; the interior was Argoat.

The Breton coast

It is extraordinarily indented; this makes it 1 200km/750mi long whereas it would be half that without its saw-teeth appearance. The jagged nature of this coastline with its islands, islets and reefs is due only in part to the action of the sea and is one of the characteristics of Brittany.

The most typical seascapes are to be found at the western tip of the peninsula. Sombre cliffs, rugged capes 50-70m/160-224ft high, islands, rocks and reefs give the coastline a grimness which is reflected in sinister local names: the Channel of Fear (Fromveur), the Bay of the Dead (Baie des Trépassés), the Hell of Plogoff (Enfer de Plogoff).

There are many other impressive features, too: piles of enormous blocks of pink granite sometimes rising as much as 20m/64ft as at Ploumanach and Trégastel; the red-sandstone promontory of Cap Fréhel standing 57m/182ft above the sea; the brightly coloured caves of Morgat. The Brest roadstead, the bay of Douarnenez, the Golfe du Morbihan and its islands are unforgettable. The successive estuaries between the Rance and the Loire offer magnificent views at high tide as one crosses the impressive bridges that span them (Pont Albert-Louppe and Pont de Térénez).

Some low-lying sections of the coast contrast with the more usual rocks. In the north, Mont-St-Michel Bay is bordered by a plain reclaimed from the sea; in the south, the inhospitable bay of Audierne, the coast between Port-Louis and the base of the Presqu'île de Quiberon, and the beach at La Baule

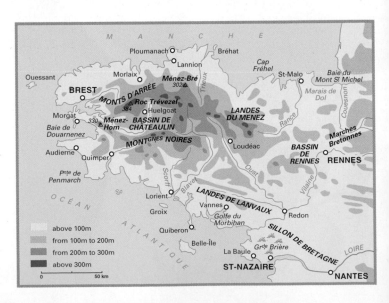

R. Mattes/MICHELIN

Low tide in Finistère

give a foretaste of the great expanses of sand which predominate south of the Loire.

Wherever the coast is directly open to the sea winds, it is completely barren. This is so on the points and on the summits of the cliffs; the salt with which the winds are impregnated destroys the vegetation. But in sheltered spots there are magnificent profusely flowering shrubs. Arum lilies, camellias, hydrangeas and rhododendrons, which would be the pride of many a skilled gardener, grace the smallest gardens.

The climate is so mild that plants which grow in hot countries flourish in the open, eg mimosa, agave, pomegranate, palm, eucalyptus, myrtle, oleander and fig trees.

Tides and Waves

Visitors should first learn the rhythm of the tides, a division of time as regular as that of the sun. Twice every 24 hours the sea advances on the coast – this is the rising tide. It reaches high water mark, where it stays for a while, and then drops back – this is the falling or ebb tide – until it reaches low water mark. It remains at this low level for a while, and then the cycle begins again.

The timetables for the tides are displayed in hotels, on quays and in local papers. Look at them before planning a trip, as they may affect the timing of your programme.

It is at high tide that the coast of Brittany is most beautiful. The waves advance on the coast, break on the rocky outspurs and surge in parallel crests into the bays; a shining liquid carpet fills the estuaries. This is the time when a journey along a coast road or a walk to the harbour is the most rewarding. At low tide the uncovered rocks, stained with algae and seaweed, are often dirty and can be disappointing. At the mouths of the great coastal rivers there is only a poor thread of water winding between mudflats. The greater the tide and the gentler the slope, the greater is the expanse of shore uncovered; in Mont-St-Michel Bay the sea retreats 15-20km/9-12mi. On the other hand, low tide is the joy of anyone fishing for crab, shrimp, clams, mussels, etc.

On the north coast, the tide sweeps in, in exceptional cases to a height of 13.50m/43ft in the bay of St-Malo and 15m/49ft in Mont-St-Michel Bay. When the wind blows, the battering-ram effect of the sea is tremendous. Sometimes the shocks given to the rocks off Penmarch are felt as far off as Quimper, 30km/18mi away. Attacking the softest parts of the cliffs, the sea makes fissures and brings down slabs of rock. In this way, caves (Morgat), tunnels and arches (Dinan "Château") are formed. Peninsulas joined to the mainland by strips of softer material are turned gradually into islands.

The waves do not only destroy; they also have a constructive effect. The sand they carry, added to the alluvial deposits brought down by the rivers, forms beaches, gradually silts up the bays (Mont-St-Michel Bay is a striking example), and connects islands with the mainland; this is the case at Quiberon and it will also be the same, in due course, at Bréhat.

SAILING

Brittany, the most maritime region of France, is home to many devoted sailors. Breton people, if one is to believe a well-known proverb, "are born with the waters of the sea flowing round their eyes and the ocean has flowed in their veins from birth". Here, sailing is more than a simple sport, it's second nature, as inevitable as sunshine and rain. For some, it is part of daily life or earning a living, for others it is an abiding passion.

Regatta, a sport for everybody — In times past, sailing used to be a sport for the elite. But now it is a popular sport, as is windsurfing, a fad that took off in the 1980s. The nautical industry abandoned craftwork to turn towards the mass production of boats made of synthetic materials. The change in production methods made recreational boats more affordable — there are now some 700 sailing schools operating within the French Federation of Sailing and

another 1000 centres which are located all around France. Sea-lovers, and not only a few of them, enjoy going on regattas along the Breton coast, examining the sky, anticipating the thermal breeze, pondering over the depressions, in order to swell the spinnakers ad the Genoa jibs better and to cleave through the waves of the big blue ocean. Things have changed a lot since the first regattas, gatherings of fishing dighies, took place around 1850. All kinds of single-hull and multi-hull ships are moored at the marinas' landing stages. If boats can dream, perhaps as they rock gently in their berths they imagine participating in a regatta, even a modest one, or perhaps the "Spi Ouest-France" which is organised every year at La Trinité-sur-Mer. Famous competitive sailors mingle with the crowd of enthusiastic wannabes and fans.

Great sailors — All the great French sailors are not Breton, of course, but Brittany represents the sea to such an extent that most of the them have a strong attachment to the region. Many are well known to "old salts" from the seas of the world: Bernard Moitessier, Yves Le Toumelin and Éric Tabarly (tragically lost at sea off Wales in June 1998). Tabarly had a reputation for fair play and love of the sea that inspired many landlubbers to consider the ocean as something more than a vast, liquid steppe without life. Among the sailors

Y. Tierny/MICHELIN

La Cancalaise

who trained by his side and are now following in his wake: Olivier de Kersauzon, Jean Le Cam, Marc Pajot, Yves Parlier, Philippe Poupon, Alain Thébault.

Sailing has grown in popularity as the number of competitive events has increased. High-performance craft are sponsored by a variety of companies eager for the visibility that media coverage of races provides. Shipyards in Lorient, Vannes and Nantes turn out racing craft made of high resistant materials such as spectra, kevlar or titanium to be captained by the likes of Florence Arthaud, Isabelle Autissier, Laurent Bourgnon, Frank Camas, Alain Gautier, Loïck Peyron or Paul Vatine. Long-distance races can be especially dangerous: besides Tabarly, sailors who lost their lives while pursing their passion include Alain Colas in 1978, Loïc Cadarec in 1986 and Gerry Roufs in 1997.

Great races — Solo and team races take place most of the year, in one corner of the world or another. The world of sailing is livened up by solo or team races and crossing records almost all the year round. Websites allow aficionados to follow the big events minute-by-minute without having to put on their rough weather gear!

Some prestigious races start or finish in Brittany. The most famous is probably the Route du Rhum race, for single-hulls and multi-hulls, which takes sailors from Pointe du Grouin to Pointe-à-Pitre in Guadeloupe. It takes place every four years (2006, 2010...); Other big events are La Baule-Dakar, (famous for the difficult crossing of the Bay of Biscay in autumn); Québec-Saint-Malo (featuring whales and icebergs); the transatlantic race Lorient-Bermuda-Lorient. The Figaro race in July occasionally starts from a Breton harbour; Round Europe race calls at main ports from the North to the South of Europe and many other races and regattas are organised in Brittany.

FISHING

Coastal Fishing

Sole, turbot, skate, bass, sea bream, crustaceans, scallops... Take your choice! Even so the catch is not nearly enough for local needs, and a town like Saint-Brieuc receives supplementary supplies from Lorient in the south. On the Atlantic coast, the season for sardine fishing lasts from June to September.

Deep-Sea Fishing

Open sea fishing takes place as far off as the coasts of Iceland, and represent the main activity of big Breton ports. For tuna fishing, both dragnets and live bait are used in the bay of Biscay and seine nets along the African coasts. White tuna is fished from June to October: the season starts somewhere between Portugal and the Azores. Tropical or albacore tuna is the quarry of a fleet of some 30 boats with refrigerated holds,

S. Sauvignier/MICHELIN

Lobster traps

Bucket and Spade

The French call it *pêche à pied,* or fishing on foot. Take care to go crabbing and shrimping in authorised areas and in season (signs are posted on beaches). There are specified sizes for each species and you are expected to gather reasonable quantities — that is, not more than you can eat! Females bearing eggs should be released and any rocks you move or turn over set back in place. Keep your catch fresh by covering it with algae (cut it, don't pull it up). Respecting these simple rules will help preserve an ecosystem that is more fragile than you might suspect.

equipped at Concarneau and operating from the ports of West Africa during the season.

"La Grande peche"

This is the name given to cod fishing in the shoals of Newfoundland, Labrador and Greenland. It made Paimpol and St-Malo famous in the past, but nowadays, it is only a modest activity practised by factory ships equipped with machines for cutting the fish into fillets that are frozen immediately.

S. Sauvignier/MICHELIN

Watch those claws!

Shellfish

Most shellfish is harvested along the rocky coasts using lobster pots and traps, but long-distance fishing is also common. Lobster boats, equipped with tanks as well as refrigeration or freezing used to leave from Camaret, Audierne for the coast of Mauritania for several months at a time.

Along the coast, in deep waters and far from home, the fishermen of Brittany have succeeded in adapting to modern techniques, despite the implementation of restrictive quotas, due mainly to the internationalisation of the fishing industry. Lorient and Concarneau make Brit-

tany the leading French region for the fishing industry.

OTHER SEAFOOD

Canning Industry

At the instigation of Louis XIV's minister of Finances, Fouquet, the method of preserving fish in barrels gradually replaced the customary drying and salting of fish. Sardines used to be preserved in oil until Nicolas Appert invented the canning process in 1810. In Brittany, the industry faces competition from developing countries, but there are still factories operating on the Presqu'île de Quiberon and in the harbours of Douarnenez and Concarneau.

Oceanography and Aquaculture

Researchers at Ifremer (French Research Institute for the Exploitation of the Sea) work to find solutions to avoid depleting the resources of the sea. Aquaculture offers promise for the future. Fish farms are already successfully breeding salmon and turbot in the Finistère.

S. Sauvignier/MICHELIN

Digging for dinner

Conchyliculture

Oyster and mussel breeding has become commercially important, which has long been the great production region for flat oysters *(belons)* and has also developed its Portuguese oyster beds (sold as *Creuses de Bretagne* or *Fines de Bretagne*). Brittany's annual oyster production amounts to 30 000t of *creuses* and 2 000t of *plates*, which is a quarter of France's national production. Mussel breeding on poles known as *"bouchots"* is carried out along the coast from Mont-St-Michel Bay to St-Brieuc Bay and in the Vilaine estuary.

Algae and Algae-Processing

Harvested and used as fertiliser for many years, then as raw materials for the chemical industry, the various types of algae are as likely nowadays to be found on restaurant tables as in sea-water spas. Wrack cultivating and harvesting, using specially equipped boats, are now subject to regulations. This activity is mainly based in the *Abers* area.

Naval Dockyards

After years of crisis, this ship-building industry is once again competitive on an international scale, with the creation of the Atlantic Dockyards at St-Nazaire. Capable of dealing with ships of up to 500 000t, they have above all turned to the production of container ships, oil rigs and cruise ships; 2003 was a red-letter year as they produced the largest ocean-liner ever, the *Queen Mary 2*. Rising to the challenge of this prestigious undertaking, the dockyards have proven their dynamism and skill.

The Land

THE ARGOAT

The Plateaux

Plains cover most of the country and although you must not expect to find great expanses extending to far horizons, the traveller crosses a series of rises that may confuse the directionally challenged! Between the uplands flow deeply sunken rivers with brown, rushing waters. The land is cut up into a chequerboard pattern by banks and dry-stone walls which form the boundaries of fields and pastures. Pollarded oaks grow on most of the banks, and it is these which make the countryside, seen from a distance, seem heavily wooded.

The Mountains

Mountains! The word rather overpowers the Breton hills. But this is what the coast dwellers call the central part of Brittany. It must be said that in many places the barrenness and loneliness of the heights, the saw-toothed crests contrasting with the undulating plains that they overshadow and the strong wind give an impression of high altitude.

In clear weather a vast expanse can be seen from the Roc Trévezel (384m/1

Les Monts d'Arrée

R. Mattes/MICHELIN

229ft), the Ménez-Hom (330m/1 056ft) and the Menez Bré (302m/966ft).

Forests and Moors

Brittany once had immense forests of oak and beech. Successive generations since the Romans have wielded the axe in these woods, and there are now only scattered strips of woodland: the forests of Paimpont, Loudéac, Huelgoat, Quénécan etc. These woodlands are very hilly and intersected by gorges, ravines and tumbled rocks. A perfect example of this type of country is to be seen at Huelgoat. Unfortunately most of the woodlands would appear to be neglected and brushwood predominates. The fine forests are rare and these Breton woodlands owe their picturesque quality more to their relief than to their trees.

Fallow moors, where the great forests once stood, now form empty stretches relieved from gloom when the gorse wears its golden cloak and the heather spreads a purple carpet on the hills. Elsewhere, moors have yielded to the efforts of the peasants and have become tilled fields. Such are the Landes de Lanvaux, where the visitor, misled by the name and expecting rough ground, finds reclaimed land, rich in promise for the future.

Agriculture

For a long time the Argoat was essentially an agricultural and stock-rearing region, but more recently industrial development has been encouraged by local authorities.

Nearly one-third of the land under cultivation is given over to cereal production together with fodder crops (mainly corn) reserved as cattle feed.

There are still many apple orchards in Ille-et-Vilaine and in the south of the Finistère but a certain decline is noticeable in Morbihan. The apples are used to make cider, apple juice and concentrate.

The Argoat has a reputation for its dairy cattle, which produce about 20% of French dairy products. Large dairies are located throughout the region. Pig rearing has been industrialised and represents half of France's production. It supplies national markets and the many firms which produce fresh, canned or salted pork products.

HISTORY

Time Line

Events in italics indicate milestones in history.

ANCIENT ARMOR

6C BC — The Celts arrive in the peninsula and name it Armor (country of the sea). A little-known people who set up many megaliths were there before them.

56 AD — Caesar destroys the fleet of the Veneti, the most powerful tribe in Armor *(see Golfe du Morbihan)*, and conquers the whole country.

For four centuries Roman civilization does its work. Then the barbarian invasions wreck Armor, which returns almost to savagery.

ARMOR BECOMES BRITTANY

460 — Arrival of the Celts from Britain, driven out by the Angles and Saxons. Immigration continues for two centuries. These colonists revive and convert Armor and give it a new name, Little Britain, later shortened to Brittany. The Breton people make saints of their religious leaders, who become the patrons of many towns in the peninsula.

The political state, made up of innumerable parishes, remains anarchic.

799 — Charlemagne subjugates all Brittany.

THE DUCHY OF BRITTANY

826 — Louis the Pious makes Nominoé, a noble of Vannes, Duke of Brittany.

845 — Nominoé throws off Frankish suzerainty by defeating Charles the Bald, near Redon. He brings all of Brittany under his authority and founds an independent ducal dynasty which lasts for more than a century.

851 — Erispoë, son of Nominoé, takes the title, King of Brittany. He is later assassinated by his cousin Salomon who reigns from 857.

874 — Salomon (the Great, or St Salomon) assassinated. During his reign the Kingdom of Brittany reached its zenith, embracing Anjou and Cotentin.

919 — Great invasion of Norsemen. Violent robbery and pillage.

939 — King Alain Barbe-Torte drives out the last Norsemen.

952 — Death of Alain, the last King of Brittany. In the fortresses built all over the country to resist the Norsemen, the nobles defy the successors of Barbe-Torte. There follows a period of disorder and poverty which lasts until nearly the end of the 14C.

1066 — *William the Conqueror lands in England.*

1215 — *Magna Carta.*

1337 — Start of the Hundred Years War ending in 1453.

1341 — The War of Succession begins on the death of Duke Jean III. His niece, Jeanne de Penthièvre, wife of Charles of Blois, supported by the French, fights her brother Jean of Montfort, ally of the English, for the duchy.

1351 — Battle of the Thirty.

1364 — Charles of Blois, though aided by Du Guesclin, is defeated and killed at Auray. Brittany emerges ruined from this war.

THE MONTFORTS

1364-1468 — The dukes of the House of Montfort restore the country. This is the most brilliant period of its history. The arts reach their highest development. The dukes are the real sovereigns and pay homage only in theory to the king of France. Constable de Richemont (*see Vannes*), the companion-in-arms of Joan of Arc, succeeds his brother in 1457 as Duke of Brittany.

1488 — Duke François II, who has entered into the federal coalition against the Regent of France, Anne of Beaujeu, is defeated at St-Aubin-du-Cormier and dies. His daughter, Anne of Brittany, succeeds him.

REUNION OF BRITTANY WITH FRANCE

1491 — Anne of Brittany marries Charles VIII (*see Rennes*) but remains Duchess and sovereign of Brittany.

1492 — *Christopher Columbus discovers America on 12 October.*

1498 — Charles VIII dies accidentally. Anne returns to her duchy.

1499 — Anne again becomes Queen of France by marrying Louis XII, who had hastily repudi-ated his first wife. The duchy remains distinct from the Crown (*see Vannes*).

1514 — Anne of Brittany dies. Her daughter, Claude of France, inherits the duchy. She marries François of Angoulême, the future François I.

1532 — Claude cedes her duchy to the Crown. François I has this permanent reunion of Brittany with France ratified by the Parliament at Vannes.

FRENCH BRITTANY

1534 — Jacques Cartier discovers the St Lawrence estuary (*see St-Malo*).

1588 — Brittany rebels against its governor, the Duke of Mercœur, who wants to profit from the troubles of the League to seize the province. Bandits like the famous La Fontenelle ravage the country (*see Douarnenez*).

1598 — By the Edict of Nantes, Henri IV puts an end to religious strife (*see Nantes*).

1675 — The "Stamped Paper" Revolt (*see Pont-L'Abbé*) develops into a peasants' rising.

1711 — Duguay-Trouin takes Rio de Janeiro.

1764 — The Rennes Parliament and its Public Prosecutor, La Chalotais, oppose Governor Aiguillon. The authority of the Crown is much weakened. The Revolution is near.

1765 — Arrival on Belle-Île of many Acadian families of French origin from Nova Scotia.

1773 — Birth of Surcouf, the Breton pirate.

1776 — *American Declaration of Independence.*

1789 — The Bretons welcome the Revolution with enthusiasm.

1793 — Carrier has thousands drowned in the Loire near Nantes.

1793-1804 — The Laws against the priests and the mass levies

"Anne de Bretagne receiving a book from its author" by Antoine du Four, Musée Dobré, Nantes

DAGLI ORTI

Surcouf

Musée de St-Malo

give rise to the *Chouannerie* (revolt of Breton Royalists).

1795 — A landing by Royalist exiles is defeated at Quiberon.

1804 — Cadoudal, who tried to revive the *Chouannerie*, is executed.

1826 — René Laënnec, the great physician, dies.

1832 — Another attempted revolt, organised by the Duchess of Berry, fails. This is the last uprising.

1861 — *Start of the American Civil War.*

1909 Strikes and riots among the Concarneau cannery workers.

1914-8 — Brittany pays a heavy toll in loss of life during the First World War.

BRITTANY TODAY

1927-8 —The Morbihan aviator Le Brix, accompanied by Costes, is the first to fly round the world.

1940 — The islanders of Sein are the first to rally to General de Gaulle's call.

1942 — An Anglo-Canadian commando raids the St-Nazaire submarine base.

1944-5 — The end of the German Occupation leaves in its wake a trail of destruction, especially at Brest, Lorient and St-Nazaire.

1951 — Formation of the organisation Comité d'Études et de Liaison des Intérêts Bretons (CELIB), to safeguard Breton interests, is an initial step towards the rejuvenation of the local economy.

1962 First transatlantic transmission by satellite of a television programme by the station at Pleumeur-Bodou.

1966 — The opening of the Rance tidal power scheme and the Monts d'Arrée nuclear station near Brennilis.

1967 — The *Torrey Canyon* disaster off the English coast causes great oil slicks to contaminate the beaches of Brittany.

1969 — Creation of the Parc naturel régional d'Armorique.

1970 — Creation of the Parc naturel régional de Brière.

1975 — First search for oil in the Iroise Sea off the Finistère coast.

1978 — Establishment of a charter and council to safeguard the Breton cultural heritage. *Amoco Cadiz* oil spill on Brittany beaches.

1985 — Introduction of bilingual road signs in French and Breton.

1994 — The Law Courts at Rennes, home to the Breton Parliament, are burned to the ground by rioting French farmers.
The opening of the Pont de l'Iroise spanning the Eloen.

1996 — Inauguration of the La Roche-Bernard bridge.

2000 — The *Erica* founders in a storm, once again, "black tides " damage the shore and wildlife.
St Nazaire receives a commission to build the *Queen Mary 2*, the world's largest ocean liner.
"Brest 2000" tall ships regatta.

2003 — Launch of the Queen Mary 2 at St-Nazaire and sea trials off the coast of Brittany.

2006 — Tall ships at St-Malo.

ART AND CULTURE

Architecture

St-BRIEUC – Ground plan of the Cathédrale St-Étienne (13C and 14C)

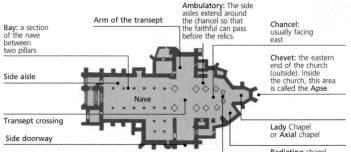

Bay: a section of the nave between two pillars

Arm of the transept

Ambulatory: The side aisles extend around the chancel so that the faithful can pass before the relics.

Chancel: usually facing east

Chevet: the eastern end of the church (outside). Inside the church, this area is called the **Apse**.

Side aisle

Nave

Transept crossing

Side doorway

Lady Chapel or **Axial** chapel

Radiating chapel or **apsidial** chapel

Round end of the chancel

ST-POL-DE-LÉON – Cross-section of the first two bays on the northern side of the cathedral nave (13C and 14C)

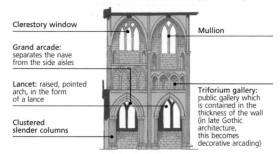

Clerestory window

Mullion

Grand arcade: separates the nave from the side aisles

Lancet: raised, pointed arch, in the form of a lance

Triforium gallery: public gallery which is contained in the thickness of the wall (in late Gothic architecture, this becomes decorative arcading)

Clustered slender columns

DINAN – Porch with three arches on the Basilique St-Sauveur (12C)

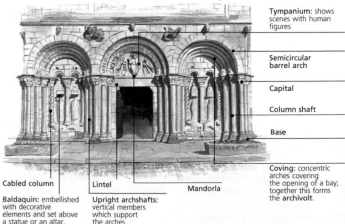

Tympanium: shows scenes with human figures

Semicircular barrel arch

Capital

Column shaft

Base

Coving: concentric arches covering the opening of a bay; together this forms the **archivolt**.

Cabled column

Lintel

Mandorla

Baldaquin: embellished with decorative elements and set above a statue or an altar.

Upright archshafts: vertical members which support the arches

R. Corbel/MICHELIN

QUIMPER – Cathédrale St-Corentin (13C and 19C)

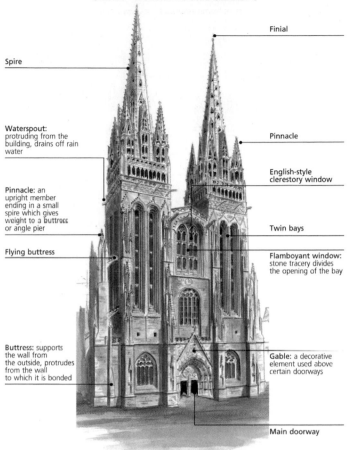

Spire

Finial

Waterspout:
protruding from the
building, drains off rain
water

Pinnacle

English-style
clerestory window

Pinnacle: an
upright member
ending in a small
spire which gives
weight to a buttress
or angle pier

Twin bays

Flying buttress

Flamboyant window:
stone tracery divides
the opening of the bay

Buttress: supports
the wall from
the outside, protrudes
from the wall
to which it is bonded

Gable: a decorative
element used above
certain doorways

Main doorway

COMMANA – Église St-Derrien – St-Anne Altarpiece

Placed behind and above the altar, this altarpiece is a jewel of Baroque art in Brittany.

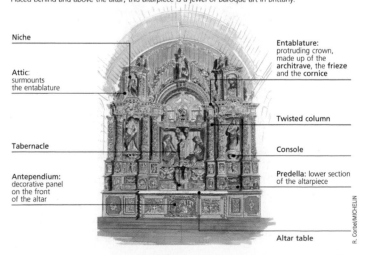

Niche

Entablature:
protruding crown,
made up of the
architrave, the frieze
and the cornice

Attic:
surmounts
the entablature

Twisted column

Tabernacle

Console

Antependium:
decorative panel
on the front
of the altar

Predella: lower section
of the altarpiece

Altar table

R. Corbel/MICHELIN

PLOUGASTEL-DAOULAS – Calvary (17C)

The words of the Evangelists are here written in stone; scenes from the life of Christ are sculpted on these imposing monuments, typical of religious expression in the region.

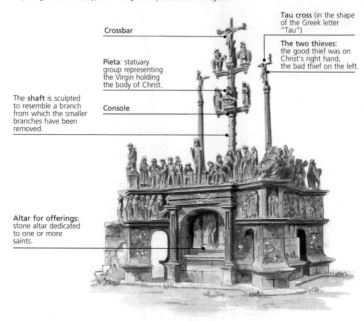

Crossbar

Tau cross (in the shape of the Greek letter "Tau")

The two thieves: the good thief was on Christ's right hand, the bad thief on the left.

Pieta: statuary group representing the Virgin holding the body of Christ.

The **shaft** is sculpted to resemble a branch from which the smaller branches have been removed.

Console

Altar for offerings: stone altar dedicated to one or more saints.

ST-THÉGONNEC – Triumphal gateway to the Parish Close (17C)

The "Gateway of the Dead", an ornately worked entranceway, marks the separation between the sacred and the profane; it was used for religious processions and funeral corteges.

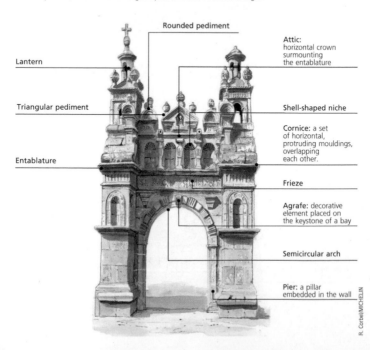

Rounded pediment

Lantern

Triangular pediment

Entablature

Attic: horizontal crown surmounting the entablature

Shell-shaped niche

Cornice: a set of horizontal, protruding mouldings, overlapping each other.

Frieze

Agrafe: decorative element placed on the keystone of a bay

Semicircular arch

Pier: a pillar embedded in the wall

R. Corbel/MICHELIN

FORT LA LATTE – Fortified castle (14C)

More than 60m/200ft above the sea, this 14C fort was modified in the 17C and restored in the 20C, but remains medieval in appearance.

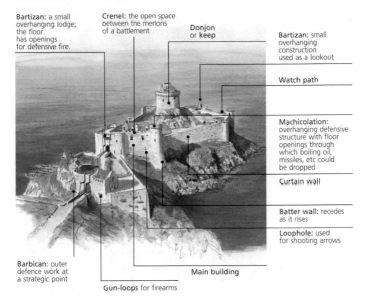

Bartizan: a small overhanging lodge; the floor has openings for defensive fire.

Crenel: the open space between the merlons of a battlement

Donjon or keep

Bartizan: small overhanging construction used as a lookout

Watch path

Machicolation: overhanging defensive structure with floor openings through which boiling oil, missiles, etc could be dropped

Curtain wall

Batter wall: recedes as it rises

Loophole: used for shooting arrows

Barbican: outer defence work at a strategic point

Main building

Gun-loops for firearms

BELLE-ÎLE-EN-MER – Vauban Citadel (17C)

Built in the 16C, the citadel was entirely redesigned by Vauban in the 17C. It is in exceptionally good condition, and a remarkable illustration of military architecture.

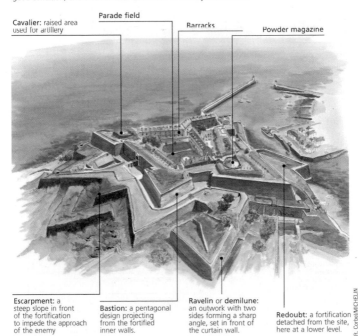

Cavalier: raised area used for artillery

Parade field

Barracks

Powder magazine

Escarpment: a steep slope in front of the fortification to impede the approach of the enemy

Bastion: a pentagonal design projecting from the fortified inner walls.

Ravelin or demilune: an outwork with two sides forming a sharp angle, set in front of the curtain wall.

Redoubt: a fortification detached from the site, here at a lower level.

JOSSELIN – Interior façade of the château (1490-1510)

Erected at the beginning of the 16C, this magnificent façade facing the courtyard illustrates the exuberance, the imagination and the abundance of sculpted dormer windows typical of the Renaissance.

Pinnacle: an upright member, which is a small, ornate spire rising from a square or polygonal base.

Gable

Polygonal roof

Finial

Dormer window: two storeys, extending out from the façade.

Flying shore

Mullion window with two crosspieces

Mullion window: the **mullion** is the vertical bar; the horizontal crossbar is the **transom**.

Mullion window (the window above it has two crosspieces)

Ogee arch

Ashlar

R. Corbel/MICHELIN

RENNES – Hôtel de ville (1730-1742)

Built by the architect Jacques Gabriel; the belfry is set off by the concave form of the building, a typically Baroque touch of the spectacular.

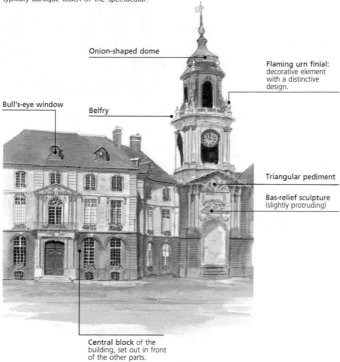

Onion-shaped dome

Flaming urn finial: decorative element with a distinctive design.

Bull's-eye window

Belfry

Triangular pediment

Bas-relief sculpture (slightly protruding)

Central block of the building, set out in front of the other parts.

JOSSELIN – Maison "Lovys Piechel" (1624)

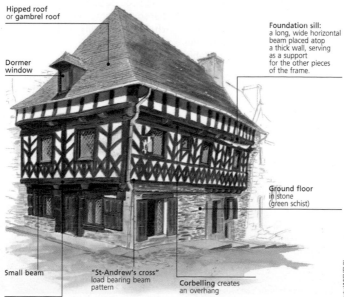

Hipped roof or gambrel roof

Dormer window

Foundation sill: a long, wide horizontal beam placed atop a thick wall, serving as a support for the other pieces of the frame.

Ground floor in stone (green schist)

Small beam

"St-Andrew's cross" load bearing beam pattern

Corbelling creates an overhang

Half-timbering

R. Corbel/MICHELIN

63

Breton Art

PREHISTORIC MONUMENTS

The megaliths or "great stones"
– More than 3 000 "great stones" are still to be found in the Carnac district alone. These monuments were set up between 5000 and 2000 BC by the little-known race who preceded the Gauls.

The **menhir**, or single stone, was set up at a spring, near a tomb and more often on a slope. It must have had a symbolic meaning. In Brittany there are about twenty menhirs over 7m/23ft high; the biggest is at Locmariaquer.

The **alignments** or lines of menhirs are probably the remains of religious monuments associated with the worship of the sun or moon. Most are formed by only a few menhirs set in line (many of the menhirs now isolated are the remains of more complicated groups). There are, however, especially in the Carnac area fields of menhirs arranged in parallel lines running from east to west and ending in a semicircle or **cromlech**. In the Lagatjar area the lines intersect. The lines of the menhirs appear also to be astronomically set, with an error of a few degrees, either by the cardinal points of the compass, or in line with sunrise and sunset at the solstices, from which it has been concluded that sun worship had something to do with the purpose of the monuments. As for the **dolmens** (the best-known is the Table

*"Callais" necklace (variscite) –
Musée archéologique de Vannes*

Société Polymathique de Morbihan, Vannes

des marchands at Locmariaquer), these are considered to have been burial chambers. Some are preceded by an ante-chamber or corridor. Originally all were buried under mounds of earth or dry stones called **tumuli** but most of them have been uncovered and now stand in the open air. The round tumuli found in the interior are of more recent date than the tumuli with closed chambers like the one of St. Michel at Carnac and the former were probably built up to 1000 BC. **Cairns** are tumuli composed entirely of stones such as the ones at Barnenez, which dates back to over 5000 BC and at Gavrinis, which is not so old. Some tumuli without burial chambers probably served as boundary markers.

Lagatjar Alignment at Camaret-sur-Mer

B. Kaufmann/MICHELIN

In northern Brittany **gallery graves** or **covered alleyways** are formed of a double row of upright stones with flat slabs laid on them, sometimes engraved. Although tumuli have never been fully excavated, some have been found to contain beautiful artefacts: polished axes made of rare stone (jadeite), or jewellery and marvellous necklaces made of *callaïs*. The museums of Carnac and Vannes contain particularly good collections of these early works of art.

Mystical tradition – For many centuries the menhirs were connected with the mystic life of the people. The Romans adapted some to their rites, carving pictures of their gods upon them. When the Christian religion became established, it acknowledged many raised stones that people still venerated by crowning them with a cross or cutting symbols on them.

CHURCHES AND CHAPELS

Nine cathedrals or former cathedrals, about 20 large churches and thousands of country churches and chapels make up an array of religious buildings altogether worthy of mystical Brittany.
The edifices were built by the people and designed by artists who transmitted to them an inspired faith. This faith appeared in a richness that was sometimes excessive - the exaggeratedly decorated altarpieces are an example - and a realism that was at times almost a caricature - as, for instance, the carvings on certain capitals and many purlins. Only affected in part by outside influences, the artists always preserved their individuality and remained faithful to their own traditions.

Cathedrals – These are inspired by the great buildings in Normandy and Ile-de-France, although they do not rival their prototypes either in size or ornamentation. The small towns that built them had limited means. Moreover, their erection was influenced by the use of granite, a hard stone, difficult to work. The builders had to be content with rather low vaulting and simplified decoration. Financial difficulties dragged out the work for three to five centuries. As a result, every phase of Gothic architecture is found in the buildings, from the bare and simple arch of early times to the wild exuberance of the Flamboyant style; the Renaissance often added the finishing touches.
The most interesting cathedrals are those of St-Pol-de-Léon, Tréguier, Quimper, Nantes and Dol-de-Bretagne.
The corresponding Gothic period in England lasted until the end of the 13C and included in whole or in part the cathedrals of Wells (1174), Lincoln (chancel and transept: 1186), Salisbury (1220-58), Westminster Abbey (c1250) and Durham (1242).

Country churches and chapels – In the Romanesque period (11C and 12C) Brittany was miserably poor. Buildings were few and small. Most of them were destroyed or transformed in the following centuries.
It was during the Gothic and the Renaissance periods, under the dukes and after the union with France, that the countryside saw the growth of churches and chapels.
Buildings constructed before the 16C are usually rectangular, though one also frequently sees the disconcerting T-plan in which the nave, usually wihout side aisles, ends in a chancel flanked by often disproportionately large chapels. The chevet is flat; there are no side windows - light comes through openings pierced right at the east end of the church.

Saint Anne

Many of the statues ornamenting the churches of Brittany provide priceless information on the history of costume, because they are faithful portraits of real people and the clothing that they wore. A common grouping is the Trinity of St Anne, the Virgin and Child, seen frequently in Central European churches, but much more rarely in the rest of France.

Stone vaulting is rare and is nearly always replaced by wooden panelling, often painted, whose crocodile headed tie-beams (cross-beams dividing the roof timbers), wooden cornices at the base of the vaulting and hammerbeams are frequently carved and painted. When there is no transept, a great stone arch separates the chancel from the nave.

From the 16C onwards there was a complete transformation in architectural design; it became necessary to include a transept which, inevitably, gave rise to the Latin Cross outline. The central arch disappeared; the east end became three-sided; the nave was lit by windows in the aisles.

Belfries – The Bretons take great pride in their belfries. The towers did not serve only to hold bells; they were also symbolic of both religious and civic life. In olden days the people prized them greatly, and it was a terrible punishment for them when an angry king laid them low.

The belfries are usually square in outline and their position on the building varies considerably. Small churches and chapels were often given the lighter and less costly gable tower in preference to a belfry. The tower was placed either on the west front gable or on the roof itself, at the intersection of the chancel and the nave. It is reached by outside steps or by stairs in the turrets that flank it and are linked to it by a gallery. Sometimes these little belfries become so reduced as only to be walls in gable form, pierced by arcades. This form of architecture, while fairly widespread in southwest France, is somewhat rare in Brittany.

Porches – Breton churches have a large porch on the south side. For a long

Southern doorway of the Commana church

period the porch was used as a meeting place for the parish notables, who were seated on stone benches along the walls.

A double row of Apostles often decorates the porch. They can be recognised by their attributes: St. Peter holds the key of Heaven; St. Paul, a book or a sword; St. John, a chalice; St. Thomas, a set square; St James the Elder, a pilgrim's staff. Others carry the instruments of their martyrdom; St. Matthew, a hatchet; St. Simon, a saw; St. Andrew, a cross; St. Bartholomew, a knife.

RELIGIOUS FURNISHINGS

Sculpture – From the 15C to the 18C an army of Breton sculptors working in stone and more particularly in wood supplied the churches with countless examples of religous furnishings: pulpits, organ casings, baptisteries and fonts, choir screens, rood screens, rood

A Myriad of Fountains

Fountains associated with the mystical or the miraculous are very common in Lower Brittany. Many are believed to produce healing waters. Almost every station of a *pardon* has a fountain for the faithful to drink from. The waters are placed under the protection of a saint or of the Virgin Mary, whose statues are found in little sanctuaries both humble and grand. In some places, such as the popular Ste-Anne-d'Auray, the fountain has been made into a grand display, with cascades and basins.

beams, altarpieces, triptychs, confessionals, niches with panels, Holy Sepulchres and statues.

These works are, as a general rule, more highly developed than the figures carved on the Calvaries, since it is much easier to work in oak, chestnut or alabaster than in granite.

Visits to the churches and chapels of Guimiliau, Lampaul-Guimiliau, St-Thégonnec, St-Fiacre near Le Faouët and Tréguier Cathedral (stalls) will give a good general idea of Breton religious furnishings.

The many **rood screens** *(jubés)* to be in the churches of Brittany are often of unparalleled richness. Some are cut in granite, as in the church at Le Folgoët, but most are carved in wood which makes them unique to Brittany.

Their decoration is very varied and is different on both sides.

The rood screen serves two purposes: it separates the chancel from the part of the church reserved for worshippers and completes the side enclosures of the chancel; the upper gallery may also be used for preaching and reading prayers. (The name derives from the first word of a prayer sung from the gallery.) The screen is usually surmounted by a large Crucifix flanked by statues of the Virgin and St John the Divine facing the congregation.

The **rood beam** or *tref*, which supported the main arch of the church, was the origin of the rood screen.

The Holy Trinity

To prevent the beam from bowing it had to be supported by posts which were eventually replaced by a screen carved to a lesser degree. It is to be seen mostly in the small chapels and churches where it serves as a symbolic boundary for the chancel; it is usually decorated with scenes from the Passion and always carries a group of Jesus Christ, the Virgin and St. John. Renaissance works are numerous and very elaborate. **Fonts** and **pulpits** are developed into richly decorated monuments.

Altarpieces, or retables, show an interesting development which can be traced through many stages in Breton churches. Originally the altar was simply a table: as the result of decoration it

Rood screen, Chapelle St-Fiacre

gradually lost its simplicity and reached a surprising size. In the 12C and 14C altars were furnished with a low step and altarpiece, the same length as the altar. Sculptors took possession of the feature and added groups of figures in scenes drawn from the Passion. From the 15C onwards, the altarpiece became a pretext for twisted columns, pediments, niches containing statues and sculpted panels, which reached their highest expression in the 17C.

Finally the main subject was lost in decoration consisting of angels, garlands, etc. and the altarpiece occupied the whole of the chapel reserved for the altar, and sometimes even, joined to the retables of side altars, decorating the whole wall of the apse as is the case at Ste-Marie-de-Ménez-Hom.

Of less importance but equally numerous are the niches which, when the two panels are open, reveal a **Tree of Jesse**. Jesse, who was a member of the tribe of Judah, had a son, David, from whom the Virgin Mary was descended. Jesse is usually depicted lying on his side; from his heart and his body spring the roots of the tree whose branches bear the figures, in chronological order, of the kings and prophets who were Christ's forebearers. in the centre the Virgin is portrayed representing the branch which bears the flower: Jesus Christ.

Among the many statues ornamenting the churches, such as the Trinity of St Anne and the Virgin and Child, portraits of real people and items of great importance in the study of the history of costume in Brittany are often to be found. Such representation, seen frequently in Central Europe, is rare in France.

Stained-glass windows – Whereas the altarpieces, friezes and statues were often coloured, paintings and frescoes, as such, were rare; almost the only exception are those at Kernascléden. In contrast there were a great many stained-glass windows, often Italian or Flemish inspired, but always made in Brittany. Some are especially fine: the cathedral at Dol has a beautiful 13C window.

The workshops at Rennes, Tréguier and Quimper produced stained glass between the 14C and 16C which should be seen: the most remarkable windows from these workshops are in the churches of Notre-Dame-du-Crann, La Roche and St-Fiacre near L Faouët.

In the 20C, the restoration and building of numerous churches and chapels has offered the possibility of decorating these edifices with colourful non-figurative stained-glass windows. The cathedral at St-Malo is a good example.

Gold and silver church plate – In spite of considerable losses, Brittany still possesses many wonderful pieces of gold and silver church plate. This was made by local craftsmen, most of them from Morlaix. Though fine chalices and

St-Thégonnec Parish Close (detail)

S. Sauvignier/MICHELIN

shrines may be hidden away for security, magnificent reliquaries, chalices, richly decorated patens and superb processional crosses may be seen at Carantec, St-Jean-du-Doigt, St-Gildas-de-Rhuys, Paimpont and Locarn.

Parish closes

The parish close (enclos paroissial) is the most typical monumental grouping in Breton communities.

Visitors should not leave Brittany without having seen a few examples. The centre of the close was the cemetery which was very small with gravestones of uniform size. Today this is tending to disappear. Around the cemetery, which is often reached through a **triumphal arch**, are grouped the **church** with its small square (placître), the **Calvary**, and the **charnel house** or ossuary. Thus the spiritual life of the parish is closely linked with the community of the dead. Death, Ankou, was a familiar idea to the Bretons who often depicted it in paintings.

The extraordinary rivalry between neighbouring villages explains the richness of the closes which were built in Lower Brittany at the time of the Renaissance and in the 17C. Competition between Guimiliau and St-Thégonnec went on for two centuries: a Calvary answered a triumphal arch, a charnel house a porch, a tower replied to a belfry, a pulpit to a font, an organ loft to a set of confessionals, an Entombment to chancel woodwork. The two finest closes in Brittany sprang from this rivalry.

Triumphal arch – The entrance to a cemetery is often ornamented with a monumental gateway. This is treated as a triumphal arch to symbolise the accession of the Just to immortality.

Some arches built during the Renaissance, like those of Sizun and Berven, are surprisingly reminiscent of the trimphal arches of antiquity.

Charnel house or ossuary – In the tiny Breton cemeteries of olden days, bodies had to be exhumed to make room for new dead. The bones were piled in small shelters with ventilation openings, built against the church or cemetery wall. The skulls were placed there separately in special "skull caskets". Then these charnel houses became separate buildings, larger and more carefully built and finally reliquaries, which could be used as funerary chapels.

Calvary – This is the name of the hill, also known as Golgotha, where Christ was crucified; its name was inspired by its skull-like shape (Skull; calvaria in Latin). Breton Calvaries representing scenes from the Passion and Crucifixion are not to be confused with wayside crosses often erected at crossroads or near churches to mark the site of a pilgrimage procession.

The unique Breton monuments illustrate episodes of the Passion, represented around Christ on the Cross. Many of them were built to ward off, as in 1598, a plague epidemic, or to give thanks after it ended. The priest preached from the dais, pointing out with a wand the scenes which he described to his congregation.

The distant forerunners of the Calvaries were the Christianised menhirs, which were still fairly common, and their immediate predecessors were the crosses, plain or ornate. Crosses along roads in this countryside are countless, certainly numbering tens of thousands at one time. In the 16C a Bishop of Léon boasted that he alone had had 5 000 put up. The oldest remaining Calvary is that of Tronoën, which dates from the end of the 15C. They were being erected as late as the end of the 17C. The most famous are those of Guimiliau with 200 figures, Plougastel-Daoulas with 180 and Pleyben.

The sculpture is rough and naive - the work of a village stonemason - but it shows a great deal of observation and is often strikingly lifelike and expressive. Many figures, notably soldiers, wear the costumes of the 16C and 17C.

CASTLES AND FORTRESSES

Breton granite is somewhat visually daunting to visitors coming to the region for the first time. Clean cut and hard, it does not age or weather and it would, therefore, not be possible to give a date to the grey buildings that

Château de Fougères

Y. Tierny/MICHELIN

blend perfectly into the landscape were it not for the architectural design and methods employed in construction. With the exception of the fortresses, most of which stood guard on the eastern border in fear of the kings of France or along the coast to ward off the raids of English invaders, there are few great castles in Brittany. This lack conveys perfectly the Breton character that turned all its artistic endeavour to the service of religion.

Nevertheless, it is easy to imagine Brittany in the Middle Ages. Few regions, in fact, had such fortresses and though many were destroyed or have fallen into ruin, a number are still standing. Before these walls the problems of war in the Middle Ages can be imagined. Although some fortresses fell at once to a surprise attack, it was not unusual for a siege to go on for several months. The attacker then sapped the ramparts, brought up machines which could hurl stones weighing over 100kg/200lb, and tried to smash the gates with battering rams before launching the final assault. In the mid-15C, artillery brought about new methods of attack and changes in military architecture.

At St-Malo and at Guérande, the stone walls that encircled these towns can be seen in their entirety. Remains of ramparts of varying extent can be seen in many other places. Vannes, Concarneau and Port-Louis have ramparts that are almost complete. There are many fortresses: those of Fougères and Vitré are among the finest in France. Dinan and Combourg have fortified castles still standing; Suscinio and Tonquédec have impressive ruins; La Hunaudaye, of lesser importance, the towers of Elven, Oudon and Châteaugiron still stand proudly upright. Fort la Latte, standing like a sentinel, boasts a magnificent site.

Buildings, half fortress and half palace, like Kerjean, Josselin and the Château des Ducs de Bretagne at Nantes, are interesting to see, but there are few of them. The fact is that the Breton nobility, except for the duke and a few great families, were poor. They included many country gentlemen who lived in very simple manors, which nevertheless retained their watchtower defences. They cultivated their own land, like the peasants, but they did not give up their rank and they continued to wear the sword.

Traditions and Folklore

BRITTANY AND ITS SYMBOLS

Like other French regions, Brittany has preserved its identity through the centuries by maintaining traditions. Costumes, religious observances, language and the arts all contribute to that identity. There is a special life-style in Brittany, a way of looking at the world. Standing on a high cliff, leaning hard into the wind to keep your footing, listening to waves crashing below. This is the stance of the Breton people in the face of the modern world

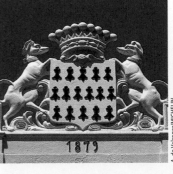

A. de Valroger/MICHELIN

that values conformity and uniformity above all else.

More changes took place in the region in the first half of the 20C than had taken place in the two preceding centuries combined. Yet in the 1980s, a movement grew for the valorisation of the old ways, despite the diminishing population of the smaller villages and the inevitable changes brought about by modern trade and services, industrial development and tourism.

One symbol the visitor is not likely to miss is the **Breton Flag**, *Gwenn ha du* (white and black). Morvan Marchal designed it in 1925. The five black stripes represent the five original bishoprics of Upper Brittany (Rennes, Nantes, Dol, St-Malo and St-Brieuc); the white bands those of Lower Brittany (Léon, Cornouaille, Vannes and Tréguier). The ermine was the symbol of the Duchy of Brittany. In the 13C, ermine fur was worn by all of the Dukes of Brittany as a symbol of authority. Another symbol is the Triskell, an ornament in the form of a revolving cross with three arms or vortexes symbolising earth, fire and water. It is Celtic symbol, and has been found on old Celtic coins in the British Isles and Ireland, Denmark and even in South and North America.

COSTUMES AND HEADDRESSES

Costumes

Brittany possesses costumes of surprising richness and variety. The fine clothes passed down from one generation to another were to be seen at every family festivity. It was customary for a girl at her marriage to acquire a costly and magnificent outfit that would last many years. Nowadays the traditional costumes are brought out only on great occasions such as *pardons*, and sometimes High Mass on feast days. In spite of attempts to modernise the dress, and the efforts of regional societies over the last few years – and they have had some success – to make the young appreciate the old finery, the tourist who travels quickly through Brittany is not likely to see many of the elaborate traditional dresses made familiar by picture postcards and books on the subject.

The most striking and attractive feature of the women's traditional costumes is their aprons which reveal how well off the family is by the abundance of their decoration. The aprons, of every size and shape, are made of satin or velvet and are brocaded, embroidered or edged with lace: at Quimper they have no bib, at Pont-Aven they have a small one, while at Lorient the bib reaches to the shoulders. Ceremonial dresses are usually black and are often ornamented with bands of velvet. The finest examples are those of Quimper which are

Folk dance

adorned with multi-coloured embroidery. The men's traditional costume includes a felt hat with ribbons and an embroidered waistcoat.

HEAD-DRESSES

The most original feature of the Breton costume is the **coiffe** or head-dress, once worn mainly in Finistère and Morbihan.

One of the most attractive is the head-dress of **Pont-Aven** which has, as an accessory, a great starched lace collar.

The **Bigouden** head-dress from the **Pont-l'Abbé** area is one of the most curious; it used to be quite small but since 1930 has become very tall.

In **Quimper** the head-dress is much smaller and is worn on the crown of the head; in **Plougastel**, where tradition is still strong, it has a medieval appearance with ribbons tied on the side.

In **Tréguier** the plainest of materials is allied with the most original of shapes. The **Douarnenez** head-dress is small and fits tightly round the bun on the back of the head, that of **Auray** shades the forehead and that of **Huelgoat** is almost like a lace hair net.

In order to get a complete picture of the richness and variety of Breton costume, the tourist should visit the museums of Quimper, Guérande, Rennes, Nantes, Dinan, Pont-l'Abbé etc all of which have fine collections of traditional dress.

THE PARDONS

The Breton pardons are above all a manifestation of popular religious fervour. They take place in the churches and chapels which may be consecrated by the tradition of a thousand years. There the faithful come to seek forgiveness, fulfil a vow or beg for grace.

The great pardons are most impressive, while the smaller events, though they may be less spectacular, are often more fervent. It is well worth tourists' while to arrange their trip so that they may be present at one of them (*see Calendar of events*). It is also one of the rare occasions when they will see the old costumes, perhaps slightly modernised.

Monsieur Saint Yves

Saint Yves is the most popular saint in Brittany. He rights all wrongs and is the patron saint of the poor. Son of a gentleman, Yves Hélori was born in Minihy-Tréguier in 1253. Magistrate and barrister, he acquired a reputation for dispensing justice quickly and fairly, achieving reconciliation, and pleading with precision. One day, a local notable

The "Tro Breiz"

Until the 16C, tradition demanded that every Breton should make a pilgrimage at least once in his or her lifetime to the seven cathedrals of Brittany. The **"Tro Breiz"**, or "Tour of Brittany", as it was known, drew people in the thousands during the 12C to the 16C, with its popularity reaching a peak in the 14C; estimates suggest that crowds numbering up to 30 000 to 40 000 pilgrims were taking to the roads! The tour covered nearly 700km/435mi, and it enabled the faithful to pay homage to the holy relics of the founding saints of Brittany; St Brieuc and St Malo

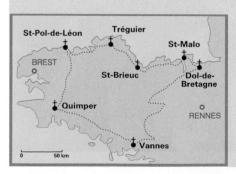

at the town of those names, St Samson at Dol-de-Bretagne, St Patern at Vannes, St Corentine at Quimper, St Paul the Aurelian at St-Pol-de-Léon and St Tugdual at Tréguier. Whoever failed to carry out this duty was supposed to have to undertake the pilgrimage after death, advancing by one coffin-length every seven years.

La grande troménie at Locronan

R. Mattès/MICHELIN

came before the Magistrate with a complaint conerning a beggar who came to stand by his kitchen window every day, to enjoy the smell of the rich man's meal in preparation. Yves jingled some coins and sent the man on his way saying "the sound of the money pays for the smell of the food". This defender of the poor died in 1303 and was canonised in 1347.

The Saints of Brittany

Brittany, with its magicians, spirits, fairies and demons – both male and female – has also claimed more haloes than any other part of France. Its saints number in hundreds and are represented by painted wooden statues adorning chapels and churches. Truth to tell, those who were canonised by the Vatican authorities (St Yves for example) can be counted on one's fingers. The most "official" among them were simply recognised by the bishops; the people themselves adopted others. Their fame goes no further than the borders of the province, or even the limits of the villages where they are venerated. (For the purposes of this guide, the names of saints revered in a particular region have been left in their local form).

Healing Saints and Protective Saints

The Bretons have always been on trusting, friendly and even familiar terms with their saints.

There are saints who are invoked on all occasions. Innumerable others are invoked against specified ailments: rheumatism, baldness etc. For centuries they took the place of doctors. Horses and oxen also have their appointed saints (St Cornely and St Herbot).

Saint Anne

Saint Anne became a popular figure around the time when the crusaders wre returning home. With the encouragement of Duchess Anne of Brittany, she became the patron saint of the region. One of the most famous *pardons* is devoted to Sainte-Anne-d'Auray and another celebrates Sainte-Anne-la-Palud. There is a saying among the faithful in Brittany: "Dead or alive, every Breton will see Saint Anne". Statues often represent her in a green cloak, the colour symbolising hope, either alone or teaching her daughter Mary.

Legends and Literature

A LAND OF LEGENDS

From East to West, North to South, Brittany is a land of marvellous tall tales. Ancient beliefs, rituals and stories have, over the centuries, woven a tapestry of folklore and mysterious legends. Many of the stories told as fables are deep-rooted myths that have endured and

Roman de Tristan: The Round Table and the Holy Grail (15C) (detail), Musée Condé, Chantilly

continue to influence contemporary writers, just as they held the imagination of those who listened to them in the dark nights of the Middle Ages.

The Breton soul has always been inclined to the dreamy, the fantastic and the supernatural. This explains the astonishing abundance and persistence of legends in the Armor country.

The Round Table

After the death of Christ, Joseph of Arimathea, one of His disciples, left Palestine carrying away a few drops of the divine blood in the cup from which the Redeemer drank during the Last Supper. He landed in Britain according to some legends, in Brittany according to others, where he lived for some time in the Forest of Brocéliande (now the Forêt de Paimpont) before vanishing without trace.

In the 6C King Arthur and 50 knights set out to find this precious cup. For them it was the Holy Grail, which only a warrior whose heart was pure could win. Percival (Wagner's Parsifal) was such a man. In the Middle Ages the search for the Grail gave rise to the endless stories of adventure which formed the Cycle of the Round Table. The most famous versions of the tale in English are, of course, Sir Thomas Malory's *Morte d'Arthur* (1471) and Alfred Lord Tennyson's *Idylls of the King* (1859).

Merlin and Viviane

One of King Arthur's companions, Merlin the sorcerer, came to the Forest of Brocéliande to live in seclusion. But he met the fairy Viviane, and love inflamed them both. To make sure of keeping Merlin, Viviane enclosed him in a magic circle. It would have been easy for him to escape, but he joyfully accepted this romantic captivity for ever.

Tristan and Isolde

Tristan, Prince of Lyonesse, was sent to Ireland by his Uncle Mark, King of Cornouaille, to bring back Isolde, whom Mark was to marry. On board their ship, Tristan and Isolde accidentally drank a philtre which was intended to bind Isolde to her husband in eternal love. Passion stronger than duty sprang up in both their hearts. There are several versions of the end: sometimes Tristan is slain by Mark, furious at his betrayal; sometimes he marries and dies in his castle in Brittany. But Isolde always follows him to the grave. Wagner's opera has made the love story famous.

The town of Is

At the time of good **King Gradlon**, about the 6C, Is was the capital of Cornouaille; finds in Trépassés and Douarnenez Bays and off the Presqu'île de Penmarch are said to have come from Is. The town was protected from the sea by a dike, opened by locks to which the King always carried the golden key.

The King had a beautiful but dissolute daughter, **Dahut**, also known as Ahès, who was seduced by the Devil in the form of an attractive young man. To test her love he asked her to open the sea gate. Dahut stole the key while the King was asleep, and soon the sea was rushing into the town.

King Gradlon fled on horseback, with his daughter on the crupper. But the waves pursued him and were about to swallow him up. At this moment a celestial voice ordered him, if he would be saved, to throw the demon who was riding behind him into the sea. With an aching heart the King obeyed, and the sea withdrew at once, but Is was destroyed.

For his new capital Gradlon chose Quimper; this is why his statue stands between the two towers of the cathedral. He ended his days in the odour of sanctity, guided and sustained by

St Corentine. As for Dahut, she turned into a mermaid, who is known as **Marie-Morgane** and whose beauty still lures sailors to the bottom of the sea. This state of affairs will persist until the Good Friday when Mass is celebrated in one of the churches of the drowned city. Then Is will cease to be accursed, and Marie-Morgane will no longer be a siren.

A Land of Literature

THE MIDDLE AGES AND THE RENAISSANCE

Learning was centred in the monasteries, the language used was Latin; the subjects studied were concerned, for the most part, with the history of the Church or of Brittany, moral philosophy and the lives of the saints. A life of St Guénolé was written by Wurdistein, Abbot of Landévennec, in the 9C, and a life of St Pol by Wromonoc, a monk from the same abbey.

Authors are rarely known by name, but there are some exceptions such as, in the 12C: the philosopher **Pierre Abélard,** one of the most brilliant figures of the Middle Ages, who was born at Le Pallet near Nantes and became Abbot of St-Gildas-de-Rhuys. **Étienne de Fougères,** who was named Bishop of Rennes in 1168, wrote *Livre des manières*, a Book of Manners, which gave him free rein to lecture his contemporaries on moral issues. **Guillaume Le Breton** was poet and historian at the court of Philippe-Auguste, whose reign he patriotically eulogised.

Students from Brittany first went to Paris University, and then to Nantes when that establishment was founded in the 15C. Schools were established to supplement the teaching provided by the churches and monasteries in out of the way parishes. However, it was not until the 15C and 16C that one began hearing of names such as those of the historians Pierre Le Baud, Alain Bouchard and Bertrand d'Argentré, of the poet Meschinot from Nantes who wrote a series of ballads entitled *Les Lunettes des princes* (The Princes' Spectacles), which became well known in his own time, of Noël du Fail,

Councillor of the Rennes Parliament, who depicted the world around him so well, and of the Dominican Albert Legrand, who wrote *Vie des Saints de la Bretagne armoricaine* (Life of the Saints of Armorican Brittany).

17C AND 18C

The best-known figures of the 17C and 18C are **Mme de Sévigné** – Breton by marriage – who addressed many of her letters from her residence, the Rochers-Sévigné Château and wrote vivid descriptions of Rennes, Vitré, Vannes and Port-Louis, **Lesage**, the witty author of *Gil Blas* who came from Vannes, and Duclos, moralist and historian, who was Mayor of Dinan. There was also **Élie Fréron**, who became known only through his disputes with Voltaire and who was the director of a literary journal published in Paris and, finally, the Benedictines Dom Lobineau and Dom Morice, historians of Brittany.

THE ROMANTICS AND CONTEMPORARY WRITERS

Three figures dominated literature in the 19C in Brittany: **François-René de Chateaubriand,** who had an immense influence on French literature. The effect he had over his contemporaries arose from his

Châteaubriand by Girodet de Roucy-Trioson, 1811, Château de Versailles

sensitivity, his passionate eloquence, his fertile imagination, all of which were displayed with brilliant and powerful style; in his *Mémoires D'Outre-Tombe* (Beyond the Tomb), he recounts his childhood at St-Malo and his youth at Combourg Castle;

Lamennais, fervent apologist of theocracy who became a convinced democrat, reflected in his philosophical works the evolution of his thought;

Ernest Renan, philologist, historian and philosopher, was a thinker who maintained that he had faith only in science. He wrote many books in an easy and brilliant prose and in one, *Souvenirs d'enfance et de jeunesse* (Recollections of Childhood and Youth), described his native Brittany.

Others who came from Brittany and should be noted though they did not write in praise of their native province are: the Symbolist poet **Villiers-de-l'Isle-Adam; Jules Verne** (1828-1905), precursor of modern scientific discoveries; Louis Hémon who became known through his *Maria Chapdelaine,* and finally Pierre Loti with his *Pêcheur d'Islande* and *Mon frère Yves.*

Henri Queffélec (1910-92) is one of the contemporary authors who has most lauded Brittany in Le Recteur de *l'île de Sein, Un homme d'Ouessant, Au bout du monde, Franche et secrète Bretagne* and *Promenades en Bretagne.* Another contemporary author, **Pierre-Jakez Hélias** (b 1917), recounts vividly in *Cheval d'orgueil* the traditions of the Pont-l'Abbé region (Claude Chabrol made a memorable film from the work).

Unfortunately, few Breton authors have been translated into English.

THE REGION TODAY

Food and Drink

Breton cooking is characterised by the high quality and freshness of the ingredients used, many of which will have been plucked from land or sea and brought almost directly to table after the briefest of interventions in the kitchen.

SEAFOOD, CRUSTACEANS AND FISH

Shellfish, crustaceans and fish are all excellent. Particularly outstanding are the spiny lobsters, grilled or stuffed clams, scallops, shrimp, crisp batter-covered fried fish morsels and crab pasties.

OYSTERS

Belon oysters, Armorican oysters from Concarneau, La Forêt and Île-Tudy, and Cancale oysters are all well known in France, but are not at their best until the end of the tourist season.

Lobster is served grilled or with cream and especially in a *coulis*, the rich hot sauce which makes the dish called *Armoricaine or à l'Américaine* (the latter name is due to a mistake made in a Paris restaurant).

Try also *cotriade* (a Breton fish soup like *bouillabaisse*), conger-eel stew, the Aulne or Élorn salmon, trout from the Monts d'Arrée and the Montagnes Noires, or pike and shad served with "white butter" in the district near the Loire. This is a sauce made from slightly salted butter, vinegar and shallots, and its preparation requires real skill. Finally, there are *civelles* (elvers), which are a speciality of Nantes.

MEAT, VEGETABLES AND FRUIT

The salt pasture sheep *(prés-salés)* of the coast are famous. Breton leg of mutton (with white beans) is part of the great French gastronomic heritage. Grey partridges and heath hares are tasty as are the chickens from Rennes and Nantais ducks. Pork butchers' meat is highly flavoured: Morlaix ham, bacon, black pudding, smoked sausage from Guémené-sur-Scorff and chitterlings from Quimperlé. Potatoes, artichokes, cauliflowers and green peas are the

Kouign-amann

This buttery Breton delight is made from 500g/1lb 2oz flour, 250g/9 oz butter, 200g/7oz sugar, 10g/1tsp baking powder, pinch of salt and an egg yolk. Work the flour, baking powder and salt into a dough with a little water and leave to rise for 30min. Form the dough into a large flat pancake about 30cm/12in in diameter, spread half the butter on this, taking care not to go right up the edge, and sprinkle

on about a third of the sugar. Fold the pancake into four, pressing the outer edges firmly together, and leave for 10min. Flatten the dough into a large pancake and cover with butter and sugar as before. Fold into four and leave for 10min. Flatten out to form a pancake of 25-30cm/10-12in in diametre and about 1-2cm/1in thick. Paint with the egg yolk and sprinkle with the rest of the sugar. Cook in a very hot oven for 30min. If the butter oozes out, use it to baste the *kouign-amann* until it has finished cooking.

S. Sauvignier/MICHELIN

glory of the Golden Belt. There are also strawberries and melons from Plougastel, cherries from Fouesnant and many other fruits.

CRÊPES, CAKES AND SWEETMEATS

Most towns have *crêperies* (pancake shops) where these very flat pancakes, called crêpes, made either of wheat or buckwheat, are served with cider or yoghurt. In some of the smaller, picturesque shops, often decorated with Breton furnishings, you may see them being made. Crêpes are served plain or with jam, cheese, eggs, ham etc. The buckwheat pancake *(crêpe de sarrasin,*

S. Sauvignier/MICHELIN

Galette de sarrasin with ham and egg

also called galette) is salted and often served as a starter while the wheat pancake *(crêpe de froment)* is sweet and served at dessert.

Also worth tasting are the Quimper wafer biscuits *(crêpes-dentelles)*, Pont-Aven butter cookies *(galettes)*, Nantes biscuits, Quintin oatmeal porridge and the far and *kouign amann* cakes. Among the sweets are the pralines from Rennes and *berlingots* (sweet drops) from Nantes.

Cider and wine – The local drink is cider *(cidre)*, of special note are the ciders from Fouesnant, Beg-Meil, and Pleudihen-sur-Rance.

The only Breton wine is **Muscadet**, which in 1936, was granted the *appellation d'origine contrôlée* (A.O.C.), literally "controlled place of origin". The people of Nantes guard it jealously and have founded a brotherhood, the Ordre des Chevaliers Bretvins, after *la petite brette* (little rapier), the nickname given to Anne of Brittany.

The grape, the *Melon de Bretagne,* has been cultivated since the early 17C, and gives a dry and fruity white wine which complements fish and seafood particularly well. Muscadet is produced in three distinct geographical areas, each with its own *appellation:* Muscadet, produced in the Grand-Lieu region; Muscadet de Sèvre et Maine, produced south of Nantes; and Muscadet des Coteaux de la Loire, produced in the Ancenis region. Other Breton drinks worth tasting are mead, also called *hydromel* or *chouchen* strawberry liqueur *(liqueur de fraises)*, a fortified cider apéritif *(pommeau)* and even a Breton whisky.

Language and Culture

THE BRETON LANGUAGE

From a linguistic point of view, Bretons are more closely related to the Irish and the Welsh than to the French. From the 4-7C, Armorica (present day Brittany) was a refuge for Britons fleeing England after the Anglo-Saxon invasion. From that time on, the Breton language rivalled French, a derivative of Low Latin. The annexation of the province to Frnach in the 15C and the French Revolution enhanced the trend in favour of French.

The **two Brittanies** – The map shows **Upper Brittany** (Haute-Bretagne), or the "Gallo" country, and **Lower Brittany** (Basse-Bretagne), or the Breton-speaking country.

French is spoken in the first, French and Breton in the second. Lower Brittany has four regions, each of which has its customs and brings shades of diversity to the Breton language – the district of Tréguier or Trégorrois, the district of Léon, the district of Cornouaille and the district of Vannes or Vannetais.

Modern Breton *(brezhoneg)*, derived from Brythonic, belongs to the Celtic languages and manifests itself in four main dialects: *cornouaillais* (south Finistère), *léonard* (north Finistère), *trégorrois* (Tréguier and the bay of St-Brieuc) and *vannetais* (Vannes and the Golfe du Morbihan). *Vannetais* distinguishes itself

from the other three, which are closely related, for example by replacing "z" with "h"; thus *Breiz (Brittany)* becomes *Breih*. In an attempt to overcome such differences, the use of "zh" has been introduced for the relevant words, thus *Breizh*.

CELTIC AND BRETON MUSIC

After the Second World War, Celtic music found a new audience with the creation of the *Bogaged ar Sonérion*, a marching band *(bagad)* playing traditional bagpipes of different sizes and shapes and percussion instruments, in the style of Scottish pipe bands. In the 1970s, Alain Stival, a musical instrument craftsman and major fan of the traditional *festounoz* (the Breton word for an evening of music and entertainment), popularised the Celtic harp and became a leading force in the new wave of Breton music. More recently, the artist Dan Ar Braz has contributed to revitalising tradtional tunes. Today, Celtic music in Brittany is a lively mixture of the traditional and the modern; many groups perform around France and their recordings are widely distributed. Festivals abound, including the **Transmusicales** and **Tombées de la Nuit** in Rennes, the **Festival de Cornouaille** in Quimper, the **Festival Interceltique** in Lorient (marching bands from around the Celtic world attend to compete). Perhaps the most famous foot-stomping get-together is the **Festival des Vieilles Charrues** in Carhaix-Plouguer. The small town in central Brittany is suddenly home to a

THE BRETON LANGUAGE
- - - Outermost limits of the linguistic region (9C)
—— Area where the language is spoken today

Place du Champ-Jacquet, Rennes

A. de Valroger/MICHELIN

crowd of happy campers who dance the nights away in a carefree and anything goes ambience.

In some places these manor farms add a great deal of character to the Breton countryside. This is the case in Léon wheere they are numerous and where Kergonadéac'h, Kerouzéré, Kergroadès and Traonjoly together form a background setting to KerJean, pride of the province. Certain other châteaux, such as Rocher-Portail, were built later, and lack all appearance of being fortresses, but impress by their simplicity of outline and the grouping of the buildings; at such places as Lanrigan and La Bourbansais, on the other hand, it is the detail that charms the visitor. Landal is one of those that gain enormously from its surroundings; others take great pride in a well laid-out garden or a fine park

- these include Bonne-Fontaine, Caradeuc and Rosanbo.

MODERN TOWNS

It is difficult to find any basis of comparison between the old towns with their historical associations and the modern towns. Nonetheless, while Dinan, Locronan, Vitré, Morlaix and Quimper, to name a few, as well as the marvellously reconstructed St-Malo, have an undeniable appeal, it is impossible not to be struck also by the planning and grouping of buildings in such towns as Brest and Lorient. The wide streets and huge, airy squares are elegant and have obviously been built to achieve harmony and unity. Visitors may well be surprised by certain buildings, but they will find something to admire in the upward sweep of a tall bell-tower, the simple lines of a concrete façade, the successful decorative effect of stone and cement combined. Above all, if they have some slight appreciation of colour harmony and go inside any building, they will be struck by the contemporary artist's skill in lighting.

S. Sauvignier/MICHELIN

HB Henriot Workshop

Port du Guilvinec

LES ABERS★★

MICHELIN LOCAL MAP 308 C/E 2/4 – FINISTÈRE (29).

The low and rocky northwest coast of Finistère, still known as the Coast of Legends, offers a magnificent sight. Life is hard here, and the enormous anchor of the Amoco Cadiz is a reminder of the violence the elements can inflict on the region. No manicured beaches here but romantic vistas, solitary coastal paths, and the smell of seaweed will feel right at home.

▶ **Orient Yourself:** The coastline from the Pointe St-Mathieu to Brignogan-Plages, wild and rugged, and is broken up by estuaries called abers (Aber-Wrac'h, Aber-Benoît, Aber-Ildut).
🐌 **Don't Miss:** The clear, calm waters of the estuaries
🕯 **Also See:** Le FOLGOËT

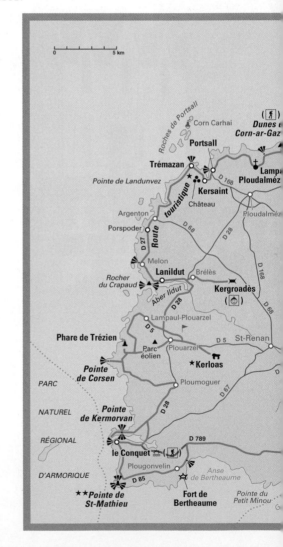

The "Coast of Legends"

195km/121mi – allow one day

This tour offers the visitor the opportunity to go off the beaten track and to enjoy nature in its unspoiled state.

▶ *Leave Brest by north road towards Roscoff.*

Gouesnou

The 17C Gothic and Renaissance **church** *(Guided tours Wed and Thur, 10am-noon; apply to the Town hall. ☎ 02 98 07 86 90)* has a polygonal chevet (1615) surmounted by three pediments. To the west, below the church, is a fine Renaissance fountain with an altar adorned with a statue of St Gouesnou.

▶ *Take the road towards Lannilis and at Boura-Blanc. turn right.*

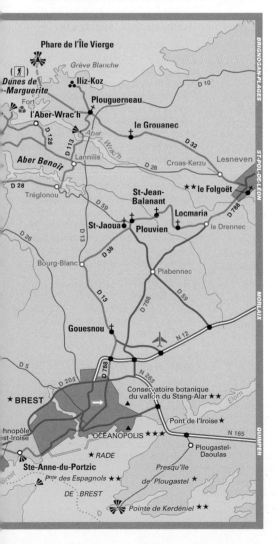

Address Book

TOURIST OFFICES

Pays d'Iroise, ☎ 02 98 84 41 15, www. pays-iroise.com.

Information on all of the towns in the area. Ploudalmézeau, 1 rue François Squiban, ☎ 02 98 48 12 88, www. ot-ploudalmezeau.com In the summer: Mon-Sat 9.30am-12.30pm, 1.30pm-6pm, Sun 10am-noon.

Pays des Abers, www.abers-tourisme. com, in **Lannilis,** 1 Place de l'Église, ☎ 02 98 04 05 43, and **Plouguerneau,** Place de l'Europe, ☎ 02 98 04 70 93. July-Aug: Mon-Sat 9.30am-12.30pm, 2-7pm, Sun 10/30am-12.30pm.

Brignogan-Plages, 7 av. du Gén.-de-Gaulle, ☎ 02 98 83 41 08, www. ot-brignogan-plage.fr In the summer: Tue-Fri 10.30am-12.30pm, 1.30-4pm, Sat 10.30am-12.30pm.

Lesneven-Le Folgoët, 14 Place du Gén. Le Flo, ☎ 02 98 83 01 47. July-Aug: Mon-Sat 9.30am-12.30pm, 2-6.30pm, Sun and holidays 10.30am-noon; off season: Mon-Fri 9.30am-noon, 2-6pm, Sat 9.30am-noon.

WHERE TO STAY, EATING OUT

ST-RENAN

⊜⊜⊜ **Hôtel-restaurant des Voyageurs**, *16 rue St-Yves,* ☎ *02 98 84 21 14 - 24 rooms* 📶 📺 ✕ Small rooms, impersonal but clean and country-style cooking or seafood (menus € 22-50) Breakfast € 8.

LANILDUT AND NEARBY

⊜⊜ **Le Clos d'Ildut**, *13 rte de Mézancou, 1 km from the centre on D 27,* ☎*02 98 04 43 02 - 3 rooms* 📶 In the heart of a peaceful garden, an old manor with slate floor and tasteful decor. The rooms have different sytles; one is in an outbuilding.

⊜⊜ **Chambres d'hôte Gwalarn**, *4 Hent Kergaradoc, follow the sign pointing right at the entrance to Lanildut when arriving from Brélès,* ☎ 02 98 04 38 41 *- 4 rooms* 📶 A lovely traditional house dating from 1800, with pretty rooms decorated on a maritime theme. Wonderful view of the surrounding area from the landscaped garden.

PLOUDALMÉZEAU AND NEARBY

⊜⊜ **Hôtel des voyageurs,** *pl. de l'Église,* ☎ *02 98 48 10 13 - 9 rooms* 📶 📺 ✕ *Closed Sun evening and Mon.* A few plain rooms in a regional-style building located on a round-about. Traditional cuisine in a rustic dining room with exposed beams and a fireplace. Breakfast € 8.30.

⊜⊜ **Hostellerie du Castel**, *Kersaint Landunvez,* ☎ *02 98 48 63 35 - 15 rooms* 📶 ✕ Rather old-fashioned rooms in a large manor covered with climbing vines; garden and private parking area. Seafood specialities. Breakfast € 6.10.

PLOUGEURNEAU AND NEARBY

⊜⊜ **Auberge de Keralloret**, *souths of D 10 between Guisseny and Plouguerneau,* ☎ *02 98 48 69 77, www. kerav3.treveon.net - 11 rooms* 📶 📺 The rooms are surprisingly lovely: unique appliques (made with beach stones) and soothing colours adorn the walls. More like a guest house than a hotel. Delicious meals (€ 15 /45), featuring regional specialities. Generous breakfast € 8.

⊜⊜ **Le Castel Ac'h**, *plage de Lilia, Kervenni,* ☎ *02 98 37 16 16.* The site is exceptionally beautiful. Choose from the bar-brasserie (moderate prices), the traditional restaurant (seafood) or fine cuisine (lobster, foie gras, etc.) served in the most elegant dining room.

PORTSALL

⊜ **Le Caïman,** *44 rue du Port,* ☎ *02 98 48 69 77.* A new restaurant serving fish in sauces from the French West Indies. Music to match the spicy food and an attractive terrace across the street.

WATER SPORTS

Diving - Aber Benoît Plongée, *quai du Stellac'h, St Pabu,* ☎ *02 98 89 75 66, www.aberbenoitplongee.com.* For neophytes, courses and underwater tours to see the flora and fauna, but also for more advanced divers, tours to wrecks of the Amoco Cadiz or the Elektra.

Chapelle St-Jaoua

Standing in the centre of a shady parish close is a charming early-16C chapel which contains the tomb and effigy of St Jaoua.

Plouvien

In the **parish church** is a tomb in Kersanton granite dating from 1555. The recumbent figure rests on 16 little monks depicted at prayer, reading or meditating.

▶ *Leave Plouvien to the east by the Lesneven road.*

St-Jean-Balanant

The 15C **chapel** *(To visit the chapel, apply to the town hall, ☎ 02 98 40 91 16)* was founded by the Order of St John of Jerusalem and was a dependant of the La Feuillée Commandery in the Monts d'Arrée.

▶ *Continue towards Lesneven and at the fourth junction turn right towards Loc-maria.*

Chapelle de Locmaria

In front of the 16C-17C chapel with its square belfry-porch, there is a fine **cross**★ with two crossbars adorned with figures.

▶ *Go to Le Drennec and take the road on the left to Le Folgoët.*

Le Folgoët★★ – ♿ *See Le FOLGOËT.*

▶ *Take the road towards Lannilis and at Croas-Kerzu, bear right towards Plou-guerneau.*

Plouguerneau

The village **church** hosts an interesting collection of 17C wooden statuettes called the little saints which can be found near the baptistery on the left on entering. Formerly carried in processions, these statuettes are the result of a wish made by villagers who had miraculously escaped the plague.

▶ *Take the D 32 towards St-Michel.*

At the exit to the village, on the right, is the **Ecomusée de Plouguerneau et du Pays Pagan** *(rte St-Michel, ☎ 02 98 37 13 35 ; ◷ July-Sep: daily except Tue 2.30-6pm; June: weekends only; ⊙ € 2.50).* From the Vierge Island lighthouse to the Koz Isle archaeological site by way of the Goemonniers and Algae ecological museum, the whole country can be explained through these natural and historic sites. Life in former times and today for the people of North Finistere developed around the coast. Regional products, stories and legends on offer, along with dispalys on the techniques of seaweed-gathering through the ages.

Ruines d'Iliz Koz

◷ *Open mid-April-mid-Sept; daily except Mon 2.30-6.30pm; rest of the year Sun only 2.30-5pm. ⊙ € 2.50. ☎ 02 98 04 66 46.*
These ruins of the church and the presbytery, which have been silted up since the early 18C, provide an excellent example of Breton funerary art at the end of the Middle Ages. A signposted route enables visitors to discover the most important elements of the site. Pay special attention to the tombs' ornamental motifs which describe the function of the tomb's occupant (knight, clerk or commoner).
Near the ruins is a good sheltered beach of fine sand in a rocky cove.

Phare de l'Île Vierge
🕐 *Take the boat from Lilia - Les Vedettes des Abers (☎ 02 98 04 74 94): July-Aug departures hourly from noon, reservations recommended, April-Sep call for schedule. Lighthouse, ﷼€2.50. ☎ 02 98 04 70 93.*
This is the tallest lighthouse in France (82.5m/270ft). From the top (397 steps) the **panorama**★ extends over the Finistère coast.

▶ *Return to Plouguerneau and take D113 towards Lannilis.*

Only 2km/1mi further on, the old road has become a lookout point (small Calvary) affording a good **view**★ of l'Aber-Wrac'h.

The tallest lighthouse in France

▶ *Turn right at Lannilis.*

L'Aber-Wrac'h
With its important sailing centre, l'Aber-Wrac'h is a very popular pleasure port. Its sailing school overlooks the village, and also livens up this seaside stay. The corniche road runs along the Baie des Anges; past the ruins of the 16C convent of Notre-Dame-des-Anges.

▶ *Bear right towards Ste-Marguerite Dunes, then right again towards Cézon Fort.*

From the platform by the roadside, there is an interesting view of l'Aber-Wrac'h estuary, the ruins of Cézon Fort on an island commanding the approach to the estuary, and the lighthouse on the Île Vierge.

▶ *Turn back and after Poulloc, bear right for the dunes.*

Dunes de Ste-Marguerite
🚶 The footpaths through the dunes afford good views. Seaweed is left to dry on the dunes for two to three days and then is sent to the processing factories.

▶ *Make for the Chapelle de Brouënnou and turn left towards Passage St-Pabu. Go to Lannilis via Landéda and then take the Ploudalmézeau road.*

Aber-Benoît
The road crosses the *aber* and runs along it for a while giving good views of the pretty setting.

▶ *After 5km/3mi, turn right for St-Pabu and after St-Pabu follow the signposts for the camp site to reach the Corn-ar-Gazel Dunes.*

Dunes de Corn-ar-Gazel
Beautiful **view** of Ste-Marguerite Peninsula, Aber-Benoît and its islets.

▶ *Turn round and follow the scenic road winding through the dunes and affording glimpses of the coast.*

Lampaul-Ploudalmézeau
The **church** has a Renaissance north door and a magnificent **belfry-porch**★ crowned by a dome with three lanterns.

Portsall
This small harbour is located in a bay sheltered by a chain of reefs called the Roches de Portsall, the rocks on which the oil tanker, Amoco Cadiz, ran aground in 1978. One of its two enormous anchors (20t) is fixed to the harbour breakwater in memory of the shipwreck, on which a legal settlement was not reached until 1992.

Kersaint
Beyond the village, towards Argenton, are the ruins of the 13C **Château de Trémazan.** Be careful! These ruins are very dangerous. However a lookout point allows one to admire the majesty of the site.
Trémazan
From the large car park past the village, the **view**★ extends over the Île Verte, the Roches de Portsall and Corn Carhai Lighthouse.

Scenic road★ *(Route touristique)*
The corniche road follows a wild coast studded with rocks; note the curious jagged **Pointe de Landunvez.** The road runs through several small resorts, Argenton, **Porspoder** – where St Budoc, Bishop of Dol-de-Bretagne is said to have landed in the 6C – and Melon.

▶ *Turn right at the entrance of Lanildut.*

Lanildut
This is Europe's foremost seaweed port. The Rumorvan quarter hosts several beautiful captain's houses from the 17C and 18C.

Rocher du Crapaud
It offers good views of the harbour and the *aber,* a picturesque estuary accessible to boats regardless of the tides. The northern bank is wooded, the southern bank has dunes and beaches.

▶ *After Lanildut, the road follows the aber as far as Brélès.*

Aber-Benoît

Château de Kergroadès

Guided tours (30min) by appointment only. ⊜ *20€.* ☎ *02 98 84 21 73.*
The main courtyard of this early-17C castle is closed by a crenellated gallery and is surrounded by an austere main building flanked by two round towers.

▶ *Return to Brélès and take 28 to Plouarzel. Drive across town heading toward Saint-Renan, and about 1km outside the town litmits, turn right toward the Menhir de Kerloas.*

Menhir de Kerloas★

This is the tallest standing stone in France, 9.5m/31ft tall, and is estimated to be 5,000 years old. The impressive menhir is knicknamed "The Hunchback" *(An Tor)* because of the two bumps, and has of course indpired many legends. A curious 19C tradition brought newlyweds here to rub their naked bodies on the bumps - the man in order to have sons, the woman in order to have authority in the home.

▶ *Return to Plouarzel and take VC 4 towards Trézien.*

You cannot miss the large **windmill field** that was built here in 200; it is made up of five large power-generating windwmill, each 60m/197ft high, with impressive propellers that are 47m/135ft in diameter.

Phare de Trézien

The lighthouse (37m/121ft high) has an average range of 35km/22mi.

▶ *Continue towards Porsmoguer Beach (Grève de Porsmoguer) and after some houses turn right.*

The road passes by the Corsen Maritime Station (Station de Corsen) and leads to a ruined house on the cliff.

Pointe de Corsen

This 50m/160ft cliff is the most westerly point in continental France. There is a fine **view** of the coast and islands.

▶ *Go to Ploumoguer passing through Porsmoguer Beach, then turn towards Le Conquet. After 5km/3mi, bear right for the Pointe de Kermorvan.*

Pointe de Kermorvan

Its central part is an isthmus which gives a pretty view on the right of Blancs Sablons Beach and on the left of the **site**★ of Le Conquet. The Groaë footbridge gives pedestrians access to the point; at the very tip, to the left of the entrance to the lighthouse, the rocky chaos makes a marvellous lookout point.

Le Conquet⌂

This town occupies a pretty **site**★, and affords a superb view of the Pointe de Kermorvan. This small fishing port is the departure point for the islands of Ouessant and Molène.
⯅ The harbour corniche road, the coastal footpaths and especially the Pointe de Kermorvan are pleasant walks offering good views of the port, the Four Channel, the Ouessant archipelago and its many lighthouses in the distance.

▶ *The road from Le Conquet to Brest is described in the opposite direction under BREST: Excursions.*

MONTS D'ARRÉE★★

MICHELIN LOCAL MAP 308 G/I 3/4 – FINISTÈRE (29)

Solitary, barren, covered in heaths, often wet, these sharp crests of quartz have been incorporated into the **Parc national régional d'Armorique** to better preserve their wild nature. In the midst of the park, the different sites which make up the **Écomusée des Monts d'Arrée** illustrate the rural way of life of times past. The mountain chain is wooded in parts, especially towards the east, but the summits are usually quite desolate. There is not a tree on them; the heath is pierced by rocky scarps; here and there are clumps of gorse with golden flowers in spring and purple heather in September.

▶ **Orient Yourself:** Dividing the Cornouaille and the Léon, the Arrée Mountains are the highest in Brittany, yet their topmost point is less than 400m/1 200ft.
- **Don't Miss:** The view from Roc Trévezel
- **Also See:** PLEYBEN

Parc Naturel Régional d'Armorique

Inaugurated in 1969, the Regional Nature Park encompasses 39 communes on 172,000 hectares (425,000 acres) of land and ocean. There are four eco-zones on the site: the Monts d'Arée, the Crozon Peninsula, the *Aulne maritime* and the islands of the Iroise Sea.

The purpose of the park is the preservation of landscapes, flora and fauna; the creation of activities to foster local economic growth; the preservation of aspects of rural civilization.

Many exhbit areas are open to the public through a network of 20 facilties: Ferme des artisans in Brasparts, open-air msuems of the Monts dArée in St-Rivoal and Commana, Museum of Lighthouses and Bouys and Niou Houses in Ouessant, Museum of Rural Schooling in Trégarvan, Mineral Museum in rozon, River House in Sizun, Wolf Museum in Cloître-St-Thégonnec.

Information from the headquarters in Le Faou ☎ 02 98 81 90 08. www-parc-naturel-armorique.fr.

Driving Tour Crossing La Montagne Pelée

122km/76mi – allow one day

In nice weather, a good way to appreciate the beauty of Brittany's interior.

▶ *Leave Huelgoat south in the direction of Pleyben.*

St-Herbot★
The **church**★ with its square tower, stands surrounded by trees. It is mainly in the Flamboyant Gothic style. A small Renaissance ossuary abuts on the south porrooms There is a fine Crucifix-Calvary in Kersanton granite (1571) in front of the building. Inside, the **chancel** is surrounded by a remarkable **screen**★★ in carved oak topped by a Crucifixion. Against this screen, on the nave side, are two stone tables for the tufts of hair from the tails of oxen and cows, which the peasants offer on the pardon to obtain the protection of St Herbot, the patron saint of horned cattle. Note also the richly decorated stalls (lift the seats) against the screen.

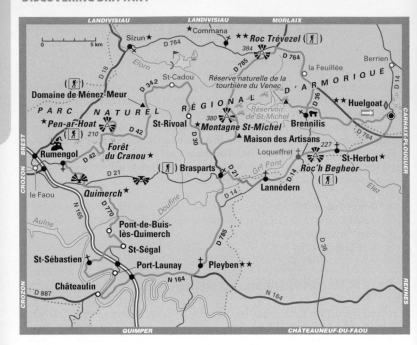

Roc'h Begheor

15min on foot. 🅿 *Car park to the right of the road.* A good **view**★ over the Monts d'Arrée and the Montagnes Noires.

Lannédern

In the **parish close** is a Cross decorated with figures; note St Edern riding a stag. Inside the **church** and six polychrome low-relief sculptures (17C) illustrating his life are of interest. *(Open during services.)*

▶ *Continue towards Pleyben and turn right after 1.5km/1mi.*

Brasparts

Perched atop a hill, this village has an interesting 16C **parish close.** Inside the church, by the nave (on the right) stands a splendid **Virgin of Pity**★ (16C).
🔣 For hikers, from the town, follow the hiking trails marked Du Méné *(11km/5.5mi)* and De Gorre *(16km/8mi).*

▶ *Make for Pleyben.*

Pleyben★★ – 🕭 *See PLEYBEN*

Châteaulin

Standing on a bend of the Aulne, in the green and deep valley through which the canalized river flows, this little town is a centre for freshwater fisherman. In fact, the tide does not reach Châteaulin but dies out a little way downstream at Port-Launay which harbours numerous pleasure boats.

Observatoir aquatique

🕙 *Open 10am-5pm,* 🕗 *closed Dec-Feb, Sun in July-Aug, weekends rest of the year.*
🔖 *No charge on pulic holidays.* ☎*02 98 86 30 68; www.smatah.fr.*

Salmon Fishing

Châteaulin is the salmon-fishing centre in the Aulne Valley; the salmon has always appeared on the town's coat of arms. Less often than in the past, the salmon come up the river to spawn, trying to leap the small waterfalls formed by the overflows from the locks. Angling (bait casting, spin casting) is done below the locks over a distance of some 100m, especially in March and April.

This centre is dedicated to the observation of the main species living in the rivers along the coast of the Finistère, such as Atlantic salmon. In summer, natue walks are orgnisaed in the Arée hills..

Chapelle Notre-Dame
Access via rue Graveran and a road to the left, opposite the cemetery. The castle's former chapel stands in an enclosure near some 17C houses. Pass through the triumphal arch, there is a 15C Calvary cross presenting a rather unusual Last Judgement. Modified in the 17C and 18C, and extensively restored in 1991, the chapel retains some vestiges of the 13C (columns, capitals), and some 17C altarpieces.

▶ *Follow the south bank of the Aulne.*

Port-Launay
This is the port of Châteaulin, on the Aulne. The long quay makes for pleasant walks.

▶ *Leave the Brest road on the right and continue along the Aulne, pass under the railway viaduct, bear right at the roundabout and 100m/110yd further on, turn left.*

Chapelle St-Sébastien
In the 16C **parish close** stand a triumphal arch surmounted by St Sebastian between two archers, and a fine Calvary with figures including the saint pierced by arrows. The chapel contains splendid 17C **altarpieces**★ in the chancel and the transept; note, to the left, the panels depicting the story of Lorette, a small Italian town where, according to legend, the house of the Virgin Mary was brought from from Nazareth by angels in the 13C.

▶ *Follow the small road over the railway line and the Quimper-Brest dual carriageway.*

Pont-de-Buis-lès-Quimerch
On leaving the village, below the road, on the left, can be seen a 300-year-old explosives factory.

▶ *Drive to Quimerch then Rumengol along D 770.*

From the Quimerch viewing table, the view extends from Ménez-Hom to the Forêt du Cranou taking in the Brest roadstead and the Presqu'île de Plougastel.

Rumengol
Rumengol dates from the time of King Gradlon who built a chapel here in the 5C, just after the town of Ys disappeared. The **church** is 16C as shown by the south porch and the magnificent west front in Kersanton granite but significant alterations were made in the 17C and 18C. The two **altarpieces**★ and altars date from 1686. In the

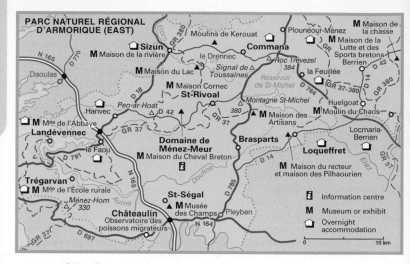

centre of the village, near the church apse, is a sacred fountain (1792), an object of devotion on *pardon* days.

Forêt du Cranou★

The road, hilly and winding, runs through the state forest of Cranou, which covers over 600ha/1 483 acres and consists mostly of oaks and beeches. *Picnic areas.*

▸ *On leaving the Forêt du Cranou, bear right towards St-Rivoal; at the entrance to Kerancuru, turn left for Pen-ar-Hoat-ar-Gorré. In the hamlet (schist houses), turn left towards Hanvec and again left onto an uphill road.*

Pen-ar-Hoat★

Alt 217m/712ft. ⊙ 45min on foot there and back.
🚶 *Walk round the farm and bear left towards the line of heights; after passing between low walls, the climb ends among gorse bushes.*

The **panorama** extends over the heath-clad hills: to the north are the hills bordering the left bank of the Elorn, to the east the nearer heights of the Arrée, to the south Cranou Forest and in the distance the Montagnes Noires and the Ménez-Hom, and lastly, to the west, the Brest roadstead.

▸ *Return to Kerancuru and bear left; 3.5km/2mi further on, left again.*

Domaine de Menez-Meur

🕐 *Open July and Aug, daily, 10am-7pm; May, June and Sep 2-6pm; Mar-April and Oct-Nov: Wed, Sun, public holidays and school holiday periods 1-5.30pm.* ⊛ *€ 3.20.* ☎ *02 98 68 81 71.* ⟿ *Guided tours of the animal park (2hr) and the Mont d'Arée landscapes (3-4hr). Picnic tables.*
The estate sprawls over 400ha/988 acres in an undulating countryside. The **Maison du Cheval breton** presents exhibitions devoted to the Parc naturel régional d'Armorique. 🚶 A nature trail *(about 1hr 30min)*, accompanied by panels giving information on the region's flora, winds through the large enclosures where ponies, sheep, deer, wild boar, horses etc roam.

▸ *Go to St-Rivoal, passing through St-Cadou.*

St-Rivoal

After the village, below the Le Faou road, to the left, is the **Maison Cornec** (🕒 *Open July and Aug, daily, 11am-7pm; June daily 2-6pm; 1-15 Sep 2-6pm except Sat; last admission 30min before closing;* 📷 *€ 1.* ☎ *02 98 68 87 76)*, a small farm dating from 1702. It is one of the many exhibits dispersed throughout the Parc d'Armorique, which makes up the open-air museum devoted to the different styles of Breton architecture. The little house, built of schist and with a fine external covered stairway going up to the hayloft, comprises a large room with the living quarters for the farmer and his family round the great chimney and the domestic animals at the other end.

▷ *Take D 30 in the direction of Brasparts.*

The road winds through a countryside of hills, and of green and wooded valleys whose freshness contrasts with the bare rocky summits.

▷ *After 5.5km/3mi, bear left onto D 785 towards Morlaix.*

Ferme des Artisans

N of Brasparts. 🕒 *Open July-Aug, daily, 10am-7pm; Jan to Mar, and Oct to Dec: weekends 10.30am-7pm; April to June and Sep, school holiday periods: Mon-Fri 2-7pm, Sat-Sun 10.30am-7pm.* ☎ *02 98 81 46 69.*
Part of the regional nature park, the centre is housed in St-Michel farmhouse; it displays the creations of over 200 Breton craftspeople.

▷ *Continue towards Morlaix; take the road which branches off to the left.*

Montagne St-Michel★

From the top of the rise (alt 380m/1 246 ft) where there is a small chapel which reaches an altitude of 391m/1 282ft at its summit, there is a **panorama** of the Monts d'Arrée and the Montagnes Noires. From the foot of the hill, a great peat bog called the Yeun Elez extends towards the east. In the winter mists, the place is so grim that Breton legend says it contains the **Youdig**, a gulf forming the entrance to Hell. Beyond it may be seen St-Michel reservoir which supplies the Monts d'Arrée thermal power station at Brennilis. Note the megalithic alignment on the rocky point to the right of the lake.

Fine views of the countryside, the mountains and Brennilis basin from the road passing by the Toussaines Signal Station *(Tuchenn Gador).*

Roc Trévezel

S. Sauvignier/MICHELIN

Roc Trévezel★★

This rocky escarpment, which juts up on the skyline (384m/1 260ft), is in a remarkably picturesque spot in a truly mountainous setting.

 *Take the path (30min on foot there and back) near a signpost. Go towards the left, cross a small heath, bearing to the right, and make for the most distant rocky point.*
From here the **panorama**★★ is immense. To the north, the Léon Plateau appears, bristling with spires; in clear weather you can see the Kreisker spire at St-Pol-de-Léon and to the east Lannion Bay; to the west, the end of the Brest roadstead; to the south, the St-Michel Mountain and, beyond it, the dark line of trees on the Montagnes Noires.

▶ *By the Roc-Tredudon pylon turn right towards Huelgoat and after 6km/4mi, bear right to Brennilis.*

Brennilis

This village has a 15C **church** topped by a delicate openwork belfry.

▶ *Return to the entrance to Brennilis and turn right, 90m/100yd further to the right, a signposted path leads to a covered alleyway partly hidden by a tumulus. Continue on the secondary road to Huelgoat.*

Réserve naturelle de la tourbière du Venec

Maison de la réserve, 2 place du calvaire, 29410 Le Cloître-St Thégonnec, ☎ 02 98 79 71 98. Nature walks and other activites are organised in July-Aug; the programme is published in June. Ramblers, wear boots and appropriate attire.
Created in 1993, covering 47 ha/175 acres, the park is mostly wetlands and peat fields covered with sphagnum moss.
Return to the edge of Brennilis and turn right. About 100 yards on, to the right, there is a marked path leading to a **covered alley**, a megalithic monument partly covered by a tumulus.

▶ *Continue on the secondary road to return to Huelgoat.*

AURAY★

POPULATION 10 911
MICHELIN LOCAL MAP 308 N9

This ancient town, built on the banks of the Loch or River Auray, is one of the eight Breton towns honoured with the title *Ville d'art et d'histoire*. Many visitors come to enjoy its attractive harbour, its old St-Goustan Quarter, and its proximity to the marvellous **Golfe du Morbihan**.

▶ **Orient Yourself:** On the banks of the River Auray, not far from Vannes
🔁 **Don't Miss:** The St-Goustan neighbourhood
Especially for Kids: Goélette St-Sauveur
🔁 **Also See:** Golfe du MORBIHAN

A Bit of History

The Battle of Auray (14C) – The town is famous in Breton history for the battle that was fought under its walls in 1364 ending the War of Succession. The troops of Charles of Blois, backed by Du Guesclin, held a bad position on a marshy plain north of Auray. Jean de Montfort, Charles's cousin, Olivier de Clisson, and the English, commanded by Chandos, were in a dominating position. Against Du Guesclin's advice, Charles attacked but was soundly defeated, before being slain by one of De Montfort's Breton soldiers.

Georges Cadoudal – A farmer's son from around Auray, he was 22 years old when the **Chouannerie**, a Breton Royalist revolt, broke out in 1793. He threw himself wholeheartedly into the cause. When the men of the Vendée were beaten, he carried on the struggle in Morbihan. He was captured, imprisoned at Brest but escaped, and took part in the action at Quiberon. He came away unhurt, submitted to Hoche in 1796 and reopened the campaign in 1799. Bonaparte offered the rebel a pardon and the rank of general, without success. The struggle ended only in 1804; Cadoudal had gone to Paris to try to kidnap Napoleon; he was arrested, sentenced to death and executed.

Sights

Église St-Gildas★
This 17C church, with its Renaissance porch, contains a very fine stone and marble **altarpiece**★ (1664) attributed to Olivier Martinet. Note the 18C woodwork in the side chapels and elegant organ loft (1761) by the Auray organ-builder Waltrin.

Chapelle du Saint-Esprit
Built by the Order of the Holy Spirit in the 13-14C, this rectangular chapel was part of a big hospital centre in Auray. It is currently under restoration.

Promenade du Loch★
There is a good **view** over the port, St-Goustan Quarter and Auray River, crossed by an attractive old stone bridge with cutwaters.
Moored in the loch is a schooner, the **Goélette St-Sauveur** (○ *July-Aug: 10.30am-12.30pm, 2.30-7.30pm, 9-11pm; off season: weekends, holidays and school holiday periods 10.30am-12.30pm, 2.30-7.30pm.* ➾ *No charge.* ☎ *02 97 56 63 38),* which has been painstakingly reconstructed from an old hull. It contains information on the way of life in St-Goustan port during the last century, including slide shows with

St-Goustan

G. Targat/MICHELIN

soundtracks. A display of tools belonging to maritime carpenters evokes the construction techniques which were once used.

Near the old bridge note the En-Bas Pavilion, an attractive 16C house.

Quartier St-Goustan★

This little port, particularly lively in the evening, still has some beautiful 15C houses and other pretty dwellings in place St-Sauveur (34) and up some of the steep, in places even stepped, little lanes leading off the square.

The quay to the left of the square is named after **Benjamin Franklin** (15). In 1776, during the War of Independence, the famous American diplomat and statesman sailed from Philadelphia to negotiate a treaty with France and landed at Auray instead of Nantes due to the unfavourable weather conditions. The house (no 8) where he stayed bears a plaque.

Mausolée de Cadoudal

Access by car from place du Loch along rue du Verger towards Le Reclus. The mausoleum, a small doomed circular building, stands opposite the general's family house.

Le Pays Alréen

Driving tour of 23km/14mi – 3hr. Leave Auray on avenue du Général-de-Gaulle.

Chartreuse d'Auray

🕓 10 April-8 May and 3 July-27 Aug: 2-5pm. 🕓 Closed Tue and the rest of the year except for school holiday periods. 👛 No charge. ☎ 02 97 24 27 02.

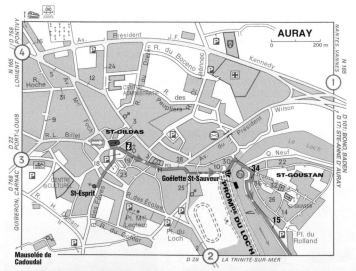

AURAY					
		Église-St-Goustan, R. de l'	14	Père-Éternel, R. du	25
		Franklin, Quai B.	15	Petit-Port, R. du	26
Abbé-Martin, R.	2	Gaulle, Av. Gén.-de	16	République, Pl. de la	28
Barré, R. J. M.	3	Joffre, Pl. du Mar.	18	St-Goustan, Pont de	30
Briand, R. Aristide	5	Lait, R. du	19	St-Julien, R.	31
Cadoudal, R. G.	9	Neuve, R.	22	St-René, R.	32
Château, R. du	10	Notre-Dame, Pl.	23	St-Sauveur, R.	36
Clemenceau, R. Georges	12	Penher, R. du	24	St-Sauveur, Pl.	34

On the battlefield where he defeated Charles of Blois, Jean de Montfort (who became Duke Jean IV) built a chapel and a collegiate church, which was later transformed into a Carthusian monastery (from 1482-1790). The funeral chapel built in the early 19C to hold the bones of exiles and Chouans who were shot on the Champ des Martyrs in 1795; in the centre, the black and white marble mausoleum bears 953 names.

Champ des Martyrs

The exiles and Chouans were shot in this enclosure during the Royalist insurrection (1793-1804). The Duchess of Angoulême had a chapel built in the style of a Greek temple on the site where they were executed and buried, before the remains were transferred to the Carthusian Monastery.

▶ *Follow the road to Ste-Anne-d'Auray.*

The road skirts the Kerzo Bog (on the right) where the Battle of Auray was fought on 29 September 1364.

▶ *After 500m/550yd bear left in the direction of St-Degan.*

St-Degan

Overlooking the deep valley of the Loch, the hamlet hosts the **écomusée** (open-air museum — ⏱ *Open July and Aug, daily 10am-7pm; Apr to June and Sept2-5.30pm; rest of the year, Sat-Sun 2-5.30pm.* ✆ *€ 26.* ☎ *02 97 57 66 00*), which contains restored thatched-roof buildings, and furniture of the Bas-Vannetais, thus rediscovering its 17C look.

Address Book

TOURIST OFFICE

Auray, 20 rue du Lait, 56400 – ☎ 02 97 24 09 75. www.auray-tourisme.com
🕐 Guided tours of the town: July-Aug, Tue-Fri 10am. € 5.

WHERE TO STAY

⊜⊜ **Hôtel Le Marin**, *1 pl. du Rolland,* ☎ *02 97 24 14 58, www.hotel-lemarin. com - 12 rooms* ⟡ 🖵 ⏱ *Closed last week of Oct and Jan.* This small, wooden hotel is quite pleasant, with its exposed beams and nautical bric-à-brac, right on the water in St-Goustan harbour. Breakfast € 6.

⊜⊜ **Hôtel du Loch**, *2 rue Guhur, La Forêt,* ☎ *02 97 56 48 33, www.hotel-du-loch.com - 30 rooms* ⟡ 🖵 ✕ This establishment has an unusual design, and is located in a quiet spot on the edge of the forest path. The rooms are spacious and comfortable, with some stylish furishings. In the restaurant, Regency decor and seafood. Breakfast € 7.50.

EATING OUT

⊜⊜ **Le Bout du quai**, *pl. du Rolland,* ☎ *02 97 50 87 17.* Next to the Hôtel du Marin, this grill offers fish and meat dishes cooked over an apple-wood fire and servied without sauce. The tuna steak is delicious! In the summer, enjoy the nice terrace on the water.

⊜⊜ **La Chebaudière**, *6 rue Abbé Joseph Martin,* ☎ *02 97 24 09 84.* ⏱ *Closed Sun evening, Tue evening and Wed.* Contemporary decor and paintings on display are the right setting for the modern cuisine that relies on seasonal availabilty of products.

⊜⊜⊜ **La Table des marées,** *16 rue du Jeu de Paume,* ☎ *02 97 56 63 60, www.latabledesmarees.com.* ⏱ *Closed Sun evening and Mon.* In this restaurant customers benefit from the chef's passion for his work. The dining room is comfortable and tasteful, the food light and fragrant. The menu depends on the day's catch and the chef's inspiration.

▶ *Go to Brech and turn right.*

Ste-Anne-d'Auray★

Ste-Anne is the outstanding Breton place of pilgrimage. The first *pardon* takes place on 7 March; then, from Easter until Rosary (the first Sunday in October); there are parish pilgrimages (especially Wednesdays and Sundays from the end of April to the end of September). The *pardon* of St Anne on 26 July is the most frequented, together with the those on 15 August and on the first Sunday in October.

In 1623 St Anne appeared to a ploughman, Yves Nicolazic, and asked him to rebuild a chapel which had been previously dedicated to her in one of his fields. On 7 March 1625, Yves unearthed, at the spot she had indicated, an old statue of St Anne. A church was built there the same year.

Basilique

Built in Renaissance style during the late 19C, the basilica took the place of the 17C chapel.

Trésor★

&🕐 *July-Aug: 10am-noon, 2.30-6pm; off season: 10.30-noon, 3-6pm except Mon.* ⊙ *€2.50.* ☎ *02 97 57 68 80.*

Located in the cloister, it contains objects devoted to St Anne, notably a relic of St Anne presented by Anne of Austria in thanks for the birth of Louis XIV. There are also gold and silver plates and the cloak of the old statue, and, in a glass case in the centre, ornaments given by Anne of Austria. A Breton art gallery contains 15C-19C statues.

Scala Sancta

Old doorway from the square with a double staircase which pilgrims climb on their knees.

Fontaine miraculeuse

The fountain consists of a basin and a column adorned with smaller basins and surmounted by a statue of St Anne.

Monument aux morts

The war memorial was raised by public subscription all over Brittany to the 250 000 Breton soldiers and sailors who died in the First World War. It has become the memorial to all dead during the wars which have occurred in the 20C.

Not far away, on the other side of the road, a Franco-Belgian cemetery contains the graves of 1 338 soldiers.

Historial de Sainte Anne

&🕐 *Open daily 8am-7pm.* ⊙ *20€.* ☎ *02 97 57 64 05.*

This retrospective exhibit presents the life of Yves Nicolazic and the origins of the annual pilgrimage.

Musée du Costume breton

To the right of the war memorial. 🕐 *Open Mar to Oct, daily, 10am-noon and 2-6pm.* 🕐 *Closed rest of the year.* ⊙ *10€.* ☎ *02 97 57 68 80.*

This museum displays a fine collection of old dolls in Breton costume and two small boats offered as ex-votos.

Maison de Nicolazic

🕐 *Open Easter to Oct, daily, 9am-7pm.* ⊙ *No charge.* ☎ *02 97 57 68 80.*

It was in this house that St Anne appeared to the pious peasant. Inside are a chapel and some 17C furniture.

Monument du comte de Chambord
Towards Brech, on the left about 500m/1 500ft from the town. This monument was erected in 1891. Each year, for St Michael's day, followers and friends made the pilgrimage to Ste-Anne. Representations of Bayard, Du Guesclin, St Geneviève and St Jeanne d'Arc frame the statue of Charles X's grandson.

▶ *Follow D 17 heading S towards Pluneret.*

Pluneret
In the cemetery, alongside the central alley, on the right, are the tombs of Sophie Rostopchine, the Countess de Ségur, the well-known author of children's books and of her son, Mgr Louis-Gaston de Ségur.

▶ *Proceed along D 101 towards Bono and after 2km/1mi turn left for Ste-Avoye.*

Ste-Avoye
Among picturesque cottages, near a fountain, stands a pretty Renaissance chapel with a fine keel-shaped **roof**★. The polychrome decoration of the carved wood **roodscreen**★ is remarkable: on the nave side, it depicts the Apostles; on the chancel side, the Virtues on the left by St Fiacre and St Lawrence; on the right by St Yves between the rich man and the poor man.

▶ *Turn back in the direction of Ste-Anne-d'Auray and bear left to Auray.*

LA BAULE ☼☼☼

POPULATION 15 831
MICHELIN LOCAL MAP 316 B4 – LOIRE ATLANTIQUE (44)

La Baule's long beach of fine sand, which boasts the title of "Europe's most beautiful beach," stretches along south Brittany. Water sports, tennis, casino and golf make this one of the most popular seaside resorts on the Atlantic coast.

Morand-Grahame/HOA-QUI

Sea, sand, sun and holiday-makers at La Baule

Address Book

TOURIST OFFICES

La Baule, Place de la Victoire, ☎ 02 40 24 34 44, www.labaule.fr.

WHERE TO STAY

Prices given are for double occupancy in high season. Prices are 20-30% lower off-season.

LA BAULE

⊜⊜ **Hôtel St-Pierre**, *124 av. de Lattre de Tassigny,* ☎ *02 40 24 05 41, www. hotel-saint-pierre.com - 19 rooms* ⎘ 📺 This hotel is typical of La Baule, nicely located between the beach and the casino. Modern rooms with a blue decor, starting at € 58. Breakfast € 7.50.

⊜⊜ **Hôtel Ty Gwenn**, *25 av. de la Grande Dune,* ☎ *02 40 60 37 07, www.hotel-tygwenn.fr - 17 rooms* ⎘ 🕐 *Closed 2 Nov-18 Feb except 16-31 Dec.* Typical 1900s decor in the public areas. Modest rooms with (€ 70 €) or without (€ 51) bath and balcony. Breakfast € 7.

⊜⊜⊜ 😊 **Hôtel St-Christophe**, *Place Notre-Dame,* ☎ *02 40 62 40 00, www. st-christophe.com - 45 rooms* ⎘ 📺 ✕ Comfortable rooms in 4 1990-style villas. Family unit for 4 people, € 206. Elegant restaurant with terrace-garden for classic cuisine, including but not limited to seafood. Half-board is obligatory in July-Aug, € 170-247/2 people.

⊜⊜⊜ **Hôtel Marini**, *22 av. Georges Clemenceau,* ☎ *02 40 60 23 29, www. hotel-marini.com - 33 rooms* ⎘ 📺 ✕ 🛏 This traditional hotel, near the station, has light, well-kept rooms. A small indoor pool and restaurant for the boarders. Half-board starts at € 59/person. Breakfast € 8. Parking € 6.

⊜⊜⊜⊜ **Castel Marie-Louise**, *1 av. Andrieu,* ☎ *02 40 11 48 38, www.castel-marielouise. com - 31 rooms* A classic Belle Époque palace, tasteful rooms with views over the ocean or the pines. The restaurant (🕐 *closed at lunch 15 Sep-15 May except Sun*) serves refined cuisine in a decor reminiscent of an English cottage.

PORNICHET

⊜⊜ **Le Normandy**, *120 av. de Mazy,* ☎ *02 40 61 03 08, www.normandy hotel.fr - 32 rooms* ⎘ 📺 ✕ The hotel is under renovation, so there are varying degrees of comfort. On the 3rd floor, the rooms without en suite amenities are € 35. Breakfast € 6.50.

⊜⊜⊜ 😊 **Villa Flornoy**, *7 av. Flornoy,* ☎ *02 40 11 60 00, www.villa-flornoy.com - 30 rooms* ⎘ 📺 ✕ A Belle Époque building with elegant rooms covered in toile de Jouy and overlooking a garden. Breakfast € 8, restaurant for hotel guests, half-board € 75/person.

EATING OUT

LA BAULE

⊜ **Beach Bar**, *on the beach, at the end of av. du Gén.-de-Gaulle,* ☎ *02 40 60 79 66.* Crepes and other assorted snack plates for € 10-12.

⊜⊜ 😊 **La Villa**, *18 av. du Gén.-de-Gaulle,* ☎ *02 40 23 06 00.* The unusual decor is reminiscent of the East and exotic travel, and there are many cosy corners for diners. Simple dishes, oysters and a good wine list. Lunch menu € 13.20.

⊜⊜ **La Croisette**, *31 Place du Mar. Leclerc,* ☎ *02 40 60 73 00.* Palm trees and a Medeterranean feel on the terrace, where you can enjoy pasta, pizza and carpaccios.

PORNICHET

⊜ **La Cabane**, *on the beach, facing the Régent hotel,* ☎ *02 40 15 20 10.* 🕐 *Open at noon all year, except Mon-Wed and Sun off season.* Mussels and crepes, your feet in the sand.

⊜⊜ 😊 **Le Danicheff**, *45 av. du Gén.-de-Gaulle,* ☎ *02 40 61 07 32.* 🕐 *Closed Sun evening Nov and Feb school holidays.* Traditional setting and cuisine, very goof value for money and good wines to enjoy in the restaurant or take away.

LE POULIGUEN

⊜ **Le Market**, *5 Place des Halles,* ☎ *02 40 62 21 02.* 🕐 *Closed Jan and 15-30 Nov.* Across from the market, inventive cuisine.

⊜⊜ **La Voile d'Or**, *14 av. de la Plage,* ☎ *02 40 31 31 68.* 🕐 *Closed Tue and Wed Oct to Mar.* Well known for its seafood and the great view.

ON THE TOWN IN LA BAULE

La Canne à Sucre, *136 av. du Gén.-de-Gaulle, ☎ 02 40 24 00 94*. Latino, zouk, salsa music and ambience.

Le Bax, *12 av. Pavic, ☎ 02 40 60 90 00*. An intimate atmosphere to start or end the evening. Popular with young professionals.

Bar M, *Place du Marché, ☎ 02 40 17 09 45*. Across from the market, lively atmosphere with oysters and tapas at noon and music in the evenings.

Casino, *24 espl. Lucien Barrière, ☎ 02 40 11 48 28*. Slot machines, games, restaurants

WATER SPORTS

Latitude, *Across from the Relais Thalasso, La Baule, 26 bd de l'Océan, ☎ 02 40 60 57 87, www.latitude-cat.com* Courses offered year round (€ 130-170); April-Sep: catamarans (€ 20-40/hr), kayaks (€ 12-16/hr) and windsurfers (€ 15/hr) for rent.

Diving - Alain 3 P, *port de Plaisance de Pornichet, ☎ 02 40 11 62 00, www.alain3p.com* Give diving a try (€ 20 without equipment), € 20 to 30 for equipment.

Seawater spa Thalgo, *av. Marie-Louise, La Baule, ☎ 02 40 11 99 99, www.*

thalasso-barriere.com ⏰ *Closed Jan.* Inside the Hôtel Royal, a wide range of treatments and packages (energizing, anti-stress, quit smoking, etc.). It is not necessary to be a guest at the hotel

Relais Thalasso La Baule, *28 bd de l'Océan, ☎ 02 40 11 33 11, www.relaisthalasso.com*. Various packages in this spa, including a weekend rate with 4 treatments and half-board in partner hotels (€ 175-209/person). "Espace underwater jets open to all, € 16-19...

SHOPPING

Markets: La Baule, covered market daily except Mon, Oct-Mar. Le Pouliguen, Tue, Fri and Sun. Pornichet, Wed and Sat morning. For a good choice of seafood, stop at the Halle aux poissons, Tue-Sun morning off season, daily mid-June to mid-Sep.

Sweet treats - Manuel, *2 av. du Gén.-de-Gaulle, La Baule, ☎ 02 40 60 20 66*. The most famous ice cream shop in town also sells chocolates and sweets. **Mignon**, *promenade du Port, Le Pouliguen, ☎ 02 40 42 35 24*. "Les Niniches", local lollypops, are always a pleasure.

▶ **Orient Yourself:** La Baule is 74km/45mi west of Nantes and 10km/6mi east of Le Croisic

⟳ **Also See:** Presqu'île de GUÉRANDE

Seafront★

Sheltered from the winds, this elegant promenade lined with modern buildings stretches for about 7km/4mi between Pornichet and Le Pouliguen, Unfortunately, the turn-of-the-century villas which were once the heart of the resort, have since fallen prey to developers.

La Baule-les-pins⌂⌂

La Baule is extended eastwards by this resort, which was built in 1930, in an area of pine forests. The attractive Allée Cavalière leads to the Escoublac Forest.

Pornichet⌂

Originally a salt-marsh workers' village, Pornichet became a fashionable seaside resort in 1860, popular with Parisian publishers. The town is composed of two distinct districts: Old Pornichet, to the southeast, which is busy all the year round, and Pornichet-les-Pins to the northwest, whose large villas surrounded by greenery are livelier in the summer. Also in the summer, horse races are held in the Côte d'Amour's racecourse. And finally the **boulevard des Océanides** runs along the beach and leads to the pleasure boat harbour which can take over 1 000 boats.

Le Pouliguen⚜

Separated from La Baule by a channel *(étier)*, this village with its narrow streets became a fashionable resort in 1854, made popular by men of letters such as Louis Veuillot and Jules Sandeau. A sheltered beach and a pleasant 6ha/15 acre wood make Le Pouliguen a very pleasant place to stop.

Chapelle Ste-Anne-et-St-Julien

Place Mgr-Freppel. ☎ *02 40 42 18 94.* 🕐 *July to mid-Sep, guided tour on Wed, 10.30am-noon.*

Standing near a Calvary, this Gothic chapel has a 16C **statue of St Anne** and a stained-glass window representing St Julian (in the chancel). At the west end, on either side of the porch are two interesting **bas-relief sculptures** depicting the Coronation of the Virgin and the Adoration of the Magi.

La Côte Sauvage★

This stretch of coast starts from the Pointe de Penchâteau. Skirted by a road and footpaths, the coastline alternates rocky parts with great sandy bays and has numerous caves which are accessible only at low tide, in particular the cave of the Korrigans, little elves of Breton legends. Geographical Brittany begins here.

BÉCHEREL

POPULATION 599
MICHELIN LOCAL MAP 309 K5 - ILLE-ET-VILAINE (35)

Bécherel, perched on a hill (alt 176m/577ft), was once a seigneurial stronghold; only a few ruins and old granite houses still stand. In former times, flax was cultivated and the purest linen thread was produced here. Now the town is known for its book market, held on the first Sunday of the month and which attracts 40 000 visitors annually. Bécherel is also among the 19 towns honoured for their typical Breton character. From Thabor Gardens the view extends as far as Dol, Dinan and Combourg.

Excursions

Château de Caradeuc

1km/0.6mi west. ♿🕐 *Park only. July-Aug daily noon-6pm; rest of the year, Sat-Sun 2-6pm.* ⊜ *€ 5 (children under 15 no charge)* ☎ *02 99 66 81 10.*

This château, the former home of a famous attorney-general, Louis-René, Marquis de Caradeuc de la Chalotais (1701-85), has a very fine **park★** dotted with statues and other monuments inspired by history and mythology. It has been nicknamed the Versailles of Brittany.

Château de Hac

8km/4mi north on D 68, D 26 and D 39. 🕐 *Aug-Sep: Sun-Thu, 1-6pm.*

This large manor house, a 14C seigneurial residence, has survived without any major alterations. The large rooms open to visitors house Gothic and Renaissance furniture; in particular an interesting collection of chests, for the most part Breton.

Église des Iffs★

7km/3.5mi southwest on D 27. Inside are nine lovely 16C **stained-glass windows★** inspired by the Dutch and Italian Schools (16C): scenes of the Passion (in the chancel),

Christ's childhood (in the north chapel), the Story of Susannah and the Two Elders (in the south chapel).

Château de Montmuran★
800m/875yd north of Les Iffs. ☎ *02 99 45 88 88.* 🕐 *June-Sep: Sun-Fri, 2-6pm.* 📷€ *4/3.*
A drawbridge across the moat leads to the narrow gateway framed by two massive round machicolated towers. Behind the entrance fort an external staircase goes to the chapel where Du Guesclin was knighted in 1354 after a skirmish with the English. He later married, as his second wife, Jeanne de Laval. From the top of the castle towers, you can admire the vast panorama extending as far as Hédé and Dinan

Tinténiac
8km/5mi east of Bécherel on D 20. The trades and tools museum, **Musée de l'Outil et des Métiers** (🕐 *June-Sep: Tue-Sat 10am-noon, 3-6pm; Sun 3-6pm.* 📷 *€ 2.* ☎ *02 99 23 09 30),* is located in a wood building near the canal. Old trades are brought back to life.

Hédé
5km/3mi south of Tinténiac in the tiny village of La Madeleine. After the bridge over the canal, bear left to the car park by the lock keeper's house. There are eleven locks, the **Onze Écluses,** three before and eight after the bridge, to negotiate a drop of 27m/89ft on the Ille-et-Rance Canal. The towpath offers a pleasant walk in a pretty setting.

BELLE-ÎLE★★★

POPULATION 4 489
MICHELIN LOCAL MAP 308 L10/11 - MORBIHAN (56)

This, the largest of the Breton islands, is a schist plateau measuring about 84km_/32sq mi; 17km/11mi long and 5-10km/3-6mi wide. Its name alone is enticing. Yet its beauty surpasses expectations. Valleys cut deeply into the high rocks, forming beaches or harbours, wheat fields alternate with patches of gorse, and whitewashed houses stand in lush fields.

A Bit of History

Fouquet, Marquis of Belle-Ile – Superintendent Fouquet bought Belle-Île in 1658, completed the fortifications and added 50 cannons. His immense wealth supported his own fleet and its flagship, the *Grand Écureuil*. But his daring behaviour, swindles and slights practised on Louis XIV, were his undoing. The final act was played out at Nantes, where the Court was visiting in 1661. D'Artagnan and the Musketeers seized Fouquet as he came out of the castle and put him in a coach which took him to Vincennes.

A fortified rock - Being the sole island between the Channel and the Mediterranean with fresh water in abundance, Belle-Île was attacked many times by British and Dutch fleets. The British captured the island twice – in 1572 and 1761 – and occupied it until the Treaty of Paris (1763) returned it to the Frenrooms The island has conserved its defensive system: in addition to Le Palais citadel, fortified by the military architect Vauban, there are several 18C and 19C isolated outworks (redoubts) around the coast.

Acadians and Bretons – In 1766, 78 Acadian families came to live on the island; they brought with them the potato many years before Parmentier introduced it to France. These Acadians were descendants of the French who had lived in Canada since the beginning of the 17C and had refused to submit to the English who had held Nova Scotia from the time of the Treaty of Utrecht, 1713. The Acadian families were moved to New England and then, after the Treaty of Paris, were moved by Louis XV to Belle-Île.

Le Palais *Allow 2hr*

The island's capital and main town is where most of the facilities are to be found. Inhabitants simply call it "Palais".

Citadelle Vauban★

Cross the mobile footbridge over the lock, go through Bourg gate and follow the path along the **huge moat,** *cut from the rock itself, as far as Donjon gate. A signposted tour takes visitors past all the sights of the citadel.* ○ *Open July and Aug, daily, 9am-7pm; Apr to June, Sep and Oct, 9.30am-6pm; Nov to Mar, 9.30am-noon and 2-5pm.* ○ *Closed public holidays;* €6.10. ☎ 02 97 31 84 17.

Built in 1549, the citadel was enlarged by the Duke Gondi de Retz and Fouquet. Its double ramparts, powerful corner bastions and outward appearance show the influence of Vauban, who resided here in 1683, 1687 and 1689. Besieged at the end of the Seven Years War, it fell into the hands of the English, who occupied it until the signing of the Treaty of Paris (1763). It was subsequently abandoned by the army and sold in 1960.

The most remarkable buildings include: the **historical museum**, set up in the Louis-Philippe blockhouses featuring "maple leaf" vaulting and displaying a host of documents on the history of Belle-Île and its illustrious visitors (Arletty, Claude Monet, Sarah Bernhardt); the **round powder magazine** and its strange acoustics; the large **arsenal** with superb oak timbering; the Louis XIII **storerooms**; the **blockhouse** which contains the map room; finally the military prison and the cells. The **Bastion**

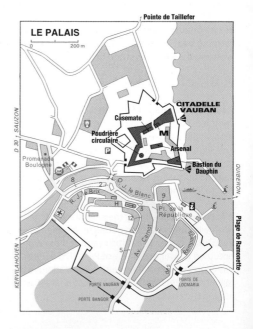

BELLE-ÎLE LE PALAIS	
Citadelle, R. de la	2
Église, R. de l'	3
Ferry, Av. Jules	5
Gambetta, Quai	8
Simon, R. J.	9
Verdun, R. de	12

de la Mer and the **Bastion du Dauphin** afford remarkable **views**★ of Le Palais, the north coast and its harbour, the Île de Houat and the Île d'Hœdic.

Driving Tours

1 La Côte Sauvage★★★

Round tour of 49km/30mi – about 3hr 30min

▷ *Leave Le Palais on Quai Gambetta and Promenade Boulogne and turn right towards the citadel. Near the coast, bear left and then right.*

Pointe de Taillefer
Near the signal station there is a fine **view** over Le Palais roadstead, the Pointe de Kerdonis, Hœdic and Houat Islands and the Presqu'île de Quiberon.

▷ *Turn round and make for Sauzon.*

Nearby is **Port-Fouque** with a pretty, sheltered beach.

Sauzon★
This small port with its busy marina lies in a pretty **setting**★ on the east bank of the River Sauzon's estuary. ⚐ A pleasant excursion *(1hr 30min on foot there and back)* starting from the port, takes you round the **Pointe du Cardinal** and affords views over the approach to the port, the Pointe de Taillefer, the Presqu'île de Quiberon and the Pointe des Poulains

Pointe des Poulains★★
30min on foot there and back. ⚐ From the car park, on the left is Fort Sarah Bernhardt, which is near the estate where the actress spent her summers. Make your way down the slip to the sandy isthmus which connects the island with the Pointe des Poulains on which stands a lighthouse and which is completely cut off at spring tide. From the point there is a vast **panorama**★.

Stêr-Vraz and Stêr-Ouen★
These *abers* cutting deeply into the coastline are at the foot of the **bird sanctuary** on the Pointe du Vieux-Château.
On Kerlédan Moor stand the menhirs **Jean and Jeanne,** said to be young fiancés punished because they wanted to meet before their wedding day.

Port-Donnant★★
30min on foot there and back; 🅿 *car park.* The setting is superb: a fine sandy beach and a rolling sea enclosed between high cliffs. ⚠ *Bathing is dangerous.*

Grand Phare
🕓 *Open July to mid-Sep, daily, 10.30am-noon and 2-5.30pm.*
The lighthouse opened near Goulphar in 1836 is 46m/150ft high and has a beam which carries 44.5km/26mi. From the balcony there is a fine **view**★★ of Belle-Île, the neighbouring islands and the coast as far as the Presqu'île de Rhuys.

Port-Goulphar★
This is one of the most charming sites on the island. After Goulphar manor house take a steep road downhill *(15min on foot there and back)* to the port, a long, narrow channel at the foot of picturesque cliffs. A group of islets marks its entrance. From the cliff is the best viewa of this curious mass of rocks.

Address Book

ARRIVAL AND DEPARTURE

The **SMN** (Société morbihannaise de navigation), ☎ *0820 056 000 (0,12 €/mn), www.smn-navigation.fr*, links **Quiberon** and **Le Palais** (passengers and vehicles), year round. 45min trip, one way aprox. € 15, round trip aprox € 25 (vehicles, one way, from € 55). In summer, speed boats (20min) for passengers to Locmaria. Mid-June through August, departures from **Lorient,** 60min, round trip € 27.

GETTING AROUND

Take the bus! *quai Bonnelle,* ☎ *02 97 31 32 32,* 4 lines run between Sauzon, Bangor and Locmaria via beaches and main sights. About 7 round trips a day in summer. 1 Ticket € 2.50/1,60.

Locatourisle, is a car rental agency at the landing stand in le Palais, ☎ *02 97 31 83 56, www.locatourisle. com.* Amusing small cars starting from € 62/day.

Roue Libre, *6 quai J. Le Blanc, Le Palais,* ☎ *02 97 31 30 45.* This agency rents off-road bikes, tandems and child trailers.

TOURIST OFFICE

Office du tourisme du Palais, quai Bonnelle, Le Palais, ☎ 02 97 31 81 93, www.belle-ile.com

WHERE TO STAY

Prices correspond to double occupancy in season. Off-season, rooms are 20-40% less expensive

LE PALAIS

⊖⊜ **Hôtel Vauban**, *1 rue des Remparts,* ☎ *02 97 31 45 42, www. hotelvauban.com - 16 rooms* 🛏 TV ✕ Calm, comfotable rooms, most facing the ocean. Seafood specialities in the restaurant. Breakfast € 8.

⊖⊜ **Hôtel de Bretagne**, *quai de l'Acadie,* ☎ *02 97 31 80 14, www.hotel-de-bretagne.fr - 33 rooms* 🛏 TV ✕ Facing the landing stage, this hotel in two buildings has comfortable rooms and a restaurant with a panormaic terrace, serving local specialities. Breakfast € 7.

EATING OUT

SAUZON

⊖⊜⊜ **Le Contre-Quai**, *rue St-Nicolas,* ☎ *02 97 31 60 60.* Lovely dishes are served here, with exquisite flavouring. Prices are a bit steep, but the delightful exeperience is worth it. Try the Belle-Île rack of lamb and the clams fricassee with ginger which could only be better if there were more of them. Finish up with a rice pudding with pineapple, served with a spicy rum and pepper sauce!

⊖⊜⊜ **Roz Avel,** *rue du lieutenant Riou,* ☎ *02 97 31 61 48.* This is a very classy restaurant serving fine cuisine: it may be worth a trip to Belle-Île just to take the "voyage autour de l'huître", an extraordinary selection of oysters prepared in different ways. Or try langoustes, lobster or lamb.

LOCMARIA

⊖⊜ **Auberge Chouk'azé**, *chemin du Petit Houx,* ☎ *02 97 31 79 69.* Chouk'azé, means something like "sit down and let's visit…" More than a restaurant, a concept! A welcoming, old-fashioned sort of place, with delicious food, and themed evenings every two weeks. Enjoy honey-mustard roast mackerel, roast prawns with pleuric butter or stuffed sardines…

ON THE TOWN

Ty Pen'Art Bar, *18 quai Gambetta,* ☎ *02 97 31 45 45, www.typenartbar. com* 🕒 *Tue-Sat noon-2am, Sun-Mon 6pm-2am.* A new club that showcases all kinds of groups (pop, rock, world music, jazz, etc.) as well as photographs and other art on its walls. Nice rum drinks, tapas and a variety of sandwhiches.

SHOPPING

Crafts - Bateaux-Moules, *Jean Guillaume, Borlagadec, Bangor,* ☎ *02 97 31 42 44.* A beautiful idea, realised with technical prowess: perfect copies of traditional ships made from mussel shells. But there's nothing camp about them! The artist works to order and none of his pieces sells for less than € 500. Real masterpeices.

A landscape to inspire legends: Aiguilles de Port-Coton

Aiguilles de Port-Coton★★

Port-Coton is called so because the sea there seems to boil and builds up a great mass of foam like cotton wool. At the end of the road loom the **Aiguilles** (Needles).

Bangor

The most primitive sites on the island are found in this village. It takes its name from the Bangor Abbey (Northern Ireland), which was one of the most well-known in Western Christianity, and from which came the first Celtic monks to settle on the island in the 6C.

In a rocky setting lies **Port-Kérel,** the most popular beach on the island.

▶ *Return to Le Palais.*

② **Pointe de Kerdonis★** *Round tour of 33km/20mi – about 2hr*

▶ *Leave Le Palais by avenue Carnot and rue Villaumez on the left.*

The first part of this tour is devoted to seeing different beaches. Backing onto the point of the same name is the **Plage de Ramonette**; this is Le Palais' bearooms

▶ *At the entrance to Port-Salio, turn left, then 250m/274yd further, turn left again to reach **La Belle Fontaine**.*

This reservoir was created under Vauban's orders, to supply fresh water to high-ranking ships.

▶ *Turn back and bear left.*

The **Plage de Bordardoué** is a fine sheltered, sandy bearooms

▶ *Turn round and bear left twice.*

The road descends towards **Port-Yorc'h** closed in by the Pointe du Bugul to the right and the Pointe du Gros Rocher to the left, which is extended by an islet on which stands an old fort. The road from Port-Yorck to the Pointe de Kerdonis commands superb **views**★★ over Houat and Le Palais roadstead.

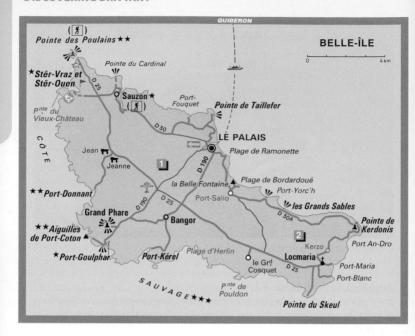

Les Grands Sables

This, the largest beach on Belle-Île, has traces of fortifications erected in 1747, as in the 17C and 18C British and Dutch forces made several attempts to land on the island.

Pointe de Kerdonis

At the southern tip of the island stands a lighthouse which commands the sea lane between Hœdic and Belle-Île. Nearby is **Port-An-Dro,** a sandy beach off a small valley where the English forces landed in 1761.

Locmaria

The village is reputed among the islanders as a place where sorcery occurs. A downhill road to the right of the church leads to **Port-Maria,** a deep cleft in the rocks which offers a fine sandy beach at low tide. Slightly farther south, the cliffs of Arzic Point overlook the small cove of **Port-Blanc.**

Pointe du Skeul

Unsurfaced road after Skeul hamlet. This headland is a semicircle of jagged rocks in a wild setting.

▶ *Return to the main road and Le Pailais, but make a slight detour to see the Acadian village, Grand-Cosquet.*

BELLE-ISLE-EN-TERRE

POPULATION 1 067
MICHELIN LOCAL MAP 309 B3 - CÔTES D'ARMOR (22)

As this old township's name indicates, it is perfect example of inland Brittany's beauty, a picturesque region of forests, hills and ravines, favorable for walking, fishing, canoeing or kayaking.

Excursions

Menez-Bré★
9km/5.5mi northeast. Take D 116, the Guingamp road. 2.5km/1.5mi after Louargat, turn left onto the steep uphill road.
The Menez-Bré, a lonely hill with an altitude of 302m/991ft, and its Chapelle de St-Hervé at the summit commands a wide **panorama**★ over the Trégorrois Plateau: to the north, the plateau slopes gently towards the sea, to the south over the maze of hills and valleys of Cornouaille; and to the southwest towards the Monts d'Arrée.

Loc-Envel
4km/2.5mi south. Leave on the Callac road, D 33, and turn right fairly soon onto a winding and picturesque road.
The Flamboyant Gothic style **church** of Loc-Envel rises from the top of a mound and dominates the village. To the left of the belfry-porch, note three small semicircular openings through which the lepers followed the services. Particularly striking features, on entering, are the Flamboyant **rood screen**★ and the rich decoration of the wood-panelled **vaulting**★: carved purlins and tie-beams, polychrome hammerbeams with the Evangelists and the two hanging keystones.

S. Sauvigrier/MICHELIN

Hanging keystone in Loc-Envel church

Gurunhuel
9km/5.5mi southeast on D 22.
Near the 16C church stands a Calvary of the same period. From the base rise three columns: the central one bears a Crucifixion with Christ between the Virgin Mary and St John on one side and a Virgin of Pity on the other. The other two crosses show the robbers; their souls are being received by an angel in the case of the good robber, and a demon in the case of the bad robber.

BÉNODET ☖ ☖

POPULATION 2 436
MICHELIN LOCAL MAP 308 G7 -FINISTÈRE (29)

This charming seaside resort lies in a pretty, verdant setting at the mouth of the Odet estuary. Bénodet offers all the summer pleasures: a small harbour, fine beaches of pale sand, open-air sports, sailing, a casino, and a new film festival. **Éric Tabarly** (1931-98), the famous yachtsman who won many solo races including the transatlantic and transpacific and was lost at sea off the coast of Ireland, had a house on the banks of the Odet.

 ⓒ **Also See:** QUIMPER

The Odet

View over the Odet
Access by avenue de Kercréven. This viewpoint affords a fine view of the river and the pleasure boat harbour.

Pont de Cornouaille
1km/0.6mi northwest on D 44.
This elegant bridge is 610m/2 001ft long, and affords a good **view**★ of the harbour, of Ste-Marine, the River Odet and its estuary.

Excursions

From Bénodet to Concarneau on the coast road
40km/25mi – about 3hr. Leave Bénodet east by D 44 towards Fouesnant and after 2km/1mi turn right.

Le Letty
A large lake sheltered by a dune provides the perfect place for sailing schools.

▶ *Return to the road to Fouesnant.*

Beach at Bénodet

Le Perguet

An unusual stone staircase on the roof of the Chapelle of Ste-Brigitte leads to the pierced bell tower.

▷ *After 2.5km/1mi, a fork to the right goes to the Pointe de Mousterlin (see FOUESNANT). Turn back; drive 2km/1mi then bear right and right again 4.5km/2.75mi further on.*

Beg-Meil and Fouesnant ⚓

The road runs along Kerleven Beach, a long beach of fine sand, in the curve of La Forêt Bay, then after a steep descent (15% or 1:7), it skirts St-Laurent Cove and crosses St-Jean Bay to Concarneau. Beautiful **views**★ especially at high tide.

Address Book

TOURIST OFFICE

Bénodet, 29 av. de la Mer, ☎ 02 98 57 00 14, www.benodet.fr

WHERE TO STAY, EATING OUT

⊜⊜ **Bains de mer,** *11 rue Kerguelen,* ☎ *02 98 57 03 41, www.lesbainsdemer. com - 50 rooms* 🍴 ▤ 📺 ✕ This is a welcoming hotel with modestly decorated rooms. The restaurant is friendly, contemporary and serves traditional dishes. Parking. Breakfast € 7.

⊜⊜⊜ **Grand hôtel Abbatiale,** *4 av. de l'Odet,* ☎ *02 98 66 21 66, www.hotel abbatiale.com - 50 rooms* 🍴 📺 ✕ In this large building in the centre of the port, the practical rooms, have a view of the ocean or the garden. In the restaurant, quality cuisine based on seafood (menus at € 20, 26 and 36). You may want to try the langoustines (prawns) or the savoury seafood crepe, followed by mackerel filets and farmer's cheese with fresh herbs. Delicious! Parking. Breakfast € 9.50.

⊜⊜⊜⊜ **Ker Moor,** *corniche de la Plage,* ☎ *02 98 57 04 48, kermoor. hotel@wanadoo.fr - 69 rooms* 🍴 📺 ✕ Surrounded by trees, this impressive building dates from the 1930s. Inside, modern rooms and and apartments for longer stays. In the dining rooms, the chairs are 1960s style, vinyl-covered, and the walls are hung with paintings by Pierre de Belay. Tasty seafood on the menu. Parking. Breakfast € 9.

ON THE TOWN

L'Alhambra, *corniche de l'Estuaire,* ☎ *02 98 57 03 41. June-Sept: daily 11am-1am.* Attractive and chic, come here at any time of day for oysters, during meal times for seafood dishes, or at the end of the evening for a drink on the terrace overlooking the River Odet.

RECREATION

Vedettes de l'Odet, ☎ *0 825 800 801, www.vedettes-odet.com* is a company offering several **cruises**. May-Sep, you can go on the river to Rosulien Manor (45min, € 12), Kérogan Bay (2hr, € 22 €) or Quimper (2hr15min, € 22). Departure from the old port, near the church. Free parking Or you can sail to the **Glénan Islands,** with a stopover on l'île de St-Nicolas (€ 26); take a guided tour through the islands (€ 34) or board the Capitaine Némo, a catamaran equipped for underwater viewing (€ 39.50).

SHOPPING

If you like beer and breweries, don't miss the brasserie Tri Martolod, ZA de Keranguyon, ☎ *02 98 66 20 22.* 🕐 *Open to visitors Fri 11am-noon, shop open in the summer Mon-Fri, 9am-noon and 1.30-6pm, Sat 9am-noon and 3-7pm.*

BLAIN

POPULATION 7 434
MICHELIN LOCAL MAP 316 F3 - LOIRE-ATLANTIQUE (44)

An old Roman crossroads, Blain plays an important commercial role between Nantes, Redon and the Anjou. The Nantes-Brest Canal separates the town from its castle (whose first construction dates from 1104).

Musée de la Fève et de la Crèche

Located in the old presidial of the dukes of Rohan, this museum revives the past of the Blain area.

Kids Two rooms are devoted to popular Christmas traditions: one room displays thousands of bean kings (lucky trinkets hidden in Twelfth Night cakes), the other about 100 Nativity cribs from all over the world.

Château

This fortress originally belonged to Olivier de Clisson, and later became Rohan family property. Despite the fact that in 1628 Richelieu razed the ramparts, impressive ruins still stand, including the 14C **Tour du Pont-Levis** topped by a pepper-pot roof and the 15C **Logis du Roi** with its pinnacled Renaissance dormer-windows. Since 1995, the château has housed the Centre de la Fresque (Workshop for the painting technique *a fresco*).

Driving Tour of the Forêt du Gâvre★

Round tour of 13km/8mi northwest on D 15, the road to Guéméné-Penfao.
The road crosses the stands of oak interspersed with beeches and pines, which cover 4 400ha/10 900 acres, to reach the Belle Étoile crossroads, the meeting point of 10 converging avenues.

▷ *Turn right towards Le Gâvre and at La Maillardais turn left.*

Chapelle de la Magdeleine

This modest 12C chapel has a charming 15C polychrome Virgin, Notre-Dame-de-Grâce (Our Lady of Grace).

▷ *Return to La Maillardais and continue straight on to Le Gâvre.*

Le Gâvre

The **Musée Benoist** (🕐 *Open May to mid-Nov, daily, 2.30-6.30pm; in Apr, Sat-Sun and holidays at the same hours.* 🕐 *Closed mid-Nov to end of Mar.* ⊜ *€1/3.* ☎ *02 40 51 25 14.*) is housed in a 17C residence flanked by a corner turret. The ground floor exhibit is concerned with the Forêt du Gâvre: its flora, forestry, fauna (stuffed animals). The upper floor is devoted to traditional crafts.
Not far from the school (*école*), the **wooden shoemaker's home** shows the life of the shoemaker who lived and worked in his workshop.

▷ *Return to Blain.*

ÎLE DE BREHAT★★

POPULATION 450
MICHELIN LOCAL MAP 309 - CÔTES D'ARMOR (22)

Bréhat is a much-frequented holiday resort. Its pink rocks stand out against the sea. Cars are not allowed; tractors are used for transportation.

▶ **Orient Yourself:** North of the Point d'Arcouest.
🤿 **Don't Miss:** The view from the Chaise de Renan.
🕐 **Organizing Your Time:** Prepare a picnic and make a day trip.

A Bit of History

A mild climate – Bréhat, which is about 3.5km/2mi long and 1.5km/1mi wide, consists of two islands joined in the 18C by a bridge built by Vauban. The coast, very broken and indented, is surrounded by 86 islets and reefs. Thanks to its mild climate (winter average 6°C/43°F), mimosa, eucalyptus and fig trees grow out in the open and the façades are bedecked with geraniums. There is little rain, the clouds generally passing over the flat island to condense over the mainland. The island's interior is a labyrinth of paths lined with honeysuckle or flower-bedecked dry stone walls, low houses with masses of hydrangea bushes, villas with vast gardens, a couple of cows in a tiny field or sheep on the heath. Its southern part is more welcoming than the rugged north. This colourful island has attracted such personalities as Prosper Mérimée, Ernest Renan and Louis Pasteur.

A varied history – Bréhat owes its name (Breiz Coat: Brittany of the Woods) to an Irish monk, St Budoc, who landed on Lavrec Island in AD 470. A medieval fortress facing this island was destroyed by the English in 1409 and local people were hanged on the sails on Crec'h ar Pot mill *(moulin)* on North Island. La Corderie Bay, on the west coast, was used as anchorage. According to local tradition, it was a sea captain from Morlaix, Coatanlem, living in Lisbon, who revealed the existence of the New World to Christopher Columbus in 1484 – eight years before its official discovery – and showed him the course taken by the island's fishermen already familiar with Newfoundland waters. In the 19C the island was frequented by privateers and during the last war, it was occupied by German troops until 4 August 1944.

Tour *allow half a day*

The island is crisscrossed by paths with arrows at ground level showing the way.

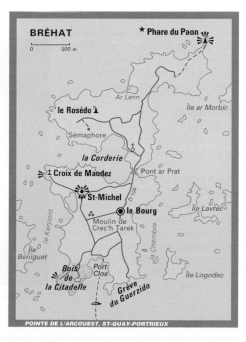

WHERE TO STAY

🍴🍴 **Hôtel Bellevue** – Port-Clos – ☎ 02 96 20 00 05 – www.hotel-bellevue-brehat. com - 🕐 *closed mid-Nov to mid-Dec, Jan and 2 weeks off season -* 🛏 📺 ✕ *– Breakfast € 9. Half-board required weekend holidays and in Aug (€ 164-180 for 2 perople).* You can enjoy the view of the port either from the large terrace or from the dining room's veranda of this attractive hotel. Its old façade hides modern rooms. Well-known and appreciated by the locals.

Port-Clos

This is a landing point for the boat service. Nearby, the **Grève du Guerzido** has two beaches of pink shingle, Petit and Grand Guerzido.

Bois de la Citadelle

Planted with conifers, the woods overlook the cliff. From the lifeboat shelter below, there is a good **view**★ of Kerpont Channel, impressive at low tide when the mass of rocks is visible, and of the Île Béniguet.

Le Bourg

The houses of the island's capital are grouped around a small square lined with plane trees.
In the 12C and 18C church, which has an unusual bell-tower, the high altar and the font grille are 17C and the lectern is 18C.

Chapelle St-Michel

High on a mound (26m/85ft; 39 steps), this chapel serves as a landmark for ships. There is an extensive **view**★ over the Île Sud the Kerpont channel and the Île Béniguet, Birlot Pool overlooked by the ruins of a once tide-operated mill, La Corderie Bay and the Île Nord and, in the distance, Talbert Spit (Sillon de Talbert).

Croix de Maudez

Erected in 1788 amid the heather and facing the ocean, the cross evokes the memory of a monk named Maudez who founded a monastery in AD 570, on a neighbouring island. There is a fine **view**★ of the islands of Béniguet to the left and Maudez to the right and the reefs.

La Corderie

Bounded by Ar Prat Bridge (Pont Vauban) this vast bay between the two islands is the main harbour. Beautiful villas.

North Island Lighthouses

Dating from 1862, the **Phare du Rosédo** stands inland, whereas the **Phare du Paon**★, was rebuilt in 1949 at the tip of North Island. The paved platform at the foot of the lighthouse affords a remarkable view of the rugged coastline, the chasm, the pink rocks and the shingles. This is the wildest part of the island.

Phare du Paon

G. Targat/MICHELIN

Boat Trips

Les Vedettes de Bréhat (☎ *02 96 55 79 50; www.vedettesdebrehat.com*) carry passengers to the island from Arcouest, and you can rent a bicycle when you arrive (round trip € 8/6.50, bikes € 15). Buy tickets at the departure point or from the Tourist Office. The company also organises day trips from Erquy, Val-André, St-Quay-Portrieux, Binic and Perros-Guirec (about € 30/20).

When planning your return from Bréhat, remember that time and tide wait for no man! There are three diffferent boarding points, depending on the tide, so be sure you know where your boat leaves from and how long it will take you to get there.

Tour of the island★★
1hr. The tour allows the visitor to admire the changing aspects of the coast: the beauty of the northern rocks and cliffs, the Mediterranean charm of the eastern shore and the ever-changing colour of the sea, which is often a deep blue.

Estuaire de Trieux★
This pleasant excursion along the Trieux Estuary, whose banks are in turn sheer, rocky and wooded and at times low-lying and under cultivation, offers views of the pretty site of Lézardrieux with its suspension bridge. The river flows at the foot of Château de la Roche-Jagu, which can be reached by a fairly steep path through woodlands.

BREST★

POPULATION 157 000
MICHELIN LOCAL MAP 308 E4

Built on the shores of a magnificent roadstead, which, nowhere less than 10m/33ft deep, is almost an inland sea in itself, Brest is by tradition a naval port which nevertheless welcomes ferries and cruising liners. Océanopolis, an impressive complex devoted to marine life, has developed near the marina and the entrance to the Elorn estuary. Every four years, the town welcomes some 2,000 traditional sailing ships from all over the world; this colourful gathering is faithfully attended by over one million sailing enthusiasts. Brest is also Brittany's second university town and a major centre of oceanographic research.

▶ **Orient Yourself:** 243km/145mi west of Rennes, 71km42mi north of Qiumper
Especially for Kids: The giant aquariums at Océanopolis
Also See: Les ABERS

A Bit of History

The English set foot in Brest (14C) – During the War of Succession which began in 1341, Montfort, ally of the English, was rash enough to let them guard the town. When he became Duke of Brittany, he tried in vain to drive out the intruders. The king of France had just as little success in his turn. At last, in 1397, Charles VI persuaded the King of England, Richard II, who had married Charles's eldest daughter, Isabella, to restore Brest to the Duke.

The Belle Cordelière – On 10 August 1513, St Laurence's Day, the English fleet of Henry VIII set out to attack Brest. The Breton fleet hurriedly set sail to meet it; however, under its panic-stricken commander it fled back to the Brest channel. The *Belle*

Cordelière, the gift of Anne of Brittany to her Duchy and on which 300 guests were dancing when the order came to weigh anchor, covered the commander's retreat and bore the brunt of the attack. Fire broke out on board the *Cordelière* as she was fighting gun to gun with an English ship. The commander, Hervé de Portzmoguer, or as he was known in France, Primauguet, knowing that his ship was lost, exhorted his crew and his guests to die bravely with the words: "We will now celebrate the Feast of St Laurence who died by fire!" The two ships blew up together.

The work of Colbert (17C) – Colbert, the greatest minister the French Navy ever had, completed the task begun by Richelieu, making Brest the maritime capital of the kingdom. To obtain good crews he set up the Inscription Maritime (marine record and administrative office), which still exists today. After completing their military service, fishermen between the ages of 18 and 48 are placed on the French Naval reserve; the Inscription Maritime looks after them and their families throughout their lives.

Colbert also founded at Brest a school of gunnery, a college of marine guards, a school of hydrography and a school for marine engineers. From this enormous effort a magnificent fleet developed. Ships reached a tonnage of 5 000 and carried up to 120 cannons; their prows and sterns were carved by such artists as Coysevox.

Duquesne improved the naval dockyard, built ramparts round the town and organised the defence of the channel (Le Goulet). Vauban, the military architect, completed the projects. Tourville improved mooring facilities in the roadstead laying down buoys to which ships could moor instead of dropping anchor.

The Belle Poule – In 1778, during the American War of Independence, the frigate *La Belle Poule* encountered the British *Arethusa* and forced her to retreat. This victory was very popular at court and all the ladies wore a new hairstyle La Belle Poule, which included, perched on their tresses, a model ship in full sail.

The Surveillante – In 1779 a British captain, George Farmer, wagered that no French frigate could destroy his Québec. Du Couëdic, who commanded the frigate *Surveillante*, challenged the wager – a furious sea duel ensued.

After a spirited battle, north of Ushant, both ships were dismasted. The sails of the Québec fell across its guns, setting the ship on fire. Du Couëdic ordered rescue action. Later the Québec blew up with the wounded Farmer. Du Couëdic also died from his wounds. The *Surveillante* was brought back to Brest in triumph, and Du Couëdic was laid to rest in the church of St Louis (destroyed in 1944).

Brest during the war – In June 1940, when the impending arrival of the German forces was announced, the French naval and commercial authorities hastily cleared the port, destroying the installations and putting several bridges and buildings and four submarines undergoing repair work out of operation. Nonetheless, the port was immediately put to use by the German navy, which built a concrete shelter for submarines at **Laninon**. The port thus occupied a highly advantageous strategic position and represented a considerable threat to Allied forces sailing between the USA and Great Britain. As a consequence, the town was heavily bombarded for four years. When the Americans finally managed to enter the town in September 1944, after a siege of 43 days, they were greeted by nothing but ruins.

Océanopolis★★★ *Allow 2hr*

&🕐 *Open Apr to early Sept, daily, 9am-6pm; 7pm in summer ; rest of the year Tue-Sat 10am-5pm, Sun and holidys 10am-6pm (last admission 1hr before closing).* 🕐 *Closed Mon except during school holiday periods, 25 Dec, 1 Jan and 2 weeks in Jan.* ⊗ *€ 15/10.50.*

Kids The enormous crab-shaped complex of Océanopolis is located east of the commercial port *(port de commerce)* alongside the Moulin Blanc marina *(port de plaisance)*.

This scientific and technical centre on marine life provides a window on all the activities linked with oceanology. Océanopolis also aims to be a living place where researchers, professional people, industrialists and the general public can be brought into contact with each other. Océanopolis expanded considerably in 2000: two new pavillons were added to the entirely renovated Pavillon Tempéré,

Fishy friends

T. Joyeux/Océanopolis

the Pavillon Tropical and Pavillon Polaire. Giant aquariums, containing some 10000 animals belonging to 1000 different species, illustrate with spectacular results the variety of submarine life in each natural habitat. Tidal movements and the swell of the sea are vividly recreated. Interactive terminals, models and films explain the history of the oceans and the extent of man's influence.

A restaurant (Vent d'Ouest) and a cafeteria (Atlantic Express) offer a pleasant break.

Town Centre *Allow 1 hr*

After the full-scale destruction of the town during the Second World War, the centre of Brest was rebuilt on a geometrical (grid) layout. The main artery linking the naval base to the enormous place de la Liberté is the wide **rue de Siam**, once a tiny street named in honour of the visit to the town of three ambassadors of the king of Siam and their colourful retinue. Running at right angles to this artery are roads leading to the River Penfeld or the Cours Dajot, from which there are good views of the roadstead. The **Église Saint-Louis**, built in 1957, was inspired by Le Corbusier's architectural style; the impression of height is increased by the vertical lines of the concrete bell-tower soaring above the rough-stone buildinng. Inside, a stained-glass window by Paul Boni is devoted to St Louis.

Naval Town *Allow 2 hr*

Cours Dajot

This fine promenade was laid out on the ramparts in 1769 by convicts from the naval prison. The Pink Tower, erected by the American Battle Monuments, commemorates the welcome offered by the people of Brest to the American troops during the First World War. Destroyed in 1941, it was rebuilt in 1958.

View of the roadstead★★

From the viewing table at the east end of the promenade, you see the Brest roadstead from the mouth of the Élorn, and past the Ménez-Hom and the Pointe de Roscanvel right over to Pointe de Portzic. The anchorage is vast (150km2/258sq mi) and deep (12-20m/6-10 fathoms – over large areas), framed between heights and connected with many big estuaries. It communicates with the Atlantic through a channel with steep banks, 5km/3mi long and about 1800m/1mi wide. This configuration explains why Brest has had such great military importance for more than 2 000 years.

To the left the Élorn estuary, spanned by Albert-Louppe Bridge (Pont Albert-Louppe), makes a safe anchorage for yachts. In the foreground is the commercial port. Beyond lies the Île de Plougastel, hiding the southeast of the roadstead. On the south side of the roadstead, at Lanvéoc, is the Naval School; nearby the nuclear submarine base

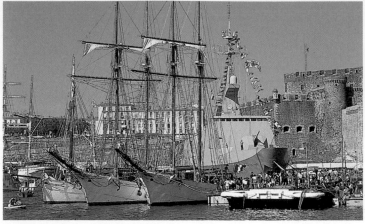

C. Chevalier

Training ships in front of the castle in Brest

is situated on the Île Longue. On the horizon to the right you see the Presqu'île de Crozon and the opening of the channel between Portzic Fort and the Pointe des Espagnols. In front of the castle, the inner harbour, protected by its breakwater, serves as anchorage for the fleet.

Port de Commerce
As seen from the Cours Dajot.
This was established in 1860, once the Penfeld became inadequate for accommodating both military and commercial shipping, for the use of the Brest Chamber of Commerce and Industry.
Traditional traffic is closely linked with the agricultural activities of west Brittany, and amounts to almost two million tonnes a year.
The commercial port imports oilseed and other products destined for livestock, as well as hydrocarbons and fertilisers; it exports mainly frozen poultry (for which it ranks as the world's number one port), potatoes and oils.
The port is also an important centre for naval repair work and encompasses three types of dry dock. The most recent of these, built in 1980, has the capacity to accommodate the largest commercial ships yet made (over 500 000t). These installations, which include wet repair docks and a gas extraction station, make Brest the foremost French naval repair complex.

Additional Sights

Musée des Beaux-Arts
🕐 *Open daily (except Sun morning and Tues), 10-noon and 2-6pm.* 🕐 *Closed public holidays.* ⊛ *€ 4. No charge 1st Sunday of the month.* ☎ *02 98 00 87 96.*
The Museum of Fine Arts' collections illustrate the Symbolist movement and in particular the Pont-Aven School (*By the Sea in Brittany* by Emile Bernard, *Green Corn at Le Pouldu* by Paul Sérusier and *Day in September* by Maurice Denis). Also well represented is 17C and 18C painting from the Italian, French and Dutch Schools (*Brest Harbour* by Van Blarenberghe, 1774). In addition, there are works by Orientalists such as Guillaumet and Fromentin, various seascapes and a noteworthy *Two Parrots* by Manet.

Château
The castle is the sole reminder of Brest's history.

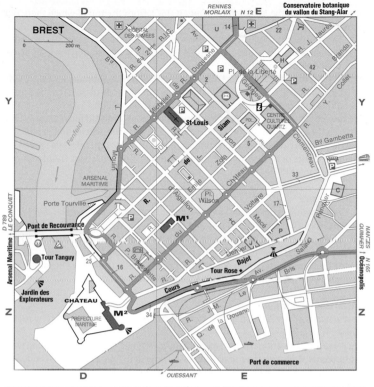

RENNES
MORLAIX N 12

Conservatoire botanique
du vallon du Stang-Alar

BREST			Français-Libres Bd des	DZ	16	Marine Bd de la	DZ	25
			Frégate-La-Belle-			Réveillère Av. Amiral	EY	33
11-Martyrs R. des	EY	42	Poule R. de la	EZ	17	Roosevelt Av. Fr.	DZ	34
Algésiras R. d'	FY	2	Jean-Jaurès R.	EY		Siam R. de	EY	
Clemenceau Av. G.	EY		Kérabécam R. de	EY	22			
Colbert R.	EY	5	Liberté Pl. de la	EY		Musée de la Marine	DZ	M²
Foch Av. Mar.	EY	14	Lyon R. de	DEY		Musée des Beaux-Arts	EZ	M¹

It was in the 11C that Brest's stronghold first put in an appearance at the mouth of the River Penfeld on a site which had already been fortified by the Romans. It was to fall victim to innumerable sieges over the centuries. Towers and fortifications were built from the 12C to the 17C. Richelieu, Colbert, Duquesne and Vauban, from 1683, were to strengthen the fortifications of the site.

The curtain wall was restored after the last war. The museum and the ramparts are all that is open to the public; the castle houses the offices of the Harbour Police (Préfecture Maritime).

R. Mattes/MICHELIN

Ships of the French fleet and Brest castle

Musée de la Marine★

🕐 Open Apr to Sept, daily 10am-6.30pm, Tues 1.30-6.30pm; rest of the year, daily (except Tues), 10am-noon and 2-6pm. 🕐 Closed 1 May and Jan. ⊕€ 4.60. ☎ 02 98 22 12 39.

Access is through the Madeleine Tower (3C-15C), from the top of which there is a good view of the port and the roadstead.

Kids This museum is an offshoot of the Maritime Museum in Paris and displays valuable models of ships, navigation instruments and charts illustrating the feats of the navy sailing ships during the 18C.

At the foot of the terrace there is a display of the 5622 pocket submarine, 11.87m/39ft long by 1.68m/5.5ft wide, and the taking aboard of the boat-people rounded up in the South China Sea by the teaching ship *Jeanne d'Arc* in 1988.

The tour continues along the watch-path of the Paradis Tower (Tour Paradis) (15C) in which there is an exhibition on the history of the castle. Interesting exhibits of ship decorations are displayed throughout, in particular **figureheads** carved by unknown artists or by famous ones such as Antoine Coysevox who sculpted many statues of Louis XIV.

Tour Tanguy

🕐 *Open June to Sept, daily, 10am-noon and 2-7pm; Oct to May, open Wed and Thur 2-5pm, Sat-Sun 2-6pm.* 🕐 *Closed 1 Jan, 1 May and 25 Dec.* ✆ *No charge.* ☎ *02 98 00 88 60.*

The tower stands opposite the castle, on the far bank of the Penfeld, overlooking the dockyard. This 14C construction, once the Quilbignon stronghold, houses the **Musée du vieux Brest,** which depicts the most significant periods of Brest's history through dioramas, town plans, modles, coats of arms, etc.

Jardin des Explorateurs

On the banks of the Penfeld, on the same side as the Tour Tanguy. Acces by rue de l'Église.

Typical of an international port that regularly welcomed naturalists returning with exotic plants, this garden reminds visitors of some of the great explorers (Bougainville, Commerson, La Billardière, Raoul), and is home to plants that are more often seen in distant lands, such as palm trees, giant ferns, Japanese anemone... There is a nice view of the castle and the arsenbal from the bridge.

Brest Naval Base (Base Navale) and Dockyard★(Arsenal)

It was in 1631 that **Cardinal Richelieu** decided to turn the city of Brest into a harbour. In 1666, **Colbert** developed the infrastructure that already existed along the banks of the Penfeld: the meandering, enclosed estuary of this river was a perfect site, able to protect the boats from heavy storms. From 1740 to 1790, **Choquet de Lindu** undertook to build a huge dockyard and, as early as 1742, the first three dry docks of Pontaniou were built. In the late 19C a pier was erected, defining the boundaries of a vast roadstead; in 1970 two **jetties** able to accommodate large-tonnage vessels (aircraft-carriers, cruisers, frigates) were added onto the pier. **Docks** no 8 (for careening only) and no 9 (construction work) were built in 1918 and extended in 1953. Their huge size (300m/985ft long by 49m/160ft wide) enables them to receive the largest ships belonging to the French fleet, over 250m/820ft long and weighing more than 35 000t. At the same time, two other quays were built: **Quai de l'Armement** (555m/1 821ft long), designed to equip and repair ships, and **Quai des Flotilles** (752m/2 468ft long), which brings together most of the war vessels that make up the Atlantic fleet.

G. Targat/MICHELIN

Arsenal

Address Book

TOURIST OFFICE

Brest, Place de la Liberté, 29200 – ☎ 02 98 44 24 96. www.brest-metropole-tourisme.fr

WHERE TO STAY

Prices are given for double occupancy in season. Prices are 20-30% lower off season.

Kyriad, 157 rue Jean Jaurès, ☎ 02 98 43 58 58, kyriadbrest@wanadoo.fr - 50 rooms ⬛ A modest establishment on a very busy avenue: the windows are double-glazed, but if possible, opt for a room in the back. Copious breakfast € 7.50.

Hôtel de la Paix, 32 rue Algésiras, ☎ 02 98 80 12 97 - 29 rooms ⬛ Family-style ambience in this little, central hotel; renovated rooms. Breakfast buffet with plenty of choice (€ 9).

Le Continental, 41 rue Émile Zola, ☎ 02 98 80 50 40, continental-brest@hotel-sofibra.com - 73 rooms. ⬛ Modern style or Art Deco in the spacious rooms of this building dating from the 50s. Breakfast € 10.

EATING OUT

Amour de pomme de terre, 23 rue des Halles St-Louis, ☎ 02 98 43 48 51. "For love of the spud" – this attractive and fun eatery served evry form of everyone's favourite root vegetable: mashed, with cheese, baked, fried, etc. To go with your potato, meat, seafood and fish grilled at your table. Tasty food in a relaxed setting.

Ma petite folie, 520 rue Eugène Berest, port du Moulin Blanc, ☎ 02 98 42 44 42. A beached fishing boat, the decks serving as dining rooms: this is a pleasant and amusing place to enjoy a seafood platter. Sit on the upper deck for a view of the beach.

Le Crabe Marteau, 8 quai de la Douane, ☎ 02 98 33 38 57. ⏱ Closed Sun and Mon. Bib around your neck, hammer in hand, go for those crabs! If you have doubts, the owner will gladly demonstrate the technique.

Aux Vieux gréements, 40 quai de la Douane, port de commerce, ☎ 02 98 43 20 48. ⏱ Closed Sun and Mon. Good value for money at this restaurant specialising in fish, decorated with a high seas theme.

Fleur de sel, 15 bis rue de Lyon, ☎ 02 98 44 38 65, www.lafleurd-esel.com ⏱ Closed Sat noon, Sun, 1-21 Aug and 1-10 Jan. Excellent cuisine in an Art Deco dining room. The menu is inspired and creative, based on fresh produce and seafood.

ON THE TOWN

Ayers Rock Café, 7 rue de l'Harteloire, ☎ 02 98 46 48 91, www.ayersrock.fr.st ⏱ Daily until the wee hours. This smokey, chummy bar programmes concerts 365 days of the year! Happy hour from 8-11pm: 3 pints for the price of 2.

La Ronde des vins, 31 rue Monge, ☎ 02 98 80 14 70. ⏱ Tue-Sun 10.30al-midnight. A pleasant wine bar, serving nice assortments of cold meats, oysters and salads.

Le Quartz, Place de la Liberté, ☎ 02 98 33 70 70, www.lequartz.com ⏱ Closed Mon and holidays. This fine national theatre welcomes more than 300 000 spectators yearly to plays, concerts and dance performances.

RECREATION

Vedettes Azenor port du Moulin Blanc, ☎ 02 98 41 46 23, www.azenor.com offers guided boat tours of the military harbour and the roadstead. 2 or 3 departures daily Tue-Sun, April through and Sep; daily in July and August. About 1hr, € 14/9.50. With a meal on board 3hr15min, € 43-59.50/25,50.

Walking tours - The Tourist Office publishes a series of leaflets showing the footpaths in the area around Brest. You can also find them on the Internet: www.brest-metropole-tourisme.fr

Watersports - The Brest roadstead is like an inland sea, and a great place to sail, windsurf, row, etc. Information from the **Station nautique Rade de Brest**, port du Moulin-Blanc, ☎ 02 98 34 64 95, station-nautique@ cub-brest.fr

Beaches - Moulin-Blanc, across from the marina, is the local favourite. The beach at **Ste-Anne-du-Porzic**, near the

Brest-Iroise Technopôle, is a beautiful natural site.

SPECIAL EVENTS

Les Jeudis du Port, *www.mairie-brest. fr/jeudis-port.* Every Thursday evening in July and August, a free concert and street fair at the port.

Brest 2008, *www.brest2008.fr.* Every four years, the Tall Ships come to Brest; the next rendez-vous is in July 2008. Concerts, events and tours of the ships.

Festival européen du film court, ☎ 02 98 44 03 94, *www.filmcourt.fr* In early Nov, the Côte Ouest association organises a festival of short films.

SHOPPPING

Markets - Halles St-Louis. The covered market is open every morning, but Sundays are most spectacular, with stalls spread out into the neighbouring streets. Marché de Siam, rue de Siam, Sun morning. This is the market where small local growers sell their wares, including cheese from the monts d'Arrée; there is also a good selection of novelties and clothing.

Chocolate - *Histoire de chocolat, 60 rue de Siam,* ☎ *02 98 44 66 09.* 🕐 *Tue-Sat 9.30am-7.30pm, Mon 2-7.30pm.* The chocalates are made on the premises and garnished with praline, caramel, honey, salted butter and even algae!

Grocery - *Roi de Bretagne, 12 quai de la Douane, port de commerce,* ☎ *02 98 46 09 00.* 🕐 *Mon-Sat 10am-noon, 2-7pm.* Specialising in products from Brittany, including beers, cider, potted fish, boating attire and celtic music!

Pastry shop - *Le Quéau, 109 rue Jean Jaurès,* ☎ *02 98 44 15 53.* 🕐 *Daily 9am-7.30pm.* This small shop is well known for its whipped cream, light and not too sweet. You can enjoy your treats in the old-fashioned tea room.

During the German Occupation in the Second World War, an underwater naval base was set up in Brest to protect the German submarines stationed in the Atlantic Ocean. As soon as the base became operational, it could accommodate up to 30 submarines. With a total area of 65 859m2/79 030sq yd covered by a 4m/13ft thick slab, it was practically invulnerable; during the bombing of 5 August 1944, the impacts made by ten 6t bombs caused only minor damage. This base is still in service today.

Visite de l'Arsenal (Tour of the Dockyard)
(Access by Porte de la Grande Rivière west of the plan by Pont de Recouvrance – 🔊 *Guided tours (90 min) in French or English by appointment. July to mid-Sept, daily, 9-11am and 2-4pm (rest of the year, call ahead for information).* 😊 *Identification papers requried as this site is only accessible by French nationals; no charge; no photographs.* ☎ *02 98 22 06 12.*
The visit offers a tour of the submarine base built by the Germans during the Second World War and of one of the warships of the French Navy, whichever is available.

Mémorial du Finistère
🕐 *Open Mon to Fri 9am-noon and 2-6pm.* 🕐 *Closed public holidays.* 🎫 *€ 4/2.50.* ☎ *02 98 05 39 46.*
Fort Montbarey, built in 1784 on the orders of Louis XVI, bears the nameof one of the king's ministers. Today it is a memorial site for the Finistère region. Visitors can see photographs, literature, objects and military equipment recalling the siege of Brest in 1944, escape routes to Braitain, deportation, etc. In the crypt is a list of local sons and daughters who dies between 3 September and 19 December 1946. Several vaulted rooms have been reconstructed as the various garrisons fo the fort (butcher's, baker's, chemist's shops).

Conservatoire botanique national de Brest, Stang-Alar★
East of the town by rue Jean-Jaurès, then by the road to Quimper. Vallon de Stang-Alar, 52 Allée du Bot, 29200 Brest. ☎*02 98 41 88 95.* 🕐 *The park is open daily from 9am-6pm; the*

greenhouses are normally accessible from 1st July to 15th September, Sunday to Thursday from 2- 5.30 pm. Free entry to the park, 🕮 € 3.50 for the tropical greenhouses.

The Vallon du Stang-Alar houses one of the most prestigious botanical gardens in the world. As well as a beautiful public **garden** (22 ha/54 acres) boasting a wide variety of both common and rare exotic ornamental plants, the **greenhouses** (1000m²/1196sq yd) and other conserva-

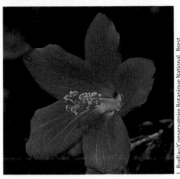

tories contain many species threatened with extinction. The role of this park is not only to preserve endangered varie- ties, but also to study them and to try to revive them in their natural environ- ment. Thus attempts have been made to resuscitate the *Hibiscus fragilis,* the *Lobelia parva,* the *Narcissus triandrus capax,* which almost disappeared from the Îles de Glénan a few years ago, or the *Limonium dendroides,* of which only four specimens remained in the wild. Playing areas for children and sports activities will delight nature lovers of all ages.

Hibiscus Boryanus

L. Ruellau/Conservatoire Botanique National, Brest

Excursions

Presqu'île de Plougastel★

Round tour of 56km/35mi – about half a day. Leave Brest along N 165 towards Quimper. You pass on the left the road leading to **Relecq-Kerhuon,** a resort nicely situated on the west bank of the Élorn.

Pont Albert-Louppe
Inaugurated by President Gaston Doumergue in 1930, this bridge crosses the Élorn estuary. It is 880m/2 887ft long and has three 186m/610ft spans. Four statues by the sculptor Quillivic stand at each end: a man and a woman from the Léon region on the Brest shore and a man and a woman from Plougastel on the opposite shore.
The bridge rises over 42m/137ft high above the river and offers a very fine viewa over Élorn Valley and the Brest roadstead.

Pont de l'Iroise
Inaugurated in 1994, this bridge has a 400m/1312ft-wide central span; it carries the main road between Brest and Quimper and is the first link of the major international highway E 60 which will eventually join Brest and the Black Sea, via Switzerland, Austria and Jungary.

▸ *1km/0.5mi after the bridge bear right towards Plougastel-Daoulas.* 👣 *See Presqu'île de PLOUGASTEL for details of the rest of the drive.*

Les Abers★

Round tour of 197km/122mi – allow 1 day. 👣 *See Les ABERS.*

Coastal drive to Pointe de St-Mathieu

56km/35mi – about 2hr. Leave Brest heading W by Pont de Recouvrance and turn left onto rue St-Exupéry to reach the cliff road overlooking the naval dockyard. At 4-Pompes drive straight on; turn left at the entrance to Cosquer.

Ste-Anne-du-Portzic

It is located along the beach in Ste-Anne Bay; walk a short distance along the coastal path to enjoy fine views.

An uphill road leads to the Pointe du Diable on the sound (Goulet de Brest). The site is occupied by the **Technopole Brest-Iroise**, a centre of technology, which includes, among others, the headquaters of IFREMER (French Institute of Research for the Exploitation of the Sea).

▶ *Join D 789.*

The road runs parallel to Trez-Hir beach, giving a good view of Bertheaume Bay, then goes through Plougonvelin.

Fort de Bertheaume

A pleasant walk along a coastal foot path leads to one of Vauban's fortified creations, at the entrance to the Brest Channel.

▶ *Carry on along D 85.*

St-Mathieu★★

Lighthouse guided tour (20min). ◷ *July-Aug, 10am-1pm and 2-7pm; May, June and Sep, weekends and holidays 3-6pm. Last admission 20min before closing.* ⊛ *€ 2.* ☎ *02 98 89 00 17*

St-Mathieu, which was an important town in the 14C, is now only a village known for the ruins of its abbey church, its site and its lighthouse.

The **lighthouse** has a considerable system of lights; two auxiliary lights are reserved for air navigation. There is also a radio beam. The main light is served by a 600-watt halogenous lamp, giving it an intensity of about 5 000 000 candlepower, with a range of 60km/38mi.

From the top *(163 steps)* there is a superb **panorama**★★; from left to right – the mouth of the Brest Sound, Presqu'île de Crozon, Pointe du Raz, Île de Sein (in clear weather), Pierres Noires reef, and the Islands of Béniguet, Molène and Ouessant. Beyond Béniguet, 30km/18.5mi away, you can sometimes distinguish Jument Lighthouse. The ruins of the **abbey church**★ are the remains of a Benedictine monastery (6C) which, according to legend, had as a relic the head of St Matthew.

The 13C chancel, which has pointed vaulting, is flanked by a square keep. The nave with rounded or octagonal pillars has a single aisle on the north side and two 16C aisles on the south side. The church has a 12C façade pierced by a round arched doorway and three narrow windows.

In front of the restored Chapelle Notre-Dame-des-Grâces, note the 14C porch, a relic of the former parish churrooms

▶ *Go round the lighthouse enclosure to reach the tip of the point.*

At the tip of the point, a column, erected to the memory of the French sailors who died in the First World War, is the work of the sculptor Quillivic. There is a magnificent view from the edge of the cliff.

Pointe de St-Mathieu

At the tip of the headland, a **column**, erected to the memory of the French sailors who died in the First World War, is the work of the sculptor Quillivic. There is a magnificent **view** from the edge of the cliff.

At a point 300m/300yd from St-Mathieu going towards Plougonvelin are two Gallic **steles** (on the left near a house) surmounted by a cross and known as the Monks' Gibbet (Gibet des Moines).

See Les ABERS for the remainder of the itinerary - the Pointe des Renards and Le Conquet which can be reached along the cliff road. You can then return to Brest by the direct road, D 789.

BRIGNOGAN-PLAGES☼

POPULATION 836
MICHELIN LOCAL MAP 308 F3

Brignogan is a seaside resort lying deep inside Pontusval Bay and framed by rock piles, sometimes curiously shaped.

Also See: Les ABERS

Pointe de Pontusval
This walk crosses a countryside dotted with blocks of granite. The Men Marz, at mid-distance, is a fine example of a menhir, 8m/25ft high, surmounted by a Cross.

Chapelle Pol
The 19C chapel, Calvary and small watchtower, built on two rocks, are worth seeing.

Keremma
10.5km/6mi south-east on the Plouescat road

La Maison des dunes
July-Aug 10.30am-5.30pm; rest of the year Mon-Fri 8.30am-5.30pm. Closed 1 Jan, 8 May and 25 Dec. €3.50 (no charge for children under 15). ☎ 05 98 61 69 69. This nature centre sits on one of the longest stretches of dunes in Brittany. Learn more about this fragile ecosystem through the exhibits and events. *Nature walk (free access).*

CÔTE DES BRUYÈRES★

MICHELIN LOCAL MAP 308 I/K 2/3– FINISTÈRE (29) AND CÔTES D'ARMOR (22)

This short section of the Channel coast, which is part of the Golden Belt and is alos known as The Heather Coast, should be seen by all tourists who visit northern Brittany. The Lieu de Grève, a long, majestic stretch of sand, is followed by steep headlands skirted from a distance by the Armorican coast road.

Also See: LANNION

From St-Michel-en-Grève to Pointe de Diben

38km/24mi – about 4hr

St-Michel-en-Grève
A small seaside resort. The church is nicely situated near the sea.

Lieue de Grève★

This magnificent beach, 4km/2.5mi long, lies int he curve of a bay which goes out 2km/1mi at low tide. Trout streams run into the sea through small green valleys. The road, which is very picturesque, follows the wooded coast and skirts the rocky mass of the Grand Rocher.

Climbing the Grand Rocher
45min on foot there and back.

A road to the left, just before the Grand Rocher, leads to a car park. From there, a path runs to the 80m/26ft-high belvedere which offers a very fine **view**★ of the Lieu de Grève. At high tide especially, and on windy days, the sight of the endless foaming waves breaking on the beach and dashing against the seawall gives you a feeling for the power of the sea.

St-Efflam

Next to the Chapelle St-Efflam, half-hidden by lush vegetation, there is a fountain, which is surmounted by a massive dome. Efflam, a hermit who came from Ireland, landed with seven companions in AD 470 on the beach of the same name.

Plestin-les-Grèves

It was here that Efflam lived, founded a monastery and died in AD 512. The 16C **church**, which burned down in 1944, has been restored; it contains the tomb of Saint Efflam adorned with his recumbant figure (1576). In the south aisle, to the left of the altar, a statue shows him vanquishing a dragon, the symbol of paganism. Note the modern stained-glass windows.

▶ *Return to the coast road.*

Corniche de l'Armorique★

Between St-Efflma and Locquirec, the road follows the indented coast. After Pointe de Plestin there is a fine view of the cove of Locquirec and its headland at high tide. Before reaching the village, you can see the Côte de Granit Rose in the distance, to the right.

Locquirec ☼

Built on a rocky peninsula, Locquirec is a small fishing port and marina as well as a seaside resort.

Once the property of the Knights of Malta, the charming **church**★ has a Renaissance turreted bell-tower. Inside, the panelled vaults of the chancel and the transept are covered with 18C paintings. At the high altar is a 16C **altarpiece**★ illustrating scenes of the Passion in high relief and simple style.

Pointe de Locquirec
30min on foot there and back.

A walk starting near the church's east end offers fine views of Lannion Bay and the coastline.

▶ *Beyond the mill, Moulin de la Rive, take the coast road along the cliff.*

Table d'orientation de Marc'h Sammet

Built on a rocky headland, the viewing table commands splendid **views**★: to the east the beaches of Moulin de la Rive and the Sables Blancs; to the north the Île de Losquet; to the west the Poul Rodou Beach (access 800m/2 265ft below).

▶ *Go to the village of Christ and turn right. Follow the signposts to the scenic road (route touristique).*

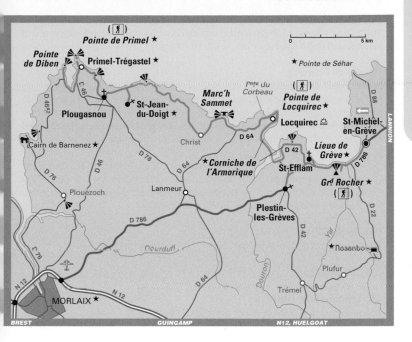

St-Jean-du-Doigt★

This picturesque village owes its name to a relic kept in the church since the 15C. It celebrates its *pardon*, which is attended In particular by those suffering from opthalmological problems, on the last Sunday in June.

The parish close has a 16C triumphal gateway and, on the left, a pretty Renaissance **fountain**★ dominated by God the Father blessing the baptism of His Son as performed by John the Baptist.

Church★

St John the Baptist's finger, which was brought to the Chapelle St-Mériadoc c 1420, worked miracles. The construction of a great church was begun in 1440, but building went slowly and it was only finished in 1513 thanks to the generosity of Anne de Bretagne. Built in a Flamboyant style, the church has a flat east end. The bell-tower has lost its spire. At the base, abutting the buttresses, are two small ossuaries; one Gothic one Renaissance.

The **treasury**★ contains several reliquaries, one of which holds the first joint of the finger of St John the Baptist. There is also a **processional cross**★. The finest piece is a silver-gilt Renaissance **chalice**★★.

Plougasnou

At the centre of this small town, the church, which is mostly 16C, has a Renaissance porch opening on the square. In the chancel are fine 17C altar pieces. In the south aisle, the Chapelle de Kéricuff, closed off by an elegant Gothic arcade in oak, contains a 16C wooden Trinity. A road from the church's east end leads (300m/330yd from the town) to the **Oratoire Notre-Dame-de-Lorette**, a granite oratory with a stone roof and two telamones framing the entrance.

▷ *Take the road past the Tourist Office and at the third crossroads turn right.*

Primel-Trégastel★

The beach of fine sand lies in a good setting near rocks comparable with those of Ploumanach and Trégastel.

Pointe de Primel★

30min on foot there and back.

🚶 The headland is a jumble of pink rocks. From the central spur, there is a fine **panorama** extending from the Baie de St-Pol-de-Léon to the Trébeurden coast. Out at sea are the Île de Batz lighthouse and the Sept-Îles. The tip of the headland is separated from the rest of the peninsula by a fissure (which can be crossed at low tide).

▶ *After 1km/0.6mi, turn right. The road passes near the fish ponds. At Le Diben, a picturesque fishing village, turn right in the direction of Les Vivier-le-Port; 100m/110yd farther on, take the road opposite the port which leads to a dike. Just before this, bear left onto a path leading to the Point de Diben*

Pointe de Diben

From here there is a fine view over the bay and of the Point de Primel.

Excursions

Château de Rosanbo

8.5km/ 5.3mi south of St-Michel-en-Grève via D 786 and D 22.

🕙 *Guided tour (40min) July-Aug, 11am-6pm; Apr, June, Sep, 2-5pm; Oct, weekends and holidays, 2-5pm.* 🕐 *Closed 2 Nov-31 March.* 💶 *€ 7.*

The château stands on the foundations of an old 14C castle, overlooking the River Bô, hence its Breton name, meaning rock *(ros)* on the *(an)* Bô.

The different periods of construction can be seen as you enter the courtyard: the 15C manor house to the west, which was enlarged in the 17C (with mansard roofs) and 18C, and finally restored in the 19C.

The rooms open to the public are furnished and decorated with good taste. Archive documents have recently made it possible to reconstruct the most authentic rooms of the residence, the dining room and the 18C drawing room.

The **library** contains over 8 000 volumes datring mainly from the 17C. The vast room overlooks a terrace and an ornamental pond.

The château is bordered by a maginificent **French-style garden**, which is the work of Achille Duchêne, the famous 19C landscape architect. Note in particular the **hedges**, almost 2 500m/2 734 yd long, and the green arbours (small clearings in the shrubbery) which once had specific functions such as horse-riding ring, training area, tennis area, etc..

Lanmeur

15km/9.3mi west of St-Michel-en-Grève via D 786 and D 22.

The small town of Lanmeur is situated in a market garden area on the Trégorrois Plateau. Only the crypt and the bell-tower of the orignal church remain; the rest of the edifice dates from 1904. Note the curious staue of St Mélar.

The pre-Romanesque **crypt**★ *(access to the left of the main altar, light switch at the foot of the stairway)* is ascribed to the 8C and is one of the oldest religious buildings in Brittany. The vaulting rests on eight massive pillars, two of which are decorated. A fountain stands to the right of the west door.

Excavations have brought to light two very rare and very old (perhaps 6C) carved gold figurines.

In the cemetery close, the impressive **Chapelle de Kernitron** has a 12C nave and transept and a 15C chancel. Inside, facing the entrance, there is a staute of Our Lady of Kernitron *(pardon on 15 August)* as well as, in a small chapel on the right, a charming statue of St Anne and the Virgin.

CAMARET-SUR-MER

POPULATION 2 668
MICHELIN LOCAL MAP 308 D5 - FINISTÈRE (29)

Also See: Presqu'ile de CROZON

An important spiny lobster port, Camaret is also a quiet, simple seaside resort, close to impressive sheer cliff and facing the entrance to the Brest Channel. On the shore, to the left of the *Sillon*, a natural dike which protects the port, is Corréjou Beach.

Sights

Chapelle Notre-Dame-de-Rocamadour

This chapel stands at the end of the dike. It was built between 1610 and 1683 and restored after a fire in 1910. It was originally a pilgrimage chapel on the pilgrims' route to Rocamadour in Quercy; from the 11C the pilgrims from the north, who came by sea, used to disembark at Camaret to continue the journey by land. A *pardon* is held on the first Sunday in September.

Château Vauban

A massive tower surrounded by walls was built by the military architect Vauban at the end of the 17C on Sillon Point. It now houses temporary exhibitions from time to time. There are fine views of the Brest Channel, Pointe des Espagnols and the port and town of Camaret.

Alignements de Lagatjar

This fine group of megaliths, whose name means hen's eye, includes 143 menhirs discovered in the early 20C.

Address Book

TOURIST OFFICE

Camaret-sur-Mer, 15 quai Kléber, on the port, ☎ 02 98 27 93 60, www.camaret-sur-mer.com ○ July-Aug: Mon-Sat 9am-7pm, Sun 10am-1pm; off season: Mon 2.15-6pm, Tue-Sat 9.15-12am, 2-6pm.

WHERE TO STAY

○ **Vauban**, 4 quai du Styvel, ☎ 02 98 27 91 36 – 16 rooms ⚑ 📺 Humble but pleasant hotel, well kept and reasonable prices. Perhaps you'll have a drink with the navigators that stop over there… Cordial welcome. Breakfast € 5.50.

○○ **Hôtel de France**, 19 quai Toudouze, ☎ 02 98 27 93 06, hotel.thalassa@wanadoo.fr – 20 rooms ⚑ 📺 ✗ Quite simple rooms but well kept and soundproofed. Those at the back are smaller. Breakfast € 7.20.

EATING OUT

○ **Chez Philippe**, 22 quai Gustave Toudouze ☎ 02 98 27 90 41. A restaurant of regulars where you eat shoulder to shoulder and for almost nothing: daily special, moules marinières, nice meat and fish dishes.

○○○ **Les Frères de la côte,** 11 quai Gustave Toudouze, ☎ 02 98 27 95 42. ○ Open Apr-Sept: daily in summer, ○ closed Wed the rest of the year. Coming from the distant island of Guadalupe, these brothers prepare Breton fishes with exotic spices: a success! Rum drinks a speciality (€ 3).

SHOPPING

Culinary specialities – Biscuiterie de Camaret, route de Crozon, ☎ 02 98 27 88 08. A huge range of regional products: preserves, candies and porcelains and faiences painted by hand. Free tasting of Breton cakes.

CANCALE★

POPULATION 5 203
MICHELIN LOCAL MAP 309 K2 - ILLE-ET-VILAINE (35)

To get a good view of the picturesque settings take the tourist road (route tour-istique – one-way) which branches off D 76 to the right 2.5km/1.5mi after the Portes Rouges crossroad. As you drive into Cancale the **views**★ of the resort and Mont-St-Michel Bay are splendid. The town has derived its gastronomic reputation for centuries from the oysters which flourish in the beds in the bay (parc à huîtres) and which oyster lovers come to eat in the hotels and bars around the port. ℹ 5, quai Kléber, 29570 – ☎ 02 98 27 93 60.

▶ **Orient Yourself:** On the coast between St Malo and the Mont-St-Michel
🐚 **Don't Miss:** Oysters!
👍 **Also See:** Côte d'ÉMERAUDE

Sights

Port de la Houle★

A bustling, animated area, the quays along the port teem with people unloading oysters, repairing nets, cleaning boats, or just waiting for the arrival of the fishing fleet at high tide.

Go to the Fenêtre jetty for a view of the bay and, at low tide, of the oyster beds. The port is surrounded by a picturesque district where sailors and fishermen lived. A street, the Vaubaudet or Val du Baudet, was the only link with the town of Cancale, the upper district, where the landsmen and traders lived.

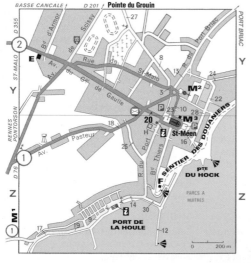

CANCALE

Bricourt Pl.	Y	3
Calvaire Pl. du	Z	4
Duguay-Trouin Quai	Z	9
Du-Guesclin R.	Y	8
Duquesne R.	Y	10
Fenêtre Jetée de la	Z	12
Gallais R.	Y	13
Gambetta Quai	Z	14
Hock R. du	Z	16
Jacques-Cartier Quai	Z	17
Juin R. du Mar.	Z	18
Kennedy Quai	Z	19
Leclerc R. Gén.	YZ	20
Mennais R. de la	Y	22
Port R. du	Z	
République Pl. de la	Z	23
Rimains R. des	Y	24
Roulette R. de la	Z	25
Stade R. du	Y	27
Surcouf R.	Y	28
Thomas Quai	Z	30

La Ferme Marine	Z	M¹	Musée de l'Huître et		Musée des Arts et		
Maison de Jeanne Jugan	Y	E	du Coquillage	Z F	Traditions Populaires	Y	M²
					Musée des Bois Sculptés	Z	M³

Address Book

TOURIST OFFICE

Cancale, 44 rue du Port,
☎ 02 99 89 63 72, www.ville-cancale.
fr Jan-Apr, Oct-Dec: Mon-Sat 9am-
12.30pm, 2-6pm; May-June, Sept:
Mon-Sat 9am-12.30pm, 2-6.30pm,
Sun 9.30am-1pm; July-Aug: Mon-Sat
9am-7pm, Sun 9am-13pm. Information
booth on the port in July-Aug: every
day 3-7pm.

Rent a bike - Les 2 Roues de Cancale,
7 rue de l'Industrie, ☎ 02 99 89 80 16.
About € 13/day.

WHERE TO STAY

Prices are given for double occupancy
in season. Prices are 10-30 % lower off
season.

☺ **La Voilerie**, *Le Chemin Neuf,* ☎ *02 99
89 88 00, www.hotel-lavoilerie.com
- 13 rooms*. Functional rooms with blue
and yellow tones, a little bit dark in the
ground floor, brighter upstairs. Numbers 3 and 6 are the more pleasant.

☺☺ **La Métairie du Vauhariot**, *66
rue des Français Libres,* ☎ *02 99 89 63 32
- 4 rooms* You reach the rooms of
this beautiful renovated old house by a
wonderful stone stairway. Modest but
tasteful setting. Good breakfast with
home made crepes and cakes.

☺☺☺☺ **La Maison de la Marine**, *23
rue de la Marine,* ☎ *02 99 89 88 53, www.
maisondelamarine.com - 5 rooms*
The former office of the sea business
has been laid out as a luxurious guest
house. Thematic rooms, all different,
with antiques and old paintings. Very
comfortable and a good restaurant.

☺☺☺ **Le Querrien**, *7 quai Duguay-
Trouin,* ☎ *02 99 89 64 56, www.le-quer-
rien.com - 15 rooms* On three
floors without lift, facing the port, you'll
find very well kept rooms, with blue,
yellow or raspberry tones. Breakfast € 8.

EATING OUT

☺ **Breizh Café**, *7 quai Thomas,*
☎ *02 99 89 61 76.* On the port, a simple
and elegant setting to savour original
crepes, such as the Cancalaise, made
with potatoes, cream and sardine
caviar. Delicious crepes with local
caramelsale made with salted butter.

Choice between 17 farmer ciders or
Breton beers on draft.

☺ **Le Herpin**, *5 quai Gambetta,*
☎ *02 99 89 86 42.* 🕐 *Closed Wed and
Thu off season, 15th Nov-1st Feb.* This
small café run by a fisherman isn't much
to look at, but the freshness of the oysters and other seafood is guaranteed.

☺ **Le Piccolo**, *6 rue Duquesne,* ☎ *02 99
89 76 13.* 🕐 *Closed Mon and Tue off
season and Jan.* Famous for its copious
meals with regional themes, such as the
Périgourdine or the Vendéenne, as well
as for its pizzas served in the garden
terrace or in a café-style room.

☺ **La Mère Champlain**, *1 quai Thomas,*
☎ *02 99 89 60 04.* In a setting and
atmosphere of pub, with terrace opposite the port, catch-of-the-day seafood
menu, starting at € 14.90.

☺☺ **Le Cancalais**, *12 quai Gambetta,*
☎ *02 99 89 61 93.* 🕐 *Closed Sun evening
and Mon off season except school
holidays, Dec-Jan.* A good address to
enjoy seafood and fish prepared in the
traditional way.

☺ **Le St-Cast**, *rte de la Corniche,*
☎ *02 99 89 66 08.* 🕐 *Closed Sun evening
and Tue except July-Aug, 2 weeks in Feb
and 16th Nov-19th Dec.* In the company
of talkative exotic birds, under the
veranda in front of the sea or in the
elegant setting room, you will enjoy
old-fashion cuisine, made with the
best regional products. Menus starting
at € 20, except during the weekends
and public holidays.

☺☺ **La Maison de la Marine**.
🕐 *Closed Mon and Tue off season and
Jan.* In a welcoming room with varnished floor, woodwork and paintings,
you will enjoy fusion cuision and "Mood
Food" that uses spices to make regional
products more exotic. Good choice of
French and foreign wines. Small terrace
giving onto the garden.

LEISURE

Windsurf - École de voile, *Port-Mer,*
☎ *02 99 89 90 22,* 🕐 *July-Aug and
weekend off season.* Lessons, trainings
and little boats and windsurfers for hire.

Old riggings - La Cancalaise, *la Halle à marée, port de la Houle*, ☎ *02 99 89 77 87, www.lacancalaise. com*, 2-5pm except Wed and Sun. A score of days per year, from Apr to Aug, you can go on a "bisquine", traditional fishing boat with sails, for a day (€ 21/42) or a half-day (€ 12/24). Departure from Port-Mer.

Walks – One of the most beautiful parts of the **GR 34**, called **"the customs officers' path"**, snakes on 11 km between Cancale and the pointe du Nid, going by the pointe du Grouin. Wonderful views on the island of the Rimains and the bay of the Mont-St-Michel, and nice beaches at Port-Mer and at the Vergers. Take a day to do it, it's easy; some precipitous ways are not advisable if you have young children with you. In season, a shuttle bus goes to and from the pointe du Grouin (information at the Tourist Office).

Fête des reposoirs- 15th Aug, Cancalais "pardon".

Fête des hites (local word for oysters), 3rd Sat of Sept, oyster tasting and parade of the fraternal society.

SHOPPING

Markets- Sat morning near the church. At the same place, Summer Flavours, in July-Aug, 5-9pm.

Oysters and sea products – On the port, along quai Thomas, a small farmers' market is held everyday in season.

Other culinary specialities - Grain de Vanille, 12 Place de la Victoire, ☎ 02 23 15 12 70. Closed Tue and Wed, mid-Jan -mid-Feb and 1 week at the end of Nov. This welcoming tea-pastry shop makes wonderful ice creams with caramel made with salted butter, cakes and all kind of desirable delicacies.

L'Épicier Breton, 6 quai Thomas, ☎ 02 23 15 19 15. Closed 15 Nov-15 Dec. This small, densely packed shop offers an amazing choice of products coming from everywhere in Brittany.

the 20C. Today visitors can take a trip round the bay aboard one of these boats, **La Cancalaise** (♿ *see below*).

Sentier des Douaniers★

This former customs officers' watch-path branches off rue du Port (after some steps) and along the coast for 7km/4mi to the Pointe du Grouin. From the war memorial there is already a fine view of Mont-St-Michel Bay and Mont-Dol. Farther on, the **Pointe du Hock** affords an extensive **view**★ over Cancale Rock (Rocher de Cancale), Mon-St-Michel Bay and the mount itself; below on the right, at the foot of the cliff, are the oyster beds. On either side of Pointe du Hock, the Sentier des Douaniers overlooks the shore. If you follow the coastline as far as Port-Mer, you will get a splendid view of Pointe de la Chaîne opposite Cancale Rock.

Église St-Méen

Apply to the tourist office. 🕐 *Open daily in summer, when the Tourist Office is open.* 🕐 *Closed Sun the rest of the year and during Christmas and New Years holidays.* From the church tower's upper platform (189 steps), where there is a viewing table, you can enjoy a wide panoramaa of Mont-St-Michel Bay, Granville and some 40 belfries. In clear weather you can see the îles Chausey.

La Ferme Marine Musée de l'Huître et du Coquillage

Via ① on the map. ♿ 🔊 *Guided tours (1 hour) from mid-June to mid-Sep: 11am, 3pm and 5pm; from mid-February to mid-June; mid-September to 1 November at 3pm (except weekends and holidays).* ⊛€ *6.10 (children € 3.10).* ☎ *02 99 89 69 99.* Kids This museum is located in St-Kerber, at the heart of an oyster-breeding farm, and has displays on the evolution of oyster-breeding techniques as well as the activities of oyster farmers through the centuries. There is a lovely collection of shellfish (more than 1500 from all over the world).

Famous Cancale Oyster

Now only young oysters brought from Auray are cultivated in the bay, for a mysterious disease around 1920 decimated the native spat. Since then spat has begun to flourish in the immense beds in the open sea, and an oyster with a particular flavour is developing due to the richness of the plankton of Mont-St-Michel Bay.

Musée des Arts et Traditions populaires

& Open July and Aug, daily, 10am-noon (except Mon morning) and 2.30-6.30pm, Thur night 8.30-10pm; June and Sept, Thur to Sun 2.30-6.30pm. € 3.50 (children 10-16 € 1.75). ☎ 02 99 89 71 26.

Housed in the old Église St-Méen (1714, now deconsecrated), the museum is devoted to the popular arts and traditions of the Cancale region (fishing, oyster-breeding, farming, costumes, furnishings...) and to the life of Jeanne Jugan. There is also a presentation relating to the sailing school (École de Navigation des Rimains), which has been located in the town for over 100 years.

Maison de Jeanne Jugan

On request only. Apply to Mme Rey. No charge. ☎ 02 99 89 62 73.

The house is the birthplace of Jeanne Jugan (1792-1879), founder of the order known as the Little Sisters of the Poor.

Excursion

Pointe du Grouin★★

4.5km/2.5mi north by the D 201 – about 30min – local map see Côte d'ÉMERAUDE. Leave Cancale by rue du Stade (Y 27), then turn right onto the road which leads straight to the Pointe du Grouin. At the end of the road, after the Hôtel de la Pointe du Grouin, leave your car in a vast parking area and take a path, to the right of the signal station, which leads directly to the point.

La Pointe du Grouin with the Île des Landes in the distance

In a fine setting, this wild, rocky headland overlooks the sea from a height of 40m/131ft and affords a **panorama** which stretches from Cap Fréhel to Granville and Mont-St-Michel Bay with, in the distance, the Îles Chausey. At low tide one can take a path to a cave in the cliffside (height 10m/32ft, depth 30m/98ft).

The Île des Landes, opposite, is an island with a bird sanctuary and nature reserve. Housed in the blockhouse is an exhibition on sea birds.

Facing the Pointe du Grouin, the Île des Landes is a bird sanctuary and nature reserve.

CARHAIX-PLOUGUER

POPULATION 7 648
MICHELIN LOCAL MAP 308 J5 FINISTÈRE (29)

In the Roman era Carhaix was an important town commanding seven main roads; even today it is still the hub of a roadway network. In the centre of a cattle-rearing district, the town is a milk production centre. Threatened, like most rural areas, by a decline in its population, the town created the *Festival des Vieilles Charrues,* a popular traditional event which attracts 200 000 visitors every year in July.

▶ **Orient Yourself:** 60km/36mi NE of Quimper.
 Don't Miss: The Vieilles Charrues music festival. A boat trip on the Nantes-Brest canal.
 Also See: Les MONTAGNES NOIRES.

La Tour d'Auvergne (1743-1800)

Carhaix's famous son is **Théophile-Malo Corret,** known as La Tour d'Auvergne. When still very young, he became keenly interested in the Breton language but he was a soldier at heart. During the Revolution his exploits were such that he, a junior captain at 46, was offered the most exalted rank; but he refused – he wanted to remain with his troops.

When there was a pause in his campaigns, he would bring his faithful Celtic grammar out. He finally retired and spent all his time studying his favourite subject.

When the son of his Celtic master was called up for the army, La Tour, moved by the old teacher's grief, took the young man's place and enlisted, at 54 years of age, as a private soldier in the 46th half-brigade. New exploits followed. Bonaparte offered La Tour a seat on the Legislative Council, but failed to overcome his modesty. He was awarded a sword of honour and the title of "First Grenadier of the Republic". He was killed in 1800, during the Rhine campaign. All the army mourned him.

Every year, on the Saturday preceding 27 June, Carhaix celebrates the name-day of La Tour d'Auvergne.

Église St-Trémeur

Rebuilt in the 19C, the church's porch opens onto the bell-tower (16C); the tympanum over the doorway is adorned with the statue of St Trémeur, whose legend dates from the 6C.

Maison du Sénéchal

No 6 rue Brizeux. *Open July and Aug, daily, 9am-12.30pm and 1.30-7pm (Sun10am-1pm); rest of the year, open daily (except Sun and holidays), 10am -noon and 2-6pm.* *No charge.* *02 98 93 04 42.*

This building has a 16C façade. The ground floor is of granite decorated with carvings and the corbelled upper storeys are faced with slate and adorned with statuettes.

Address Book

TOURIST OFFICE
Carhaix-Plouguer, Rue Brizeux, ☎ 02 98 93 04 42, www.poher.com July-Aug: Mon-Sat 9am-12.30pm, 1.30-7pm, Sun and public holidays 10am-1pm; off season: Mon-Sat 10-12am, 2-5.30pm except Thur morning. Information on the guided visits offered by volunteers or professional guides (slate quarried, old town, canal from Nantes to Brest, rail network, etc.): everyday in July-Aug, € 3/1.

WHERE TO STAY
Prices are given for double occupancy in season. Prices are 20-30 % lower off season.

⊜⊜ **Noz-Vad,** 12 bd de la République, ☎ 02 98 99 12 12, www.nozvad.com – 43 rooms 🗍 📺 Comfortable and quiet rooms; the fancy decoration has been made by regional artists: armchairs and sofas embroidered with flowery designs, warm colours and beautiful bedding. Small garden. Breakfast € 7.

EATING OUT
⊜ **Crêperie Ty Gwechall,** 25 place des Halles, ☎ 02 98 93 17 00. 🕐 Closed Sun evening and Mon. Take care to lower your head as you enter this lovely house made of stones where the crepes are prepared with the best products of the region: andouille of Guéméné, goat cheese, etc.

⊜⊜ **La Ronde des Mets,** 5 Place de la Mairie, ☎ 02 98 93 01 50. 🕐 Closed Mon and Thur evening. Comfortably seated among the paintings made by regional artists, you will enjoy flavourful traditional cuisine.

LEISURE
Festival des Vieilles Charrues, www.vieillescharrues.asso.fr, end of July. One of the biggest festivals of French music (varieties, rock, world, etc.). At this time of the year, the fields around the town are full of spectators.

SHOPPING
Culinary specialities – Saveurs, 37 rue Brizeux, Carhaix-Plouguer ☎ 02 98 93 23 97. Tue-Sat 10-12am, 1.30-7pm. This very small grocery in the town centre abounds with products from the Brittany and other regions of France: sardines, cakes, caramels made with salted butter, foies gras, eaux-de-vie, flavoured teas, etc., but also tableware and a selection of amusing teapots.

Chatillon Chocolat, 46 Place Charles-de-Gaulle, Pleyben, ☎ 02 98 26 63 77, www.chatillon-chocolat.com Apr-Sept: 🕐 everyday 9am-12.30pm, 2-7pm; off season: Mon-Sat 9am-12.30pm, 2-6.30pm. Enjoy the "florentin": a subtle biscuit made with honey, almonds, oranges and chocolate, that Michel Chatillon makes with perfection. Dozens of other typically Breton treats – chocolates, cakes and biscuits – are offered in this small shop.

The tourist office (syndicat d'initiative) has its premises here (temporary exhibitions), and a small **museum** of local ethnography is open to the public on the first floor.

Plateau du Huelgoat

Round tour of 80km/50mi – 4hr. Leave Carhaix by rue Oberhausen and rue des Abattoirs in the direction of Plounevézel. Turn right at Croissant Marie-Joffré. 3km/1.2mi further on, past the Lesquern hamlet on the left, take a bend on the right onto an unsurfaced road.

Chapelle St-Gildas
The beacon of St-Gildas (238m/781 ft) stands to the right of the chapel (view of Monts d'Arrée).

⚡ The road leads through woodlands to the 16C chapel which has a square bell-tower crowned by a stone spire and grotesques at the east end. The beacon of St-Gildas (238m/781ft) stands to the right.

▸ *Return to the main road and turn right. Bear left towards Plourac'h.*

Église de Plourac'h

The Renaissance church in the form of a T was built largely in the 15C and 16C. The south face is the most ornate. The porch, which is Gothic in character, contains statues of the Apostles surmounted by canopies. A beautiful Renaissance doorway with windows on either side is crowned by three gables adorned with coats of arms. Near the font is an 18C altarpiece depicting the mysteries of the rosary and statues of St Adrian and St Margaret. Among the many statues ornamenting the church should be noted those of St Guénolé and St Nicodemus, dressed as a doctor of law, and a Descent from the Cross in which the Virgin wears a Breton cloak of mourning.

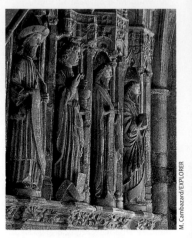

M. Cambazard/EXPLORER

Plourac'h – Apostles on the south doorway

▸ *Continue towards Callac.*

Callac

This town is dominated by the ruins of Botmel Church. In front of the stud farm stands a bronze statue of the stallion Naous, by Guyot. The town is also the home of the Breton spaniel, a pointer.

▸ *Take the road towards Guingamp and after 4km/2.5 mi turn right.*

Bulat-Pestivien

This former pilgrimage centre has retained a fine **church**★ built in the 15 and 16C with remarkable porches. The Renaissance tower, had a spire added in the 19C. Inside is a monumental sacristy – adorned with a frieze of macabre design – with a loggia which projects into the church. There is a curious lectern representing a peasant in the local Vannes costume; and a massive table dating back to 1583; offerings used to be placed there during the **pardon** which still takes place every year on the Sunday following 8 September.

There is a fine Calvary (1550) with a striking Entombment at *Pestivien (1km/0.6mi north of Bulat).*

▸ *Drive to Burthulet along the Rostrenen road.*

Chapelle de Burthulet

The simple 16C chapel, with wall belfry, stands in melancholy surroundings; one does not question the legend that says: "The devil died of cold here".

▸ *Make for Ty-Bourg and bear right.*

St-Servais

The writer Anatole Le Braz was born here. Note the 16C church.

▶ *Take the road opposite the church towards St-Nicodème. After 2km/0.6mi turn right.*

Gorges du Corong★

1hr on foot there and back. 🚶 *From the roundabout at the end of the road follow the path leading to the gorges.* The path runs along the river and into the Duault Forest. The river disappears beneath a mass of rocks to reappear as a series of cascades.

▶ *Turn round and bear right and right again in the direction of Locarn.*

Église de Locarn

📷 *Guided tours daily 10am-noon and 2-5pm.* ☎ *02 96 36 66 11.*
The **church** contains 17C furnishings (altarpiece, pulpit, statues), a remarkable 16C stained-glass window, a carillon wheel and the panels of a Flemish altarpiece, also of that period. Displayed in the presbytery is the **treasury**★. Note the following objects made of silver-gilt: St Henrin's bust and reliquary (in the form of an arm) both 15C, a processional cross (late 16C) and a 17C chalice.

▶ *Return to Carhaix-Plouguer via Trebrivan.*

CARNAC★

POPULATION 4 444
MICHELIN LOCAL MAP 308 M9 - MORBIHAN (56)

Carnac has always been known as a prehistoric capital. The name of Carnac is often associated with megalithic monuments.

▶ **Orient Yourself:** Though famous, it is not very big, located at the base of the Quiberon Peninisula.
😊 **Don't Miss**: The Petit-Ménec alignments

Megalithic Monuments★★ (Mégalithes)

A tour of the numerous megalithic monuments (alignments, dolmens, tumuli) to the north of Carnac makes a fascinating excursion.
Since the footsteps of innumerable visitors pose a serious threat to the soil (which is essential for the study of the mysterious origins of the megaliths) the public authorities have had to take action to protect the Ménec, Kermario and Kerlascan Alignments. If plant life is allowed to grow again, this will prevent any further erosion of the soil, which will in turn prevent the foundations of the menhirs from becoming exposed. At Kermario, if conditions are favourable, a temporary footbridge enables visitors to observe the alignment in its entirety, while reflecting that it is an example of Western Europe's first ever architecture.

Alignements du Ménec★★

The Ménec Alignments, over 1km/0.8mi long and 100m/330ft wide, include 1170 menhirs arranged in 11 rows. The tallest is 4m/12ft high.
They begin with a semicircle of 70 menhirs partly surrounding the hamlet of Ménec.

Address Book

TOURIST OFFICE

Carnac, Place de l'Église, ☎ 02 97 52 13 52, www.carnac.fr July-Aug: Mon-Sat 9.30am-1pm, 2-7pm, Sun 10am-1pm; off season: Mon-Sat 9.30am-12.30pm, 2-6pm. **Carnac-Plage,** 74 av. des Druides. July-Aug: Mon-Sat 9am-7pm, Sun 3-7pm; Sept-June: Mon-Sat 9-12am, 2-6pm. The office distributes a very precise map of the megaliths of the region and of the paths around.

GETTING AROUND

On bus – The local shuttle **Tatoovu** operates from the 15th of June to the 15 of Sept between Carnac-Ville, Carnac-Plage and the alignments. Information at the Tourist Office.

Rent a bike or a scooter – Marie-France et Christian Besret, 2 bis av. des Salines, ☎ 02 97 52 88 92. Bike for around € 5.35/day, scooters and mopeds for around € 21/day.

WHERE TO STAY

Prices are given for double occupancy in season. Prices are 20-40 % lower off season.

⊜⊜ **Chambres d'hôte Plume au vent,** *Élisabeth Rabot, 4 venelle Notre-Dame, Carnac-Ville,* ☎ 06 16 98 34 79, *rabot.carnac@wanadoo.fr – 2 rooms* This renovated family house shelters two large, beautiful rooms: "Marée haute" and "Marée basse", tastefully decorated.

⊜⊜ **Le Ratelier,** *4 chemin du Drouet, Carnac-Ville,* ☎ 02 97 52 05 04, *www.le-ratelier.com – 8 rooms* 🛏 📺 ✕ A former hostelry, low and vine-covered, in the centre of Old Carnac. Comfortable rooms (some with toilets outside), but the food is not equal to the reputation and the atmosphere is overrated. Breakfast € 8.

⊜⊜⊜ **La Marine,** *4 Place de la Chapelle, Carnac-Ville,* ☎ 02 97 52 07 33 *– 31 rooms.* 🛏 📺 ✕ Wonderfully located at the heart of the town, this hotel has just been bought by two very nice young couples. Rooms well kept. The restaurant (🕐 *closed Sat evening-Mon*) has a fixed-price menu starting at € 11. Breakfast € 6.70.

⊜⊜⊜⊜ **Le Diana,** *21 bd de la Plage, Carnac-Plage,* ☎ *02 97 52 05 38, www.lediana.com – 31 rooms* 🛏 📺 ✕ 🕐 *Closed in winter.* This luxury hotel offers rooms with all the comforts (staring at € 232), with view of the sea or the hotel's miniature golf. At the restaurant: fish, seafood and lobster. Breakfast € 19.

EATING OUT

⊜ **Chez Céline,** *among the alignments of Kermario,* ☎ *02 97 52 17 31.* 🕐 *In summer, daily 10am-9.30pm.* Pottery, leather, jewels, watercolour paintings, books, blown glass, candles, granite, sculptures, pixies… promises the leaflet. But you will also be able to enjoy a delicious buckwheat crepe on the terrace, among the standing stones. Perhaps you'll have the luck to meet the navigator Eugène Riguidel.

⊜ **Le Baobab,** *3 allée du Parc, Carnac-Plage,* ☎ *02 97 52 29 96, www.baobab-cafe.net.* 🕐 *Until 1am.* It's a pub, a café and an ice cream parlour rolled into one, set back from the shore. Savour some fish, a dish of oysters or a salad, or have a drink at night.

🐚 **Kreiz An Avel,** *plage de St-Colomban, 1 av. de la Chapelle,* ☎ *02 97 52 74 52.* 🕐 *Everyday until midnight.* A restaurant and a creperie, located in a pleasant place. The fish is fresh from the front bay. You can also order a beautiful seafood platter (crab, oysters, scampi…)

⊜⊜⊜ **Le Cornely,** *40 bd de Légenèse, Carnac-Plage,* ☎ *02 97 52 76 24.* 🕐 *Wed-Sun 11am-1am.* A very nice terrace in front of the Légenèse beach, a beautiful, shaded place full of green plants, where you will savour oyster stuffed with bacon or a frying pan full of Saint-Jacques with smoked duck filet

⊜⊜⊜⊜ **La Calypso,** *parc à huîtres du Pô,* ☎ *02 97 52 06 14.* 🕐 *Closed Mon in July-Aug.* You will not regret the walk to this little remote place on the waterfront where the food is prepared over wood fire grills: fish, lobsters or meat. The small village of St-Colomban, near, is a wonder. Booking advised.

The Menec Alignments

Alignements de Kermario★
🔹 *Guided tours organised in July and August, reservations required.* 🔸 *€25.* ☎ *02 97 52 29 81.*
990 menhirs in 10 rows occupy an area similar to the Ménec Alignments.

Alignements de Kerlescan★
In this field (880 x 139m/962 x 153yd), 540 menhirs are arranged in 13 rows and the whole is preceded by a semicircle of 39 menhirs.

▶ *From Kerlescan, take D 186 on the left, then turn right on the Chemin de la Métairie.*

Alignements du Petit Ménec
🕐 *Open all year.* Barely visible from the road, tucked amid the woods, this site, which has not been developed for tourism, is an enchanted place.

Tumulus St-Michel★
🔑 *Closed for restoration.* The tumulus is 120m/395ft long and 12m/38ft high (395 x 38ft), a mound of earth and stones covering two burial chambers and some 20 stone chests. Most of the artefacts found there are now in Carnac's Musée de Préhistoire and the Musée archéologique du Morbihan in Vannes. The galleries were first explored in the early 20C, but for safety reasons visitors are no longer allowed inside.
Surmounting the tumulus are the Chapelle St-Michel, decorated with fine frescoes (1961) by Alic Pasquo, a small 16C calvary and a viewing table. The **view**★ extends over the megaliths, the coast and the islands.

Dolmens de Mané-Kerioned
A group of three dolmens; the first has eight uprights with stylised engravings: axes, spirals, coats of arms etc.

Tumulus de Kercado
Leave the car at the entrance to Kercado Castle. 🕐 *Open Apr to Oct, daily 9am-7pm (5pm rest of the year).* 🔸 *Donations accepted.* 🛈 *Information at the crêperie nearby.*
This tumulus (3800 BC) is 30m/98ft across and 3.50m/11ft high and covers a fine example of a dolmen. A menhir stands on the summit. Note the carvings on the table and four uprights.

Additional Sights

Musée de Préhistoire J.-Miln-Z.-Le-Rouzic★★

&. ⏱ *Open mid-Sep to mid-June: 10am-12.30 and 1.30-6pm; mid-June tà mid-Sep: 10am-12h30 and 1.30-7pm.* ⏱ *Wed morning, January, 1 May and 25 Dec.* ⬥€ 5 (children € 2.50). ☎ 02 97 52 22 04. www.museedecarnac.com.

This Museum of Prehistory was founded in 1881 by the Scotsman James Miln (1819-81), who had excavated in Carnac and Kermario, and enriched by Zacharie Le Rouzic, native of Carnac.

In its new surroundings, these exceptional, beautifully displayed collections, cover prehistory from the Lower Paleolithic (450 000 BC) to the early Middle Ages.

The tour starts on the ground floor with an audio-visual presentation positioning the region's prehistory and archeology in world prehistory; the stratigraphic column presents, via the different strata, the different civilizations.

Proceeding chronologically, the visitor is presented: Lower Palaeolithic (chipped stone, scrapers, points); Middle and Upper Paleolithic (panels and documents); Mesolithic (primitive tools in wood or bone, shell ornaments, a reconstructed burial chamber); Neolithic Period, when man lived in settled communities and turned to crop growing and stock raising, marked by the realisation of megalithic tombs: dolmens or collective burial tombs (placed with the dead were pottery, polished axes, jewellery); menhirs and alignments. Also exhibited here are necklaces made of variscite (a green semiprecious stone), fine polished axes in jadeite or fibrolite, beads and pendants, pottery, engraved stones, dolmens and objects related to daily life. The first floor covers the Bronze Age (socketed axes, gold

Venus (1C)

N. Hautemanière/SCOPE

jewellery), Iron Age (reconstructed burial tomb, salt oven, Celtic gold coins), to the Roman era (model of a villa, statuettes of Venus, coins, objects related to daily life).

Church★

This 17C church is dedicated to **St Cornely,** the patron saint of horned cattle; his statue stands on the façade between two oxen. A massive bell-tower topped by an octagonal spire dominates the building. The porch on the north side is surmounted by a canopy in the form of a crown. Inside, the wooden vaults are covered with curious 18C **paintings** depicting the lives of the saint, Christ and St John the Baptist, and the Virgin. The communion table, pulpit and chancel screen are of the 18C and in wrought iron. In the chancel entrance, on the left, is a reliquary bust of St Cornely (18C gilt wood). The church's treasury is exhibited in the south aisle: chasuble, cross, chalices, monstrance etc.

Carnac-Plage ⚓

Carnac-Plage, with its gently shelving beach, has been developed in the shelter of the Presqu'île de Quiberon. It boasts several beaches: Grande Plage to the south (2km/1.2mi long); Légenès, Ty Bihan and St-Colomban to the west; Beaumer and Men-du to the east. Windsurfers meet at St-Colomban Beach the whole year.

DISCOVERING BRITTANY

140

Excursions

Other Megaliths★
To the NW along D 781 towards Lorient.

Dolmens de Rondossec
To the left on leaving Plouharnel. Three underground chambers.

Menhirs du Vieux-Moulin
After the level crossing. These stand in a field to the right of the road.

Alignements de Ste-Barbe
Near the road on the left in the direction of Kersily camp site. Four menhirs on the edge of a field.

Dolmen de Crucuno
Take a road to the right. It rises against a farm in the centre of the hamlet of Crucuno. Only one chamber remains with the great table supported by 11 uprights.

Dolmen de Mané-Croch
500m/0.7mi beyond Crucuno, on the left. A typical dolmen with side chambers.

Alignements de Kerzerho
To the right of the road at the entrance to Erdeven. The 10 rows here include 1 130 menhirs.

Plouharnel
Strategically located on the Qiberon Bay, this town has some lovely old houses and a charming 16C chapel, Notre-Dame-des-Fleurs. Inside, there is a 15C Tree of Knowledge carved in alabaster. A path behind the chapel leads to a 16C fountain.
An old blockhouse houses the **Musée de la Chouannerie** (&. ◷ *Open mid-June to mid-Sep, daily, 10am-noon and 2-5.30pm Sat, Sun and Mon afternoons only; Easter to mid-June 2-6pm.* ∞ €5. ☎ *02 97 52 31 31).* The Chouannerie movement, a Breton Royalist revolt, is recounted with dioramas peopled with terracotta figures, depicting the movement's main antagonists and Chouan arms, costumes, guillotine etc.
Outside Plouharnel, on the road to Auray, you can see the abbey of **Ste-Anne-de-Kergonan**, founded in 1897. Benedictine monks live and work here. There is a ceramic shop open to the public.

Abbaye St-Michel-de-Kergonan
3km/1.9mi by D 781 towards Plouharnel.
This Benedictine abbey, founded in 1898, is part of the Abbaye St-Pierre in Solesmes (& *see The Michelin Green Guide Chateaux of the Loire).* An imposing granite building includes a plain church with wooden vaulting held up by granite pillars.
Beyond the abbey shop (books, produce and objects made by the nuns), a gallery houses an exhibit on the Benedictine Order: its origin, Cistercian Law, expansion, the height of its power with Cluny etc and Gregorian chants.

CHÂTEAUBRIANT

POPULATION 12 065
MICHELIN LOCAL MAP 316 H1 - LOIRE-ATLANTIQUE (44)

This old fortified town with its imposing castle stands on the border of Brittany and Anjou, surrounded by woods dotted with lakes. By preserving and enchancing its historic and cultural heritage, Châteaubriant has become a lively tourist destination.

Sights

Château★

🕐 *Open all year.* 🚶 *Guided tour mid-Sep to mid-June Sat and Sun 3pm; mid-June to mid-Sep daily (except Tuesday) 11am, 2.30 and 4.30pm.* 👁€ 3. ☎ 02 40 28 20 90. *chateau.briant@cg44.fr.*

A part of the castle, which has been remodelled several times, is feudal while another part, dating from the Renaissance, was built by Jean de Laval. You can stroll round it along the esplanade and the gardens which go right down to the Chère.

All that remains of the feudal castle is a large keep on a height, connected with the entrance fort and the chapel by walls against which the two wings of the main building stand. The three wings of the Seigneurial Palace (Palais Seigneurial), opposite, are connected by elegant Renaissance pavilions. The roof is ornamented with dormer windows, which are emblazoned with the coats of arms of Châteaubriant, Laval and Montmorency.

The tour takes you up the central staircase (**1**) to a balcony from where there is a lovely view onto the Main Courtyard, embellished with gardens and a huge chestnut tree, the keep, and the city's rooftops. Continue on to the room (**2**) of Françoise de Foix with its coffered ceiling and monumental early-17C carved wood chimney. Next to it is the oratory (**3**) with the tombstone of Françoise de Foix on which is carved an epitaph by Clément Marot (French Renaissance poet).

The Magistrate's Court (Tribunal d'Instance – **J**) occupies a part of the palace while the public library (**B**) is housed in the south wing.

There are only two sections left of the colonnade which surrounded the Main Courtyard: the covered gallery (**4**) which ends at a charming staircase-pavilion and the other section (**5**) enclosing the Main Courtyard.

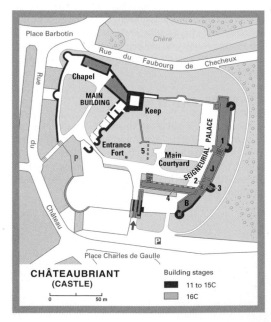

CHÂTEAUBRIANT
(CASTLE)

Building stages
⬛ 11 to 15C
⬜ 16C

0   50 m

Église de St-Jean-de-Béré

The church's oldest parts comprising the chancel and the transept crossing, which are built of fine red sandstone, date from the end of the 11C; the nave is 12C. Outside, near the picturesque south porch (16C), is a rustic altar from which services were held at the time of the plague.

Inside you will see the ornately decorated altarpiece at the high altar (1665).

La Sablière

At the ton gates, on the road to Pouancé, the Carrière des Fusillés is a memorial to the 27 hostages executed byt he Nazis on 22 Ocotber 1941. The recesses at the base contain soil from all the areas where the Resitance movement was particularly active.

Excursion

Abbaye de Melleray

21km/12mi south via D 178; turn left on D 18 at La Meilleraye-de-Bretagne (towards Riallé).

Founded in 1142 near a lovely lake, this Cistercian abbey has buildings which date from the 18C. The **Église Notre-Dame-de-Melleray,** completed in 1183, has been restored to its Cistercian severity, including a series of grisaille windows. Note the pointed white-stone arches resting on square pink-granite pillars. In the flat chevet, admire the gracious 17C wood polychrome **statue of the Virgin**.

COMBOURG★

POPULATION 4 850

MICHELIN LOCAL MAP 309 - ILLE-ET-VILAINE (35)

This picturesque old town stands at the edge of a great pool and is dominated by an imposing feudal castle. The tourist office is on place Albert-Parent, inside the restored 16C Maison de la Lanterne. Tourists who only want to take a quick look at the castle from the outside should walk along the local road which branches off the Rennes road and runs beside the pool, facing the castle and the village.

R. Mattes/MICHELIN

The perfect setting for a Romantic author

Chateaubriand at Combourg

The castle, which was built in the 11C, was enlarged in the 14C and 15C and restored in the 19C. It belonged first to the Du Guesclin family, and then in the 18C to the Count of Chateaubriand, father of François-René, the great Romantic writer.

In his *Memoirs*, Chateaubriand recalled the two years he spent at Combourg in his youth, adding still more to their romantic nature. The Count, a sombre and moody man, lived very much in retirement; when the family met he would walk up and down for hours in the drawing room, in silence, while no one dared to speak. The Countess, who was unwell, kept only a distant eye on the children. Months passed without a visitor. Left to themselves, the young Chateaubriand and his sister Lucile grew close, sharing their boredom, their dreams and their fears.

The old castle, almost deserted, was gloomy; the pool, the woods and the surrounding heath exuded melancholy. The Cat Tower (Tour du Chat), in which François-René had his lonely room, was haunted; a former Lord of Combourg was said to return there at night in the form of a black cat, which the boy watched for anxiously. The owls fluttering against the window and the wind rattling the door and howling in the corridors made him shiver.

It was there that the dreamy and melancholy soul of one of the great Romantic writers, was formed, or perhaps confirmed.

▶ **Orient Yourself:** North of Rennes.
🕐 **Organizing Your Time:** Combine your visit with a trip to Mont-St-Michel.
Especially for Kids: Cobac amusement park and pool.

Château★

🕐 *Open April-Oct: 9am-noon and 2-6pm (park only).* ✎ *Guided tours (45min) 2-5.30pm.* 🕐 *Closed Sat (except July and Aug).* ☎ *02 99 73 22 95. www. combourg.net.*
The exterior of the castle appears like a powerful fortress: its four massive towers, with pepper-pot roofs, its crenellated parapet walk, and its thick walls slit by narrow openings. The interior was rearranged in 1876. The tour takes you to the chapel, the drawing room (now divided in two), the Archives, where souvenirs of the author are displayed: autographs, awards, furniture etc and to François-René's austere bedroom in Cat Tower.

From the parapet walk there are views of the locality, the lake and the pretty, sweet-smelling park.

Excursions

Cobac Parc

10km/6mi northwest on D 73. At Lanhélin, follow the signs for the Parc de Loisirs. ♿🕐 *Open July and Aug, daily, 10am-7pm; Apr to June and first fortnight in Sept, 10.30am-6.30pm.* 🕐 *Closed mid-Sept to Easter.* ⊜ *€ 13/€ 11.* ☎ *02 99 73 80 16. www.cobac-parc.com.*
This open-air park, covering 10ha/25 acres, is a family recreation area with more than 30 leisure attractions, including a swimming pool with giant slide, quads, a small train, merry-go-rounds. There is a picnic area and a restaurant.
🌁 Check out the package deals that include attractions in St Malos, cruises, hotel discounts, etc.

Antrain

21km/10.5mi east on D 796 and D 313.
High on a promontory, Antrain is a market town with steep little streets and 16C and 17C houses. **Église St-André** (for the most part from the 12C) hosts an imposing 17C bell-tower, topped by a dome with lantern turrets.

Address Book

COMBOURG AND SURROUNDINGS

EATING OUT

⊜⊜ **Restaurant du Château**, Combourg, ☎ 02 99 73 00 38. 🕐 *Closed Sun evening off season, Sat noon and Mon from Oct to Apr, a week in Apr and 20th Dec-20th Jan*. Rustic and comfortable setting for classic cuisine of very high level, made with fresh regional products.

⊜ **L'écrivain**, 20 Place St-Gilduin, Combourg, ☎ 02 99 73 01 61. 🕐 *Closed Wed evening, Thur and Sun evenings off season, Thur in summer, Feb and Nov school holidays*. Light and flavourful cuisine, basically traditional but with a contemporary flair. Bright room giving onto a garden or rustic room with woodwork, more intimate.

⊜⊜ **Auberge de la Tourelle**, 1 Place de la Mairie, Sens-de-Bretagne, ☎ 02 99 39 60 06. 🕐 *Closed Mon, Tue.* In a rustic decor, enjoy simple but delicious cuisine, inspired by the region. During the week, at noon: fixed-price menu € 11.

Château de Bonnefontaine

1.5km/1mi south. Leave Antrain by Rues Général-Lavigne and Bonne-Fontaine. 🕐 *Park open Easter to All Saints' Day, daily, 9am-6pm.* ⊜ *€3.* ☎ *02 99 98 31 13; www.bonnefontaine.com.*

Built in 1547 as a feudal manor-house and remodelled in the 19C, this castle rises in the centre of a beautifully maintained park. The elegant turrets adorning the massive main range, the tall windows and the carved dormer windows balance the severity of the squat, machicolated pepper pot towers.

Bazouges-la-Pérouse

8km/5mi SW of Antrain on D 313, which intersects D 155.

This pleasant village is an artists' haven, where painters sculptors and others display their work and organise workshops in summer.

Château de la Balue

Visit of the gardens on reservation and from 1-5.30pm from 1 May to 30 Sep. ⊜ *€ 8.* ☎ *02 99 97 47 86. www.la-ballue.com.*

In the eyes of some Romantic writers, this residence symbolised the royalist rebellion, and for this reason was visited by Musset, Balzac and Hugo. The **garden**★ holds many surprises for the visitor.

CONCARNEAU★★

POPULATION 18 630
MICHELIN LOCAL MAP 308 H7 - FINISTÈRE (29)

Concarneau offers a fascinating picture of a bustling fishing port, the charm of a walled town, enclosed in granite ramparts, and the facilities of a popular resort. France's first fishing port, it is the leading market for tunny caught in African waters and in the Indian Ocean, and possesses three fish canneries and holds a colourful **fresh fish auction** *(criée)*. There is an attractive **general view**★ of Concarneau, its fishing port and the bay from Moros Bridge (Pont du Moros).

▶ **Orient Yourself:** South of Quimper.
👁 **Don't Miss:** *La Criée* - the fish auction.

⏱ **Organizing Your Time:** Visit the walled town early ine th morning, when it is less crowded

Walled Town★★ (Ville Close) *Allow 2hr*

Narrow alleys cover the islet of irregular shape (350 x 100m/1 150 x 330ft) linked to the mainland by two small bridges between which stands a fortified building. Massive ramparts, built in the 14C and completed in the 17C, surround the town. Cross the two small bridges and pass under a gateway leading to a fortified inner courtyard. There is a fine well.

Musée de la Pêche★

♿⏱ *Open early July to early Sept, daily, 9am-8pm; rest of the year, open 9am -noon and 2-6pm.* ⏱ *Closed last three weeks of January, 1 Jan and 25 Dec.* ✉ *€ 6/€ 4.* ☎ *02 98 97 10 20.*

This fishing museum is located in what used to be the arsenal which also served as barracks and a fishing school. In the courtyard *Commandant Garreau*, a lifeboat built in 1894, is exhibited. Accompanying notices, models, photographs, dioramas, and some 10 boats explain the history of Concarneau, its evolution as a port, traditional and modern fishing techniques (whale, cod, sardine, tuna, herring), boats, canning industry, shipbuilding, navigational equipment and rescue operations.

Outside (via Major's Tower – Tour du Major) a fishing boat is moored; climb aboard *Hémérica*, a trawler put out of commission in 1981, and relive the hard life of the fishermen.

Walk round the ramparts

⏱ *Mid-June to mid-Sept, daily, 10am-8pm; rest of the year, 10am-5pm.* ⏱ *Closed during school holidays in Feb and Nov. Access to the ramparts may be forbidden in adverse weather conditions or during the Blue Nets Festival.* ✉ *No charge off season.*

▶ 🚶 *Follow the signs. For the first part of the tour, go up a few steps on the left and follow the wall walk.*

Glimpses of the inner harbour and the fishing fleet can be caught through the loopholes. You also get an overall impression of the New Tower (Tour Neuve).

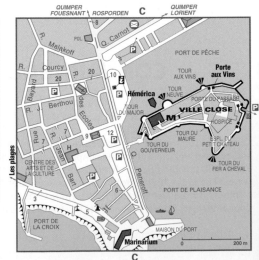

CONCARNEAU	
Bougainville Bd	C 3
Croix Quai de la	C 5
Dr-P.-Nicolas Av. du	C 6
Dumont-d'Urville R.	C 7
Gare Av. de la	C 8
Gaulle Pl. Gén.-de	C 9
Guéguin Av. Pierre	C 10
Jean-Jaurès Pl.	C 12
Morvan R. Gén.	C 20
Vauban R.	C 29
Musée de la Peche	C M¹

Concarneau

▶ *For the second part of the tour, return by the same path to the starting-point and descend the steps.*

After skirting Esplanade du Petit Château, giving onto the marina, you overlook the channel between the two harbours.

▶ *Return to the town by Porte du Passage. By the corner of the Hospice take rue St-Guénolé, which bears left towards place St-Guénolé.*

From place St-Guénolé a short alley to the right leads to **Porte aux Vins** (Wine Gateway) through the ramparts. As you go through the gate *(porte)* you will get a typical view of the trawlers moored in the harbour.

▶ *Rue Vauban brings you back out of the walled town.*

The Harbours

By way of avenue Pierre-Guéguin and Quai Carnot, take a quick look at the **Port de pêche** (fishing port), where the main fishing fleet (trawlers and cargo boats) is moored; you may see the day's catch being unloaded. Then follow avenue du Dr-P.-Nicolas and walk round the **marina**. The embarkation point for excursions is at the end of this quay, on the left.

On the left of Quai de la Croix is the marine laboratory (Laboratoire Maritime) of the Collège de France. Inside visit the **Marinarium** (& Open July and August, daily, 10am7pm; Apr to June and Sept, 10am-noon and 2-6pm. Closed January. €5. 02 98 97 06 59. www.mnhn.fr), an exhibition devoted to the sea world: aquariums, dioramas and audio-visual displays.

After passing the picturesque old fish market where fish used to be sold by auction, the 15C Chapelle Notre-Dame-de-Bon-Secours and a small lighthouse, you may skirt **Port de la Croix** (follow boulevard Bougainville), which is sheltered by a jetty. Looking back, there is a good view of the Pointe du Cabellou and, further on, of the Pointe de Beg-Meil. Out at sea are the Îles Glénan.

Address Book

TOURIST OFFICE

Concarneau, Quai d'Aiguillon, ☎ 02 98 97 01 44, www.tourismeconcarneau.fr July-Aug: everyday 9am-6.45pm; off season 9-12am and 2-6pm.

WHERE TO STAY

☕🛏 **Hôtel des Halles**, *Place de l'Hôtel de ville*, ☎ *02 98 97 11 41, www.hoteldeshalles.com – 22 rms* 📶 📺 Nearby the walled town, this very pleasant establishment has just been renovated and offers attractive rooms, some with pine floorboards and others with beech wood parquet. Breezy welcome. Breakfast € 8.

☕🛏💶 **Kermoor**, *plage des Sables Blancs*, ☎ *02 98 97 02 96, kermoor@ lespiedsdansleau.com – 12 rooms* 📶 📺 ☂ The discreet facade of this 1900 villa hides a very beautiful hotel. The atmosphere is reminecent of a ship's cabin: onboard furniture, portholes, painted wainscots, model ships. All rooms have a view on the sea, and 3 have a terrace. Parking. Breakfast € 12.

☕🛏🍴 **Océan**, *plage des Sables-Blancs*, ☎ *02 98 56 53 50, hotel-ocean@ wanadoo.fr – 53 rooms* 📶 📺 ✕ 🛏 In a modern neighbourhood along the coast, this imposing new building shelters big rooms facing either the sea or the swimming pool. The comfortable dining room (🕐 closed Sun evening, Mon noon and Sat from Oct to Apr) has a nice view over the beach and the bay; seafood holds pride of place on the menu. Parking. Breakfast € 13.

EATING OUT

☕ **Xtra Kfé**, *8 av. du Dr Nicolas*, ☎ *02 98 50 54 21.* 🕐 *Everyday 11am-1am.* Here's a lively spot that doesn't serve chips, mayonnaise or ketchup, but rather home made bread with good meat and fresh vegetables, tortillas, paninis and home made pizzas. It's delicious!

☕🛏 **Le Buccin**, *1 rue Duguay-Trouin*, ☎ *02 98 50 54 22, www.le-buccin.com.* 🕐 *Closed Sun evening, Thur and Sat noon.* A dining room with a simple and fresh setting located on the ground floor of an old house, appetizing recipes that adapt everyday the sea products,

very warm and attentive service and reception: perfect harmony!

☕🛏 **Grill l'Océania**, *3 rue Alfred Le Ray*, ☎ *02 98 50 81 58.* 🕐 *Tue-Sun 7pm-midnight, Fri-Sat until 2am.* The specialities of the place: delicious and copious dishes cooked over a wood fire. Fish (swordfish, bluefin tuna) but also meat, and not only beef but African-style frogs' legs, ostrich and even kangaroo!

☕🛏 **L'Amiral**, *1 av. Paul Guéguin*, ☎ *02 98 60 55 23.* 🕐 *Closed Mon and Sun evening off season.* A big pub, a restaurant and an ice-cream parlour with a pleasant marine setting. Generous cuisine made from the catch of the day: sea bream, red mullet, lobster, scampi, etc.

☕🛏💶 **La Coquille**, *quai du Moros*, ☎ *02 98 97 08 52.* 🕐 *Tue-Sun noon: 12am-1.30pm, 7-9pm.* If you have no car, use the ferry boat at the far end of the walled town and cross the fishing port basin to reach this gastronomic restaurant serving seafood specials, in a room full of Breton furniture.

☕🛏 **Chez Armande**, *15 bis av. du Dr Nicolas*, ☎ *02 98 97 00 76.* 🕐 *Closed Tue and Wed in July-Aug, mid-Dec-early Jan, 2 weeks in Feb.* Enjoy your meal on the terrace, in front of the marina: lobsters stew with mushroom sauce or a "cotriade Concarnoise". If you like leg of lamb, try the "gigot de 7 heures", or you may prefer of filet of fine "Salers" beef.

LEISURE

Tour of the criée (fish auction) – In summer, the guided tours (€ 5) are carried out daily by **Video-mer**, ☎ 02 98 97 01 44, www.videomer. fr, and by **À l'assaut des remparts**, ☎ 02 98 50 55 18, www.alassautdesremparts.fr. Films on life as a fisherman and trips on board a trawler.

Beaches – Along the boulevard Katherine Wylie, that offers beautiful views of the bay of Concarneau, the ledge is lined with the beaches of **Rodel**, Les **Dames** and **Miné**. Farther on, the beach of **Cornouaille** and the **Sables-Blancs** are reachable from the centre by urban bus BUSCO (n° 2).

Boat trips and cruises – In July-Aug, the **Vedette Jeanne-Yvonne links-up.**

Environs

Beuzec-Conq

1.5km/0.9mi N. Follow rue Jules-Simon and cross D 783. Once in rue de Stang, go through the entrance gate on the left.

The **Kériolet Mansion**, built in the 15C, was transformed in the 19C into a medieval-style fantasy dwelling by the wealthy Russian princess Zenaïde Narischkine-Youssopoff.

Rosporden

13km/8mi NE along D 70.

The church **bell-tower**★ is reflected in a pool formed by the River Aven. There are many canning factories in the town which is also famous for its mead (*chouchen* in Breton).The **church,** dating from the 14C-15C, was remodelled in the 17C. The square **belltower**★ is surmounted by an octagonal spire.

Excursions

From Concarneau to Pont-Aven by the coast road

45km/28mi – about 2hr. Leave Concarneau by S on the town plan towards Quimperlé and after 2.5km/1.25mi bear right.

Pointe du Cabellou★

▶ *Go round the point starting from the right.*

The car park affords a fine **view**★ of the site of Concarneau and the walled town. The road skirts the rocky coastline amid the villas and pine trees and offers pretty views of Baie de la Forêt and the Îles de Glénan.

▶ *Return to the main road and make for Quimperlé. Turn right at Pont-Minaouët and right again at Kermao.*

The road goes through **Pouldohan** (fine beach and large sailing school) and Pendruc.

Pointe de la Jument

▶ *15min on foot there and back.*

Enjoy the fine rocky site and view of Cabellou, the bay and Beg-Meil, and the coast of Loctudy in the distance.

▶ *Make for the Pointe de Trévignon going via Lambell where you turn right, Lanénos and Ruat.*

Pointe de Trévignon

An old fort stands at the tip of the headland; fishing boats and the lifeboat are berthed in the tiny port to the west. Fine **view**★ to the right of La Forêt Bay and Beg-Meil, Bénodet Bay, and on the left of the Îles de Glénan and near the coast of Verte and Raguenès Islands.

▶ *Follow the road along Kersidan Beach and turn left to Kercanic.*

Kercanic

This picturesque hamlet has several traditional thatched farmhouses.

▶ *Turn back and bear left.*

The road runs through the charming village of **Kerascoët** (thatched cottages) towards Port-Manech. In Trémorvezen, turn right beyond the chapel.

◔ *The remainder of the excursion is described in the opposite direction under PONT-AVEN: Excursions.*

LA CORNOUAILLE★★

MICHELIN LOCAL MAP 308 F/H 5/7 - FINISTÈRE (29)

Historic Cornouaille, the kingdom and then the duchy of medieval Brittany, extended far to the north and east of its capital, Quimper, reaching Landerneau, the neighbourhood of Morlaix and Quimperlé.

The area included in our tour is much smaller and is limited to the coastal districts of Cornouaille, west of Quimper. This very extensive coastline is marked by two rocky peninsulas, Cap Sizun, "Le Cap", and the Presqu'île de Penmarch, which are its main tourist attractions. This is a maritime country in which fishing plays an important role; the ports of Guilvinec, Audierne and Douarnenez specialise in sardines and spiny lobster.

The interior is densely cultivated (potatoes and early vegetables), and the countryside with its tranquil horizons is covered with small hamlets of whitewashed houses.

Cap Sizun★★

1 From Quimper to Plozévet

158km/98mi – allow one day

Quimper★★ – ◔ *See QUIMPER.*

▶ *Leave Quimper northwest by rue de Locronan and rue de la Providence.*

The road goes up the rural valley of the Steïr with its wooded slopes and then through undulating countryside.

Plogonnec

The 16C **church**, remodelled in the 18C, has a fine Renaissance bell-tower; it also has 16C stained-glass windows; in the chancel to the left of the high altar the windows recount the Transfiguration, above the altar the Passion and to the right the Last Judgement.

Locronan★★ – ◔ *See LOCRONAN.*

▶ *The Douarnenez road with Forest of Nevet on its left, leads to the sea.*

Kerlaz

Note the 16C and 17C church with an openwork bell-tower.
There is a good view of Douarnenez, which is reached after skirting the fine Ris Beach.

Douarnenez★ – ♿ *See DOUARNENEZ.*

▸ *Leave Douarnenez, go through Tréboul and make for Poullan-sur-Mer where you turn left and then right and right again.*

Chapelle Notre-Dame-de-Kérinec

The chapel, surrounded by trees, dates from the 13C and 15C; the elegant bell-tower was struck by lightning in 1958 but an exact replica, as it appeared in the 17C, has

---

Address Book

WHERE TO STAY

⬭⬭ **Hôtel Sterenn** – *Route phare d'Eckmühl, 29760 Penmarch* – ☏ 02 98 58 60 36 – 🕐 *closed 11 Oct-14 Apr and Mon except from 21 June to 20 Sept* – 🅿 – *16 rooms.* Facing the sea, between Saint Guénolé and the Eckmühl lighthouse, this modern hotel is very welcoming. Almost all of its well-kept rooms have bay views. And its restaurant is well known to food lovers from near and far!

⬭⬭ **Hôtel Roi Gradlon** – *On the beach, 29700 Audierne* – ☏ 02 98 70 04 51 – 🕐 *closed 5 Jan-20 Feb* – 🅿 – *19 rooms* Breakfast € 8.50. All the rooms in this little hotel look onto the sea. It offers simple comforts, but is beautifully situated and provides a good starting point for discovering the Cournouaille. Its dining room serves seafood with a good view. Children's menu.

⬭⬭ **Hôtel La Baie des Trépassés** – *29770 La Baie des Trépassés, 3km/1.8mi from the Pointe du Raz via D 784* – ☏ 02 98 70 61 34 – 🕐 *closed 5 Jan-12 Feb* – 🅿 – *27 rooms.* Breakfast €8. The location of this hotel alone is worth making a detour. It stands on the beach, 3km/6mi from the Pointe du Raz, and offers a unique view over the bay, the Pointe and the Île de Sein. Its rooms resemble the rest of the establishment: functional and clean. There is a bar, an ice-cream salon, and a restaurant.

EATING OUT

⬭ **L'Étrave** – *Route de la pointe du Van sur D 7, 2km/1mi, 29770 Cléden-Cap-Sizun* – ☏ 02 98 70 66 87 – 🕐 *closed 2 Nov-27 Mar and Wed.* Opposite the Pointe de Brezellec, this restaurant looks like a private home. Inside, it is decorated with a touch of maritime decor, which is reinforced by the ceiling in the shape of an inverted boat's hull. The food is simple and fresh. Children's menu.

⬭ **La Pêcherie** – *15 rue Pasteur, 29770 Audierne* – ☏ 02 98 75 01 26. "No meat, no French fries, no frozen food": that's the motto of this nice little bistro located slightly back from the port. Its fresh fish, garden vegetables and its convivial atmosphere make it an essential stop. Whether you come for a full course meal, or just one dish, you will always receive a warm welcome.

SPORT AND RECREATION

Scuba diving at Cap-Sizun – *Club des plongeurs du cap Sizun* – 🕐 *Open year round* – ☏ 02 98 70 24 10. This club organises diving outings for novices and for the more advanced. (A medical certificate certifying no physical counter-indications to scuba-diving is required).

Surfing at La Torche – *École de surf de Bretagne "Beg An Torchen" – La Torche* – ☏ 02 98 58 53 80 – open Easter-Oct.

Deep-sea fishing – *On board the Yannick –At Lechiagat (near Guilvinec)* – ☏ 02 98 58 10 10. The excursion lasts half a day.

Wind-surfing – *At Esquibien* – ☏ 02 98 70 21 69. Le Club Nautique de la Baie d'Audierne is open all year.

been rebuilt. Note the flat east end and to the left the rounded pulpit dominated by a Calvary.

Église Notre-Dame-de-Confort

The 16C church with its galleried bell-tower dating from 1736, has 16C **stained-glass windows** in the chancel, one of which is a Tree of Jesse. Over the last arch in the nave, on the north side, hangs a carillon wheel with 12 little bells. The chimes are rung to beg the Virgin for the gift of speech for children who have difficulties in speaking.

▸ *Leave Confort in the direction of Pont-Croix and turn right, then left onto D 307 towards Beuzec-Cap-Sizun and again right after 2km/1mi.*

Pointe du Millier★

A small lighthouse stands on this arid site.

🚶 From the point *(15min on foot there and back)* there is a **view**★ of Douarnenez Bay and Cap de la Chèvre.

▸ *On leaving Beuzec-Cap-Sizun bear right.*

Pointe de Beuzec★

From the car park there is a **view**★ of the approach to Douarnenez Bay, the Presqu'île de Crozon and in fine weather, of the Pointe de St-Mathieu.

Réserve du Cap Sizun★

🕐 10am–6pm. *Apply to the Maison de la Réserve, Chemin de Kérisit, 29770 Goulien.* ☎ *02 98 70 13 53.*

The most interesting time for a visit is at nesting time in the spring. Starting in March, most birds finish nesting by mid July. The adults and chicks then leave the sanctuary progressively through the month of August. In the magnificent and wild setting of the Castel-ar-Roc'h, more than 70m/230ft above sea level, such sea-birds as guillemots, cormorants, common herring gulls, lesser black-backed gulls, great black-backed gulls, which are the rarest of all, and black-legged kittiwakes can be seen, sitting on their nests and feeding their young.

Herring gull

M. Guillou/MICHELIN

Pointe de Brézellec★

Park the car by the lighthouse enclosure. Go to the rock platforms nearby. There is a magnificent **view**★ along an exceptionally long stretch of coast of saw-tooth rocks and sheer cliffs: Presqu'île de Crozon, Pointe de St-Mathieu, Pointe du Van and Pointe de Tévennec can be seen.

▸ *Turn back and turn right towards Pointe du Van.*

Pointe du Van★★

1hr on foot there and back.

🚶 The 15C **Chapelle St-They** stands on the left of the path. On the point itself follow the half-hidden path, bearing always to the left, which goes right round the headland. The Pointe du Van, which is too big to be seen all in one glance, is, nevertheless, less spectacular than the Pointe du Raz, but it has the advantage of being off the tourists' beaten track. There is a **view**★★ of the Pointe de Castelmeur, the Pointe de Brézellec, the Cap de la Chèvre, the Pointe de Penhir, the Pointe de St-Mathieu and the Tas de

B. Kaufmann/MICHELIN

Pointe du Van

Pois rocks on the right; the Île de Sein, the Vieille Lighthouse and the Pointe du Raz on the left. It is recommended that you do not climb down the cliffs.
The landscape becomes ever harsher: no trees grow; stone walls and barren moss cover the final headland.

▶ *Turn round and take, immediately on the right, a small road which hugs the coast leading to the Baie des Trépassés and affording fine views of the jagged coastline from the Pointe du Raz to the Île de Sein.*

Baie des Trépassés
It was once thought that the drowned bodies of those who had been shipwrecked, and which the currents brought to the bay, gave the bay its name of Bay of the Dead. Another, less macabre explanation, based on the existence of a stream that flowed in the marshes, was that the original Breton name for the bay was *boe an aon* (bay of the stream), which became *boe anaon* (bay of the troubled souls). Now it is believed that the bay was the embarkation point from the mainland for Druids' remains which were taken over to Île de Sein for burial. According to local legend, the town of Is once stood in the little valley which is now covered in marshes.
The swell runs unimpeded into the bay, where it breaks with an impressive display of force.

Pointe du Raz★★★ –   *See Pointe du RAZ.*

▶ *Take the road in the direction of Audierne and after 10km/6mi, turn right towards St-Tugen.*

St-Tugen★
The nave and the tower of the **chapel** are in the 16C Flamboyant Gothic style, the transept and the east end in the 17C Renaissance style. There is a fine south porch surmounted by an elegant pierced tympanum, containing six statues of Apostles in Kersanton granite and three 16C statues of Christ, the Virgin and St Anne.
Inside may be seen interesting 17C furnishings, including several altarpieces and a curious catafalque flanked at each end by statues of Adam and Eve.

Audierne★
This pleasure port and fishing village (mainly lobster and crabs) lies on the estuary of the Goyen, at the foot of a wooded hill in a **pretty setting**★.

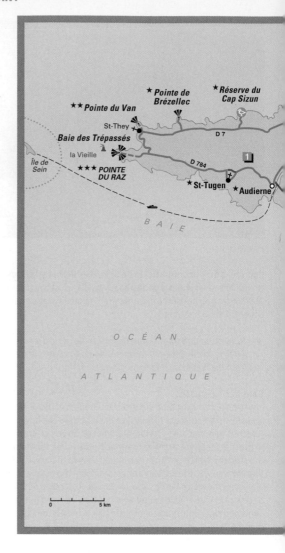

Aquashow★

Kids ⏰ *Apr-Sep: daily 10am-7pm; Oct: 2-5pm except Fri-Sat; school holidays: daily 2-5pm.* ∞ *€ 10.50/€ 7. www.aquarium.fr.*

More than 180 species of fish and various sea creatures live here in this aquarium than is well worth a two-hour visit. There are "petting" areas where you can touch different fish and crustceans. The sharks are favourites, and the the demonstration of diving and fishing birds is fascinating.

Pont-Croix★

A small town built up in terraces on the south bank of the Goyen, also known as the River Audierne. Its narrow streets, hemmed in between old houses, slope picturesquely down to the bridge. A great procession take place there on 15 August. Take Petite and Grande-Rue-Chère; the latter is a charming stepped street. The church, **Notre-Dame-de-Roscudon★,** is interesting with its Romanesque nave dating from the early 13C. The chancel was enlarged in 1290 and the transept was built in

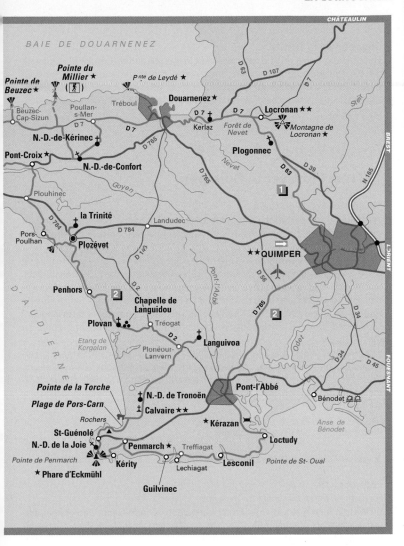

BAIE DE DOUARNENEZ

1450 and crowned by the very fine belfry with a steeple 67m/223ft high. There is an elegant south porch (late 14C) with three tall decorated gables.
Inside, the church contains fine furnishings: in the apsidal chapel is a **Last Supper** carved in high relief in wood (17C); on the right of the chancel, the Chapel of the Rosary (Chapelle du Rosaire) has fine **stained glass** (c 1540).

▶ *Go to Plouhinec, the native town of the sculptor Quillivic, the on to Pors-Poulhan.*

Pors-Poulhand
This tiny port is sheltered by a pier. Before Plozévet, there are fine views of Audierne Bay and the Phare d'Eckmühl.

Plozévet
There is a 15C porch to the Gothic church. A menhir, decorated by Quivillic, stands nearby as a First World War memorial.

▷ *Follow the route 1km/0.6mi further north.*

Chapelle de la Trinité

The chapel is T-shaped; the nave was built in the 14C and the remainder added in the 16C. Outside note the charming Louis XII decoration (transitional style between Gothic and Renaissance with Italian influence) of two walls on the south transept side. Inside, the nave arches come down onto groups of columns with florally decorated capitals.

Presqu'île de Penmarch★

② From Plozévet to Quimper

100km/62mi – allow half a day

The journey is made through bigouden country, which has become known through the women's local costume, in particular their unique headdress in the shape of a little lace menhir.

The **Presqu'île de Penmarch** was one of the richest regions in Brittany up to the end of the 16C: cod-fishing (the "lenten meat") brought wealth to the 15 500 inhabitants. But then the cod deserted the coastal waters, and a tidal wave brought devastation. Final disaster came with the brigand **La Fontenelle** who took the locality by surprise in spite of its defences. He killed 5 000 peasants, burned down their houses and loaded 300 boats with booty which he then took back to his stronghold on the Île Tristan.

From Plozévet to the tip of Penmarch Peninsula the sea breaks against a great sweep of shingle, continually rolling and knocking the stones of the some 20km/12mi arc. The even coastline is altogether inhospitable and desolate. The little villages with their white houses, which lie back from the coast, turn to the hinterland for their livelihood.

Plozévet – ⚇ *See description above.*

▷ *Leave Plozévet south towards Penhors; the road then follows the coastline.*

Penhors

For access to the chapel, make for the beach.

On the first Sunday in September the great pardon of Notre-Dame-de-Penhors, one of the largest of Cornouaille (⚇ *see Calendar of events*) takes place. The night before (Saturday) there is a procession with torches. On Sunday afternoon the procession walks through the countryside until it comes to the shore line and back to the chapel where the benediction of the sea takes place.

Maison de l'Amiral

Kids ♿ ⏰ *July-Aug: 10.30am-7.30pm; May-June and Sep: daily excep Mon: 2-7pm; rest of the year Sun and holidays 2-7pm.* 🚗 *€ 4.95/€ 2.50 (children under 5 free of charge)* ☎ *02 98 51 52 52. www.maison-de-l-amiral.com.*

This is an interesting place to take a break and admire the collection of thousands of sea shells. Two rooms are devoted to displays of stuffd and mounted birds. There are five very short films on local sealife, and children are free to roam the park.

▷ *Proceed to Plovan.*

Plovan

A small 16C church adorned with beautifully coloured modern (1944) stained-glass windows and a fine turreted belfry. Nearby is a 16C Calvary.

Chapelle de Languidou
The ruined 13-15C chapel still has some interesting elements, particularly the fine rose window.

▶ *Make for Plonéour-Lanvern via Tréogat then bear left to Languivoa.*

Chapelle de Languivoa
1.5km/1mi to the east of Plonéour-Lanvern.
This 14C and 17C chapel (restored) forms an imposing ensemble adorned by rose windows and Gothic arcading. The dismantled belfry porch still dominates the devastated nave and Classical style entrance with its engaged Doric columns. The chapel contains the Virgin of Notre-Dame-de-Languivoa suckling her child. A pardon is held on 15 August.

▶ *At Plonéour-Lanvern take the road to Plomeur and after 2km/1mi turn right.*

Calvaire and Chapelle Notre-Dame-de-Tronoën★★
The Calvary and Chapelle of Notre-Dame-de-Tronoën stand beside Audierne Bay, in the bare and wild landscape of the dunes.
The **Calvary**★★ (1450-60) is the oldest in Brittany. The childhood and Passion of Christ are recounted on two friezes. The intensity and originality of the 100 figures are remarkable. Details of the sculpted figures, although worn by exposure, can be fully appreciated. The scenes are depicted in the round or in high relief in a coarse granite from Scaer, which is friable and tends to attract lichen (the Last Supper and the Last Judgment on the south face are greatly damaged). Three scenes on the north face are in Kersanton granite: the Visitation, an unusual Nativity with a sleeping Joseph and the Magi in 15C vestment. Christ and the thieves are also carved in hard granite.
The 15C **chapel** has a pierced belfry, flanked by turrets. Beneath the vaulted roof are old statues. The ornate south door opens on to the Calvary. A pardon takes place annually *(see Calendar of events)*.

▶ *Continue along the road bearing right and right again.*

Pointe de la Torche
The name is a corruption of the Breton Beg an Dorchenn: flat stone point. Note the fine **view**★ of the St-Guénolé rocks and Audierne Bay. There is a tumulus with a large

Surf's up at Pointe de la Torche

dolmen. The two beaches, which are dangerous for swimming, are the rendezvous of surfing enthusiasts.

Plage de Pors-Carn

This great sandy beach along La Torche Bay is the terminal point of the telephone cable linking France and the USA.

St-Guénolé

Behind the fishing port (coastal fishing) are the famous **rocks** against which the sea breaks furiously.

Musée préhistorique finistérien★

At the entrance to St-Guénolé. ♿ ⏰ *Open June to mid-Sept, daily (except Tues), 11am-12.30pm and 2.30-6.30pm; rest of the year by appointment.* ⌨ *€ 3/€ 2.* ☎ *02 98 58 60 35.*

A series of megaliths and Gallic steles or obelisks called *lec'hs* stand around the museum. Start the visit from the left to see the exhibits in chronological order, from the Stone Age to the Gallo-Roman period. On display are, in the first gallery, a reconstruction of an Iron Age necropolis, Gallic pottery with Celtic decorations and a Gallic stele with spiral carving; in the south gallery, polished axes of rare stone, flint arrowheads, bronze weapons and chests with grooves.

The museum contains all the prehistorical antiquities discovered in Finistère except for the rich collection displayed in the Musée des Antiquités Nationales at St-Germain-en-Laye (see the Michelin Green Guide to Flanders, Picardy and the Paris Region).

Chapelle Notre-Dame-de-la-Joie

This 15C chapel with its pierced bell-tower is flanked by turrets. The 16C Calvary is adorned with a *Pietà*. A *pardon* is held on 15 August.

Phare d'Eckmühl★

Tours of the lighthouse depend on the availability of the keepers. ☎ *02 98 58 61 17.*

Eckmühl Lighthouse stands at the very end of the Pointe de Penmarch. The lighthouse is 65m/213ft tall and its light of 2 million candle-power has a range of 54km/33.5mi. From the gallery at the top of the tower (307 steps) there is a **view**★★ of Audierne Bay, the Pointe du Raz, the lighthouse on Île de Sein, the coast of Concarneau and Beg-Meil and the Îles de Glénan. Passing to the left of the lighthouse, you will reach the very tip of the point on which the old lighthouse – it now serves as a marker for ships at sea – a small fortified chapel and a signal station stand. The sea is studded with reefs covered in seaweed.

S. Sauvignier/MICHELIN

The lighthouse

Kérity

This small fishing port leaning more and more towards pleasure boating. The Église Ste-Thumette (1675) has an elegant gabled front flanked by a turret.

Penmarch★

The parish includes several villages: St-Guénolé, Kérity, Tréoultré and St-Pierre.

Église St-Nonna★ (*⛵ Guided tours mid-July to mid-Aug, daily, 10am-noon and 3-6pm. ☎ 02 98 58 60 30*) was built in the 16C in the Flamboyant Gothic style. At the east end and on the buttresses on either side of the doorway, ships and caravels are carved into high or low-relief sculptures, recalling that the church was built with donations from shipowners. A gabled bell-tower crowns the roof. Inside there are several old statues: in the south chapel, St Michael and St Anne carrying the Virgin and Child; in the south aisle hangs the Vow of Louis XIII.

▶ *Proceed to Guilvinec by the coast road.*

Guilvinec

This very active fishing port (ranked number one for local fishing) has an impressive fleet of some 130 boats. It forms, with **Lechiagat**, where numerous pleasure boats anchor, it forms a well-sheltered harbour. Beaches unfold behind the dunes as far as Lesconil. The Haliotika Discovery Centre is a charming place to learn more about seafaring fishermen.

Haliotika

Kids *Visit of the auction sale :* 🕐 *Mon-Fri from 4.50pm (except public holidays).*
Follow your guide through the wholesalers fish market, watch the daily fish auction. 30 minutes typical atmosphere guaranteed! Audio guided tours in English are available on request for € 1 each at Haliotika's desk. *⛵ Guided tours in English.* 🕐 *Monday to Friday: 2.30pm (also 10.30 am to 12.30 in July and Aug).Sun: 3-6pm from April to Aug. Sat: 3- 6.30pm in July and Aug. www.leguilvinec.com*
The guided tour of the auction sale is complementary with the visit to the Centre (from Monday to Friday except public holidays).
Learn how to recognize the fishing boats, the techniques of fishing, the species of fish, the professional activities of the port. A new exhibition called "Grandfather, tell me about sea fishing" involves a retired fisherman talking about the history of fishing in Brittany. From the panoramic terrace, witness the return of the colourful coastal trawlers bringing back the daily fish and crustaceans.

Lesconil

Small but bustling trawler fishing port. A picturesque scene occurs when the boats come in around 5.30pm.

▶ *Make for Loctudy via Palue-du-Cosquer and Lodonnec.*

Loctudy – ♿ *See PONT-L'ABBÉ.*

Manoir de Kérazan★ – ♿ *See PONT-L'ABBÉ.*

Pont-l'Abbé – ♿ *See PONT-L'ABBÉ.*

▶ *Leave Pont-l'Abbé by R on the town plan and return to Quimper.*

LE CROISIC★

POPULATION 4 428
MICHELIN LOCAL MAP 316 A4 - LOIRE ATLANTIQUE (44)

This pleasant fishing port is located on a peninsula and overlooks the Grand Traict lagoon which feeds the salt marshes of Guérande. It is only accessible by N 171. Originally one of the first seaside resorts, today Le Croisic still attracts many summer holiday visitors. Two companies offer **boat trips** to Belle-Île, Houat and Hoedic. A ferry service crosses the roadstead to La Turballe.

Especially for Kids: The Oceanarium aquarium.
Also see: Presqu'île de Guérande.

Sights

Port

It extends between Mont Esprit and Mont Lénigo, two mounds formed by ballast unloaded by ships in former days (*see below*), and is well protected by the Tréhic jetty; 17C houses with wrought-iron balconies line the quayside over a distance of more than 1km/0.6 mi. It is a picturesque and busy scene in winter with the arrival of prawn boats, and in summer is enlivened by tourists.

Hôtel d'Aiguillon

The pretty 17C building houses the town hall. Dumas' D'Artagnan stopped here.

Église Notre-Dame-de-Pitié

This unusual 15C and 16C church, with its 17C **lantern tower** (56m/84ft), overlooks the port. Inside it has a short nave, with a flat east end illuminated by a window with Flamboyant tracery and three side aisles. The doorway pier is adorned with a statue of Notre-Dame-des-Vents.

Old houses

To admire the beautiful corbelled and half-timbered houses, walk through the little streets near the church. Note nos 25, 20 and 28 in rue de l'Église, no 4 place du Pilori and nos 33 and 35 in rue St-Christophe.

Mont-Lénigo

Ships at one time unloaded their ballast here and in 1761 trees were planted. The **view**★ goes over the roadstead, the Tréhic jetty (850m/2 789ft long), and its lighthouse (1872) at the entrance to the port; the Pen Bron dike (1724) is across the way as is its marine centre. A shaded walk goes down to the esplanade where there is the memorial (1919) by René Paris, erected to Hervé Rielle, the coxswain, who saved 22 ships of the French fleet from disaster in 1692, by directing them to St-Malo.

Océarium du Croisic

Océarium★

Open June to mid-Sept, daily, 10am-7pm; rest of the year, open 10am-noon

Tropical guest

and 2-6pm. Last entrance 1hr before closing. 🕐 Closed Jan. ☞€ 10/€ 7. ☎ 02 40 23 02 44. www.oceanarium-croisic.fr.

This star-shaped marine centre houses a collection of wonders of the deep from both temperate and tropical waters. Not to be missed is the amusing colony of penguins, the nursey, the marvellous 11m/36ft-long tunnel which goes through an aquarium containing 300 000l/66 000gal of seawater and the pool where visitors can look at and touch starfish, shellfish and...crabs.

Côte Sauvage★

Driving tour of 26km/16mi – 2hr – 🚶 *local map see Presqu'île de GUERANDE.*

▶ *Leave Le Croisic by D 45, the coast road.*

After St-Jean-de-Dieu, the road follows the coast passing St-Goustan and its salt-marsh where eels are raised. The Côte Sauvage (meaning wild coastline) with oddly shaped rocks (appropriately named the Bear, the Altar) ends at the **Pointe du Croisic**. Further on the view opens out over Pornichet, the Loire estuary and the coast as far as the Pointe St-Gildas.

Batz-sur-Mer⌂
Against a background of the ocean and the salt-marshes, Batz's tall church bell-tower acts as a landmark for the town. The rocky coastline is broken by the sandy beaches of Valentin, La Govelle (fun-board) and St-Michel, a small strand where locals gather to watch the waves crashing on the dike.

Église St-Guénolé★
The church was rebuilt in the 15C-16C. Its **bell-tower**, 60m/190ft high, surmounted by a pinnacled turret, dates from 1677. In the **interior**, you will notice at once that the chancel is off-centre, that massive pillars support Gothic arches and that the wooden roof is shaped like the keel of a boat; note the remarkable **keystones** in the north aisle. The top of the **bell-tower** (182 steps) offers an extensive **panorama**★★ along the coast from the Pointe St-Gildas to the shores of the Presqu'île de Rhuys and, at sea, to Belle-Île and Noirmoutier.

Chapelle Notre-Dame-du-Mûrier★
Legend has it that this fine Gothic chapel, now in ruins, was built in the 15C by Jean de Rieux de Ranrouët to keep a vow he made when in peril at sea. He was guided to safety by a burning mulberry bush (hence the name *mûrier*).

Musée des Marais salants
This museum of popular arts and traditions contains a 19C Batz interior, salt workers' clothes, and other exhibits covering all aspects of working with salt. The tour ends with an audio-visual presentation on the salt-marsh and its fauna. **Guided tours**★ of the salt-marshes are available.

Grand blockhaus
🕐 Open April to mid-Nov: 10am-7pm ☎ 02 40 23 88 29. ☞ € 5.50/€ 4.
This is one of the largest bunkers of the Atlantic Wall defences. During the Second World War, it was camouflaged as a villa in order to avoid being bombed. It now houses the Musée de la Poche de Saint-Nazaire (St-Nazaire pocket), the last European area to be liberated in 1945. The atmosphere of a bunker has been recreated: sleeping area, radio station, ammunition store, engine room, etc..

Le Pouliguen⚐⚐ – 🏌️ *See La BAULE.*

▶ *Take D 45 back to Le Croisic.*

PRESQU'ILE DE CROZON★★★

MICHELIN LOCAL MAP 308 E5 - FINISTÈRE (29)

The Crozon Peninsula affords many excursions typical of the Breton coast. Nowhere else, except perhaps at Raz Point, do the sea and coast reach such heights of grim beauty, with the giddy steepness of the cliffs, the colouring of the rocks and the fury of the sea breaking on the reefs. Another attraction is the variety of views over the indentations and estuaries of the Brest roadstead, the Goulet, the broken coast of Toulinguet, Penhir, Dinan Castle, Cap de la Chèvre and Douarnenez Bay. From the summit of the Ménez-Hom all these features can be seen arrayed in an immense panorama.

▶ **Orient Yourself:** The peninsula sprawls into the sea between the Brest road-steads and the Douarnenez Bay. On the coast between St Malo and the Mont-St-Michel.
🏵 **Don't Miss:** Sunset viewed from the Pointe de Penhir.
🥾 A great place for walking!

1 From Pointe de Penhir to Pointe des Espagnols★★★

Driving tour starting from Crozon – 45 km/28mi – 2hr 30min

Crozon
The town stands in the middle of the peninsula of the same name. The **church** is modern. The altar to the right of the chancel is ornamented with a large 17C **altar-piece**★ depicting the martyrdom of the Theban Legion on Mount Ararat during the reign of Emperor Hadrian.

Address Book

TOURIST OFFICE
Crozon, Bd de Pralognan-la-Vanoise, Crozon ☎ 02 98 27 07 92, www.crozon.com All year 9.15-12am, 2-6pm. **Bureau de Morgat**, Place d'Ys, ☎ 02 98 27 29 49, July-Aug: 10am-1pm and 3-7pm.

WHERE TO STAY
◔◔◙ **Grand Hôtel de la Mer**, av. de la Plage, ☎ 02 98 27 02 09 – 78 rooms 🔕 📺 ✗ This Belle Époque building shelters functional rooms, with view on the ocean or on the park full of palm trees. Big dining room facing Douarnenez bay (off season 🕐 closed Tue noon, Sat noon and Mon evening). Breakfast € 11.

EATING OUT
CROZON
◔◔ **Le Mutin Gourmand,** *Place de l'Église,* ☎ 02 98 27 06 51. 🕐 *Closed Mon noon in summer, Sun evening and Tue noon off season.* Small Breton house. The catch of the day is served to guests in one of the three dining rooms decorated with watercolour paintings.

▶ *Leave Crozon by D 8, west of town and make for Camaret.*

Camaret-sur-Mer – 🖐 *See CAMARET-SUR-MER.*

An isthmus bounded by Pen-Hat Beach leads to the **Pointe du Toulinguet** on which a French Navy signal station stands. There is a view of the Pointe de Penhir to the south.

▶ *Return to the entrance to Camaret and bear right.*

Pointe de Penhir★★★

Penhir Point is the finest of the four headlands of the Presqu'île de Crozon. A memorial (150m/164yd off the road) to the Bretons of the Free French Forces has been erected on the cliff.

▶ *Leave the car at the end of the surfaced road. Go onto the platform at the end of the promontory for a view of the sea 70m/229ft down below. Telescopes. 45min.*

The setting is magnificent as is the **panorama**: below are the great isolated rocks called the **Tas de Pois** (literally, pile of peas!); on the left is the Pointe de Dinan; on the right, Pointe de St-Mathieu and Pointe du Toulinguet, the second with its little lighthouse, and at the back the Ménez-Hom. In the distance, the Pointe du Raz and the Île de Sein can be seen on clear days to the left, and Ouessant over to the right.

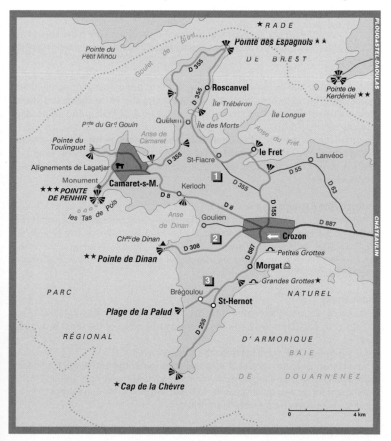

R. Mattes/MICHELIN

A prosaic name (Tas de Poise) for a poetic site

Tourists who enjoy scrambling over rocks should take a path going down to the left of the platform and monument. Halfway down the sheer drop of the cliff there is a view of a little cove. Here take the path on the left which climbs towards a cavity covered with a rock beyond which is the **Chambre Verte,** a grassy strip. From here there is an unusual view of the Tas de Pois Rocks and the Pointe de Penhir.

▶ *Return to the car and take the Camaret road again. Turn right after 1.5km/1mi towards Crozon, to avoid the town; then take the road to Roscanvel, once a strategic road.*

The view opens out to show Camaret Bay on the left and, on the right, the Brest roadstead. The road enters the walls which enclose the Presqu'île de Roscanvel before Quélern. These fortifications date from the time of Vauban and the Second Empire.
This road running west is picturesque. The curious contrast between the slopes on either side of the peninsula is striking: the western slope, facing the west wind and the sea, is moorland and lacks vegetation; the eastern slope is covered with trees and meadows.

Pointe des Espagnols★★
From here one can see a remarkable **panorama** which includes the Brest Sound, the town and harbour of Brest, the Elorn estuary, the Pont Albert-Louppe, the Presqu'île de Plougastel, and the end of the roadstead. The point owes its name to the Spanish garrison which occupied the area for a brief period in 1594 and built a fort on the headland.

Roscanvel
The church was rebuilt after a fire in 1956 and now possesses fine dark stained-glass windows by Labouret, and a coloured terracotta Stations of the Cross by Claude Gruher.
Note the hedges of fuschia between the gardens.
The road, which to the south of Roscanvel goes round the end of the roadstead, affords fine views of Île Longue (nuclear submarine base – ⚷ no entry), and in the foreground, of the two smaller islands, Trébéron and Morts. You leave the peninsular territory once more by the ruined fortifications.

▶ *About 500m/545yd beyond St-Fiacre, turn left.*

Le Fret

This small port provides a regular boat service to and from Brest and has a view of the Presqu'île de Plougastel from the jetty.

The road runs along the jetty bordering Le Fret Bay.

▶ *When you come to a fork, leave the Lanvéoc road on your left and turn right to Crozon.*

Enjoy a last look back at the roadstead.

2 FROM CROZON TO POINTE DE DINAN★★

6km/4mi – 2hr

Crozon – ◔ *See* 1 *above.*

▶ *Leave Crozon west by D 308.*

Windswept heathland follows after the pine groves.

Pointe de Dinan★★

Allow 1hr. Leave your car at the car park; continue on foot, by the path on the left for about 500m/545yd.

A fine **panorama** can be seen from the edge of the cliff; on the left are Cap de la Chèvre, the coast of Cornouaille and Pointe du Raz; on the right, Pointe du Penhir and the Tas de Pois. Skirting the cliff to the right you will see the enormous rocky mass of **Dinan Castle** (Château de Dinan), joined to the mainland by a natural arch.

R. Mattes/MICHELIN

▲ Take the footpath over the natural arch to explore the rock which looks like a fortified castle in ruins (*30min on foot there and back, over rocky ground; wear non-slip soles*).

The coastline at Crozon

3 From Crozon to Cap de la Chevre★

11km/7mi – allow 2hr

Crozon – ◔ *See* 1 *above.*

▶ *Leave Crozon by D 887 southwest.*

Morgat⚓

Morgat is a well-sheltered seaside resort. The great sandy beach is enclosed to the south by a point covered with pine woods, Beg-ar-Gador. On the north side, a rocky spur separates Morgat Beach from that of Le Portzic. Fishing boats go out from the **harbour,** sheltering behind a jetty where 400 pleasure craft can also anchor. Morgat offers all types of fishing to the keen sportsman.

Les grandes grottes★

🛥 *Guided tour (40min) April-Sep: daily depautures scheduled according to the tides, leaving from the port.* 🎫 *€ 9(adult), € 7 (child). Vedettes Rosmeur Croisières* ☎ *02 98 27 10 71 or Vedettes Sirènes* ☎ *02 98 96 20 10.*

The first group of big caves, situated beyond Beg-ar-Gador, includes Ste-Marine and the Devil's Chamber (Chambre du Diable). The second group is at the other end of the bay. The finest grotto is that of the Altar (l'Autel), 80m/262ft deep and 15m/49ft high. One of its attractions is the colouring of the roofs and walls.

Les petites grottes

Small caves at the foot of the spur between Morgat and Le Portzic beaches can be reached at low tide.

From Morgat to Cap de la Chèvre the road runs through an austere landscape of rocks and stunted heath, open to the ocean winds, with little hamlets of houses huddled together which seem to hide in the folds of the ground. To the left, the view gradually opens out over Douarnenez Bay, with the massive outline of the Ménez-Hom in the distance.

A short distance past **Brégoulou**, leave the car in the car park from which you can enjoy a good view of the Tas de Pois and Pointe du Raz.

Plage de la Palud

This splendid beach offers fine views of the rocky coastline. Bathing is forbidden owing to the powerful waves breaking on the shore.

St-Hernot

The former school houses the **Maison des Minéraux** containing over 500 items which testify to the geological wealth of the area.

Cap de la Chèvre★

From the former German observation point there is a fine **view** over the Atlantic and the advanced points of Finistère: (left to right) Pointe de Penhir and the Tas de Pois, the Île de Sein, Cap Sizun and its headlands, Pointe du Van and Pointe du Raz to the south of Douarnenez Bay.

A **monument**, representing the wing of an aircraft stuck into the ground, is dedicated to the aircrew personnel of Aéronautique Navale killed or missing in active service in the Atlantic and Scandinavian regions. The names of the people concerned are engraved on the sides of a circular trench.

DAOULAS★

POPULATION 1 794
MICHELIN LOCAL MAP 308 F4 - FINISTÈRE (29)

This small town is located on the banks of the river which shares its name. The river's estuary forms one of the many inlets in the Brest roadstead. The town owes its development largely to the presence of the abbey built here; the fates of both have been closely linked over the centuries. Daoulas has inherited many artistic features which bear witness to its past. There are still some 15C and 17C houses along rue de l'Église.

Parish Close★ (Enclos paroissial)

The old abbey buildings are to the left. Opposite, and slightly to the right, a 16C **porch**★ takes the place of a bell-tower and leads into the cemetery. It is both Gothic and Renaissance in style and is richly carved (remarkable vine). The **old abbey** church still has the original 12C west door, nave and north side aisle. In the east end the ossuary has been converted into a sacristy.

Ancienne abbaye

🕐 ♿ *July-Aug: 2-7pm; April-June and Sep to mid-Nov: 10am-6pm (last entrance 1hr before closing).* 🚶 *Guided tours available (1hr).* 🕐 *Closed 1 Jan and 25 Dec.* ✺€ 6/€ 3. ☎ *02 98 25 84 39. www.abbaye-daoulas.com.*

The abbey was founded around the year 500 and, until the 10C, played a major part in the history of Daoulas. It was razed by the Vikings, then rebuilt in the 12C by Augustinian canons, under whose care it flourished until the Revolution.

The abbey now belongs to the Conseil Général of Finistère, which has converted it into a cultural centre, more particularly a venue for international archeological exhibitions.

The Romanesque **cloisters**, built in 1167 to 1173 (only three walls are still standing), is the only surviving example of this style of architecture in Brittany. The decoration consists of geometric designs and leaf motifs.

A path leads to a garden where herbs and medicinal plants are cultivated and to a fountain dating from 1550. Set back is the 16C **Oratoire Notre-Dame-des-Fontaines** with 19C additions.

Cloisters

DINAN★★

POPULATION 10 907

MICHELIN LOCAL MAP 309 J4 – CÔTES D'ARMOR (22)

Dinan's old town is a small gem; its old houses and streets are girt by ramparts and guarded by an imposing castle. Enhanced by trees and gardens, it stands on a plateau overlooking the Rance and the marina 75m/279ft below.

▶ **Orient Yourself:** About 30km/18mi south of St-Malo, Dinan is at the top of the Rance estuary.
😊 **Don't Miss:** A boat trip on the Rance estuary.
🕐 **Organizing Your Time:** Plan to spend two days to visit Dinan and the Rance Valley.
Kids **Especially for Kids:** The zoo in the park of the Château de la Bourbansais.
👀 **Also See:** Vallée de la RANCE.

A Bit of History

Du Guesclin against Canterbury

In 1357 the Duke of Lancaster besieged Dinan, which was defended by Bertrand Du Guesclin and his brother Olivier. After several encounters with the superior English forces, Bertrand asked for a 40-day truce, after which, he promised, the town would surrender if it were not relieved. In violation of the truce, Olivier, who had gone out of the town unarmed, was made prisoner by an English knight, Canterbury, who demanded a ransom of 1 000 florins. Bertrand challenged the Englishman to single combat. The encounter took place at a spot now called place du Champ; a stele marks the spot. Lancaster presided. Canterbury lost and had to pay Olivier the 1 000 florins he had demanded and surrender his arms to Bertrand. He was also discharged from the English army.

Du Guesclin's tombs

After more than 20 years of campaigning for the King of France, Bertrand du Guesclin died on 13 July 1380, at the gates of Châteauneuf-de-Randon, to which he had laid siege. He had asked to be buried at Dinan. The funeral convoy, therefore, set out for that town. At Le Puy the body was embalmed and the entrails buried in the Jacobins' church (now the Église St-Laurent). As the embalming was inadequate, the remains were boiled at Montferrand and the flesh was removed from the skeleton and buried in the Franciscans' church (destroyed in 1793). At Le Mans an officer of the King brought an order to bring the body to St-Denis; the skeleton was then handed over to him. Only the heart arrived at Dinan, where it was deposited in the Jacobins' church. It has since been transferred to the Église St-Sauveur. So it was that, while the kings of France had only three tombs (for the heart, entrails and body), Du Guesclin had four.

Walking Tour

Old Town★★ (Vieille Ville)

A medieval atmosphere can be felt as you walk through Dinan's old streets with their beautifully restored, picturesque half-timbered houses.

Place Du-Guesclin

In this square, bordered with 18C and 19C town houses, stands the equestrian statue of Du Guesclin; the square, with place du Champ, served as a fairground during the Middle Ages.

▸ *Bear right on rue Ste-Claire, then left on rue de l'Horloge.*

Hôtel Kératry

This attractive 16C mansion with three granite pillars, houses the tourist office.

Maison du Gisant

During the restoration of this 17C house, the 14C recumbent figure (exhibited outside) was found.

Tour de l'Horloge

🕐 *Open April-May: 2-6.30pm; June-Sep: 10am-6.30pm.* €2.70/1.70.
Exhibited in the belfry are the clock, bought by the town in 1498. From the top of the Clock Tower (158 steps), there is a vast **panorama**★★ of the town and its principle monuments and the surrounding countryside. Exhibition on Anne of Brittany.

The marina on the River Rance

G. Targat/MICHELIN

Place des Merciers★

The old well and lovely old triangular-gabled houses with wooden porches paint a pleasant scene. Different types of half-timbered houses, characteristic of 15C to 17C Dinan architecture, can be seen in rue de l'Apport: houses with the upper floor resting on thick wooden pillars, under which the merchants and tradesmen exposed their wares, houses with overhanging upper storeys and houses with large projecting display windows.

Glance into nearby rue de la Cordonnerie and rue du Petit-Pain lined with corbelled houses. At no 10 rue de la Mittrie, Théodore Botrel (1868-1925), the songwriter, was born.

▶ *Cross place des Cordeliers and take the Grande-Rue on the left to reach St-Malo Church.*

Église St-Malo

This Flamboyant Gothic church was begun in 1490 and finished in the 19C. The late-15C transept, chancel and chevet make a striking impression. The **stained-glass windows** date from the 20C and depict life in the various districts of Dinan during major religious festivals.

▶ *Walk back along Grande-Rue and continue along rue de la Lainerie*

Rue du Jerzual★

This lovely cobbled street slopes steeply downhill. The 15C and 16C **shops** lining the street are now occupied by artists: glass-blowers, sculptors, weavers etc. This was once the main street leading down to the port; imagine the constant comings and goings of the bourgeois, the hawkers with their overflowing carts and the tradesmen and apprentices running about.

Maison du Gouverneur

No 24 rue du Petit-Fort. This is a fine 15C mansion in which a weaving and high-warp tapestry workshop has been installed.

Walk down the street to the marina. On your way back, take the pretty walk along the watch-path of the ramparts *(stairs by the Porte de Jerzual)*. The walk leads past Tour due Gouverneur which offers a lovely **view**★★ of the Rance Valley.

▶ *Walk up rue Michel then rue du Rempart to the Jardin Anglais.*

Jardin Anglais

The terraced garden offers a good overall **view**★★, especially from Tour Ste-Catherine, of the River Rance, the port, the enormous viaduct, 250m/820ft long and 40m/128ft high, and the ramparts.

Basilique St-Sauveur

This basilica features a Romanesque porch surmounted by a Flamboyant Gothic gable opening off the façade. Construction stretched from the 12C (the wall to the right) to the 16C. The original dome of the tower, which was destroyed by lightning, was replaced in the 18C by a timber steeple covered with slate.

Inside, the building's lack of symmetry is striking; the south side is Romanesque, while the north side, the transept and the chancel are Flamboyant Gothic. In the north transept, the heart of Du Guesclin is preserved behind a 14C tomb stone incorporated in a 19C tomb. The modern stained-glass windows were made in the Barillet workshop.

As you leave the basilica, on place St-Sauveur, there is a house with pillars on the left, in which Auguste Pavie, diplomat and explorer of Indochina, was born in 1847.

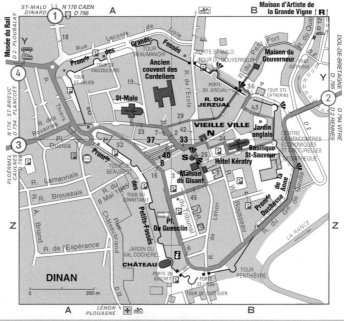

DINAN						
		Gambetta R.	AY 18	Michel R.	BY 36	
		Garaye R. Comte de la	AY 19	Mittrie R. de la	AZ 37	
Apport R. de l'	ABY 2	Grande-R.	AY 23	Petit-Pain R. du	AZ 40	
Champ Clos Pl. du	ABZ 3	Haute-Voie R.	BY 24	Poissonnerie R. de la	BY 42	
Château R. du	BZ 6	Horloge R. de l'	BZ 25	Rempart R. du	BY 43	
Cordeliers Pl. des	AY 7	Lainerie R. de la	BY 29	Ste-Claire R.	BZ 45	
Cordonnerie R. de la	AZ 8	Marchix R. du	AYZ 32	St-Malo R.	BY 44	
Ferronerie R. de la	AZ 15	Merciers Pl. des	BYZ 33			

| Ancien Hôtel | | | Maison de la Rance | BY R |
| Beaumanoir | BYZ N | | Tour de l'Horloge | BZ S |

Address Book

TOURIST OFFICE

Dinan, 9 rue du Château, ☎ 02 96 87 69 76, www.dinan-tourisme.com; July-Aug: Mon-Sat 9am-7pm, Sun and public holidays 10am-12.30pm, 2.30-6pm; Sept-June: Mon-Sat 9am-12.30pm, 2-6pm. Special weekend and short-stay offers. Guided tours of Dinan and Léhon,departure at 3pm daily July-Aug, Sat in June, variable the rest of the year, €5/3.

GETTING AROUND

Dinan can be explored on foot. Ask for the car park list at the tourist office

On small train – Guided tours of the town, ☎ 02 99 88 47 07. Departure from the théâtre des Jacobins, from the place Duclos and from the marina, 45min, Easter-Oct daily 9am-7pm, €5/3.50.

Rent a bike- Cycles Gauthier, 15 rue Déroyer, ☎ 02 96 85 07 60. About €17/day. Be careful on the many cobblestone streets of Dinan!

WHERE TO STAY

Les Grandes Tours, 6 rue du Château, ☎ 02 96 85 16 20, www.les-grandestours.com - 34 rooms, 🅿 ☐ €5. Ⓒ Closed Jan and 1st week of Feb. Simple but clean, close by the Old Town.

La Ville Ameline, Tressaint, Lanvallay, ☎ 02 96 39 33 69, www.lavilleameline.com - 4 rooms. Meals by reservation (☐). Authentically rustic atmosphere in the colourful rooms of this beautiful farm. Two connecting rooms available. Cottages also available for rent.

Le Challonge, 29 Place Du Guesclin, ☎ 02 96 87 16 30, www.lechallonge.fr.st - 18 rooms, ☐ €7.50, ✕ Comfortable establishment in town centre. Rooms with green and ochre walls. View over the square or, more pleasant, over the back.

Hôtel de la Porte St-Malo, 35 rue St-Malo, ☎ 02 96 39 19 76, www.hotelportemalo.com - 15 rooms. Charming small hotel in an old house away from the centre. Comfortable rooms with an English country house feel about them, and pleasant inner courtyards.

Le Logis du Jerzual, 25-27 rue du Petit-Port, ☎ 02 96 85 46 54, www.logis-du-jerzual.com - 4 rooms. In the port district, this hotel provides very comfortable rooms, with a refined decor that mixes Breton antiques and Asian souvenirs. Enjoy breakfast on the veranda with a view of a wonderful garden.

La Villa Côté Cour, 10 rue Lord Kitchener, ☎ 02 96 39 30 07, www.villa-cote-cour.fr - 4 rooms. Outside the centre of town, this big house (built 1900) has spacious, bright guest rooms, lavishly laid out with a bath or shower with hydro-jets. Tasteful contemporary decor.

EATING OUT

Crêperie Ahna, 7 rue de la Poissonnerie, ☎ 02 96 39 09 13. Ⓒ Closed Sun, 2 weeks in Aug and 3 weeks in March. In the Old Town of Dinan, this creperie with orange walls offers tasty crepes such as the agénoise, made with streaky bacon and prune cream.

Crêperie du Beffroi, 3 rue de l'Horloge, ☎ 02 96 39 03 36. Don't just stare at the blue facade, enter to find a good choice of omelettes and a beautiful selection of crepes.

Chez le Gaulois, 9 rue de l'Apport, ☎ 02 96 39 11 60. Ⓒ Closed Sun afternoon and Mon. Besides some good regional specialities, this fine grocery offers small handcrafted breads served with toasted cheese, ham and dried tomatoes. Perfect for a quick bite on the run.

Le Léonie, 19 rue Rolland, ☎ 02 96 85 47 47. Ⓒ Closed Sun evening, Mon and Thu evening off season; Sun and Mon in July-Aug; 3 weeks in Aug-Sept. Bright colours light up the unsophisticated décor. The food is made with ingredients fresh from the market or the sea.

Le Saint-Louis, 9 rue de Léhon, ☎ 02 96 39 89 50. Ⓒ Closed Tue off season and Wed. Hors-d'œuvre and home-made pastry buffets, appreciated by those with big appetites as well as gourmets.

🍴 **Auberge des Terre-Neuvas**, *25 rue du Quai, le port*, ☎ *02 96 39 86 45.* 🕐 *Closed Wed and Sun evenings.* Traditional nautical decor, good seafood dishes, regional cuisine and wines at good prices.

🍴 **Le Cochon Grillé**, *Taden, near the camping de la Hallerais*, ☎ *02 96 39 96 67.* 🕐 *Closed Mon off season and Feb.* The weekend, the smell of spit roasted suckling pig coming from this charming place draws people from the camp ground next door. Also serves some regional dishes.

🍴 **L'Atelier Gourmand**, *4 rue du Quai, le port*, ☎ *02 96 85 14 18.* 🕐 *Closed Sun evening and Mon off season.* Rustic room with checked tableclothes or small terrace along the River Rance, where you can savour a haddock with cream potpourri, mussels with chips, brochettes or an apple upside-down tart.

🍴 **La Courtine**, *6 rue de la Croix*, ☎ *02 96 39 74 41. In summer,* 🕐 *closed Sun, Tue lunch, Wed and Sat evenings; off season, closed Sat noon, Sun evening, Tue evening, Wed evening, a week at the end of June and 15-30 Nov.* Traditional cuisine inspired by the region, served in a quaint 19C house. Home-smoked salmon, sweetbreads. Wine €10.

🍴🍴 **La Fleur de Sel**, *7 rue Ste-Claire*, ☎ *02 96 85 15 14.* 🕐 *Closed Sun evening, Mon and Wed evenings.* Refined cuisine spiced with a touch of Asia, to be enjoyed in an elegant, contemporary setting.

🍴🍴 **Chez la mère Pourcel**, *3 Place des Merciers*, ☎ *02 96 39 03 80.* 🕐 *Closed Sun evening, Mon off season and 4 weeks in Feb-March.* In one of the older and most beautiful houses of Dinan, enjoy a subtle gastronomic mix of tradition and creativity.

🍴🍴🍴 **Le Bistrot du Viaduc**, *22 rue du Lion d'Or, Lanvalllay*, ☎ *02 96 85 95 00.* 🕐 *Closed Sat noon, Sun evening, Mon, 2 weeks in June and 20 Dec-1 Jan.* Enjoy the beautiful view from this restaurant located at the entrance of the Rance viaduct. The view over your meal is nice, too, featuring creative cuisine made with fresh regional products.

ON THE TOWN

La **rue de la Cordonnerie**, is the centre of night life in Dinan. **À la Truye qui file** - *n° 14*, ☎ *02 96 39 72 29.* The owner, known to regulars as "Nounours" (teddy bear), sometimes seranades with song here. In the same street, **La Lycorne** and **Le Saut de la Puce** are popular with a younger crowd. **Le Poche Café** (*1 bis rue Haute-Voie*, ☎ *02 96 39 98 60*) is home to a bookstore with 8 000 paperback books, a pub and an exhibition gallery. Thematic nights organised one Sat each month. On the port, the **Rive Gauche** is a cool place to savour a late-night cocktail.

WATER SPORTS

Boat trips - La Compagnie Corsaire, the port, (☎ *08 25 13 81 20 (€0.35/mn), www.compagniecorsaire.com*) organises guided cruises (2hr 45min) on the River Rance to St-Malo. Departures from Apr to Sep daily in accordance with the tides. In July-Aug, this company provides a return trip by bus from St-Malo. Off season, you'll have to take a regular bus or the train. If you leave Dinan after 5pm, you will not have time to visit St-Malo and catch a bus in time. About €15/25 there and back; €7.50/bike.

Le Jaman IV, the port, (☎ *06 07 87 64 90 or 02 96 39 28 41, www.vedettejamaniv.com*) takes you on a 1hr cruise to Léhon and the St-Magloire abbey. Departures July-Aug: daily 11am, 1.15pm, 2.30pm, 4pm and 5.30pm; during the rest of the year: information at the company. About €7/9.

Danfleurenn Nautic (*rue du Quai, the port*, ☎ *06 07 45 89 97*) rents boats without license for 4-8 people, from Easter to Nov, €25-30/hour or €129-141/day.

Canoë-kayak - Maison de la Rance- Guided trips on the Rance.

SHOPPING

Market – Markets take place Thu mornings on rue du Petit-Pain, promenade des Petits-Fossés and rue de l'Espérance. The rest of the week, you can find regional products at the halles.

Culinary specialities - Le Rucher Fleuri, *16 rue de l'Horloge*, ☎ *02 96 85 92 01. Tue-Sun 10am (11am Sun) to 12.30pm,*

2.30-7pm; July-Aug: daily 10am-7.30pm; ● closed Jan-Mar. Products from the beehive and Breton cakes.

Boulangerie-pâtisserie Monnier, *the port*, ☎ *02 96 85 03 12.* ● *Closed Wed.* Home-made shortbread with plums, Dinan "pave", apple far and **kouign amann**. All in the best tradition.

Arts and crafts –Old Dinan is full of workshops of all kind. The **Circuit des artistes et des artisans d'art** is a map showing their locations, available at the **Tourist Office**. The association **Art Di**, ☎ *02 96 87 59 88 or 06 88 28 63 32,* organises guided tours of the workshops during the summer.

LEISURE

Festival des Terre-Neuvas, *beginning of July, at Bobital, 8.5 km at the South of Dinan. Information* ☎ *02 96 87 69 76, www.festival-terre-neuvas.com.* Created in 1998, the festival has become the incontrovertible rendezvous of all kinds of music: rock, reggae, techno, salsa, French songs, etc.

Fête du blé (celebration of wheat), *Pleudihen-sur-Rance, about 15 Aug,* ☎ *02 96 83 35 43, www.feteduble.com* Hundreds of volunteers give life to the old rural jobs and the old traditions.

Fest-Noz - Events, meals.

Ancien hôtel Beaumanoir

A beautiful Renaissance porch, called the Pelican, adorns the entrance of this old mansion. In the courtyard, note the decoration of the windows and a 16C turret, which houses a lovely staircase.

Tour of the Ramparts

Promenade de la Duchesse-Anne

From this promenade along the ramparts, there is a lovely **view**★ of the Rance, the viaduct and the port.

Promenade des Petits-Fossés

This promenade skirts the outside of the 13C-15C ramparts. Looming above are the castle, and the Connétable and Beaufort Towers.

Promenade des Grands-Fossés

This magnificent avenue is embellished by the St-Julien, Vaucouleurs and Beauma-noir Towers and the Porte St-Malo.

Banks of the Rance

🚶 *Allow 1hr on foot. Go down to the Rance and cross the Gothic bridge (Pont Gothique).*
On the right, take the old towpath which passes under the viaduct and follows the river in a green and sheltered **setting**, where it is pleasant to stroll.

Additional Sights

Château★

● *Open Oct-May: 1;30-5.30pm; June-Sep: 10am-6.30pm;* ● *Closed Jan.* 🕐 *Guided tours July-Aug, daily at 11am.* €4/1.60. ☎ *02 96 39 45 20.*
The 13C Porte du Guichet is framed by towers pierced with arrow slits. The 14C dungeon, with its bold machicolations, houses a **museum** of the history of Dinan from prehistoric times to the early 20C. It also contains exhibits of local crafts. The top room displays works by painters who have drawn inspiration from the town and surrounding area, and by late-19C sculptors who worked in Dinan. From the

terrace overlooking the watch-path there is a lovely **panorama**★ of the region. The Tour de Coëtquen, the old artillery tower, exhibits tombstones in a ground floor room.

Musée du Rail

🕐 *Open Easter holidays, Nov school holidays, and June to 15 Sep: daily 2-6pm.* ✆€4/3.25. ☎ 02 96 89 81 33. www.museedurail-dinan.com

The railway museum contains two model railway networks and a Vignier signal box dating from 1889. Railway enthusiasts will love the posters, clocks, lamps, engine plates, etc.

Ancien Couvent des Cordeliers

🕐 *Open July and Aug, Mon-Fri 10am-6pm. No charge.* ☎ 02 96 85 89 00.

The 15C Gothic cloisters and the 13C turreted (pepper-pot roofs) main courtyard are all that remain of the monastery.

Maison d'Artiste de la Grande Vigne

🕐 *Open 20 May-20 Sep: 2-6.30pm; July-Aug: 10am-6.30pm.* ✆ €2.70/1.70. ☎ 02 96 87 90 80.

The former house of **Yvonne Jean-Haffen** (1895-1993), a friend and student of the painter Mathurin Méheut, displays several hundred paintings and drawings depicting the Brittany of bygone days.

Maison de la Rance

📍 ♿🕐 *Open July-Aug 10am-7pm; Apr-June; Sep-Oct and school holidays, daily except Mon 2-6pm.* ✆€3.90 (children 12-18 €3). Quai Talard, on the port. ☎ 02 96 87 00 40.

The Rance estuary is popular with recreational boaters. But the RIver Rance has a long and interesting history, as this exhibit shows. Interactive displays help visitors learn about the flora and fauna of this ecosystem.

The castle keep

Excursions

Léhon

2km/1mi S 45min. In this village, nestled in the Rance Valley, stands the **Prieuré St-Magloire,** a priory built in the 12C.

Church

The church, rebuilt in the 13C and restored in the late 19C, has a rounded doorway adorned with small columns and surmounted by a horizontal string-course decorated with heads. The Angevin-style pointed vaulted nave contains the tombs of the Beaumanoir family and a 13C stoup, where harvesters came to sharpen their sickles.

Conventual Buildings

A small **museum** exhibits capitals of the old Romanesque cloisters. The 13C **refectory**, the oldest room in the Abbey, has been beautifully restored. Note the reader's chair with its staircase and rostrum. The dormitory houses several treasures including the reliquary of St-Magloire.

Gardens
Excavations have uncovered an underground passage which was, in fact, a covered canal linking the abbey to the Rance running down below.

Corseul
11km/7mi W. Leave Dinan towards St-Brieuc, then bear right onto D 794 to Plancoët. Already known to the Celts, Corseul was conquered and extensively modified by the Romans, as was most of the Armor area. Many artefacts from those periods are gathered here, notably in the Garden of Antiquities (Jardin des Antiques), (columns and capitals) and in the **Musée de la Société archéologique de Corseul** (⏱ *Open Mon-Fri: 8am-noon and 2-5.30pm; Sat 8am-noon; July-Aug: 10am-noon and 2-6pm; Sat 8am-noon.* ☎ *02 96 82 73 14.)* On the second floor of the town hall are fossils from the Falun Sea, polished and dressed stones, funerary urns, coins, Roman murals and everyday implements from Gallo–Roman times.
The most remarkable vestige is the **Temple du Haut-Bécherel,** said to be the Temple of Mars *(1.5km/1mi on the road to Dinan and right on an uphill road).* It is a polygonal tower with masonry in small courses, dating from Emperor Augustus's reign.

Château de la Bourbansais★
14km/8.5mi SE. Standing in an immense park, this impressive late-16C building was embellished by three generations of the Huart family, counsellors to the Breton Parliament.

Parc zoologique et Jardin
[Kids] ♿ ⏱ *Open Apr to Sep, daily, 10am-7pm; the rest of the year open 2-6pm.* ☞ €18 *(children €12) garden, zoo and château, €14/10 zoo only.* ☎ *02 99 69 40 07. www. zoo-bourbansais.com.*
The zoo protects more than 500 animal species from the five continents. *After the zoo go to the château.* The main building is flanked by pinnacled turrets and saddle-back-roofed pavilions characteristic of the 18C.

Château interior
🔊 *Guided tours (40min) Apr to Sep: Mon-Sat, 4-6pm.*
On the ground floor the rooms are decorated and furnished in the 18C style and contain 17C Aubusson tapestries and a fine collection of porcelain from the Dutch India Company. In the peristyle, there is a display of documents, archives and personal objects belonging to the past owners that evoke the château's history.

DINARD

POPULATION 10 430
MICHELIN LOCAL MAP 309 J – ILLE-ET-VILAINE (35)E

This smart resort, which lies in a magnificent setting on the estuary of the Rance, opposite St-Malo, is frequented by the international set and in particular by the British and Americans. The place was "launched" about 1850 by an American named Coppinger and developed by the British. Before that it was a small fishing village and an offshoot of St-Énogat.

▸ **Orient Yourself:** On the left bank of the Rance estuary, across from St Malo.

🕑 **Organizing Your Time:** This popular resort is especially enjoyable in late spring.

👣 **Also See:** Côte d'EMERAUDE, Vallée de la RANCE.

Walking Tour

North

Pointe du Moulinet★★

▸ *Start from Grande Plage.*

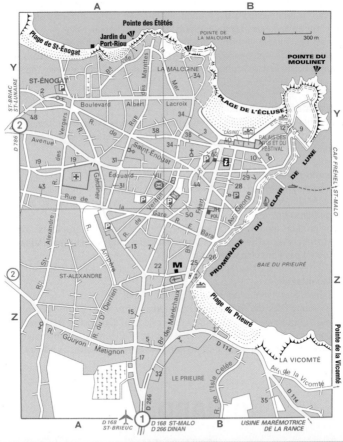

A walk round this point offers a series of magnificent views of the coast from Cap Fréhel, on the left, to St-Malo on the right and, a little further on, of the Rance estuary.

Grande Plage or Plage de l'Écluse★

This beach of fine sand, bordered by luxurious hotels, the casino and convention centre (Palais des Congrès), extends to the end of the cove formed by Moulinet and Malouine Points.

Following the promenade along the beach to the left you will reach a terrace from which you can see St-Malo.

East

Promenade du Clair de Lune and Plage du Prieuré★

This walk (pedestrians only) lies along a sea wall which follows the water's edge and offers pretty views over the Rance estuary. Lovely multicoloured flower beds and remarkable Mediterranean vegetation embellish the promenade.

The **Plage du Prieuré** is at the end of the Promenade. It owes its name to a priory founded here in 1324.

Promenade du Clair-de-Lune

Pointe de la Vicomté★★

The Vicomté, a fine estate divided into lots, is becoming one of Dinard's most fashionable quarters.

Walk along the circular road (chemin de ronde), which starts at Avenue Bruzzo and offers splendid vistas towards the roadstead, the Rance estuary and the Usine marémotrice de la Rance.

Additional Sights

Musée du Site Balnéaire

⌐ Closed for restoration. ☎ 02 99 46 13 90.

The regional museum is housed in Villa Eugénie, built in honour of Napoleon III's wife, who was to have inaugurated the season in 1868.

The museum illustrates late-19C and early-20C resort life, an era of opulence, when magnificent villas and great hotels (Grand Hôtel, Grand Hôtel des Terrasses, Crystal Hôtel, to name a few) were built and excellent food was served.

Excursions

St-Lunaire♨♨

4km/2.5mi along D 786. This smart resort, not far from Dinard, has two fine beaches: St-Lunaire to the east, which is the more frequented as it faces St-Malo, and Longchamp (the larger of the two that face Cap Fréhel) to the west.

Pointe du Décollé★★

The point is joined to the mainland by a natural bridge crossing a deep fissure and is known as the Cat's Leap (Saut du Chat); the Décollé promenades are laid out beyond the bridge.

DISCOVERING BRITTANY

Address Book

TOURIST OFFICES

Dinard, 2 bd Féart, ☎ 02 99 46 94 12, www.ot-dinard.com July-Aug: daily 9.30am-7.30pm; off season: Mon-Sat 9.30am-12.30pm, 2-6pm; 1st Apr-15 Sept: Sun 10am-12.30pm, 2.30-6pm. Organises thematic guided tours, departure 2.30pm, every day in July-Aug, weekends in June and Sep, €2/5.

St-Lunaire, 72 bd du Gén.-de-Gaulle, ☎ 02 99 46 31 09, www.saint-lunaire.com July-Aug: daily 9.30-7pm; Easter-June, Sep: Mon-Tue 10-12am, 2.30-5.30pm, Wed 10-12am, Thu-Sat 2.30-5.30pm; off season: Mon-Tue, Fri 2-5pm.

St-Briac, 49 Grande Rue, ☎ 02 99 88 32 47, www.saint-briac.com; July-Aug: daily 10am-12.30pm, 2.30-6.30pm; mid-Apr-June, Sept: Mon, Tue and Thu 9am-12.30pm, Wed 2-5pm, Fri-Sat 10-12am, 2-5pm; off season: Tue, Fri 10-12am, 2-5pm, Sat 10-12am.

Rent a bike - Cycles Duval, 43 rue Gardiner, ☎ 02 99 46 19 63. **Breizh Cycles**, 8 rue St-Énogat, ☎ 02 99 46 27 25.

WHERE TO STAY

DINARD

◔◔ **Hôtel des Bains**, *38 av. George V*, ☎ *02 99 46 13 71, www.dinard.hotel.plus.com - 39 rooms* ☐ *€6.90.* ◷ *Closed 16 Nov-5 Feb.* Near the beaches. Simple rooms in blue tones, some have a view over the sea.

◔◔◔ **Hôtel Émeraude**, *1 bd Albert ler*, ☎ *02 99 46 15 79, www.hotelemeraudeplage.com - 47 rooms* ✕ ◷ *Closed Jan-Feb holidays.* You will have to book to enjoy the beautiful rooms on the corner, with view and balcony. The others are simpler, with views over the beach or the piazza.

◔◔◔ **Hôtel de la Plage**, *3 bd Féart*, ☎ *02 99 46 14 87, hotel-de-la-plage@wanadoo.com - 18 rooms,* ☐ *€8.50* ✕. Near Écluse beach , rooms decorated with English style giving onto a piazza, or onto the sea with balcony.

◔◔◔ **Hôtel Améthyste**, *pl. du Calvaire, St-Énogat*, ☎ *02 99 46 61 81, hotel-amethyste@wanadoo.fr - 19 rooms* ☐ *€7.50.* ◷ *Closed mid-Nov to early March.* Modest rooms on three floors, or 5 fully equipped studios.

◔◔◔ **Hôtel Printania**, *5 av. Georges V*, ☎ *02 99 46 13 07, www.printaniahotel.com - 57 rooms,* ☐ *€8.50.* ◷ *Closed 21 Nov-19 March.* The common rooms are very well decorated with furniture, faiences and paintings evoking Brittany. Guest rooms have a view over the sea or over the avenue. Breakfast on a pleasant veranda.

ST-LUNAIRE

◔◔ **Hôtel Kan-Avel**, *pl. de l'Église*, ☎ *02 99 46 30 13, www.kan-avel.fr - 11 rooms and 3 studios* ☐ *€6.* Modest but pleasant and well decorated hotel. View over the church from the balcony of the rooms.

◔◔◔ **La Pensée**, *35 rue de la Grève*, ☎ *02 99 46 03 82, www.la-pensee.fr.* Large range of rooms tastefully decorated and giving onto an English garden along the sea. Locations in summer starting at €352/week.

LA RICHARDAIS

◔◔ **Le Berceul**, *24 rue de la Théaudais*, ☎ *02 23 17 06 00, www.berceul.com - 3 rooms* ✄. 18C shipowners' house and garden. Elegant country setting. Family unit for 4 people in duplex.

EATING OUT

DINARD

◔ **Le Full Time**, *plage de l'Écluse*. Ice-cream, sandwiches and waffles to nibble while wiggling your toes in the sand.

◔ **Crêperie Wishbone**, *8 Place du Calvaire, St-Énogat*, ☎ *02 99 46 94 92.* ◷ *Closed Mon and Tue off season.* Traditional crepes served under exposed beams or on the terrace.

◔ **Altaïr**, *18 bd Féart*, ☎ *02 99 46 13 58.* Family restaurant appreciated for its traditional cuisine. Some rooms also available.

◔ **Castor-Bellux**, *5 rue Winston Churchill*, ☎ *02 99 46 25 72. Closed Tue and Wed off season.* Pizzas, mussels and mixed salads in a lively atmosphere.

◔◔ **La Gonelle**, *promenade du Clair de Lune*, ☎ *02 99 16 40 47.* ◷ *Closed*

Tue and Wed off season. Pleasant terrace above the hold, where diners enjoy shellfish, seafood and fish.

⊜⊜ **Le Printania,** *5 av. Georges V,* ☎ *02 99 46 13 07, www.printaniahotel. com.* In the dining room or on the terrace, food is served by Bretons in costumes and traditional headdresses.

ST-LUNAIRE

⊜ **L'Amirauté,** *1 pointe du Décollé,* ☎ *02 99 46 33 38.* 🕐 *Closed Wed and Thu from Apr to Oct and mid-Nov to ealy Feb; open daily July-Aug and weekends during Feb and Easter school holidays.* Wonderful panoramic view over the sea and St-Lunaire from this creperie.

⊜⊜ **La Pensée Gourmande.** Tea room and English garden set up on the premises of an an old grocery store.

⊜⊜⊜ **Le Décollé,** *pointe du Décollé,* ☎ *02 99 46 01 70.* 🕐 *Closed Mon and Tue off season, Mon in July-Aug, and mid-Nov to mid-Feb.* Seafood and wonderful view over the bay of St-Malo.

ON THE TOWN

DINARD

Yacht Club de Dinard, *9 promenade du Clair de Lune,* ☎ *02 99 46 67 62.* Open to everyone for a drink or a lunch in a moderately formal atmosphere.

L'Escale à Corto, *12 av. George V,* ☎ *02 99 46 78 57.* 🕐 *Closed Mon off season.* Step into the world of Corto Maltese and enjoy the hip atmosphere of this pub-restaurant.

Casino de Dinard, *4 bd Wilson,* ☎ *02 99 16 30 30.* Slot machines, seafood restaurant and pub on Écluse beach.

IN THE SURROUNDINGS

La Chaumière, *pointe du Décollé,* ☎ *02 99 16 61 12, from midnight to daybreak, daily in summer, weekends off season.* Perched above the waves, the only nightclub in the area.

LEISURE

DINARD

Beaches- Bathing is supervised 10am-1pm and 3-7pm on **Prieuré and Écluse beaches** (the busiest beaches) and at **St-Énogat** and **Port-Blanc.**

Sea kayak and windsurf- Centre nautique de Port-Blanc, rue Sergent-Boulanger, ☎ 02 99 88 23 21, www. voiledinard.com Windsurf lessons for children from 7 years old (€110-180/ week); kayaks and windsurfer rentals (€10-15/h). **Wishbone Club,** plage de l'Écluse, ☎ 02 99 88 15 20, www. wishbone-club-dinard.com, 🕐 closed Dec-Feb. Lessons for children from 6-8 years old (€120-145/week). **Point Passion Plage**: windsurfer (€15-21/h), catamarans (€30-42/h) rentals.

Diving - Club subaquatique Dinardais, 25 rue Barbine, ☎ 02 99 46 25 18. Apr-Oct and weekend. Level 1 and equipment required (€17/diving).

Olympic sea water swimming pool- Digue de l'Écluse, ☎ 02 99 46 22 77. All year, open-air and heated swimming pool, sauna, jacuzzi, paddling pool.

▶ *To the left of the entrance to the Décollé Pavilion, take the road leading to the point, on which stands a granite cross.*

From here the vantage point affords a very fine **view**★★ of the Côte d'Émeraude, from Cap Fréhel to Pointe de la Varde.

Grotte des Sirènes★
From the bridge crossing the cleft through which it opens to the sea, you can see the bottom of the grotto. The wash of the sea at high tide is spectacular.

Vieille église St-Lunaire
🕐 *Open Easter to Sept.* ☎ *02 99 46 30 51 (Town Hall).*
The church stands among the trees in a former cemetery. The nave is 11C; the side aisles and canted chancel were rebuilt in the 17C. In the middle of the nave lies the tomb of St Lunaire with the recumbent figure of the saint (14C) resting on a Gallo-Roman sarcophagus. The transept contains seven tombs; in the Chapelle des

Pontbriand in the north arm, note the tombs of a squire and a lady (15C), and in the Chapelle des Pontual in the south arm, the tomb of a lady of the Pontual family (13-14C), richly carved in high relief.

DOL-DE-BRETAGNE★

POPULATION 4 629
MICHELIN LOCAL MAP 309 L3 - ILLE-ET-VILLAINE (35)

Dol, a former bishopric and proud of its fine cathedral, is now the small capital of the "Marais" (marsh) district. It stands on the edge of a cliff, about 20m/64ft high, which was washed by the sea until the 10C, when marine deposits began forming; the deposit enabled the construction of the sea dike, now a section of the Pontorson-St-Malo tourist road.

Sights

Cathédrale St-Samson★★ – *Allow 30 min.*
The cathedral is a vast structure, built of granite in the 12C and 13C and completed during the next three centuries. It gives an idea of the importance that the bishopric of Dol then enjoyed.

On the outside, the most interesting part is the south wall, which includes two porches: the splendid **great porch**★ (14C) and the little porch (13C) with its fine pointed arcade. Seen from the north, the cathedral looks like a fortress; its crenellated parapet was linked to the old fortifications of the town.

The interior, 100m/328ft long, is impressive. Notice in the chancel: the medallion-glass **window**★★ (13C restored), the eighty stalls (14C), the carved wood Bishop's throne (16C) and, above the high altar, the 14C wooden Statue of the Virgin, coloured in 1859. In the north arm of the transept, is the tomb of Thomas James, Bishop of Dol (16C); it is the work of two Florentine sculptors, Antoine and Jean Juste. In the north aisle note the Christ Reviled.

Cathédraloscope★
Kids ⏰ *Open Easter-Oct, 10am-7pm.* 📷 *€7.50/4.90.* ☎ *02 99 48 35 30.*
This exhibit, installed in the former residence of the bishops of Dol, is devoted to the subject of cathedrals, and is especially attractive to children. In a modern and uncluttered setting, which lends itself to contemplation, various models of cathedrals and the machines used to build them are on display, as well as items relating to the craftsmanship of stained-glass windows and sculpture.

Walking Tour

Promenade des Douves
This public garden (also known as Promenade Jules Revert) has been traced along the north part of the old ramparts. One of the 12 defence towers, the large Tour des Carmes, can still be seen. Its offers a fine **view**★ of the Mont Dol and the Marais de Dol.

Old Houses
The streets near the cathedral precincts have interesting old half-timbered houses, town houses, and shops.

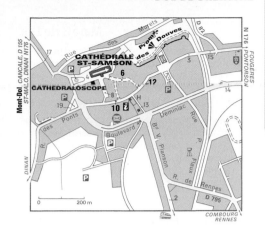

Grande-Rue des Stuarts

No 17 dates from the 11C and 12C and has Romanesque arcading; no 27 (antique-dealer) is 13C; no 33 is a 1617 dwelling with fine dormer windows; no 18, a former Templars' inn with a 12C vaulted cellar, is now transformed into a bar crêperie; a charming 16C courtyard is at no 32.

Rue Le-Jamptel

No 31 (now a hardware store) dates from the 12C or 13C; no 27 is a 15C house decorated with pillars.

Rue Ceinte

This street formerly claimed home to the chapter-house. No 1, an old shop with a granite counter, and no 4, now a crêperie, are both 15C; no 16 dates from 1668.

Driving Tour

Mont Dol★

▶ *Leave Dol-de-Bretagne heading for Cancale (2km/1.2mi).*

This granite mound, though only 65m/208ft high, overlooks a great plain and resembles a small mountain. The remains of many prehistoric animals – mammoth, elephant, rhinoceros, reindeer etc – and flint implements have been unearthed on its slopes. *It is possible to go round the mound by car on of the surface road.*

Panorama★

To the north, from the top of the tower, there is a view of the Îles Chausey and Cancale and Grouin Points; to the northeast, Mont-St-Michel, Avranches and Granville. From the Calvary, to the south, on the edge of the Dol Marsh, Dol and its fine cathedral can be seen with the Hédé heights in the background; and below, the Dol Marsh.

The Countryside – *30km/18.5mi – allow 1hr 45min.*

▶ *Leave Dol southeast of the town plan on D 795. Leave the road to Épiniac on your left; 600m/0.3mi further turn left then turn right onto a tarmac road.*

Marais de Dol

This is the name given to land reclaimed from the marshes and the sea in Mont-St-Michel Bay. Seen from the mound the countryside looks strange and monotonous; it extends for about 15 000ha/40 000 acres from the mouth of the River Couesnon to near Cancale. The old shoreline ran through Cancale, Châteauneuf, Dol and St-Broladre and along the stretch of road between Pontorson and St-Malo.

This former marshy area consists of two land-types: white marsh, made up of silt from a marine deposit and black marsh, made up of peat bogs. Some 12 000 years ago the sea covered the Marais de Dol; it then receded, uncovering a large part of the bay. Bit by bit, forest and vegetation took possession of the land abandoned by the sea. Drainage went on for centuries and today the marais is fertile plain devoted to mixed agriculture.

Menhir de Champ-Dolent

The dolmen, one of the finest in Brittany, stands 9.50m/30ft high (width: 8.70m/31ft). The granite comes from Bonnemain located 5km/3mi south. The name Champ-Dolent ("Field of Pain") refers to a legendary struggle which is supposed to have taken place here.

▷ *Return to the road to Combourg.*

Baguer-Morvan, Musée de la Paysannerie

Kids ♿ 🕐 *Open July-Aug: 10am-7pm; May-June and Sep: Mon and Thu 10am-7pm. ⊗€4/2. ☎ 02 99 48 04 04.*

Champ-Dolent menhir

M. Gurfinkel/MICHELIN

Housed in three large buildings. This museum retraces the past 100 years in the life of the peasant farmer: reconstructed furnished interiors, photographs and postcards, farming equipment (tractors, threshers, harvesters) and tools (rakes, knives, hammers). Cider tasting is offered at the end of the tour.

▷ *Continue on D 795 and then left towards Épiniac.*

Épiniac

In the north aisle of the **church**, on the altar, is a 16C polychrome high relief representing the Dormition of the Virgin.

▷ *Follow D 85 then bear left onto D 285.*

Broualan

In the centre of the village near a small yet remarkable Calvary stands a 15C church, enlarged in the 16C. The east end is decorated with pinnacled buttresses and lovely Flamboyant windows. The small columned bell tower rests on the large arch which separates the nave from the chancel. Inside, several small granite altars and finely worked credenzas (side tables) can be seen. The tabernacle of the high altar is supported by angels. Note the 16C polychrome stone Pietà.

▷ *Via La Boussac return to Dol-de-Bretagne.*

DOUARNENEZ★

POPULATION 16 457
MICHELIN LOCAL MAP 308 F6 – FINISTÈRE (29)

The four localities of Douarnenez, Ploaré, Pouldavid and Tréboul have merged to form the *commune* of Douarnenez, known today as a port city (the museum-port, fishing port and sailing harbour), a European centre for fish canning, a seaside resort and a thalassotherapy spa. The town itself, nestled in a prettily curved bay, presents colourful, picturesque façades that have seduced many an artist, including: Auguste Renoir, Eugène Boudin and Emmanuel Lansyer. Although "the era of the sardine" now belongs to the past, visitors will appreciate the old-fashioned atmosphere which permeates the maze of narrow streets encircling the port.

According to local tradition, Douarnenez was the original site of the palace belonging to King Marc'h; the island located at the entrance to the estuary of Pouldavid bears the name of his nephew Tristan. Before being called Douarnenez in 1541 (*douar an enez* means the land of the island), the harbour was known as Hameau de St-Michel (St-Michael's Hamlet) and then, in 1520, Bourg de l'Île Tristan (Village of Tristan's Island).

- ▶ **Orient Yourself:** The town is divided by a waterway: on one side the centre and Les Dames beach, on the other the marina and Tréboul beach.
- **Don't Miss:** This is the sardine capital of Brittany.
- **Organizing Your Time:** A good place to explore the northern coast of Cornouaille, including the Sizun reserve and Pointe du Raz.
- **Also See:** CORNOUAILLE.

La Fontenelle (16C)

In the 16C this island was the lair of Sire Guy Eder La Fontenelle, the most dangerous of the robber barons who devastated the country during the conflicts of the League.

La Fontenelle seized the Île Tristan. To obtain materials for fortifications he demolished those of Douarnenez. His cruelty was legendary. In 1598 he agreed to lay down his arms on condition that he be allowed to keep the island; a request

Douarnenez and the port

G. Couraud/MICHELIN

DISCOVERING BRITTANY

granted by Henri IV. But in 1602 the King took his revenge: involved in a plot, La Fontenelle was sentenced to be broken on the wheel in Paris.

Walking Tour

Chapelle St-Michel
If the chapel is closed, apply to the presbytery: 10, rue Ernest-Renan. ☎ *02 98 92 03 17.*
Built in 1663, this chapel contains 52 panels from the 16C painted by Don Michel Le Noblets (1577-1652) who evangelised lower Brittany.
Half way between Chapelle St-Michel and Chapelle Ste-Hélène, at the heart of the city, stands place Gabriel-Péri where a convivial, bustling open-air market takes place very morning.

Chapelle Ste-Hélène
This chapel, in the Flamboyant Gothic style, was remodelled in the 17C and 18C. Note, for instance, the two 16C stained-glass windows at the end of the nave, .
The west front is decorated with three low-relief sculptures representing a fishing boat, a gannet and a shoal—perhaps a hint at the fact that fishermen partly financed the church.

▶ *Take rue Hervé-Julien opposite the chapel.*

Address Book

TOURIST OFFICE

Douarnenez, 1 rue Dr Mével, ☎ 02 98 92 13 35, www.douarnenez-tourisme. com, July-Aug: everyday 9am-7pm; off season: Mon-Sat: 10-12am, 2-5pm. Offers guided visits of the island of Tristan.
Rent a bike - La Bécane, *42 av. de la Gare*, ☎ 02 98 74 20 07.

WHERE TO STAY

⊜⊜ **Le Bretagne**, *23 rue Duguay-Trouin*, ☎ 02 98 92 30 44, contact@ le-bretagne.fr - 23 rooms, ⊠ €6.00, ✗ Very near the Port-Musée, This hotel has progressively renovated rooms and a restaurant decorated with many knick-knacks.

⊜⊜⊜ **Ty Mad**, *22 Place Gambetta, Tréboul*, ☎ 02 98 74 00 53, www.hotelty-mad.com - 17 rooms, ⊠ €7.50, ✗ Just above the St-Jean beach, this old presbytery overlooks the bay and promises beautiful surprises. Very pleasant and airy contemporary setting that favours natural materials: plain wood or sea rush floors, stone walls, etc. The cuisine is fresh and the welcome is as warm as at a guest house. As an added attraction, there is a contemporary art gallery.

EATING OUT
DOUARNENEZ

⊜ **Le Bigorneau amoureux**, *bd Richepin, plage des Dames*, ☎ 02 98 92 35 55. 🕐 *Daily except Mon and Sat noon.* Hearty meals of potatoes with meat and fish. Facing the gulf, along the coast road, the view from the terrace is unsurpassed. It's better to book if you want a table overlooking the water. If it's too late for dinner, stop in for a drink at the Bistrot du Bigorneau.

RECREATION

Yachting - Centre nautique municipal de Douarnenez-Tréboul, *rue du Birou*, ☎ 02 98 74 13 79, www.centre-nautique-douarnenez.fr. Kayaks (€10/h), windsurfers (€15/h), day sailers (€23/h) and catamarans (€42/h). Trips on board a schooner or traditional longboat (€20.75).

Thalassa - Thalass-Santé, *Tréboul-Plage*, ☎ 08 25 00 42 30, www.thalasso. com Mon-Sat 8.30am-12.30pm, 2-5pm. Seawater spa treatments a la carte or half-day pass on reservation.

Port du Rosmeur★

Rue Hervé-Julien leads to a tiny square surrounded by fishermen's cottages. **Rue Anatole-France** runs down to the harbour that was once filled with sardine-fishing boats. When the sardine trade was at its peak, **rue du Rosmeur** was lined with canneries such as Capitaine Cook. You can see where the former canning plant, now a private residence, stood: it is easily identifiable by its bright façade and the old sign.

Port de pêche

Built in 1951 on ground reclaimed from the sea, behind a 741m/800yd-long jetty, the fishing port boasts an important *criée* (fish auction) where the boats unload at about 11pm and bidding starts at 6.30am. A walk along the jetty offers a good **view**★ of the bay beneath the towering Menez-Hom.

▸ *Walk along boulevard Jean-Richepin to Port-Rhû and admire the splendid view of Douarnenez Bay.*

The walk takes you past **Plage de Porscad**, then **Plage des Dames** and along boulevard Camille Réaud, whith picturesque views of Tristan Island.

▸ *A footbridge and a metal bridge for cars span the Port-Rhû estuary, linking Douarnenez to Tréboul.*

Tréboul

It is in this district with its cluster of narrow streets that the **marina** is located, which can accommodate up to 700 boats. Further away is **Plage St-Jean** followed by the vast **Plage des Sables-Blancs** near Pointe de Leydé and opposite Coulinec Island.

Additional Sights

Port-Musée★★

& ◷ *Open mid-June to Sept, daily, 10am-7pm; Apr to mid-June and mid-Sep-first week Nov: 10am-12.30pm and 2-6pm.* ◷ *Closed Mon except during school holidays. Combined ticket with visit to "Musée à flot" ships on the water:* ⊶ *€6.20/3.80 (€17 group rate for families).* ☏ *02 98 92 65 20. www.port-musee.org.*

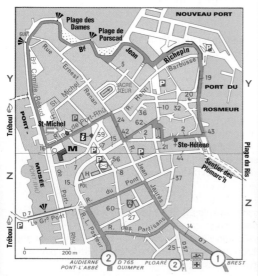

DOUARNENEZ		
Anatole-France R.	Y	2
Baigneurs R. des	Y	5
Barré R. J.	YZ	7
Berthelot R.	Z	8
Centre R. du	Y	10
Croas-Talud R.	Z	14
Duguay-Trouin R.	YZ	15
Enfer Pl. de l'	YZ	16
Grand-Port R. du	Y	20
Grand-Port Quai du	Y	19
Jaurès R. Jean	YZ	
Jean-Bart R.	Y	24
Kerivel R. E.	YZ	21
Laënnec R.	Z	25
Lamennais R.	Z	27
Marine R. de la	Y	32
Michel R. L.	Y	36
Monte-au-Ciel R.	Z	37
Péri Pl. Gabriel	Y	42
Petit-Port Quai du	Y	43
Plomarc'h R. des	YZ	44
Stalingrad Pl.	Z	65
Vaillant Pl. E.	Y	59
Victor-Hugo R.	Z	60
Voltaire R.	Y	62

This Port Museum is both a centre of conservation of boats and a permanent workshop where expertise in this field is passed on. It offers a good opportunity to rediscover the recent maritime past. The various elements of the Port Museum, established on the wonderful site of Port-Rhu, once the commercial harbour of Douarnenez, contain displays on all aspects of maritime and harbour life, from ships afloat, to construction sites and an onshore museum containing some 100 boats.

Musée du Bateau

This Boat Museum is located in an old canning factory and contains an **outstanding collection**★ of fishing, transport and pleasure boats from France and abroad. The Irish curragh can be found beside the Welsh coracle or the Norwegian *oselvar*; clinker-built ships are next to carvel-built ships. Most of the exhibits are of wood; however, there are some boats made from the skins of horses, deer, seals or even whales. Many of the craft are displayed in full sailing rig. There are reconstructed scenes and short black-and-white files of famous rescues, as well as an exhibition of Douarnenez's canning tradition.

 In summer, craftsmen are at work along the quayside, in an effort to keep alive traditional maritime crafts; various activities are scheduled (*programme of events available at the Port-Musée*).

Musée à flot

This comprises about 40 boats, 26 of which are open to visitors, moored in three harbour docks. In the first basin, fishing boats include: trawlers, lobster boats, shellfish boats, sardine boats and tuna boats. Visitors can go aboard one of the lobster boats, the *Notre-Dame-de-Rocamadour*. In another basin are larger coastal vessels such as the Saint-Denys, the *Anna Rosa* or the Northdown. The variety of boats displayed encompasses a British steam tug, a Norwegian coaster and a Breton sablier (used for transporting sand). Pleasure craft include the Ariane, built in 1927, the Viviane, dating from 1859, as well as cruising vessels and modern racing boats moored on the premises.

Excursions

Sentier des Plomarc'h and Plage du Ris★

E of town 2hr 30min on foot there and back. Access via rue des Plomarc'h east of the town plan.

 The path begins at Port du Rosmeur, runs along the side of a slope, affording some very picturesque **views**★ of Douarnenez, and leads to Plage du Ris. Return by the Locronan road.

Sentier des Roches-Blanches★

At Sables-Blancs Beach (Tréboul district), turn left on the road to Roches-Blanches and leave the car in the parking area just after the Village de Vacances.

 This hiking trail forms a loop of 6km/4mi. The coast path is marked by orange blazes, and runs along the sea to **Pointe de Leydé**★. The point affords a lovely **view**★ of the bay of Dournenez. If you are interested in a longer hike, continue on to Poullan-sur-Mer from here instead of taking the road back to Tréboul.

Église de Ploaré

Rue Laënnec. Access by ② on the town plan, D 57. ◐ Open July and Aug, daily, 10am-noon. Rest of the year: Sun 10am-noon.

The church dates from the 16C and 17C. It is crowned by a fine Flamboyant and Renaissance **tower**★, 55m/180ft high, with a crocketed steeple with four pinnacles at the corners (two Gothic, two Renaissance).

The façade is flanked with Gothic buttresses surmounted by pinnacles, while the buttresses of the apse and transept are crowned with small Renaissance lanterns. Inside note the high altar's carved altarpiece and a 17C painted wooden group representing the Holy Trinity.

Laënnec (1781-1826), the inventor of the stethoscope, is buried in the cemetery. Kerlouarnec, the country house where this eminent physician died, can be seen at the end of a fine avenue leading to the Chapelle de Ste-Croix (1701).

Le Juch
8km/5mi. Leave Douarnenez by S on the town plan, D 765. 6km/4mi further on, turn left for Le Juch.

Fine **view** of Douarnenez Bay, the Presqu'île de Crozon and Ménez-Hom. Inside the 16C-17C **church** *(If the church is closed, apply to Mme Pennanéac'h. ☎ 02 98 74 73 21 and ☎ 02 98 74 71 38.)*, the old 16C stained-glass window at the east end shows scenes from the Passion; to the left and right of the chancel are statues depicting the Annunciation, placed in niches with 16C painted shutters. To the right of the sacristy door, in the north aisle is St Michael overcoming a dragon known as the Devil of Le Juch. *Pardon* on 15 August.

Église de Guengat
14km/9mi by ② on the town plan, D 765. 11km/7mi further on, turn left 11km/7mi further on, for Guengat.

In the Gothic church at the entrance to the choir is, on the left column, a Flemish statue of St Barbara and, on the right column, a 16C Virgin and Child. In the choir itself are 16C **stained-glass windows**★ depicting the Passion (centre), the Last Judgment (right) and the Virgin between St John the Baptist and St Michael (right), and a carved frieze with animals (hare, fox, wild boar), people and floral decoration. It is worth going into the cemetery to see the fine Calvary.

CÔTE D'ÉMERAUDE★★★

EMERALD COAST

MICHELIN LOCAL MAP 309 F/M 2/3/ ILLE-ET-VILAINE (35) AND CÔTES D'ARMOR (22)

The "Emerald Coast" is the part of the coast between the Pointe du Grouin and Le Val-André, which includes some famous beaches: Dinard, St-Lunaire, Paramé etc and the city of the privateers: St-Malo. Rocky, heavily indented and very picturesque, the Côte d'Émeraude is a series of points from which fine panoramas can be seen, project into the sea. The coast is bisected by the Rance estuary. An enjoyable boat excursion between Dinan and St-Malo can be made on the estuary.

Driving Tours

1 From Cancale to St-Malo *23km/14mi – allow 5hr*

The scenic road along the Emerald Coast is among the major tourist attractions of Brittany's north coast. Although it does not hug the coastline all the way, it offers many excursions to the points, enabling the visitor to enjoy spectacular sites with views and panoramas typical of this jagged coastline.

Cancale★ –  *See CANCALE.*

▷ *Leave Cancale by ② on the town plan, turn right towards Pointe du Grouin 300m/0.2mi further on.*

Pointe du Grouin★★ – *See CANCALE: Excursion.*

The coast road follows the cliffs as far as Le Verger and offers lovely views.

▷ *Bear right towards the beach.*

Chapelle Notre-Dame-du-Verger
This small chapel, rebuilt in the 19C, is venerated by the sailors of Cancale (pilgrimage 15 August). Inside there are models of different kinds of sailing vessels: sloops, three-masted ships, schooners, etc.

La Guimorais
Chevrets Beach stretches between Pointe du Meinga and the Presqu'île Bénard near this quiet seaside resort. The road skirts the harbour of Rothéneuf, where low tide almost completely empties the harbour. The flow of the tides was once used to work a mill.
On the right, the elegant 17C **Château du Lupin**, a malouinière built by a wealthy St-Malo shipowner, is of interest.

Rothéneuf and Le Minihic – *See ST-MALO: Rothéneuf.*

The road here offers fine glimpses of the Bay of St-Malo.

Paramé – *See ST-MALO: Paramé.*

St-Malo★★★ – *See ST-MALO.*

② From Dinard to Cap Frehel *73km/45mi – allow 4hr*

Dinard – *See DINARD.*
Unfortunately, the road does not follow all the indentations of the coast between Dinard and Cap Fréhel. However, it has interesting overhanging sections and opens

A magic moment on the Emerald Coast

R. Mattes/MICHELIN

Address Book

WHERE TO STAY

Manoir de la Salle – *Rue du Lac, 22240 Sables-d'Or-les-Pins, 1km/0.6mi southwest via D 34* – ☎ *02 96 72 38 29.* 🕐 *Closed 1 Oct-31 Mar.* 📇 *– 14 rooms 250/700F,* 🍽 *40F.* Despite being entirely renovated, this 16C Breton manor house has retained its character: its stone façades are superb. Inside, except for one large salon with a fireplace, all the rooms are modern and functional.

Manoir St-Michel – *At La Carquois, 22240 Sables-d'Or-les-Pins, 1.5km/1mi east via D 34* – ☎ *02 96 41 48 87.* 🕐 *Closed 3 Nov-31 Mar.* 📇 *17 rooms 280/600F,* 🍽 *42F.* In this old manor house with rose-coloured sandstone walls, you can enjoy the large garden overlooking the sea and a duck-pond.

The rooms are slightly out-of-date, but nonetheless are welcoming. Duplex for families; attractive prices off-season.

Hôtel Les Pins – *22240 Sables-d'Or-les-Pins* – ☎ *02 96 41 42 20* – 🕐 *closed 1 Oct-31 Mar – 22 rooms 290F,* 🍽 *36F,* 🍴 A large establishment in a garden planted with pines, of course! This hotel is well-kept and has retained its familial atmosphere, which accounts for its simple and welcoming decor: the rooms are light and the dining room is warm and inviting.

SPORT

Golf de St-Briac-sur-Mer – *54, boulevard Houle* – ☎ *02 99 88 32 07.* This 18-hole golf course is open all year, and is one of the oldest in France.

up fine panoramas and remarkable scenery. Many fashionable and family resorts lie along the coast.

St-Lunaire♨♨ – 👤 *See DINARD.*

Pointe de la Garde Guérin★

15min on foot there and back. 🖼 After crossing the point at its base, turn right onto a road as it descends to the foot of the hill, which is honeycombed with casemates *(car park)*. Climb on foot to the top of the promontory, from which a fine **panorama**★★ extends from Cap Fréhel to Pointe de la Varde.
The road traverses the Dinard golf course (60ha/148 acres).

St-Briac-sur-Mer♨

This pleasant resort with its picturesque and varied sites, has a fishing harbour, a marina, and many good beaches. There are good views of the coast from the Emerald Balcony (Balcon d'Émeraude) and the Sailors' Cross (Croix des Marins – *access: from the Emerald Balcony by a path on the left, just before a bridge).*

▶ *As you come out of St-Briac cross River Frémur on a bridge 330m/984ft long.*

Lancieux

This village has a very extensive beach of fine sand, from which there is a lovely view of Ebihens Island and the advanced points of the coast: St-Jacut-de-la-Mer, St-Cast and Cap Fréhel. In the centre of the village stands the old bell-tower of the former church. The square tower is capped by a dome and its lantern turret.

▶ *In Ploubalay take the road towards Dinard and 800m/0.5mi further on turn left.*

St-Jacut-de-la-Mer♨

The road follows a long peninsula and goes through St-Jacut-de-la-Mer, a small fishing port and seaside resort. After skirting the beach of Le Rougeret, you will reach the high and picturesque cliff of the **Pointe du Chevet;** there is a fine **view**★ of the Île Ebihens, opposite, and its tower, of the Bay of Arguenon (note the upstan-

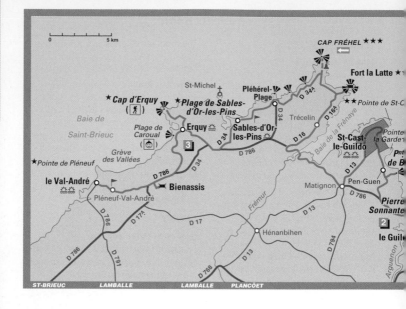

ding poles – *bouchots* – where mussels mature), to the left, and of St-Cast, to the right of the Bay of Lancieux.

Le Guildo

This village lies in a picturesque setting on the shore of the Arguenon estuary. From the bridge across it you will see the ruins of Le Guildo Castle on the east bank. In the 15C this was the seat of Gilles de Bretagne, a carefree and gallant poet, who led a happy life at Le Guildo. However, Gilles was suspected of plotting by his brother, the reigning duke, and was thrown into prison. As he did not die fast enough, he was smothered. Before Gilles died he summoned his brother to the judgement of God. A short time later the Duke died, supposedly of remorse.

Les Pierres Sonnantes

Opposite the ruins of the castle *(to the right, on the far bank)*, you will find a pile of rocks known as "the ringing stones" which emit a metallic note when you strike them with a stone of the same type. This resonance is due to the perfectly even grain of the rocks.

▶ *Go towards St-Cast by the coastal road.*

Pointe de Bay

A good road on the right leads to a large car park. The **view**★ includes the Arguenon estuary with its lines of mussel poles and the Presqu'île de St-Jacut and the Île Ebihens.
The road skirts the fashionable fine sandy beach of **Pen-Guen.**

St-Cast-le-Guildo⚐⚐ – ⬤ *See ST-CAST-LE-GUILDO.*

Leaving St-Cast the road makes a big loop round the head of the bay of La Frênaye.

▶ *After Trécelin, take D 16A which leads to the fort (car park).*

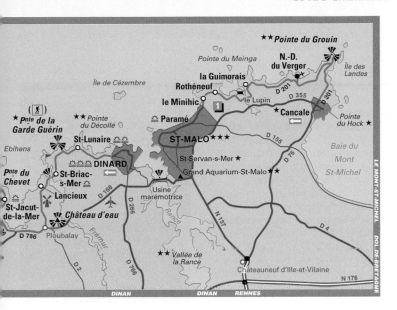

Fort la Latte★★ – 👣 *See Cap FRÉHEL*

Cap Fréhel★★★ – 👣 *See Cap FRÉHEL.*

③ **From Cap Frehel to Le Val-Andre**

34km/21mi/ – about 2hr 30min

The tourist road, which twists and turns in the moor, affords striking **views**★★ of the sea, cliffs and golden beaches. The road also goes through a pine forest.

Pléhérel-Plage

The beach is on the right after a forest of conifers. A scenic view of Cap Fréhel and, in the foreground, a succession of tiny coves carved into the dunes may be enjoyed.

Sables-d'Or-les-Pins⌂

This seaside resort, created in 1922 and immediately fashionable, boasts opulent villas and Anglo-Norman-style hotels. The channel can be seen through the pine forest. From the vast sandy **beach**★, one of the finest in Brittany, a group of small islands can be distinguished, especially that of St-Michel and its chapel.

After the Plurien intersection, the St-Quay coastline comes into view across St-Brieuc Bay.

▶ *As you enter Erquy go towards the cape.*

Cap d'Erquy★

30min on foot there and back.

From the point where the road ends, there is an extensive view of grey-pink shingle beaches lapped by clear waters, opposite Caroual Beach, Vallées seashore, the Pointe de Pléneuf and Verdelet Islet and beyond St-Brieuc Bay, the Pointe de l'Arcouest and the Île de Bréhat.

Pleasant footpaths bordered by bracken cross the heath dotted with patches of yellow and mauve and afford glimpses of the reefs. *Guided tours of this area are organised in July and August.*

Erquy⌂

In the 19C, a number of historians believed that Erquy was located on the alleged site of Reginea, a former Gallo-Roman settlement. It now appears they may have been mistaken. However, due to this misunderstanding, the inhabitants of Erquy have retained the charming name of "Réginéens".

Set against a backdrop of rugged cliffs, this busy fishing port (2 000t of scallops in 1993) is gradually extending its influence. Its fishing fleet is made up of around 80 boats specialised in coastal fishing: fish (sole, turbot, gurnard, John Dory) and shellfish (scallops but also clams and queen scallops). Among the many beaches, that of Caroual stands out on account of its **view** of the bay and Cap d'Erquy, as well as its natural

The fishing port at Erquy

topography, which ensures safe bathing for children.

On the edge of the road leading to Cap d'Erquy stand two small guard-rooms – the vestiges of Vauban's fortifications – along with a curious-looking cannon-ball foundry; its purpose was to manufacture cannon-balls for the batteries of artillery to fire at the approaching English, sailing forth in their 17C wooden ships.

▶ *Via Pléneuf-Val-André return to Le Val-André.*

Le Val-André⌂⌂ – ♿ *See Le VAL-ANDRÉ.*

LES ENCLOS PAROISSIAUX★★

MICHELIN LOCAL MAP 308 F/I 3/4 - FINISTÈRE (29)

Parish **closes**, which are a special feature of Breton art, are to be found mostly in Lower Brittany. The route runs through the picturesque Élorn Valley and the foothills of the Monts d'Arrée and includes only a few of the more interesting ones. There are many others, especially that of Pleyben, further to the south.

Driving Tour

Starting From Morlaix

130km/81mi – one day

Morlaix★ – ♿ *See MORLAIX.*

▶ *Leave Morlaix W along N 12.*

St-Thégonnec★★ – ⚫ *See ST-THÉGONNEC.*

▶ *Go round the east end of the church and bear left.*

Guimiliau★★ – ⚫ *See GUIMILIAU.*

Lampaul-Guimiliau★ – ⚫ *See LAMPAUL-GUIMILIAU.*

Landivisiau

Landivisiau is a busy town. Its cattle fairs are among the largest in France. The **Église St-Thivisiau** is a modern church in the Gothic style, which still has the bell-tower and the fine granite **porch**★ of a former 16C church. Note the elegant canopies above the statues of the Apostles and the delicate ornamentation round the doors.

Chapelle Ste-Anne in middle of the churchyard was an ossuary in the 17C. The façade is adorned with six caryatids. Death is represented to the left of the west doorway
In the village of *Lambader*, 8km/5mi north, the Chapelle Notre-Dame has a lovely rood screen in the Flamboyant Gothic style (1481).

▶ *Head towards Landerneau, then turn right via the intersection at La-Croix-des-Maltotiers.*

Bodilis

The **church**★ (16C) is preceded by a Flamboyant bell-tower pierced with three openings at the base. The large 17C sacristy, jutting out from the north aisle, is very handsome, with a roof in the shape of an inverted hull, a richly decorated cornice and buttresses ornamented with niches. A porch opens on the south side. The interior has remarkable **decorations**★: purlins, tie-beams, hammerbeams, statues and gilded altarpieces. The font canopy is carved from Kersanton granite. There is also a colourful Entombment in high relief on the porch wall.

▶ *Rejoin D 712 Landerneau and bear right.*

S. Sauvignier/MICHELIN

Sculpture on St-Thégonnec Calvary

Moulin de Brézal

The mill, which has an interesting façade with a Flamboyant doorway, stands in a pleasant setting below a pool. On the opposite side of the road is the ruined Chapelle de Pont-Christ (1533).

▶ *3.5km/2.2mi farther on, turn left to La roche-Maurice.*

La Roche-Maurice★

The village, situated on a hillside and dominated by the ruins of a castle, has a fine **parish close**, featuring three crosses with Christ and the thieves.

Church

An elegant, twin-galleried belfry crowns the 16C building. The **south porch**★ is delicately carved with bunches of grapes and statuettes of saints. Inside, note the Renaissance **rood screen**★ decorated on the side facing the nave with 12 statues carved in the round, including nine Apostles and three Popes, and on the chancel side with low-relief sculptures of saints. Behind the high altar, a large **stained-glass window**★ (1539) illustrates the Passion and the Resurrection of Christ. Also of interest is the panelled ceiling adorned with angels and coats of arms, carved purlins and beams.

Ossuary★

This ossuary dates from 1640 and is one of the largest in Brittany. Above the outside font, Death is shown armed with an arrow, threatening small figures framed in medallions representing all social classes: a peasant, a woman, a lawyer, a bishop, St-Yves, a pauper and a rich man; an inscription reads *Je vous tue tous* (Death comes to all).

Landerneau – See LANDERNEAU.

▶ *Leave Landerneau by S on the town plan, towards Sizun.*

La Martyre★

This **parish close**★, the oldest in the Léon region, opens onto a triumphal arch with a Flamboyant balustrade and a small Calvary. The ossuary (1619) is adorned with a curious caryatid and macabre motifs. The 14-16C church has a fine historiated **porch**★ (c 1450) on its south side. Inside, note the carved purlins, tie-beams, altarpieces and 15C chancel screen. The chancel is lit by 16C **stained-glass windows**★.

Ploudiry

The village, formerly the largest parish of the Léon region, has an interesting close. On the façade of the ossuary (1635), Death is depicted striking down men of all social classes. The church, rebuilt in the 19C, retains a fine south **porch**★ dating from 1665. The high altar, adorned with polychrome high-relief carvings and the side altars are good specimens of 17C Breton art. In the chancel is a 17C window depicting the Passion.

▶ *Pass through Le Traon and turn left towards Sizun.*

Sizun★ – See SIZUN.

▶ *Proceed to Carhaix.*

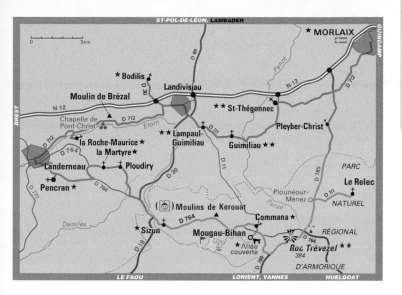

Moulins de Kerouat

🕐 *Open July and Aug, daily, 11am-7pm; in June, 10am-noon and 2-6pm, Sat-Sun afternoons only; mid-Mar to May and Sept to Oct, daily (except Sat), 10am-noon and 2-6pm, Sun and holidays afternoons only.* ⚌ €4.50 (children €2.10). ☎ 02 98 68 87 76.
Under the auspices of the Parc naturel régional d'Armorique, the 19C village of Kerouat has been revived and is now **Écomusée des Monts d'Arrée**. You will see its mills, dwelling house, outbuildings (stable, barn) and bread oven; learn how a water mill functioned with its scoop wheel and mechanism (gears on the ground floor, millstone on the upper floor), and how the miller lived.

▷ *Continue onto Carhaix and at Ty Douar bear left.*

Commana★

The village stands on an isolated foothill of the Monts d'Arrée. Within the close is a 16C-17C **church**★ with a fine south porch. Inside, there are three interesting altarpieces. Note the **altar**★ to St Anne (1682) in the north aisle and an Ecce Homo in wood on a pillar in the transept, to the right. The canopied font is ornamented with five statues: Faith, Hope, Charity, Justice and Temperance.
In the summer there is an exhibit of sacred art in the charnel-house.

Commana church, altar screen

Mougau-Bian

Beyond the hamlet, to the right, is a **covered alleyway**★, 14m/46ft long; some of the uprights are carved on the inside with lances and daggers.

▷ *Return to D 764 and turn right; 1km/0.7mi further on, take an uphill road to the right (D 11) to join the Morlaix road, and turn left onto D 785.*

Roc Trévezel★★ – ⏱ *See Monts d'ARÉE*

▶ *Near Plounéour-Ménez, turn right.*

Le Relec

Nestled in the valley, a 12C-13C church and the ruins of the monastery buildings, are all that remain of the former Cistercian abbey. It is a simple, austere building, although the façade was restored in the 18C. Concerts take place in the abbey on the *Dimanches du Relec,* from May to September, and during the *Rencontres de Musique Vocale* in August. The pardon of Notre-Dame-du-Relec is on August 15.

▶ *Turn back and bear right towards Morlaix.*

Pleyber-Christ

Here, the Gothic-Renaissance **church** is preceded by a triumphal arch (1921) dedicated to the dead of the First World War. Inside the building, which has fine carved purlins and remarkable beams, are some old pews and three lovely altarpieces.

▶ *Continue towards Ste-Sève; after 3.5km/2mi, take the road on the right to return to Morlaix.*

RIVIÈRE D'ÉTEL

MICHELIN LOCAL MAP 308 K/L 8/9 - MORBIHAN (56)

This very short river, which forms a bay west of the Quiberon Peninsula, follows a course that covers 15km/9mi from its source to the sea, yet the banks are so winding that they would measure 100km/60mi if stretched straight. These endless curves make the river banks a lovely place to enjoy nature.

Sights

Étel

The River Étel is known for its treacherous bank of quicksand *(barre)*, which offers a spectacular scene in bad weather. Navigation is difficult and requires constant surveillance. The view extends over Groix Island, Belle-Île and the Quiberon peninsula. The small fishing port of **Étel** lies on the river's south bank. It is home to a fleet of about 10 fishing boats, which sail to the Azores, and a small fleet of trawlers, which fish along the coast.

Pont-Lorois

This short and pretty run gives a glimpse of the wide estuary, which on the left opens out into a bay and on the right narrows into a deep channel which winds down to the sea.

Left Bank

St-Cado

Located on an island linked to the mainland by a dike, this hamlet with its little fishermen's houses make a charming Breton **scene**★, especially at high tide. Chapelle St-Cado is one of the few Romanesque buildings in the Morbihan with unornamented rounded arches, plainly decorated capitals and dim lighting. It is in this chapel that the deaf sought help from St Cado, whose stone bed and pillow can still be seen.

Pointe du Verdon

As with all the points of the bay, the far end of the Pointe du Verdon is devoted to oyster farming; after crossing the isthmus and before taking the uphill road through the pines, bear right to reach a platform from which there is a fine view over the oyster beds. At low tide it is possible to walk round the point.

St-Cado

R. Mattes/MICHELIN

Right Bank

Presqu'île de Nestadio

This village has some 16C houses. At the end of the peninsula, stands a small chapel dedicated to St-Guillaume.

Pointe de Mané-Hellec

▶ *By a small transformer station, turn left onto a surfaced road.*

Lovely view of St-Cado and its chapel, Pont-Lorois, the River Étel and the Forêt de Locoal-Mendon.

Merlevenez★

This little town's **church**★ is one of the few Romanesque churches in Brittany which has kept intact its elegant doorways with chevron and saw-tooth archivolts, its depressed arches in the nave, its historiated capitals and dome on squinches rising above the transept crossing. Modern stained-glass windows by Grüber illustrate scenes from the Life of the Virgin.

There is a fountain in Sainte-Hélène where local seamen used to come and pray before going to sea. Each one would throw a piece of soft bread into the fountain and, according to popular belief, if the bread floated, then the seaman would come back.

LE FAOUËT

POPULATION 3 110
MICHELIN LOCAL MAP 306 E3 - FINISTÈRE (29)

This village is the centre of a very picturesque district extending between the Stêr Laër and the Ellé, two rivers flowing from the Montagnes Noires.The 16C covered market with its great slate roof supported by a domed pinnacle houses a lively market. In the shady square in front of the market, stands a monument to **Corentin Carré,** the youngest soldier of France. In 1915 he enlisted at the age of 15, and died in aerial combat in 1918. He was then a sergeant-major.

Excursions

Chapelle St-Fiacre★

2.5km/1.5mi southeast on D 790. ◷ *Open April to mid-Nov, 10am-noon, 2pm-6pm; mid-Nov to March, Sat-Mon 2pm-5pm.* ☎ *02 97 23 23 23.*

The chapel is a fine 15C building. The façade has one of the best gable-belfries in Brittany. Inside, the **rood screen**★★ of lace-like woodcarving is a Flamboyant work of 1480. On the nave side, scenes of the Temptation of Adam and Eve, the Annunciation and the Calvary are related. The most curious figures are on the chancel side; they picture theft (a man picking fruit from a tree), drunkenness (a man vomiting a fox), lust (a man and a woman) and laziness (a Breton peasant playing bagpipes and a bombard). The decoration of the panels of the gallery and the corbels is quite varied.

Rood screen

H. Le Gac/MICHELIN

The stone altarpiece against the left pillar shows the martyrdom of St Sebastian. There are fine 16C stained-glass windows in the chancel and transept: the Passion (chancel), the Life of St John the Baptist (south transept), the Tree of Jesse and the Life of St Fiacre (north transept).

Chapelle Ste-Barbe

3km/1.8mi northeast of Le Faouët via D 790. ◷ *Open April to mid-Nov, 10am-noon, 2pm-6pm; mid-Nov to March, Sat-Mon 2pm-5pm.* ☎ *02 97 23 23 23.*

This Flamboyant-style chapel is built in a rocky cleft on the side of a hill. The **site**★ is very pretty; from a height of some 100m/300ft, it overlooks the small Ellé Valley. The great stairway (78 steps), built in 1700, leading up to the chapel, is linked by an arch to the St Michael Oratory (Oratoire St-Michel) crowning a rock spur. Nearby, in a small building, is the bell tolled by pilgrims to call down blessings from heaven. Owing to its position and orientation, the chapel has only a single aisle and a small apse.

Paths lead down to the sacred fountain, below the chapel.

From a rocky platform reached by a path starting on the right half-way along the car park, there is a good view of the sunken, wooded Ellé Valley.

LE FOLGOËT★★

POPULATION 3 094
MICHELIN LOCAL MAP 58 FOLD 4 OR 230 FOLDS 3 AND 4 – LOCAL MAP SEE ABERS

You should see this little village and its magnificent Basilica of Our Lady (Notre-Dame) during the *grand pardon*. It is the best known in the Léon region and one of the largest in Brittany. The ceremonies begin at 6pm the day before and continue the next day. The pardon of St Christopher with the blessing of cars is on the fourth Sunday in July.

Basilique★★

A great esplanade with inns on each side leads up to the basilica, but is not even wide enough to hold the crowd on pardon days. The **north tower**★ of the façade supports one of the finest bell-towers in Brittany.

The basilica is square in shape, which is unusual; the Chapel of the Cross, whose east wall is an extension of the flat east end, branches off the chancel. This chapel has a fine **porch**★. Salaün's fountain, where pilgrims come to drink, stands outside, against the east wall. The water comes from the spring under the altar.

Inside is a masterpiece of Breton art of the 15C, the admirably carved granite **rood screen**★★. Five 15C Kersanton granite altars stand in the east end. The Chapel of the Cross and the apse

The north tower

R. Mattes/MICHELIN

are adorned by fine rose windows. There is a 15C statue of Our Lady of Folgoët. Left of the basilica the little 15C manor house of Le Doyenné, though much restored, forms an attractive group with the pilgrim's inn and the church.

The Legend of the Fool's Wood

The name Folgoët (Fool's Wood) recalls the legend attached to the foundation of the shrine. In the mid 14C, a poor half-wit named Salaün lived in a hollow oak in a wood, near a spring not far from Lesneven. He knew only a few words, and he constantly repeated them: "Itron Gwerc'hez Vari" (Lady Virgin Mary). After his death a lily grew on his grave; the pistil made the words "Ave Maria" in gold letters. Men dug up the earth and found that the lily sprang from Salaün's mouth. News of the miracle spread in Brittany. The War of Succession was raging at the time. The Pretender Montfort vowed that if he won he would build a sumptuous chapel to the Virgin. After his victory at Auray, he gave orders for the building to begin. The altar was to stand over the spring where the simpleton used to drink. The work was completed by Montfort's son in 1423.

The chapel was pillaged during the Revolution. To save it from being demolished, 12 farmers joined together to buy it. It was returned to the parish at the Restoration, and has been gradually repaired since.

In the inn, a small museum (♿🕐 *Open mid-June to mid-Sept, daily (except Sun and public holidays in the morning), 10am-12.30pm and 2.30-6.30pm. €3. ☎ 02 98 83 03 78*) contains a collection of 15C, 16C and 17C stone statues, archives and 15C furnishings.

Excursion

Lesneven
NE of Folgoët. Lesneven was founded in the 5C by the Breton chief Even. There are several 17C and 18C granite houses.

Musée de Léon
Located in the Ursuline convent's chapel, this museum is devoted to the history of the Léon region. Note the authentic decree signed by Louis XIV authorising the creation of an Ursuline convent in Lesneven.

FOUESNANT-LES-GLÉNAN★

POPULATION 8 076
MICHELIN LOCAL MAP 308 G7

This town is in the middle of one of the most fertile areas in Brittany; the villages stand among cherry and apple orchards. This is also where the best Breton cider is produced. The costumes and headdresses of Fouesnant are a very pretty sight at the feast of the apple trees and at the pardon of St Anne. Its beaches and small ports make it a popular seaside resort. Built in the 12C, the church, remodelled in the 18C, was restored. Inside, the tall granite pillars are adorned with fine Romanesque capitals. An unusual stoup is built into an engaged pillar.

Excursion

La Forêt-Fouesnant
3.5km/2.2mi E. This village possesses
a parish close and a 16C Calvary with
four corner pilasters. The church porch,
dating from 1538, is adorned with two
old, rough-hewn statues of St Roch and
St Mélar. Inside, at the high altar are an
altarpiece and, on either side, two 17C
statues. The chapels at the far end of the
church contain, to the right, a wooden
statue of St Alan and to the left, a font
(1628) with a piscina and a basin hewn
from the same block. In the chapel on
the south side of the chancel stands a
Pietà. Breton and Celtic music is played
in the background all day.

Port-la-Forêt
This port for pleasure craft has been built
near La Forêt-Fouesnant; it can hold 800
boats. There are boat services to the Îles
de Glénan and up the Odet.

Commemorative monument, La Forêt-Fouesnant

Cap-Coz 🏊
2km/1.2mi ESE. This small resort is built on a sandy spit, between the cliffs of Beg-Meil and the channel to Port-la-Forêt. The view extends on one side over La Forêt Bay, Beg-Meil and Concarneau and on the other side over Port-la-Forêt and La Forêt-Fouesnant.
A pleasant excursion can be enjoyed by taking the **coastal path** which runs along La Forêt Bay as far as La Roche-Percée, overlooking or crossing small coves and affording fine views of the coastline from Kerleven to the Pointe de Trévignon.

Beg-Meil 🏊
5.5km/3.5mi S. Beg-Meil (meaning the Point of the Mill) is located at the mouth of Baie de La Forêt and opposite Concarneau. This resort has beaches both on its bay and ocean front. On the bay side there are small rocky wooded coves: Oiseaux Beach and La Cale Beach. On the ocean side there are dunes and the well-equipped Sémaphore Beach. From the vast Dunes Beach (or Grande Plage), the Glénan archipelago is visible in the distance. From **Pointe de Beg-Meil** (Beg-Meil Point), there is a 7m/23ft-high menhir, which was laid on its side by the Germans during the Second World War.

Boat trips to Concarneau and Île St-Nicolas are organised in season. There are also cruises round the Glénan Islands aboard boats with underwater viewing.

Pointe de Mousterlin
6.5km/4mi SW. From the end of the point, there is an extensive view of the coast from the Pointe de Lesconil to the Pointe de Trévignon, with in the distance the Île aux Moutons and the Îles de Glénan. The Eckmühl Lighthouse can be seen on the right after dark.

Îles de Glénan★
Access by boat: Apr-Sep from Beg-Meil, Bénodet, Concarneau and Loctudy (1hr crossing). The Île St-Nicolas where you disembark is a natural reserve with a fragile ecosystem. The

Glénan Islands

local narcissus has been given special protection, but all of the flora should be observed only. 🐾 *It is forbidden to pick the flowers. Stay on the marked paths.*

The archipelago consists of nine islets surrounded by reefs and lies off Concarneau. It is home to a unique plant species, the narcisse des Glénan (narcissus), discovered in 1803 by a chemist from Quimper, which flowers briefly in mid-April.

Boats go to the Île St-Nicolas which has a few houses, a skin diving school (Centre International de Plongée) and a breeding pool for crustaceans. A footpath goes round the island, affording good views of the coast from Penmarch to Le Pouldu.

To the north lies the **Île Brunec** and to the south the **Île du Loch,** which can easily be distinguished from a being former seaweed factory by its chimney. Both are privately owned.

Penfret with its lighthouse, **Cigogne** (The Stork), identified by its 18C fort and the annexe of the marine laboratory of Concarneau, **Bananec**, which is linked to St-Nicolas at low tide, and **Drénec** are islands from which the internationally famous sailing school, the Centre Nautique de Glénan, operates.

FOUGÈRES★★

POPULATION 21 779

MICHELIN LOCAL MAP 309 O4.

This former stronghold is built in a picturesque setting on a promontory overlooking the winding valley of the Nançon. Below it, on a rocky height almost entirely encircled by the river, stands a magnificent feudal castle whose walls and 13 big towers are among the most massive in Europe. The town centre (place Aristide-Briand, place du Théâtre, rue Nationale and the neighbouring streets) has been transformed into a pedestrian precinct. The Classical buildings in this area are the works of Gabriel.

▶ **Orient Yourself:** On the eastern edge of Brittany, 49km/30mi NE of Rennes.
🐾 **Don't Miss:** The view of the château from the public gardens.
🕐 **Organizing Your Time:** A leisurely day is enough time to walk the town.
🅿 **Parking:** Free in July and August.

A Bit of History

A frontier post – Standing on the border of Brittany and France, Fougères acquired great military importance in the early Middle Ages, when its barons were very powerful. The most famous was Raoul II. He lived in the mid 12C under Conan IV, known as "the Little", Duke of Brittany. This weak duke submitted to Henry II Plantagenet, King of England and Duke of Normandy, but the proud Raoul revolted against the English yoke. He formed a league with some of the Breton nobles and rebelled against Henry II. In 1166 Henry II surrounded Fougères, which capitulated after three months' siege. The castle was completely demolished, but Raoul immediately began to rebuild it, and part of his work still stands.

In the 13C the fief passed to some Poitou noblemen, the Lusignans. They claimed to be descendants of the fairy Mélusine and gave her name to the finest of the towers that they added to the walls.

Fougères is an example of a formidable fortress which was often taken. Among those who fought their way into it were St Louis, Du Guesclin, Surienne, a leader from Aragon in the service of the English (at night without striking a blow), La Trémoille, the Duke of Mercœur and the men of the Vendée.

After the union of Brittany and France, there was a succession of governors at Fougères; 10 of its towers bear their names. The castle was then mainly used as a prison. In the 18C it became private property. The town bought it in 1892.

The Castle★★

♿ ⏱ *Open 12 Sep-7 May: 10am-12.30pm and 2-5pm; rest of the year: 9.30am-12.30pm and 2-6.30pm. Last entrance 30min before closing.* ⏱ *Closed Tue from Oct-March, 1 Jan, 1 May, 1 Nov, 11 Nov and 25 Dec.* ⚇ *€4.10/3.60.* *Guided tours available.* ☎ *02 99 99 79 59.*

The castle is a fine example of military architecture of the Middle Ages. There is an interesting general view from the public garden.

The site is curious. A loop in the river, washing a rocky eminence, shaped like a very narrow peninsula, formed an excellent defensive position. Military architects took advantage of this site to build ramparts and towers and turn the peninsula into an island by a short diversion of the Nançon at the base of the loop. As the castle was connected with the upper town by the city ramparts, the garrison could take part in its defence; they also had the advantage

Fougères

R. Mattes/MICHELIN

of being able to retire into the fortress and hold it as a frontier post for the Duchy of Brittany should the town fall. The fortress, as we see it, has suffered greatly over the centuries. The wall is complete, with its curtains closely following the lie of the land and its 13 towers. Unfortunately, we can no longer see the high keep that commanded all the defences; it was razed in 1166 by King Henry II of England and there are now only traces which can be seen when visiting the castle's interior. The main buildings which occupied part of the inner court were also demolished down to their foundations, in the beginning of the 19C. History tells us that the defenders often succumbed and that attackers were able to seize these high walls, either by surprise attack or after long sieges. An outer tour of the castle shows the attackers' point of view; an inner tour, that of the defenders.

Address Book

TOURIST OFFICE

Fougères ,2 rue Nationale, antenne au château in July-Aug, ☎ 02 99 94 12 20, www.ot-fougeres.fr; July-Aug: Mon-Sat 9am-7pm, Sun and public holidays 10-12am, 2-4pm; Easter-June and Sept-Oct: Mon-Sat 9.30am-12.30pm, 2-6pm, Sun and public holidays 1.30-5.30pm; Nov-Easter: Mon 2-6pm, Tue-Sat 10am-12.30pm, 2-6pm. Offers guided tours of the town and of the castle. The office sells a guide to hiking trails in the area (€3). The card **Passe-Portes** (€4.70), available for 2 days, enables you to visit all the monuments in the town.

& *For coin ranges, see the Legend on the cover flap.*

WHERE TO STAY

FOUGÈRES

⊜⊜ **Balzac Hôtel**, *15 rue Nationale,* ☎ 02 99 99 42 46, balzachotel@wanadoo.fr - 22 rooms, ⌙ €6. Traditional hotel with elegant rooms, most are equipped with a bath. Cordial welcome.

⊜⊜⊜ **Hôtel des Voyageurs**, *10 Place Gambetta,* ☎ 02 99 99 08 20, hotel-voyageurs-fougeres@wanadoo.fr - 37 rooms, ⌙ €6.50. Well-kept and functional rooms, opening onto the street or the back, in the upper town.

SURROUNDINGS

⊜ **Chambres d'hôte La Haute Bourdière**, *Landéan,* ☎ 02 99 97 21 52, www.haute-bourdiere.com - 5 rooms, ⌙✕. Renovated farm with individualized rooms, including a unit for up to 6 people. Crepes and white wine cakes for breakfast. The dining room is well known in the area; be sure to reserve if you would like to have dinner there.

⊜⊜⊜⊜ **Château de la Foletière**, *Parc floral de haute Bretagne,* ⌙. Five very elegant guest rooms.

EATING OUT

FOUGÈRES

⊜ **Ti Vabro**, *13 Place du Marchix,* ☎ 02 99 17 20 90. 🕐 *Closed Sun evening and Mon.* In a half-timbered house in the mediaeval district, this creperie offers a menu of 15 ciders to enjoy with nicely made crepes.

⊜ **Les Remparts**, *102 rue de la Pinterie,* ☎ 02 99 94 53 53. Traditional creperie with terrace offering a beautiful view over the castle.

⊜⊜ **Les Voyageurs**, ☎ 02 99 99 14 17. 🕐 *Closed Sat noon and Sun evening.* Haute cuisine made with regional products by a chef with a creative touch. Beautiful desserts.

⊜⊜ **Haute Sève**, *37 bd Jean Jaurès,* ☎ 02 99 94 23 39. 🕐 *Closed Sun evening and Mon, 25 July-25 Aug, 1st-9 Jan and 22 Feb-6 March.* Behind the half-timber façade, you will find a welcoming dining room where inventive, market-fresh cuisine is served.

SURROUNDINGS

⊜⊜ **La Petite Auberge**, *La Templerie, 9 km in direction of Laval by the N 12,* ☎ 02 99 95 27 03. 🕐 *Open at noon Tue-Thu and Sun, noon and evening Fri-Sat,* 🕐 *closed Mon except public holidays.* Country-style cooking in a traditional setting.

ON THE TOWN

La Table de Cueillette, *1 rue Lesueur,* ☎ 02 99 99 60 38. 🕐 *Closed Wed and Sun from July to Sept.* Welcoming tea shop to enjoy sweet or savoury tarts and excellent English teas.

Le Coquelicot, *18 rue de Vitré,* ☎ 02 99 99 82 11. 🕐 *Closed Sun, Mon and mid-July-mid-Aug.* The liveliest night-spot in Fougères, this warm pub regularly schedules musical nights.

Café de Paris, *9 Place Aristide Briand,* ☎ 02 99 94 39 38. Small pub in the town centre with musical nights in summer.

Les Oubliettes, *71 rue de la Pinterie,* ☎ 02 99 94 15 62. 🕐 *Closed Mon.* Concerts are often organized Fri night in this beer pub with mediaeval decor.

SHOPPING

Market – In the streets of the upper town Sat morning.

Culinary specialities - Lecourtiller, *21 Place Aristide Briand,* ☎ 02 99 99 38 70. 🕐 *Closed Mon and Sun afternoon.* La Gâche, a flat cake made with bread pastry, and the Beffroi, a meringue with hazelnut cream, are the specialities of this well known pattisserie.

La Galette du Beffroi, *41 rue Nationale, ☎ 02 99 99 31 23.* 🕐 *Closed Sun and Mon.* Cakes, Breton far, cupcakes and apple cakes.

Charcuterie Plessis, *14 rue de la Forêt,* ☎ *02 99 99 06 96.* 🕐 *Closed Sun and Mon.* Good home-cooked meats for a picnic.

Around the fortifications★
Park your car in place Raoul-II, skirt the fortifications, then left along rue Le Bouteiller.
As you circle the walls you will see the splendid towers in all their variety of appearance and structure. At the start you will also see, in the middle of the north rampart, the 14C **Guibé Turret**, a corbelled sentry-post built onto the wall.

Going round the spur formed by the ramparts towards the west, you will see how massively the defences are concentrated at this point. The whole forms a triangle with two towers at the base and a postern at the apex. The 15C postern today looks out on empty space, but it was once connected with a double arcade that crossed the moat to communicate with an outwork. The 13C and 14C **Gobelin Tower,** to the left of the postern, and the 14C **Mélusine Tower,** to the right, are round and overlook the walls from a height. Stripped of their machicolations and with their upper parts probably rebuilt, they have lost much of their proud aspect. The Mélusine Tower is regarded as a masterpiece of military architecture of the period; it is over 13m/41.5ft in diameter, with walls 3.50m/11ft thick and rising 31m/99ft above the rock.

Further on are two squat, horseshoe-shaped towers, the **Surienne** and the **Raoul**, which mark the last stage in the building of the castle (15C). Built to serve as platforms for artillery, they contain several storeys of very strong and well-preserved gun platforms. To resist enemy artillery fire, their walls are 7m/22ft thick. At the end of the 15C, artillery had been in use for nearly a century and a half, and siege warfare often took the form of an artillery duel at short range.

▷ *Opposite the two towers stands the Église St-Sulpice. On the right is the Marchix District (see The Medieval District below).*

Still following the walls, you will see the 13C Cadran Tower, two centuries older than the others. It is small, square and badly damaged, not nearly as strong as its neighbours and recalling the time when firearms had not yet taken the place of bows and arrows. Further on, **Our Lady's Gate** is the only one left of the four rampart gateways preceding the four gates in the walls which encircled the town. The left-hand tower, which is higher and is pierced with narrow loopholes, dates from the 14C; that on the right, with very ornamental machicolations, dates from the 15C.

▷ *Go under the gate and follow rue de la Fourchette, then turn a sharp right onto rue de la Pinterie.*

Walk *(50m/55yd to your right)* through the gardens laid out along the reconstructed watch-path; there is a fine overall view of the Nançon Valley and the castle.

▷ *To leave the garden, go under the ruins of a beautiful chapel doorway and go once more onto rue de la Pinterie on the left. This leads to the castle entrance.*

Inside the castle★★
The entrance, preceded by a moat filled from a diversion of the Nançon, is through the **square tower of La Haye-St-Hilaire**. To reach it, you first had to go through a town gate and the wall before it. The castle has **three successive walls.** The *Avancée* (advanced wall) was guarded by three 13C towers pierced with loopholes. When

this line of resistance had been crossed, attackers would enter a small courtyard on the island formed by a second diversion of the river, and would come under the converging fire of defenders posted on the four sides. Thus exposed, the attackers had to cross a second moat before reaching the main ring of fortifications, guarded by four towers dating from the 12C and 15C.

When both lines had been stormed, they would burst into the main inside courtyard where the **living quarters** and the **chapel** stood; but the defenders still had a chance to rally. A third position, the redoubt, girt with a wall and two towers, and the keep (demolished after the 12C), made a long resistance possible, and from these positions the garrison could still seek safety in flight through the postern.

Entering the main inside courtyard, go round the walls on the wall walk. This enables one to appreciate the might of such a fortress and also to enjoy some good views of Fougères.

At the end of the highest wall of the castle is Mélusine Tower, which from the top (75 steps) commands a fine view of the castle and the town. Further on are the remains of the keep and north wall, and beyond, the Guibé Turret and the Coigny Tower (13C and 14C), whose second and third storeys were turned into a chapel in the 17C. The summit was disfigured by the addition of a loggia during its first restoration in the 19C.

The Medieval District

Église St-Sulpice★

A Gothic building in the Flamboyant style; although erected between the 15C and the 18C, it has great homogeneity. It has a slim 15C slate-covered steeple. The inside is enriched with 18C woodwork; nonetheless the 15C granite **altarpieces**★ in the chapels are the most noteworthy. The Lady Chapel (on the left) contains the altarpiece dedicated to Anne of Brittany, the church's donor. In the niche, underneath Brittany's coat of arms, is the miraculous 12C statue of the Nursing Virgin (Notre-Dame des Marais).

Y. Boëlle/ANDIA

The "Anne of Brittany" altarpiece

Quartier du Marchix

This area around place du Marchix (the site of the former market at the heart of the old town) (**AY**), with its picturesque old houses, has always been of interest to painters. On place du Marchix are two fine 16C houses, nos 13 and 15.

▶ *Take rue Foskeraly.*

From rue Foskeraly, which skirts the Nançon, there are good views of the old ramparts now converted into a public garden. Take a walk along rue du Nançon with its 16C houses. There are other interesting houses at the corner of rue de la Providence and rue de Lusignan as well as in rue de Lusignan.

On place du Marchix are two fine 16C houses, nos 13 and 15. Take rue des Tanneurs to cross the bridge over the Nançon; looking back, you will see a picturesque group formed by the backs of the houses of place du Marchix.

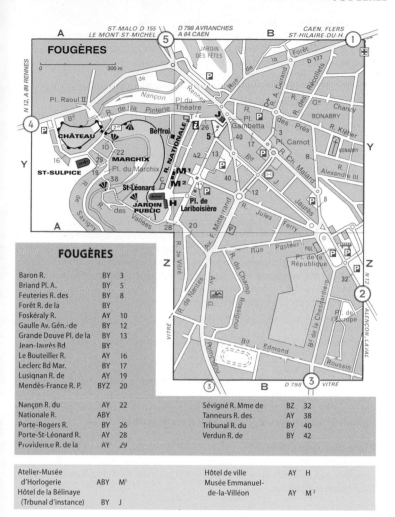

Upper Town

Place Aristide-Briand
Hôtel de la Belinaye, which presently houses the Magistrates' Court, was the birthplace of **Armand Turffin de la Rouërie.** A statue was erected in 1993 to commemorate the bicentenary of his death.

Rue Nationale★
This is the town's most attractive street, with its 18C granite façades decorated with wrought-iron balconies.

Beffroi
On the right as you walk down the street.
Rising proudly above the ramparts, this octagonal belfry was built in the 14C and 15C. It is decorated with gargoyles and topped by a slate-covered steeple.

L'Artisan du Temps – Musée d'horlogerie
37 rue Nationale. 🕐 *Open 15 June-15 Sep: Tus-Sat 9am-noon and 2-7pm; Sun and Mon until 6.30pm.* 🕐 *Closed last week of August.* ⌨ *€4.50/3.70.* ☎ *02 99 99 40 98.*
This small museum displays some 200 items presented by an enthusiastic clockmaker who keeps himself busy in his workshop.

Musée Emmanuel de la Villéon
🕐 *Open mid-June to mid-Sept, daily, 10am-12.30pm and 2.30-6pm;rest of the year, contact the Tourist Office for information* 🕐 *Closed Jan, 1 May and 25 Dec.* ⌨ *No charge.* ☎ *02 99 94 88 00.*
The museum, located in a 16C house (restored), displays works (drawings and water-colours) by **Emmanuel de la Villéon** (1858-1944), an Impressionist painter, born in Fougères. He was inspired by the landscape people of his native Brittany.

Jardin Public★
This lovely garden, at the foot of St-Léonard and the town hall, is laid out partly in ter-races on the site of the former town walls and partly on the slopes down into the valley of the River Naçon. Follow the low wall that elongates the balustrade to the entrance for an extensive view of the woodlands typical of the Fougères region. From the terrace closed off by the balustrade, there is an interesting general **view**★ of the castle.

▶ *Steps lead to the castle and the river banks.*

Hôtel de Ville
A 16C building with a Renaissance doorway (partly walled up).

Église St-Léonard
The 15C-16C church has a richly decorated 16C north façade and a 17C tower. It is lit through modern stained-glass windows by Lorin; however, in the Chapel of the Cross, on the left as you go in, are two 12C scenes of St Benedict's life, and in the baptismal chapel pieces of 16C **stained-glass windows**★.

Place de Lariboisière
This square is named after the **Comte de Lariboisière** (1759-1812), a native of Fougères and one of Napoleon's valiant officers, who died of exhaustion during the Russian campaign.

Excursions

Forêt domaniale de Fougères
3km/1.8mi NE. Leave Fougères on ① on the town plan, the road to Flers.
Those who like walking in a forest will spend hours strolling in the fine beech woods, along the forest roads. Spy the two dolmens in ruins and a line of megalithic stones called the Druids' Cord (Cordon des Druides) near the Chennedet crossroads (Car-refour de Chennedet).
At Landéan, on the edge of the forest, near the Recouvrance crossroads (Carrefour de la Recouvrance) are the 12C cellars (⌚ *now closed*) once used as a secret hideout by the lords of Fougères.

Parc floral de Haute-Bretagne★
Le Châtelier, 10m/6mi NW. Leave Fougères heading N on D 798 (towrds St-James) until you reach D19, then turn left and follow the signs.
The grounds of the Château de la Folletière have been laid out as a floral park. A discovery trail links the dozen gardens with evocative names (Knossos labyrinth, Valley of the Kings, etc), offering a year round festival of colour and fragrance.

CAP FRÉHEL ★★★

MICHELIN LOCAL MAP 309 I2 - CÔTES D'ARMOR (22)

The **site** of this cape is one of the grandest on the Breton coast. Its red, grey and black cliffs rise vertically to a height of 70m/229ft and are fringed with reefs on which the swell breaks heavily.

▶ **Orient Yourself:** Between St-Brieuc and Dinard, on the Emerald Coast.
Parking: June to Sept: €2 for private cars.
Also see: Côte d'EMERAUDE.

Panorama

The coastal panorama is vast in clear weather: from the Pointe du Grouin, on the right, with the Cotentin in the background, to the Île de Bréhat, on the left. The famous outline of Fort la Latte is visible on the right.

Boat trips *(Departures from Dinard and St-Malo (2hr45min). For information apply to "Emeraude Lines" in St-Malo.* ☎ *08 25 13 80 35. www.compagniecorsaire.com)*, provide a great view of Cap Fréhel from the sea.

Round tour – *30min walk.*

At the extremity of the headland stands the **lighthouse** *(145 steps – Guided tours July to mid-Sept, daily, 2-6pm.* ☎ *02 96 41 40 03)*, built in 1950 and lit by a xenon flash lamp; the light carries only 200m/656ft in foggy weather but it can be seen 120km/74.5mi away when it is clear. From the gallery at the top of the tower, there is an immense view of the horizon: you may see Bréhat to the west, Jersey to the north, Granville, a part of the Cotentin Peninsula and the Îles Chausey to the northeast. At a point 400m/437yd from the lighthouse a siren mounted in a shelter gives two blasts every minute in foggy weather.

After passing the extreme point where the siren stands, you can look down on the **Fauconnière rocks,** crowded with seagulls and cormorants; the contrast between the mauvish-red of the rocks and the blue or green of the sea is striking. Near the Restaurant de la Fauconnière take a steep path on the right; halfway down, it reaches a platform from which there is another fine view of the Fauconnière rocks and the deep blue sea.

The cape is an ornithological reserve

Y. Tierny/MICHELIN

Excursion

Fort de la Latte★★

🕐 *Open 11 April 11- 30 Sep, 10am-12.30pm and 2-6pm; Oct-March, weekends and school holidays, 2-5.30pm.* 🔐 *€4.30 (children under 12, €2.40; under 5, no charge).* ☎ *02 99 30 38 84. www.castlelalatte.com.*

This stronghold, built by the Goyon-Matignons in the 14C, remodelled in the 17C and restored in the early 20C, has kept its feudal appearance. It stands on a spectacular **site**★★, separated from the mainland by two gullies, which are crossed by drawbridges.

A gate marks the entrance to the park. Follow the lane to the fort; you will pass a menhir known as Gargantua's Finger. You will visit in succession: the two fortified enclosures, the inner courtyard, around which are located the guard-room, the Governor's living quarters, the cistern and the chapel. Cross the thick walls made to shield the defender from cannon-balls and go to the Échauguette

A vision of the past

Tower (Tour de l'Échaugette) and the cannon-ball foundry. A look-out post takes you to the keep. From the parapet walk, there is a **panorama**★★ of Sévignés Cove, Cap Fréhel, the bay of La Frênaye, Pointe de St-Cast, the Hébihens archipelago, the resorts of St-Briac and St-Lunaire, Pointe du Décollé, St-Malo, Paramé and Rothéneuf, the Île de Cézembre, the Pointe du Meinga and the walls of the fort. It is possible to walk up to the top of the tower (🔐*difficult steps).*

LA GRANDE BRIÈRE★★

MICHELIN LOCAL MAP 316 C/D 3/4 - LOIRE-ATLANTIQQUE (44)

Also known as **Grande Brière Mottière,** this region covers 7 000ha/17 297 acres of the total 40 000ha/98 840 acres belonging to the **Parc naturel régional de Brière.** Lying to the north of St-Nazaire, the area is renowned for its wildfowling, fishing and interesting boat trips.

A Bit of History

Brière in the past – In early geological times the area was a forested, undulating basin which reached the hills of Sillon de Bretagne. Neolithic man (7500 BC) was expelled from the area, when there was a momentary maritime incursion. Marshes formed behind the alluvial banks deposited by the Loire. The trees died and were submerged and vegetable matter decomposed to form **peat bogs,** often entrapping fossilized tree trunks, known as **mortas,** over 5 000 years old.

Brière from the 15C to the 20C – This swampy area was subdivided, water pumped and the drainage improved. In 1461, the Duke of Brittany, François II, decreed the area the common property of all Briérons, an act which was to be confirmed by several royal edicts. For centuries the Briérons (17 parishes divided into 21 communes) have

Address Book

WHERE TO STAY

BUDGET

⊜ **Chambre d'hôte Ty Gwen** – *25 Île d'Errand, 44550 St-Malo-de-Guersac, 3km/2.4mi from St-Malo, after the church go straight – ☎ 02 40 91 15 04 – ⊘ closed Oct-Mar- ⌿ – 4 rooms.* Incredibly romantic, this pretty thatched cottage welcomes its guests with cozy comfort. Ceiling beams, fireplace and well-chosen fabrics create a refined atmosphere. Its charming garden and swimming pool add to the pleasure of stopping here.

EATING OUT

⊜⊜ **Auberge de Kerbourg** – *In Kerbourg, 44410 St-Lyphard, 6km/3.6mi southwest of St-Lyphard via D 51 (road to Guérande) – ☎ 02 40 61 95 15 – ⊘ closed 15 Dec-15 Feb, Sun evening off-season, Mon (⊘ but open evening in season), Tues lunch.* The authentic details of this old thatched cottage have been scrupulously preserved. The owners welcome their clients as if they were personal friends in the two meticulously decorated dining rooms, where the meal is also congenial and tasty.

⊜⊜ **Auberge du Parc** – *44720 St-Joachim, Île de Fedrun – ☎ 02 40 88 53 01 – ⊘ closed Mar, Sun evening and Mon off-season.* You will be well-received in this attractive inn, with its blue shutters and thatched roof. In the muted dining room, you can enjoy a refined meal, or simply spend a peaceful night in one of its lovely rooms. A very charming stop!

⊜ **Auberge de Breca** – *Road to Breca (follow the signs to the restaurant) – ⊘ July-Aug, daily 10am-6pm; Sept-June Fri-Wed.* This restaurant and ice-cream salon, located in an old hunting lodge, offers a quick bite or a little refreshment to those enjoying long row-boat outings.

BARGE TOUR

Barge outings★★ are available all year; refer to the map of the park to find embarking points. The Brière is delightful in every season: abloom in the spring, lush green in the summer, orange and red in the autumn, and silver in the winter.

cut the peat, gathered the reeds and rushes for thatching, woven baskets with the buckthorn, tended their gardens and kept poultry. They have trapped leeches, harpooned eels, placed eel-pots in the open stretches of water and wickerwork traps to catch pike, tench and roach; and hunted with their dogs in a boat hidden by a clump of willow trees. For ages the Briéron has propelled with a pole his **blin,** a flat-bottomed boat, loaded with cows or sheep going to pasture. In spite of these activities, the Briéron women also had to work to make ends meet. In the 19C and early 20C, two workshops in St-Joachim employed approximately 140 women to make wax orange blossoms. These flowers were used to make splendid brides' headdresses exported throughout Europe (⊘ *see Bride's House below*).

The Briéron of the 20C has remained closely attached to the land but, by force of circumstance, he is turning more to local industries: metallurgy in Trignac and dockyards and aeronautics at St-Nazaire. Nevertheless, he continues to fish, shoot, graze animals or cut reeds and pay his annual fee. Change is inevitable, roads now link the islets, locks have been built, marsh has become pastureland but despite it all, La Grande Brière has retained its charm and when the Briéron returns home he fishes and shoots for his own pleasure. Many of those who have boats will take visitors on trips along the canals and smaller channels beautiful with yellow irises (mid-May to mid-June) and pearl-white water lilies (mid-June to late July).

Parc Naturel Régional de Brière

Created in 1970, the **Brière Regional Nature Park** organises events celebrating regional traditions and folklore, and offers opportunities for rambling, cycling and canoeing It is a haven for bird-watching.

Tour from St-Nazaire

83km/52mi – half a day

St-Nazaire – 👁 *See ST-NAZAIRE.*

▷ *Leave St-Nazaire by N 171, the road to Nantes. Take the Montoir-de-Bretagne exit and turn onto D 50.*

St-Malo-de-Guersac

This, the largest of the islets (13m/43ft high), offers a **view** from Guérande in the west to the hilly region, Sillon de Bretagne, to the east.

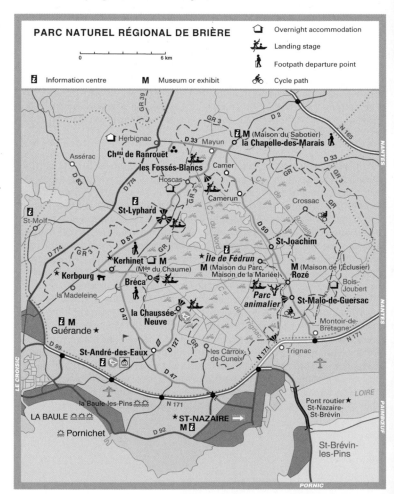

Rozé
A boat-building centre, this small port, was the former departure point for the boats plying upstream to Nantes and Vannes.

Maison de l'Éclusier
Guided tours (1hr) early July to mid-Sep, 10.30am-1pm; 2.30-6.30pm; April-June, 2-6pm. Closed the rest of the year. €5/2.50. 02 40 66 85 01. www.parc-naturel-briere.fr
The house is located on Rosé Canal. The lock keeper operated the two locks which regulated the water level of the marsh. There is an exhibit devoted to the fauna (stuffed animals) and flora to be found in the marshland. An aquarium contains the main species of Brière fish. Slides and various documents illustrate the formation and evolution of the marsh. Docked alongside the canal is a reconstruction of the Théotiste, which was used to transport peat.

Parc animalier
Field-glasses can be hired. Cross the bridge over the canal and take the path to the right to the reception building (pavillon d'accueil) 800m/875yd further on. The park can also be reached by boat (landing-stage to the right of the bridge). Open July to mid-Sep, 10.30am-1pm; 2.30-6.30pm; April-June, 2-6pm. Closed the rest of the year. €5/2.50. 02 40 66 85 01. www.parc-naturel-briere.fr
A path *(about 1.8km/1mi)* cuts through this nature reserve (26ha/64 acres), with observation posts where silence and patience will be rewarded. There are descriptive panels to help you identify the flora and fauna. In a wood and reed building Brière activities are displayed.

▶ *Bear left before St-Joachim.*

Île de Fédrun★
Linked to the St-Joachim road by two bridges, this, the most attractive of the islets, is entirely surrounded by marshland. The islet has two roads: one which divides it in two and the other which runs around it. At no 130 of the circular road is the **Maison de la Mariée (Bride's House (** *Open July to mid-Sep: 10.30am-1pm; 2.30-6.30pm; April-June 2-6pm. Closed the rest of the year. €5/2.50. 02 40 66 85 01).* The interior of the house, arranged in typical Brière style, displays a collection of bridal headdresses decorated with wax orange blossoms and an explanation of how they are made.

St-Joachim
The village, once a wax orange blossom manufacturing centre, extends along the two islets of **Brécun** (alt 8m/26ft) and **Pendille**, dominated by the tall white spire of its 19C **church**.
The road crosses the sparsely populated islets of **Camerun** and **Camer**.

La Chapelle-des-Marais
At the entrance to the village, on the right, is the **Maison du Sabotier** (Sabot-Maker's House), where the last Briéron craftsman lived. In the **church**, the granite pillars stand out against the white stone; in the chapel to the right of the chancel, there is a polychrome statue of St Corneille, protector of horned cattle.
▶ *Take the road in the direction of Herbignac and after 4km/2.5mi turn left.*

Château de Ranrouët
Leave the car in the car park (grassy) and go behind the old farm buildings. Open July and Aug, daily, 10am-7pm; Apr to June and Sept, Tues to Sat, 2.30-6.30pm, Sun and holidays 2-7pm. Closed Oct to Mar and 1 May. €2.50/1.50. 02 40 88 96 17. www.herbignac.com.

This 12C-13C fortress, dismantled in 1618 by Louis XIII and burnt during the Revolution, is spectacular with its six round towers and moat (dried-up). Note in particular the 16C modifications designed to counter improved artillery (barbican, fortified curtain wall). Cannon-balls embedded in the right tower wall recall that the castle once belonged to the Rieux family, whose coat of arms included 10 gold cannon-balls.

▷ *Turn around and bear right towards Pontchâteau; at Mayun, turn right.*

Les Fossés-Blancs
From a landing-stage on the canal to the north, there is a fine view of the Brière. A tour of the marsh provides an opportunity to study the flora and, occasionally, the fauna.

St-Lyphard
In the **church's belfry** *(135 steps – Guided tours (30min) July and Aug, daily, 10am-noon and 1.30-6pm (Sat 5.30pm), Sun 10.30am-noon and 1.30-5pm; Feb to June and Sept, 10.30am-noon and 1.30-5pm; Oct to Jan, Wed, Fri and Sat only, 11am-noon and 2-5pm.* ○ *Closed 1 May and Christmas school holiday.* €3/2. ☎ *02 40 91 41 34.)* a lookout point has been set up. A **panorama**★★ extends onto the Brière and from the Loire estuary to the mouth of the Vilaine encompassing Guérande and its salt-marshes.

▷ *Follow the road towards Guérande and turn left.*

Dolmen de Kerbourg★
This covered alleyway stands on a mound near a windmill.

▷ *Continue in the direction of Le Brunet.*

Kerhinet
One of the thatched cottages of this charming hamlet presents a modest **Brière interior** (dirt floor, meagre furnishings and kitchen utensils) and houses the **Musée du Chaume** *(Guided tours (1hr) Apr and June to Sept, daily, 10.30am-1pm and 2.30-6.30pm; Feb and Nov school holidays, 2.30-6.30pm; 8 and 9 May, Ascension Day, Whitsun, Sun and holidays from Oct to Dec, 2.30-6.30pm.* €3. ☎ *02 40 66 85 01).* In the shed are tools used for peat harvesting, farming and fishing.
Go onto Le Brunet and from there continue to **Bréca** offering a good view over the Brière and Bréca Canal.

Thatched cottage

▷ *Return to Le Brunet and follow D 47.*

St-André-des-Eaux, Parc ornithologique de Ker Anas
○ *Open Jul & Aug 10am - 6:30pm. Apr-Sept 2:30pm-6:30pm. Mar weekends 2pm-5:30pm.*
○ *Closed Nov-Jan except school holidays.* 5,80€. www.ornithopark.com.
The nature trail of this park extends over a kilometre. Along the way visitors can see a great variety of birds from different continents: geese, barnacle geese, teals, swans and ducks from all over the world.

▶ *Follow D 127 to La Chaussée-Neuve.*

La Chaussée-Neuve
It was from this former port that the boats loaded with peat used to leave. From here there is a wide **view**★ over the Brière.

▶ *Return to St-André-des-Eaux, and bear left to return to St-Nazaire.*

Excursions

Pontchâteau
12km/7.5mi NE of St-Joachim along D 16. The church of Pontchâteau, which is perched on a hill in a region of windmills, now no longer in use, overlooks the little town with its houses built in terraces on the banks of the River Brivet.

Calvaire de la Madeleine
4km/2.5mi W. Leave Pontchâteau on D 33 towards Herbignac. Leave the car in the car park on the left side of the road.

St Louis-Marie Grignion de Montfort (1673-1716), a famous preacher, had the Calvary built in 1709 on the heath of the same name. Destroyed under Louis XIV, it was rebuilt in 1821.

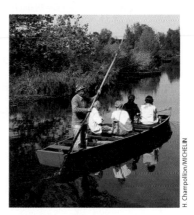

Boat trip

From the Temple of Jerusalem, a fortress-type oriental palace, an alley crosses the park and leads to Pilate's Court or Scala Sancta, the five high-relief sculptures of which represent the Passion. It is the first station in the Stations of the Cross which, further on (on the left) are continued by large white statues derived from the local folklore. From above the Calvary the view extends to the Brière, St-Nazaire and Donges.

Fuseau de la Madeleine
800m/875yd from the Calvary. Take the road to the left of the statue of the Sacred Heart, cross the park and bear left at the first crossroads.
This menhir, 7m/23ft tall and 5m/16ft in circumference, stands in the middle of a field.

CÔTE DE GRANIT ROSE★★

MICHELIN LOCAL MAP 309 A/B 2 CÔTES D'ARMOR (22)

The scenic Breton coast road that joins Perros-Guirec and Trébeurden, following the "Pink Granite Coast" from Pointe de l'Arcouest, is one of the most interests-ing drives in Brittany.

From Perros-Guirec to Trébeurden

27km/17mi – about 6hr

Ploumanach

Perros-Guirec♨♨ – 🚺 *See PERROS-GUIREC.*

▶ *Leave Perros-Guirec heading W.*

Chapelle Notre-Dame-de-la-Clarté – 🚺*See PERROS-GUIREC.*

Ploumanach – 🚺 *See PERROS-GUIREC.*

Trégastel-Plage♨♨ – 🚺 *See TRÉGASTEL-PLAGE.*

As you leave the village, on the right, at the end of a short rise, look behind you to admire the view of Sept-Îles.

▶ *At Penvern, bear left after the Café du Menhir, and take the road to Pleumur-Bodou.*

Menhir de St-Uzec★
A giant standing stone is surmounted by a Crucifixion with instuments of the Pasion surrounding the figure of a praying woman.

▶ *Take the road below the menhir to rejoin the Pleumur-Bodou road, then turn left and 400m/437yd further on, left again.*

Pleumeur-Bodou
This village, located between Lannion and Penvern, has given its name to the radar dome, near which a telecommunications museum and plaentarium have been set up.

Radôme and Musée des Télécommunications★
🚺🕐 *Open July-Aug: daily 11am-7pm; April-Sep: Mon-Fri, 11am-6pm;* 🕐 *Closed the rest of the year except school holidays (Mon-Sat 2-6pm).* 🎟 *€7/5.60 (includes one show).* ☎ *02 96 46 63 08. www.leradome.com.*
The Pleumeur-Bodou telecommunications centre, inaugurated in 1962, is the historic site of the first transatlantic communication between France and the United States (Andover), via the **Téléstar** satellite, on 11 July 1962. Besides the radar dome and the museum, the Pleumur-Bodou site is occupied by a dozen or so giant antennae which communicate with the five continents.

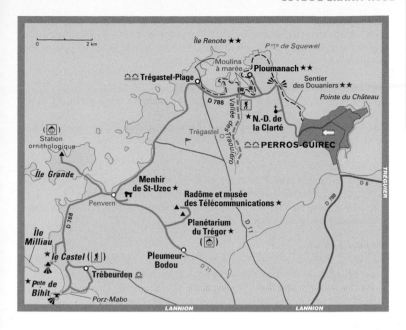

The **Telecommunications Museum**, in a buidling shaped like an immense Delta wing, retraces one and a half centuries of inventions, progress and continuously updated technology.

Planétarium du Trégor★

Kids ⏱ *Closed Jan and 24,25, 26 Dec.* ⊚ *€7/5.60.* ☎ *05 96 15 80 32; www. planetarium-bretagne.fr.*

Beneath a dome (20m/66.5ft in diameter, the visitor travels through the universe. In the entrance hall is an exhibit on astronomy and astrophysics.

Île Grande *(across the bridge)*

The island offers a landscape of heath bordered by blue granite shores. This granite was used for building as far away as London and Antwerp. There are megalithic vestiges, in particular a passage tomb *(allée couverte)* north-east of the village.

Kids A sort of hospital for seabirds, the **Station Ornithologique** presents different bird species (guillemot, herring gull, black-headed gull, puffin, northern gannet and razorbill) on Sept-Îles. An audio-visual system provides a glimpse of the northern gannet in its natural habitat.

▷ *Return to the coast road and turn right towards Trébeurden.*

"Granite Rose"

The strange forms of the enormous pink granite rocks along this part of the coast are the result of erosion. Granite is composed of quartz, mica and feldspar. The feldspar turns into kaolin (china clay), which is washed away by water, and the residue of the quartz grains makes sand, which is carried away by rain and waves. Little by little, the stone changes shape and takes on surprising forms: almost perfect spheres. Erosion here has been very severe because the rocks are coarse-grained and easily broken.

Local imagination has given names to some of the rocks dotted along the shore: Napolean's hat, St Yves, the Gnome, the Witch, the Death's Head, the Elephant, the Whale, the Ram, the Rabbit, the Tortoise, the Hare, the Thimble, the Torpedo, the Armchair, the Umbrella, the Corkscrew – you can use your own imagination too!

Trébeurden ⌂

This seaside resort has several beaches. The two main ones are well situated and separated by the rocky peninsula of Le Castel: Pors-Termen Beach is opposite the harbour; Tresmeur Beach is larger and more popular.

Le Castel★ –*Allow 30min on foot there and back.*

🚶 Follow a path along the isthmus (car park) between the two beaches of Trozoul and Tresmeur.
Le Castel commands an extensive **view**★ of the coast and the Milliau (access by boat or on foot at low tide), Molène, Grande and Losquet Islands.

Île Milliau

Access on foot at low tide (see above). The Tourist Office at Trébeurden can provide tide tables. It is possible to stay overnight in a "gîte d'étape," a 16C farmhouse.
This little emerald island is home to no less than 280 species of flora. There is a lovely panoramic view from the far end of the island.

Pointe de Bihit★

Round trip of 4km/2.5mi. The Porz-Mabo road overlooks Tresmeur Beach and offers views of Grande, Molène and Milliau Islands. Take the road to the right.
From the viewing table there is a fine **view**★ of the coast from Île de Batz and Roscoff right over to Île Grande and Triagoz Lighthouse out to sea with Trébeurden and its beaches down below.
The raod goes on to Porz-Mabo, a nice sand beach. From there, you can take the road to Trébeurden.

ÎLE DE GROIX★

MICHELIN LOCAL MAP 308 K - MORBIHAN (56)

Groix Island is smaller than its neighbour, Belle-Ile, but has the same geological form – a mass of schist rock. The coast to the north and west is wild and deeply indented: there you will see cliffs and giant rocks, valleys and creeks. The east and south sides are flatter, with many sheltered sandy creeks along the coast. Small villages dot some of the still cultivated fields and the vast expanses on which gorse and heather grow.

Address Book

ARRIVAL AND DEPARTURE

By boat– The **SMN** (Société morbi-hannaise de navigation), ☎ 08 20 05 60 00 (€0.12/mn), www.smn-navigation.fr, serves Groix (Port-Tudy) all year, departing from Lorient (45min, about €23 there and back). 9 daily trips in summer. From €105 to 200 there and back for a vehicle.

A taxi cab / boat, ☎ 02 97 65 52 52, www.bateautaxi-iledegroix.com, is doing, In July-Aug, 6 There and back/day (€23) between the continent and Groix. Sat on reservation only.

GETTING AROUND

In minibus – In July-Aug, the **Taxico** shuttle serves the island 4 times a day, departures in town: Primiture (Eastwards of the island) and Piwisy (Westwards). Single ticket €1.10.

Rent a bike or a scooter – Coconut's Location, Port-Tudy, ☎ 02 97 86 81 57. Rental of bikes, off-road bikes, scooters and cars (Jeep and Mehari).

TOURIST OFFICE

Île de Groix, Port-Tudy, ☎ 02 97 86 53 08, www.lorient-tourisme.fr July-Aug: daily 9am-1pm, 2.30-7pm except Sun afternoon; Mon-Fri 9am-12.30pm, 2-5pm and Sat morning.

WHERE TO STAY

◒◒ **Chambres d'hôte les Alizés**, *Élisabeth Goumon, 8 rue du Gén.-de-Gaulle,* ☎ 02 97 86 89 64 or 06 21 79 64 45, elisabeth_goumon@hotmail.com – *3 rooms.* Bright, comfortable and quiet rooms facing the garden. Individual toilets but shared baths.

◒**L'Escale**, *5 quai de Port-Tudy,* ☎ 02 97 86 80 04 – *7 rooms,* ⌣. Located in front of the landing stage, this small establishment offers rooms with views over the harbour. Breakfast is served on the terrace in summer.

◒◒ **Hôtel de la Marine**, *Le Bourg,* ☎ 02 97 86 80 05, *www.hoteldelamarine. com – 22 rooms,* ⌣ €8.50, ✗. Wood interior with a refined decor, rooms giving onto the terrace, the garden or the sea. The restaurant is popular and the welcome warm.

EATING OUT

◒ **L'Ocre Marine**, *22 rue de Tromor, Locmaria,* ☎ 02 97 86 53 98. A pleasant terrace where you can order a bottle of excellent cider to accompany crepes made with organic flour.

◒◒ **Les Courreaux**, *rue du Gén.-de-Gaulle, Port-Tudy,* ☎ 02 97 86 82 66. «Surf and Turf» specialities prepared with creative flair, (try a dish served with their famous sweet-and-sour sauce), have made the reputation of this popular establishment.

◒◒ **Auberge du Pêcheur**, *Port-Tudy,* ☎ 02 97 86 56 92, *www.auberge-dupecheur.free.fr*. Tasteful seafood cuisine served in an old house decorated with a collection of traditional coffee pots. A few rooms are available at a reasonable price.

ON THE TOWN

Ty Beudeff, *rue du Gén.-de-Gaulle, Port-Tudy,* ☎ 02 97 86 80 73. ◷ *Daily at 6pm.* This café, open since 1972, is the island's hot spot. The uninhibited, festive, cordial and sometimes hedonistic atmosphere makes this the place to meet people. Occasionally, Celtic music groups are featured.

LEISURE

Walks – The coastal path, exclusively for pedestrians, goes all around the island (30km/18mi). To discover the rest of the island, nothing is better than a bike! Ask for the map "Itinéraires de Découverte" (for walkers and cyclists) at the Tourist office.

Nature and heritage visits – L'écomusée de Groix offers different events all year long, devoted to discovering the island, the shipping trades and traditional fishing communities. You can learn about digging for shellfish, working on a sailing ship, rowing, etc.

La Maison de la réserve François Le Bail, *au Bourg,* ☎ 02 97 86 55 97, *www. groix.fr/sepnb*, offers various thematic trips and walks on the 2 sites of the game reserve: geology, ornithology, algae and fauna of the littoral, etc.

Driving Tour *1 day*

Port-Tudy

Sheltered by two piers, this port offers a direct link with Lorient, on the mainland. Former tunny fishing port, it is now a safe harbour for trawlers and pleasure boats.

Housed in an early-20C canning factory, the **Ecomusée de l'Île de Groix** presents interesting exhibits (explanatory panels, photographs) on the island's geography, history and ethnography.

The *Kenavo*, the last coastal fishing cutter built on the Île de Groix, can be hired for a boat trip round the island; contact the tourist office, for details.

St-Tudy (le Bourg)

This is the island's capital with its low slate-roofed houses grouped round the church. The bell-tower is crowned by a tunny fish weather vane, recalling the island's great tunny fishing days of the early 1900s.

From **Port-Mélite**, a rocky cove with a beach, the view extends from the Étel Bar to the Pointe du Talut. The island's largest beach, **Plage des Grands Sables** is situated south-east of Port-Mélite, along a convex section of coastline.

Locmaria

Facing the open sea, this village, with its winding streets, has a small harbour, where fishing and pleasure boats seek shelter behind a jetty.

Pointe des Chats

On this point, the lowest part of the island, stands a small lighthouse; fine view of the south coast. There is a **mineralogy reserve** where visitors can see garnets, needles of blue glaucophane and green lepidolite, but of course the taking of samples is strictly forbidden.

Trou de l'Enfer★

This deep opening (the Devil's Hole) in the cliff face, into which the sea surges with great force, is a wild barren site with a beautiful **view** of the Pointe St-Nicolas and the rocky coast.

Beyond Trou de l'Enfer, to the north-west, is **Port-St-Nicolas**, a large bay with deep, clear waters hemmed in by cliffs.

Pen-Men

The western tip of the island, to the right of Pen-Men Lighthouse, is a rocky headland, offering splendid views of the Morbihan coast extending from Talut Point to Port-Manech. This, the **Réserve naturelle François Le Bail,** is home to thousands of birds.

Plages des Grands Sables – This is the island's largest beach; garnets can sometimes be found in the sand.

Pointe de Bileric

Near the Beg-Melen signal station (⊶ *not open to the public)*, many black-legged kittiwakes can be seen nesting in this bird sanctuary.

Port-Melin

The little creek can only be reached on foot down a steep slope. Note the statue of the Breton poet, J.-P. Calloc'h, native of the island (1888-1917), who wrote in Celtic, under the pseudonym of Bleimor.

Port-Lay

This safe anchorage, where trawlers used to shelter, lies in a beautiful **setting**★.

PRESQU'ÎLE DE GUÉRANDE★

MICHELIN LOCAL MAP 316 B4 - LOIRE-ATLANTIQUE (44)

This is a very interesting district in which you may see, besides the curious landscape of salt-marshes, several beaches, of which La Baule is the finest, the picturesque Côte Sauvage, busy fishing ports, Guérande and its ramparts, and Batz and its church.

The former gulf – In the Roman era, a great sea gulf stretched between the rocky Île de Batz and the Guérande ridge. A change of level of approximately 15m/50ft turned the gulf into marshland.

Sand brought down by the currents linked the Île de Batz with the mainland through the strip on which La Baule and Le Pouliguen stand. To the west the sandy Pen Bron Point has not quite reached the island; a channel remains open opposite Le Croisic through which the sea flows at high tide into the Grand and Petit Trait, vestiges of the former gulf. At low tide it retreats, exposing mud flats on which the coast dwellers raise oysters and mussels, clams and periwinkles. The rest of the marsh is used for salt pans.

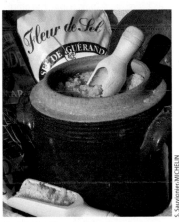

Salt-marshes – The salt-marshes cover 1 800ha/4 448 acres divided into two basins: Mesquer and Guérande, forming a huge quadrilateral delimited by clay embankments.

The sea, brought in by the tides through canals (*étier*), irrigates the salt-marsh. Every 15 days, during the salt harvest, the salt pan worker allows the seawater to flow through a gate into a type of settling pond (*vasière*) used for removing the impurities (sand, clay etc). Then with the drop in water level the water flows through a series of evaporating ponds

Guérande salt

S. Sauvignier/MICHELIN

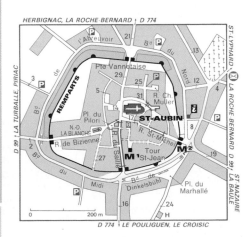

GUÉRANDE

Bizienne Fg	2
Bouton d'Or R. du	3
Brière Av. de la	4
Capucins R. des	5
Marché-au-Bois Pl.	8
Peupliers R. des	12
Pourieux Bd Émile	13
Psalette Pl. de la	14
Saulniers R. des	24
Sœurs-Grises R. des	25
St-Armel Fg	16
St-Aubin Pl.	17
Ste-Anne Fg	21
St-Michel R.	
St-Michel Fg	19
Tricot R. du	27
Vannetaise R.	29
Vieux-Marché Pl. du	31

Musée de la Poupée	M¹
Porte de St-Michel, Château-musée	M²

where the wind and sun cause the water to evaporate, producing brine. In the 70m²/853sq ft pools called *œillets* the brine finally rests and crystallises.

From June to September the salt-pan worker harvests two kinds of salt: table or white salt collected (3-5kg/7-11lb per day per *œillet*) with a flat spade *(lousse)* and coarse or grey salt collected (40-70kg/88-154lb per day per œillet) at the bottom of the pond with a large flat rake *(lasse)* onto a tray. The salt is put to dry on little platforms *(trenet)* built on the banks, then piled in large heaps *(mulons)* at the edge of the salt-pans before being stored in sheds in September.

Address Book

TOURIST OFFICE

Guérande, 1 Place du Marché au Bois, ☎ 02 40 24 96 71, www.ot-guerande. fr July-Aug: Mon-Sat 9.30am-7pm, Sun 10am-1pm, 3-5pm; off season: Mon-Sat 9.30am-12.30pm, 1.30-6pm, Sun in June and Sept 10am-1pm, 3-5pm. The office organises **concerts** in the Old Town on Thu evening in July-Aug, offers thematic tours and a historical tour, Mon-Sat in Apr-Oct, and tours featuring dramatised scenes, Wed at 6pm in July-Aug.

Rent a bike – Bicycle Repair, 6 rue Gustave Flaubert, Guérande, ☎ 02 40 62 39 95. Off-road and touring bikes. **Garage Patalane**, 3 rue du Calvaire, Piriac-sur-Mer, ☎ 02 40 23 50 62. Touring bikes and and bikes for children €10/day.

WHERE TO STAY

🍽 **Les Voyageurs**, *Place du 8 Mai 1945*, ☎ 02 40 24 90 13 – 12 rooms, 🛏 €6.20, 🍴. ⏰ *Closed 23 Dec-21 Jan*. In front of the ramparts, old-fashioned but well-kept rooms and good regional cuisine. Half board compulsory in July-Aug €99/2 people.

🍽🛏 **La Guérandière**, *porte Vannetaise*, ☎ 02 40 62 17 15 or 06 86 77 84 43, www.guerandiere.com – 4 rm, 🛏 €9. Inside the spacious, distinguished house there are comfortable rooms decorated in pastel tones.

EATING OUT

GUÉRANDE AND NEARBY

🍽 **La Flambée**, *12 rue de Saillé*, ☎ 02 40 47 382. In front of the old LU biscuit factory counter enjoy good crepes with caramel made with salted butter or with organic flour.

🍽 **La Salorge**, *12 rue de la Croix Sérot Saillé*, ☎ 02 40 15 14 19. Beside the blue shutters of this village house, in a room decorated with embroideries, crepes reach new levels of culinary refinement. Nice terrace in summer.

🍽🍽 **Les Remparts**, *14-15 bd du Nord*, ☎ 02 40 24 90 69. ⏰ *Closed Sun evening, Mon except public holidays and Augt, 1st Dec-10 Jan and 1 week in Feb*. Contemporary setting for genuine regional cuisine and seasonal seafood.

🍽🍽 **La Comère**, *18 rue de Keroman*, ☎ 02 40 23 53 63. ⏰ *Open Feb-Nov;* ⏰ *Closed Mon and Tue except July-Aug*. Crepes, mussels, oysters, sardines and seafood sauerkraut keep guests happy in this pub.

LEISURE

Fête médiévale, 3rd weekend of May, procession and festive events. Grand **Festival celtique**, 2nd weekend of Aug, with Breton dances, concerts by Breton and foreign bands. **Marché du livre et du papier ancien (book and old paper fair)**, Mon evening place St-Aubin in July-Aug. **Festival du livre (book festival)**, 3rd weekend of Nov.

SHOPPING

Markets – Guérande, Wed and Sat morning, in the halles and Place St-Aubin in July-Aug. **La Turballe**, Wed and Sat under the halles, Wed evening in July-Aug, arts and crafts market, quai St-Pierre. **Piriac-sur-Mer**, Tue off season, Mon, Wed and Sat from the 15 June to the 15 Sept.

Salt – L'œillet de Guérande, 1 Place St-Aubin, ☎ 02 40 62 12 95, www. oeilletdeguerande.com A family of salt marsh harvesters offers all sorts of products made with salt from Guérande. Quite expensive.

When not harvesting salt, the salt-pan worker looks after the salt-marsh: repairing the dikes, raking the settling pond (October-March), cleaning and preparing the salt pans (April-May) and removing the salt before the next harvest.

A hard struggle – The salt pans of Guérande were very prosperous until the Revolution, for, thanks to a relic of the former rights of the province, the salt could be sent all over Brittany without paying the *gabelle* or salt tax. Dealers or salt makers could exchange it in neighbouring provinces for cereals. Trafficking by "false salt makers" or smugglers often occurred.

Today about 7 000 *œillets* are harvested, they produce an average of 10 000t of coarse salt a year. Guérande salt is rich in sodium chloride and weak in magnesium, potassium and other trace elements.

Cliffs and dunes – The cliffs and rocks of the Côte Sauvage, between the Pointe de Penchâteau and Le Croisic, offer a striking contrast to the immense sandy beach at La Baule.

In 1527 a violent wind spread the sand accumulated in the Loire estuary over the village of **Escoublac**. After this gale, which lasted for several days, sand continued to accumulate, and in the 18C the last inhabitants finally left. The village was rebuilt several miles further back. The pines planted to fix the dunes form the Bois d'Amour of La Baule. The coast, which became very popular in the 19C, took the name of **Côte d'Amour.**

Guérande★

Standing on a plateau overlooking the salt-marshes and surrounded by ramparts, the town has retained its medieval appearance. A colourful market takes place on Wednesday and Saturday mornings inside the covered market and on place St-Aubin. Every year in August there is a three day Interceltic Festival at the foot of the fortifications.

Porte St-Michel – Chateau-Musée

🕐 *Open Apr to Sept, daily, 10am-12.30pm (noon in Oct) and 2.30-7pm (6pm in Oct). Nov to Mar, by appointment.* 🕭 *€3.50.* ☎ *02 40 42 96 52.*

The gatehouse was once the governor's house (15C) and is now a local museum; a spiral staircase goes up to the different floors. Note the two reconstructred interiors: that of the Briéron inhabitant with its waxed furniture and that of the sal-marsh worker with its furniture painted a deep plum-red colour, as well as porcelain from Le Croisic, pottery and other everyday objects typical of the area, part of the collegiate church's rood screen and old bourgeois, salt-marsh worker and farm tenant costumes. Particularly interesting is the relief map of a salt-marsh which illustrates the salt-gathering process.

Walk round the ramparts★

The ramparts, in which there is still no breach, were built in the 14C and 15C. They are flanked by six towers and pierced by four fortified gateways. In the 18C the Duke of Aiguillon, Governor of Brittany, had the moats filled in (although the north and west sections still contain water) and arranged the present circular promenade, which the tourist can follow by car or on foot. They can walk along the **watch-path** from Porte St-Michel to beyond St-Jean Tower.

Collégiale St-Aubin★

This collegiate church, built from the 12C to the 16C on the site of a baptistery, features a granite west façade decorated with bell turrets and crocketed pinnacles. To the right a 15C outside pulpit is embedded into a buttress. The **interior** is imposing with large 15C pillars in the transept. The Romanesque columns of the nave support Gothic arches with **capitals** portraying grotesque and floral decoration. The 15C chancel, with aisles opening onto four 16C chapels, is lit by a magnificent 18C **stained-glass window** showing the Coronation of the Virgin and the Assumption. On the left, the small 14C lancet window shows the life of St Peter. The chapel to the right, oddly enough called the **crypt**, contains a Merovingian sarcophagus (6C) discovered under the chancel, a recumbent figure and a tombstone, both 16C. In the nave is a 16C carved wooden Christ.

Musée de la Poupée

Kids The museum houses hundreds of dolls made of porcelain or wood displayed in an old-world setting including miniature furniture, china and accessories.

Driving Tour

62km/39mi starting from Guérande – allow half a day

Guérande★ – 🕭 *See above.*

▶ *Head for La Turballe then Piriac.*

From D 99, as it runs along the Guérande ridge, there is a fine view of the salt-marshes and the harbour of Le Croisic. In the evening, the light effects on the marshes are remarkable.

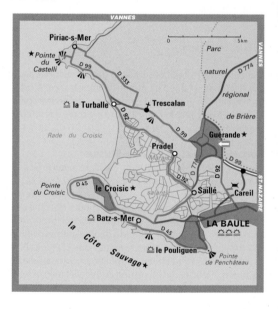

Trescalan

The main square is dominated by a small Calvary topped with a pediment. The **church** flanked by buttresses has fine columns with capitals and a statue of St Bridget in the south aisle.

Piriac-sur-Mer

A small resort and fishing village. In the square, in front of the church, there is a fine group of 17C houses.

A path along the cliff ridge leads to **Pointe du Castelli**★.

There is a nice view of the rocky creeks. On the right Île Dumet and the low shore of Presqu'île de Rhuys are visible. On the left are the roadstead and peninsula of Le Croisic with the church towers of Batz and Le Croisic.

Around Piriac and at Lerat, there are several small beaches which are suitable for families and to the south of La Turballe there is another vast sandy beach facing due west.

La Turballe⌂

The town stretches along the seafront. The fish auction (La Criée) stands in the middle of the busy artificial port which receives both pleasure craft and sardine boats. The **view** is beautiful along the coast from Lerat onwards.

In Pradel, situated on D 92 between La Turballe and Saillé, the organises guided tours of the salt-marshes (commentary given by salt-marsh workers or members of the association for the protection of birds).

Saillé

Built on an island amidst the salt-marshes, this town is the salt capital. A former chapel contains the **Maison des Paludiers** (&⊙ *Open Mar to Oct, daily, 10am-12.30pm and 2-6pm.* ⚶ *€5.60. Guided tours (2hr) of a salt marsh July and August, daily at 4.30pm (except in rainy weather).* ⚶*€6.* ☎ *02 40 62 21 96).* Engravings, tools, furnishings and costumes illustrate the life of the salt-marsh worker.

Le Croisic★ – &*See Le CROISIC.*

Côte Sauvage★ – &*See Le CROISIC: Excursion (opposite direction).*

Batz-sur-Mer⌂ – &*See Le CROISIC.*

The road hugs the coast and there is soon a fine view of the shore south of the Loire as far as Pointe de St Gildas and Banche Lighthouse.

Le Pouliguen⌂ – &*See La BAULE.*

La Baule⌂⌂⌂ – &*See La BAULE.*

▶ *Take D 99ᵉ toward Guérande and turn right.*

Château de Careil

☜ *Guided tours (30min) June to Aug, daily, 10.30am-noon and 2.30-7pm. In July and Aug, guided tours by candlelight Wed and Sat at 9.30pm.* ⚶ *Guided tour €5/4; tour by candlelight €10/6.* ☎ *02 40 60 22 99.*

The first fortified castle was built in the 14C; renovated in the 15C-16C, it is still inhabited today. Note the elegant Renaissance façade, as well as the guard-room and drawing room with their fine beams.

LA GUERCHE-DE-BRETAGNE

POPULATION 4 095

MICHELIN LOCAL MAP 309 O7 - ILLE-ET-VILAINE (35)

This small town, once a manorial estate with Du Guesclin as its overlord, still retains some old houses and an interesting church. An important fair and market has been held since 1211 around the town hall and the squares in the town centre.

A Bit of History

Church (Église) – Only the chancel, with its triple-sided apse, and the Romanesque tower, with its massive buttresses, remain from the original building erected in 1206. The nave and south aisle were rebuilt in the 16C; the north aisle and the bell-tower, with openings at the top, date from the end of the 19C. The splendour of this church lies in its 16C stalls with their amusing Gothic misericords – the carved decoration of the woodwork is clearly of the time of Henri II (1547-59) a more advanced period – and the remains of the 15C and 16C stained-glass windows in the south aisle. Note the purlins embellishing the nave's wooden vaulting and at the rear of the apse a stained-glass window depicting the Assumption.

Old houses – About 15 porched and half-timbered houses dating from the 16 and 17C can be found on place du Général-de-Gaulle, near the church, and in the neighbouring streets of rue du Cheval-Blanc and rue de Nantes.

Driving Tour

Peninsula

▷ *Round-trip of 43km/27mi – about 2hr 30min. Leave La Guerche W on the Rennes road, D 463. At Visseiche turn left.*

You soon reach an arm of Marcillé Lake (Étang de Marcillé) formed by the junction of the Seiche and Ardenne Valleys; hence its curved shape.

▷ *On leaving Marcillé-Robert, cross the Seiche and bear left towards Retiers which follows the bank of the other arm of the lake. Turn right after 800m/0.5mi to Theil and then right again 3km/2mi further on. On the right, a short distance from the road, stands La Roche-aux-Fées (Fairies' Rock).*

La Roche-aux-Fées★

This is one of the finest megalithic monuments in Brittany, dating from the Middle Neolithic period (fourth millennium BC). Built in purple schist, it consists of 42 stones, of which half a dozen weigh between 40 and 45t each. There is a massive portico entrance and then a low ceilinged corridor leading to a large, very high compartmented room (14m/46ft long, 4m/13ft wide, 2m/6.5ft high). Scientists have established that these huge stones were moved over a distance of 4km/2.5mi. According to legend, this was done by fairies who simply put the stones in their aprons!

▷ *Turn round and go to Le Theil then turn left towards Ste-Colombe.*

G. Targat/MICHELIN

La Roche-aux-Fées

The road affords a view of **Lac des Mottes**, a charming artificial lake amid magnificent trees.

▶ *When within sight of Ste-Colombe, turn left.*

Retiers
Pretty small town where the church contains five paintings and three 17C and 18C altarpieces in carved wood.
Cross Arbrissel, the birthplace of Robert d'Arbrissel who founded the famous abbey of Fontevraud where he is buried.

▶ *Return to La Guerche via Rannée.*

LAC DE GUERLÉDAN★★

MICHELIN LOCAL MAP 309 D5- CÔTES D'ARMOR (22)

At the heart of the Argoat, the waters of the River Blavet form a winding reservoir known as Guerlédan Lake, a magnificent stretch of water surrounded by trees. It is one of the finest sights of inland Brittany and a lovely place for water sports.

- **Don't Miss:** A boat trip on he lake
- **Organizing Your Time:** The months from June to September are the best for taking advantages of the water sports opportunities on the lake

Lake

Round-trip of 44km/27mi starting from Mur-de-Bretagne – allow 3hr 30min.

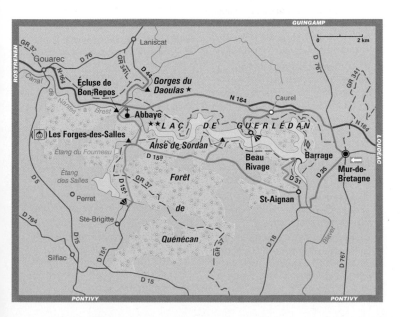

Mur-de-Bretagne

This is one of the liveliest towns in the interior of Brittany.

Chapelle Ste-Suzanne stands to the north of the town in a very pretty wooded setting. The splendid oak trees which surround it are several centuries old and inspired the painter Corot (1796-1875) on several occasions. The chapel's elegant **belfry-porch** dates from 1760. Inside, the remarkable 18C **painted ceiling**★ is dedicated to St Suzanne.

In the village, a road to the right leads to a roundabout, which affords a lovely **view**★ of Guerlédan Lake and dam.

Address Book

TOURIST OFFICE

Guerlédan, Place de l'Église, Mûr-de-Bretagne, ☏ 02 96 28 51 41. 🕐 Open Easter-Jun, Sep: Mon-Sat 10am-12.30pm, 2-5.30pm; Jul-Aug: Mon-Sat 10am-12.30pm, 2-6pm, Sun and public hols. 10.30am-12.30pm. 🕐 Closed Oct-Easter: Sat afternoon.

Centre Bretagne, 1 rue St-Joseph, Loudéac, ☏ 02 96 28 25 17, www.centrebretagne.com; 🕐 Open Mon-Fri 9am-12.30pm, 1.30-6pm, Sat 11am-12.30pm (2-5pm Jul-Aug); mid-Jul to mid-Aug: Sun 10am-12.30pm.

🛈 For coin ranges, see the Legend on the cover flap.

WHERE TO STAY

AROUND THE LAKE

⊜⊜ **Pear Blossom House**, 14 rue de la Résistance, Mûr-de-Bretagne, ☏ 02 96 26 05 79 - 2rm ⇥ A big house with rooms decorated in the owner's English style.

⊜⊜ **Chambres d'hôte du Pont-Guern**, Mûr-de-Bretagne. Take the Pontivy road, then follow the signage on the right. ☏ 02 96 28 54 52 - 3rm ⇥ Along the Blavet, picturesque farmhouses offer rustic rooms looking out onto a beautiful garden. Guest table.

EATING OUT

AROUND THE LAKE OF GUERLÉDAN

⊜ **Les Pêcheries**, St-Aignan, ☏ 02 97 27 50 12. 🕐 Closed evenings. Familial cuisine and atmosphere.

⊜ **Restaurant La Chapelle**, 37 rue Ste-Suzanne, Mûr-de-Bretagne, ☏ 02 96 26 05 67. 🕐 Closed Nov-Mar; Sat off season. Big-eaters will have plenty to

choose from with three buffets of hors-d'oeuvres, main dishes and desserts.

⊜⊜ **Merlin**, anse de Sordan, ☏ 02 97 27 52 36. Take a seat either on the terrace above the lake or in the elegant dining room before deciding on tapas, salads or several traditional courses for your meal.

RECREATION

Sail and canoe-kayak - Base de plein air de Guerlédan, Mûr-de-Bretagne, ☏ 02 96 67 12 22, http://base-plein-air-guerledan.com. 🕐 Open Easter; Jul-Aug. Supervised activities €12/session.

Club canoë-kayak de Guerlédan, plage Beau Rivage, Caurel, ☏ 02 96 26 30 52. Rental €18-25/day.

Camping Tost-Aven, Gouarec, ☏ 02 96 24 85 42, baxter.david@wanadoo.fr. Canoe and kayak rental €16-23/day.

Cruises on the lake - Vedettes de Guerlédan, Beau Rivage, Caurel, ☏ 02 96 28 52 64, www.guerladan.com. Operates Jul-Aug daily at 3pm, €5.30/8.20. Reservations required for dinner cruises mid-Mar to 1 Nov, starting at €28.90.

Walks – Check out the IGN map, série bleue n° 0818 (1: 25 000), for details on the walks around the lake. Another good option includes Balades en pays du Centre Bretagne (on sale at the Tourist Office of Loudéac). For easy access to the **Guerlédan-Argoat region**, head to the train station, Gouarec, west of the lake, ☏ 02 96 24 85 83, guerledan-argoat@wanadoo.fr.

Horse riding - Centre équestre de Guerlédan, Mûr-de-Bretagne, ☏ 02 96 26 02 02 or 06 19 83 22 99. 🕐 Closed Christmas hols. Enjoy the lake on horseback or pony. €12-15/h.

▷ *Take D 35 southwest and after crossing two bridges over the canal and the Blavet, turn right.*

St-Aignan

In the charming 12C **church** note in particular a beautiful carved wooden image of the Tree of Jesse to the north of the chancel and a depiction of the Trinity surrounded by Evangelists, in the same medium, to the south. There is also a statue of St Mark and a Pietà.

Barrage de Guerlédan

A viewpoint overlooks this dead-weight dam (45m/147ft high, 206m/240yd long along the top and 33.50m/109ft thick at the base) and extending over 12km/7mi in the Blavet Gorges.

▷ *Come back by the same road and bear right. Before entering the Forêt de Quénécan bear right.*

Anse de Sordan

Pleasant site on the edge of the Lac de Guerlédan.

Forêt de Quénécan

The forest of 2 500ha/6 175 acres stands on an uneven plateau overlooking the Blavet Valley. Apart from beech and spruce around Lake Fourneau (Étang du Fourneau) and Les Forges des Salles, the forest, abounding in game (deer, wild boar), consists of pine, scrubland and heath.

Les Forges-des-Salles

Kids Guided tours (1hr) July to August, daily, 2-6.30pm; Easter to June and Sept to Nov, Sat-Sun 2-6.30pm. €5/3. ☎ 02 96 24 90 12.
Les Forges Hamlet, tucked at the bottom of a wooded valley, was the site of an iron and steel industry in the 18C and 19C. Quite apart from the site's remarkable testimony to a complete period of industrial history, the setting itself is charming. Since the mining and processing of iron ore was stopped, in 1880, this collection of well-designed buildings has not been altered.
The buildings of schist, which are arranged around the ironmaster's house, include some which are open to visitors; these are the former homes of blacksmiths (arranged as exhibition rooms). Some have been furnished according to their original style and function: the school, the accounts office, the canteen, the chapel, the joiner's workshop and a small smithy.
East of the castle, at the top of the terraced pleasure garden (the **Thabor**), there is a lovely view over the valley and the various stretches of water in it.

▷ *Continue in the direction of Ste-Brigitte.*

There are fine views on the right of Lake Fourneau.

▷ *Via Les Forges des Salles return to the main crossroads, then bear left. Leave the car in the car park before the bridge to the left.*

Écluse de Bon-Repos

The lock on the River Blavet, the old corbelled bridge, the former lock keeper's house and the overflow form a pretty picture.

▷ *Go over the bridge and take the towpath to the right.*

Abbaye de Bon-Repos
🕐 *Open Easter to Sept, daily; rest of the year, Sun–Fri.* ✍€3. ☎ *02 96 24 82 20.*
This 12C Cistercian abbey, a dependent of the Abbaye de Boquen, rebuilt in the 14C and embellished in the early 18C, was sacked and destroyed during the Revolution. The fine façade of the abbot's lodging, the sober architecture of the conventual buildings and the vast size of the church may still be admired.

▶ *Make for N 164 and turn left towards Gouarec; immediately after the bridge bear right to Daoulas Gorges.*

Gorges du Daoulas★
Go up the gorges. The fast-flowing waters of the Daoulas run in a narrow, winding valley with steep sides covered with gorse, broom and heather. To join the Blavet, which has become the canal between Nantes and Brest, the river has made a deep cut through a belt of schist and quartzite. The slabs of rock rise almost vertically; some end in curious needles, with sharp edges.

▶ *Continue for 2km/1mi, reverse into a lane before two houses at the place known as Toulrodez and turn back. Follow N 164 towards Loudéac and turn right after 5km/3mi.*

After dropping down into a small pine wood, the road provides a beautiful **view**★ of the Lac de Guerlédan.

Beau-Rivage
Leisure and sailing centre.

▶ *Proceed to Caurel and turn right towards Loudéac. After 3.5km/2mi turn right to return to Mur-de-Bretagne.*

GUIMILIAU★★

POPULATION 814
MICHELIN LOCAL MAP 308 H4 - FINISTÈRE (29)

The fame of the small village of Guimiliau is due to its remarkable parish close and to the magnificently ornamented furniture of its church.

▶ **Orient Yourself:** Between Morlaix and Landvisiau.
🕐 **Organizing Your Time:** Visit the parish colose of St-Thégonnec nearby.
Also See: Les ENCLOS PAROISSIAUX.

Parish Close★★

Calvaire★★
The Calvary, the most curious and one of the largest in the region, dates from 1581-8 and includes over 200 figures. On the upper part stands a large cross with a thorny shaft bearing four statues: the Virgin and St John, St Peter and St Yves. On the platform are 17 scenes from the Passion and a composition representing the story of Catell-Gollet above the Last Supper. The figures on the frieze are numerous and depict, in no chronological order, 15 scenes from the life of Jesus. The four Evangelists stand at the corners of the buttresses.

B. Kaufmann/MICHELIN

Guimiliau parish close

Church★

This 16C building was rebuilt in the Flamboyant Renaissance style at the beginning of the 17C.

South porch★★

The recessed arches adorned with statuettes give an interesting picture of the Bible and the Gospels. Above the triangular pediment over the porch is the statue of St Miliau, King of Cornouaille and patron saint of the area. To the left of the porch is a small ossuary with low-relief sculptures depicting scenes from the life of Christ. The inside of the porch is a fine example of a form of decoration frequent in Brittany. Under the usual statues of the Apostles is a frieze ornamented with rose medallions, strapwork and scenes from the Old Testament. Note on the left side, near the date 1606, the Creation of Woman.

Interior

To the left of the entrance is a fine carved oak **baptistery**★★ dating from 1675. In the **organ loft** are three 17C **low-relief sculptures**★; on the nave side, David playing the harp, and St Cecilia at the organ; opposite the baptistery, the Triumph of Alexander. The **pulpit**★, dating from 1677, is ornamented at the corners with statues of the four Sibyls.

The chancel with its central stained-glass window (1599) is closed by a 17C altar rail. Note from right to left: the colourful **altarpiece of St Joseph,** on which can be seen St Yves, the patron saint of barristers between a rich man and a poor one, and the blind St Hervé with his wolf; the **altarpiece of St Miliau,** representing scenes from the saint's life; the **altarpiece of the Rosary,** with 15 mysteries in medallions, is surmounted by a Trinity.

Chapelle funéraire

The funerary chapel in the Renaissance style, dating from 1648, has an outdoor pulpit set in one of the windows.

GUINGAMP

POPULATION 8 008
MICHELIN LOCAL MAP 309 D3 - CÔTES D'ARMOR (22)

Located on the edge of Armor and Argoat, Guingamp is a commercial and industrial town that has greatly developed in the last decades.

Sights

Basilique Notre-Dame-de-Bon-Secours★

This church was built in the Gothic style in the 14C (a Romanesque part remains at the transept crossing); but two centuries later the south tower collapsed, demolishing the nave's south side. The town asked several architects to plan its reconstruction. One old master presented a purely traditional Gothic design; but a young man named Le Moal submitted plans in which the Renaissance style, almost unknown in Brittany at that time, appeared. Quite unexpectedly the people of Guingamp awarded the prize to the innovator. Since then the church has had the unusual feature of being Gothic on the left and Renaissance on the right.

Inside, the church is unusual with its numerous pillars and graceful flying buttresses in the chancel. The triforium is adorned with trilobed arches with a quadrilobed balustrade while lower down the nave has striking Renaissance decoration.

A great *pardon* draws thousands of pilgrims. After the torch-lit procession, three bonfires are lit on place du Centre in the company of the bishop, who also presides over the ceremony.

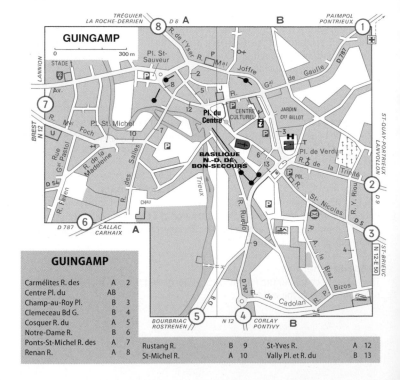

GUINGAMP

Carmélites R. des	A	2
Centre Pl. du	AB	
Champ-au-Roy Pl.	B	3
Clemeceau Bd G.	B	4
Cosquer R. du	A	5
Notre-Dame R.	B	6
Ponts-St-Michel R. des	A	7
Renan R.	A	8

Rustang R.	B	9	St-Yves R.	A	12
St-Michel R.	A	10	Vally Pl. et R. du	B	13

Place du Centre

On the square are a few old houses (nos 31, 33, 35, 39, 48) and at the corner of rue St-Yves and rue du Cosquet. The fountain called **la Plomée,** with three lead and

Address Book

TOURIST OFFICES

Guingamp, Place du Champ-au-Roy, ☏ 02 96 43 73 89, www.ot-guingamp. org Open Jul-Aug: Tue-Sat 10am-noon, 2-6pm; Jun, Sep: Tue-Sat 10.15am-noon, 2.15-6pm; Oct-May: Tue, Thu-Sat 10.15am-noon, 2.15-5.30pm (except Thu from Dec to Feb). Free guided tours in summer.

Châtelaudren, rue des Sapeurs-Pompiers, ☏ 02 96 79 77 71, www.cdc-chatelaudren-plouagat.com ⏰ Open Jul-Aug: Mon-Sat 9am-7pm, Sun 10am-noon; Sep-Jun: Mon-Wed 9am-noon, 1.30-5.30pm.

Rent a bike - Ets Lancien, 3 bd Gambetta, Ploumagoar, ☏ 02 96 95 60 33. *For coin ranges, see the Legend on the cover flap.*

WHERE TO STAY

⊖⊖ **Hôtel de l'Arrivée**, *19 bd Clemenceau*, ☏ *02 96 40 04 57, www.hotelarrivee.com – 27rm*, ⊑ *€6.50*. Near the train station: renovated, functional and well kept rooms.

⊖⊖⊜ **La Demeure**, *5 rue du Gén.-de-Gaulle*, ☏ *02 96 44 28 53, www.demeure-vb.com – 6rm*, ⊑ *€8*. Located in the town centre, this stately home offers bright and very comfortable rooms, with balcony or terrace. All are equipped with kitchenettes.

SURROUNDINGS

⊖⊖ **Au Char à Bancs**, *Plélo*, ☏ *02 96 74 13 63, www.aucharabanc. com – 5rm*, ✖. Rustic-chic defines these guest rooms located in an old mill (2 to 4 persons/room). Museum, second hand trade, and all farm-related activites (horse and pony riding) abound. Guest table with rustic hotpot on reservation.

EATING OUT

GUINGAMP

⊖ **Crêperie Saint-Yves**, *27 rue St-Yves*, ☏ *02 96 44 31 18*. ⏰ *Closed Mon and*

Thur evenings. Good variety of crêpes served in a room decorated with tasteful reproductions of famous works of art.

⊖ **Les Perchamps**, *11 rue de Rustang*, ☏ *02 96 44 28 66.* This rustic room overlooking a garden is a good place to enjoy crêpes, pizzas or grilled selections.

⊖ **L'Express**, *26 bd Clemenceau*, ☏ *02 96 43 72 19.* ⏰ *Closed Sat lunch; Sun evening; Mon.* Located near the train station, this pub offers everyday fare at reasonable prices with good service.

⊖⊜ **Le Clos de la Fontaine**, *9 rue du Gén.-de-Gaulle*, ☏ *02 96 21 33 63.* ⏰ *Closed Sun evening; Mon; 15 days in Feb; 1 week in Jul.* Good maritime cuisine, to be enjoyed in an elegant setting.

⊖⊖⊜⊜ **Le Relais du Roy**, *42 Place du Centre*, ☏ *02 96 43 76 62.* ⏰ *Closed Sun evening; Mon lunch; end of Dec to mid-Jan.* Located in a former post relay, this hotel-restaurant offers regional cuisine served in a refined setting with blue flax tablecloths. Very comfortable rooms.

ENTERTAINMENT

Campbell's Pub, *14 Place St-Michel*, ☏ 02 96 43 85 32. The most animated café in town is open late at night. Young and enthusiastic atmosphere.

FESTIVALS

Le Festival de la St-Loup, ☏ 02 96 43 87 10, assembles the children of Brittany for the **Bugale Breizh**, a big gathering of Breton dances held on the first Sun of Jul. The festival continues on weekdays, about the 15 of Aug. **Le pardon N.-D.-de-Bon-Secours**, first Sat of Jul, is dedicated to the Black Virgin, patron saint of the basilica.

SHOPPING

Markets- Guingamp, Fri, Place du Vally; Sat, Place du Centre. **Bourbriac**, Tue **Châtelaudren**, Mon in summer.

stone basins dating from the Renaissance is popular.

Hôtel de Ville

🕐 *The Town hall is open daily (except Sat afternoon and Sun), 8.30am–noon and 1.30–5.30pm. No charge.* ☎ *02 96 40 64 40. www.guingamp.fr.*

The town hall (1699) housed in the old hospital (Hôtel-Dieu), was formerly an Augustinian monastery. The cloisters, great staircase and fine Italian-style chapel (1709) may be visited. In the chapel, in season, temporary exhibitions are held.

Among the permanent collection are paintings by Sérusier (in the great hall) and the Pont-Aven School.

Ramparts

Standing on place du Vally are all that remains of the castle (1438-42). Ruins of the fortifications which once surrounded the town can be seen not far from rue du Maréchal-Joffre and place St-Sauveur.

Excursions

Grâces

3.5km/2mi. Leave Guingamp on D 54, west on the town plan. Turn right after 2km/1mi; in the village centre stands the large church.

Originally **Église Notre-Dame** (Church of Our Lady) would appear to have been a pilgrims' chapel, probably founded by Queen Anne. Built in the 16C, it was slightly altered in the 17C and restored in the 19C. The four gables of the single aisle give it a saw-tooth silhouette from the south.

Inside, note the nave's tie-beams and the superb carved purlins. A satirical picture of drunkenness is the main theme; but there are also hunting scenes, monsters, and a poignant Holy Face surrounded by little angels.

Châtelaudren

14km/8.mi E along N 12. This little town stands on a bend of the Aulne, in the green and deep valley through which the canalised river flows. Two lines of shady quays are its most decorative feature. There are camping and fishing facilities on the edge of the lake which replaced the former fortifications.

Driving Tour

Valleé du Trieux

Round-trip of 39km/24mi – 2hr. Leave Guingamp on ⑤ on the town plan.

Bourbriac

Rising in the centre of the town and surrounded by gardens, is the church with its soaring bell-tower 64m/210ft high. There have been several buildings erected on the site: of the first there remains a crypt probably of the 10C or 11C; of the Romanesque church which followed, there is the very high transept crossing – the tower above it was burnt down in the fire of 1765 and has been replaced by a pinnacle. In 1535 building on the west tower began; it is a remarkable example of the style that was to come: while the big pointed arched porch and all the lower floor are in the Flamboyant style, the remainder of the tower is definitely Renaissance. The spire was added in 1869. Inside, the sarcophagus of St Briac, dating from Merovingian times, is invoked as a cure for epilepsy.

▶ *Go towards Plésidy and then in the direction of St-Péver.*

After 2km/1mi, note on the left below the road the small **Manoir de Toul-an-Gollet,** a pleasant 15C granite with a pepper-pot turret and mullioned windows.

▶ *Turn left at the crossroads and before the bridge over the Trieux, take a small road to the right.*

Chapelle Notre-Dame-de-Restudo

🕐 *By appointment, key at the Town Hall in St-Péver (Mon, Tue, Thu and Fri).* ☎ *02 96 21 42 48.*

This 14C-15C chapel retains traces of 14C frescoes depicting the Last Supper and chivalric scenes in the nave and chancel which are separated by a great pointed arch. *Pardon* on 30 June in honour of St Eligius.

▶ *Turn back and take the road back to Guingamp.*

The Trieux Valley offers varied scenery.

▶ *After 2km/1mi bear right to Avaugour.*

Chapelle d'Avaugour

🕐 *By appointment, key at the Town Hall in St-Péver (Mon, Tue, Thu and Fri).* ☎ *02 96 21 42 48.*

The chapel stands in an attractive setting and contains a finely carved wood sacrarium (shrine) of the 16C and interesting statues of the Apostles.

▶ *Return to Guingamp along D 767.*

ÎLE D'HOUAT AND ÎLE DE HŒDIC

MICHELIN LOCAL MAP 308 N10 - MORBIHAN (56)

These islands in the Ponant archipelago lie some 15km/8mi from the mainland. Their coastline is fringed by sandy beaches alternating with cliffs and rocky headlands. Tourism and fishing are the main activities. Peace and quiet guaranteed.

▶ **Orient Yourself:** The islands are 14km/8.4mi off shore from Qiberon
🅿 **Parking:** Leave your car on the mainland: no motor vehicles allowed!
🕐 **Organizing Your Time:** In the summer, be sure to reserve your lodging and your boat trip to the islands

Houat

This island (5km/3mi long and 1.3km/1mi wide) is a granite ridge fringed by cliffs. Because of its location commanding the access to Quiberon Bay, it was occupied three times by the English in the 17C and 18C. The boats dock in the new harbour on the north coast. A road leads uphill to the town.

Town

Pretty houses, whitewashed and flower-bedecked, line the winding streets and alleyways leading to a square in the centre of the town in which stands the communal well, and to another square next to the church.

  For coin ranges, see the Legend on the cover flap.

WHERE TO STAY / WHERE TO EAT

HOUAT

La Sirène, *rte du Port,* ☎ *02 97 30 66 73, www.houat-la-sirene.com* – 20rm, €10, ✗ Bright rooms with standard comfort; meals focus on seafood with a daily fish special. In July and August, rates are for demi- and full-pension exclusively.

HŒDIC

Les Cardinaux, ☎ *02 97 52 37 27, lescardinaux@aol.com* – 10rm ✗ Demi-pension only. The only hotel of the island offers comfortable rooms and a delicious menu featuring specialties such as seafood sauerkraut and roasted lobster.

The church, built in the 19C, commemorates St Gildas, an English monk and patron of the island, who visited Houat prior to founding the monastery of St-Gildas-de-Rhuys.

▶ *Go round the church and follow the path skirting the cemetery.*

From the look-out point, there is a fine **view**⋆ of the harbour and of the Presqu'île de Rhuys.

Beaches

There are numerous beaches located in small creeks but the loveliest extends to the west, facing the Île de Hœdic, near the old harbour.

Hœdic

Separated from the Île d'Houat by the Sœurs Channel, Hoedic is the smaller of the two (2.5 x 1km/1.5 x 0.5mi); it has the same granite formation with beaches and rocky headlands. Two lagoons extend east of the town while the island is covered in sparse heathland where wild carnations, a few cypresses, fine fig trees and tamarisks grow. Fresh water is supplied by an underground water bearing bed.
The boats dock at Argol Harbour.

Town

The south-facing houses stand in groups of three or four. Near the former beacon is the **Église St-Goustan** named after a Cornish hermit, who came to the island for a few years. It has fine 19C **furnishings**; note the two angels in white marble by the high altar.

Ancien fort

The old fort, built in 1859 and partly hidden by the dunes, can be seen on the road to Port de la Croix.
Kids Footpaths by the sea take you round the island to discover the beaches and admire the lovely **view** of the mainland, Houat Island, Belle-Ile and of the reefs.

HUELGOAT★★

POPULATION 1 687
MICHELIN LOCAL MAP 308 I4 – FINISTÈRE (29)

The forest, lake, running water and rocks make Huelgoat one of the finest sites★★ in inner Brittany which come under the aegis of the Parc natural régional d'Armorique. Huelgoat is a favourite place for anglers (especially for carp and perch in the lake and trout in the river) and a good excursion centre.

▶ **Orient Yourself:** East of the Monts d'Arée, in the heart of a wooded region
🕑 **Organizing Your Time:** This is the perfect place to plan a picnic
👣 **Also See:** Monts d'ARRÉE

Walking Tour

The town

The 16C **church** with a modern belfry stands near the main square in the town centre. Inside there are sculpted purlins and to the left of the chancel is a statue of St Yves, the patron saint of the parish, between a rich man and a pauper.

Overlooking Huelgoat, this Renaissance **Chapelle Notre-Dame-des-Cieux** with its 18C bell tower, has curious painted low-relief sculptures depicting scenes from the life of the Virgin and the Passion around the chancel and the side altars. A pardon takes place on the first Sunday in August.

The Rocks – *Allow 1hr 30min on foot*
🚶 *From rue de Berrien past the lake, follow the signposted path.*

Chaos du Moulin

The path cuts through the rocks dominating the course of the River Argent. This pile of rounded granite rocks, surrounded by greenery, is very picturesque.

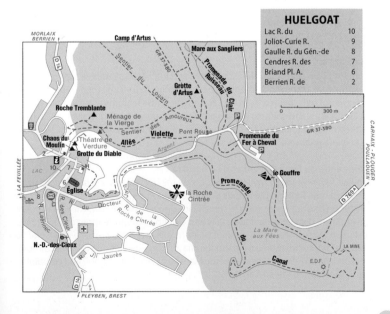

HUELGOAT	
Lac R. du	10
Joliot-Curie R.	9
Gaulle R. du Gén.-de	8
Cendres R. des	7
Briand Pl. A.	6
Berrien R. de	2

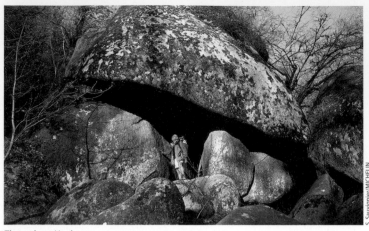

S. Sauvignier/MICHELIN

The rocks at Huelgoat

Grotte du Diable

▶ *To reach this, climb down an iron ladder. A brook babbles under the rocks.*

Roche Tremblante

North bank. By leaning against this 100t block at a precise point, you can make it rock on its base.

▶ *An uphill path, known as Lovers' Walk* (Sentier des Amoureux), *leads directly through the woods to Artus's Cave and to Boars' Pool (see The Forest below).*

Allée Violette

A pleasant path in the woods along the left bank of the River Argent ends this ramble through the rocks.

▶ *To return to the centre of Huelgoat, at Pont-Rouge, turn right oto the road from Carhaix and then take rue du Docteur-Jacq.*

The Forest

Extending over 1 000ha/2 471 acres, the Forest of Huelgoat lies at the foot of the southern slope of the Monts d'Arrée mountain range. Its tortured topography consists of a series of hills divided by deep valleys. The forest features a great many different landscapes and colours; it also contains strange, picturesque sites which have inspired many traditional tales and legends. (*Visitors can discover these sites with the help of signposts and car parks; see below*).

Promenade du Fer à Cheval and Le Gouffre

Allow 30min on foot. After Pont-Rouge, take the Horseshoe Walk on the right.
A pleasant walk through the woods along the River Argent. *Then return to the Carhaix road for 300/328yd.* A stairway *(39 steps)* leads down to the chasm. The River Argent flowing from the Lac d'Huelgoat, falls into a deep cavity to reappear 150m/164yd further on. A path leads to a lookout point *(15min there and back – difficult and no security ramp)* commanding a view of the chasm. You can continue this walk through the woods by the river passing near the Mare aux Fées (Fairies Pool) and combining it with the Promenade du Canal.

▶ *Follow the signposts to the mine (La Mine), turn right at the bridge into an unsurfaced road and at the former mine, continue along an uphill path to the right to the power station (usine électrique). A footbridge spans the canal and leads to the opposite bank.*

Promenade du Canal

🚶 *2hr on foot there and back on rue du Docteur-Jacq.*

This walk follows the bank of the upper canal. A reservoir and two canals were dug in the 19C to work the silver-bearing lead mines, already known to the Romans. The waters were used to wash the ore and drive a crusher. From the far end of the canal walk you may continue on to the chasm. (*This walk is described in the opposite direction see below.*)

Promenade du Clair-Ruisseau

🚶 *1hr 30min on foot there and back. From the car park after Pont-Rouge, take Allée du Clair-Ruisseau.*

TOURIST OFFICE

Huelgoat, moulin du Chaos, ☎ 02 98 99 72 32; In season: Mon-Sat 10am-12.30pm, 2-5.30pm; off season: Tue-Sat 10-12am, 2-5.30pm.
Communauté des communes des monts d'Arrée, Place Alphonse Penven, Huelgoat, ☎ 02 98 99 81 50, www.lesmontsdarree.com

WHERE TO STAY / EATING OUT

🍽️ **Auberge du Youdig**, *Kerveguenet, Brennilis*, ☎ 02 98 99 62 36, www.youdig.fr - 4 rm. At the "hell door", there is a passion for Breton legends and heritage. Stay in the guest rooms, bright and well equipped, or in a cottage, and enjoy a night of tales, a nature walk or a thematic weekend. In the restaurant, savour traditional regional cuisine, notably the kig ha farz savoury or sweet (order ahead of time). By the end of your stay, you'll be dancing a gig to the tune of the pipes!

This path half-way up the slope affords fine views of the rock-strewn stream bed. A stairway *(25 steps)* on the left leads down to the **Mare aux Sangliers** (Boars' Pool) in a pretty setting of rocks shaped rather like boars' heads, hence the name. Cross over the rustic bridge to Allée de la Mare on the left.

After the great stairway *(218 steps)*, which provides the quickest access to **Camp d'Artus** (Artus's Camp), you can see up above, on the right, the entrance to **Grotte d'Artus** (Artus's Cave).

▶ *Continue up the path which after 800m/0.5mi takes you to the camp. Boulders mark the entrance which was dominated by an artificial mound.*

The cave is an important example of a Gallic fortified site, bordered by two enclosures. In spite of the encroaching vegetation, it is possible to go round the camp by a path *(1km/0.6mi)* following the remaining second elliptical enclosure which is fairly well preserved.

Northeast of Huelgoat (13km/8mi), in the 🔲 **Maison de la faune sauvage**, you can learn more about the animals living free in the Armorique Regional Nature Park. Set up in the former railway station at Scrignac, it houses exhibits on recognizing animal tracks and contains about 70 stuffed and mounted specimens.

JOSSELIN★★

POPULATION 2 419 - MICHELIN LOCAL MAP 308 P7 - MORBIHAN (56)

This small town stands in a picturesque setting. Its river, the Oust, reflects the famous castle of the Rohan family. Behind the fortress-castle, on the sides and the summit of a steep ridge, old houses with slate roofs are scattered around the Basilique Notre-Dame-du-Roncier (Our Lady of the Brambles).

A Bit of History

The Battle of the Thirty (14C) – By the middle of the 14C Josselin Castle had already been razed and rebuilt. It belonged to the Royal House of France; Beaumanoir was its Captain; the War of Succession was raging. Josselin supported the cause of Blois; the Montfort party held Ploërmel, where an Englishman, Bemborough, was in command. At first the two garrisons had frequent encounters as they ravaged the countryside; then the two leaders arranged a fight between 30 knights from each camp: they would fight on foot, using sword, dagger, battle-axe and pike.

After taking Communion and praying all night at Our Lady of the Brambles, Beaumanoir's men repaired, on 27 March 1351, to the rendez-vous on the heath at Mi-Voie, between Josselin and Ploërmel (5km/3mi from Josselin at a place called Pyramide; a stone column marks the spot today). In the opposite camp were 20 Englishmen, six Germans and four Bretons. The day was spent in fierce hand-to-hand fighting until the combatants were completely exhausted. Josselin won; the English captain was killed with eight of his men, and the rest were taken prisoner. During the struggle, which has remained famous as the Battle of the Thirty, the Breton leader, wounded, asked for a drink. "Drink your blood, Beaumanoir, your thirst will pass!" replied one of his rough companions.

Constable de Clisson (14C) – Among the owners of Josselin the greatest figure was Olivier de Clisson, who married Marguerite de Rohan, Beaumanoir's widow. He acquired the castle in 1370. He had a tragic childhood; for when he was only seven

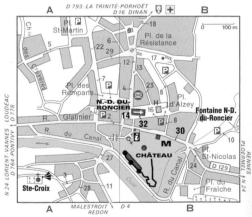

JOSSELIN		
Beaumanoir	A	2
Chapelle R. de la	A	3
Clisson R. O. de	B	4
Coteaux R. des	A	5
Devins R. des	A	6
Douves-du-Lion-d'Or R.	A	7
Douves-du-Noyer R. des	B	8
Duchesse-Anne Pl.	B	9
Fontaine R. de la	B	10
Gaulle R. Gén.-de	A	11
Le-Berd R. Georges	B	12
Libération Pl. de	B	13
Notre-Dame Pl.	B	14
Rohan Pl. A.-de	B	16
Rohan Cours J.-de	B	17
Ste-Croix R.	A	28
Ste-Croix Pont	A	27
St-Jacques R.	B	18
St-Martin R.	A	22
St-Michel R.	B	23
St-Nicolas R. et Pl.	B	24
Texier R. Alphonse	A	29
Trente R. des	B	30
Vierges R. des	B	32

his father was accused of betraying the French party in the War of Succession and beheaded in Paris. His widow, Jeanne de Belleville, who had been quiet and inconspicuous hitherto, became a fury. She hurried to Nantes with her children and, on the bloody head of their father nailed to the ramparts, made them swear to avenge him. Then she took the field with 400 men and put to the sword the garrisons of six castles which favoured the French cause. When the royal troops forced her to flee, she put to sea and sank every enemy ship that she met.

The Rohans at Josselin (15 and 17C) – In 1488, to punish Jean II de Rohan for having sided with the King of France, the Duke of Brittany, François II, seized Josselin and had it dismantled. When his daughter Anne became Queen of France she compensated Jean II, who was able in the rebuilding of the castle to create a masterpiece worthy of the proud motto of his family: *"Roi ne puis, Prince ne daigne, Rohan suis"* (I cannot be king, I scorn to be a prince, I am a Rohan). The owner of Josselin showed his gratitude to the Queen in the decoration of the palace; in many places, the letter A is carved in the stone, crowned and surmonted by the girdle which was Anne's emblem, and accompanied by the royal fleur-de-lis. In 1629, Henri de Rohan, the leader of the Huguenots, Richelieu's sworn enemies, met the Cardinal in the King's antechamber where the cleric, who had just had the keep and five of the nine towers of Josselin razed, announced with cruel irony: "I have just thrown a fine ball among your skittles, Monsieur."

Château★★ *45min*

🕐 *Guided tours (45min) daily July and Aug, daily, 10am-6pm; June and Sept 2-6pm; Apr, May and Oct, Wed, Sat-Sun, public holidays and during school holidays 2-6pm.* €7 (children €4.80). ☎ *02 97 22 36 45.*

Josselin castle

To get a good **view**★ of the castle stand on Ste-Croix Bridge, which spans the River Oust. From this point the building has the appearance of a fortress, with high towers, curtain walls and battlements. The windows and dormer windows appearing above the walls belong to the palace built by Jean II in the 16C.

The castle is built on a terrace of irregular shape, surrounded by walls of which only the bases remain, except on the side which is seen from the bridge. The isolated "prison tower" marked the northeast corner of the enclosure.

The delightful **façade**★★ of the main building which looks out onto the old courtyard, now the park, makes a striking contrast with the fortifications of the outer façade. Nowhere else in Brittany has the art of the sculptor in that hard material, granite, been pushed to such limits: brackets, florets, pinnacles, gables, crowns and curled leaves adorn the dormer windows and balustrades.

Only the ground floor, restored in the 19C, is open. to the public. In the panelled dining room stands an equestrian statue of Olivier de Clisson by Frémiet. After the antechamber, in which are hung portraits of the Rohan family, is the richly furnished drawing room with its delicately carved chimney which bears the current Rohan motto, *"A plus"* (To more). There are over 3 000 books and some portraits in the library.

Musée des Poupées

🕐 *Same hours as the castle.* ✺€6.20 (children 7-14: €4.40). ☎ 02 97 22 36 45.

In the castle's old stables, 500 dolls from the Rohan collection are exhibited. These come from many different countries (France, Netherlands, Austria, North America etc) and date from the 17C to the 20C. The dolls (in wood, wax, celluloid, porcelain) are dressed in religious or traditional costumes. Miscellaneous doll accessories are also exhibited. There are temporary exhibitions here in summer.

Walking Tour

Basilique Notre-Dame-du-Roncier★

🕐 *Guided tours available.* ☎ 02 97 22 20 18.

The name is based on a very old legend: around the year 800 a peasant, cutting brambles in his field discovered a statue of the Virgin and the site became one of pilgrimage and prayer. Founded in the 11C on the site of an oratory made of branches and several times remodelled (east end's spire built in 1949), the basilica is, generally speaking, Flamboyant in style; note the wonderful gargoyles which adorn its three sides and the stone statue of the Virgin at the entrance door. It is famous for its great pardon (ℰ *see Calendar of events*). Inside, in the south chapel, is the **mausoleum**★ of Olivier de Clisson and his wife Marguerite de Rohan (15C).

Top of the tower

Access from place A.-de-Rohan. 🕐 *Open July and Aug, daily, 10.30am-12.30pm and 2.30-6pm; apply to the Town Hall. No charge.* ☎ 02 97 22 24 17.

The tower commands a view of the north-east façade, the castle's inner courtyard and the countryside beyond.

Old houses

There are many old houses around the basilica, especially on rue des Vierges and place Notre-Dame. Some of the most picturesque are in rue des Trente; note the former residence at no 7 (1624), now the Tourist office, and beside it a house built in 1663.

Fontaine N.-D.-du-Roncier

Built in 1675, the fountain is still a place of pilgrimage.

Chapelle Ste-Croix

Built on the side of the hill is this chapel with its 11C nave. After a visit to the chapel, stroll in the picturesque Ste-Croix district with its narrow streets and old corbelled houses.

Excursions

Guéhenno

10km/6mi SW along D 24 then D778. The village has retained fine 16C and 17C stone houses. The **Calvary**★ stands in the cemetery near the church. It dates from 1550, was destroyed in 1794 and restored in the last century. All its beauty lies in its perfect composition. Carved in the shaft of the central cross is Jesse, father of David. In front of it stands a column, with the instruments of the Passion, on which a cock is perched, in allusion to the denial of St Peter. Behind this monument is a small ossuary, whose entrance is protected by the figures of two guards on duty.

Lizio *– 10km/6mi S via D 4 then right onto D 147.*

Écomusée des Vieux Metiers

&🕔 *Open April-Sep: 10am-noon and 2-7pm; Oct, Feb-Mar and school holidays: 2-6pm; rest of the year, by prior request. Guided tours available (1hr 30min).* 🕔 *Closed Sat-Sun mornings.* ☞ *€5.50 (children €4).* ☎ *02 97 74 93 01.*
More than 60 obsolete crafts and trades are illustrated in a large exhibition area. There are reconstructions of shops, farmhouse interiors, workshops and a wealth of tools and objects from by-gone days.

Insectarium

Rue du Stade. 🔲 & 🕔 *Open 10am-12.30pm and 1.30-6.30pm; Oct-Mar during school holidays: 1.30-6.30pm.* ☞ *€5.50 (children under 4 no charge).* ☎ *02 97 74 99 12.*
Dozens of different speies of insects are displayed here: centipedes, stick insects, moths, crickets, scoprions, trapdoor spiders. Two videos films are shown and a microscope is available for observation of insects.

Univers du Poète ferrailleur

On the road to Roc-St-André. & 🕔 *Open July to mid-Sep: 10.30am-12.30pm and 2-7pm; April-June and mid-Sep-Oct: Sun and holidays 2-6pm.* ☞ *€5.50 (children €4.50).* ☎ *02 97 74 97 94.*
Enter into the world of "the poet-junkman", a fantastic artist whose unbridled imagination has breathed life into a collection of 60-odd strange and intriguing sculptures.

Ploërmel

13km/8mi E along D 24. This little town, in the centre of an agricultural area at the limit of Upper Brittany, was once the seat of the dukes of Brittany and it was from Ploërmel that the Englishman, Bemborough, set out for the Battle of the Thirty (1351).

Église St-Armel★

The church is dedicated to St Arthmael, who founded the town in the 6C; he is shown taming a dragon which he leads away with his stole.
The church dates from the 16C. The Flamboyant Gothic and Renaissance north **portal**★ presents two finely carved doors. The scenes depicted take both religious (Christ's Childhood, Virtue Trampling on Vice) and comic themes. The Apostles have been sculpted on the door panels.
The magnificent 16C and 17C **stained-glass windows**★ have been restored: Tree of Jesse (in the side aisle), life of St Arthmael (in the north transept); there are also modern windows by Jacques Bony.

In the chapel to the north of the chancel are white marble statues of Duke Jean II and Duke Jean III of Brittany (14C). In the south transept, behind the Kersanton granite tomb of Philippe of Montauban and his wife, is a fine 14C recumbent figure in white marble. Below the wood vaulting the purlins are worth noticing *(light switch)*.

Old houses
Rue Beaumanoir, so-called in memory of the hero of the Battle of the Thirty, contains (at no 7) the 16C **Maison des Marmousets**★ adorned with woodcarvings, and opposite the 16C former house of the dukes of Brittany. Other old houses may be seen in rue des Francs-Bourgeois.

Maison-Mère des Frères de Ploërmel
The order was founded in 1819 by the abbot Jean-Marie de La Mennais (1780-1860), brother of the famous author Lamennais.

▶ *Enter the abbey's courtyard via place J.-M.-de-La-Mennais.*

Horloge astronomique (Astronomical Clock)
The clock, protected by a glass case, was created between 1850 and 1855 and was intended for the instruction of the future teachers of the schools situated along the coast.

Lac au Duc
2.5km/1.5mi north. Leave Ploërmel by boulevard du Maréchal-Foch west of the plan.
This lake (250ha/718 acres) has an artificial beach, a water sports centre and fishing facilities.
A 3km/1.3mi footpath, starting from the parking area of the King Arthur hotel, runs along the edge of the lake through an arboretum planted with 2 000 hydrangea of 220 different types. They flower from May to October.

La Trinité-Porhoët
15.5km/9.3mi N on D 793.
This town owes its name to the intersection of three Roman roads and to the lords of Porhoët, powerful counts of Brittany.

Église de la Sainte-Trinité
This massive church was built to serve as a priory for the St-Jacut brothers. An unusual feature of the interior is the slanting floor, which rises towards the choir. A spectacular **Tree of Life**★ from the 17C embellishes the altar screen.

Malestroit
25km/15mi south-east along D 4 and D 764. Near the Lanvaux Moors, this picturesque town, built along the Oust Canal, contains interesting Gothic and Renaissance houses. Malestroit was, during the Middle Ages, one of Brittany's nine baronies.

Old houses
Half-timbered or in stone, these houses are located mostly in the St Gilles precincts. On place du Bouffay one of the residences has humorous carvings on its façade, another has a pelican in wood. Stroll along rue au Froment, rue aux Anglais, rue des Ponts and the rue du Général-de-Gaulle.

Église St-Gilles
This 12C and 16C church is curious for the juxtaposition of styles and the double nave. Notice the south doorway, with its two doors with 17C carved panels, flanked by massive buttresses adorned with the symbolic attributes of the four Evangelists. The lion of St Mark is mounted by a youth symbolising St Matthew, and St Luke's ox

rests on a pedestal adorned with the eagle of St John. About 3pm the shadows of the ox and the eagle between them suggest the well-known profile of Voltaire.

Musée de la Résistance bretonne
In St-Marcel, 3km/2mi W of Malestroit via D 321. 🚻🕐 *Open mid-June to mid-Sept, daily, 10am-7pm; rest of the year, daily (except Tues), 10am-noon and 2-6pm.* 🕐 *Closed 1 Jan and 25 Dec.* 💶 *€6.30 (children €4.80).* ☎ *02 97 75 16 90.*

Spread over a forested park is the Museum of Breton Resitance, which vividly retraces this very important part of local Breton history.

The visit starts with a film which summarises the important events in the Second World War: German war effort, invasion of Europe, Allied preparation of the landing and the landing itself, and the Liberation.

Audio-visual presentations, explanatory panels, slides and films, models, arms, uniforms etc evoking the war and its effect on Brittany. To illustrate wartime rationing, a street has been reconstituted, with its local grocery, petrol pump and restaurant; the black market and the collaboration are also explained. In the park part of the Atlantic Wall has been rebuilt; further on there is a garage, during the Occupation, with its gas-run cars, an American Army camp and finally a collection of military vehicles and weapons belonging to both the German and Allied armies.

Bear left 1km/0.5mi on leaving, to find a monument commemorating the battle which occurred between members of the Maquis (French Resistance Movement) Free French commandos and the Germans on 18 June, 1944, soon after D-day.

DOMAINE DE KERGUÉHENNEC

MICHELIN LOCAL MAP 308 O7 - MORBIHAN (56)

The Kerguéhennec **estate**, in a pleasant, verdant setting, includes a Classical-style château, wooded park and lake. It was acquired by the Morbihan département in the 1970s and transformed into a **Contemporary Art Centre** .

Visit

Park and Sculptures
🚻🕐 *Open mid-Jan to mid-Dec, daily (except Monday), 10am-6pm (7pm mid-June to mid-Sept).* 🕐 *Closed mid-Dec to mid-Jan. No charge.* ☎ *02 97 60 44 44. www.art-kerguehennec.com*

An arboretum with fine trees is located in the 195ha /482 acre park. Dotted throughout the park are some 30 sculptures by artists including Giuseppe Penone, François Morellet, Tony Cragg, Michelangelo Pistoletto, Richard Long and Jean-Pierre Raynaud (*1 000 Cement Pots*, 1986)

To find your way in the maze of the park and to identify the sculptures which are scattered in it, ask for a map at the château or at the Café du Parc next to it.

Richard Long, Un cercle en Bretagne

L. Sillau/Centre d'Art Contemporain de Kerguéhennec

Château and outbuildings
The château, built in the early 18C by local architect Olivier Delourme, consists of a main building, with two projecting wings and symmetrically opposed outbuildings, the whole enclosing a vast court of honour, closed by a fine grille. It houses temporary exhibitions and conferences.

Excursion

Locminé
8km/5mi W along D 123 and D 1. The name of this town (*lieu des moines* meaning a place where the monks are), derives from the abbey founded here in the 6C, which had two churches identical in plan: Église St-Sauveur (16C) and Chapelle of St-Colomban. Only their façades remain; behind is a modern church (1975) built on the site of the naves.

Chapelle Notre-Dame-du-Plasker
To the left of the east end of the modern church. This 16C rectangular chapel is decorated in the Flamboyant style.

KERNASCLÉDEN★★

POPULATION 355
MICHELIN LOCAL MAP 308 L6 MORBIHAN (56)

This small village possesses a beautiful church built by the Rohan family.

Church★★

Though the church at Kernascléden was consecrated in 1453, 30 years before the Chapelle de St-Fiacre (*see Le FAOUËT*), there is a legend that they were built at the same time and by the same workmen. Every day, angels carried the men and their tools from one site to the other.
A characteristic feature of this church is the striving for perfection that appears in every detail. The very slender tower, the foliated pinnacles, rose carvings and delicate tracery help to adorn the church without overloading it. Two porches open on the south side. The left **porch**★, which is the larger, is ornamented with statues (restored) of the twelve Apostles.

15C frescoes on the vaulted ceiling

Inside, the church has pointed stone vaulting. The vaults and walls surmounting the main arches are decorated with 15C **frescoes**★★ representing episodes in the lives of the Virgin and Christ. The finest are the Virgin's Marriage, Annunciation (left of chancel) and Burial (right of chancel). In the north transept are eight angel-musicians; over the triumphal arch (on the chancel side), the Resurrection of Christ. On the walls of the south arm are fragments of a dance of death and a picture of Hell (facing the altar), which is remarkable for the variety of tortures it depicts.
There are many 15C statues in wood and stone: Our Lady of Kernascléden to the left of the high altar, St Sebastian and a Pietà in the nave.

Excursions

Château de Pont-Calleck
4km/2mi south. Take D 782 in the direction of Le Faouët and at Kerchopine, turn left. ◷ *Open all day (park only).* ◷ *Closed late July and Aug. No charge.* ☎ *02 97 51 61 17.*
The road skirts the site of Notre Dame-de-Joie, a children's home housed in **Château de Pont-Calleck** (Pont-Calleck Castle) which was rebuilt in 1880 (only the park is open to visitors). The tiny Chapelle Notre-Dame-des-Bois stands at the entrance to the park.

▸ *Continue towards Plouay.*

The road runs through the **Forêt de Pont-Calleck** (Forest of Pont-Calleck). A small road to the left runs down steeply and leads to a lake which affords a lovely view of the castle's site. Return to the Plouay road for a pleasant drive through the narrow valley of the Scorff.

Ploërdut
11km/6mi N along D 782 towards Guéméné-sur-Scorff, then left in Lignol. Situated at the heart of inland Brittany, the village has retained an interesting architectural heritage (manor houses and traditional farms of the 16C and 17C). The **church** (13C-17C) has a fine Romanesque nave and side aisles. The rounded arches rest on solid square **capitals**★ adorned with geometrical designs. Note the charnel-house abutting the south side of the church, which has a granite enclosure.

LAMBALLE

POPULATION 10 5634
MICHELIN LOCAL MAP 309 G4 - CÔTES D'ARMOR (22)

Lamballe, once the capital of the duchy of Penthièvre, is a picturesque commercial town built on the slope of a hill crowned by the church of Notre-Dame-de-Grande-Puissance. It is an important market centre, slightly off the tourist track.

Walking Tour

Collégiale Notre-Dame
☞ *Guided tours July and Aug, daily (except Sun), 10am-noon and 2-6pm; rest of the year, apply to the tourist office or the presbytery.* ☎ *02 96 31 02 55.*
The Gothic collegiate church has Romanesque features. On the south side of the church with its buttressed gables, there is a terrace, built in the 19C, which affords a fine view of the town and the Gouessant Valley. A shady esplanade is located left of the church.

S. Sauvignier/MICHELIN

The Executioner's House is now the Tourist office

Place du Martray

Old half-timbered houses. The most remarkable is the 15C Maison du Bourreau (Executioner's House) which now contains the tourist office and two museums (see Additional Sights).

Église St-Martin

The old priory of Marmoutier Abbey was remodelled many times in the 15C to the 18C. In front of the church is a small, shady square. On the right is an unusual little porch (11C-12C) with a wooden canopy (1519). The handsome bell-tower has an 18C steeple.

Additionial Sights

Musée du Pays de Lamballe

Ground floor of the Maison du Bourreau. 🕒 *Open July and Aug, daily, 9.30am-6.30pm, Sun 10am-noon; Apr to June and Sept, daily (except Sun) 10am-12.30pm and 2-6pm (5pm the rest of the year).* 🕒 *Closed Jan, 1 and 8 May, 14 July, 15 Aug.* ⊜ *€2/1.* ☏ *02 96 34 77 63.*
Devoted to popular arts and traditions, displays of pottery from Lamballe, etchings of the old town, headdresses and regional costumes.

Musée Mathurin-Méheut

First floor of the Maison du Bourreau. 🕒 *Open June to Sept, daily (except Sun), 10am-noon and 2.30-6pm; spring school holiday, 10am-noon and 2.30-5pm; rest of the year,*

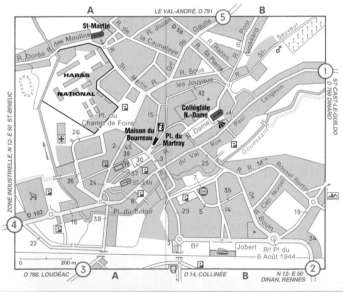

LAMBALLE		Dr-Lavergne R. du	A 16	Mouëxigné R.	B 31
		Foch R. Mar.	B 19	Poincaré R.	B 34
Augustins R. des	A 2	Gesle Ch. de la	A 23	Préville R.	B 35
Bario R.	A 3	Grand Bd R. du	A 24	St-Jean R.	A 37
Blois R. Ch. de	B 5	Hurel R. du Bg	B 25	St-Lazare R.	A 38
Boucouets R. des	B 7	Jeu-de-Paume R. du	A 26	Tery R. G.	A 39
Cartel R. Ch.	A 8	Leclerc R. Gén.	B 29	Tour-aux-Chouettes R.	B 42
Charpentier R. Y.	B 14	Marché Pl. du	A 30	Val R. du	AB
Dr-A.-Calmette R. du	A 15	Martray Pl. du	A	Villedeneu R.	A 45

Address Book

TOURIST OFFICE

Lamballe, Place du Martray, ☎ 02 96 31 05 38. July-Aug: 10am-6pm except Sun and public holidays; Apr: 10am-12.30pm, 2-4.30pm except Sun and public holidays; off season: 10am-12.30pm except Sun and public holidays. Information booth at the Haras National. July-Aug: daily 10am-6.30pm; Apr: daily 2-6pm; off season: daily 2-5.30pm.

WHERE TO STAY

LAMBALLE AND SURROUNDINGS

☕☕ **Hôtel Le Lion d'Or**, *3 rue du Lion d'Or*, ☎ 02 96 31 20 36, leliondorhotel@ wanadoo.fr - 🄿 – *17 rooms*, ☕ €7. In a calm district, this is a well-kept and traditional hotel with elegant, colourful rooms.

EATING OUT

LAMBALLE

☕ **Crêperie Ty Coz**, *35 Place du Champ de Foire*, ☎ 02 96 31 03 58. 🕐 *Closed Tue evening, Wed and Sun noon.* Big room, with stones and exposed beams, where you will be served all kind of crepe specialities such as the Cassoulett with sausage and white beans from Paimpol.

☕☕ **La Tour des Arch'Ants**, *2 rue du Dr Lavergne*, ☎ 02 96 31 01 37. 🕐 *Closed Sat in winter.* Regional cuisine in a rustic decor. Modest rooms available (☕).

Tues, Fri and Sat, 2.30-5pm. 🕐 *Closed January and all public holidays.* ☜ *€3 (children €1).* ☎ *02 96 31 19 99.*
This museum contains works by the local painter M Méheut (1882-1958).

Haras National★ (Stud Farm)

Founded in 1825, the stud contains 70 stallions (draught horses). From the beginning of March to mid-July, all the stallions are sent out to breeding stands in the Côtes d'Armor and the north of Finistère. The stud houses a school of dressage (40 horses) and a riding centre (20 horses).
The visit includes the stables, blacksmith's shop, carriage house, harness room, riding school and main court.

Excursions

Château de la Hunaudaye★

15km/9.3mi E along D 28 towards Pléven then D 28E to the right.
🔎 *Tours with guides in period costume July and Aug, daily, 11am-12.30pm and 2.30-6pm, on Sat-Sun 2.30-6pm; in June, Sun 2.30-6pm. Guided tours July and Aug, Sat 2.30-6pm; Apr, May and Sept, Sun and public holidays 2.30-6pm; Easter school holiday, daily (except Mon), 2-5.30pm.* ☜ *€3.80 in July-Aug;* ☜ *€3 April-Sep.* ☎ *02 96 34 82 10.*
The ruins of La Hunaudaye Castle rise in a lonely, wooded spot. Still impressive and severe, they reflect the power of the great barons, equals of the Rohans, who built the castle.
Built in 1220 by Olivier de Tournemine, it was partly destroyed during the War of Succession. Rebuilt and enlarged by Pierre de Tournemine in the 14C, enriched in the early 17C by Sébastien de Rosmadec, husband of one of the Tournemine heiresses, it was dismantled and then burnt by the Republicans at the time of the Revolution.
The shape is that of an irregular pentagon with a tower at each corner. The two smallest derive from the first building, the other three were built in the 14C-15C. A bridge, replacing the original drawbridge, gives access to a large rounded doorway surmounted by a coat of arms.

Tour de la Glacière

This 15C tower is north facing, hence its name (glacière meaning ice-house). Go up the spiral staircase to admire the elegant structure and chimneys, and the view of the moat.

Logis seigneurial

15C-16C. The walls and the splendid Renaissance stairway give some idea of the lay-out of this great manor house.

Donjon seigneurial

This 15C tower of this manorial keep with its spiral staircase (73 steps) is the best preserved. The monumental chimney-pieces and loopholes in the walls are noteworthy. View of the courtyard and moat.

This site is the setting for a performance, in period costume, of various aspects of life in a medieval castellany. The actors belong to the Compagnie Médiévale Mac'htiern.

St-Esprit-de-Bois-en-Plédeliac

Beyond Plédéliac, 11km/6mi E along D 28, D 52ᴬ, D 52 and D 55.

Ferme d'antan

Kids ⏱ *Open June-Aug: 10am-6pm, Sun and holidays 2-6pm; April-May and Easter holidays: daily except Mon and Sat: 2-6pm; Sep: daily except Mon: 2-6pm (last entrance 1hr 30mon before closing)* ⏱ *Closed 1 Jan and 25 Dec.* ⊶ *€4.50 (children (€2.50)* ☎ *02 96 34 80 77. www.ferme-dantan22.com.*

This traditional farmhouse is surrounded by outbuildings with their usual implements. The communal living room is furnished in typical Breton style. The tour ends with a film projection illustrating the everyday life of a peasant family in this very farm at the beginning of the 20C.

Moncontour and sub-sights

16km/10mi SW on D 769 , heading towards Loudéac.

Montcontour was built in the 11C on a rocky promintory, at the junction of two valleys. Picturesque **streets**★ and stairs lead to the gates built in the ramparts, partly dismantled by order of Richelieu in 1626. The Château des Granges, rebuilt in the 18C, stands on a hilltop north of the town.

Église St-Mathurin – The 16C church, considerably remodelled in the 18C, contains remarkable stained-glass windows: in the north aisle, they illustrate scenes from the life of St Yves, St Barbe and St John the Baptist; in the south aisle, they depict the Tree of Life and the life of St Mathurin. The restored window lighting the marble high altar (1768) evokes Christ's childhood.

Château de la Touche-Trébry

17km/10.6mi S along D 14 then D 25 right towards Moncontour just beyond Penguily. The château has recently changed ownership. ⓘ *For information, contact the Tourist Office.* ☎ *02 96 73 49 57.*

Although built at the end of the 16C, La Touche-Trébry looks like a medieval castle. It stands, facing a pond, protected by its defensive walls forming a homogeneous whole, unaltered in character by the restorations that have taken place.

The courtyard is regular in shape with the main building, with its symmetrical façade, at the far end. On either side, at right angles, are the two wings with pointed roofs; next to them are the outbuildings, not as tall, extending all the way to the two entrance pavilions.

Inside the castle there are some fine fireplaces.

Jugon-les-Lacs
16km/10mi SE on N 12 then N 176 heading towards Dinan.
The town is near the dam forming the large Jugon reservoir, a 70ha/173-acre **lake** with sailing and water sports facilities. The church, partly rebuilt in the 19C, has retained a 12C porch and an intersting carved doorway on the south side. Note, in rue du Château, the **Hôtel Sevoy** (1634), built on rock.

LAMPAUL-GUIMILIAU★

POPULATION 2 037
MICHELIN LOCAL MAP 308 G4 – FINISTÈRE (29)

This village has a complete parish close. The church is especially noteworthy for its rich decoration and furnishings.

▶ **Orient Yourself:** 4km/2mi SE of Landivisiau on D 11.
  Also See: Les ENCLOS PAROISSAUX.

Parish Close★

Recently restored, it is entered via the **porte triomphale** (triumphal arch) surmounted by three crosses (1669). The **chapelle funéraire** (funerary chapel), a former ossuary (1667), abuts on the arch and has buttresses crowned with small lantern turrets. Inside is the altar of the Trinity, with statues of St Rock, St Sebastian and St Pol and his dragon. The **Calvaire** (Calvary), dating from the early 16C, is older than the rest of the close.

Église★
The church is dominated by a 16C bell-tower, whose steeple was struck by lightning in the early 1800s. The apse, with a sacristy added in 1679, forms a harmonious whole in which the Gothic and Classical styles are blended. The porch on the south side dates from 1533. Under it are statues of the twelve Apostles.

Interior★★
A 16C **rood beam** spans the nave, bearing a Crucifix between statues of the Virgin and St John. Both its faces are adorned with sculptures representing, on the nave side, scenes from the Passion and, on the chancel side, the twelve Sibyls separated by a group of the Annunciation. The pulpit dates from 1759. At the end of the south aisle is a **font** surmounted by a fine canopy dating from 1651. Higher up, on the right of the St Lawrence altarpiece, is a curious stoup (17C) representing two devils writhing in holy water; above, the Baptism of Christ.

G. Biollay/PHOTONONSTOP

The Last Supper (detail)

In the **chancel** are 17C stalls, and on each side of the high altar, carved woodwork: on the left, St Paul on the road to Damascus and his escape; on the right, St Peter's martyrdom and the divine virtues. The side altars have 17C altarpieces.

The altar of St John the Baptist, on the right of the chancel, is adorned with low-relief sculptures of which the most interesting (left) represents the Fall of the Angels after Rubens. The altar of the Passion, on the left of the chancel, has an **altarpiece** in eight sections in high relief with lifelike figures and, on the top, the Resurrection. On either side are two panels showing the Birth of the Virgin (left), a rare theme in Brittany, and the Martyrdom of St Miliau (right), King of Cornouaille beheaded by his jealous brother. In the north side aisle is a 16C **Pietà** with six figures carved out of a single piece of wood and also a 17C **banner**, embroidered in silver on a velvet ground (in an open cupboard). The impressive 1676 **Entombment** in polychrome tufa was carved by the naval sculptor Anthoine. Note the expression of the Christ figure in particular. The organ case is 17C. The sacristy contains a 17C chest.

Maison du patrimoine
🕐 *Open mid-June to mid-Sep: daily except Sat, 10am-1pm and 2.30-6pm; Sun 10am-12.30pm; rest of the year,* 🔎 *guided tour of the parish close (1hr) available by appointment.* 🎟 *No charge.* ☎ *02 98 68 76 67.*
Facing the parish close, this old house built in the traditional regional style is a little museum featuring figures dressed in historical costumes, antique furnishings; in tourist season, there are exhibits of local artists' work.

LANDERNEAU

POPULATION 14 281
MICHELIN LOCAL MAP 308 F4– FINISTÈRE (29)

Located between Léon and Cornouaille, this small port is an active market town; the Élorn abounds in salmon and trout, making Landerneau the paradise of anglers. 🛈 *Tourist Office: Pavillon Pont-de-Rohan, 29800.* ☎ *02 98 85 13 09. www.pays-landerneau-daoulas.fr.*

▸ **Orient Yourself:** Mid-way between Brest and Landivisiau.
🕭 **Also See:** Les ENCLOS PAROISSAUX.

Sights

Pont de Rohan
Built in the 16C, this picturesque bridge, lined with houses with overhanging upper storeys, is one of the last inhabited European bridges.
Walk to the front of the town hall and enjoy the scene of the bridge, with its slate-covered houses with overhanging upper storeys.

Old houses
These are to be found mainly on the right bank of the River Élorn: no 9 place du Général-de-Gaulle, the turretted house (1664) known as the house of Duchess Anne; the façade at no 4 rue de la Fontaine-Blanche; at no 5 rue du Commerce, house with decorated turret and dormer windows (1667) and at the corner of the Pont de Rohan and Quai du Cornouaille is the so-called Maison des Rohan (Rohan House) (1639) with its sundial.

Église St-Houardon
The granite porch (1604) on the south side of this church served as a model for many parish closes along the Élorn Valley.

▶ *Walk across to the south bank.*

Église St-Thomas-de-Cantorbéry
🐾 *Guided tours mid-July to mid-Aug, Mon to Fri, 9.30am-noon and 2-6pm.*
This 16C church has a belfry-porch (1607) with three superimposed balconies. Inside, note the amusing decoration of the purlins in the north aisle and the great 18C altarpiece at the high altar.
Note the **ossuary chapel** erected as an annexe to the church in 1635.

LANDÉVENNEC★

POPULATION 371
MICHELIN LOCAL MAP 308 F5 - FINISTÈRE (29)

Situated on the Presqu'île de Landévennec, which is part of the Parc naturel régional de l'Armorique, the village of Landévennec stands in a pretty **site**★ at the mouth of the River Aulne, which is best seen by taking the steep downhill road to the right from Gorréquer. A lookout point to the right offers a fine **view**★ of Landévennec. Below is the course of the River Aulne, with the Île de Térénez; beyond, the Presqu'île de Landévennec and the River Faou.

Visit

Église Notre-Dame
Inside the church, you can see intersting statuary and some fine 17C **paintings**★.

Nouvelle abbaye bénédictine St-Guénolé

▶ *Halfway down the slope, bear right onto a tree-lined alley and follow the signposts.*

The very plain church contains a polychrome wood statue of St Guénolé (15C), in sacerdotal vestments and a monolithic pink granite altar. Services are held.

Ruines de l'ancienne abbaye
🕐 *Open mid-June to Sept, daily, 10am-7pm, Sun and holidays 2-7pm; rest of the year, Sat-Sun and school holidays 2-6pm.* €4. ☎ 02 98 27 35 90.
The monastery founded by the Welsh St Guénolé (Winwaloe) in the 5C and remodelled several times ceased to exist in the 18C and only the ruins of the Romanesque church remain. The plan can be deduced from the column bases, wall remains and doorway: a nave and aisles with six bays, transept, chancel and ambulatory with three radiating chapels. At the entrance to the south transept, there is a monument thought to be the tomb of King Gradlon.
An **abbey museum** of a very modern design was inaugurated on this site. It houses objects unearthed during excavations, including a wooden sarcophagus predating the 10C and models illustrating the different stages of construction of the abbey.

Excursions

Pont de Térénez
Spanning the River Aulne, this graceful bridge, whose central span 272m/893ft, offers a fine view of the valley.

Le Faou
The town, at the head of the Faou estuary, occupies a **site**★ which is full of character at high tide.

Rue Principale
The main street is flanked, on one side, by old houses with overhanging upper storeys and slate-covered façades. The 16C **church** stands on the river bank. It has an elegant 17C domed bell-tower, a double transept, a canted east end and an ornately sculpted south porch.

LANNION★

POPULATION 18 368
MICHELIN LOCAL MAP 309 B2 - CÔTES D'ARMOR (22)

Lannion, spread out on both banks of the River Léguer, has retained its typical Old Brittany character; from the bridge, there is a good view of the port an d of the vast Monastère Ste-Anne. The Centre de Recherches de Lannion and the Centre National d'Études des Télécommunications, where research is undertaken in telecommunications and electronics, have been built 3km/2mi north of Lannion at the crossroads of the road to Perros-Guirec and that of Trégastel-Plage. Lannion's annual organ festival takes place in Église St-Jean-du-Baly (16C-17C).

- 🐾 **Don't Miss:** The Thursday morning market
- 🕐 **Organizing Your Time:** This lively city, nestled between the coast and the countryside, is a good home base for touring the Granite Rose coast

Sights

Old houses★
The beautiful façades of the 15C and 16C houses, half-timbered, corbelled and with slate roofs, may be admired especially at place du Général Leclerc (nos 23, 29, 31, 33), rue des Chapeliers (nos 1-9), rue Geoffroy-de-Pont-Blanc (nos 1 and 3) and rue Cie-Roger-de-Barbé (nos 1 and 7). At the corner of the latter, on the left, a granite cross has been sealed in the wall at the spot where the Chevalier de Pont-Blanc distinguished himself in the heroic defence of the town during the War of Succession.

Église de Brélévenez★
Escalier de la Trinité (140 steps). The church was built on a hill by the Templars in the 12C and remodelled in the Gothic period.
Before entering look at the curious **Romanesque apse** which is decorated with engaged round pillars, carved capitals and modillions.
The bell-tower, crowned by a granite spire, dates from the 15C. From the terrace, there is an attractive view of Lannion and Léguer Valley.
Under the chancel, the Romanesque crypt, which was remodelled in the 18C, contains a marvellous 18C **Entombment**★, in which the subjects, carved in polychrome stone, are depicted life-size.

Address Book

TOURIST OFFICE

Lannion, Quai d'Aiguillon,
☎ 02 96 46 41 00, www.ot-lannion.fr
July-Aug: Mon-Sat 9am-7pm, Sun and
public holidays 10am-1pm; off season:
Mon-Sat 9.30am-12.30pm, 2-6pm.
Guided tours of the Old Town Sat at
2.30pm, by night Thu from June to Sep.

WHERE TO STAY

LANNION

Chambres d'hôte Noëlle Roger,
14 rue Jean Savidan, ☎ *02 96 46 40 12 -
3 rooms* In the town centre, elegant
rooms on three floors in an old house.
Ask for one on the first floor.

IN THE SURROUNDINGS

Chambres d'hôte Beeckmann,
*20 rte de Kerhervrec, Ploulec'h, ask
your way,* ☎ *02 96 46 42 33, nadia.
beeckmann@wanadoo.fr - 3 rooms* In
the countryside, this old but renovated
house shelters pretty rooms in the English country-house style. You can enjoy
dinner here by reservation.

Manoir du Launay, *Servel,
de Lannion,* ☎ *02 96 46 40 12, www.
manoirdulaunay.com - 5 rooms.* Surrounded by a park, this manor offers
thematic rooms decorated with a lot
of imagination. The "Nordique", with
a mezzanine, can accomodate up to
4 people (€ 150).

EATING OUT

LANNION

Le Moulin Vert, *15 rue Duguesclin,*
☎ *02 96 37 91 20.* Under exposed
beams, you will enjoy copious flat cakes
au gratin, but also big mixed salads and
20 sorts of crepes.

La Légende, *18 rue Jean Savidan,*
☎ *02 96 37 19 59.* The decor has an auto-
motive theme, and the meals change
with the season. One of the region's
best restaurants in this price range.

Le Serpolet, *1 rue Félix Le Dantec,*
☎ *02 96 46 50 23.* ⏰ *Closed Sat noon,
Sun evening and Mon.* In a rustic setting,
the menu features local vegetables and
seafood, prepared in an inventive way.

La Flambée, *67 rue Georges Pom-
pidou,* ☎ *02 96 48 04 85.* ⏰ *Closed Mon
off season.* Fish specialities prepared
with all kind of sauces, served in a
traditional setting.

IN THE SURROUNDINGS

Hôtel-restaurant de la Baie,
Trédrez-Loquemeau, in the village,
☎ *02 96 35 23 11.* Cosy restaurant where
you will be served regional meals and
copious seafood sauerkraut. Some
simple rooms.

Les Filets Bleus, *pointe de Séhar,
6 km Westwards of Ploulec'h,* ☎ *02 96
35 22 26. Apr-Nov,* ⏰ *closed Mon-Wed
except July-Aug.* From the panoramic
room, enjoy the view over the sea and
savour the cuisine.

La Ville Blanche, *5 km towards
Tréguier by the D 786,* ☎ *02 96 37 04 28.*
⏰ *Closed Sun evening and Wed except
July-Aug, Mon all year, and 27 June-4 July
and 18 Dec-27 Jan.* In an elegant setting,
top quality cuisine made with seasonal
Breton products.

ON THE TOWN

Les Valseuses, *opposite the church of
Brélévenez,* ☎ *02 96 48 75 19.* ⏰ *Closed
Mon.* ⏰ *Open until 1am, 2am in summer.* Concerts two Thu per month, and
theatrical improvisations. Breton beers,
parlour games and good atmosphere.

Le Flambart, *7 Place du Gén. Leclerc,*
☎ *02 96 37 40 72.* Good choice of Breton
beers and lively atmosphere during the
weekend, musical nights sometimes.

LEISURE

**Kayak and raft - École française
de canoë-kayak**, *8 rue de Kermaria,*
☎ *02 96 37 43 90* and, in July-Aug, **Base
de canoë-kayak**, *rue St-Christophe,*
☎ *02 96 37 05 46.* Kayak and raft on the
Léguer or on the river all year. Sea kayak
in the bay of Lannion in July-Aug.

Walks - The Tourist Office of Lannion
offers guided tours of the Old Town
*(14.30pm or at night in the sum-
mer)* and has maps showing trails in the
are. From the **château de Tonquédec**,
there is a very beautiful 11km/6.6mi
walk (half a day).

1 Castles and chapels

Round-trip of 50km/31mi – 3hr.

▷ *Leave Lannion on ④ on the town plan, the road to Plouaret. 1.5km/1mi after Ploubezre, bear left at a fork where five granite crosses stand and 1.2km/1mi further on, turn left.*

Chapelle de Kerfons★
🕐 *Open July to Sept, daily, 10am–noon and 2-6pm; rest of the year, apply to the Town hall (Mairie) in Ploubezre.* ☎ 02 96 47 15 51.

In a lovely setting, the chapel in front of which is an old Calvary, is surrounded by chestnut trees. Built in the 15C and 16C, it has a flat east end, a modillioned cornice along the south wall and a pinnacle turret decorated with telamones crowning the gabled south transept. It contains a late-15C carved **rood screen**★.

▷ *Turn back and take the road on the left.*

Soon the road starts to wind downhill providing good views over the ruins of Tonquédec in the Léguer Valley. After crossing the swiftly flowing river you will see the castle on the left (🅿 *car park).*

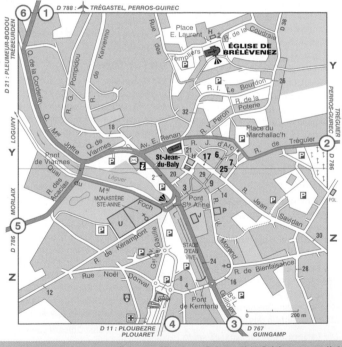

LANNION					
		Clemenceau Allée	Z 8	Mairie R. de la	Y 21
		Du Guesclin R.	Z 9	Palais-de-Justice Allée du	Z 24
Aiguillon Quai d'	Z 2	Frères-Lagadec R. des	Z 12	Pont-Blanc R. Geoffroy-de	Z 25
Augustins R. des	Z 3	Kériavily R. de	Z 14	Pors an Prat R. de	Y 26
Buzulzo R. de	Z 4	Kermaria R. et Pont	Z 16	Roud Ar Roc'h R. de	Z 28
Chapeliers R. des	Y 6	Leclerc Pl. Gén.	Y 17	St-Malo R. de	Z 29
Cie-Roger-de-Barbé R.	Y 7	Le-Dantec R. F.	Y 18	St-Nicolas R.	Z 30
		Le-Taillandier R. E.	Z 20	Trinité R. de la	Y 32

Château de Tonquédec★

🕐 *Open June to Aug, daily, 10am7pm; Easter to May and 1 to 30 Sept, 3-7pm.* ☎ *02 96 47 18 63 or* 🖷 *02 96 47 15 47. www.chateau-tonquedec.com.*

The ruins of the castle stand in very fine surroundings on a height overlooking the Léguer Valley. The castle, which was built in the early 13C, was dismantled by order of Jean IV in 1395; rebuilt at the beginning of the 15 C, it was again razed by order of Richelieu in 1622.

The entrance gate is opposite a pool now run dry. Enter a fortified outer courtyard. On the right, two towers connected by a curtain wall frame the main entrance to the second enclosure. Pass through a postern into the second courtyard. Opposite, standing alone, is the keep with walls over 4m/13ft thick. Go up a stairway *(70 steps)* to a platform to admire the plan of the castle and the local countryside: a wide, fertile and populous plateau intersected by deep, wooded valleys.

▷ *Turn back and at the first crossroads bear left to join the road to Plouaret, then turn left again; and after 1km/0.5mi turn left.*

Château de Kergrist

🕐 *Open June to Sept, daily, 11am-6.30pm; spring school holidays and public holidays in May, 2-6pm.* ⊜ *Combined ticket château and gardens €10, gardens only €5.* ☎ *02 96 38 91 44.*

One of the principal attractions of the château lies in the variety of its façades. The north façade is Gothic with dormer windows set in tall Flamboyant gables; the main building, which belongs to the 14C and 15C, nevertheless features an 18C façade on the opposite side, while the wings running at right angles, which were built at an earlier date, have Classical fronts overlooking the gardens. The formal French gardens extend as far as the terrace which overlooks a landscaped English garden and the woods.

▷ *Return to the Plouaret road and bear left; after 2.2km/1.5mi, turn left.*

Chapelle des Sept-Saints

This 18C chapel, surrounded by greenery, is unusual in that it is built in part on top of an imposing dolmen. From the outside, a small door in the south arm of the transept

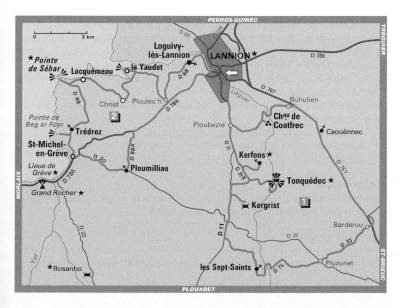

leads under the dolmen which has been turned into a crypt for the cult of the Seven Sleepers of Ephesus. According to legend, seven young Christians walled up in a cave in the 3C woke up 200 years later. Every year, an Islamic-Christian pilgrimage (👣 *see Calendar of events*) is held in this Breton chapel.

▷ *Via Pluzunet and Bardérou you will reach the road to Lannion, then bear left. Drive past Caouënnec-Lanvézéac and continue toward Lannion and at Buhulien bear left in the direction of Ploubezre and 100m/110yd after a farm at Pont-Keriel, turn left onto an unsurfaced path through the woods.*

Château de Coatfrec
There are fine ruins of this large 16C mansion.

▷ *Make for Ploubezre and turn right to Lannion.*

② Towns in the Léguer Estuary

Round-trip of 32km/20mi – 2hr.

▷ *Leave Lannion by Quai du Maréchal-Foch.*

The south bank of the River Léguer is very picturesque, especially at high tide.

Loguivy-lès-Lannion
This town on the outskirts of Lannion clings to the hillside in a pleasant setting. The **church**, nestled in a verdant landscape along the banks of the Léguer, is 15C. A curious outdoor stairway leads to the wall-belfry (1570).
Inside the church, in the chapel to the right of the chancel, there is a 17C wooden **altarpiece** depicting the Adoration of the Three Wise Men with shepherds in Breton costume playing the bagpipes and the bombardon. The fine wooden balustrade in the chancel dates from the same period.
In the cemetery, a granite fountain, dating from 1577, plays beneath yew trees which are several centuries old.

Le Yaudet
This hamlet, in its beautiful setting, was the episcopal seat in the early centuries of our era and was destroyed by the Danes (c 848); it has remains of Roman walls and an interesting **chapel** overlooking the bay. Inside, above the altar, is a curious sculpted panel depicting the Trinity: a recumbent figure of the Virgin with the Infant Jesus at her side; God the Father is sitting in an alcove at the foot of the bed over which hovers a dove symbolising the Holy Spirit.
From the car park, the Corps de Garde footpath leads to a viewpoint, which affords a lovely **view** of the Léguer.

▷ *Return to the centre of Le Yaudet and turn right. At Christ, bear right towards Locquémeau.*

Locquémeau
The town overlooks the beach and the fishing harbour which are reached by a corniche road to the left at the entrance to the town.

Pointe de Séhar★
Leave your car near the port of Locquémeau and make for the point. The **view**★ extends westwards as far as the Pointe de Primel and eastwards to the resort of Trébeurden.

Trédrez

St Yves was Rector of Trédrez from 1284-92. The **church** was completed in 1500 by Philippe Beaumanoir to whom we owe many of the region's churches, with their characteristic wall belfries. Note inside the 14C granite font crowned with a beautifully carved wood canopy (1540).

▶ *Leave Trédrez by the road going towards Kerbiriou and follow the road that leads to the Beg-ar-Forn headland.*

Shortly before the car park there is a good view of the bay and the Lieue de Grève.

▶ *Turn round and at the second junction turn right towards St-Michel-en-Grève.*

St-Michel-en-Grève – 🚻 *ee Côte des BRUYÈRES.*

▶ *Take the road to Lannion on leaving St-Michel-en-Grève, then bear right.*

Ploumilliau

The 17C **church** (*Guided tours during the high season, daily, 2-6pm; off season, apply to M. Maurice L'Escop. ☎ 02 96 35 44 44*) contains, in the south transept, 13 wooden **panels**, carved and polychrome, which illustrate scenes from the Life of Christ (Last Supper, the Passion, the Resurrection). There is also, on the wall opposite the sacristy, a curious portrayal of Ankou (Death), so often mentioned in Breton legend.

▶ *Return to the Morlaix-Lannion road to the N; turn right towards Lannion.*

LOCMARIAQUER★★

POPULATION 1 404
MICHELIN LOCAL MAP 308 N9 – MORBIHAN (56)

The village, which commands the entrance to the Golfe du Morbihan, has retained several important megaliths.

Sights

Ensemble mégalithique de Locmariaquer★★

By the cemetery, take the signposted path to the car park. Kids ◷ Open June to Sept, daily, 10am-7pm (last admission 30min before closing); Apr and May 10am-1pm and 2-6pm; rest of the year 2-5pm. ◷ Closed mid-Dec to mid-Feb. ⊛ High season €5, low season €4. ☎ 02 97 57 37 59.
This group of three megaliths is an important part of a programme of conservation and restoration of megalithic sites.

Grand Menhir brisé

This menhir was probably broken on purpose as long ago as the Neolithic period, when it measured 20m/64ft and weighed almost 350t. It is made of a type of gneiss which can only be found 12km/7.5mi away and an axe carved on one of its sides, which seems to reinforce its symbolic meaning within an important group of megaliths.

Note the massive lintel above the entrance to the tumulus, a covered tomb

G. Targat/MICHELIN

Table des Marchands

The origin of the name of this dolmen has provoked considerable dispute, and experts are not sure whether the dolmen in fact bears the name of the family to which it belonged. It has been restored recently, and its tumulus has been rediscovered. A 7m/23ft corridor leads to a funerary chamber in which the base stele is decorated with crooks arranged symmetrically. The slab which forms the ceiling is in fact part of a large menhir, the two other parts of which can be found at the Tumulus d'Er-Grah, not far from here, and in the Cavin de Gavrinis, 4km/2.5mi from here. This slab features axe and crook motifs and part of a bovine figure.

Tumulus d'Er-Grah

This very elongated monument is situated north of the other megaliths. It is thought that its original length was more than 170m/558ft. The tumulus is currently the object of examination.

Dolmen de Mané-Lud★

It stands surrounded by houses on the right at the entrance to the village. The stones which remain standing inside the chamber are carved.

Dolmen de Mané-Rethual★

In the centre of the village and to the right of the former town hall, take a path which passes by a group of houses and gardens. A long covered alleyway leads to a vast chamber, the supports of which are carved.

TOURIST OFFICE

Locmariaquer,1 rue de la Victoire, ☎ 02 97 57 33 05, www.ot-locmari-aquer.com.

Rent a bike – Station Élan, rte d'Auray, ☎ 02 97 57 32 52.

WHERE TO STAY / EATING OUT

🍴🍴🍴 **Hôtel des 3 Fontaines,** *rte d'Auray,* ☎ *02 97 57 42 70, www.hotel-troisfontaines.com – 18 rooms.* At the entrance of Locmariaquer, a charming establishment with a terrace and a garden. Breakfast €11.

🍴🍴 **Retour de la marée,** *Scarpoche,* ☎ *02 97 57 30 22.* 🕐 *Daily 11am-1am.* Catch-of-the-day, pan-fried squid, locally raised meat dishes cooked just right—a good address to share with your best friends. Fridays, musical nights until 2am or later.

Megalithic Monuments   *5km/3mi*

▶ *From place Évariste-Frick, follow rue Wilson.*

On leaving the village take the road on the right leading to **Kerlud** village, a remarkable group of small farms built in granite. Opposite the last house is the partly hidden **Dolmen de Kerlud.**

▶ *Return to the main road and bear right; beside the beach turn right again.*

Dolmen des Pierres-Plates★

A menhir indicates the entrance to this dolmen. Two chambers are linked by a long alleyway. Remarkable engravings decorate the supports. A terrace affords a fine view of the Pointe de Port-Navalo and the Pointe du Grand-Mont, the Île d'Houat with Belle-Île in the distance, and the Presqu'île de Quiberon.

▶ *Turn round and follow the shoreline as far as the Pointe de Kerpenhir.*

Pointe de Kerpenhir★

Continue past the blockhouse. The point where a granite statue of Our Lady of Kerdro stands protecting sailors (*kerdro* is Breton for safe return), affords a **view**★ onto the Morbihan channel.
The road to the left offers a fine glimpse of the bay.

Tumulus de Mané-er-Hroech★

At Kerpenhir take a path to the left of the road which climbs up to the tumulus. A stairway *(23 steps)* gives access to the funerary chamber and to the dry-stone structure forming the tumulus.

▶ *Return to Locmariaquer.*

LOCRONAN★★

POPULATION 799
MICHELIN LOCAL MAP 308 F6 – FINISTÈRE (29)

The little town once prospered from the manufacturing of sailcloth. Traces of its golden age are to be found in its fine **square**★★, with its granite houses built during the Renaissance, old well, large church and pretty chapel. The hill or mountain of Locronan, which overlooks the town, presents a very unique sight on days devoted to *pardons*, which are known here as *Troménies*.

▶ **Orient Yourself:** East of Douarnenez and Northeast of Quimper.
 **Parking:** You must leave your car (⊜ €3) in the car park outside the village.
🍴 **Don't Miss:** The beautiful main square.
🔥 **Also See:** CORNOUAILLE.

Sights

Place centrale

The main square of Locronan is emblematic of the city. It has been featured in films (*Tess d'Urberville,* for example) for the beauty and authenticity of the granite, Renais-

The buildings on the main square were once the homes of makers and traders of sailcloth

sance townhouses. Listed as a historic monument in 1936, it was formerly inhabited by merchants.

Église St-Ronan and Chapelle du Penity★★

The adjacent and intercommunicating church and chapel form a harmonious ensemble. The 15C church is remarkable for its unity of style and stone vaulting. The decoration of the **pulpit**★ (1707) relates the life of St Ronan, and the 15C **stained-glass window**★ in the apse depicts scenes of the Passion. Among the old statues note that of St Roch (1509). The 16C chapel houses the tomb of St Ronan (the recumbent figure dates from the early 16C and is one of the earliest works in Kersanton granite). Note too a 16C Descent from the Cross in polychrome stone with six figures. The base is decorated with two beautiful **bas-relief sculptures**★, depicting the apparition of the resurrected Jesus to Mary Magdalene and the disciples of Emmaus, and two 15C statues (Christ in Fetters and St Michael weighing souls).
From the cemetery behind the church there is a good view of the church's flat east end.

Chapelle Notre-Dame-de-Bonne-Nouvelle

300m/328yd along rue Moal, which starts from the square and leads down the slope of the ridge. ◔ *Open Easter to All Saints' Day, daily, 10am-7pm.*
With the Calvary and the fountain (1698), this 14C chapel forms a typically Breton scene.

The Troménies

The **Petite Troménie** (◔ *see Calendar of events*) consist of a procession that makes its way to the top of the hill, repeating the walk that St Ronan, a 5C Irish saint, according to tradition, took every day, fasting and barefooted.

The **Grande Troménie**★★ takes place every sixth year on the second and third Sundays in July *(next in 2007)*. Carrying banners, the pilgrims go round the hill (12km/7.5mi), stopping at 12 stations. At the different stations each parish exhibits its saints and reliquaries. The circuit follows the boundary of the former Benedictine priory – built on the site of the sacred forest, the "Nemeton", which served as a natural shrine – founded in the 11C – which was a place of retreat. Hence the name of the pardon *Tro Minihy* or Tour of the Retreat, gallicised as Troménie.

Museum

On the Châteaulin road. 🕐 *Open mid-June to mid-Sept, daily, 10am-7pm; Easter to mid-June and mid-Sept to 1 Nov 10am-noon and 2-6pm; 1 Nov to Easter, 2-6pm.* 🕐 *Closed Jan and Feb.* ⊛ €2. ☎ *02 98 91 70 14.*

The museum houses Quimper faience, sandstone objects, local costumes exhibits relating to the *Troménies (see above)* and to ancient crafts, pictures and engravings by contemporary artists of Locronan and the surrounding area.

Excursions

Montagne de Locronan★

2km/1mi E. 🕐 *Open only during the "Troménies": the "Petites Troménies" are held every year on the 2nd Sun in July; the "Grandes Troménies" are held every six years from the 1st to the 2nd Sun in July.* ☎ *02 98 91 70 93.*

From the top (289m/948ft), crowned by a **chapel** (note the stained-glass windows by Bazaine), you will see a fine **panorama**★ of Douarnenez Bay. On the left are Douarnenez and the Pointe du Leydé; on the right Cap de la Chèvre, the Presqu'île de Crozon, Ménez-Hom and the Monts d'Arrée.

Ste-Anne-la-Palud

8km/4mi NW. Leave Locronan by D 63 to Crozon. After Plonévez-Porzay, turn left. 🕐 *Open Easter to All Saints' Day, daily, 9am-7pm.* ☎ *02 98 92 50 17.*

The 19C **chapel** contains a much-venerated painted granite statue of St Anne dating from 1548. The *pardon* on the last Sunday in August, one of the finest and most picturesque in Brittany, attracts thousands.

On the Saturday at 9pm the torchlit procession progresses along the dune above the chapel.

MANOIR DE L'AUTOMOBILE À LOHÉAC★★

MICHELIN LOCAL MAP 309 K7 - ILLE-ET-VILAINE (35)

This **Motor Museum**, set up in La Courneuve manor house, contains a collection of over 160 cars of all types, ages and nationalities, specialising particularly in private and sports cars.

Visit

Motor Museum

From Lohéac, take D 50 towards Lieuron. 🕐 *Open daily (except Mon), 10am-noon and 2-7pm.* ⊛ €8.50 (children age 10-16 €7). ☎ *02 99 34 02 32.*

The tour begins in the old manor house, taking in a collection of "golden oldies" from the turn of the century, before moving on to an impressive line-up of Alpines (A 210 Le Mans, Coach A 106, Berlinette Tour de France A 108, A 110 GT4, A 310 1600 VE). Further on, there are examples of essentially the whole Lamborghini production (from the 350 GT to the Diablo). Dozens of Maseratis, Ferraris, Porsches and Rolls-Royces rub fenders with Dauphine Renaults, R8s or R12s, Citroëns, Peugeots (convertibles 301-403, from the 1960s and 70s) and Volkswagens.

The next stop on the tour is the **Chapelle des Moteurs** (Engine Chapel), an original display of several vintage engines in an old chapel. Other features of the museum include the reconstructions of a forge, a garage and an old-fashioned filling station fully equipped with tools, materials and authentic equipment connected with vehicle repair and maintenance.

The spacious first floor houses an exhibition of lavish foreign cars known as the *belles étrangères* and at the end of it is a wall of illuminated signs bearing the names of leading manufacturers associated with the motor industry.

The area devoted to miniature models relates the glorious history of the steam engine, illustrated by over 3 000 exhibits.

Espace hippomobile is devoted to some 50 horse-drawn carriages of all types: travelling coaches, omnibus, etc.

To finish your visit, take a seat in the projection room, and imagine yourself behind the wheel.

LORIENT

POPULATION 116 174

MICHELIN LOCAL MAP 308 KB - MORBIHAN (56)

The modern city of Lorient boasts proudly of being the site of 5 ports: the fishing port of Keroman, a military port, with dockyard and submarine base (capacity: 30 submarines), a passenger port, with ships crossing the roadstead and sailing to the Île de Groix, the Kergroise commercial port, which specialises in the importing of animal foodstuffs, and the Kernevel pleasure boat harbour, with a wet dock located in the centre of the city; it is the starting point for transatlantic competition. An annual Interceltic Festival (Festival Interceltique, *see Calendar of events*) is held in Lorient. *6, quai de Rohan, 56100 –* 02 97 21 07 84.

▶ **Orient Yourself:** At the confluence of the RIvers Blavet and Scorff, the port is a well-protected harbour.

 Don't Miss: The great parades and festivities during the Interceltic fesstival, the first two weeks of August: bring your bagpipes!

 Organizing Your Time: Use the *Batobus*, very practical and pleasant "boat-buses" with 6 itineraries to serve you.

Pipers at the Interceltic Festival

R. Mattes/MICHELIN

Kids Especially for Kids: *La Thalassa.*

Mast pond

On your way into Lorient, coming from Lanester, after taking the Pont St-Christophe, skirt the River Scorff and you will see black posts sticking out, particularly striking at low tide. They are probably the remains of the mast pond started in 1826.
The wood, used for naval construction, was plunged into the muddy sand to protect it from rotting and from ship worms.

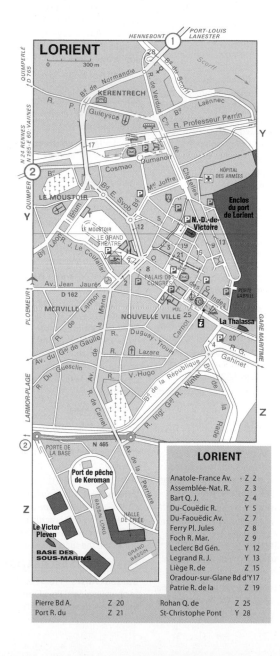

Address Book

GETTING AROUND

On bus – The CTRL (Compagnie des transports de la région lorientaise), ☎ 02 97 21 28 29, www.ctrl.fr, serves 19 villages of Lorient and its surroundings.

On Batobus – The CTRL also offers 6 boat links, very useful to go from one shore to the other of the harbour. Everyday of the year, except for line 5 (Sun only). One way ticket €1.10. Batobus 1: from the quai des Indes (Lorient) to Pen Mané (Locmiquélic), 7mn; Batobus 2: fishing port (Lorient) to the Pointe (Port-Louis), 11mn; Batobus 3: fishing port (Lorient) to Ste-Catherine (Locmiquélic), 6mn; Batobus 4: Le Lohic (Port-Louis) to Gâvres, 3mn; Batobus 5: quai des Indes (Lorient) to the Pointe (Port-Louis), 22mn.

Taxis – Radio Taxis Lorientais, 27 bd de Normandie,☎ 02 97 21 29 29. Taxis verts-Taxico, 1 Place de l'Église, ☎ 06 07 87 95 93 or 02 97 86 81 81.

On bike – 62 km of bicycle paths in Lorient and its surroundings! The rentals can be made at the Tourist Office or at the shop "Transports et Déplacements", gare d'échange, cours de Chazelles, ☎ 02 97 21 28 29.

TOURIST OFFICE

Lorient, Maison de la mer, quai Rohan, ☎ 02 97 21 07 84, www.lorient-tourisme.fr July-Aug: Mon-Sat 9am-7pm, Sun 9-12am; Mon-Sat 9am-12.30pm, 1.30-5pm, Sat 9am-12.30pm.

☺ *For coin ranges, see the Legend on the cover flap.*

WHERE TO STAY

◡◡ **Astoria**, *3 rue Clisson,* ☎ *02 97 21 10 23, www.hotelastoria-lorient.com – 35 rooms,* □ *€7. Functional and redecorated rooms in the town centre. In the top floor, attic rooms in rustic style.*

◡◡ **Central**, *1 rue Cambry,* ☎ *02 97 54 22 19, www.lorient-tourisme.com/central-hotel – 24 rooms,* □ *€6. Nearby the Town Hall, the pedestrian streets and the yachting harbour, the Central offers quiet, comfortable rooms.*

◡◡◨ **Cleria**, *27 bd Maréchal Franchet d'Esperey,* ☎ *02 97 21 04 59, www.hotel-cleria.com – 33 rooms,* □ *€8.50. Bright rooms with contemporary furniture, new bedding and small sparkling bathrooms. You will also enjoy the breakfast, served in the patio.*

EATING OUT

◡ **Crêperie St-Georges**, *14 rue Paul Bert,* ☎ *02 97 64 28 11.* ⏱ *Closed Sun all year and Mon off season.* Big, beautiful wooden tables, copious salads, sweet and savoury crepes.

◡◡ **Victor Hugo**, *36 rue L. Carnot,* ☎ *02 97 64 26 54.* ⏱ *Closed Sun and Mon.* Market cuisine, with an occasional guest of honour: the lobster. Comfortable dining rooms and pleasant fireplace.

◡◡ **Le Jardin gourmand**, *46 rue Jules Simon.* ☎ *02 97 64 17 24.* ⏱ *Closed Sun and Mon.* A beautiful dining room with caramel-coloured furniture and a small terrace at one end. The cuisine is light and delicious! Nice wine list.

◡◡◨ **Le Pic**, *2 bd du Maréchal Franchet d'Esperey,* ☎ *02 97 21 18 29.* Behind an elegant facade, old-fashioned setting and pub atmosphere for a traditional cuisine based on the catch of the day.

◡◡◨ **Le Pécharmant**, *5 rue Carnel,* ☎ *02 97 21 33 86.* ⏱ *Closed Sun, Mon and 3-25 July.* The salmon facade decorated with copper saucepans should not pass unnoticed, but it's for the cuisine, generous and fine, that one should come here. Or, stop in for a glass of wine.

ON THE TOWN

Tavarn Ar Roue Morvan, *17 rue Poissonnière,* ☎ *02 97 21 61 57.* ⏱ *Mon-Sat 11am-1am.* 100% Breton tavern – you may even hear French spoken! Enjoy regional cuisine with Celtic music.

Café du Port, *52 rue du Port,* ☎ *02 97 21 87 41.* ⏱ *Mon-Sat 11am-1am.* Despite its name, this café is actually on a pedestrian street. Breton beers and rum drinks are the specialities.

LEISURE AND RECREATION

Guided cruises – From Lorient, Larmor-Plage and Port-Louis, several themes for the cruises: in the harbour with, in summer, legendary and story-telling nights; on the Blavet with a stop at the market of Hennebont on Thu; and up to Groix. Information and ticket booth at the Tourist Office.

Paddle on the Scorff – **Canoë-Kayak du Scorff**, *base nautique, Bas Pont-Scorff-Cléguer*, ☎ *02 97 32 56 87.* 🕐 *Everyday in July-Aug, Sat off season.* **Aviron du Scorff**, *rue Amiral-Favereau, Lorient*, ☎ *02 97 84 04 96.* All year. Initiation, leisure, rides and challenges.

Yachting – **Centre nautique de Kerguelen**, *parc Océanique, Larmor- Plage*, ☎ *02 97 33 77 78, www.sellor-nautisme. com* Windsurf, diving and sea kayak, all year. Rentals and lessons. **Centre nautique de Port-Louis**, *plage des Grands Sables*, ☎ *02 97 82 18 60.* Sea garden from 4 years old in summer, lessons and rental of catamaran, windsurf, sea kayak.

Diving – **Blue Live**, *rue des Frères Leroy-Quéret, Larmor-Plage*, ☎ *02 97 65 44 69, www.bluelive.net* A team of professionals invites you to discover the sea beds of l'île de Groix and elsewhere.

FESTIVALS
Festival interceltique, *2 rue Paul Bert*, ☎ *02 97 21 24 29, www.festival-interceltique.com, 1st fortnight of Aug.* The big annual gathering of the Celtic cultures attracts hundreds of thousands of spectators and thousands of artists from everywhere.

A Bit of History

The India Company – After the first India Company, founded by Richelieu at Port-Louis, failed, Colbert revived the project in 1664 at Le Havre. But as the Company's ships were too easily captured in the Channel by the British, it was decided to move its headquarters to the Atlantic coast. The choice fell on "vague and vain" plots of land located on the right bank of the Scorff. Soon afterwards, what was to be known as the "Compound of the India Company" was born. Since all maritime activities were focused on India and China, the installations built on that site bore the name *l'Orient* (French for the East). In those days, the arrogant motto of the India Company – *Florebo quocumque ferar* (I shall prosper wherever I go) – was fully justified by the flourishing trade which it exercised. But a new naval war loomed ahead. So Seignelay turned the "Compound" into a royal dockyard patronized by the most famous privateers (Beauchêne, Duguay-Trouin).

In the 18C, under the stimulus of the well-known Scots financier Law, business grew rapidly; 60 years after its foundation, the town already had 18 000 inhabitants. The loss of India brought the Company to ruin, and in 1770 the State took over the port and its equipment. Napoleon turned it into a naval base.

The war years – Lorient was occupied by the Germans on 25 June 1940. From 27 September 1940 the city was subject to bombardments, which intensified as the war raged on, and was destroyed in August 1944. The fighting between the entrenched German garrison and the Americans and locally based Free French Forces which encircled the Lorient "pocket" devastated the surrounding area so that when the townspeople returned on Mya 8, 1945, all that greeted them was a scene of desolation.

Sights

Ancien arsenal
Until 2000, the naval dockyard was located in the former India Company's area: four docks were used for the repair of warships. Abandoned by the navy, the area is being modernised. The Breton television channel Breizh has located its headquarters along quai du Péristyle.

Église Notre-Dame-de-Victoire

Better known to the locals as the church of St-Louis, it stands in place Alsace-Lorraine, which is itself a successful example of modern town planning. The church is built in reinforced concrete and has very plain lines. It is square with a flattened cupola roof and a square tower flanking the façade. The beauty of the church lies in its **interior**★. Little panes of glass, yellow and clear, reflect the outside light into the building from the top of the rotunda and the bays in the lower section consist of brightly coloured splintered glass.

Enclos du Port de Lorient

🕐 *Enter through the "Porte Gabriel". Information on tours available from the Tourist Office:* ☎ *02 97 21 07 84. www.lorient-tourisme.fr*

A tour of the dockyards recalls the heyday of the India Company: the Hotel des Ventes, built by Gabriel in 1740, has been entirely restored in the original style. There are four dry docks designed for battleship repair. The **Tour de la Découverte** (1737), flanked by the Admiralty mills (1677), once served as a watchtower. Climbing its 225 steps is a small price to pay to enjoy the superb **view**★ of the roadstead.

La Thalassa *(Quai de Rohan)*

Kids ♿🕐*Open July-Aug: 9am-7pm; Sep-June: daily (except mornings of Sat-Mon and public hols) 9am-12.30pm and 2-6pm. Last entrance 1hr 30min before closing.* 🕐 *Closed 1 Jan and 25 Dec.* ✒€6.60 (children €5.10). ☎ *02 97 35 13 00. www.sellor. com*

After sailing the seas of the world (nearly 38 times round the globe), this ship, launched in 1960 by Ifremer, is enjoying well-deserved retirement in Lorient. A tour of the three decks gives visitors a good idea of life on board, techniques of navigation, trawler fishing and oceanographic research. The tour continues on land with an exhibit devoted to the fishing industry in Lorient.

Port de pêche de Keroman

👁 *Best seen in the morning when the fishermen return with the day's catch (depending on the tide).* Partly reclaimed from the sea, the port of Keroman is the only French harbour designed and equipped for commercial fishing; it is the leading port in France for the value and variety of fish unloaded. It has two basins set at right angles: the Grand Bassin and the **Bassin Long** (totalling 1 850m/6 070ft of docks). The **Grand Bassin** is sheltered by a jetty 250m/265yd long which is used as a loading and unloading quay for cargo steamers and trawlers. The basin has two other quays, one with a refrigerating and cold-storage plant for the trawlers and fish dealers; and the other, as well as the quay at the east end of the Bassin Long, where the trawlers unload their catch. In front of the quays is the 600m/650yd long **market hall** (*criée*) where auctions are held, and, close behind it, the fish dealers' warehouses which open onto the car park, where lorries destined for the rest of France are loaded. There is also a **slipway** with six bays where trawlers can be dry-docked or repaired.

The port of Keroman sends out ships for all kinds of fishing all the year round. The largest vessels go to sea for a fortnight, especially to the Irish Sea for coalfish and carry their own ice-making equipment (which can make up to 400t a day) to the fishing grounds.

Ancienne base de sous-marins Stosskopf★

Entrance by the "Porte de Keroman". 👁 *Guided tours (1hr15min) July and Aug, school holidays: daily 12.30-5.30pm; rest of the year inquire in advance.* 🕐 *Closed 1 May and 25 Dec.* ✒€6. ☎ *02 97 21 07 84. www.lorient-tourisme.fr.*

The submarine base is named in honour of the Second World War maritime engineer who, by appearing to collaborate with the Germans, was able to keep abreast of activities on the base and inform Allies. When he was discovered, he was executed.

The three blocks were built in record time. The first two (1941) have slots for 13 submarines. The third (1943) has a protected reinforced concrete roof 7.5m/25ft thick.

At the end of the war, the French Navy took over the base for their Atlantic submarine operations, but have since abandoned it for this purpose. The last dry-dock operation took place in December 1996, and the Sirène, the last active submarine, left the base for the Toulon port in February 1997. The Flore is the only ship remaining; it has no military purpose but is kept up for display between blocks one and two. The Navy has progressively turned over the dockyards to the city of Lorient and various projects for the use of the area are underway or being considered.

Driving Tours

The Coast Between Scorff and Laïta
Round-trip of 47km/29mi 2hr 30min.

▶ *Leave Lorient by ② on the town plan passing the Kernével road on the left.*

Larmor-Plage⌂
Looking out over the ocean, across from Port-Louis, Larmor-Plage has lovely, fine, sandy beaches much appreciated by the people of Lorient.

The parish **church**, built in the 12C, was remodelled until the 17C. The 15C porch, uncommonly situated on the north façade because of the prevailing winds, contains statues of the Apostles and above the door a 16C painted wood Christ in Fetters.

The inside contains interesting furnishings: a 17C altarpiece at the high altar and in the north aisle, at the Jews' altar, a Flemish-style 16C altarpiece, which portrays 40 small figures on the slopes of the Calvary; to the right is a 16C polychrome statue of Our Lady of the Angels and in the south aisle a 16C *Pietà* in stone; from the same period are statues of St Efflam and St Barbara, in the chancel.

Every year, on the Sunday before or after 24 June, there is a blessing of the Coureaux (the channel between the Île de Groix and the coast). By tradition, warships leaving Lorient salute the Church of Our Lady of Larmor with three guns, while the priest blesses the ship, has the church bells rung and hoists the flag.

▶ *The old road from Larmor follows the coast fairly closely, passing many small seaside resorts. Note the kaolin quarries on the right. After Kerpape the drive affords extensive views of the coast of Finistère, beyond the cove of Le Pouldu and over to the Île de Groix.*

In the foreground are the coastal inlets in which lie the little ports of Lomener, Perello Kerroch and Le Courégant and the large beach of **Fort-Bloqué** dominated by a fort. Go through **Guidel-Plages** on the Laïta estuary. From Guidel make for the Pont de St-Maurice (6km/4mi there and back) over the Laïta. The **view**★ up the enclosed valley is magnificent.

▶ *From Guidel continue on via Coatermalo and Gostel to Pont-Scorff. At Pont-Scorff take the road towards Quéven.*

Pont-Scorff & Odyssaum
Port-Scorff, on the banks of the river of the same name, is renowned for salmon fishing.

Odyssaum
At Moulin des Princes.
Having spent two winters in the Atlantic, **wild salmon** swim up the Scorff to spawn and then die. An exhibition space devoted to salmon has been laid out inside the mill. It explains the life-cycle of this species and the evolution of fishing techniques. On summer mornings, you may be able to see a salmon trap being raised.

Zoo

🧒 🕐 *Open Apr to mid-July and mid-Aug to end of Sept, daily, 9.30am-6pm; mid-July to mid-Aug, 9.30am-10pm; the rest of the year 9.30am-5pm (last admission 1hr before closing).* 🚌*€12.80 (children €7.80).* ☎ *02 97 32 60 86.*

In a woodland setting on the steep banks of the Scarve, the zoo, which specialises in breeding big cats, contains 13 species from the cat family: lions, tigers, leopards, ocelots, snow leopards, lynxes, pumas etc as well as many other types of animal from all over the world: bears, wolves, llamas, bison, hippopotamuses, web-footed animals, birds and monkeys.

▶ *Return to Lorient passing through Quéven.*

Hennebont

▶ *Leave Lorient by* ① *toward Hennebont.*

Hennebont is a former fortified town on the steep banks of the River Blavet (*good fishing!*). The 16C basilica, **Basilique Notre-Dame-de-Paradis**, has a big **bell-tower**★ and is surmounted by a steeple 65m/213ft high. At the base of the tower is a fine flamboyant porch ornamented with niches leading into the nave, which is lit up by a stained-glass window by Max Ingrand.

Porte Broëc'h and ramparts

This restored gateway, a vestige of the 13C fortifications, was once used as a prison.

▶ *Go through the gate and take a stairway on the left up to the watch-pa*th.

The 15C ramparts completely encircled the old fortified town. **Gardens** are laid out along the walls. 🕐 *Open June-Sep: 10.30am-12.30pm and 1.30-6.30pm; May: Sat-Sun and holidays 2-6pm.* 🚌*€4 (children under 12 no charge).*

Haras

🕐 *Open July-Aug 9am-7pm (horse show in the eveneing); Sep-June: daily (except mornings of Sat-Sun and public hols) 9am-12.30pm and 2-6pm. Last entrance 1hr 30min before closing.* 🕐 *Closed 1 Jan, 25 Dec.* 🚌*€6.60 (children €5.10).* ☎ *02 97 89 40 30.*

Housed in a former abbey, the stud farm breeds a variety of stallions used throughout southern Brittany.

Parc de Kerbihan

Access by rue Nationale and rue Léo-Lagrange (the latter for pedestrians only).

The botanical park, bordered by the St-Gilles stream, is planted with species (all labelled) from the five continents.

Écomusée industrial de Inzinzac-Lochrist

🕐 *Open July-Aug: 10am-6.30pm; Sat-Sun 2-6.30pm; June: 10am-noon and 2-6pm; Sat-Sun and holidays 2-6pm; Sep-May daily except Sat 10am-noon and 2-6pm, Sun 2-6pm. Last entrance 1hr 30 min before closing.* 🕐 *Closed 1 Jan, Easter Mon and 1 May.* 🚌*€4.* ☎ *02 97 36 98 21.*

The open-air museum occupies the site of the Hennebont ironworks, one of Brittany's most important companies, which operated between 1860 and 1966.

Musée des Métallurgistes des Forges d'Hennebont

Located on the RIver Blavet's north bank, int he old research laboratory, the museum is devoted to the history of Brittany's main iron and steel industrial centre (technology, social conditions and family life, the rise of trade unions, historic strikes, etc).

Maison de l'Eau et de l'Hydraulique
Near the dam, in the Hennebont ironworks caretaker's house, is an exhibit devoted
to the canalisation of the River Blavet.

LOUDÉAC

POPULATION 9 371
MICHELIN LOCAL MAP 309 F5 - CÔTES D'ARMOR (22)

This little town, at the heart of Brittany, still holds some large fairs and markets. The region specialises in intensive farming, mainly chicken and pigs, and
the countryside is dotted with large hangars flanked by tall silos. Loudéac is
also well known for its race meetings. With the second-largest **race track** in
Western France, Loudéac remains faithful to a history of horse breeding which
began in the Middle Ages. The Rohan family kept a stud farm of about 100 fine
horses here. Today, tourists can still discover the unspoiled landscapes astride
a traditional mount.

Excursions

Querrien
11km/7mi E along N 164 then left on D 14 beyond Loudéac Forest.
The little village of Querrien was the site of the miraculous apparition of the Virgin
to a young shepherdess in the 17C. There is an annual pilgrimage in the sanctuary
in honour of Our Lady of Infinite Succour (Notre-Dame-de-Toute-Aide).

La Chèze
10km/6mi SE on the D 778.
In this village, which has preserved the vestiges of a 13C castle, is the **Musée régional
des Métiers de Bretagne** (Breton Crafts Regional Museum). The centre evokes
the crafts and trades of yesteryear with reconstituted workshops of the slate roofer,
harness-saddle maker, cartwright, wooden shoemaker and blacksmith.

MÉNEZ-HOM★★★

MICHELIN LOCAL MAP 308 F5 - FINISTÈRE (29)

Ménez-Hom (alt 330m/1 082ft), a detached peak at the west end of the Montagnes Noires, is one of the great Breton viewpoints and a key position commanding the approach to the Presqu'île de Crozon. On 15 August a folklore
festival is held at the summit.

▶ *Travelling from Châtelain towards Crozon along D 887 and D 83, you can see the
mount above you. The final 2km/1mi climb is along a road which branches off,
1.5km/1mi after the Chapelle Ste-Marie-du-Ménez-Hom.*

Sights

Panorama★★★

Viewing table. In clear weather there is a vast panorama. You will see Douarnenez Bay, bounded on the left by the Cornouaille coast as far as the Pointe du Van, and on the right by the coast of the Presqu'île de Crozon as far as Cap de la Chèvre. To the right the view extends to the Pointe de St-Mathieu, the Tas de Pois Rocks, the Pointe de Penhir, Brest and its roadstead, in front of which you will see the Île Longue on the left, the Île Ronde and the Pointe de l'Armorique on the right. The nearer valley – that of the Aulne – follows a fine, winding course, spanned by the suspension bridge at Térénez. In the distance are the Monts d'Arrée, the Montagne St-Michel crowned by its little chapel,

The viewing table on a cold winter day

the Châteaulin Basin, the Montagne de Noires Montagnes, Locronan, Douarnenez and Tréboul.

Go as far as the mark of the Geographical Institute *(Institut géographique)* to get a view of the horizon from all sides.

Chapelle Ste-Marie-du-Ménez-Hom

🕐 *Open April-Sep: 10am-6pm. In the event that it is locked, apply to the Town Hall.*
The chapel stands in a small parish close at the entrance to Presqu'île de Crozon. The close has a very plain rounded doorway, dated 1739, and a Calvary with three crosses rising from separate bases. The chapel, which has a twin-gabled façade, is entered through a doorway beneath the elegant galleried belfry, topped by a cupola which gives an upward sweep to the massive building. Inside, the ornate **altarpieces**★ take up the whole of the east wall, without covering over the window apertures. While both the central altarpiece, with the family and life of the Virgin as its theme, and the north altarpiece, depicting the saints, have figures which are rather heavy and expressionless, the figures of the Apostles on the south altarpiece show life and elegance. The skill with which they were carved marks a step forward in Breton sculpture. The lovely purlins in the north transept, adorned with animals and various scenes, a remarkable St Lawrence and a graceful St Barbara in wood, are also noteworthy.

Trégarvan, Musée de l'École rurale en Bretagne

7km/4.3mi N of Ste-Marie-du-Menez-Hom. 🚸 🕐 *Open July-Aug: 10.30am-7pm; otherwise by appointment.* 🕐*Closed 1 Jan, 1 Nov and 25 Dec.* ➔€4 *(children €2.30).* ☎ *02 98 26 04 72.*
This museum, set up by the parc naturel regional d'Armorique, recreates the atmosphere of an early 20C country schoolhouse. It includes a large classroom and the schoolmaster's living quarters.

MONTAGNES NOIRES★★

MICHELIN LOCAL MAP 308 I/J5 - FINISTÈRE (29 AND MORBIHAN (56)

With the Monts d'Arrée, the Montagnes Noires form what Bretons call the spine of the peninsula. These two little mountain chains, mainly of hard sandstone and quartzite, are not quite alike. The Montagnes Noires are lower (326m/1 043ft as against 384m/1 229ft); their crest is narrower; their slopes are less steep and their heaths are less extensive. The chain's name (*noire* means black) suggests that it was once covered with forest. As in all inland Brittany, the ground became bare with time. Since the end of the last century reafforestation has been going on, and the fir woods, now numerous, once more justify the name of Black Mountains. Quarrying of Breton slate carried out on a large scale in the past, is now concentrated on the eastern end of the chain, in the district of Motreff and Maël-Carhaix.

Driving Tour

From Carhaix-Plouguer *585km/53mi – allow half a day*

Carhaix-Plouguer – 🕭 *See CARHAIX-PLOUGUER.*

▶ *Leave Carhaix-Plouguer west towards Pleyben and after 2.5km/1.5mi turn left.*

The road then enters the picturesque valley of the Hyère.

▶ *At Port-de-Carhaix, after crossing the Nantes-Brest Canal, bear right.*

Some 1.5km/1mi further on, note the **Calvaire de Kerbreudeur** on the left, parts of which are thought to date from the 15C.

St-Hernin
In this place, where Ireland's St Hernin is said to have settled, is a 16C parish close. The church and charnel house were remodelled in the 17C. On the beautiful slender Calvary note St Michael slaying the Dragon.

▶ *Take the road to Moulin-Neuf and bear right on the road Carhaix-Plouguer to Gourin. Old slate quarries can be seen to the right and left.*

Chapelle St-Hervé
Access via a road to the left. This small 16C building with a pierced pinnacle is decorated in the Flamboyant Gothic style. A *pardon* is held on the last Sunday in September.

▶ *Head for Gourin via Minetoul.*

La Trinité-Langonnet
This village possesses a fine Flamboyant-style **church**. The **timbering**★ inside, dated 1568 and decorated with Renaissance designs, shows great craftsmanship and enhances the lofty, well-lit nave. In the richly ornamented chancel, note the carved recesses, corbels and purlins.

Gourin
Once a centre of slate production, Gourin also has white stone quarries and raises horses, cattle and poultry.

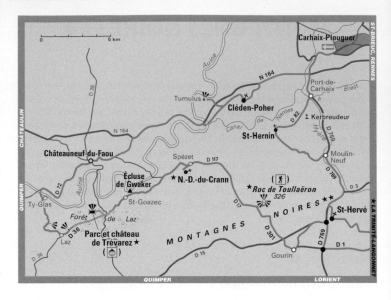

▶ *Follow D 301 N. The road climbs towards the crest of the Montagnes Noires.*

Roc de Toullaëron★

🔺 *5km/3mi from Gourin – allow 30min on foot there and back. Leave your car and take a stony lane bordered with oak trees (⊘ private property, no picnicking) to the right. At the end of the lane, climb up the rocks.*
From the top, which is the highest point in the Montagnes Noires (326m/1043ft), a wide **panorama**★ may be enjoyed in clear weather: to the west is the densely wooded valley of Châteaulin; to the north, the Monts d'Arrée; to the south, in the distance, the Breton plateau slopes gently down to the Atlantic.

▶ *Make for Spézet; on leaving Spézet take the Châteauneuf-du-Faou road, bear left.*

Chapelle Notre-Dame-du-Crann★

🔎 *Guided tours May to Sept, daily, 1.30-6.30pm; rest of the year, apply to M. Unvoas.* ☎ *02 98 93 86 03.*
The chapel, built in 1532, stands on the side of the road in a verdant setting. It contains some remarkable 16C **stained-glass windows**★★.
In the south aisle you will see the window illustrating the legend of St Eligius, who is the patron of farriers. In the south transept are the Death and Coronation of the Virgin. Above the south aisle, is the stained-glass window of St James the Greater, in three bays. The window in the chancel depicts scenes of the Passion in 12 bays.

▶ *Return to Spézet and before entering bear left and after 2km/1mi, left again. At the entrance to St-Goazec, turn right.*

Écluse de Gwaker

This is one of the many locks on the Nantes-Brest Canal. There is a pretty waterfall at the end of the large pool, forming a pleasant setting.

▶ *After St-Goazec, bear right towards Laz. The road climbs into the lovely forest of Laz, which is mostly coniferous.*

Park and Château de Trévarez★

Kids ⏱ *Open July and Aug, daily, 11am-6.30pm; Apr to June and Sept 1-6pm; rest of the year, Wed, Sat-Sun and public hols, 2-5.30pm; Christmas school hols 1.30-5.30pm. ◉€4.30 (children under 11 no charge). ☎ 02 98 26 82 79.*

This 85ha/210 acre forest park is laid out around an imposing neo-Gothic château built in the "Belle Epoque" style. The signposted paths wind their way through the woods, making for a pleasant stroll whatever the season: admire the camellias (April), the azaleas and hydrangeas (July), fuchsias and rhododendrons. A pond, a water garden and several fountains add a refreshing touch. The château terrace offers a **splendid view** of the Châteauneuf-du-Faou region. The former stables, whose original design was extremely modern for their time, have kept their stalls and loose-boxes; these have been converted into a small museum and are used for exhibitions and other educational activities organised throughout the year. This charming outing can be complemented by a train ride.

P. Le Corre/Domaine de Trévarez

Beyond the eccentric façade, the lovely bright gardens of Trévarez

▶ *At Laz, turn right towards Kerohan.*

The picturesque downhill road, hemmed in by rocky ridges, affords a fine view over the Aulne Valley.

▶ *After Ty-Glas, bear right towards Châteauneuf-du-Faou. The road crosses and then follows the Aulne.*

Châteauneuf-du-Faou

This village is built in very pretty surroundings on the slope of a hill overlooking the Aulne. It is an angler's delight with salmon swimming up the Aulne from the sea and also pike. In the church, the baptismal chapel decorated in 1919 with scenes from the life of Christ by **Paul Sérusier** (1865-1927), a painter of the Nabis group, is of interest. A pardon is held on the third Sunday in August at the Chapelle Notre-Dame-des-Portes.

The road from Châteauneuf to Carhaix-Plouguer is charming for the short distance that it follows the Aulne.

▶ *After 1.5km/1mi beyond the confluence with the Nantes-Brest Canal, bear left towards La Roche and then right after some 500m/547yd.*

The road runs past farmyards to a hillock. From the top of the tumulus, there is a fine **view** of a loop of the Aulne.

▶ *Return to the road to Carhaix-Plouguer.*

Cléden-Poher

The village has a fine **parish close**★ dating mainly from the 16C. The 15C-16C church contains interesting altarpieces: three Flemish-style 16C panels at the high altar; the altarpiece of the Rosary (1694) in the south aisle; the altarpiece of the Pentecost

(17C) in the north aisle. Much of the vaulting has preserved its panelling painted in 1750. In the cemetery are an ossuary turned into a chapel with a fine timber roof, a Calvary (1575) and two curious sacristies with keel vaulting.

▶ *Return to Carhaix-Plouguer.*

MONT-ST-MICHEL★★★

POPULATION 72
MICHELIN LOCAL MAP 59 303 C8 - MANCHE (50)

The Mont-St-Michel has been called "the Marvel of the Western World" owing to its island setting, its rich history and the beauty of its architecture; at any season of the year it leaves an indelible impression. The rock and the immensity of nature around it, the Bay with both sand and grassy flats are all parts of a magical whole, which made it among the fist sites to be included on UNESCO's World Heritage List (1979).

As the bay is already partially silted up *(◐ see DOL-DE-BRETAGNE: Marais de Dol)*, the mount is usually to be seen surrounded by huge sand banks which shift with the tides and often reshape the mouths of the neighbouring rivers.

The course of the Cousenon, which used to threaten the dikes and polders with its wandering, has been canalised and the river now flows straight out to sea to the west of the mount. Its former course, northwest from Pontorson, used to mark the frontier between the duchies of Normandy and Brittany.

A Bit of History

Foundation – The abbey's origin goes back to the early 8C, when the Archangel Michael appeared to Aubert, Bishop of Avranches, who founded an oratory on the island, then known as Mont Tombe. In the Carolingian era, the oratory was replaced

Mont-St-Michel

by an abbey and from then until the 16C a series of increasingly splendid buildings, in the Romanesque and then the Gothic styles, succeeded one another on the mount which was subsequently dedicated to the Archangel.
The well fortified abbey was never captured.

Pilgrimages – Even during the Hundred Years War, pilgrims flocked to the mount. The English, who had possession of the area, granted safe conduct to the faithful in return for payment. People of all sorts made the journey: nobles, rich citizens and beggars, who lived on alms and were given free lodging by the monks. Hotels and souvenir shops flourished even then. The pilgrims bought medals bearing the effigy of St Michael and amulets which they filled with sand from the beach.
Of the many thousands of people crossing the bay, some were drowned and others were lost in quicksand. This gave rise to the longer dedication: St Michael in Peril from the Sea.

Decline – In the 17C, the Maurists, monks from St Maur, were made responsible for reforming the monastery. They made only deceptive architectural changes, tinkering with the stonework. Used as a local facility before the Revolution, the abbey suffered further when it became a national prison in 1811 and took in political prisoners including Barbés and Blanqui. In 1874, the abbey and the ramparts passed into the care of the Historic Monuments Department (Service des Monuments Historiques). Since 1969 a few monks have again been in residence, conducting services in the abbey church.

Stages in the abbey's construction – The construction is an amazing achievemnt. The blocks of granite were transported from the Îles Chausey or from Brittany and

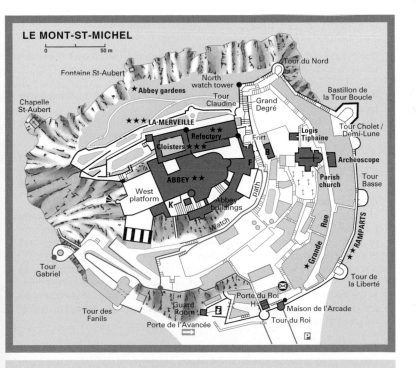

LE MONT-ST-MICHEL

"La Truie-qui-file" old house......**B**   Guard room or Gatehouse............**F**   "Le Saut Gautier" terrace....**K**

277

The Movement of the Tides

The movement of the tides in the bay is very great and the difference in sea level between high and low water can be over 12m/40ft, the highest in France. As the sea bed is flat, the sea retreats a long way exposing 15km/9mi of sand. The tide comes in very rapidly, not quite at the speed of a galloping horse, as has been said, but of a person walking at a brisk pace. This phenomenon, which is aggravated by numerous currents, can spell danger for the unwary.

hoisted up to the foot of the building. As the crest of the hill was very narrow, the foundations had to be built up from the lower slopes.

Romanesque Abbey – 11C-12C. Between 1017 and 1144 a church was built on the top of the mount. The previous Carolingian building was incorporated as a crypt —Our Lady Underground (Notre-Dame-sous-Terre)—to support the platform on which the last three bays of the Romanesque nave were built. Other crypts were constructed to support the transepts and the chancel which projected beyond the natural rock.

The conventual buildings were constructed on the west face and on either side of the nave. The entrance to the abbey faced west.

Gothic Abbey – 13C-16C. This period saw the construction of::
♦   the magnificent Merveille buildings (1211-28) on the north side of the church, used by the monks and pilgrims and for the reception of important guests;
♦   the abbatial buildings (13C-15C) on the south side comprising the administrative offices, the abbot's lodging and the garrison's quarters;
♦   the fort and the outer defences (14C) on the east side, which protected the entrance, moved to this side of the mount.

The chancel of the Romanesque church had collapsed and was rebuilt more magnificently in the Flamboyant Gothic style (1446-1521) above a new crypt.

Alterations – 18C-19C. In 1780 the last three bays of the nave and the Romanesque façade were demolished.

The present bell-tower (1897) is surmounted by a beautiful spire which rises to 157m/515ft and culminates in a statue of St Michael (1879) by Emmanuel Frémiet.

The Town

Outer Defences

The Outer Gate is the only breach in the ramparts and opens into the first fortified courtyard. On the left stands the **Citizens' Guard-room** (16C) which presently houses the tourist office; on the right are the "Michelettes", English mortars captured in a sortie during the Hundred Years War.

A second gate leads into a second courtyard. The third gate (15C), complete with machicolations and portcullis, is called the **King's Gate** because it was the lodging of the token contingent maintained on the mount by the king in assertion of his rights; it opens into the Grande-Rue where the abbot's soldiers lodged in the fine arcaded house (right).

Grande-Rue★

This picturesque narrow street climbs steeply between old (15C-16C) houses, several of which have retained their original name – **Logis Saint-Etienne, Vieux logis, Sirène, Truie qui file** – and ends in a flight of steps. In summer it is lively and crowded with restaurants and the stalls of souvenir merchants, as it was in the Middle Ages at the height of the most fervent pilgrimages.

Ramparts★★
These are 13C-15C. The sentry walk offers fine views of the bay; from the North Tower the Tombelaine Rock, which Philippe Auguste had fortified, is clearly visible.

Abbey Gardens★
🕒 *Open to the public in summer only (ask at the abbey entrance).*
A pleasant place for a stroll with a view of the west side of the mount and the Chapelle St Aubert.

Archéoscope
🕒 *Open early Feb to mid-Nov, 9am-6pm (15min show, last admission 5.30pm).* 🎫 €7 *(€4.50 child).* ☎ *02 33 48 09 37.*
This magical mystery tour takes you back in time to the mount's origins. The seismic phenomenon of Scissy Forest, the Archangel Michael's appearance before Bishop Aubert, the different stages of the mount's construction and its architectural splendour are all explained by sophisticated special effects coordinated by a computer: models emerge out of water, slides flash on screens and the whole show is accompanied by light and sound effects.

Église paroissiale St-Pierre
The building, which dates from the 11C, has been much altered. The apse spans a narrow street. The parish church contains a Crucifix and other furnishings from the abbey; the chapel in the south aisle contains a statue of St Michael covered in silver; in the chapel to the right of the altar there is a 15C statue of the Virgin and from the gallery hang numerous pilgrim banners.

Logis Tiphaine
🕒 *Open July and Aug, daily, 9.30am-10pm or 11pm; Feb school hols to June, Sept to mid-Nov, Christmas school hols, daily 9.30-6pm; school hols and public hols, 9am-7pm.* 🎫€7. ☎ *02 33 60 23 34.*
When Du Guesclin was captain of the mount, he had this house built (1365) for his wife, Tiphaine Raguenel, an attractive and educated woman from Dinan, while he went off to the wars in Spain: the Constable's room (tester bed, chest), dining room (six-door sideboard, chimney bearing the arms of Du Guesclin, 17C copperware) and Tiphaine's room (cupboard, tester bed, wax figure).

St Michael's Mount, Cornwall

In the 4C BC ships came from the Mediterranean to the **Island of Ictis,** as they named it, to trade in tin, copper and gold; in AD 495, according to Cornish legend, fishermen saw St Michael standing on a westerly ledge of the granite rock which rises high out of the sea, whereupon the island became a place of pilgrimage. By the 8C, it is said, a Celtic monastery had been founded upon it which endured until the 11C.

In AD 708 in France, St Michael appeared three times in a vision to Bishop Aubert of Avranches, who then built an oratory to the saint on the island from then known as Mont-St-Michel. By the time of the Battle of Hastings, the oratory in France had developed into an important Benedictine community to which St Michael's Mount passed as a dependency. The English house, always modest by comparison with the French monastery, was ultimately appropriated during the course of the Hundred Years War by Henry V as alien property and was finally suppressed in 1535.

The Abbey★★★

🕓 *Open May to Sept, daily, 9am-5.30pm; rest of the year 9.30am-4.30pm (5pm during school hols). Guided tours also available at the same dates and times.* 🕓 *Closed 1 Jan, 1 May, 1 and 11 Nov, and 25 Dec. ∞€7 (guided tour included), ∞€10 (visit-conference by appointment):* ☎ *02 33 60 14 14.*

The tour of the abbey does not go from building to building nor from period to period but from floor to floor through a maze of corridors and stairs.

Outer Defences of the Abbey

A flight of steps, the Grand Degré, once cut off by a swing door, leads up to the abbey. At the top on the right is the entrance to the gardens; more steps lead up to the ramparts.

Through the arch of an old door is a fortified courtyard overlooked by the fort, which consists of two tall towers shaped like mortars standing on their breeches and linked by machicolations. Even this military structure shows the builder's artistic sense: the wall is attractively constructed of alternate courses of pink and grey granite. Beneath a pointed barrel vault, a steep and ill-lit staircase, known as the Pit Steps (Escalier du Gouffre), leads down to the beautiful door which opens into the Guard-room, also called the Gatehouse (Porterie).

Omelette de la Mère Poulard

Annette Boutiaut was born in Nevers in 1851. She was employed as a lady's maid by the architect Édouard Corroyer, a disciple of Viollet-le-Duc, who was commissioned by the Monuments Historiques (a State-run organisation) to restore Mont-St-Michel Abbey. Annette followed her employers there and met the son of a local baker. They married and took over the running of the St-Michel Tête d'Or Hotel. At that time (around 1875), the causeway had not been built yet so that tourists and pilgrims reached Mont-St-Michel on foot, on horseback or aboard a *maringotte* (a small two-wheeled horse-drawn cart), tide permitting. They were usually very hungry and could not bear to wait for food to be prepared. Annette knew that a good innkeeper should not be taken unawares. She therefore always had eggs in store and quickly beat up an omelette for her guests while they waited for more substantial dishes. Her welcome and the quality of the food she served gradu-

ally brought her fame. When Annette Poulard died in 1931, food critics speculated on the secret recipe of the omelette. Some talked about fresh cream, specially selected eggs and butter, others argued it was all due to fast cooking; Annette herself explained in a letter dated 1922: "I break the eggs in a bowl, I beat them up well, I put a nice knob of butter in the frying pan, I throw the eggs in and stir continuously."

Curnonsky (1872-1956), the "Prince of gourmets", said that the secret lay in the recipe of Dr Rouget, the hero of Balzac's *La Rabouilleuse,* who beat up the yolks and whites separately before mixing them in the frying pan!

G. Targat/MICHELIN

Guard-room or Gatehouse

This hall was the focal point of the abbey. Poor pilgrims passed through on their way from the Merveille Court to the Almonry. The abbot's visitors and the faithful making for the church used the Abbey Steps.

Abbey Steps

An impressive flight of 90 steps rises between the abbatial buildings (left) and the abbey church (right); it is spanned by a fortified bridge (15C). The stairs stop outside the south door of the church on a terrace called the Gautier Leap (Saut Gautier) after a prisoner who is supposed to have hurled himself over the edge. The tour starts here.

The **West Platform** is a spacious terrace, which was created by the demolition of the last three bays of the church, providing an extensive **view**★ of the bay of Mont-St-Michel.

Church★★

The exterior of the church, particularly the east end with its buttresses, flying buttresses, bell turrets and balustrades, is a masterpiece of light and graceful architecture. The interior reveals the marked contrast between the severe and sombre Romanesque nave and the elegant and luminous Gothic chancel.

The church is built on three crypts which are visited during the tour.

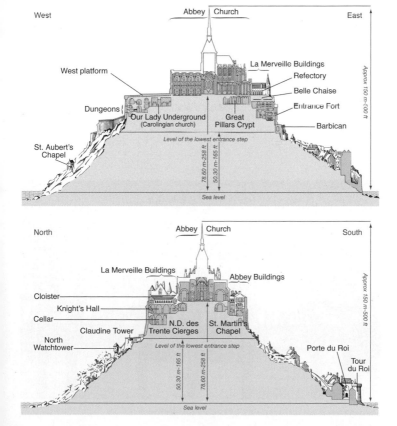

La Merveille★★★

The name, which means "The Marvel," applies to the superb Gothic buildings on the north face of the mount. The eastern block, the first to be built between 1211 and 1218, comprises from top to bottom, the Refectory, the Guests' Hall and the Almonry; the western block, built between 1218 and 1228, consists of the cloisters, the Knights' Hall and the cellar.

From the outside the buildings look like a fortress although their religious vocation is suggested by the dignity and purity of their line. The interior is a perfect example of the evolution of the Gothic style, from a simplicity which is almost Romanesque in the lower halls, through the elegance of the Guests' Hall, the majesty of the Knights' Hall and the mysterious luminosity of the Refectory, to the cloisters which are a masterpiece of delicacy and refinement. The top floor comprises the cloisters and the Refectory.

Cloisters★★★

The cloisters seem to be suspended between the sea and the sky. The gallery arcades display heavily undercut **sculpture** of foliage ornamented with the occasional animal or human figure (particularly human heads); there are also a few religious symbols. The double row of arches rests on delightful slim single columns arranged in quincunx to enhance the impression of lightness. The different colours of the various materials add to the overall charm. The *lavatorium* (lavabo), on the right of the entrance, recalls the ceremonial "washing of the feet" which took place every Thursday.

Refectory★★

The effect is mysterious; the chamber is full of light although it appears to have only two windows in the end wall. To admit so much light without weakening the solid side walls which support the wooden roof and are lined with a row of slim niches, the architect introduced a very narrow aperture high up in each recess. The vaulted ceiling is panelled with wood and the acoustics are excellent.

Old Romanesque Abbey

The ribbed vaulting of this former abbey marks the transition between Romanesque and Gothic. The tour includes the **Monk's Walk** (Promenoir des Moines) and part of the old dormitory.

G. Targat/MICHELIN

The graceful arcades are supported by elegant colonnettes

Address Book

TOURIST OFFICES

Mont-St-Michel, corps de garde des Bourgeois, through the main doors and on the left, ☎ 02 33 60 14 30; www.ot-montsaintmichel.com. ◷ Open Jul-Aug: 9am-7pm; shorter hours off season. ◷ Closed 1 Jan and 25 Dec.

Pontorson, Place de l'Hôtel de Ville, ☎ 02 33 60 20 65, www.mont-saint-michel-baie.com. ◷ Open Jul-Aug: Mon-Fri 9am (10am Sat)-6.30pm, Sun 10-12am; shorter hours off season.

♿ *For coin ranges, see the Legend on the cover flap.*

WHERE TO STAY

MONT-ST-MICHEL

⊜⊜ **Le St-Michel**, *Grande Rue*, ☎ 02 33 60 14 37 – 6rm. *Reception at the restaurant.* ◷ *Closed 2pm-6pm.* Located near the church these rooms are simple and functional with two rooms boasting views over the bay.

⊜⊜⊟ **Le Du Guesclin**, *Grande Rue*, ☎ 02 33 60 14 10 – 10rm. ◷ *Closed 1 Nov to end-Mar.* The comfortable and brightly coloured rooms of this hotel have views over the sea or the street. Ask for the sought after third floor for the best place to rest your weary body. Breakfast €8.

⊜⊜⊟ **Le Mouton Blanc,** *Grande Rue*, ☎ 02 33 60 14 08 – 15rm, ⚏ €7.50. Half-timbering and stained glass windows create a mediaeval atmosphere in the rooms of the main building.

NEARBY

⊜⊜ **Ferme St-Joseph**, *polders St-Joseph*, ☎ 02 33 60 09 04, www.chez.com/fermesaintjoseph – 5rm Wonderful views over the Mont, a copious breakfast with home-grown ingredients and great value at this working farm. The kitchen area is at the disposal of the guests; bike rental (€5/day).

⊜⊜ **Chambres d'hôte La Bourdatière**, *Beauvoir, follow the arrows between the town hall and the church*, ☎ 02 33 68 11 17 – 4rm. The owner of this old farm offers a warm welcome and nicely renovated rustic rooms (2-5 people). Reservations required.

⊜⊜⊟ **Le Petit Manoir**, *21 rue de la Pierre du Tertre, Servon, follow the arrows on the D 113*, ☎ 02 33 60 03 44 – 5rm ♿ Antique beds and views of the garden or Mont St. Michel in elegant rooms.

⊜⊜⊟⊟ **Hôtel Montgoméry**, *13 rue du Couesnon, Pontorson*, ☎ 02 33 60 00 09, www.hotel-mont gomery.com – 32rm, ⚏ €10, ✕ Whether you choose utilitarian or luxurious, the accommodations at this beautiful Renaissance establishment, formerly the property of the duke of Montgomery, are designed to fit all budgets.

EATING OUT

MONT-ST-MICHEL

⊜ **La Sirène**, *Grande Rue*, ☎ 02 33 60 08 60. Admire 14C architecture while you delve into a modern-day crêpe.

⊜⊜ **Le Chapeau Rouge**, *Grande Rue*, ☎ 02 33 60 14 29. Despite its touristy feel, the restaurant and its mediaeval setting, warm reception and good food for the price make for a fun evening.

⊜⊜ **Le Mouton Blanc**. Enjoy a view of the bay and a lunch of crepes and galettes on the terrace located on the ramparts.

⊜⊜⊟ **La Mère Poulard**, *Grande Rue*, ☎ 02 33 89 68 58. Don't miss the spectacle of delicious omelettes prepared out in the open over a wood fire. The traditional cuisine is complemented by the rustic and cosy setting.

NEARBY

⊜⊜ **Auberge de la Baie**, *La Rive, Ardevon*, ☎ 02 33 68 26 70. ◷ *Closed Wed (except Jul-Aug and Nov to mid-Feb.* This small and welcoming hostelry serves regional cuisine at reasonable prices.

RECREATION

🐎 Crossing the bay of Mont-St-Michel on foot or horseback to experience the big tides is unforgettable, but dangerous and should never be attempted without an authorized guide (list of recommended guides at the Tourist Offices Mont-St-Michel and Pontorson).

FESTIVALS

Several festivals take place around **St-Michel** (29 Sep), the most popular being the classical music concerts in the abbey. The Pilgrimage across the bay takes place the last Sun of Jul.

Returning Mont-St-Michel to the Sea

Mont St-Michel has been silting up for several decades. Every year, the sea deposits tons of sediment in the bay. In part, this can be blamed on mankind, since between the mid-19C and 1969 a number of regional building initiatives were taken that accelerated the formation of polders (canalisation of the River Couesnon, building of a dike then a dam). In 1995, a joint project was commissioned by the State and local authorities, intended to return the Mount to the sea. Ideally, this would make it possible to replace the dike by a footbridge under which cross-currents could once again flow between the mainland and the island. It would also help restore the scouring action of the coastal rivers and streams.

Grande Roue

This huge wheel brings back the days in which the abbey served as a prison. Operated by five to six prisoners who would tread inside it, the wheel was used for hoisting provisions and pieces of equipment.

Crypts

The chancel and transepts of the church are supported by three undercrofts or crypts; the most impressive is the **Crypte des Gros Piliers**★ (Great Pillared Crypt) with its 10 pillars 5m/16ft round, sculpted in granite coming from the Îles Chausey.

Guests' Hall★

Here the Abbot received royalty (Louis IX, Louis XI, François I) and other important visitors. The hall, which is 35m/115ft long, has a Gothic ceiling supported on a central row of slim columns; the effect is graceful and elegant.

At one time it was divided down the middle by a huge curtain of tapestries; on one side were the kitchen quarters (two chimneys) and on the other the great dining hall (one chimney). One can easily imagine the opulence of the banquets held in the Guests' Hall.

Knights' Hall★

The name of this hall may refer to the military order of St Michael which was founded in 1469 by Louis XI with the abbey as its seat.

The hall is vast and majestic (26 x 18m/85 x 58ft) and divided into four sections by three rows of stout columns. Functionally, the hall was the monks' workroom, where they illuminated manuscripts, and was heated by two great chimneys.

Cellar

This was the storeroom; it was divided in three by two rows of square pillars supporting the groined vaulting.

Almonry

This is a Gothic room with a Romanesque vault supported on a row of columns.

Baie du Mont-St-Michel★★

The coastline extands 100m/62mi around the bay, which has been on UNESCO's World Heritage List since 1979. Islands, cliffs, beaches and dunes form a succession of natural areas with a wealth of fauna and flora.

🔼 The coastal footpath provides wonderful views of the Mont and is a pleasant ramble across polders and grassland.

Le Vivier-sur-Mer

The miles of wooden posts that you see in the bay and the curious aluminium boats on wheels that roam around them are sure signs of mussel beds. To learn more about how mussels are collected and more generally about the ecology of the bay, visit the **Maison de la baie.** ⏱ *Open July-Aug 9am-12.30pm and 2-6.30pm, Sun 2-6.30pm; rest of the year: daily except Sun and holidays 9am-12.30pm and 2-5.30pm.* ⏱ *Closed 1 Jan, 25 Dec.* €2.50. ☎ *02 99 48 84 38. www.maison-baie.com.*

There is a also small train, the **Mytili-mobile** (☎ *02 99 48 84 38 – advance booking required),* that will take you through the labyrinth of mussel posts on a two-hour tour.

Cherrueix

The windmills along the coast here have mostly lost their sails, but the beaches provide are lively with sand-sailers who make the most out of wind-power on the long flat stretches of sand.

The town holds a garlic festival in July, and you will find garlic in various guises for sale in local shops.

For more information on touring the area around the Mont St-Michel, 🚶 *see The Michelin Green Guide Normandy.*

GOLFE DU MORBIHAN★★

MICHELIN LOCAL MAP 308 N/O9 - MORBIHAN (56)

The Morhiban Gulf, an inland sea dotted with islands, offers some of the most unusual scenery in Brittany. It has the most delicate light effects, and its sunsets are unforgettable. A visit, especially by boat, is essential.

A Bit of History

In 1C BC the Veneti – after whom Vannes is named – lived around the Golfe du Morbihan. They were the most powerful tribe in Armor and when Caesar decided to conquer the peninsula he aimed his main effort at them. It was a stiff task, for the Veneti were fine sailors and had a fleet which made it useless to attack them by land. The decisive struggle, therefore, had to be waged afloat. The Roman leader had a large number of galleys, built and assembled at the mouth of the Loire which were under the command of his lieutenant, Brutus.

The encounter, which took place before Port-Navalo, is said to have been watched by Caesar from the top of the Tumulus de Tumiac. On the other hand, geologists declare that the gulf did not exist at the time of the Gallic War. In all events, it is certain that the battle took place off the southeast coast of Brittany.

The Gauls put to sea with 220 large sailing ships, with high, strong hulls. The Romans opposed them with their large flat barges, propelled by oarsmen. The total and unexpected victory of Brutus was due to several causes: the sea was smooth and this favoured the galleys, which could not face bad weather; moreover, the wind dropped completely during the battle, becalming the Veneti in their sailing ships. Finally the Romans had sickles tied to long poles. When a galley drew alongside an enemy sailing ship, an agile sailor heaved the sickle into its rigging. The galley rowed on at full speed, the rope drew taut and the blade cut the rigging; mast and sails came tumbling down. Two or three galleys then attacked the ship and boarded it.

After this victory Caesar occupied the country of the Veneti and made them pay dearly for their resistance. All the members of their Senate were put to death, and the people were sold into slavery.

Geographical Notes

Mor-bihan means "little sea", while *Mor-braz* means "great sea" or ocean. This gulf, which is about 20km/12mi wide and 15km/9mi deep from the sea to the inner shore, was made by a comparatively recent settling of the land. The sea spread widely over land already despoiled by river erosion leaving inlets and estuaries which run far into the interior, and innumerable islands which give the Morbihan its special character. The River Vannes and River Auray form the two largest estuaries. About 40 islands are privately owned and inhabited; the largest are the Île d'Arz and the Île aux Moines, both communes. The gulf is tidal; at high tide the sea sparkles everywhere around the low, flat and often wooded islands; at low tide, great mud-banks lie between the remaining channels. A narrow channel, before Port-Navalo permits passage both at high and low tide.

Morbihan is thronged with boats fishing between the islands, as well as with pleasure boats and oyster barges using Auray and the port of Vannes. There are many oyster beds in the rivers and along the islands.

The Gulf by Boat★★★

The best way to see the gulf is by boat. About 40 islands are privately owned and inhabited; the largest are Île d'Arz and Île aux Moines, both *communes*.

Île d'Arz
The island, 3.5km/2mi long, has several megalithic monuments. A footpath runs along the coast, right round the island.

Île aux Moines★
Departures every 30 min (time: 5 min) in July and Aug, 7am-10pm; rest of the year, 7am-7.30pm. €4 there and back. ☎ 02 97 57 23 24.
This former monastic fief is the largest of the Morbihan Islands (7km/4mi long) and the most populous. It is a particularly quiet and restful seaside resort where mimosas and camellias grow among palm trees, lemon and orange trees. Its woods have poetic names: Bois des Soupirs (Wood of Sighs), Bois d'Amour (Wood of Love), Bois des Regrets (Wood of Regrets). The beauty of the island women, often sung by Breton poets, is no doubt responsible for these gallantries.

Abélard

A love story with his brilliant student, Héloïse, ended tragically when her outraged family had Abélard emasculated. The learned philosopher tried to find peace in this Breton solitude. His disillusion was quick and cruel: "I live", he wrote to Héloïse, "in a wild country whose language I find strange and horrible; I see only savages; I take my walks on the inaccessible shores of a rough sea; my monks have only one rule, which is to have none at all. I should like you to see my house; you would never take it for an abbey; the only decorations on the doors are the footmarks of various animals—hinds, wolves, bears, wild boars—or the hideous remains of owls. Every day brings new dangers; I always seem to see a sword hanging over my head."

However, the monks used poison, not a sword, to get rid of their abbot. It was a wonder he survived and managed to escape through a secret passage in 1132.

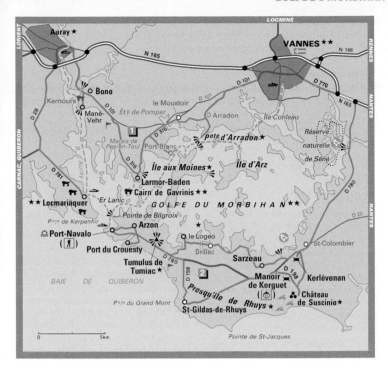

There are several sights worth visiting: the town with its picturesque alleyways; from Pointe du Trech, north of the island, there is a good view of Pointe d'Arradon and the gulf – note the odd-looking Calvary, its base composed of different levels and with stairs on its right side; southwards are the Boglieux and Penhap dolmens; and Pointe de Brouël, east of the island, affords a view of the Île d'Arz.

The Shores of the Gulf★

1 From Vannes to Locmariaquer

49km/30mi – 3hr 30min

Vannes★★ – *2hr 30min.* 🕭 *See VANNES.*

▷ *Leave Vannes on D 101. After 5km/3mi bear left towards Pointe d'Arradon. The road skirts Arradon.*

Pointe d'Arradon★
Turn left towards Cale de la Carrière. From here there is a very typical **view**★ of the Golfe du Morbihan in which you can distinguish, from left to right: the Îles de Logoden; in the distance, the Île d'Arz; then the Île d'Holavre, which is rocky and the Île aux Moines. To reach the point take the path bordering the rocks, behind the hotel.

▷ *Turn round and go to Le Moustoir and bear left.*

At the place called **Moulin de Pomper** note on the left the old tidal power mill (🕭 *see Vallée de la RANCE*).

287

Larmor-Baden

A little fishing port and large oyster-farming centre. From the port there is a fine view of the other islands and the entrance to the gulf.

Cairn de Gavrinis★★

During the visit, you will be able to glimpse lovely views of the River Auray. The Gavrinis Tumulus is the most interesting megalithic monument in Brittany. It is situated on the

Address Book

♦ *For coin ranges, see the Legend on the cover flap.*

WHERE TO STAY

⌒ **Vacation village Île de Berder** – *56870 Île de Berder* – ☎ *02 97 57 03 74* – ◯ *closed Nov-Feb* ⌐ *90 rooms, full board.* Comforts are very modest (shared sanitary facilities) at this former convent, situated on a 57-acre island. The conviviality, calm and events organised in the summer, however, will make you quickly forget the spartan accommodation. Boarding only.

⌒⌒ **Kerdelan** – *56870 Larmor-Baden, Locqueltas, 2km/1mi along the road to Vannes* – ☎ *02 97 57 05 85* – ◯ *closed 15 July-30 Aug* –⌐ *4 rooms.* In a beautiful park facing a golf course and the Île aux Moines, this white villa is especially for those who delight in luxurious idleness! All the rooms open onto a terrace, and the library, billiard room, and salon create a true holiday ambience.

⌒ **Glann Ar Mor** – *27 rue des Fontaines, 56640 Port-Navalo* – ☎ *02 97 53 88 30* – *8 rooms,* ⌷ *€6.50.* A nice establishment near the golf course. The restaurant has marine accents, and the white rooms have been simply renovated. Full or half-board in-season.

⌒⌒⌒⌒ **Hôtel Miramar** – *56640 Port du Crouesty* – ☎ *02 97 67 68 00* – ◯ *closed 29 Nov-26 Dec* – ☐ – *120 rooms* The imposing white façade of this beautiful hotel looks like a cruise liner. Gangways and rails on the outside, nice wood furniture and bay windows inside invite you into a dream-world.

⌒⌒⌒⌒ **Résidence Pierre et Vacances** – *56640 Port du Crouesty* – ☎ *02 97 53 85 35* – ◯ *closed 15 Nov-19 Dec and 6 Jan-6 Feb* – *350 apartments, suitable for 4/5 persons.* Well situated between the pleasure port and the ocean, this modern village rents apartments that are functional, if slightly lacking in charm. Services specially adapted for families. Private swimming pools and thalassotherapy close by.

EATING OUT

⌒⌒ **Grand Largue** – *At the landing-stage, 56640 Port-Navalo* – ☎ *02 97 53 71 58* – ◯ *closed 13 Nov-20-Dec, 3 Jan-7 Feb, Mon lunch in summer, Mon evening and Tues Sept-June.* Located at the end of the wharf, this restaurant looks out over the sea. Surround yourself by hortensias on the terrace or amid the dainty, flowered decor of the interior.

⌒⌒ **San Francisco** – *At the port, 56780 Île aux Moines* – ☎ *02 97 26 31 52* – ◯ *closed 15 Nov-24 Mar.* The stone-walled dining room and covered terrace, with a beautiful view of the port, make this hotel worth a visit. Two of its rooms also offer beautiful views.

SPORTS

Discover the gulf in a kayak – *Base nautique Varec'h, in Baden,* ☎ *02 97 57 16 16.* For beginners or experienced practitioners. Outings with a monitor are available in July and August.

Swimming – There are numerous small beaches on the gulf, notably on the Île aux Moines. The pretty beach at Suscinio (near its château), however, has two advantages: it is 3km/2mi long, and although the water may be cooler than in the gulf, it is also much clearer.

MARKETS

At Port du Crouesty, every Monday morning in the summer. At Port-Navalo, Tuesday and Friday mornings. At Sarzeau, Thursday mornings, as well as a market-fair on the third Wednesday of each month.

island of Gavrinis, at the mouth of the Golfe du Morbihan, south of Larmor-Baden, from which it can be reached. The tumulus – 6m/20ft high and 50m/164ft around, is made of stones piled on a hillock. It was discovered in 1832 and comprises a covered gallery 14m/46ft long with nine tables held up by 23 carved supports; the funeral chamber, probably a royal tomb (2.50m/8ft on one side), with a ceiling made of a single granite slab, resting on supports is also covered with carvings.

From the top of the tumulus there is a wide view of the Golfe du Morbihan.

On the tiny island of **Er Lanic,** a little south of Gavrinis, are two tangent circles of menhirs (cromlechs) in the form of a figure eight, half of which is submerged. This gives evidence of the subsidence of the soil which created the gulf in prehistoric times. At low tide the menhirs reappear.

Le Bono

As you leave **Kernours**, on the right in a small pine forest is a right-angled dolmen. On this same road continue to **Mané-Verh** which offers glimpses of the River Auray.

▶ *Go back to Le Bono.*

From the new bridge is a picturesque **view**★ of Bono, its river and harbour and the old suspension bridge. You will notice piles of whitewashed tiles used to collect oyster spat (& *see CANCALE).*

Auray★ – & *See AURAY.*

▶ *Leave Auray by ② on the town plan, then after 8km/5mi bear left.*

The road skirts megalithic monuments.

Locmariaquer★★ – & *See LOCMARIAQUER.*

② From Vannes to Port-Navalo and Back

79km/49mi – about 4hr – local map right

Vannes★★ – *2hr 30min.* & *See VANNES.*

▶ *Leave Vannes on the Nantes road on the town plan. After St-Léonard, turn right.*

The road runs along the east bank of the bay; there are several viewpoints.

Presqu'île de Rhuys★

At St-Colombier you enter the peninsula, which encloses the Golfe du Morbihan to the south. Its flora is reminiscent of that of the south of France.

Sarzeau

Birthplace of **Lesage** (1668-1747), satirical dramatist and author of *Turcaret* and *Gil Blas*. On the small square, to the right of the church, stand two lovely Renaissance houses.

▶ *From Sarzeau go towards Brillac, the road follows the coast for some distance.*

Le Logeo

A pretty little port sheltered by the Gouihan and Stibiden Islands.

▶ *Go as far as Le Net and bear right.*

Tumulus de Tumiac★

15min on foot. Leave your car in the car park and take a dirt track to the right. From the top of the tumulus there is an extensive **view**★ of the gulf, Quiberon Bay and the islands. This was the observatory from which Caesar is supposed to have watched the naval battle agains the Veneti.

Arzon

In obedience to a vow made to St Anne in 1673, during the war with Holland, the sailors of Arzon march in the procession of Ste-Anne-d'Auray every year on Whit Monday. Two stained-glass windows (1884) in the chancel of the church recount the story of this vow.

Port-Navalo⚓

A small port and seaside resort. The roadstead is enclosed to the south by a promontory on which stands a lighthouse (benches and telescope), and to the north by Bilgroix Point which offers a good **view**★ of the Golfe du Morbihan. The beach faces the open sea.

Port du Crouesty

Located on the bay of the same name and southeast of Port-Navalois lies this pleasure boat harbour. Alongside it is a large residential complex. The four docks are well sheltered and can hold over 1 100 boats. From the tourist car park there is a good view of the site. Fine walk along tåhe quayside.

St-Gildas-de-Rhuys

🕐 *Open daily (except Mon morning, Sat afternoon and Sun). Guided tours available. Apply to the presbytery.* ☎ *02 97 45 24 71.*

This village owes its origin to a monastery founded by St Gildas in the 6C. The most famous of the abbots who governed it was Abélard in the 12C.

Church★

This is the former abbey church built at the beginning of the 11C and largely rebuilt in the 16 and 17C.

The Romanesque chevet has pure, harmonious lines; it is ornamented with modillions; note a small carving depicting a tournament. Inside, the Romanesque **chancel**★ is remarkable. Behind the Baroque high altar is the tomb of St Gildas (11C). In the north transept lies the 11C gravestone of St Goustan and in the ambulatory, lit by modern stained-glass windows, 13C and 14C gravestones of Breton children and gravestones of abbots and knights. At the end of the nave is a stoup made up from two carved capitals. Another capital is found in the south aisle.

The **treasury**★ contains valuable antique objects, well displayed: 14C and 18C shrines, reliquaries (15C) containing the arms and legs of St Gildas, and his embroidered mitre, a 17C silver-gilt cross bejewelled with emeralds etc.

Château de Suscinio★

🕐 *Open Apr to Sept, daily 10am-noon and 2-7pm (June to Sept, 10am-7pm); rest of the year, daily (except Tues), 2-5pm, Sat-Sun and holidays10am-noon and 2-5pm.* 🕐 *Closed 20 Dec to 10 Jan.* ☎ *€6 (adult), €3 (child). Sagemor* ☎ *02 97 41 91 91.*

The impressive ruins stand in a wild setting by the seashore, where they are buffeted by sea winds. It was the sea which used to fill the moat. The castle was built in the 13C and modified by the dukes of Brittany in the 15C, prior to becoming one of their favourite residences. It was confiscated by François I and fell into the hands of the French Crown which used it to house faithful servants and the current Royal favourite. In ruins at the end of the Ancien Régime, the castle was sold to a private individual during the Revolution and was used as a stone quarry. Six of the towers have survived. In 1955, the roofing of the New Tower (Tour Neuve) and the West Pavillion (Logis Ouest) were restored to its former glory. The rooms in the entrance pavilion, also restored, house a small **museum** devoted to the history of Brittany.

Restoration has saved the castle from complete ruin

Having crossed the moat, enter the guard-room and the adjoining tower in which the history of the castle and its restoration are explained.

On the upper floors, the history of Brittany is described with the aid of literature, portraits, paintings and locally produced artefacts (*Scène de pardon* by Camille Chazal and a relief depicting Olivier de Clisson on horseback by Fremiet). Several rooms are devoted to splendid 13C and 14C **floor coverings** in varnished ceramic, which came from a chapel outside the castle's curtain wall, on the banks of the moat, which has since disappeared. The variety and quality of the decoration, which has been excellently preserved, make these an eloquent witness to medieval decorative art.

The Ceremonial Hall (Salle des Cérémonies), which opens onto a small chapel, provides access to the north façade and to the terraces, offering a lovely **panorama** of the peninsula and nearby ocean.

▶ *From St-Colombier return to Vannes on the road on which you came.*

BAIE DE MORLAIX★

MICHELIN LOCAL MAP 308 H2- FINISTÈRE (29)
– LOCAL MAP SEE LES ENCLOS PAROISSIAUX

The first thing the tourist will notice at Morlaix is its colossal viaduct. This structure bestrides the deep valley in which lies the estuary of the Dossen, commonly called the River Morlaix. The town is busy but the port, though it is used mostly by yachts, has only limited commercial activity (sand, wood, fertilisers). 🛈 *Place des Otages, 29600 – ☎ 02 98 62 14 94.*

Old Morlaix *2hr*

Viaduc★
From place des Otages there is a good view of the viaduct, an imposing two-storeyed structure, 58m/190ft high and 285m/935ft long.

291

Église St-Mélaine

🕐 *Daily except Sat-Sun*. The present church, which dates from 1489, is in the Flamboyant Gothic style with an interesting porch on the south side.

Rue Ange-de-Guernisac

This street is lined with fine corbelled and half-timbered houses: the Hôtel du Relais de France at no 13, and the houses at nos 9, 6 and 5 are of interest. Take a look in the picturesque alleyways, Venelle du Créou and Venelle au Son.

Grand'Rue★

Pedestrian precinct. Here you will see picturesque 15C houses adorned with statues of saints and grotesques, and low-fronted shops with wide windows, especially at nos 8 and 10. Originally these old houses, called **skylight houses,** comprised a large central area with skylights onto which opened the other rooms, linked by a spiral staircase supported by a lovely carved newel post. Queen Anne's House (👃 *see below*) has a fine collection and many illustrations of newel posts.

Maison de la Reine Anne

🕐 *Open July and Aug, daily (except Sun), 10am-6.30pm; May and June, 10am-noon and 2-6pm; Sept, 10am-noon and 2.30-5pm; Apr, daily (except Sun and Mon), 10am-noon and 2.30-5.30pm.* 🕐 *Closed Oct to Mar and public holidays.* €3. ☎ 02 98 88 23 26. This 16C corbelled mansion, three storeys high, has a façade adorned with statues of saints and grotesques. With its courtyard lit by a skylight, the interiora is a perfect example of the skylight house. In one of the courtyard's corners, there is a magnificent spiral staircase, 11m/36ft high, carved from one piece of wood. The newel post is adorned with saints carved in the round: St Roch, St Nicholas, St Christopher and St Michael. Between the first and second floors, note the fine sculpture of an acrobat with his barrel. There is a monumental stone chimney-piece opposite the staircase.

Address Book

com - 25 rooms, 🛏 €8. In front of the marina, this Breton house provides simple rooms; some have a view over the docks and the viaduct.

😊😊 **Europe**, *1 rue d'Aiguillon,* ☎ 02 98 62 11 99, www.hotel-europe-com. fr *- 56 rooms,* 🛏 €8. Insdide this 200-year-old building, the hall and stairway are decorated with beautiful sculpted woodworks. Modern rooms.

EATING OUT

😊 **Le Bibliophage**, *15 rue Ange de Guernisac,* ☎ 02 98 62 65 45. *Tue-Sat 11am-6.30pm.* A "library" to feed the soul and the stomach. Small dishes of salads and pastries.

😊 **Le Bistrot de Marie,** *2 rue Basse,* ☎ 02 98 88 47 26. *Mon noon and Tue-Sat 11am-1am.* A pleasant pub that prepares seasonal dishes and serves them with charm. .

😊😊 **L'Hermine**, *35 rue Ange de Guernisac,* ☎ 02 98 88 10 91. 🕔*Closed 13-22 June and 29 Aug-4 Sep and Sun noon and Wed except July-Aug.* This nice creperie along a pedestrian street offers good specialities, such as the crêpes made with fresh algae.

😊😊 **Marée bleue**, *3 rampe St-Mélaine,* ☎ 02 98 63 24 21. 🕔*Closed Sun eve. and Mon except July-Aug.* Enjoy traditinal seafood dishes in a room with a schist floor and blue and yellow furniture.

😊😊 **Les Bains Douches**, *45 allée du Poan-Ben,* ☎ 02 98 63 83 83. 🕔*Closed Mon evening, Sat noon, Sun.* Traditional meals carefully presented in the wonderful setting of the former municipal baths.

ON THE TOWN

Le Tempo, *cours Beaumont,* ☎ 02 98 63 29 11. In front of the marina, this pub is a meeting place for old salts and landlubbers, who can share a drink or a daily meal (salads, stews, and tarts). Terrace in summer.

Péniche Le Sterne, *quai de Léon,* ☎ 02 98 15 12 12. 🕔*Closed Mon.* This barge in its berth is home to a small pub. Savour a beautiful meal on the deck.

DISCOVERING THE COAST

Le Léon à Fer et à Flots, *Place des Otages,* ☎ 02 98 62 07 52, www. aferaflots.org This association offers guided tours of the town and of the coast between Morlaix and Roscoff: on foot, on board a train or boat. There are opportunities to discovery sites that are usually off-limits to the general public, such as the first floor of the viaduct of Morlaix (spectacular view!). About €10-20/person for the day.

YACHTING

École de voile de Terenez, *Plougas-nou,* ☎ 02 98 72 33 25, www.srtz.com In a small cove sheltered off the harbour of Morlaix, catamaran, day sailer and windsurfing lessons, €92-149/week. Numerous classes for children.

DIVING

Groupe Subaquatique Morlaix Trégor (GSMT), *18 rue de Kernehelen, Plouezoc'h,* ☎ 02 98 79 50 95, http:// plongee.gsmt.free.fr Everyday in summer. Evening dives are followed by a barbecue at the club. Neophytes can dive for €25.

FESTIVALS

Festival des arts de la rue (FAR), ☎ 02 98 46 19 46, www.artsdanslarue. com Twelve days from the end of July to the beginning of August.

SHOPPING

MARKET

Place Allende, contiguous streets and place des Otages. A big market all day on Saturdays. Livelier in the morning.

BAKERY

Au Four St-Mélaine, *1 venelle Four St-Mélaine,* ☎ 02 98 88 10 22. *Daily 6am-7pm in July-Aug; Tue-Sun in May-June and Sep-Oct; Tue-Sat Nov- Apr.* One of the house specialities is the "armoricain," cake without butter but with almonds. Pastries and various breads.

WINES

La Maison des vins, *Place des Viarmes,* ☎ 02 98 88 72 43. *Tue-Sat 9.30-12am, 2-7pm.* An exceptional establishment, for high quality wines and for the glass roof and corbelled façade of the shop itself.

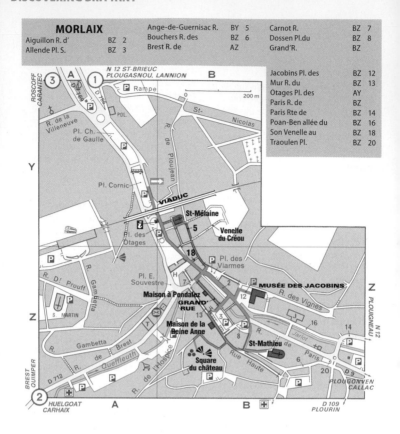

MORLAIX		Ange-de-Guernisac R.	BY	5	Carnot R.		BZ	7
Aiguillon R. d'	BZ 2	Bouchers R. des	BZ	6	Dossen Pl.du		BZ	8
Allende Pl. S.	BZ 3	Brest R. de	AZ		Grand'R.		BZ	

Jacobins Pl. des	BZ	12
Mur R. du	BZ	13
Otages Pl. des	AY	
Paris R. de	BZ	
Paris Rte de	BZ	14
Poan-Ben allée du	BZ	16
Son Venelle au	BZ	18
Traoulen Pl.	BZ	20

Musée des Morlaix – Couvent des Jacobins★

&♿🕐 *Open July and Aug, daily, 10am-12.30pm and 2-6.30pm; Easter to June, Sept and Oct, daily (except Sat morning and Tues), 10am-noon and 2-6pm; rest of the year, daily (except Sat morning and Tues), 10am-noon and 2-5pm, Sun 10am-noon and 2-6pm.* 🕐 *Closed 1 Jan, 1 May and 25 Dec.* 💶 *€5.* ☎ *02 98 88 68 88.*

The museum is housed in the former church of the Jacobins, which has a fine early-15C **rose window★** at the east end. The exhibits include the finds from archeological digs in the region, mementoes of Morlaix's famous citizens and of Old Morlaix with its skylight houses: 16C carved newel posts. Also on display are a large collection of 13C-17C religious statues, typical 17C furniture of the Léon region (chests, tester beds), household objects, farming and craft implements, and a collection of **modern paintings★**. On display is an old cannon from the privateer's ship *Alcida*, which sank at the mouth of the River Morlaix in 1747 (found in 1879).

Église St-Mathieu

The church was rebuilt in 1824 but the tower is 16C. Inside, it has a basilical plan and Doric columns supporting a pointed barrel vault. To the left of the high altar is an unusual wood statue of the **Virgin★** (c 14C) which opens. When closed it represents the Virgin suckling the Infant Jesus; open, it contains a group of the Holy Trinity.

Excursions

Plougonven★

12km/7mi southeast on D 9 towards Callac. This village, nestling at the foot of the Arrée Mountains, has an interesting parish close. The **Calvary**★★ was built in 1554; the cross in two tiers, carries, above, the statues of the Virgin and St John, and, below, two guards; the thieves' crosses stand on either side. At the foot of the main cross there is a Descent from the Cross. On the platform and around the base are scenes depicting various episodes in the life of Christ: the Temptation in the Desert, His Arrest etc. The charnel house presents a trefoil arcade and a basket-handle arched doorway.

The **church**, built in 1523 and badly damaged by fire in the early 20C, is dominated by a graceful belfry with a balcony, a turreted staircase and striking gargoyles.

Le Cloître-Saint-Thégonnec

13km/8mi S via Plourin-lès-Morlaix then along D111.

Musée du Loup

1 rue du Calvaire. ♿🕒 *Open July-Aug: 2-6pm; mid-Feb to June and Sep to mid-Dec: Sun 2-6pm.* ⊛ *€ 3.50 (children € 2.20).* ☎ *02 98 79 73 45.*

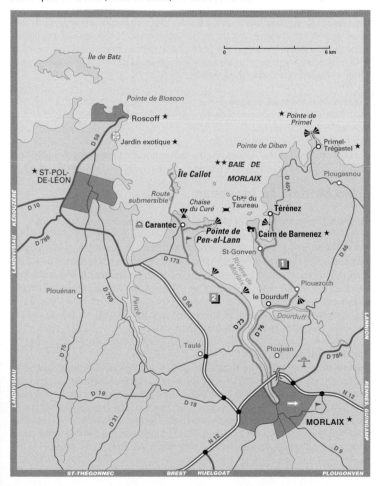

Summer twilight on the bay

This village's former school houses the Muséee du Loup (wolf museum), which illustrates the lifestyle of wolves and the long struggle faced by the region's inhabitants at the turn of the 20C as they sought to chase this mythic beast from their presence. In 1885, an inhabitant of Le Cloître-Saint-Thégonnec was the last person to receive a bounty for killing a wolf in the Arée hills.

Réserve des landes de Cragou

Walking tours leave from the car park across from the wolf museum . ◷ July-Aug: Mon and Fri 3pm (return 5pm). ∞ € 4 (children under 12 no charge). Bring appropraite shoes and clothes. ☎ 02 98 79 771 98.

Buzzards are king in this nature reserve that is home to many species. The lfora includes rare orchids and primitive ferns.

From Morlaix to Térénez★

☐ *19km/12mi round tour NE of Morlaix. Leave Morlaix via ① on the town plan.*

The cliff road runs along the RIver Morlaix and gives views of the sand dredging port, the marina and the lock, the charming setting of the town, river and viaduct. After the bridge, it reaches the small oyster port of **Le Dourduff** where the fishmerchants' boats are moored. Further on, the pleasant road goes through the picturesque Dourduff Valley.

The coast road offers glimpses of Morlaix estuary, the Château du Tareau and the peninsula topped by the Cairn de Bernenez.

Cairn de Barnenez

This imposing tumulus on the Kernéléhen peninsula overlooks the bay of Térénez and the estuary of the RIver Morlaix. Eleven funerary chambers were discovered under stone slabs between 1955 and 1968. The south-facing entrances are all preceded by a passage varying in length from 8m/26ft to 12m/39ft. The clour of the stones has revealed two distinct construction periods. The first cairn (46000 BC) is built of dolerite, a green stone found in the area. The second cairn, located nearer the slope, is more recent by 200 years and is built of light granite from Stérec Island.

▸ *Turn back, then left as you leave St-Gonven.*

Térénez
This small, very pleasant and typically Breton port is a sailing centre.

From Morlaix to Île Callot★★

[2] *14 km/8.7mi round tour from Morlaix. Leave Morlaix via ② on the town plan.*

Carantec⌂
This family seaside resort lies on a peninsula between the estuary of the Penzé and the River Morlaix, is a. There are several beaches suitable for bathing; the most important are Grève Blanche and Grève du Kélenn, the larger of the two.
A number of pardons are held at Carantec (& *see Calendar of events)*. The apse of the modern **church** contains a fine silver **processional cross**★ (1652) and a less ornate one in front of the altar.

Musée maritime
🕓 *Open Apr and mid-June to early Sept, daily (except Thur), 10am-noon and 3-6pm.*
€ 3. ☎ 02 98 67 00 43.
The exhibits in this small maritime museum show the region's link with the sea (oyster breeding, privateering, Morlaix Bay's flora and fauna and seaweed collecting).

La Chaise du Curé
From this rocky platform, the **view**★ extends from left to right over the Porspol and Blanche Beaches with St-Pol-de-Léon and Roscoff in the background, as far as the Pointe de Pen-al-Lann.

Pointe de Pen-al-Lann
1.5km/1mi east, plus 15min on foot there and back. Take rue de Pen-al-Lann and leave your car at a roundabout. Take the downhill path through pine trees to a rocky height.
The **view**★ extends along the coast from the Pointe de Bloscon crowned by the Chapelle Ste-Barbe, near Roscoff, to the Pointe de Primel; opposite you can see the castle on **Taureau Island**, which guarded the mouth of River Morlaix.

Île Callot
From Grève Blanche port you can reach the island by car (car park) at mid-tide.
The **Chapelle Notre-Dame** on the island was founded in the 16C and rebuilt in the 17C and 19C. Inside is a 16C statue of the Virgin. Pardon on the Sunday after 15 August. The island is excellent for fishing.

NANTES★★★

POPULATION 492 255

MICHELIN LOCAL MAP 318 G4 – LOIRE-ATLANTIQUE (44)

Nantes is many cities combined: a city of the arts, a great industrial city, and the seat of a big university. Located at the confluence of the rivers Loire, Sèvre and Erdre, Nantes is the historic capital of the dukes of Brittany and has now become the capital of the region called Pays de la Loire. The three ports of Donges, Nantes and St-Nazaire have merged and follow the estuary from Nantes up to the Atlantic Ocean. Nantes is the birthplace of Jules Verne (1828-1905) and Éric Tabarly (1931-98).

▸ **Orient Yourself:** Capital city of the Loire-Atlantique region
▣ **Parking:** Traffic in town is heavy. Leave your car in one of the many central car parks during your visit
☺ **Don't Miss:** The Royale de Luxe theatre company is famous for its spectacular street shows using giant puppets – check for performances!
⊙ **Organizing Your Time:** The "Pass Nantes" gives a good bargain on public transport, musuems and attractions
▣ **Especially for Kids:** Natural History Museum, Planetarium, Hespérides gardens

A Bit of History

Nantes, capital of Brittany – Nantes, first Gallic and then Roman, was involved in the bloody struggle between the Frankish kings and the Breton noblemen. But it was the Vikings who did the most damage. In 843 the pirates landed, rushed into the cathedral, where the Bishop was saying Mass, and put the prelate, the clergy and the congregation to death. In 939, young **Alain Barbe-Torte** (Crookbeard), a descendant of the great Breton chiefs, who had taken refuge in England, returned to the country and drove the invaders out of Brittany. Having become duke, he chose Nantes as his capital and rebuilt it. Nantes was the capital of the Duchy of Brittany several times during the Middle Ages, in rivalry with Rennes. The dukes of

Along the Loire

A. de Valroger/MICHELIN

the House of Montfort, especially **François II,** governed as undisputed sovereigns and restored the prestige of the town and its title of capital.

Edict of Nantes (13 August 1598) – In 1597, Brittany, tired of disorder and suffering caused by the League and also of the separatist ambitions of its Governor, Philip of Lorraine, sent a pressing appeal to Henri IV, asking him to come and restore order. Before the castle he whistled with admiration. "God's teeth", he exclaimed, "the dukes of Brittany were no small beer!" The royal visit was marked by a great historic event: on 13 August 1598, Henri IV signed the Edict of Nantes, which, in 92 articles, settled the religious question – or so he thought.

Sugar and ebony – From the 16C to the 18C, Nantes had two main sources of revenue: sugar and the slave trade, known discreetly as the ebony trade. In the Antilles, the slaver would sell the slaves bought on the Guinea coast and buy cane sugar, refined at Nantes and sent up the Loire. The ebony trade made an average profit of 200 percent.

Philosophers inveighed against this inhuman traffic, but Voltaire, whose business acumen is well known, had a 5 000 livres share in a slave ship from Nantes. At the end of the 18C the prosperity of Nantes was at its height: it had become the first port of France; its fleet included 2 500 ships and barques. The big shipowners and traders founded dynasties and built the fine mansions on Quai de la Fosse and the former Feydeau Islet.

All drowned – In June 1793, Nantes numbered many royalists. The Convention sent **Carrier,** the Deputy of the Cantal, there as its representative in early October. Carrier had already spent some time at Rennes. His mission was "to purge the body politic of all the rotten matter it contained".

Address Book

NANTES FOR TOURISTS

Thematic guided tours – In the summer, the tourist office organises a variety of thematic tours, which last 2hr-2hr 30min. For information or reservations, call ☎ 02 40 20 60 00, or stop by the tourist office.

Horse-drawn carriage tours – Facing the château entrance – ☎ 02 40 38 34 16 – 1 Apr-30 Sept, carriages depart every hour (11am-5pm); the rest of the year, by reservation only.

URBAN TRANSPORT

By tramway – Getting around by tramway is quick and convenient (operational all year, except on 1 May). There are two existing tramway routes (27 km/18mi, the longest tramway network in France) and another under construction. An individual ticket is valid for 1hr on both buses and tramways, and can be bought from automatic vending machines at tramway stops, from TAN

establishments and TAN kiosks (the main one is at the stop known as Commerce). The best way to visit the town is to buy a daily pass, called a "ticket 24hr" which permits unlimited travel for one entire day. Info Allô TAN ☎ 0 801 444 444.

By bus – You may buy bus tickets from the bus driver, from automatic vending machines, or in TAN kiosks.

Regional information in the media

For information about events, cultural activities and movies, consult the newspaper Ouest-France (Nantes edition), the magazine Nantes-Poche, and the tourist office's monthly program, "Des Jours et des Nuits ". You may also consult 3615 Nantes (booth at the tourist office) for other information about cultural activities and sports.

Radio stations – Radio Sud-Loire 88.8 mhz ; Radio Nantes 100.9 mhz, Radio-France Bretagne Ouest 101.4mhz.

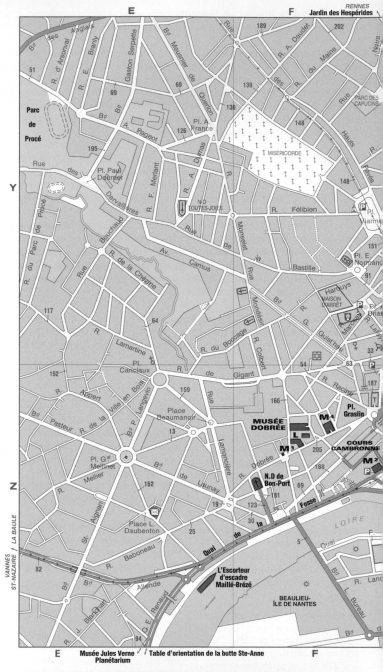

RENNES
Jardin des Hespérides

Parc
de
Procé

MISÉRICORDE

VANNES / ST-NAZAIRE / LA BAULE

Musée Jules Verne / **Table d'orientation de la butte Ste-Anne**
Planétarium

NANTES

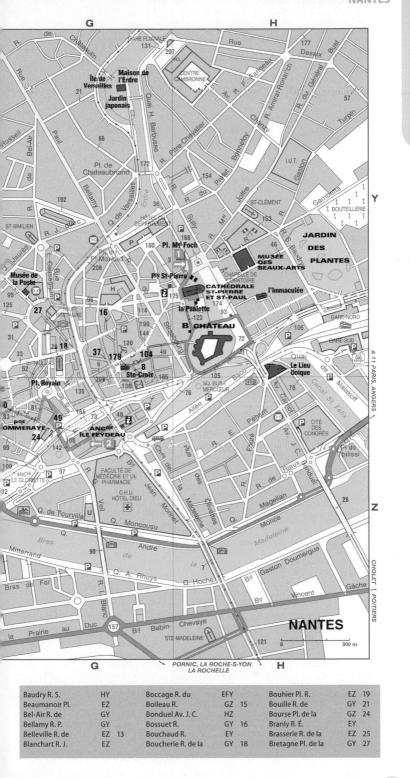

The revolutionary tribunal had filled the prisons with Vendéens, priests and suspects, and a problem arose: how to make room for new arrivals. Carrier chose drowning. Condemned people were put into barges which were scuttled in the Loire, opposite Chantenay. When informed, the Convention immediately recalled its delegate. He was put on trial and was sent before the Nantes Revolutionary court, sentenced to death and guillotined in December.

The duchess' hiding place – In 1832 tragedy gave way to farce. The **Duchess of Berry**, a mortal enemy of Louis-Philippe, was convinced that Brittany was still legitimist and scoured the Nantes countryside. Her failure was complete. She took refuge at Nantes but was betrayed. The police invaded the house and found it empty, but kept it under surveillance. Feeling cold, they lit a fire in one room. Their surprise was great when the chimney-shutter fell open and out on all fours came the duchess and three of her followers, black as sweeps and half suffocated. They had spent 16hr in the thickness of the wall.

A new vitality – In the 1980s the shipyards closed down, threatening the town's economic prosperity but Nantes promptly turned to service industries (insurance, communications) which now represent the bulk of its economic activity. Nantes has also become an important university town with a large student population.

Walking Tour

1 **Around the Castle**★★ *allow 3hr*

Place Maréchal-Foch
Two fine 18C hotels, built from the plans by Ceineray, flank the Louis XVI Column which was erected in 1790. From the square, commonly called place Louis-XVI, which is prolonged by Cours St-André and St-Pierre, you can readily appreciate the dimensions of the cathedral, in particular its soaring height.

Porte St-Pierre
This 15C gateway stands on the remains of a 3C Gallo-Roman wall. The gateway is built into an elegant turreted building.

Cathédrale St-Pierre-et-St-Paul★
This imposing building, begun in 1434, completed in 1893 and restored after serious fire damage in 1972, is remarkable for its austere façade restored in 1930: two plain towers frame a Flamboyant window; note the 15C canopied niches which decorate the pillars supporting the towers. The three portals reveal finely sculpted recessed arches and on the central portal stands a statue of St Peter.

Interior★★
Here, at Nantes, white stone replaces the granite used in purely Breton cathedrals. Being less heavy, this stone made it possible to build vaults 37.50m/123ft high (the vaulting of Westminster Abbey is 30.50m/100ft high).
As you enter you will be struck by the nave's pure, soaring lines, a fine example of Flamboyant work. Stand under the organ loft to appreciate the effect; you will see a double row of vertical lines springing from the ground and shooting without a break up to the delicately carved keystones of the vaults, where they cross.
Everything is based on elevation and the dimension of 37.50m/123ft loses significance. Seen from this angle, the slender ribs of the pillars mask not only the flat wall surfaces that separate them but all the lines, curved or horizontal, of the arcades, the triforium or the upper windows which could break the harmony of this vista, composed entirely of parallel vertical elements.

Address Book

TOURIST OFFICE

Nantes, cours Olivier de Clisson, ☎ 08 92 46 40 44 (€0.33/min), www. nantes-tourisme.com. ○ Open Mon-Sat 10am-6pm, annexe Place St-Pierre, Tue-Sun 10am-1pm, 2-6pm, (Thur 10.30am). Organises guided tours, notably a Jules Verne visit: "Nantes, the town is a novel". ○ The Office offers a **Pass Nantes** that provides free access to public transportation, bicycles, cruises-trips, and to more than 20 tourist sites, €14/24h, €24/48h, €30/72h, free for children under 12 accompanied by an adult.

ⓘ *For coin ranges, see the Legend on the cover flap.*

WHERE TO STAY

○ Booking your hotel by the reservation exchange of the Tourist Office entitles you to a 25 % off discount on the *Pass Nantes*.

○ The formula **Bon week-end en villes** entitles you to two nights in a hotel for the price of one for Fri or Sat evening arrivals. Information www. bon-week-end-en-villes.com.

○○ **Hôtel Cœur de Loire**, *3 rue Anatole Le Braz*, ☎ 02 40 74 37 61, *www.coeurdeloirehotel.com; 16 rooms.* ○ *Closed 10 days in Jan.* A bit off the beaten path, this family-run hotel offers elegant rooms that bear the name of vineyards.

○○ **Grand Hôtel**, *2 bis rue Santeuil*, ☎ 02 40 73 46 68, www.grandhotel-nantes.com; 41rm, 🛏 ☎ €7.50. Located in the town centre, this hotel boasts pastel coloured rooms that are functional, quiet and bright.

○○ **Hôtel des Colonies**, *5 rue du Chapeau Rouge*, ☎ 02 40 48 79 76, www. hoteldescolonies.fr - 38rm, 🛏 €8. Traditional and exotic décor complement each other in this contemporary hotel. The pleasant breakfast room also serves as an exhibition space for local artists.

○○ **Hôtel Graslin**, *1 rue Piron.* ☎ 02 40 69 72 91, www.ifrance.com/graslin - 47rm, 🛏 €8. ○ *Closed two weeks in Aug; 25 Dec-1 Jan.* Charming and well

kept, this hotel features cheerful, quiet and colourful rooms.

○○○ **Hôtel de France**, *24 rue Crébillon*, ☎ 02 40 73 57 91,*www.hotelfrancenantes.com; 74rm,* 🛏 €10, 🅿✕ This old mansion of the 18th century offers comfortable rooms, decorated in Louis XVI style. In the restaurant, take a step back into old France with its traditional décor and cuisine.

○○○ **Domaine d'Orvault**, *24 chem. des Marais-du-Cens, Orvault*, ☎ 02 40 76 64 02, www.domaine-orvault.com; 41rm ✕🛏 Situated in a garden setting, this hotel offers bright and individually-decorated rooms; some even come with a balcony and bay-windows. Heated swimming-pool, fitness, sauna and rental of bikes.

EATING OUT

Explore rue de la Juiverie for a multitude of crêperies, pizzerias and other inexpensive restaurants.

○ **Fleur de Sel**, *rue de la Bâclerie*, ☎ 02 40 12 44 36. Take a seat in the rustic dining room or on the terrace to enjoy the nice choice of crêpes and galettes made with certified organic flour.

○ **L'Île Mystérieuse**, *15 rue Kervégan*, ☎ 02 40 47 42 83. Enjoy gourmet galettes and crêpes in a warm setting on the ground floor of this 18C mansion.

○○ **La Vache nantaise**, *11 rue du Bon Secours*, ☎ 02 40 89 59 69. ○ *Closed Sat lunch; Sun.* Grilled meats, regional meals and rustic setting.

○○ **Au P'tit Beurre**, *18 rue Richebourg*, ☎ 02 40 74 11 61. ○ *Closed Sat-Sun lunch; Mon.* An unpretentious and warm atmosphere; regional cuisine with a menu that changes daily.

○○ **La Palombière**, *13 bd Stalingrad*, ☎ 02 40 74 05 15. ○ *Closed Sun evening; Oct-May: Mon evening; May-Oct: Sat-Sun lunch; 3 weeks in Aug.* Reasonable and ambitious cuisine featuring the bounty of the sea and land. Good value for the price.

○○○ **L'Esquinade**, *7 rue St-Denis*, ☎ 02 40 48 17 22. ○ *Closed Sun-Mon; 3 weeks in Aug.* Elegant and private setting - perfect for a candlelight supper of refined and seasonal cuisine.

L'Océanide, *2 rue Paul Bellamy*, ☎ *02 40 20 32 28*. ⏱ *Closed Sun evening; Mon; 3 weeks Jul-Aug*. With a 1950s décor and good value for the price, this restaurant features cuisine that honours the flavours of the ocean. Nice selection of muscatels.

Félix, *1 rue Lefèvre-Utile*, ☎ *02 40 34 15 93*. Situated on the canal near the Cité des Congrés, this contemporary pub pleases patrons with its electic menu. Sun brunch.

ENTERTAINMENT

La Maison Café, *4 rue Lebrun*, ☎ *02 40 37 04 12*. The name means what it says – enjoy drinks in the bathroom or in the kitchen.

L'Univers, *16 rue J.-J. Rousseau*, ☎ *02 40 73 49 55*. Cosy atmosphere perfect for before or after dinner; jazz bands every second Thursday.

Le Café Flesselles, *3 allées Flesselles*, ☎ *02 40 47 66 11*. A Nantaise institution, this bar also features exhibitions on the first floor.

Fées maison, *3 rue Pré Nian*, ☎ *02 40 48 44 42*. The setting is original and the witch potions will make your head spin.

Le Marlowe, *1 Place St-Vincent*, ☎ *02 40 48 47 65*. Located in a former chapel, this dancing pub takes you to 1960s America (*not* because of the location).

RECREATION

Boat trips- Bateaux Nantais, *gare fluviale, quai de la Motte Rouge, tram n° 2, stop Motte Rouge*, ☎ *02 40 14 51 14, www.bateaux-nantais.fr*. This 1h45min cruise lets you discover the manors and sites of the Erdre. Operates Jul-Aug: Sat-Sun, hols 3pm and 5pm, Mon-Fri 3.30pm; Apr: Sat-Sun, hols, 3.15pm; May, Jun, Sep: daily 3.15pm; €4.50/7/10. Discover the port of Nantes, on the Loire (2hr) May-Aug, departures in accordance with the lock times, (ask for information) €6/8/12. Dinner or lunch cruises by reservation €59-80.

Marine et Loire Croisières, *quai Ernest Renaud, near the Maillé-Brézé*, ☎ *02 40 69 40 40*. Nantes to St-Nazaire guided cruises on board a speedboat.

Reservations only. ⏱ Operates Apr-Oct (except Jul-Aug), departure at 10am, arrival St-Nazaire at noon; depart at 4pm with arrival at Nantes at 6pm; One-way ticket €10/16, There and back €13.50/25.50.

Ruban Vert, ☎ *02 51 81 04 24, www.rubanvert.fr*.

Rental of electric boats - (no license required) to discover the Erdre or the Sèvre Nantaise. Departures from l'île de Versailles, Vertou or Sucé-sur-Erdre. Boat for 4 people €23/1h, €68/4h.

FESTIVALS

Aside from the festivals listed below, be sure to find out about the performances of the Royal de Luxe, one of France's most well-known street-theatre companies. Between its trips around the world, the company regularly comes back to Nantes, its home town, to invade the streets with articulate giants and legendary stories.

Carnaval de Nantes, ☎ *02 40 35 75 49, Mar-Apr*. One of France's most nighttime parades.

Festival I.D.E.A.L, ☎ *02 40 12 14 34, Apr*. Featuring unclassified, eclectic, acoustic and electronic music.

Printemps des Arts, ☎ *02 40 20 03 00, May-Jun*. Baroque theatre, music, dance and painting.

Sardinantes, *Quai Ernest Renaud*, ☎ *02 40 35 75 49, Jun*. Snacking on grilled sardines of the Turballe, singing songs of sailors and of fest noz.

Festiv'île, *sur les îles de Loire*, ☎ *02 40 80 86 05, a week around the 20 June*. Festival of street art.

Rendez-Vous de l'Erdre, *sur les Quais de l'Erdre*, ☎ *02 51 82 37 70, www.rendezvouserdre.com, last weekend of Aug*. Jazz festival that gathers musicians from 5 continents.

Festival International de Science Fiction, ☎ *02 51 88 20 00, Nov*. Cinema, literature and comic strips.

Festival des Trois Continents, ☎ *02 40 69 74 14, Nov*. Movies from Africa, Asia and South America.

▶ *Go around the building to the right.*

In the south transept is the decorative masterpiece of the cathedral and a very great Renaissance work: the **tomb of François II**★★. It was carved between 1502 and 1507 by Michel Colombe, a sculptor who was born in Brittany but settled in the Touraine. It was commissioned by Anne of Brittany to receive the remains of her father, François II, and her mother, Marguerite of Foix, and it was placed in the Church of the Carmelites. The Revolutionary Tribunal ordered it to be demolished, but the courageous town architect of the time, instead of obeying the order, hid various pieces of the tomb in his friends' homes. It was reconstructed after the Revolution and transferred to the cathedral in 1817.

The Duke and Duchess recline on a black marble slab placed on a rectangular one in white marble. The statues grouped round them are symbolic: the angels supporting their heads represent their welcome to Heaven; the lion crouching at the feet of François stands for power, and Marguerite's greyhound for fidelity. The four large corner statues personify the four Cardinal Virtues: for the Duke, Justice (crowned and holding a sword) and Strength (helmeted and armed and expelling a dragon from a tower); Prudence and Temperance guard the Duchess. Prudence has two faces: in front, a young girl with a looking glass, symbolising the future, and behind, an old man representing the past. Temperance holds a bridle to signify control over passions, and a clock representing steadiness.

Below the recumbent figures are 16 niches containing the statues of saints interceding for the deceased, notably St Francis of Assisi and St Margaret, their patrons. Below the saints, 16 mourners, partly damaged, represent their people's sorrow.

This magnificent group is lit by a superb modern **stained-glass window**, 25m/80ft high and 5.30m/14ft wide devoted to Breton and Nantes saints, the work of Chapuis. The impression of height at the transept crossing is especially astonishing.

In the north arm of the transept is the **Cenotaph of Lamoricière**★, the work of the sculptor Paul Dubois (1879). The General is shown reclining under a shroud. Four bronze statues represent Meditation and Charity (at his head) and Military Courage and Faith (at his feet). Lamoricière (1806-65), a great African campaigner who came from Nantes, captured the Arabian Emir Abd-el-Kaderin 1847 during the wars in Algeria. He later fell into disgrace and when exiled by Napoleon III commanded Papal troops against the Italians. It is the Catholic paladin who is honoured here.

▶ *Skirt the cathedral façade; go through the portal to the left.*

La Psalette

This 15C building with a polygonal turret formerly contained the chapter-house but is now part of the sacristy.

▶ *Take the vaulted passageway on the right.*

From the small square you can see the other side of La Psalette.

▶ *Bear right on Impasse St-Laurent then left into rue Mathelin-Rodier (the name of the architect of the cathedral and part of the castle).*

It was in the house at no 3 that the Duchess of Berry was arrested (⌂ *see A Bit of History*).

Château des ducs de Bretagne

⊶ *Restoration ongoing at press time. Contact the Town Hall or* ☎ *02 51 17 49 00.*
The golden age of the castle was the age of Duke François II, when court life was truly regal: five ministers, 17 chamberlains and a host of retainers attended the Duke. Life was sumptuous and morals liberal.

The present building was begun by Duke François II in 1466 and continued by his daughter, Anne of Brittany. Defence works were added during the League by the Duke of Mercœur. From the 18C onwards the military took possession, destroyed some buildings and erected others lacking in style. The Spaniards' Tower (1), which had been used as a magazine, blew up in 1800 (the north part of the castle was destroyed – the sites of the destroyed buildings are indicated by a broken line on the plan). From Charles VII to Louis XIV, nearly all the kings of France spent some time at the castle: Louis XII married Anne of Brittany in its chapel (1499); it was here that Henri IV signed the Edict of Nantes in 1598. Chalais, Cardinal de Retz, Gilles de Rais (Bluebeard) and the Duchess of Berry were imprisoned in its towers.

If these stones could speak, what stories they would tell

An arm of the Loire washed the south, east and northeast walls until the building of a quay in the 19C and the filling up in the 20C of a branch of the Loire.

The fortress

The moat has now been re-established; the ditches which guarded the north and west sides have been turned into gardens and the old ditches have been restored on the other sides. An 18C bridge leads to the former drawbridge which is flanked by two massive round towers dating from the time of Duke François.

Inside the courtyard

Behind the massive defensive walls, the court was used for jousting and tournaments, also for the performance of mystery plays and farces.

The 15C **Bakery Tower** *(Tour de la Boulangerie;* ⊶ *not open to the public)*, also called Tower of Hell, was used as a prison, a theory confirmed by the graffiti visible on the walls.

The elegant **Golden Crown Tower**★ (Tour de la Couronne d'Or), whose name may be explained by the presence of a nearby well, presents fine Italian-style loggias and connects two pavilions pierced by rows of windows The 15C **Jacobins Tower** (Tour des Jacobins) was also used as a prison (carved graffiti).

The main building, built by François II and extended two storeys by Anne of Brittany,

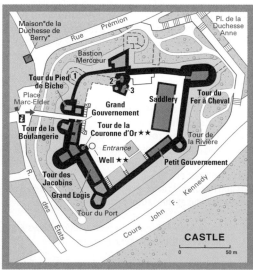

Maison"de la Duchesse de Berry"

Rue Prémion

Pl. de la Duchesse Anne

Bastion Mercœur

Tour du Pied de Biche 1

Place Marc-Elder

Tour de la Boulangerie

Grand Gouvernement

2

3

Saddlery

Tour du Fer à Cheval

Tour de la Couronne d'Or ★★

Tour de la Rivière

Entrance

Well ★★

Petit Gouvernement

Tour des Jacobins

Grand Logis

Tour du Port

Cours John F. Kennedy

CASTLE

0   50 m

was the ducal palace. It is decorated by five tall Gothic dormer windows with ornate pinnacles.

This part of the castle took the name **Governor's Major Palace** (Grand Gouvernement) after the 1670 fire, which destroyed a whole wing of the castle. It then became the home of the governor of Brittany. During the reign of the dukes, it had been their palace and had been used for meetings concerning the duchy.

Over the **well**★★, which probably dates back to the days of François II, there is a wrought-iron framework, which represents the ducal crown. The seven-sided curb of the well has seven pulleys and seven gargoyles for the overflow.

The Renaissance **Governor's Lesser Palace** (Petit Gouvernement) was built under François I; the military Saddlery, dating back to 1784 was the armoury.

The **old keep (2)** is, in fact, one of the four polygonal towers, which enclosed the original castle built in the 13C and enlarged in the 14C; it is part of an 18C mansion, which houses the **porter's lodge (3)**.

The Horseshoe Tower is 16C. In the restored rooms, special lighting enhances the vaulting with armorial-decorated keystones. Temporary exhibitions are held alternately, presenting the works formerly displayed in the Musée des Salorges.

Nantes derives its name from the Namnètes, a Gallic tribe who made the town their capital. The Romans developed it as a trading centre; the Vikings pillaged then occupied Nantes. In the early 20C, a plan for urban renewal greatly altered the face of the town, as did the massive destruction of the Second World War. The cathedral, striking for its Gothic unity despite the long building period, was bombed during the war, and had been nearly completely restored in 1972 when fire largely destroyed the roof. The medieval castle is remarkable for its contrasts: outside, a fortress with its crenellated towers; inside, a typical Renaissance palace. These rare historic buildings are the architectural pride of Nantes.

Le Lieu Unique

🕐 *Tower open Wed-Sun 3-7pm.* 📷 *€2 (children under 12 no charge).* ☎ *02 40 82 15 00. www.lelieuunique.com.*

Across from the Château, on the other side of the rail lines, there stands a blue, white and red cupola. It s the last remaining trace of the biscuit manufactory founded by Jean Romain Lefèvre, husband of Pauline Isabelle Utile in 1885. They joined their initials and created **Lu**, probably the best known of all bicuits in France, especially famous for the "Petit Beurre". In 1986, the machinery moved to premises south of town. In 1999 the former factory was redesigned by architect Patrick Bouchain and renamed Lieu Unique. In the stripped-down space with concrete and brick walls, a culture research centre was born. You can see performances of dance, theatre or music, attend exhibits, browse in the book shop, have a drink or visit the famous **tower** for a view over town and a look back at the former factory.

Plateau Ste-Croix

This is an area where 15C and 16C half-timbered houses still stand: no 7 **rue de la Juiverie**, no 7 **rue Ste-Croix**, nos 8 and 10 **rue de la Boucherie,** no 5 **rue Bossuet** and **place du Change**.

The 17C **Église Ste-Croix** is surmounted by the former town **belfry**★ crowned with trumpeting angels. The palm tree decoration of the chancel vaulting contrasts with the round vaulting of the nave. Large Flamboyant windows open onto the aisles. The furnishings are 18C.

Bars and restaurants liven up the district in the evening and pavement cafés welcome visitors as soon as the eather turns mild.

▶ *To return to the historic city centre, follow cours Franklin-Roosevelt then cours Olivier-de-Clisson to rue Kervégan.*

2 Old Nantes *allow 3hr*

Ancienne île Feydeau★

Between 1926 and 1938 the islet was linked to the mainland and a second island, the Île Gloriette, by filling in several arms of the Loire. The islet has retained its 18C appearance, especially between place de la Petite Hollande and cours Olivier-de-Clisson (no 4 was the birthplace of Jules Verne). It was here that rich shipowners used to build their vast mansions which stretch from the central street, rue Kervégan, right back to one of the outer avenues, Allées Turenne or Duguay-Trouin. Curved wrought-iron balconies and grotesque masks, probably the work of seafaring craftsmen, adorn the façades. The inner courtyards have staircases with remarkable vaulting.

Quartier Graslin★

It was the financier **Graslin**, Receiver Gerneral for farmlands at Nantes, who was responsible for the creation of this area in the late 18C. The Stock Exchange, built by Crucy in 1811-13, stands on Place du Commerce. It now houses the Tourist Office. Further on, **Place Royale**, designed by Crucy, is adorned by a fountain represetning Nantes (1865)

Opening onto rue Santeuil is a curious stepped shopping arcade on three levels. **Passage Pommeraye**★, built in 1843, leads to the Stack Exchange. Great fluted columns support galleries lined with elegant shops and rows of statues serve as pedestals for the lamps.

Passage Pommeraye is a popular place to meet

R. Dechamps/MICHELIN

Quai de la Fosse

Several 18C mansions line this quay (nos 17, 54, 70), including no 86, Hôtel Durbé, whose outbuildings served as a warehouse for the India Company.

Église Notre-Dame-de-Bon-Port

Also known as **Église St-Louis,** this unusual building overlooks Place Sanitat. The great cubic mass (1846-58) is adorned by a frescoes and a triangular pediment topped by a majestic dome. Massive hexagonal pillars support the dome decorated alternately with panels of stained glass and frescoes.

Parks and Gardens

Nantes took an interest in botany as early as the 17C and exotic plants such as magnolias adorned the town's gardens which today cover an area of 800ha/1 977 acres.

Jardin des Plantes★

Entrance: boulevard de Stalingrad (opposite the station) or place Sophie-Trébuchet. This very fine garden which was created in 1807. It is beautifully landscaped and contains, in addition to the masses of white, pink, purple and yellow camellias, magnolias, rhododendrons and splendid trees, several fine ponds and wooden sculpture. A statue of Jules Verne is a reminder that Nantes was the writer's native town. The greenhouses contain an extensive collection of cacti.

Île de Versailles

Entrance: quai de Versailles or quai Henri-Barbusse. Once covered with marshland, the islet was landfilled during the building of the Nantes-Brest Canal. A charming Japanese garden has been landscaped with rock gardens, waterfalls, and lanterns.

Maison de l'Erdre (🕐 *Open Wed - Mon, 11.30am to 6pm, Sat-Sun and holidays, 10am-noon and 3pm to 6pm. 🚫 No charge.* ☎ *02 40 29 41 11.*) displays the river's flora and fauna; the river, until the 19C, flowed into the canal.

Parc de Procé

Entrance: boulevard des Anglais, rue des Dervallières or boulevard Clovis-Constant. It is a pleasure to stroll through this undulating park (16ha/40 acres) landscaped with perspectives and rhododendrons, azaleas, oaks etc.

Additional Sights

Musée des Beaux Arts★★

♿🕐 *Open daily (except Tues), 10am-6pm, Fri 10am-9pm, Sun 11am-6pm.* 🕐 *Closed all public holidays.* 🎟€3.10 (children under 18 no charge. ☎ 02 51 17 45 00.
The museum is housed in an imposing late-19C building, the main part of which is flanked by projecting wings. The collections, enriched by exhibits from the depository, cover the 13C to the present. A central patio is surrounded by large galleries with works exhibited in chronological order.

15C-18C

Note Perugino's (1448-1523) *Saint Sebastian* portrayed as an elegant page holding an arrow; *Saint Peter's Denial, The Angel Appearing to Joseph in His Dream* and *The Hurdy-Gurdy Player* the 17C is represented by Georges de La Tour (1593-1652), *The Guitarist* by Greuze (1725-1805) and *Harlequin, Emperor of the Moon* by Watteau (1684-1721).

19C

Classicism and Romanticism are represented by Ingres' fine portrait *Madame Senonnes,* Delacroix's *The Moroccan Chief* and Courbet's *The Winnowers*.

Modern and Contemporary Art

The 20C collections are displayed in seven large galleries. In the first, works illustrating the period from Impressionism to the Fauves include Monet's *Venitian Gondolas*, Émile Bernard's *Apple Tree Beating,* representing the Pont-Aven School, Sonia Delaunay's *Yellow Nude,* a Fauve work, and *Transatlantic Roll* by Nantes artist Émile Laboureur. The second gallery contains a collection, which must be unique in a provincial museum, of paintings by Vasili Kandinsky executed during the years he taught at the Bauhaus (1922-33). The homogeneity of this collection, which features in particular Black Frame and the bright Évènement doux, revolves around the idea of a "microcosm".
The third gallery exhibits different artistic movements from the period 1913-45, notably two works by the Constructivist Gorin, Two Women Standing by a Magnelli at the intersection of Futurism and Cubism, as well as two paintings by Chagall executed at a particularly testing time in his life, Red Horse and Obsession.
The fourth gallery plunges the viewer into the cultural context of the period 1940-60, with figurative works by Lapicque (Sunset on the Salute), Hélion (Still Life with Pumpkin) and abstract works by Poliakoff, Hartung, Bissière and the Nantes artist Camille Bryen.

The fifth gallery covers the period 1960-75. It focuses principally on the Nantes artist Martin Barré, but also exhibits the interesting work of François Morellet, representing Kinetic art.

The sixth gallery is largely given over to the 1970s and 80s. Note in particular Promenade of the Blue Cavalier, a charming abstract work by Thiéval, large "canvases" by Viallat and above all two Picassos, among the master's last works, *Couple*★ and *Man Seated with Walking Stick*. Finally, there are three works by Dubuffet, including Setting with two Figures F 106.

The final gallery devotes a large area to contemporary European artistic expression. Rebecca Horn's Hydrapiano, with the bizarre behaviour of its long column of mercury, is particularly eye-catching.

Muséum d'Histoire naturelle★★

Kids ♿ 🕐 *Open daily (except Sun morning and Mon), 10am-noon and 2-6pm.* 🕐 *Closed public holidays.* 💶 *€3.10 (under 18: no charge), no charge on 3rd Sun of every month.* ☎ *02 40 99 26 20.*

Originally set up in the Cabinet Dubuisson in 1799, this Natural History Museum was later moved to the former Mint (Hôtel de la Monnaie) and inaugurated in 1875. It houses several important collections in such varied areas as zoology, regional fauna, osteology, paleontology, prehistory, sciences of the earth, mineralogy and ethnography. The section devoted to shells is remarkable on account of the sheer beauty and variety of the exhibits. A vivarium presents reptiles and batrachians from all over the world.

Musée Dobrée★

🕐 *Open daily (except Mon), 10am-noon and 1.30-5.30pm.* 🕐 *Closed public holidays.* 💶 *€3, no charge on Sun.* ☎ *02 40 71 03 50.*

This Romanesque-style mansion was built in the 19C by the Nantes shipowner and collector **Thomas Dobrée** (1810-95).

The museum contains Romanesque and Gothic sculptures from Nantes and the Val de Loire medieval ivories and alabasters, champlevé enamels (12C-14C) from the Limousin, Rhine and Moselle regions, paintings and jewellery.

On the first floor are Chinese collections, Dobree family memorabilia.

Musée archéologique★

Entrance rue Voltaire. 🕐 *Open daily (except Mon), 10am-noon and 1.30-5.30pm.* 🕐 *Closed public holidays.* 💶 *€3, no charge on Sun.* ☎ *02 40 71 03 50.*

The first floor of this archeological museum concentrates on Greek and Etruscan pottery and all that is Egyptian (sarcophagi, canopic vases – funerary urns, the covers of which are in the form of an animal or human head – bronze and painted statuettes).

The second floor concentrates on local civilizations covering prehistory to the invasion of the Norsemen, with displays of arms, tools, terracotta and bronze vases, jewellery, items from St-Nazaire dating from the neolithic to the Bronze Age, and Gallo-Roman objects excavated at Rezé (Loire-Atlantique).

Musée Jules-Verne★

No 3 rue de l'Hermitage. ♿🕐 *Open daily (except Sun morning and Tues), 10am-noon and 2-5pm.* 🕐 *Closed public holidays.* 💶 *€3 (children free), no charge 4th Sun of the month.* ☎ *02 40 69 72 52.*

A 19C mansion houses the museum devoted to Jules Verne (1828-1905), one of the first to write science fiction novels such as *Five Weeks in a Balloon*, *A Journey to the Centre of the Earth* and *Around the World in Eighty Days*.

Musée de la Poste

No 2 bis rue du Président-Herriot. ◐ *Open daily (except Sat afternoon and Sun), 8am-7pm.* ◐ *Closed public holidays.* ✆ *No charge.* ☎ *02 51 83 39 39.*

Located in the post office's regional headquarters, the museum recounts the history of the postal system from the mounted couriers to the post office box to private messenger services. Displays include the model of a 19C relay post, uniforms worn by the postilion and postman, scales, stamp-making machines, telephones, calendars etc.

Musée de l'Imprimerie

&♿◐ *Open Mar to July, Mon to Fri 2-5pm; Sept to Feb, Tues to Sat 2-6pm, Sat 10am-noon and 2-5pm.* ◐ *Closed August and all public holidays.* ✆ *€5 (children €3.20).* ☎ *02 40 73 26 55. www.musee.imprimerie.free.fr.*

Book cover of an original Hertzel edition

Musée de Jules Verne, Nantes

Before entering the workshop, visit the gallery with its lithographs, illuminated manuscripts and engraved wood. In the workshop, composition and printing techniques are illustrated with machines – lithographic and typographic presses, copper-plate engraving press, type-setting and casting machines – all in perfect working order.

Escorteur d'escadre Maillé-Brézé

🐦 *Guided tours (1hr or 90min including machinery) June to Sept, daily, 2-6pm; rest of the year, Wed, Sat-Sun, school holidays and public holidays 2-5pm.* ✆ *€4.60/2.30 (✆€7/4 including machinery).* ☎ *02 40 69 56 82. www.maillebreze.com.*

Docked on the Loire, this escort ship (132.65m/434ft long and 12.70m/40ft wide) was launched in 1957 and served until 1988. The visit includes anti-submarine and anti-aircraft weapons and detection systems, the command post and the officers' and sailors' living quarters.

In the officers' quarters, a small museum evokes the life of French Admiral Jean Armand de Maillé (1619-46) through literature and various exhibits.

A Visionary's Childhood

The 20 years that Jules Verne spent in Nantes from his birth on Feydeau Island in 1828 until he set up house in Paris in 1848, undoubtedly helped to strengthen his vocation as a writer of fiction, whose exceptional talent and boundless imagination successfully combined dream, scientific fact and adventure. The sight of the great port crowded with ships, their holds giving off all kinds of smells, or the equally fascinating scene of the steam-driven machines at the Indret factory, the tales of voyages he listened to from his uncle Prudent, once a privateer, lessons in reading and writing with Madame Sambin, the widow of the captain of an ocean-going vessel, or imaginary shipwrecks conjured up while playing among the little islands of the Loire, all played a part in inspiring the author's imaginative genius when he came to write Voyages extraordinaires, which earned him the acclaim of more than 25 million teenagers even before he was universally acknowledged to be a great writer.

Planétarium

Access by Quai E.-Renaud and rue de l'Hermitage. No 8 rue des Acadiens. 🎫 ♿ 🕐 *Shows (1hr), daily (except Sat) at 10.30am, 2.15pm, 3.45pm; Sun at 3pm and 4.30pm.* 🕐 *Closed public holidays.* ⟨€5 (children €3).* ☎ 02 40 73 99 23.

In the planetarium, the visitor discovers the mysteries of the universe: the sun, moon, stars and planets are projected onto the dome. Each show takes a different theme.

View from Ste-Anne Lookout point★

Access via Quai E.-Renaud and rue de l'Hermitage.

From the terraced lookout point there is a good view of the port installations with cranes in the foreground and shipyards and Île de Nantes in the distance.

A viewing table *(table d'orientation)* helps the visitor pinpoint Nantes' main sights and its new buildings.

Excursions

Boat Trip on the Erdre★

Landing stage: Quai de la Motte Rouge. Cruises at various times depending on the season. 👟 *See Address book for details.*

This is a favourite trip for the Nantais in a pleasantly green countryside dotted with manor houses; the 16C Château de la Gascherie with its ornate windows is notable. The Erdre widens beyond Sucé to form Lake Mazerolles.

Château de Goulaine

13km/8mi southeast on N 149, then D 119 towards Haute-Goulaine. 🚶 *Guided tours (1hr) mid-June to mid-Sept, daily (except Tues), 2-6pm; late Mar to mid-June and mid-Sept to end of Oct, Sat-Sun and public holidays 2-6pm.* 🕐 *Closed Nov to Mar.* ⟨€7 (children €3.50; under 4 no charge).* ☎ 02 40 54 91 42. http:/chateau.goulaine.online.fr.

The château, surrounded by vineyards, was built between 1480 and 1495 by Christophe de Goulaine, Groom of the Bedchamber to Louis XII and François I. He built it on the foundations of an old medieval fortress which, with those at Clisson and Nantes, had been used to defend the Duchy of Brittany against France.

Remains from this military past include a machicolated tower and a small castle in front of a bridge spanning a moat. This handsome residence consists of a Gothic 15C main building of calcareous tufa from the Saumur region, and two wings added in the early 17C.

Interior

A spiral staircase leads to the first floor, which opens into the **Great Hall,** in which the most striking feature is the richly sculpted, monumental Renaissance chimney-piece. A beautiful 16C Flemish tapestry depicting the Fall of Phaethon adorns the wall. The **Blue Room** still has its early-17C decor intact: blue and gold coffered ceiling, chimney-piece with Corinthian columns and caryatids, panelling decorated with pastel landscapes, and a large majestic Gobelins tapestry. The **Grey Room** has interesting panelling and mythological scenes on its piers.

Volière à papillons

🎫 An enormous greenhouse next to the castle's curtain wall contains tropical flowers and shrubs and is an aviary for butterflies.

Les jardin des Hespérides

Ferme de la Hautière, 3km/1.9mi N via the ring road, exit: La Chapelle-sur-Erdre. 🎫 ♿ 🕐 *Open early May to mid-Oct:* 🚶 *guided tour (1hr 30min) at 4pm; Sun and holidays at 10.30am, 3pm and 5pm.* ≈€7.50 (children €4.10). ☎ 02 4072 03 80. www. jardinhesperides.free.fr.

This fruit-growing farm, run by the same family since 1810, has set aside a 1.5ha/4-acre theme area which includes a strawberry garden, a Loire-Atlantique garden, a World garden (fruit from faraway countries), a New-Fruit garden (hybrids), a Wild-Fruit garden, a Neolithic garden, a Mediterranean garden and a Botanists' garden.

ÎLE D'OUESSANT★★

USHANT – POPULATION 932
MICHELIN LOCAL MAP 308 A4 FINISTÈRE (29)

An excursion to the Île d'Ouessant by sea is of the greatest interest, since it enables you to see Brest Channel, Pointe de St-Mathieu, Four Channel, the famous Black Stones (Pierres Noires) reef and the Green Stones (Pierres Vertes) reef, the islands of Béniguet and Molène, and Fromveur Channel. The island itself is extremely curious. On the way to Ouessant the boat usually anchors off and sometimes calls at Molène. There the pastures on the rare patches of earth in this archipelago are so small that, according to a local jest, a Molène cow which has all four feet in one field grazes from another and manures a third.

▶ **Orient Yourself:** 20km/12mi off the coast of Le Conquet, in the Iroise Sea.
☺ **Don't Miss:** The tour of the lighthouses.
🕐 **Organizing Your Time:** Be sure to reserve your boat trip and lodging in advance.
Kids **Especially for Kids:** The Écomusée.

Geographical Notes

Nature – Ouessant is 7km/4mi long and 4km/2.5mi wide and its highest point is 60m/197ft above sea level. It is famous in marine history for the danger of its waters due to frequent fog, strong currents (the Fromrust to the northwest and the Fromveur to the southeast) and countless reefs.

In winter the wind is master and hurls the waves against the broken and rocky shores with the utmost fury for as much as 10 days on end. The scene is often sinister when the fog comes down and the mournful howl of the foghorns mingles with the roar of the storm.

Few tourists know the island in this inhospitable guise, for the summer season brings calm and a quieter atmosphere, similar to that of the coasts of Brittany. The climate is mild. In January and February, Ushant has the highest mean temperature in France. The colonies of sea birds that nest on the island's cliff and on the neighbouring islets are particularly numerous in the autumn when the migrants from Northern Europe fly in, attracted by the beams of the two lighthouses.

Economic Notes

The people and their work – The majority of the island's population is made up of women and men who have retired from the Navy or the merchant marine. Their principle occupations are stock raising and food crops.

Vegetables and potatoes grow in beautifully maintained lots. The grain cultivated on larger parcels of land is used as feed for poultry and also as a supplementary fodder crop for the cattle's diet. The livestock (sheep, dairy cows, horses) consists mainly of sheep with brown wool, which graze on meagre tufts of salt grass; the result is meat with a splendid flavour, comparable to the famous prés salés of Mont-St-Michel Bay.

They live in the open and take shelter from northwesterly or southwesterly gales behind low dry-stone walls built in a star formation or wood shelters. Though from early February (first Wednesday: a great cattle fair) before lambing to late September they are tethered in twos to a stake; they wander freely the rest of the year, their owner's mark being nicked on their ears.

A few dairy cows are raised and two riding centres have reintroduced horse breeding. The cultivation of algae and the raising of mussels have developed into very promising enterprises.

Driving Tour

Roads from Lampaul lead to the best sites but many paths and tracks enable the visitor to crisscross the island, to reach the fine cliffs, the pretty little creeks and to discover the flora as well as the marine fauna: herring gulls, cormorants, oyster catchers, puffins and terns.

Lampaul

This is the island's capital. Note the old houses kept in excellent repair; the shutters are painted in green or blue, the island's traditional colours. A small monument containing the Proëlla crosses (see above) stands in the cemetery.

The tiny port, west facing, is picturesque, while the sandy beach of Le Corz nearby extends to the south.

La Côte Sauvage★★★

▶ *Leave Lampaul west by an uphill road; after 500m/547yd, bear right.*

Address Book

ARRIVAL AND DEPARTURE

By flight - Finist'air, ☎ 02 98 84 64 87, www.finistair.fr, 2 flights/day between Ouessant and Brest airport. 15min of flight; one-way ticket €36/62.

By boat - Compagnie Penn Ar Bed, ☎ 02 98 48 80 13, www.pennarbed. fr. In summer, 3 trips daily from Brest, 4 from Le Conquet (about 1hr). Round trip: €18.20/30.40. Bikes allowed onboard. Reservations required 48 hours in advance. **Compagnie Finist'Mer**, ☎ 02 98 89 16 61 www.finist-mer.fr Links with Brest (€30) Le Conquet (€25.50), Camaret (€26.50) or Lanildut (€27), on speedboats (around 30min from Le Conquet).

TOURIST OFFICE

Lampaul, ☎ 02 98 48 85 83, www.ouessant.org, ⏰ Open Mon-Sat 10am-noon, 1.30pm-5pm, Sun 10am-noon.

Shopping - Groceries, bakeries, butchers, seafood shops at Lampaul.

For coin ranges, see the Legend on the cover flap.

WHERE TO STAY

⬤⬤ **Ti Jan Ar C'hafé**, Kernigou, ☎ 02 98 48 82 64 – 8rm, ⬤ €6.10. Tasteful and well laid-out rooms define this charming hotel. After a hard day of touring, take a break in one of the deckchairs on the veranda. Call ahead of time to announce your arrival.

EATING OUT

⬤⬤ **Roc'h-Ar-Mor,** ⏰ *Closed Sun evening and Mon.* Known for beautiful meals with a focus on Ouessantin regional products; don't miss out on the lamb.

⬤⬤ **Ty Korn**, *Place de l'Église,* Lampaul, ☎ *02 98 48 87 33.* Savour local seafood such as fresh bass while seated with a view of an artist's rendition of the shore of Ouessant. After dinner, head downstairs to sample the fine variety of Breton beers.

Écomusée de l'île d'Ouessant

Kids ⏱ *Open June to Sept and school holidays, daily 10.30am-6.30pm; Apr and May, daily (except Mon), 2-6.30pm; rest of the year, daily (except Mon), 2-4pm.* ⊗ €3.30 (children €2.10). ☎ 02 98 48 86 37.

At the hamlet of **Niou Uhella,** two traditional houses have been restored and rearranged by the Parc naturel régional d'Armorique. Visitors will see in one of them furniture typical of the island built of wood from wrecked vessels, painted in blue, symbol of the Virgin's protection, and in the second a display of farm and domestic implements and costumes etc which depicts aspects of life on Ouessant; an exhibit on the island's geology and population is upstairs.

▶ *Carry on towards the coast.*

Moulin de Karaes

This is the island's last mill (restored) with its round stone base. It was used to mill barley from which bread was still made at the beginning of the 20C.

Phare de Créac'h

This lighthouse, with that at Land's End, marks the entrance to the English Channel; it has two tiers of revolving beams. The light is cast by four lamps giving a total of 20 million candlepower and an average range of more than 60km/37mi.

In the old machine room, there is a small **Centre d'Interprétation des Phares et Balises (Lighthouse Museum –** ⏱ *Open May to Sept and during school holidays, daily, 10.30am-6.30pm; Apr, daily (except Mon), 2-6.30pm; rest of the year, daily (except Mon), 2-4pm.* ⊗ €4.10 children under 8 no charge. ☎ 02 98 48 80 70.**)** retracing their history from Antiquity to the present. It shows how the original lighthouse was a tower, with, at its summit, a light fuelled by burning coal, wood or oil. The exhibit includes turbines, lens, lamps, beams and recounts the life of the lighthouse keeper. An audio-visual show completes the tour.

▶ *Go around the lighthouse to the right to view the coast.*

Its extraordinarily jagged **rocks**★★★ *(rochers)* pounded by the sea are very impressive. A gangway in front of the lighthouse gives access to Pointe du Créac'h where the foghorn stands. Cargo boats and oil tankers can be seen on the horizon; some 300 ships pass daily in the area which is patrolled day and night by the French Navy.

Ph. Plisson/La Trinité

Whitecaps at the entrance to the Channel, Créac'h lighthouse

▷ *Turn back and bear right towards Pointe de Pern.*

Chapelle Notre-Dame-de-Bon-Voyage
Also known as the Chapelle St-Gildas after the English saint who came here in the 5C, it was built at the end of the 19C. The people of Ouessant come to the chapel every year for the island's pardon on the first or second Sunday in September.

Pointe de Pern★
This, the western-most point of the island, extends into the sea in a series of rocks and reefs lashed by the rollers. In the distance is the unmanned Nividic Lighthouse (Phare de Nividic).

Crique de Porz Yusin

▷ *Leave Lampaul north by a road running past the island's electricity generating plant.*

The road passes several hamlets with white houses adorned with brightly coloured shutters and surrounded by small gardens, on the way to Porz Yusin, one of the few sheltered spots on the north coast. This pretty, rocky setting is ideal for birdwatching. There are also very fine varieties of seaweed.

Presqu'île de Feunteun Velen

▷ *At Lampaul, take the road skirting the cemetery.*

Pass near the small port of Lampaul, where the boat from Brest sometimes drops anchor. The jetty gives shelter to the fishing boats.
The road goes round the deep Lampaul Bay bounded by the Corz and Le Prat Beaches, with the Le Grand Truk and Youc'h Corz rocks in the centre, then descends gently towards the Pointe de Porz Doun. Note on the left the white pyramid of Le Runiou (Pyramide du Runiou), a landmark for shipping; on the right is the great cove of Porz Coret.

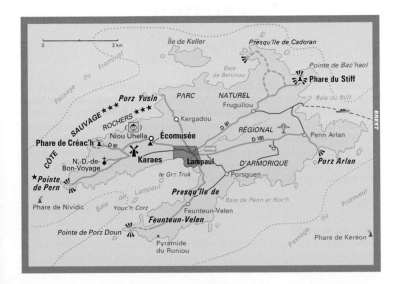

Pointe de Porz Doun

The cliff-lined point at the southern tip of the island affords a fine **view** over Lampaul, the Pointe de Pern and Jument Lighthouse (built from 1904-12; unmanned) which reaches a height of 42m/138ft and houses a foghorn.

Phare du Stiff

▶ *Leave Lampaul by the road running along the north side of the church.*

The road rises gently to the island's highest point (alt 60m/197ft), the **Pointe de Bac'haol.** The lighthouse, built by the military architect Vauban in 1695, comprises two adjoining towers, one containing a spiral staircase (126 steps) and the other three small superposed rooms. The light has a range of 50km/31mi thanks to a lamp of 1 000W giving a total of 600 000 candlepower. From the top a vast **panorama**★★ unfolds over the islands and the mainland from Vierge Lighthouse to the Pointe du Raz.

Nearby stands the new radar-tower (height 140m/459ft) which controls the sea lane off the island.

Paths lead to the tip of the **Presqu'île de Cadoran** (Cadoran Peninsula) from which may be enjoyed a pretty view of Beninou Bay, sometimes frequented by a seal colony, and Keller Island, favoured by nesting birds.

Crique de Porz Arlan

▶ *Leave Lampaul by the road skirting the cemetery, then turn left.*

The road runs across the plateau, leaving on the right the 1863 Chapelle Notre-Dame-d'Espérance and on the left the airfield, before bearing right towards picturesque Porz Arlan.

In this creek nestle a tiny sandy beach and a small port sheltered by a jetty. From this charming site the beautiful **view** extends over the rocky coastline, Fromveur and Kéréon Lighthouse, and the Île de Bannec.

PAIMPOL

POPULATION 7 932
MICHELIN LOCAL MAP 309 D2

Pierre Loti's novel *Pêcheur d'Islande* (Fisherman of Iceland, 1886) and Botrel's song *The Paimpolaise* (the cliff mentioned in the song is located near the town, towards the Pointe de Guilben) brought both literary fame and popularity to Paimpol. Life has changed a great deal, however, since those days when deep-sea fishing was done off the banks of Iceland. The fishermen now tend to fish along the coast; the port, large and impersonal, contains mostly pleasure boats. The town retains a certain prosperity as a market for early vegetables. Oyster farming has brought wealth to the region.

Visit

Place du Martray

In the centre of the town, the square retains fine 16C houses; note at the corner of rue de l'Église the house with a square corner turret where Loti used to stay and where Gaud, the heroine of *Pêcheur d'Islande,* lived.

Address Book

TOURIST OFFICES

Goëlo-Paimpol, Place de la République, Paimpol, ☎ 02 96 20 83 16, www.paimpol.net ◷ Open 15 Jun-15 Sep: Mon-Sat 9.30am-7.30pm, Sun and public hols 10am-6pm; low season: Mon-Sat 9.30am-12.30pm, 1.30pm-6.30pm. ☛ Guided tours and ticket booth for the Vapeur du Trieux and Bréhat.

Pointe de l'Arcouest, ◷ Open 15 Jun-15 Sept: Mon-Sat 9.30am-12.30pm, 2.30pm-6.30pm, Sun and public hols 10am-1pm.

Plouézec, rue du Colonel Henri Simon, ☎ 02 96 22 72 92. 15 Jun-15 Sep: Mon-Sat 9.30am-12.30pm, 2.30pm-6.30pm, Sun and public hols 10am-1pm; school hols: Mon-Sat 10am-1pm.

Pontrieux, la Maison Eiffel, ☎ 02 96 95 14 03. July-Aug: daily 10am-7pm; off season: Tue-Sun 1pm-5pm.

Rent a bike - Cycles du Vieux Clocher, Place de Verdun, ☎ 02 96 20 83 58. ◷ Open Mon-Sun lunch, €10/day
For coin ranges, see the Legend on the cover flap.

WHERE TO STAY

PAIMPOL AND ENVIRONS

⊜⊜ **L'Origano**, *7 bis rue du quai, Paimpol*, ☎ *02 96 22 05 49 – 9rm*, ⊑ €5. Well-kept and located near the port, this modest hotel even has a family unit for 5 people.

⊜⊜ **La Maison de Kervig**, *Kervig*, ☎ *02 96 20 78 46, charles.villerbu@wanadoo.fr – 2rm* ⊟ ◷ *Closed Nov-Feb.* This beautiful 19C edifice has been beautifully decorated by its artist-gardener owners.

PONTRIEUX AND ENVIRONS

⊜⊜ **Chambres d'hôte Kergoc**, *Quemper-Guézennec*, ☎ *02 96 95 62 72 – 2rm* ⊟ Located in the middle of the countryside, this bed and breakfast offers a variety of accommodation possibilities - two simple rooms on the farm, a well-equipped rest house and a manor for 6 people.

⊜⊜⊜ **Les Korrigann'ès**, *10 rue des Fontaines, Pontrieux*, ☎ *02 96 95 12 46, http://monsite.wanadoo.fr/korrigannes*

– 6rm. The refined setting of this spacious house owned by artists is a blend of rustic and eastern influences. Tea room.

EATING OUT

PAIMPOL AND ENVIRONS

⊜ **Crêperie Morel**, *11 Place du Martray*, ☎ *02 96 20 86 34.* ◷ *Closed Sun; Nov; 10 days in Feb.* Try this address to savour crêpes and galettes made in the Breton tradition.

⊜⊜ **Restaurant du Port**, *17 quai Morand*, ☎ *02 96 20 82 76.* ◷ *Closed Mon in summer; Tue-Wed low season.* Take a seat either in the panoramic room facing the port or on the terrace, in order to enjoy traditional Breton cuisine and impeccable seafood.

⊜⊜ **Le Bellevue**, *Port-Lazo*. ◷ *Closed Mon low season; Jan.* Pub atmosphere with a view of the water. Seafood tray and good wine menu. Evening Jazz on the weekend.

PONTRIEUX

⊜ **Les Jardins du Trieux**, *22 rue St-Yves*, ☎ *02 96 95 06 07.* ◷ *Closed Mon off season.* On a terrace above the Trieux, enjoy crêpes that represent all the provinces of France.

SHOPPING

Markets - Paimpol, Tue, beautiful stands of seafood products; **Plouézec**, Sat morning; **Ploubazlanec**, Sun morning.

RECREATION

Beaches – Near the yachting harbour of Paimpol, **La Tossen** is supervised and offers a sea water swimming-pool.

Windsurf and sea kayak - Centre nautique du Trieux, ☎ 02 96 20 92 80, www.pole-nautique-paimpol.com Lessons and initiations starting at €150. **Force 8**, *rte de Lézardrieux*, ☎ 02 96 22 03 31. Rental of kayaks and windsurfing equipment, €35-50/24h.

Diving - Association subaquatique Paimpolaise, ☎ 06 96 20 92 80. ◷ *Open Apr-Nov.* Explorations and lessons around the island of Bréhat.

Old riggings - Initiation to sailing and fishing, on board the Eulalie, an old sardine boat (€30/day). Information at the pub Le Cargo in Paimpol, ☎ 02 96 55 99 99, www.eulalie-paimpol.com

Walks - The **GR 34 boasts wonderful landscapes between the** pointe de l'Arcouest, Loguivy-de-la-Mer and the mouth of the Trieux. There are also 4 loops around Pontrieux. Information at the Tourist Office.

FESTIVALS

Every two years, Paimpol welcomes the big **Fete of the chant de marin**, with various concerts and animations. The next festival is scheduled for 2-5 Aug 2007. Information ☎ 02 96 55 12 77.

Square Théodore-Botrel

In the square stand an isolated 18C bell-tower, all that remains of a former church, and a monument to the popular singer Théodore Botrel, who died in Pont-Aven in 1925.

Musée de la Mer

Rue de la Benne. 🕐 *Open mid-June to mid-Sept, daily 10.30am-1pm and 3-7pm; Easter school holiday and mid-May to mid-June, 3-6pm.* 🕐 *Closed the rest of the year.* ☞ *€4.30 (children €2.10).* ☎ *02 96 22 02 19.*

Paimpol's seafaring activity, from the time of the Icelandic fishing expeditions to the present day, is recalled by models, photographs and navigational instruments.

La Vapeur du Trieux

Ave du Général-de-Gaulle. 🔲 🕐 *Open late May to late Sep: 1 or 2 departures daily (sometimes does not operate on Mon or Tue).* ☞*€21 (children €10.50).* ☎ *02 96 20 52 06. www.vapeurdutrieux.com.*

A blast from the past when the whistle blows on this old steam locomotive. The train carries passengers on a round trip (4hr 30min) from Paimpol to Pontrieux and back (one-way trips also possible) along the Trieux estuary. Choose the option *avec halte* and stop for 40 minutes at the manoir de Traou Nez for cider and crêpes and some local colour (music, art exhibits). The website is very complete and offers an English version.

Paimpol marina

Excursions

Plourivo, Labyrinthe végétal

2km/1.2mi SW along D 15. Kids ♿ 🕐 *Open July-Aug: daily except Sun 1.30-8pm (last entrance 6.30pm).*👁 €6 *(children €4.50).* ☎ *02 96 20 44 06. www.chez.com/tourisma.*

"Get lost" takes on new meaning here. A maze laid out in a 6ha/15-acre corn field provides ample opportunity for adventure. Every year the theme of the maze varies, with new enigmas to solve and clues to find and actors to make the experience complete (and find your children before closing time).

Tour de Kerroc'h

This tower stands in a pretty wooded setting. From the first platform there is a fine **view**★ of Paimpol Bay.

Ploubazlanec

In the cemetery is a wall on which the names of men lost at sea are recorded.

Pointe de l'Arcouest★★

On the way down to the creek of Arcouest there are remarkable **views** of the bay and of the Île de Bréhat at high tide. Each summer the place is invaded by a colony of artists and men of science and letters. A monument – two identical pink blocks of granite set side by side – has been erected to the memory of Frédéric and Irène Joliot-Curie, who were frequent visitors to Arcouest (below the car park, before the point's larger car park).

Loguivy-de-la-Mer

5km/3mi north. Leave Paimpol towards the Pointe de l'Arcouest, then take D 15.
This fishing port, the second in the Côtes d'Armor departement, is simply a creek in which boats are grounded at low tide.
Climb the promontory that encloses the creek on the left to get a view of the mouth of the River Trieux, Bréhat and the many islands.

Île de Bréhat★★ – 👁 *See Île de BRÉHAT.*

La Cote du Goëlo★

Round-trip of 47km/24mi – 4hr

▷ *Take D 786 south towards St-Quay-Portrieux and on leaving Paimpol, turn left.*

Pointe de Guilben

This is the cliff mentioned in the song by Botrel. From the point which ends in a long spur cutting the cove of Paimpol in two, there is a lovely view of the coast.

▷ *After Kérity, a road to the left leads to the Abbaye de Beauport.*

Abbaye de Beauport★

Founded in the 13C by the Premonstratensians, the abbey was seen as an important spiritual and economic centre for the St-Brieuc diocese. Of the 13C and 14C church only the façade, open-air nave, north aisle and north arm of the transept remain. The long chapter-house with its polygonal apse, lying to the east of the cloisters, is an excellent example of the Anglo-Norman Gothic style, in the pure Mont-St-Michel tradition.

In the northwest corner of the cloisters, to the right of the three fine depressed arches, which stood above the lavabo, is the elegant entrance to the large refectory which looks out over the sea. Pass into the lower court overlooked by the Duc building, a huge hostelry for receiving the pilgrims, and the cellar underneath the refectory, whose groined vaulting rests on eight massive granite columns.

The tour ends with the almonership, the room in which the monks collected the tax on salt and cereals, and the visitor's hostel, with its two naves, where you can see an unusual box bed open on two sides.

The *Conservatoire du Littoral*, a national body in charge of preserving France's coastal heritage, has acquired the abbey estate and implemented a programme aimed at protecting the premises and organising guided tours for visitors.

▷ *Return to the St-Quay road, turn left and past the pool, turn left again onto an uphill road.*

Ste-Barbe

The sea can be seen from the small square of the chapel, the porch of which is decorated with a statue of St Barbara. A path (car park), 250m/274yd further on takes you to a viewing table from where one can see beyond the meadow, Paimpol Bay and its nearby islands, the oyster beds, Port-Lazo and Mez du Goëlo Lighthouse.

▷ *At Plouézec, turn left and at St-Riom left again to Port-Lazo.*

Port-Lazo

At the end of the road there is a view of Paimpol Bay.

▷ *Return to St-Riom; bear left.*

Pointe de Bilfot★

From the viewing table, the **view** extends westwards to the Île de Bréhat and eastwards to Cap Fréhel. Between the small lighthouse at Mez du Goëlo nearby and Paon Lighthouse at Bréhat in the distance, the bay is studded with rocks.

▷ *Turn back and at the entrance to Plouézec, bear left (D 54C).*

Pointe de Minard★★

Make for this rocky platform which affords a wide view over St-Brieuc Bay and Cap d'Erquy, the Paimpol Cove and the Île de Bréhat.

▷ *After a picturesque run along the coast to Le Questel, bear left twice after the hamlet. Make a detour via Pors Pin, a small creek with rocks curiously shaped by erosion, then return to the first junction an dmake a left turn.*

The road runs along the edge of the bare cliff offering glimpses of St-Brieuc Bay and leads to a **viewpoint** *(car park)*. The **view**★ extends over the site of Bréhec-en-Plouha, Pointe de la Tour, St-Quay rocks and the coast from Erquy to Le Val-André.

Bréhec-en-Plouha
A small harbour sheltered by a dike and a modest seaside resort at the bottom of a cove bounded by the Pointe de la Tour on the right and the Pointe de Berjule on the left. St Brieuc and the first emigrants from Britain landed at Bréhec in the 5C.

▶ *Go up the green valley of the Kergolo stream.*

Lanloup
The 15C-16C church has an interesting south porch (♿ *see Introduction: Breton Art*) flanked by buttresses with niches and with St Lupus and St Giles standing on the pediment. The twelve Apostles, carved in granite, on ornate corbels precede the doorway topped by a 14C Virgin. In the cemetery are a cross (1758) and the tomb of the composer Guy Ropartz (1864-1955) in an alcove to the right of the porch.

▶ *Return to Paimpol via Plouézec.*

FORÊT DE PAIMPONT★

MICHELIN LOCAL MAP 309 I6 ILLE-ET-VILAINE (35)

The Forest of Paimpont – the ancient "Brocéllande" where, according to the songs of the Middle Ages, the sorcerer Merlin and the fairy Viviane lived (see Introduction: Tradition and Folklore) – is all that remains in the east of the great forest which, in the early centuries of our era, still covered a large part of inner Brittany extending almost 140km/85mi. The cutting and learing that went on for centuries have reduced the forest so that it now covers an area of only 7 067ha/27sq mi where 500ha/2sq mi belong to the state. Recently great areas have been replanted with conifers which will increase the industry of the massif. A few charming corners remain, especially in the vicinity of the many pools.

Walking Tour

This route leaves from St Léry and follows a round-trip through the forest of Paimpont, past the best-known sites. In the wake of the great fire of September 1990, nature is gaining the upper hand, and, although some trees many centuries old have been lost forever, gorse, heather, broom and ferns are composing a new landscape, which clearly has its own charm. The reforestation of the areas destroyed by the fire will be completed this year.

St-Léry
On the south side of the 14C **church** is a Renaissance porch with two elegant basket-handle arched doors surmounted by delicately carved ogee mouldings. Sculpted figures frame the door on the right: the Virgin, the Angel Gabriel, St Michael slaying the dragon, and one of the damned. The leaves of the door are beautifully carved. Inside, in the nave, is the 16C tomb of St Léry, and opposite it is a little bas-relief in sculpted wood depicting the life of the saint. The lovely Flamboyant chapel in the south side aisle is illuminated through a stained-glass window dating from 1493

which is dedicated to the Virgin Mary. Beneath the gallery, the clock can be seen through a glass door.

Near the church, note a 17C house decorated with three lovely dormer windows.

Château de Comper

🕐 *Open June to Aug, daily (except Tues), 10am-7pm; Apr, May and Sept, daily (except Tues and Fri), 10am-7pm.* ✆ €5 . ☎ *02 97 22 79 96.*

The Montforts, the Charettes, the Rieux, the Lavals, the Colignys, the La Trémoilles and the Rosmadecs are the great families who have at some point been the owners of this site where the fairy Viviane is supposed to have been born. This is also where she is said to have brought up Lancelot, the gallant Knight of the Round Table. The castle was destroyed twice, in the 14C and in the 18C, and all that now remains of it are two sections of curtain wall, the postern and a huge tower; the body of the main building was restored in the 19C. The castle is the headquarters of the Centre Arthurien, which organises exhibitions and events every year on the Celtic world, Arthurian legend or the Middle Ages.

Tombeau de Merlin

Merlin's tomb is indicated by two schist slabs and some holly.

Fontaine de Jouvence

Ordinary looking fountain said to have magic powers.

Étang du Pas-du-Houx

This lake is the largest in the forest (86ha/212 acres). Two châteaux were built on its shores in 1912; Brocéliande, in the Norman style, and Pas-du-Houx.

Paimpont

This market town, deep in the forest near a pool amid tall trees, dates back to the Revolution. It owes its origins to the founding of a monastery in the 7C which, raised

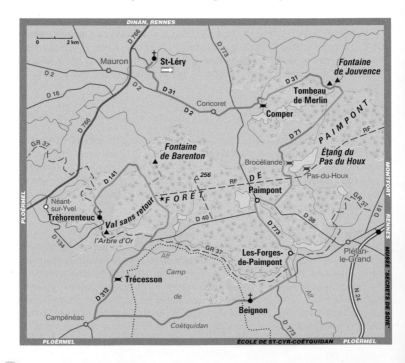

to the status of abbey in the late 12C, survived until the Revolution. The 17C north wing houses the town hall and the presbytery.

The 13C **abbey church** was decorated in the 17C with richly ornate **woodwork**. Busts, carved medallions and festoons of fruit and flowers have been executed with remarkable skill. Note in particular the 15C and 16C statues, including one of St Judicaël, in stone, and a St Méen, in wood, the 16C high altar and some beautiful 17C woodwork. The **treasury** (♿🕐 *Open July and Aug, daily, 10am-noon and 3-6.30pm; Easter to June and Sept, Sat-Sun and holidays, 10am-noon and 3-6.30pm. No charge.* ☎ *02 99 07 81 37)*, in the sacristy, displays a statue of St Anne carrying the

Address Book

TOURIST OFFICES

Syndicat d'initiative de Paimpont, 5 espl. Brocéliande, ☎ 02 99 07 84 23, www.broceliande-tourisme.info July-Aug: daily 10-12am, 2-6pm; off season: 10-12am, 2-5pm, 🕐 closed Mon and Jan. **Tréhorenteuc**, Place de l'Abbé Gillard, ☎ 02 97 93 05 12, www.valsanretour.com June-Sep: daily 9am-7pm; off season: Mon-Sat 9.30-12am, 2-5.30pm, Sun 2-5.30pm.

GUIDED TOURS

In July and August, the Paimpont tourist office organises tours of the main legendary sites of the **Brocéliande Forest**. The guide comes with you in your personal car. About €5/10 per person, no charge for children under 10

Le Centre de l'imaginaire arthurien, at the Comper castle, also offers guided tours focusing on **Arthurian legends** on Mon and Tue from mid-July to mid-Sep.

For coin ranges, see the Legend on the cover flap.

WHERE TO STAY

⊜⊜ **Relais de Brocéliande**, *5 rue des Forges, Paimpon*t, ☎ *02 99 07 84 94, www.le-relais-de-broceliande.fr - 24 rooms* ✗ 🕐 *Closed 15 Dec-1st Jan.* In this former 19C coaching inn, you will find modest but well-kept rooms and a good restaurant. If you enjoy fishing, ask the owner for advice on the best spots.

⊜⊜ **La Corne de Cerf**, *Le Cannée, take the direction of Beignon*, ☎ *02 99 07 84 19 - 3 rooms*, 🕐 *Closed Jan.* This elegant house offers bright and fresh rooms, giving onto a delightful English

garden. Home made jams and breads for the breakfast.

⊜⊜ **Le Val sans retour**, *Tréhorenteuc*, ☎ *02 97 93 08 08, gite-valsansretour@hotmail.com - 31 rooms*, 🍴 *€5*. This old presbytery welcomes walkers and lovers of nature. Some rooms offer more comfort than others (2 to 6 beds per room).

⊜ **La Hulotte**, *St-Malon-sur-Mel*, ☎ *02 99 07 57 21, lahulotte35@yahoo.fr - 20 beds*. You will have the choice between guest rooms for 1 and 2 people in the comfortable rooms of an old farm.

EATING OUT

⊜ **Au Temps des Moines**, *16 av. du Chevalier Ponthus, Paimpont*, ☎ *02 99 07 89 63*. 🕐 *Closed Mon-Wed off season*. Creperie with a rustic setting, facing Paimpont Lake.

⊜⊜ **Le Relais des Diligence**s, *Place de l'Église, Plélan-le-Grand*, ☎ *02 99 06 81 44*. 🕐 *Closed Mon*. At the heart of the village, this small family hostelry serves authentic regional cuisine. Menu with roast rabbit and cider parfait, served at noon and in the evening.

Relais de Brocéliande, Paimpont. This address is worth it for its ultra-kitsch decoration and its good and copious regional cuisine.

DISCOVER THE COUNTRYSIDE

The Brocéliande country is full of paths you can take on foot, on bike or on horseback. Several guides and maps are for sale at the Tourist Office of Paimpont or at the Pays touristique de Brocéliande, 1 rue des Korrigans, à Plélan-le-Grand, ☎ 02 99 06 86 07. Experienced ramblers can also pick up the IGN map Brocéliand (€7.50).

Virgin and Child (15C), an interesting arm reliquary of St Judicaël (15C) and, most importantly, a magnificent ivory Christ (18C).

Les Forges de Paimpont

This pretty hamlet, next to a lake, owes its name to the forges which were here between the 16C and late 19C. They were fuelled by iron ore and local wood and produced a highly valued metal.

Beignon

The church contains some beautiful 16C stained-glass windows. In the chancel, behind the altar, there are a representation of the Crucifixion of St Peter, and, in the north transept, that of the Tree of Jesse.

Château de Trécesson

Access is limited to the interior courtyard.

This castle, surrounded by a pool, was built at the end of the 14C in reddish schist and still has its original medieval appearance. A striking gatehouse flanked with corbelled turrets commands the entrance.

Fontaine de Barenton

Accessible on foot only. Endowed with supernatural powers (according to legend), this fountain could generate violent storms when water from the spring was poured onto the **Perron de Merlin** (Merlin's threshold), a nearby stone slab.

Tréhorenteuc

In the **church** (🕐 *Open daily (except Sun morning), 9.30am-noon and 2-5.30pm.* ☎ *02 97 93 05 12.)* and sacristy, mosaics and pictures illustrate the legend of the Val sans retour and the Barenton fountain. In the chancel: stained-glass window of the Holy Grail; painting of the Knights of the Round Table.

Val sans retour

Known as the "Valley of No Return", this is one of the places most heavily steeped in legend in the Forêt de Paimpont. It can be found by taking the unsurfaced track, for pedestrians only, after the second car park. This leads to the Fairies' Mirror and False Lovers' Rock (Miroir des Fées et Rocher des Faux Amants). Legend has it that Morgana the witch, jealous of a knight who had been unfaithful to her, cast a spell over the valley preventing anyone who had done wrong from leaving it. Only Lancelot, who remained faithful to Guinevere, was able to break the spell. At the Fairies' Mirror, note the splendid **Golden Tree** (Arbre d'Or), the work of François Davin, which marks the furthest spot reached by the fire of 1990.

The Golden Tree

M. Gurfinklel/MICHELIN

Additional Sights

École de St-Cyr-Coëtquidan

Coëtquidan military academy houses the training schools for elite officers of the land forces: the École Spéciale Militaire, founded in 1802 by Napoleon Bonaparte, commonly known as St-Cyr or Coët in military circles; the École Militaire Interarmes, founded in 1961 by Général de Gaulle; the École Militaire du Corps Technique et Administratif, founded in 1977 by President Giscard d'Estaing and the Bataillion des Élèves-Officiers en Réserve (EORs – Reserve Officers' Training Cadet Corps).

Musée du Souvenir★

○ Open daily (except Mon), 10am-noon and 2-6pm. ○ Closed 1 May and mid-Dec to mid-Feb. €5. ☎ 02 97 73 53 06.
This museum, famed for its memorial ("France" by Antoine Bourdelle) in honour of 17 000 officers killed in action, is to the right of Cours Rivoli. It retraces the history of officer training from the Ancien Régime to the present and contains numerous documents, uniforms and military decorations connected with this elite.

Site mégalithique de Monteneuf

○ Open July and Aug, daily, 10.30am-6.30pm; Apr to June, Sept and Oct, Sat-Sun and holidays, 2.30-6pm. €3. ☎ 02 97 22 04 78.
Located on the moor lying between Guer and Monteneuf, this megalithic site is seen as one of the most important in central Brittany; it is currently being excavated and restored. More than 20 huge blocks of purple schist have been raised with the help of the Engineers from the nearby military college of Coëtquidan.
Two 7km/4.3mi long pedestrian itineraries takes you past the Loge Morinais (schist gallery graves), the menhirs of Chomet, Coëplan and Pierres Droites (standing stone), the Pièce Couverte, the Rocher Maheux and the Bordoués (gallery graves). Over 420 officially listed menhirs, thought to have been knocked down towards the end of the first millenium on the orders of the Church, line D 776.

St-Méen-le-Grand

In the 6C, St Méen (Mewan), a monk from Great Britain, founded an abbey on this site, which was reconstructed several times from the 11C to the 18C. The abbey buildings now contain flats. The church retains a fine 12C square **tower**. Inside, note in the south aisle, the tombstone, and in the south transept, the statue and funerary monument of St Méen, all from the 15C. Some 13C and 14C frescoes recently discovered beneath the plasterwork are currently undergoing restoration.

Musée Louison Bobet

○ Open 2-5pm ○ Closed Tue (Oct-June, 1 Jan and 25 Dec. ☎ 02 99 06 67 86.
A small museum is dedicated to the career of Louison Bobet, the legendary cycling champion, native of St-Méen, who won the famous Tour de France race several times in the early 1950s.

PERROS-GUIREC ≈≈

POPULATION 7 614
MICHELIN LOCAL MAP 309 B2

This much-frequented seaside resort (casino, seawater therapy centre), built in the form of an amphitheatre on the pink granite coast, overlooks the fishing and pleasure boat harbour, the anchorage and the two gently sloping, fine sand, sheltered beaches (Kids *ideal for children*) of Trestraou and Trestignel.

Also See: Côte de GRANITE ROSE.

Sights

Church

Open Mon to Fri, 9.30-noon and 2.30pm-5.30pm. Presbytère de Perros-Guirec ☎ 02 96 23 21 64.

A porch with delicate trefoil arches abuts onto the massive 14C belfry topped by a dome (1669) crowned by a spire. Go into the **Romanesque nave**★, all that remains of the first chapel built on the spot. Massive pillars, cylindrical on the left and with engaged columns on the right, support capitals which are either historiated or adorned with geometrical designs. It is separated by a diaphragm arch from the Gothic nave built in the 14C at the same time as the chancel. In this arch is a rood beam on which Christ is surrounded by the Virgin and St John. The church has a 12C granite stoup decorated with small figures and several old statues: an Ecce Homo (15C), St Lawrence and St Catherine (16C), St James, patron of the parish (17C). The round-arched south porch is richly ornamented.

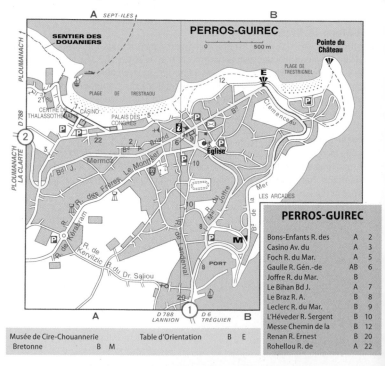

PERROS-GUIREC		
Bons-Enfants R. des	A	2
Casino Av. du	A	3
Foch R. du Mar.	A	5
Gaulle R. Gén.-de	AB	6
Joffre R. du Mar.	B	
Le Bihan Bd J.	A	7
Le Braz R. A.	B	8
Leclerc R. du Mar.	B	9
L'Héveder R. Sergent	B	10
Messe Chemin de la	B	12
Renan R. Ernest	B	20
Rohellou R. de	A	22

Musée de Cire-Chouannerie Bretonne	B M	Table d'Orientation	B E

Viewing Table (Table d'orientation)

A splendid **view**★ of the Pointe du Château, Trestrignel Beach, Port-Blanc, Trélevern, Trévou, the Île de Tomé, Sept-Îles and of the rocks below.

Pointe du Château

From this steep little viewpoint, there is a lovely **view**★ over the site of Perros-Guirec, Sept-Îles, the Île Tomé and the coast as far as Port-L'Épine.

Musée de Cire Chouannerie Bretonne

🕐 *Open June to Aug: 9.30am-6.30pm; April-May and Sep: 10am-12.15pm and 4-6pm.*
🕐 *Closed the rest of the year.* ☞ *€3 (children €1.50).* ☎ *02 96 91 23 45.*

This wax museum has reconstituted historical scenes with figures dating from La Chalotais to Auguste Renan. Note the collection of regional headdresses from Lower Brittany.

Excursions

La Clarté

3km/2mi by ② on the town plan.

The pretty rose granite **Chapelle Notre-Dame-de-la-Clarté**★ stands 200m/219yd back from the road. In the 16C the lord of Barac'h, whose ship was in danger in fog off the coast, vowed to build a chapel to Our Lady at whatever spot on the coast that first emerged from the fog. The promised chapel was built on the height which enabled him to take his bearings; to commemorate the circumstances, it was called Our Lady of Light (Notre-Dame-de-la-Clarté). The south doorway is adorned with sculptures in low relief: on the lintel, an Annunciation and *Pietà*; two coats of arms and a Virgin and Child frame the mullioned window in the registry; under the porch are two 17C wood statues and 16C door panels. The tall nave includes three bays decorated with carved roses and foliage; the 15C stoup ornamented with three Moorish heads and the Stations of the Cross by Maurice Denis (1931) are noteworthy. A pardon is held every year *(👣 see Calendar of events).*

Take Rue du Tertre which starts on the north side of the chapel, leading to the top of a rocky knoll which affords a good **view**★.

Sémaphore★★ (Signal Station)

3.5km/2.5mi west. Leave Perros-Guirec by ② on the town plan.

From the roadside look-out point the **view**★ extends to the rocks of Ploumanach, seawards to Sept-Îles and behind to the beaches of Perros-Guirec, and in the distance along the Port-Blanc coastline.

Le Sentier des Douaniers★★

🚶 *3hr on foot there and back.* 👣 *The best time to go is in the morning, and if possible, at high tide.*

Follow the edge of the cliff as far as Pors-Rolland to reach the lighthouse via the Pointe de Squéouel, the Ploumanac'h lighthouse and the Maison du Littoral information centre. Bring your camera!

Ploumanac'h★★

This little fishing port on the pink granite coast, belonging to the municipality of Perros-Guirec and well situated at the mouths of the two picturesque Traouiéros valleys, has become a well-known seaside resort, famous for its piles of **rocks**★★. You will get a good view of them by going to the lighthouse. The **Parc municipal**★★ extends from Pors-Kamor, where the lifeboat is kept, to Pors-Rolland. It is a sort of reserve where the rocky site is kept in its original state. The most interesting feature

Address Book

TOURIST OFFICE

Perros-Guirec, 21 Place de l'Hôtel-de-Ville, ☎ 02 96 23 21 15, www.perros-guirec.com ◷ Open Jul-Aug: Mon-Sat 9am-7.30pm, Sun 10am-noon, 4pm-7pm; off season: Mon-Sat 9am-12.30pm, 2pm-6.30pm. Ticket booth for Bréhat Island and the Sept-Îles.

For coin ranges, see the Legend on the cover flap.

WHERE TO STAY

PERROS-GUIREC

◌◌ **Le Suroît**, *81 rue Ernest Renan*, ☎ 02 96 23 03 55 – 10rm ✕ ◷ *Closed Feb.* Near the port, these small, nice, clean rooms are a good value for the price.

◌ **Les Sternes**, *rond-point de Perros-Louanec*, ☎ 02 96 91 03 38, www.sternes.com – 20rm ⅋ An old fisherman's house with simple, bright and well kept rooms.

◌◌ **À la Corniche**, *41 rue de la Petite-Corniche*, ☎ 02 96 23 28 08, www.perso.orange.fr/corniche/ - 2rm and a rest house ⊨ ◷ *Closed Christmas hols.* The upstairs of this house overlooks the sea and contains very elegant rooms with beautiful views. Adjoining rest house also available.

◌◌ **Le Gulf Stream**, *26 rue des Sept-Îles*, ☎ 02 96 23 21 86, www.gulf-stream-hotel-bretagne.com – 11rm, ⊠ €7.50, ✕ ◷ *Closed mid-Nov to 25 Dec.* Small and simple rooms are available some with and some without a view, or for an even more pleasant stay, reserve the bungalow with balcony.

◌◌ **L'Hermitage**, *20 rue des Frères Le Montréer*, ☎ 02 96 23 21 22, www.hotel-hermitage-22.com – 23rm, ⊠ €6, ✕ ◷ *Closed Oct-25 Mar.* Near the church, traditional hotel with small garden. Simple but bright and well kept rooms.

◌◌◌ **Le Morgane**, *92 av. du Casino*, ☎ 02 96 23 22 80, www.hotel-morgane.com – 29rm, ⊠ €6.50, ⤢✕ ◷ *Closed 10-28 Feb; Christmas holidays.* Very well located near the beach of Trestraou, this hotel dates to the beginning of the 20C and offers comfortable rooms, with or without balcony.

◌◌ **Villa Cyrnos**, *10 rue du Sergent l'Hévéder*, ☎ 02 96 91 13 36, villa-cyrnos22@wanadoo.fr – 5rm ⊨ This 1950s home in pink granite provides big, bright and comfortable rooms; some have views of the sea, others of the garden. Family unit for 4 people also available.

◌◌◌ **Le Beauséjour**, *plage du Coz-Pors*, ☎ 02 96 23 88 02 – 16rm, ⊠ €9, ✕ ◷ *Closed 5 Jan to mid-Feb; 15 Nov-18 Dec.* Rooms of variable sizes, decorated in a maritime theme, boast views of the water, while others have a terrace. Around back, the rooms are simpler with a view of the rocks. Pleasant restaurant with a traditional cuisine (◌◌◌).

EATING OUT

PERROS-GUIREC

◌ **Les Blés Noirs**, *105 av. du Casino*, ☎ 02 96 91 19 47. Set back from the beach of Trestraou, a crêperie well-known for its culinary skill. Terrace and room with a maritime setting.

◌ **Les Vieux Gréements**, *port de plaisance*, ☎ 02 96 91 14 99. ◷ *Closed Tue low season and Mon year-round.* Crêperie-mussels shop located in an old Breton house with terrace. Very lively on summer nights.

◌◌ **La Bonne Auberge**, *Place de la Chapelle, La Clarté*, ☎ 02 96 91 46 05. A pleasant site, where you can dine with a view of the water. The freshness of the seafood is guaranteed by the owner (a fish merchant). Provides very simple rooms in half-board during the summer (◌).

La Crémaillère, *Place de l'Église*, ☎ 02 96 23 22 08. Dine on inventive regional cuisine and seafood under the beams of this rustic room. Located in the town centre.

◌◌◌ **Le Gulf Stream**. ◷ *Closed Sat lunch; Sun evening low season; Mon in season; Jan.* Pleasant panoramic room with view over the sea. Regional cuisine and seafood inspired by international flavours. Good but expensive wine list.

◌◌◌ **Les Feux des Îles**, *53 bd Clémenceau*, ☎ 02 96 23 22 94. ◷ *Closed*

Oct-Apr: Mon-Thu lunch; Sun evening; Mon (except public holidays); 3 weeks Sept-Oct; 20 Dec-15 Jan. Comfortable room and wonderful terrace leading to a garden where diners enjoy meticulously prepared regional cuisine.

ENTERTAINMENT

Casino de Perros-Guirec, *plage de Trestraou*, ☎ *02 96 49 80 80*. Games of chance begin at 9.30pm.

SHOPPING

Markets – Fri in **Perros-Guirec** and Tue in **Trébeurden**.

Honey - Lossouarn, *20 rue du Mar. Joffre,* ☎ *02 96 23 14 43*. Honey of heather, chestnut tree, bramble and other flavours of Brittany.

RECREATION

Windsurf, surfboard and sea kayak - Centre nautique de Perros-Guirec, *plage de Trestraou,* ☎ *02 96 49 89 21, www.perros-guirec.com*. Windsurfing lessons of windsurf and rentals at the Point Passion Plage in summer. Trips and individual kayaking lessons (must be 14yrs). **Base nautique de l'Île Grande**, *Pors Gelen,* ☎ *02 96 91 92 10, www.bnig.maline.org Mar-Nov.* **Club nautique de Trégastel**, *La Grève Rose,* ☎ *02 96 23 45 05*. With lessons even for the kinder-crowd (must be 5 yrs), you can take a stab at learning to pilot an Optimist and sailer; windsurfing rentals and funboards. Kayaking trips from an hour to a whole day (must be 14yrs); lessons in Jul-Aug.

Old riggings – Participate as a crew member on board the Sant C'hireg, ☎ *06 85 92 60 61,* €22/36 entire day. **Le centre nautique de Perros-Guirec** also offers trips along the Côte de Granit Rose on board the Ar jentilez, €17/22, half day.

Diving - Lodan Glaz, *Barnabanec, Perros-Guirec,* ☎ *06 80 45 81 93.* ⏰*Open Easter-Nov.* Trips and explorations on Ploumanach and the reserve of the Sept-Îles. **Centre Activités Plongée de Trébeurden**, 54 corniche de Goas Treiz, ☎ 02 96 23 66 71, www.plongeecap. com ⏰ Open Apr-15 Nov. Explore between Trébeurden and Trégastel (must be 14yrs).

Surf – For surf/tide information, contact **Thierry Deniel** ☎ 02 96 91 46 20. **Seven Island Surf Club**, Perros-Guirec, plage de Trestraou, ☎ 02 96 23 18 38. ⏰ Open Oct-May. Surf, bodyboard and longboard.

Thalasso - Thermes marins de Perros-Guirec, plage de Trestraou, ☎ 02 96 23 28 97. Stress therapy, sauna, jacuzzi. **Forum de Trégastel**, ☎ 02 96 15 30 44. Water games, paddling pools and warm sea water swimming pool.

Walks and hikes –The Perros-Guirec tourist office publication details three easy walking itineraries in the area as well as a 23-km marked circuit for all terrain vehicles. Guided walks on the path between Perros-Guirec and Ploumanach are organized by the Maison du littoral in Ploumanach, 15 Jun-15 Sep: Mon - Sat.

Horse riding - Poney-Club de Rulan, rte de Lannion, Trégastel, ☎ 02 96 23 85 29 ⏰ Closed Sep. Ponies and horses for all levels (1hr – Full day available).

FESTIVALS

Perros-Guirec - Festival of chamber music, Jul-Aug. **Grand pardon N.-D.-de-la-Clarté**, 14-15 Aug, followed by fest-noz.

---

is the Pointe de Squewel, formed of innumerable rocks separated by coves. The Devil's Castle (Château du Diable) also makes a fine picture.

The park is studded with curiously shaped rocks: note a turtle by the sea, and inland, a mushroom, a rabbit, etc.

Maison du Littoral

♿ ⏰ *Mid-June to mid-Sept, 10.30am-7pm; school hoidays: daily except Mon 2.30pm-5.30pm.* ⏰ *Closed Nov-Jan, 1 May and 25 Dec.* ⊗ *No charge.* ☎ *02 96 91 62 77.* This information centre has a variety of exhibits related to the formation of granite and the different methods for extracting and using this stone.

Beach

The beach lies in the bay of St-Guirec. At the far end on the left, on a rock washed by the sea at high tide, stands the oratory dedicated to St Guirec, who landed here in the 6C. A granite statue of the saint has taken the place of the original wooden effigy which had suffered from a disrespectful tradition: girls who wanted to get married stuck a pin into his nose.

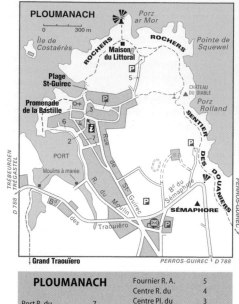

Sept-Îles

Boats tour the islands. Four companies use a central reservation service at the Trestaou Gare Maritime. Some boats are "glass bottomed". Excursions (1hr30min to 3hr30min) round various islands (with or without stopovers of variable length) from Feb to early Nov. ☎ 02 96 91 10 00.

This archipelago has been an ornithological centre since 1912. You can observe more sea birds in the morning and in the evening: choose the first or the last departure.

Rouzic

⊘ Landing forbidden. The boat goes near the island, also known as Bird Island, where a large **colony**★ of northern gannets, some 12 000 pairs, settle from February to September; they can be observed from Grande Island's ornithological centre *(closed-circuit remote control television)*. One can see guillemots, razorbills, lesser and great black-backed gulls, puffins, crested cormorants, black-legged kittiwakes, oyster catchers and petrels all of which reproduce in March and leave at the end of July. Another interesting feature is the presence of a small colony of grey seals (around a dozen).

The boat then skirts Malban and Bono Islands.

Île aux Moines

The boat stops at the island *(1hr)* where you may visit the old gunpowder factory, the **lighthouse** (83 steps; range 40km/25mi – *Guided tours (30min) June to Sept, daily, depending on arrival time of the boats. No charge. ☎ 02 96 23 92 10.)* which offers a fine panorama of the islands and the coast, the ruined fort erected by Vauban on the far tip and below the former monastery with its tiny chapel and well.

On the return journey, the curious pink granite rocks at the Pointe de Ploumanach come into view.

Puffins nest in colonies on cliffs and grassy islands

PLEYBEN★★

POPULATION 3 397
MICHELIN LOCAL MAP 308 H5

The great feature of Pleyben is its magnificent parish close, built from the 15C to the 17C. *Pardon* on the first Sunday in August.

ⓒ **Also See:** Monts d'ARRÉE.

Parish Close★★

The monumental door was rebuilt in 1725.

Calvary★★
Built in 1555 near the church's side entrance, it was displaced in 1738 and given its present form in 1743. Since then new motifs and scenes have been added to the monument: the Last Supper and Washing of the Disciples' Feet date from 1650. The huge pedestal with triumphal arches enhances the figures on the platform.
To follow the life of Christ start at the corner with the Annunciation and move in an anticlockwise direction to discover the Nativity, the Adoration of the Shepherds etc.

Church★
The church, dedicated to St Germanus of Auxerre, is dominated by two belfries, of which that on the right is the more remarkable. It is a Renaissance **tower**★★ crowned with a dome with small lantern turrets. The other tower has a Gothic spire linked to the corner turret at the balustrade level. Beyond the arm of the south transept is a curious quatrefoil sacristy, dating from 1719, with cupolas and lantern turrets.
Inside, the nave has 16C panelled **vaulting**★; the ribs and the remarkable purlin are carved and painted with mythological and religious scenes.
At the high altar is an altarpiece with turrets and a two storey tabernacle (17C). At the centre of the east end is a 16C **stained-glass window**★ depicting the Passion. Note the pulpit, the organ case (1688), the Baptism of Christ over the font and the many coloured statues including St Yves between the rich man and the pauper.

Chapelle funéraire
A former 16C ossuary where exhibitions are held.

PRESQU'ÎLE DE PLOUGASTEL★

MICHELIN LOCAL MAP 308 E4 FINISTÈRE (29)

Lying away from main roads, Plougastel Peninsula is a corner of the Breton countryside, which may still be seen in its traditional guise. Narrow, winding roads run between hedges through farming country, characteristically cut up into squares. There are few houses apart from occasional hamlets grouped round their little chapels. Here everything seems hidden away; you are deep in the strawberry country, but you will not see the strawberries, which grow in open fields, unless you get out of your car and look through the gaps in the hedges. Vast glassed-in areas shelter vegetables and flowers. In May and June, however, when the strawberries are picked, there is plenty of life on the roads.

Plougastel-Daoulas

Calvary★★

(⌖ See illustration in Introduction: Art and Culture) Built in 1604 to commemorate the end of the Plague of 1598, the Calvary is made of dark Kersanton granite and ochre stone from Logonna. It is more harmonious than the Guimiliau Calvary but the attitude of the 180 figures seems more stiff. On either side of the Cross, the two thieves (do not appear at Guimiliau) are surmounted by an angel and a devil respectively. On the Calvary base an altar is carved under a portico; above is a large statue of Christ leaving the tomb.

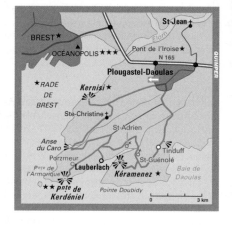

The church is built of granite and reinforced concrete; inside it is brilliant with blue, green, orange and violet, all used in its decoration.

Musée du Patrimoine et de la Fraise

This museum of local history, traditions and ethnology contains various documents, objects, tools and items of furniture and clothing relating to everyday life from the 18C until the present. Displayed in more detail are the cultivation of flax and **strawberries** (fraises), and marine activities linked with exporting these two crops, as well as trawling for scallops in Brest Bay.

Chapelle St-Jean

▶ *4.5km/3mi northeast on D 29 towards Landerneau and after crossing the Brest-Quimper expressway bear left then right.*

The 15C chapel, remodelled in the 17C, stands in a verdant **site**★ on the banks of the Élorn.

Peninsula★

Round-trip of 35km/22mi – allow 3hr

▷ *Leave Plougastel-Daoulas by a road to the right of the church; follow the signposts to Kernisi.*

Panorama de Kernisi★
At the entrance to the hamlet of Kernisi, leave the car and make for a knoll. From here you will see a panorama of the Brest roadstead, the outer harbour and town of Brest, the Élorn estuary and the Pont Albert-Louppe.

▷ *Turn round and at the second main junction, bear right towards Langristin.*

Drive past the 16C **Chapelle Ste-Christine** and its small Calvary dating from 1587. From the **Anse du Caro** there is a fine view of Brest and Pointe des Espagnols.

▷ *Go back in the direction of Plougastel-Daoulas and after 3km/2mi, turn right.*

Pointe de Kerdéniel★★
Allow 15min on foot there and back. Leave the car at the bottom of Kerdéniel and after the houses turn right and take the lane on the left (signposts) to the blockhouse. The view extends, from left to right, over Le Faou estuary, the mouth of the Aulne, Ménez-Hom, Île Longue, Presqu'île de Crozon's east coast to Pointe des Espagnols and Brest Sound.

▷ *Turn back and after 3km/2mi, bear right.*

Lauberlach
This small fishing port and sailing centre is set in a pretty cove.

▷ *Take the road on the right towards St-Adrien.*

From the hillside, the road gives fine glimpses of Lauberlach cove and passes the Chapelle St-Adrien (1549) on the right.

▷ *Next turn right towards St-Guénolé. At Pennaster, go round Lauberlach Cove.*

At Pennaster, go round Lauberlach cove. The Chapelle St-Guénolé (1514) stands in a wooded setting on the left side of the road.

▷ *At the first junction beyond St-Guenolé, take an uphill road on the right; turn right, then left onto a stony lane.*

Keramenez Viewing Table★
An extensive panorama over the Presqu'île de Plougastel and the southern section of Brest roadstead.

▷ *Return to Plougastel-Daoulas by the fishing port of Tinduff, then Lestraouen and Lanriwaz.*

WHERE TO STAY
◷◷ **Kastel Roc'h**, at the interchange of D 33A, ☎ 02 98 40 32 00, *kastel-roch@wanadoo.fr* – 45rm, 🍽 €8, ✕ Located at a crossroads in the countryside, these well-insulated rooms offer a break from the buzz of the city. Traditional cuisine is served in the rotunda accented by a king-sized fireplace.

EATING OUT
◷◷ **Le Chevalier de l'Auberlach**, *rue Mathurin Thomas*, ☎ 02 98 40 54 56. 🕐 *Closed Sun evening.* This is the right place for all you knights-in-shining armour. Try out the traditional cuisine served in a romantic mediaeval atmosphere complete with stained glass windows, exposed beams and, of course, armour.

PONT-AVEN★

POPULATION 2 960
MICHELIN LOCAL MAP 308 I7 – FINISTÈRE (29)

The town lies in a very pleasant setting at the point where the River Aven, after flowing between rocks, opens out into a tidal estuary. The Aven used to drive numerous mills, hence the saying: "Pont-Aven, a famous town; 14 mills, 15 houses". Today only one mill remains in operation. Pont-Aven is also famous for Galettes de Pont-Aven (butter cookies) and as a favourite resort of painters; the Pont-Aven School, headed by Gauguin, was formed in about 1888. The poet and songwriter Théodore Botrel spent a great part of his life in Pont-Aven and is buried here. Botrel started the Festival of the Golden Gorse.

Pont-Aven School

Between 1886 and 1896 more than 20 painters (Charles Laval, Paul Sérusier, Charles Filiger, Maurice Denis) grouped around Paul Gauguin seeking to invent new forms of artistic expression. The meeting between **Paul Gauguin** and **Émile Bernard** in 1888 was the beginning of the Synthetist group. Rejecting the Impressionist and Pointillist movements, their work was characterised by painting from memory, two-dimensional patterns, bright vivid colours and spiritual subjects.

The Caisse Nationale des Monuments Historiques has set up La Route des Peintres, which includes five itineraries of one or two days each, described in a book of the same name (available in English). The tours start in an art gallery, concentrating on the works of local and visiting artists in Cornouaille, 1850-1950, then take the visitor off to discover the landscapes which inspired the art.

Sights

Promenade Xavier-Grall

Access via rue Émile-Bernard.

This promenade (named after the poet and reporter **Xavier Grall**, 1930-81), along the Aven, passes by the mill course and gates, which regulated the water to the

Breton Women by Gauguin

Musée d'Orsay, Paris/RMN

mills, and old wash-houses scattered on either side of the river. Footbridges span the river, which winds between the Porche-Menu rocks.

Bois d'Amour★

Access via Promenade Xavier-Grall.

🚶 A footpath follows the meanders of the Aven and climbs the hillside. With the aid of maps produced by the tourist office, this pleasant walk unfolds to visitors the places which inspired the painters of the Pont-Aven School.

The Banks of the Aven

Allow 30min on foot there and back. Walk to the right of the bridge towards the harbour.

🚶 Follow the river bank lined with rocks and ruined watermills. On the river's east bank, there is an enormous rock called Gargantua's shoe *(soulier de Gargantua)*.
In the square, beside the harbour, is a statue of Botrel and on the opposite bank, amid the greenery, stands the house where he lived. About 800m/875yd further on, there is a view of the fine stretch of water formed by the Aven. The once prosperous port (oysters, wine, salt and grain) is now used by pleasure boats.

Chapelle de Trémalo

Access via rue Émile-Bernard and right on D 24, the Quimper road (signposted).

This characteristic early-16C Breton country chapel is set amid fine trees. It has a lopsided roof, with one of the eaves nearly touching the ground. Inside is a 17C wooden Christ, which was the model for Gauguin's *Yellow Christ* where, painted in the background, is the village of Pont-Aven and Ste-Marguerite Hill.

Musée de Pont-Aven

♿🕐 *Open July and Aug, daily, 10am-7pm; Apr to June, Sept and Oct, 10am-12.30pm and 2-6.30pm; Feb, Mar, and Nov and Dec, 10am-12.30pm and 2-6pm.* ⌛ *The museum closes for four days between temporary exhibitions.* ✎ *€4.* ☎ *02 98 06 14 43.*

The modern wing is for temporary exhibits and the old wing recounts with photographs and documents the history of Pont-Aven: the town, port, Gorse-Bloom Festival, and the Pont-Aven painters and their lodgings (Pension Gloanec).
The first floor houses the permanent collection concentrating on the Pont-Aven School *(see above)*: Maurice Denis *(Midsummer Bonfire at Loctudy)*, Émile Jourdan *(Lanriot Chapel)*, Rouillet *(The Port in Pont-Aven)*, Gustave Loiseau *(View of Pont-Aven)*, and works by Paul Sérusier, Charles Filiger, Émile Schuffenecker. An audio visual presentation illustrates the environment which favoured the development of the Pont-Aven School: the Golden Gorse Festival, the Gloanec boarding house where the painters lived.
Temporary exhibits present artists who worked in Brittany at the end of the 19C as well as contemporary artists, who are once more being welcomed in Pont-Aven.

Driving Tour

▶ *Leave Pont-Aven by D 24 towards Rosporden. Nizon lies 3km/2mi NW.*

Nizon

The small **church** (restored) with its squat pillars dates from the 15C and 16C and contains many old statues. The colours of the stained-glass windows by the master glazier Guével are remarkable. The Romanesque Calvary was used as a model by Gauguin for his *Green Christ*.

Address Book

TOURIST OFFICE

Pont-Aven, 5 Place de l'Hôtel de ville, ☎ 02 98 06 04 70. July-Aug: everyday 9.30am-7.30pm; off season: 10am-12.30pm, 2-6pm.

For coin ranges, see the Legend on the cover flap.

WHERE TO STAY

⊜⊜ **Les Ajoncs d'or**, *11 quai Théodore Botrel*, ☎ *02 98 06 13 06 - www.hotel-pontaven.online.fr – 17 rooms*, ⇌ *€7*. In the centre of Pont-Aven, a very pleasant place with elegant rooms (choose one in the main building) equipped with bright wood furniture and sea rush floors.

⊜⊜⊜ **Roz Aven**, *11 quai Théodore Botrel*, ☎ *02 98 0613 06, www.hotelpontaven.online.fr – 17 rooms*, ⇌ *€7*, ✕ A good occasion to sleep in a cottage, really near the centre! Nice rooms with very different styles (Louis XVI, Voltaire, Breton); most of them have a view on the sailing harbour.

EATING OUT

⊜ **Le Talisman**, *4 rue Paul Sérusier*, ☎ *02 98 06 02 58.* ◷ *Closed Mon in summer.* Owned and operated by the same family since 1920, this good crêperie bears the name of a small painting by Sérusier (1888) describing the Bois d'Amour.

⊜⊜ **Le Rive gauche**, *13 rue du Gén.-de-Gaulle (take the passage)*, ☎ *02 98 09*

14 94. ◷ *Closed Wed, Tue evening and Sat noon.* Fish and meat dishes served on a covered terrace above the River Aven. The speciality: grilled sparerib of pork.

⊜⊜⊜ **Le Moulin de Rosmadec**, ☎ *02 98 06 00 22.* ◷ *Closed Wed.* An unusual sight in the centre of town, this mill provides 4 charming rooms, but is best known for the exceptional setting of the dining room, featuring copper pans, faiences and Breton furniture. Try the grilled "Saint-Pierre" (John Dory) with artichokes and then crêpes souf-flés with lemon.

LEISURE

River cruises – Vedettes Aven-Bélon, ☎ *02 98 71 14 59.* From Apr to Sep, guided tours on the Aven and the Bélon (1h to 2h): small ports, castles, beaches and sea birds. €10-15/person.

SHOPPING

Crêpes – *Penven, 1 quai Théodore Botrel*, ☎ *02 98 06 05 87. Daily 9am-7.30pm in summer.* The shop bears the name of the inventor of the famous crepes with fresh butter from Pont-Aven, which you can choose thick or thin.

Aboriginal art– *Le temps du Rêve, 19 rue du Gén.-de-Gaulle*, ☎ *02 98 06 02 58. Daily 2.30-6.30pm in summer.* A change of pace from the Pont-Aven school, this gallery is devoted to the art of the native Australians."

From Pont-Aven to Concarneau on the Coast Road

▷ *45km/28mi – 1hr 30min. Leave Pont-Aven west on D 783, the Concarneau road and after 2.5km/1.5mi, turn left.*

A 15C tide mill stands next to the miller's house, in the picturesque site of Le Nénant on the banks of the Aven.

Kerdruc

In a pretty **setting** ★ overlooking the Aven, this small port still has some old thatched cottages.

▷ *Drive W to Névez.*

Névez

This village has retained a number of 18C granite houses built of 2m/6.6ft-high standing stones. In the **Chapelle Ste-Barbe** there are some old wooden statues and a 17C high altar.

▶ *Take D 77 SE to Port-Manech.*

Port-Manech

Facilities. A charming resort with a well-sited beach on the Aven-Belon estuary.
◪ A path cut in the hillside links the port to the beach and offers fine views of the coast and islands.

▶ *Make for Rospico Cove via Kerangall. The rest of the driving tour is described in the opposite direction: ◔ see CONCARNEAU.*

PONTIVY

POPULATION 13 140
MICHELIN LOCAL MAP 308 N6 – MORBIHAN (56)

The old capital of the Rohan owes its name to the monastery founded in the 7C by St Ivy. The older part of the town has narrow, winding streets, in contrast with the geometrical town plan laid out by Napoleon.

Sights

Old Houses★

To admire the old half-timbered and corbelled houses of the 16 and 17C, walk along **rue du Fil**, place du Martrat, the centre of Old Pontivy, rue du Pont and rue du Docteur-Guépin. At the corner of rue Lorois and rue du Général-de-Gaulle, not the turreted house (1578), which is presumed to be the hunting pavilion of the Rohan family, and the elegant 18C buildings in place Anne-de-Bretagne.

Château des Rohan

◷ *Open mid-June to mid-Sep: 10.30am-6.30pm; April to mid-June: 10am-noon and 2-6pm; Feb to Mar and mid-Sep to end Nov: daily except Mon and Tue 2-6pm. ◷ Closed Dec-Jan.* ◉ *€1.30; €4.10 for special exhibits.*

The castle was built in the 15C by Jean II de Rohan. The façade is flanked by two large machicolated towers with pepper-pot roofs, all that remains of the four towers of the perimeter wall. The main building, remodelled in the 18C, is adorned with cusped pediments and a spiral staircase. The tour includes the guard-room, the first-floor rooms, the duke's bedroom with its fine ceiling and the chapel. In the west tower, note the emblazoned fireplaces.

Driving Tour

From Pontivy to Hennebont

90km/45mi about 4hr. Leave Pontivy on rue ALbert-de-Mun, driving towards Auray and turn right at Talvern-Nénez.

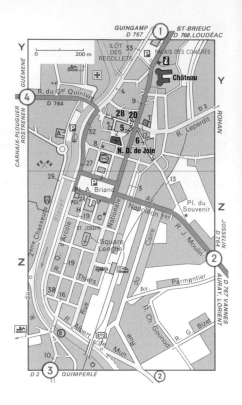

PONTIVY		
Anne-de-Bretagne Pl.	Y	2
Caïnain R.	Z	3
Couvent Q. du	Y	4
Dr-Guépin R. du	Y	5
Fil R. du	Y	6
Friedland R. de	Y	8
Gaulle R. du Gén.-de	Y	9
Jean-Jaurès R.	Z	10
Lamennais R. J.-M. de	Z	13
Le Goff R.	Z	16
Lorois R.	Y	17
Marengo R.	Z	19
Martray Pl. du	Y	20
Mitterrand R. François	Z	24
Nationale R.	YZ	
Niémen Q.	Y	27
Plessis Q. du	YZ	29
Pont R. du	Y	28
Presbourg Q.	Y	32
Récollets Q. des	Y	33
Viollard Bd	Z	38

Chapelle St-Nicodème

This 16C chapel is preceded by a massive tower with a granite steeple. A Renaissance doorway leading to a 16C staircase opens at the base of the tower.

To the left of the chapel, a Gothic fountain empties into three piscinas in front of three niches surmounted by richly carved gables. There is a *pardon* on the first Sunday in August.

You may notice that many of the chapels in the Blavet Valley hold art exhibits in the summer, featuring contemporary works.

St-Nicolas-des-Eaux

The little town is built on the side of a hill. The chapel sits above the town and is surrounded by picturesque thatched-roof houses.

Site de Castennec★

This Celtic site became an oppidum and then a fortified Roman camp. A small tower to the left of the road offers a magnificent view of the valley.

▶ *Turn left after Castennec .*

Bleuzy

To the left of the **church**, note the two Renaissance houses with a bread oven and a well. Inside the church, the stained-glass windows and the woodwork and beams are worth looking at. A ringing stone located next to the pulpit, once used in guise of a bell, is beleived to be a meteorite.

Many farms in the area have graceful 17-18C wells.

▶ *Go to Melrand passing through La Paule.*

Pleasure craft moored at St-Nicolas-des-Eaux

Melrand, Le Village de l'An Mil
🕐 *Open May-Aug: 10am-7pm; Sep-April: 11am-5pm, weekends 11am-6pm.* 👓 €3.
☎ *02 97 39 57 89; www.melrand-village-an-mil.info*
Deep in the countryside, excavations have brought to light the vestiges of the village of Lann Gouh ("old land"), which date back to around the year 1000. The village illustrates rural medieval architecture and the daily life of people and animals, who lived under one roof.

▶ *Return to the centre of the town. Behind the church, take D 142 towards St-Barthélemy, where you will turn right towards St-Adrien.*

Chapelle St-Adrien
The 15C chapel stands below the road, between two fountains: the one on the right is surmounted by a calvary. Inside, there is a simple rood screen, carved on the nave side and painted on the other.

▶ *The road (D 237) follows the Blavet Valley through delightful countryside. Turn left towards Baud (D 3)*

Baud
Some 30km/17mi from the the sea, the Baud region offers many pretty walks which show the more traditional side of Brittany. In the lower town, below the Locminé road, at the far end of the large car park, is the **Fontaine Notre-Dame-de-la-Clarté**.

Cartopole
🕐 *Open mid-June to mid-Sep: 9.30am-12.30pm and 2-6pm (July-Aug until 7pm); mid-Sep to mid-June: Wed, Thu and Sat 2.30-5.30pm, Sun 2-6pm.* 👓 €4 (children €2). ☎ 02 97 51 15 14. www.cartolis.org
Here you will find a treasure chest of some 30 000 post cards that show the heritage of Brittany and the evolution of its society in the early 20C. There is a film, you can view 3 000 cards in the centre and all of them are available on a data base.

▶ *Leave Baud by the road to Hennebont. At Coët Vin bear left; 500m/550yd further on, leave your car in the car park on the right.*

Venus de Quinipily and Park
🕐 *Open May-Oct: 10am-7pm; Nov-April: 11am-5pm.* 🕐 *Closed mid-Dec to end Jan.* 👓 *€2.50.* ☎ *02 97 39 04 94.*

From the other side of a wooden gate, a steep path leads up to the Venus, placed above a fountain, set in the park of the restored Château de Quinipily. The origins of the statue are uncertain. It has been taken for a Roman idol or an Egyptian Isis. As it was the object of much reverent speculation, it was thrown into the River Blavet several times by zealous clergymen. The Count of Lannion installed it here in 1696.

▶ *Return to Baud and go towards Poule Fetan*

Poul Fetan★
15km/9mi W along D3. In Quistinic, turn onto the Hennebont road. 🐾 *Open July-Aug for guided tours in the morning (10.45am-1pm) and individual visits in the afternoon (1-7pm); June and Sep, guided tour 11am, open to visitors 2-6pm; April-May, 2-6.30pm.* 🕐 *Closed Oct-March.* 👓 *€7.* ☎ *02 97 39 51 74.*

In a setting high above the Blavet Valley, a quaint little 16C hamlet has been painstakingly reconstructed from the ruins abandoned during the 1970s. Among the charming thatched cottages, note the Maison du Minour (The Chief's House), the inn (auberge) where you may enjoy a typical Breton meal, the former bakery and an écomusée. In the summer, craftspeople attired in regional costume demonstrate trades from tupical peasant life of yesteryear: washerwome rub steaming linens; a baker is busy at his oven; a farmer is making millet porrideg while another is churning butter. A pottery workshop illustrates the traditional sculpting and firing techiniques. Various farm animals include the "magpir", a small cow typical of the Breton region.

Hennebont
👣 *See: LORIENT: Excursions*

PONT-L'ABBÉ

POPULATION 7 849
MICHELIN LOCAL MAP 308 F7 – FINISTÈRE (29)

This town, which stands at the head of an estuary, owes its name to the first bridge *(pont)* built by the monks *(abbés)* of Loctudy between the harbour and the lake *(étang)*. It is the capital of the Bigouden district which is bounded by the estuary of the Odet, the coast of Penmarc'h and Audierne Bay. Bigouden costume is distinctive and is still worn, for example, during the Embroidery Festival *(Fête des Brodeuses)*.

👣 **Also See: CORNOUAILLE.**

Sights

Église Notre-Dame-des-Carmes
Former 14C chapel of the Carmelite monastery. On the right going in, stands an 18C font; the canopy comes from the Église de Lambour. Above the high altar is a 15C stained-glass window with a rose 7.7m/25ft in diameter. To the left, the Chapelle Ste-Anne is a modern processional banner; in the nave statues of the Virgin and St John, both of the 16C, flank Christ. As you come out, turn right to go round the

Address Book

TOURIST OFFICE

Pont-l'Abbé-Plobannalec-Lesconil,
10 Place de la République, Pont-l'Abbé,
☎ 02 98 82 37 99, www.ot-pontlab-
be29.fr In summer: Mon-Sat 9.30am-
12.30pm, 2-7pm; off season: Mon-Sat
9.30-12am, 2-5pm.

🖑 *For coin ranges, see the Legend on the
cover flap.*

WHERE TO STAY

PONT-L'ABBÉ

⊜⊜ **La Tour d'Auvergne**, *22 Place
Gambetta,* ☎ 02 98 87 00 47, *www.
tourdauvergne.fr - 21 rooms,* ⊐ €6, ✗
Standard rooms, a little bit hold-fash-
ioned, but pleasant wine bar.

⊜⊜ **Hôtel de Bretagne**, *24 Place de la
République,* ☎ 02 98 8/ 17 22 - 18 rooms,
⊐ €7.80, ✗ In this establishment
located on the market place, it's not the
little rooms with pastel tones that will
seduce you most, but the welcoming
family atmosphere, notably at lunch.

COMBRIT

⊜⊜⊜⊜ **Villa tri Men**, *16 rue du
Phare,* ☎ 02 98 51 94 94 - 17 rooms,
⊐ €12, ✗ Between Pont-Aven and
the pointe de Combrit Eastward, a big
family home dating from 1900 has been
totally renovated with care. The result is
elegant, with a beautiful terrace above
the estuary of the River Odet.

EATING OUT

⊖ **Crêperie bigoudenne**, *33 rue
du Gén.-de-Gaulle,* ☎ 02 98 87 20 41.
🕐 *Closed Sun and Mon except school
holidays.* The country-style décor and
traditional crêpes are just right after a
visit to the Musée Bigouden. Eat your
way from theory to practice.

⊖ **Le Bistrot gourmand,** *wine bar of
the Tour d'Auvergne.* The décor features
slate, wainscoting and dried grape
vines. Have a drink and enjoy a quick
snack: kidneys, fresh sea scallops, etc.

⊖⊖⊖ **Hôtel de Bretagne**, regional
specialities principally made with
seafood products (crunchy blue lobster
and julienne of vegetables), but also
meats (delicious roast duck filet with
peaches and ginger).

---

church and look at the flat chevet crowned by an unusual domed belfry. *Pardon* on
the Sunday after 15 July.
In the garden, on the north side of the church, note the **Bigouden monument**
(1931) by Bazin which stands among greenery on the river's edge.

Château

🄺 This 14C-18C fortress has a large oval tower or keep with a building attached.
Go round the tower to see the turret overlooking rue du Château. Inside the keep
you may visit the **musée Bigouden** (taped commentary on each floor) housed
on three floors *(79 steps)*, which has collections of Bigouden costumes, beautifully
embroidered headdresses and 19C furniture (box beds, dressers, chests), models
of boats, sailing equipment.

Ancienne Église de Lambour

The ruined church retains a fine 16C façade and some bays of the 13C nave. The
bell-tower was razed during a peasant revolt *(🖑 see below).*

Excursions

Chapelle N.-D.-de-Tréminou
2km/1mi west on rue Jean-Moulin.
Standing in a shaded close this 14C and 16C chapel (restored) has a belfry which is
set above the nave.

Near this chapel, in 1675, the Cornouaille peasants in revolt adopted the "peasant code". Closely linked with the "stamped paper" revolt, this mass uprising was severely crushed and many bell-towers in the vicinity were razed to the ground in reprisal. A pardon takes place on the fourth Sunday in September.

Maison du Pays bigouden
2km/1mi on S via the road to Loctudy.
A fine alley bordered by chestnut trees leads to the Ferme de Kervazégan. Built around the courtyard are the farmhouse and outbuildings (sheds, cowshed, pigsty, stable). The farmhouse is a solid squat building with dressed stone covered with lime; inside, the two rooms, which were lived in, are furnished with Bigouden furnishings (cupboards decorated with copper studs, box beds, longcase clock) and utensils (churn, creamer, salting tub).
In the outbuildings are the farm tools (apple crusher, press).

Manoir de Kérazan★
3km/1.9mi on S along the Loctudy road.
The manor house is situated in a large park full of tall trees and consists of a main building with large windows, which was rebuilt in the 18C, and a wing set at right-angles, dating from the 16C. The estate was bequeathed to the Institut de France by Joseph Astor in 1928. The rooms, richly decorated and furnished, bear witness to the luxurious setting the Astors aimed to create.
Louis XV woodwork, both authentic and reconstructed, adorns the great hall, the billiards room, the corner room and the green hall. The dining room, decorated with painted panelling, contains a display of a number of works by **Alfred Beau** (1829-1907). This ceramic painter, who was associated with the Porquier de Quimper faience works (hence the well-known PB insignia), created many works of art from plates and trays, as well as by painting works on enamel which was then framed in either plain or carved wood, giving the impression that they were real paintings. The true masterpiece has to be the life-size cello made from polychrome faience, for which the manufacture process involved 15 different firings. The library is as it was arranged by Joseph Astor's father, mayor of Quimper and a great admirer of Beau; the furniture and the layout of the shelves have not been changed. As a whole, the rooms contain a collection of paintings and drawings in which Brittany and the Breton way of life in days gone by play an important role. Various Schools are represented, from the 16C to the 20C (Frans Francken, Charles Cotter, Lucien Simon, Maurice Denis). The tour ends in the blue hall, once a chapel, which houses the Astor family's memorabilia and a collection of 19C weapons.

Loctudy
Loctudy is a quiet little seaport and resort at the mouth of the River Pont-l'Abbé.

Port
An animated fishing port on week-day evenings, when the fishing fleet (prawns, burbot, sole and sea bass) comes sailing in.
A pretty view of the Île Chevalier, in Pont-l'Abbé estuary and Île-Tudy and its beach can be had from the quays.

S. Sauvignier/MICHELIN

"Young ladies of Loctudy"

Church

Dating from the beginning of the 12C and remodelled several times: the porch added in the 15C, its façade and belfry built in the 18C. In spite of the additions, the **interior**★ is elegant and well proportioned with its nave, chancel, ambulatory and radiating chapels in pure Romanesque style. Admire the capitals and column bases carved with small figures, animals, scrolls, foliage and crosses.

In the cemetery to the left of the church, near the road, is the 15C Chapel of Pors-Bihan. Left of the lane leading to the church is a **Gallic stele** 2m/6ft high surmounted by a cross.

Boat trips to Île-Tudy

The peninsula can be reached by CD 144 or by sea, with departures from Loctudy. There are several round-trips a day (except Sun mid-Sept to mid-June). €2 there and back From Loctudy, cyclists and pedestrians can sail to Île-Tudy, a fishing port which, despite its name, is not on an island, but a peninsula.

PORT-LOUIS★

POPULATION 2 808
MICHELIN LOCAL MAP 308 8K – MORBIHAN (56)

Port-Louis is a small fishing port and seaside resort where many of the inhabitants of Lorient may be found. It still has its 16C citadel, 17C ramparts, as well as several interesting old houses (rue de la Poste, rue des Dames, Petite Rue, rue du Driasker). The town also has two fishing harbours: Locmalo in Gâvres cove and, opposite Lorient, La Point, a marina which has been equipped with 200 moorings for yachts.

A Bit of History

Port-Louis was originally called Blavet. During the League, the Duke of Mercœur captured it with the help of the Spaniards. Forty young girls fled in a ship, but the Spaniards saw them and gave chase. Rather than be taken by the victorious enemy, all 40 girls joined hands and jumped into the sea.

It was under Louis XIII that Blavet took the name of Port-Louis in honour of the King. Richelieu made it a fortified port and the headquarters of the first India Company, which failed. When Colbert founded the second India Company, Lorient was built to receive it. From that time on, Port-Louis declined. Under Louis-Philippe the town found new life in sardine fishing and canning in oil.

Sights

Citadelle★

The citadel is at the entrance to the Lorient roadstead. Its construction occurred in different stages: in 1591, during the Spanish occupation by Juan del Aguila; continued in 1616-22, by Marshal Brissac and completed in 1636 under Richelieu. Built on a rectangular plan, the citadel is bastioned at the corners and sides; two bridges and a demilune protect the entrance. The citadel has always been a prison – among its "occupants" was Louis Napoleon, the future Emperor Napoleon III.

A signposted path directs you to the parapet walk (note the cannons facing the Île de Groix) which looks onto two courtyards and the different parts of the edifice of

Musée de la Compagnie des Indes, Port-Louis

Porcelain bowl

which some contain museums, the **Musées de la Citadelle** (*⊙ Open June to Sept, daily, 10am-6.30pm; Apr to May, daily (except Tues), 10am-6.30pm; Jan to Mar, Oct and Nov, 1.30-6pm. ⊙ Closed December, 1 Jan and 1 May. ⊕ €5.50 (children under 18 no charge). ☎ 02 97 82 56 72. www.musee-marine.fr).*

Musée de la Compagnie des Indes★★
Housed in the new wing of the Lourmel barracks, this India Company Museum traces the history of this prestigious company from the founding of Lorient, its expansion in the 18C, its crews, cargoes, trading posts (in India, Africa, China), maps, furnishings and engravings.
One gallery concentrates on the theme of the India Company's fleet: shipbuilding, cargoes, models of *Comte d'Artois* (with cargo and passengers) and *Comte de Provence* (both built in the Lorient shipyards).

Salle de l'Arsenal★
Housed in the Arsenal, in a room which has fine woodwork, ship's models (corvettes, frigates, merchant ships, cruisers etc), portraits of seamen, paintings and documents pertaining to navigation on the Atlantic are on display. Reduced model of the Napoleon's (launched in Cherbourg in 1850) engine room.

Poudrière
The former Powder Factory contains 17C to 20C arms (torpedoes, mines, mortars, munitions etc) and documents on naval artillery.

Conservatoire de Bateaux
The Boat Museum focuses on a lifeboat, *Commandant Philippes de Kerhallet,* manned by 12 oarsmen, built in Le Havre in 1857 and used between 1897 and 1939 at Roscoff.

Ramparts
Built between 1649 and 1653 by Marshal Meilleraye, these ramparts envelop the town on two sides. On Promenade des Pâtis, a door in the wall leads to a fine sandy beach from where there is a pleasant view onto the Pointe de Gâvres, Île de Groix, Larmor-Plage.

Old houses
It is well worth walking along rue de la Poste, rue des Dames, Petite Rue and rue du Driasker lined with interesting old houses.

Excursion

Riantec
This village lying on the shores of Gâvres lagoon is the favourite haunt of people keen on looking for shellfish. The **Maison de l'île de Kerner** offers an insight into the local natural environment, which shelters numerous migrating birds and where oyster beds thrive. The botanical gardnes contain an intersting selection of salt-meadow and dune plants (&🕐 *Open July-Aug: 10am-7pm; April-June and Sep: daily except Sat, Sun and Mon mornings 10am-12.30pm and 2-6pm. Rest of the year: Sun afternoons only.* 🕐 *Closed 1 Jan and 25 Dec.* ⌕ *€3.80.*

PRESQU'ÎLE DE QUIBERON★

MICHELIN LOCAL MAP 308 M10 MORBIHAN (56)

This former island is now attached to the mainland by a narrow isthmus, offers a varied landscape: sand dunes fixed by maritime pines, a wild coast (Côte Sauvage) with an impressive jumble of cliffs, rocks, caves, reefs and wide sunny beaches.

A Bit of History

Hoche repels the exiles (July 1795) – Quiberon saw the rout of the Royalists in 1795. The French exiles in England and Germany had made great plans; 100 000 men, led by the princes, were to land in Brittany, join hands with the Chouans and drive out the "Blues". In fact, the British fleet which anchored in the Quiberon roadstead carried only 10 000 men, commanded by Puisaye, Hervilly and Sombreuil. The princes did not come.

The landing began on the beach at Carnac on 27 June and continued for several days. Cadoudal's Chouans joined them. But the effect of surprise was lost; long preparations and talk among the exiles had warned the Convention; **General Hoche** was ready, and he drove the invaders back into the peninsula. Driven to the beach at Port-Haliguen, the exiles tried to re-embark. Unfortunately, the British ships were prevented by a heavy swell from getting near enough to land and the Royalists were captured. The Convention refused to pardon them. Some were shot at Quiberon and others were taken to Auray and Vannes and shot there.

Quiberon⚓
At the far end of the peninsula, Quiberon is a popular resort with its fine south-facing sandy beach and proximity to the Côte Sauvage.

Port-Maria
This departure point for boat services to Belle-Île, Houat and Hœdic is a busy harbour and a fishing port.

Address Book

TOURIST OFFICES

Quiberon, 14 rue de Verdun, ☎ 02 97 50 45 17, www.quiberon.com Jul-Aug: Mon-Sat 9am-noon, 1.30-7pm, Sun 10am-noon, 3-5pm; off season: Mon-Fri 9am-12.30pm, 2-6pm (5pm Sat). A guidebook of the peninsula walking trails (€2). Information point **St-Pierre-Quiberon**, rue Curie, ☎ 02 97 30 88 86 Jul-Aug.

♿ *For coin ranges, see the Legend on the cover flap.*

WHERE TO STAY

☕☕🛏 **Au bon Accueil**, *6 quai de Houat, Quiberon*, ☎ *02 97 50 07 92 – 16rm*, 🍽 €7, ✕ A recently renovated establishment that offers comfortable rooms with a view of the sea.

☕☕🛏 **Navirotel**, *Place du Vieux Port, Port-Haliguen*, ☎ *02 97 50 16 52, navirotel@wanadoo.fr – 16rm*, 🍽 €6.80. Well-located next to the sailing marina, the Navirotel provides a cordial welcome and modern decor; it's also a bargain for the area.

☕☕🛏 **La Baie**, *13 rue de la Petite Côte, St-Julien*, ☎ *02 97 50 08 20, www.hotellabaie.com – 19rm*, 🍽 €7. Only 50m from the beach, this 1930s-style hotel offers old-fashioned rooms and a familial atmosphere.

☕☕ **Hôtel de l'Océan**, *7 quai de l'Océan, Port-Maria*, ☎ *02 97 50 07 58, www.hotel-de-locean.com – 37rm*, 🍽 €6.50. Behind a façade of soft-hued shutters nestle small, well-kept rooms oriented toward the port.

☕☕🛏🛏 **Hôtel de la Plage**, *quai d'Orange, St-Pierre-Quiberon*, ☎ *02 97 30 92 10, www.hotel-la-plage.com – 43rm*, 🍽 €9.80, ✕ All you see is ocean out of every window, and at the restaurant you can enjoy the bounty of the sea.

EATING OUT

☕ **La Ferme Bretonne**, *2 rue du Manoir, St-Pierre-Quiberon*, ☎ *02 97 30 95 23*. Opposite the town hall, this creperie gets inventive with its outdoor seating options – a cosy garden where customers get comfortable under parasols in the loggia or next to the olive trees.

☕☕ **Le Neptune**, *4 quai de Houat, Quiberon*, ☎ *02 97 50 09 62*. ⏰ *Closed Mon low season*. The restaurant focuses on fish and other types of seafood. Don't miss the tournedos of St Jacques.

☕☕ **Le Jules Verne**, *21 bd de la Plage, Quiberon*, ☎ *02 97 30 55 55*. Just a glance at the the desserts on display and you know you've made the right choice. The other menu items and service are also on par.

☕☕☕ **La Chaumine**, *36 Place du Manémeur, Quiberon*, ☎ *02 97 50 17 67*. ⏰ *Closed Sun evening low season; Mon*. This restaurant is known for its inventive cuisine: oysters au gratin with Muscatel and hazelnuts, ray wing with balsamic dressing, crêpes and potatoes with crab and coulis of crustacean.

RECREATION

Windsurf – Windsurfing clubs abound all around the peninsula (information at the Tourist Office). **Centre nautique Quiberonnais**, ☎ *02 97 30 56 19, http://cnquiberon.ifrance.com* The bay of Quiberon or the bay of Morbihan, on board a catamaran or a single hulled vessel (half day, €50/person; full day, €85/person; 2 person minimum).

Sea kayak – Slipstreams, *St-Joseph-de-l'Océan beach, Portivy*, ☎ *02 97 30 95 29 or 06 81 26 75 08, www.perso.orange.fr/kayakmersillages* Initiations (half day, €30), trips (full day €53) or training.

Diving – École française de Plongée, *3 quai de Houat, Quiberon*, ☎ *02 97 50 00 98; www.plongee-rivier.com Operates Apr-Nov*.

Surfing – Surf Paradise, *rte de Port-Blanc, ZA de Kergroix, St-Pierre-Quiberon*, ☎ *02 97 50 39 67 or 06 14 40 16 74, www.quiberonsurfparadise.com Operates Apr to 1 Nov*. Lessons (2hr, €20-45) and lessons (week, €160) all levels.

École de surf et de skateboard de Bretagne, *6 av. de l'Océan, Plouharnel*, ☎ *02 97 52 41 18, www.bretagnesurf.net* Initiation or surf and skate trainings, children and adults. Training 5 day (€110), 3 lessons (€80), collective lessons (€30), individual lessons (€60).

Thalasso – Thalassa Quiberon, *pointe de Goulvar*, ☎ *02 97 50 48 88, www.accorthalassa.com* The Sofitel hotel offers sea-water swimming pools and all the spa-treatments you desire.

Driving Tours

La Cote Sauvage★★ ☐1 *18km/11mi round-trip – allow 2hr*

▶ *Go to Port-Maria and bear right onto the coast road (signposted route côtière).*

This wild coast is a succession of jagged cliffs where caves, crevasses and inlets alternate with little sandy beaches with crashing rolling waves (🚫 bathing prohibited; ground swell). Rocks of all shapes and sizes edge the coast, forming passages and labyrinths in which the sea boils and roars.

Beg er Goalennec

Go around the Café Le Vivier and over the rocks to reach the tip of the promontory from where there is a pretty view over the whole length of the Côte Sauvage.

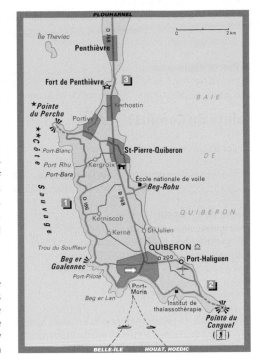

▶ *After Kroh-Kollé, bear left.*

The road runs downhill towards **Port-Bara,** a cove prickling with rocks, before going inland. Surfaced roads lead to Port-Rhu and Port-Blanc; the latter has a nice white sandy beach.

Spectacular waves crash on the "wild coast"even in calm weather

G. Targat/MICHELIN

Pointe du Percho★

Go on foot to the tip of the point. A lovely **view**★ opens out, on the left, to the Côte Sauvage, on the right, to the Isthme de Penthièvre, its fort and beach, and beyond the islands of Belle-Île and Groix.

The last stele indicates Beg en Aud, the furthest point on this coastline.

▶ *Cross Portivy and drive to St-Pierre-Quiberon.*

St-Pierre-Quiberon

This resort has two beaches on either side of the small port of Orange. Take rue des Menhirs to see the St-Pierre lines made up of 22 menhirs on the right.

Pointe du Conguel ② *6km/4mi round-trip – allow 1hr 30min*

▶ *Leave Quiberon to the E by boulevard Chanard.*

Drive round the **Institut de Thalassothérapie** – salt-water cures for arthrosis, rheumatism, over-exertion and the after-effects of injuries.

Pointe du Conguel

Viewing table. Allow 30min on foot there and back.

From the tip of the point there is a view of Belle-Île, Houat and Hœdic Islands, the Morbihan coast and Quiberon Bay. Teignouse Lighthouse, near which the battleship *France*, which sank in 1922 after striking a reef.

▶ *Drive to Port-Haliguen.*

On the left there is an aerodrome with a runway for light aircraft. Beyond Fort-Neuf, note the bustle created on the beach by the various sailing clubs and schools. The view opens out over the bay and the Morbihan coastline. Pass on your right, an obelisk commemorating the surrender of the exiles in 1795.

Port-Haliguen

A small fishing and pleasure boat harbour hosts summer regattas.

Isthme de Penthievre ③

This provides road and rail links between the former island and the mainland.

▶ *Leave Quiberon via D 768 towards St-Pierre-de Quiberon.*

Fort de Penthièvre

Rebuilt in the 19C, it commands the access to the peninsula. A monument and a crypt commemorate 59 members of the Resistance shot here in 1944.

Penthièvre

This small resort has two fine sandy beaches on either side of the isthmus.

QUIMPER★★

CONURBATION 68 000

MICHELIN LOCAL MAP 308 G7 FINISTÈRE (29)

The town lies in a pretty little valley at the junction (*kemper* in Breton) of the River Steir and River Odet. This used to be the capital of Cornouaille, and it is here, perhaps, that the traditional atmosphere of the province can best be felt. The **Festival de Cornouaille**★ is an important folk festival.

▶ **Orient Yourself:** Quimper is the Préfecture of the Finistère.
🅿 **Parking:** Use the central car parks, the one near St-Mathieu church is convenient.
🕭 **Don't Miss:** The regional art works in the Beaux-Arts museum.
🕭 **Also See:** CORNOUAILLE.

Famous Residents

The statue of **Laënnec** (1781-1826) commemorates the most illustrious son of Quimper – the man who invented the stethoscope *(🕭 see DOUARNENEZ: Ploaré)*.
Streets are named after Kerguelen, Fréron and Madec, three other famous men of Quimper. **Yves de Kerguelen** (1734-97) was a South Seas explorer; a group of islands bears his name. **Élie Fréron** (1718-76) was a critic, bitterly opposed to Voltaire and other philosophers. **René Madec** (1738-84) was a hero of adventure. As a cabin boy in a ship of the India Company, he jumped overboard and landed at Pondichéry. He served a rajah and became a successful man. The British found a relentless enemy in him. When he returned to France, enormously rich, the king gave him a title and the Cross of St-Louis, with a colonel's commission.
Quimper was also the birthplace of **Max Jacob** (1876-1944), a poet and illustrator, friend of Picasso.

A Bit of History

A dynasty of faience makers – In 1690, a southerner, Jean-Baptiste Bousquet, a faience maker from St-Zacharie near Marseilles, settled on the site which was to become Locmaria, a suburb of Quimper on the banks of the Odet, where it has been revealed that potters were active as early as the Gallo-Roman era. Bousquet founded the first Quimper faience works, where he adopted his favoured style from Moustiers faience ware. His son Pierre succeeded him in 1708 and associated himself with a faience maker from Nevers, Pierre Belleveaux, and later on with a faience maker from Rouen, Pierre-Clément Caussy. Both these were to play an important role in the evolution of Quimper faience, one by enriching it with new shapes, colours (yellow) and Nevers decorative motifs, the other by introducing rich iron red to the Quimper palette and adding some 300 decorative designs (tracings). It is this blend of expertise and working methods handed down to Quimper "painters" over the centuries which has made Quimper, now a real guild centre for this craft, the seat of an artistic production distinguished by the diversity of style it encompasses. Two more faience works were established in Quimper towards the end of the 18C, **Porquier** faience works, founded by François Eloury c 1772 and with which the name of **Alfred Beau** is linked in the 1870s, and **Dumaine** faience works, over which Jules Henriot assumed directorship in 1891.

Address Book

TOURIST OFFICE

Quimper, Place de la Résistance, ☎ 02 98 53 04 05, www.quimper-tourisme.com ⏰ Open Jul-Aug: Mon-Sat 9am-7pm, Sun 10am-12.45pm, 3-5.45pm; Apr-June, Sep: Mon-Sat 9.30am-12.30pm, 1.30-6.30pm, Sun 10am-12.45pm; Oct-Mar: Mon-Sat 9.30am-12.30pm, 1.30-6pm. Organises guided tours of the town (90min) and nocturnal tours of the town's "stories and legends" (ask for the full calendar). The cultural passport (€11.50) enables you to visit four of the main sites of Quimper at a reduced rate.

For coin ranges, see the Legend on the cover flap.

WHERE TO STAY

TGV, *4 rue de Concarneau,* ☎ 02 98 90 54 00, www.hoteltgv.com; 22rm, €5.60. A small hotel with the rosy façade; simple and useful, it is located opposite the train station.

Hôtel de la Gare, *17 ter av. de la Gare,* ☎ 02 98 90 00 81, www.hoteldelagarequimper.com; 27rm, €6, ✕🅿 Near the train station too, this establishment offers colourful and functional rooms, sometimes equipped with kitchenettes. Breakfast served in a flowery patio in summer.

Mascotte, *6 rue Théodore Le Hars,* ☎ 02 98 53 37 37, www.hotel-sofibra.com; 63rm, €8, ✕ Near the docks of the Odet, comfortable and quiet rooms come standard.

Océania, *2 rue du Poher, rte de Bénodet,* ☎ 02 98 90 46 26, www.hotel-sofibra.com - 92rm, €11, 🖿✕🅿 Lacking Breton charm, this comfortable hotel compensates with an enormous swimming-pool and lovely terraces.

Gradlon, *30 rue de Brest,* ☎ 02 98 95 04 39, www.hotel-gradlon.com - 22rm, €11. One of the most pleasant hotels in town, the Gradlon features distinctive rooms with antique furniture as well as a copious breakfast served in the tranquil winter garden.

EATING OUT

Ti Cass' d'Halles, *3 Halles St-François, rue Astor,* ☎ 02 98 95 87 56.

⏰ *Open Mon-Wed 10am-3pm, Thur-Sat 10am-7pm.* Ideal for a quick snack, this takeaway stand prepares salads and excellent sandwiches: chicken curry, tuna with peaches, vegetarian (carrots tartar) or seafood (salad of crab and prawns with garlic). Don't forget the home-made desserts. Soup is for sale by the litre.

Le Bistro à lire, *18 rue des Boucheries,* ☎ 02 98 95 30 86. ⏰ *Open Mon Noon-2pm, 7.30pm-10pm, Tue-Sat 7.30pm-10pm.* ⏰ *Closed Aug.* Savour excellent vegetable crumbles while you browse the library of detective stories (Tue-Sat 9am-7pm) collected at this unique pub-restaurant.

La Krampouzerie, *Halles St-François, 9 rue du Sallé (Place au Beurre),* ☎ 02 98 95 13 08. ⏰ *Open daily 11.45am-3.45pm, 6.45-11.30pm.* ⏰ *Closed Sun-Mon in off season.* Savour unexpected specialities such as crepes with algae from Ouessant, or onion jam from Roscoff paired with caramel and ginger--or even with *gros lait.* Leave room for a dessert of Basque sheep's milk cheese and black-cherry jam.

Le Jardin d'été, *15 rue du Sallé,* ☎ 02 98 95 33 00. *Last service at 2pm and 10pm.* ⏰ *Closed Sun-Mon.* At the Summer Garden, epicureans may choose the "menu dégustation" with foie gras, oysters and snails, while the less adventurous may sample the fish and seafood from the à la carte selections. For lighter meals, take a seat on the terrace and enjoy a tasty salad.

L'Ambroisie, *49 rue Élie Fréron,* ☎ 02 98 95 00 02. *Last service at 2pm and 9.30pm.* ⏰ *Closed Sun evening and Mon in off season.* In a narrow street leading to the cathedral St-Corentin lies l'Ambroisie with its bright and contemporary dining room. Enjoy refined cuisine that emphasizes the quality of regional products.

ENTERTAINMENT

Stargames Café, *17 rue des Gentilshommes,* ☎ 02 98 95 71 97. ⏰ *Open Tue, Thu-Fri 1pm-midnight; Wed, Sat noon-midnight.* Relax with Berber, mint, or jasmine tea, or take a hit of the chicha (€5.50-8) while checking your e-mail (€4/h).

Ceili, *4 rue Aristide Briand*, ☎ *02 98 95 17 61*. ○ *Open Mon-Sat 10.30am-1am, Sun 5pm-1am*. This Celtic pub organises year-round concerts - the perfect occasion to share a Breton beer with your neighbour and listen to bagpipes. Yec'hed mad!

RECREATION

Walk - From the place de la Résistance, follow the path (15min walk) that leads to the summit of Mont Frugy (70m) where you can enjoy a panoramic view of the town.

Hikes – I.D., Itinéraires découverte, available at the Tourist Office (€8.50), is a helpful compilation of the hikes on the 225 km of paths in the region.

Cruises on the Odet – Travel by waterway from Quimper to Bénodet on board one of the **Vedettes de l'Odet**, ☎ *08 25 80 08 01, www.vedettes-odet.com* About 75min and €16/adult. Departures from Jun to Sep from the Port du Cap Horn (opposite the Faïenceries) or from the Port du Corniguel, 3 km from the town centre (car transfer guaranteed, free parking). Make reservations at the Tourist Office.

Kayak to Bénodet – Discover the Odet by taking a kayaking class with l'**École de canoë-kayak**, rue du Chanoine Moreau, at the yachting marina of Locmaria, behind the Faïenceries H.B. Henriot, ☎ *02 98 53 19 99, kayak.quimper@ wanadoo.fr* You can also sign up for an 18km tour (return by shuttle). One- to four-person kayaks (€20-45/day).

SHOPPING

Faience - Boutique de la **Faïencerie H.B. Henriot**, *Place Bérardier, Locmaria*, ☎ *02 98 52 22 52*. ○ *Open Mon-Sat 9.30am-7pm*.

Modern Artists – From 1920 onwards there was a long succession of artists. One of the first, **René Quillivic** (1879-1969), sculptor and ceramic painter, produced some striking works with designs based on woodcuts. The Odetta trademark, registered in 1922, produced works in sandstone, in dark tones made iridescent with enamel. Artists whose signatures adorn such work include Georges Renaud, René Beauclair, one of the most prolific, Louis Garin, Paul Fouillen and Jacques Nam.

The **Ar Seiz Breur** (Seven Brothers – a reference to seven Breton heros) movement was founded in 1923 by René-Yves Creston, Jeanne Malivel and Jorg Robin with the aim of modernising traditional Breton folk art by combining it with Art Deco and Cubism. Many of the works produced by the artists who were members of this movement can be seen in exhibitions on this period.

Cathédrale St-Corentin★★

🐟 *Guided tours July and Aug, daily, 10am-noon and 2-6pm. SPREV (Sauvegarde du Patrimoine Religieux en Vie).* ☎ *02 98 95 06 19.*

This fine Gothic cathedral was built from the 13C (chancel) to the 15C (transept and nave). The two steeples were only erected in 1856, being modelled on the Breton steeple of Pont-Croix.

After seeing the north side of the building make for the façade. Between the spires stands the statue of a man on horseback: this is King Gradlon. Until the 18C, on 26 July each year, a great festival was held in his honour. A man would climb up behind him, tie a napkin round his neck and offer him a glass of wine. Then he drank up the wine himself, carefully wiped the King's mouth with the napkin and threw the empty glass down on the square. Any spectator who could catch the glass as it fell received a prize of 100 gold écus, if the glass was not broken.

QUIMPER

4 Chemins Les	BX	Boucheries R. des	BY 6	Douarnenez R. de	AY
Astor R.	AYZ 2	Brest R. de	BY	Douarnenez Rte de	AV
Bécharles Av. de	BV 3	Brest Rte de	BV	Douves R. des	BY
Bénodet Rue de	ABX	Briand R. A.	BZ	Dupleix Bd	BZ
Beurre Pl. au	BY 4	Chapeau-Rouge R. du	AY 9	Ergué-Armel Bd d'	BX
		Concarneau R. de	BX 10	Flandres-Dunkerque	
		Créac'h Gwen Bd de	BX 12	-1940 Bd	BX

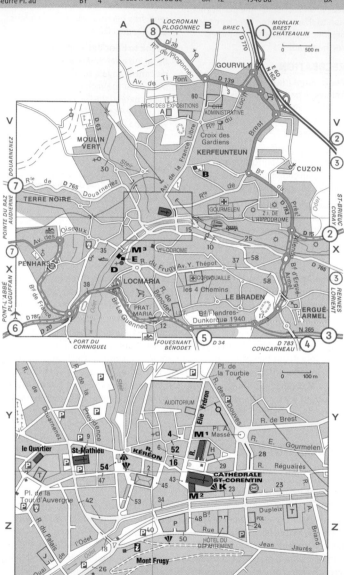

Nave and chancel

Enter through the main door. On the right, note the 17C pulpit adorned with low-relief sculptures relating the life of St Corentine. Notice that the choir is quite out of line with the nave; this is due to the presence of a previous building. One theory is that in the early 13C, the cathedral craftsmen incorporated a small sanctuary set off to the left. The new chancel linked this chapel to the nave.

Side chapels

Visitors, going round the fine 92m/302ft long building, will see in the side chapels, tombs (15C), altars, frescoes, altarpieces, statues, old (St John the Baptist, 15C alabaster) and modern **works of art** and, in the chapel beneath the south tower, an Entombment copied from that in Bourges Cathedral and dating from the 18C.

The decoration of one of the chapels to the left of the chancel reltes the legend of St Corentine, Quimper's first bishop (5C), who lived on the flesh of a single, miraculous fish. Every morning he took half the fish to eat and threw the other half back into the river. When he came back the next day the fish was whole once more and offered itself to be eaten again.

Stained-glass windows★★

The cathedral has a remarkable set of 15C **stained glass**★★ in the upper windows, mainly in the nave and transept, depicting canons, lords and ladies surrounded by their patron saints. It is interesting to note the marked evolution from the stained glass decorating the chancel, which dates from the early 15C, and that adorning the nave and transept which was only completed at the end of the 15C, when artists had considerable skill in drawing and in the use of subtle colours.

Old Quimper★ *Allow half a day*

The old district stretches in front of the cathedral between the Odet and the Steir. Rue du Parc along the Odet leads to Quai du Steir. This small tributary has now been canalised and covered before its confluence with the Odet, to form a vast pedestrian precinct.

Rue Élie-Fréon

North of place St-Corentin. Walk up the no 22 to admire a 17C corbelled house with a slate roof, and a Renaissance porch at no 20.

Rue du Sallé

Note the beautiful old house of the **Mahault de Minuellou** family at no 10.

Rue Kéréon

Cross the tiny place au Beurre to reach rue Élie-Fréron; walk up to no 22 to admire a corbelled house with a slate roof, and a Renaissance porch at no 20.
Make a detour to the left via rue des Boucheries to **rue du Guéodet** where a house with caryatids and figures of men and women in 16C costume stands.

Rue Kéréon★

A busy shopping street. The cathedral and its spires between the two rows of old corbelled houses make a delightful picture.

Place Terre-au-Duc

A picturesque square lined with old half-timbered houses. This was the lay town opposite the episcopal city and included the Law Courts, prison and the Duc de Bretagne market.
Take **rue St-Mathieu** which has some fine houses to reach **Église St-Mathieu.** This church, rebuilt in 1898, retains a fine 16C stained-glass window of the Passion half way up the chancel.

Additional Sights

Musée des Beaux-Arts★★

Open July and Aug, daily, 10am-7pm; Apr to June, Sept and Oct, daily (except Tues), 10am-noon and 2-6pm; rest of the year, daily (except Sun morning and Tues), 10am-noon and 2-6pm. Closed 1 Jan, 1 May, 1 and 11 Nov and 25 Dec. €4. 02 98 95 45 20. www.beauxarts.quimper.fr.
This Fine Arts Museum contains a collection of paintings representing European painting from the 14C to the present. The museum has its own unique atmosphere, largely due to the mixing of natural and artificial lighting, in which it is possible to view the works in – quite literally – a new light.
On the ground floor, two rooms are devoted to 19C Breton painting: *A Marriage in Brittany* by Leleux; *A Street in Morlaix* by Noël; Potato Harvest by Simon; *Widow on Sein Island* by Renouf; *Flight of King Gradlon* by Luminais and *Fouesnant Rebels* by Girardet. One room is devoted to **Max Jacob** (1876-1944), who was born and grew up in Quimper. His life and work are evoked through literature, memorabilia, drawings, gouaches, and in particular a series of portraits signed by his friends Picasso, Cocteau and others.

Musée des Beaux-Arts, Quimper

Le Pardon de Kergoat by Jules Breton

At the centre of the first floor, the architect J-P Philippon designed an area fitted in pale beech wood to set 23 paintings from the dining room of the Hôtel de l'Épée, executed by the painter Lemordant (1878-1968). The area around the edges displays the work of different European Schools up to the contemporary period: Flemish (Rubens, Van Schriek); Italian (Bartolo di Fredi); Spanish; and French. Note in particular works by Boucher, Fragonard, Van Loo, View of the Château de Pierrefonds by Corot and View of Quimper Harbour by Boudin.

Musée départemental breton★

🕐 *Open June to Sept, daily, 9am-6pm; rest of the year, daily (except Sun morning, Mon and holidays), 9am-noon and 2-5pm.* 🎟 *€3.80, no charge on Sun, Jan-May and Oct-Dec.* ☎ *02 98 95 21 60.*

This museum, devoted to regional history (archeology, ethnology, economy), occupies what used to be the episcopal palace, a large edifice built from the 16C to the 19C adjoining the cathedral.

After a brief display on prehistory, the visitor enters the first rooms devoted to the environment and way of life in one of the Gallo-Roman cities of the Osismes: coins, monumental mosaics, vases and funerary urns, silverware, figurines of Venus and mother-goddesses etc.

The medieval section displays, among other things, a stone likeness of King Marc'h, Romanesque capitals, and tomb stones, including the magnificently sculpted tombstone of Grallon of Kervaster.

The galleries of medieval and modern statues bring to mind the various religious cults which inspired this art form. The display includes two large 16C stained-glass windows.

The galleries which contain furniture retrace the history (17C-20C) of the domestic space occupied by folk furniture and the use to which it was put, from the grain and linen chests of Léon to the "petits meubles" mementoes by Plovézet. It is particularly interesting to see the role played by the cupboard in both the marriage ritual and in the attempt to create a "modern Breton piece" between the World Wars.

The final section is devoted to Quimper faience and displays a rich collection of exhibits dating from the 18C to the present, illustrating the evolution of this decorative art form which reflects at once everyday life, creative spirit and perhaps even the dreams of an entire region.

Jardin de l'évêché

Between the cathedral and ramparts, the garden offers a good **view**★ of the cathedral chevet and spires, the Odet lined by the Préfecture with its ornate dormer windows, the former Ste-Catherine hospital and Mont Frugy.

Some vestiges of the old ramparts can be seen in boulevard de Kerguélen and rue des Douves.

Musée de la faïence★

Open mid-April to Oct, daily (except Sun), 10am-6pm. Closed public holidays. €4 (children €2.30). ☎ 02 98 90 12 72.

This faience museum contains a rich collection of almost 2 500 items which it displays in rotation, retracing several centuries of the history of Quimper and its faience. The tour also explains the craft itself, giving details of techniques, artists and anonymous craftsmen (throwers, kiln-chargers and painters), to whom the museum pays homage in the form of a tall, colourful bas-relief.

The first two rooms are given over to the sequence of stages in the manufacturing process and to the tools and materials used. The marvellous works displayed In the following two rooms illustrate the blend of different styles from Rouen and Nevers.

Jean-Yves Uguet/Musée de la faïence

Dish decorated with Breton figures, HB faience works (late 19C)

The ground floor is reserved for 20C production concentrating on that from the period between the World Wars, which was particularly varied and prolific: from the shapes, colours and complex motifs by Quillivic or **Mathurin Méheut** to the highly refined ones of René Beauclair, or even the very original works by Giovanni Leonardi, to name but four artists.

The final gallery houses exhibitions on various themes.

Faïenceries de Quimper HB Henriot

Guided tours (45min) July and Aug, Mon to Fri, 9-11.15am and 2-4.45pm (3.45pm Frid); rest of the year Mon to Fri 9-11.15am and 2-4.15pm (3pm Fri). Closed mid-Dec to end of Dec. €3 (children €2). ☎ 02 98 90 09 36; www.quimper-faiences.com.

Rue Haute. The 300-year-old faience workshops were bought in 1984 by Paul Janssens, an American citizen of Dutch origin. Earthenware is still entirely decorated by hand with traditional motifs such as Breton peasants in traditional dress, birds, roosters, plants. A tour of the workshops enables visitors to discover in turn the various manufacturing stages, from the lump of clay to the firing process. A few concessions have been made to modern practices: the clay mixture is no longer prepared in house and the ovens are electrically heated.

Église Notre-Dame-de-Locmaria

This Romanesque church, rebuilt in the 15C and then later restored, is on the banks of the Odet. The plain interior contains, in the north side aisle, three tombstones dating from the 14C, 15C and 17C, and, on the rood beam, a robed Christ. In the south side aisle, a door leads to the garden of the old Benedictine priory (16C-17C) which has a cloistral gallery dating from 1669 and two 12C arches.

Mont Frugy

🚶 *Allow 30min on foot there and back.* From place de la Résistance a path (30min on foot there and back) leads to the top of this wooded hill, 70m/22ft high. From the look-out point there is a good **view**★ of the city.

Excursions

Boat Trips down the Odet★★

April-Sep: up to 5 cruises daily (2hr 30min); luncheon cruises daily except Mon. Possible stop-over in Bénodet, depending on the tide, or extended excursion to the Glénan Islands. Information at the Tourist Office or from Vedettes de l'Odet ☎ 02 98 57 00 58.

Baie de Kérogan★

The woods and castle parks, which lie along the river form a fine, green landscape. The Port du Corniguel, at the mouth of Kérogan Bay, adds a modern touch to the picture.

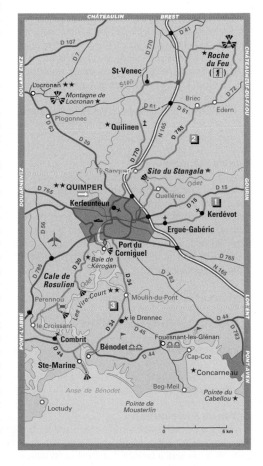

Les Vire-Court★★

The Odet here winds between high, wooded cliffs. This wild spot has its legends. Two rocks at the narrowest point of the gorge are called the Maiden's Leap (Saut de la Pucelle). Another rock is called the Bishop's Chair (Chaise de l'Evêque). Angels are said to have made it in the shape of a seat for the use of a saintly prelate of Quimper who liked to meditate in this lonely place. A little further on, the river bends so sharply that a Spanish fleet, coming up to attack Quimper, did not dare go through. Having taken on water at a fountain now called the Spaniards' Fountain, the ships turned back. On the west bank, before Le Perennou, ruins of Roman baths can be seen.

1 **From the Banks of the Jet to the Odet**

Round-trip of 27km/17mi – 2hr 30min. Apr to Sept, up to 5 cruises a day (2hr30min). Luncheon cruises Tuesday to Sunday. Stopover in Bénodet, depending on tides, or longer trips out to the Îles Glénan. 🛈 *For information apply to the tourist office in Quimper or to "Les Vedettes de l'Odet".* ☎ *02 98 57 00 58.*

▶ *Leave Quimper on avenue de la Libération (**BX 25**), at the first major roundabout, turn left on the road to Brest and take the second road to the right to Coray. 700m/766yd further on, take the road towards Elliant.*

The road runs beside the River Jet and offers views of the wooded countryside and pastureland.

Ergué-Gabéric
In the chancel of the early-16C church there is a stained-glass window depicting the Passion (1571) and a 17C group of the Trinity. The organ loft dates from 1680.

▶ *Bear right after the church towards the Chapelle de Kerdévot.*

Chapelle de Kerdévot
🕐 *Open July to Aug, daily, 2-6pm; May, June and Sept, Sun only 2-6pm.*
The 15C chapel stands in an attractive setting near a Calvary, which is of a later date and unfortunately somewhat damaged. Inside, a late-15C Flemish **altarpiece**★ standing on the high altar depicts six scenes from the life of the Virgin. There is a 17C statue of Our Lady of Kerdévot in painted wood in the nave.

▶ *Leave Kerdévot by the road on the left of the chapel, then turn left towards Quimper. After 3km/2mi turn right towards the hamlet of Lestonan. Go through Quellénec, turn right onto a partly surfaced road 600m/656yd to the Griffonès car park.*

Site du Stangala★
After crossing an arboretum (red oak, copper beech etc), bear left through woodland to reach two rocky platforms. The site is a remarkable one: the rocky ridge overlooks the Odet from a height of 70m/230ft as the river winds between wooded slopes. Opposite and slightly to the right, the hamlet of Tréouzon clings to the slopes. Ahead, in the distance, to the left of the television tower, Locronan Mountain, with its characteristic outline and the chapel perched on its summit, can be picked out easily. On the way back to the car park, a road to the left leads down to the bank of the Odet *(30min there and back)*.

▶ *To return to Quimper, bear right as you leave the narrow road.*

2 **Chapels and Calvaries**

Round-trip of 57km/35mi – 3hr

▶ *Leave Quimper on rue des Douves (BY). Shortly after a cemetery at the entrance of Kerfeunteun, turn right.*

Église de Kerfeunteun
A small square belfry with a stone spire surmounts the west façade.
The church was built in the 16C and 17C but the transept and chancel were rebuilt in 1953. It has kept a beautiful stained-glass window (16C) above the high altar, depicting a Tree of Jesse with a Crucifixion above.

▷ *Continue 800m/875yd further on, turn right towards Brest, then left in the direction of Briec and at Ty-Sanquer, left again.*

Calvaire de Quilinen★

Near the main road, hidden by the trees, stands the **Chapelle Notre-Dame-de-Quilinen** (*Guided tours available, apply to the Landrévarzec Town Hall. ☎ 02 98 57 90 44*) with its unusual Calvary. Built c 1550 on two superposed triangular bases with the points opposite one another, the Calvary reveals a rough and naïve style. As the Cross rises to the figure of Christ above the two thieves who are placed close together, the statues become more and more slender. The other side of the Cross represents Christ resurrected. The south portal of the 15C chapel is decorated by a graceful Virgin between two angels.

▷ *Return to the main road and bear right; after 5km/3mi, turn right towards the nearby Chapelle de St-Venec.*

Chapelle de St-Venec

Visit by appointment, apply to the tourist office. ☎ 02 98 57 70 73.
In front of this Gothic chapel is a Calvary (1556) on a triangular base similar to that of Quilinen and on the other side of the road stands a charming 16C fountain.
Take the chapel road, pass under the Quimper-Brest motorway and turn left towards the Chapelle Notre-Dame-des-Trois-Fontaines.
This large chapel was built in the 15C-16C; the Calvary is badly damaged.

▷ *Take the chapel road, pass under the Quimper-Brest dual carriageway and turn left towards Chuelle Notre-Dame-des-Trois Fontaines. Proceed to the Gouézec road and turn right.*

La Roche du Feu★ (Karreg an Tan)

30min on foot there and back.
🔼 From the car park, take a path to the summit (28m/899ft): an extensive **panorama**★ over the Montagnes Noires, Ménez-Hom and the Aulne Valley.

▷ *Return to Quimper via Edern and Briec.*

③ Along the Banks of the Odet

Round-trip of 48km/30mi – 2hr 30min

▷ *Leave Quimper on the boulevard de Poulguinan to Pont-l'Abbé. After the roundabout, uphill, bear left.*

Port du Corniguel

This is the port of Quimper from which wine, timber and sand are exported. Fine view of the Odet and the Baie de Kérogan.

▷ *Return to the Pont-l'Abbé road, and then turn left towards Plomelin. At the next junction, bear left towards the Cale de Rosulien.*

Cale de Rosulien

Road unsurfaced at the end. A ruined mill stands on the right. From the dock, there is a good view of the **Vire-Court**★★ (Ⓒ *see above*).

▷ *Return to the junction, turn left and after the entrance to Perennou Castle, bear left towards the Odet (signposts).*

From the car park, take a path *(15min on foot there and back)* to the banks of the Odet with good views of the river.

Before the Croissant junction where you bear left for Combrit, the road crosses the deep Combrit Cove, which presents a fine sight at high tide.

Combrit

The 16C **church** has a square domed belfry flanked by two turrets. An ossuary (17C) stands next to the south porch.

Pacr Botanique de Cornouaille

After you have visited this very beautiful 4ha/10-acre park, which constitues one of the most important botanical colection in Brittany, you can buy bedding plants in the nursery, located at the entrance, where some of the 3,500 vrieties of plants found in the garden are for sale. This is a magical place in March, when the 550 varieties of camellias and the 85 kinds of magnolias are in full bloom.

▶ *Proceed in the direction of Bénodet, then bear right for Ste-Marine.*

Ste-Marine

This small resort on the west bank of the Odet has a good sandy beach with a fine view over Loctudy and Pointe de Lesconil, the Île aux Moutons and the Îles Glénan, and a small pleasure boat harbour, from which you can enjoy a lovely view of Bénodet and the Odet (*see BÉNODET*).

 In season, a ferry for pedestrians links only Ste-Marine and Bénodet.

▶ *Go over the Pont de Cornouaille.*

Bénodet≜≜ –   *See BÉNODET.*

The return road *(D 34)* is further inland from the east bank of the Odet and runs through **Le Drennec**. Standing in front of the chapel, beside the road, is a charming 16C fountain. A trefoil niche beneath a crocketed gable contains a *Pietà*.

▶ *Pass through Moulin-du-Port to return to Quimper.*

QUIMPERLÉ★

POPULATION 10 850
MICHELIN LOCAL MAP 308 J7– FINISTÈRE (29)

This little town is prettily situated at the confluence (*kemper*) of the River Ellé and River Isole, which join to form the Laïta. It consists of an upper town, dominated by the Église Notre-Dame-de-l'Assomption, and a lower town grouped about the former Abbaye of Ste-Croix and rue Dom-Morice. Quimperlé was once a fairly important harbour but today it is chiefly used for small pleasure craft which sail along the Laïta to discover the Forêt de Carnoët and Le Pouldu.

▶ **Orient Yourself:** 20km/12mi NW of Lorient.

 Don't Miss: Eating oysters on the banks of the River Belon.

 Organizing Your Time: There are not many restaurants in Quimperlé, so book ahead when possible.

Sights

Église Ste-Croix★★

The church, which is interesting archeologically, was built in the 12C, but had to be rebuilt in 1862, except for the apse and the crypt, when its bell-tower collapsed. The new bell-tower stands alone.

The plan is copied from that of the Holy Sepulchre at Jerusalem. It includes a rotunda with three small apsidal chapels opening into it and a porch, the whole forming a Greek cross.

The **apse**★★, with its blind arcades, columns, capitals and windows, is the finest specimen of Romanesque art in Brittany. A Renaissance stone **altarpiece**★ (part of an old rood screen) stands against the façade.

The **crypt**★★ has remarkable capitals and two 15C tombs with recumbent statues.

On leaving the church, take rue Ellé which skirts the north side and affords a good view of the east end and the bell-tower.

Rue Brémond-d'Ars

There are some half-timbered and old 17C houses at nos 8, 10, 11 and 12. At no 15 bis note the staircase of the Présidial, a former Law Court. Note, also, the ruins of the Église St Colomban.

Rue Dom-Morice★

This narrow alley is lined with 16C half-timbered and corbelled houses; no 7, the **Maison des Archers** (1470) is noteworthy; it stages interesting temporary exhibits.

Église Notre-Dame-de-l'Assomption

This 13C and 15C church, surmounted by a large square tower, is also known as St-Michel. Pass under the archway on the right, built into one of the buttresses, to get a glimpse of the fine carved porch (1450). Inside, look at the oak-panelled vault with a sculpted cornice.

Driving Tours

Rochers du Diable★

▷ 12km/7mi northeast, plus 30min on foot there and back. Leave Quimperlé on D 790 towards Le Faouët and after 4.5km/3mi turn right and go through Locunolé.

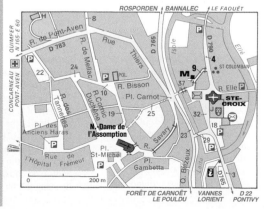

There is a pretty run as the road descends towards the Ellé.

▶ *Cross the bridge and turn left towards Meslan; after 400m/437yd, leave the car in the car park to the left.*

Address Book

TOURIST OFFICE

Quimperlé, 45 Place St-Michel, ☎ 02 98 96 04 32, www.ville-quimperle.fr; Jul-Aug: Mon-Sat 9.30am-7pm, Sun 10am-noon; Sep-June: Mon-Sat 9am-12.30pm, 2-6pm. 🗨 Organises guided tours of the town. Jul-Aug: Mon, Thu and Fri at 3pm. Sep-June: by reservation; 🚶 €1.55.

🕯 *For coin ranges, see the Legend on the cover flap.*

WHERE TO STAY

QUIMPERLÉ

🍽🍽 **Maison d'hôte La maison d'Hippolyte,** *2 quai Surcouf,* ☎ *02 98 39 09 11 – 4 rm* Located on the banks of the Laïta, this centenary house welcomes contemporary art exhibitions. The bathrooms are tiny, and the rooms simple, equipped with period parquet and wooden furniture. Hippolyte? A well-known fisherman of Quimperlé.

🍽🍽🥂 **Le Vintage,** *20 rue Brémond d'Ars,* ☎ *02 98 35 09 10 – 9 rm,* 🛏 *€9.* The keynote is wine at this beautiful contemporary hotel, deceptively masked by a 19C facade. Bright, simple and quiet rooms come furnished with comfortably large beds and, in some rooms, incredible leather armchairs.

SURROUNDING AREAS

🍽🍽 **Auberge de la Pigoulière,** *3 rue de Kérou, Le Pouldu,* ☎ *02 98 39 92 69 – 7 rm* ✕ 🕐 *Open Jul-Aug: daily.* 🕐 *Closed Apr-Nov: Wed evening, Thu; Dec-Mar: Mon-Wed evenings, Thu.* Only 100m away from the beach at Kérou, this recently renovated establishment offers simple but well-kept rooms. The restaurant is widely known, and the service is attentive.

🍽🍽🥂🥂 **Manoir de Kertalg,** *rte de Riec-sur-Belon, Moëlan-sur-Mer,* ☎ *02 98 39 77 77, www.manoirdekertalg.com – 9rm,* 🛏 *€12.* Located on 85ha of timbered property, this charming "castle-hotel" offers gorgeous and refined accomodations. The rooms of the manor display painting exhibitions for a clientele in love with art.

EATING OUT

QUIMPERLÉ

🍽🍽 **La Cigale égarée,** *La Villeneuve-Braouic,* ☎ *02 98 39 15 53.* A Mediterranean menu and resolutely inventive cuisine deliver dishes such as chicken brochettes in vanilla wood, prepared with grated coconut and served with a piña-colada.

🍽🍽 **Le Bistro de La Tour,** *2 rue Dom-Morice,* ☎ *02 98 39 29 58.* 🕐 *Closed Mon; Sat afternoon; Sep-Jun: Sun evening.* A lovely address located in a pleasant alley of the Old Quimperlé. More evocative of a wine store than of a restaurant, the facade here takes its cue from the owner, chairman of the Sommeliers de Bretagne. In addition to sampling the regional menus served in two dining rooms, oenophiles can also purchase and taste their favorite wines.

RECREATION

Walks – The Tourist Office organises thematic walks for everyone from casual ramblers to avid walkers. You may learn about the inshore flora, the difficulties facing heritage and conservation efforts or the lost villages of the Carnoët forest.

Fluvial cruises– Vedettes Aven-Bélon, *Moëlan-sur-Mer,* ☎ *02 98 71 14 59, vedettes.aven.belon@free.fr.* From the port of Bélon, speedboats offer two circuits: the first, a trip to discover the estuaries of Bélon and of the Aven (Jul-Aug, 1h, €8, only a few departures per month), the second, a round-trip to Pont-Aven and back (Jul-Aug, 1 departure/day, 90min + short-stop, €13).

⊞ Paths leading up to the top of the Devil's Rocks drop vertically to the fast-flowing waters of the Ellé.

① Domaine de Clohars-Carnoët

Round-trip of 43km/27ml – 2hr 30min.

▶ *Leave Quimperlé via Quai Brizeux.*

Forêt de Carnoët
Bordered by the River Laïta, the forest offers pretty sites and pleasant walks (⟨⟩ *some paths are reserved for walking and riding*).

▶ *Some 500m/547yd beyond Toulfoën, turn left towards the Rocher Royal.*

The road winds through the forest to the banks of the Laïta where the **Rocher Royal** can be seen, a rocky ridge towering above the river, and the ruins of the Château de Carnoët. This is the legendary dwelling of the Count of Commore, the Bluebeard of Cornouaille. After hearing a prediction that he would die by the hand of his son, he put his first four wives to death as soon as they conceived. The fifth wife, Triphine, before she died, was able to save her son, who became **St Trémeur**. Commore, on meeting the saint, was struck by his resemblance to his mother and immediately had him beheaded. Then, according to the legend, Trémeur picked up his own head, walked towards his father's castle and threw a handful of earth against the building, which then collapsed, burying Commore alive.

▶ *Return to the Le Pouldu road, turn left and at a major junction, left again.*

The **Pont de St-Maurice** over the Laïta gives a fine **view**★ of the river and its steep banks.

▶ *Turn round and after 700m/766yd, turn right.*

St-Maurice
This stands in a green and pleasant **site**★: the Laïta is on the right with a lake on the left. Nearby are remains of the chapter-house of the former **Abbaye St-Maurice,** founded in the 12C.

Le Pouldu
This small port lies at the mouth of the River Laïta.

Maison Marie-Henry
10 rue des Grands-Sables. Reconstruction of the inn which Gauguin and members of the Pont-Aven School decorated with paintings and drawings; the furniture dates from the 1880s. Temporary exhibitions devoted to these artists illustrate their influence on the Nabis movement in Paris and on other artists abroad.

The Chapelle Notre-Dame-de-la-Paix
Situated near Grands Sables Beach, stands in a grassy close, the entrance of which is flanked by a monument to Gauguin. The chapel escaped ruin by being transported 26km/16mi and rebuilt here. The bays have flame and lily shaped tracery with stained glass by Manessier and Le Moal. Below the timber roof, the rood beam carries a Christ with a red loincloth and a second group depicting a *Pietà*.

▶ *Drive along Grands Sables Beach then turn left towards Doëlan.*

Doëlan

A small fishing port commanding the entrance to a deep, sheltered estuary.

▶ *Return to Quimperlé via Clohars-Carnoët.*

2 The Bélon Region

Round-trip of 37km/23mi – 1hr 30min.

▶ *Leave Quimperlé to the southwest on D 16 and at Gare-de-la-Forêt, bear right.*

Moëlan-sur-Mer

The peaceful port of Doëlan

Several small harbours. In the **church** (🕐 *Open Mon-Fri, 9am-6pm*), note the four 18C confessional boxes in the Italian style.

▶ *Continue SW to Brigneau.*

Brigneau

A tiny fishing port where pleasure craft also find shelter.
The road follows the coastline. Thatched-roofed houses are found along the way.

▶ *At Kergroès, bear left.*

Kerfany-les-Pins

On the River Bélon, this small seaside resort has a pretty site and a sandy beach. Fine view over Port-Manech and the Aven estuary.

▶ *Take the uphill road beyond the beach and at Lanriot, turn left.*

Bélon

This locality, on the south bank of the Bélon, is famous as an oyster-farming centre. The oyster beds on the north bank can be seen at low tide.

▶ *Return to Quimperlé via Moëlan-sur-Mer.*

QUINTIN

POPULATION 2 611
MICHELIN LOCAL MAP 309 E4 – CÔTES D'ARMOR (22)

In the past, Quintin was well known for its fine linen which was used for headdresses and collars. In the 17C and 18C the industry expanded to the manufacture of Brittany cloth which was exported to America but decline set in at the Revolution when there were 300 weavers in the town. The old houses of Quintin rise in terraces on a hill; the River Gouët forms a fine stretch of water below.

Sights

There are fine 16C-17C corbelled houses lining the picturesque place 1830, rue au Lait (nos 12, 13) and Grande Rue (nos 37 and 43). In place du Martray, the Hôtel du Martray, the town hall and the house at no 1 date from the 18C.

Basilica (Basilique)

Built on the site of a collegiate church in 1887. The relics of St Thuriau and a piece of the Virgin's girdle, brought from Jerusalem in the 13C by a lord of Quintin (Geoffroy Botrel or Botherel), are kept in the basilica. There are also four stoups made of shells from Java and the old crowned statue of Notre-Dame-de-Délivrance (Our Lady of Safe Delivery), especially venerated by expectant mothers; a 14C font in the north transept and two 14C recumbent figures in the chancel. At the east end of the basilica stands the 15C New Gate (Porte Neuve), all that remains of the ramparts which surrounded the town.

Château

Access via place 1830. ♿ 🚗 *Guided tours (1hr15min; last admission 30min before closing) mid-June to mid-Sept, daily, 10.30am-12.30pm and 1.30-6.30pm; May to mid-June and last two weeks of Sept, Easter and Nov school hols, 2-5pm; Apr and Oct, Sat-Sun 2.30-5pm.* 🕘 *Closed the rest of the year.* ⊛ *€5 (children 8-14: €2.50).* ☎ *02 96 74 94 79.*
The château is made up of an older 17C building and a grand 18C building, flanked by a low-lying wing at a right angle, visible once through the entrance gate.
The **museum**, housed in the 18C part of the château, recounts Quintin's history and that of the chateau's previous owners. Displayed inside are: hand-painted India Company plates, Meissen tableware, archives and Quintin linen. In the kitchen is an unusual piece: an 18C granite oven with seven holes (used for slow cooking).

Excursion

Menhir de Roche-Longue

800m/875yd farther on by the road beyond the Calvary which skirts the lake.
At the top of the hill, a menhir 4.70m/14ft high stands in a field to the left.

VALLÉE DE LA RANCE★★

MICHELIN LOCAL MAP 309 J/L 2/6 – CÔTES-D'ARMOR (22)

The Rance estuary, lying between St-Malo and Dinard, is among the places most frequented in Brittany. Upstream, Dinan is a typical old inland town. The Rance is a perfect example of a Breton river. It forms a deep gulf between Dinan and the sea, flowing with many branches and inlets over a level plateau. This curious gulf is due to the flooding by the sea of an ordinary but steep-sided valley: the stream itself and the bottom of the valley have been "drowned" by a mass of tidal water. All that remains visible of the original valley is its steep sides, sloping into the sea. The Rance proper is a small river without much water, which winds along above Dinan.

Boat Trip★★

Allow 5hr there and back – not counting the stop and tour of Dinan. ▣ *For information, apply to the Tourist Offices of St-Malo, Dinard or Dinan.*

The boat follows the Noires breakwater (Môle des Noires) and crosses the Rance estuary for a brief stop at Dinard. It enters the Rance, leaving the Corniche d'Aleth on the left (St-Servan), passes in front of Pointe de la Vicomté and Rocher Bizeux and then enters the lock of the Rance dam. You will go up the river, between its great banks, through a series of narrow channels and wide pools. After Chatelier Lock (Écluse du Chatelier), the Rance gets narrower and narrower and becomes a mere canal just as you come within sight of Dinan, perched on its ridge.

Address Book

For coin ranges, see the Legend on the cover flap.

WHERE TO STAY

TADEN

◌◌ **Le Petit Paris**, *signed from the Intermarché,* ☎ 02 96 39 17 24 - 2rm ▱ This beautiful Breton farm with flowery surroundings harbors bright rooms, decorated with souvenirs brought back from Bali by the owner. A large unit with space for 4 people is very pleasant. Guest table by reservation.

PLEUDIHEN-SUR-RANCE

◌◌ **La Châtaigneraie**, *Les Rouchiviers (ask for directions),* ☎ 02 96 83 39 63, *lachataigneraie@bretagne-heberge-ment.com* – 3 suites. The owners of this immense farm in the middle of the countryside have decorated guest rooms with objects they brought back from their trip around the world. Large units with space for 3 to 4 people are distributed among the different build-ings. Home-made foods for breakfast and guest table by reservation.

ST-SULIAC

◌ **Les Mouettes**, *17 Grande Rue,* ☎ 02 99 58 30 41, *www.les-mouettes-saint-suliac.com* – 5rm ▱ The owner, who makes and sells scrumptious jams, offers simple accomodations in a rustic setting, upstairs or on the ground floor of her house. Be sure to pick a room looking out into the garden.

◌◌ **La Goélette**, *2 rue Besnier,* ☎ 02 99 58 47 03 – 3rm ▱ Surrounded by a peaceful garden, this former residence houses spacious rooms—one with enough room for six people.

EATING OUT

LA VICOMTÉ-SUR-RANCE

◌◌ **Le Ty Corentin**, *port de Lyvet,* ☎ 02 96 83 21 10. ⏲ *Closed Jan: Wed; 2 weeks in Nov.* Traditional cuisine and seafood served in a dining room or on a terrace in front of the port of the Lyvet.

PLOUËR-SUR-RANCE

◌◌ **La Vieille Auberge**, *Place de l'Église,* ☎ 02 96 86 89 86. ⏲ *Closed Sun evening; Mon.* In this old village house with a crackling fireplace, delicioius regional cuisine or seafood and wines at good prices can be found year round.

ST-SULIAC

◌◌ **La Ferme du Boucanier**, ☎ 02 23 15 06 35. ⏲ *Closed Tue and Wed noon.* Enjoy fresh market cuisine here as it is prepared with Breton products and the graceful note of Belgian creativity.

ON BOARD IN THE RANCE

From St-Malo-Dinard - Croisières Chateaubriand, *boom of the Rance, from the South exit of St-Malo, travel toward Dinard and get out at the boom,* ☎ 02 99 46 44 40, *www.chateaubriand. com* Choose any of several possibili-ties: guided tours of 1hr (€7-14), 90min (€10-17) or 3hr (€19-28); cruise (3hr) on board a restaurant-boat, afternoon and evening, (€45-53, children €28).

SHOPPING

Farm products - Potager des Bords de Rance, *La Ville-Ger, rte de Mordreuc, Pleudihen,* ☎ 02 96 83 37 03. ⏲ *Closed Sun afternoon; Tue morning.* Fruits and vegetables among other farm products fill the stalls of Pleudihen's Tuesday morning marketplace all year long.

Dinan★★

 See DINAN. Your boat will stop for a longer or shorter time according to the tide – from 8hr to only 15min.
The scenes on your way back will change depending on the direction and intensity of the light.

Along the Banks of the Rance★

Round-trip Starting from St-Malo
87km/54mi – allow one day

St-Malo★★★ – *See ST-MALO.*

▶ *Leave St-Malo by ③ on the town plan. Turn right towards* **La Passagère**.

From this landing-stage, there is a fine view over the Rance.

▶ *Make for St-Suliac via Chapelle du Boscq and St-Jouan-des-Guérets.*

On the right notice the **Moulin du Beauchet**, once a tidal mill.

St-Suliac

This charming fishing village has retained a number of old granite houses along its meandering streets overlooked by the massive bell-tower of the church (13-17C). Note the fine parish close nearby. A steep street leads donw to the bank of the Rance; the local sailing school is active in fine weather.

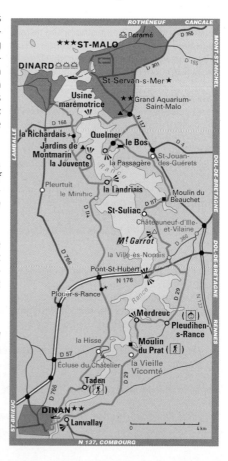

▶ *In St-Suliac, before the church, bear left in the direction of Mont Garrot. 1km/0.5mi farther on leave the car near an old crenellated watchtower.*

From the foot of the tower, there is a wide **panorama**★ of St-Suliac Cove, St-Malo, the Dol countryside, the River Rance and Pont St-Hubert.

Mont Garrot

Allow 15min on foot there and back. A path to the right leads to the point, passing behind a farm. Notice the views of the Vallée de la Rance on the way.

▶ *From La Ville-ès-Nonais continue onto the Pont St-Hubert.*

Tidal Power

The use of tidal power is nothing new to the Vallée de la Rance. As early as the 12C, riverside dwellers had thought up the idea of building little reservoirs which, as they emptied with the ebb tide, drove mill wheels. To double the output of a modern industrial plant, it was tempting to try to work out a means of using the flow as well as the ebb tide. The French electricity board (EDF), therefore, searched for new technical methods of producing electricity and successfully set up, between the headlands of La Briantais and La Brebis, a Usine hydro-électrique (hydroelectric power station) operated by both the flow and ebb of the tide. A 750m/820yd-long dam extends across the Rance estuary; it forms a rservoir covering 22km2/8.5sq mi. The road linking St-Malo and Dinard runs along the top of the dam and across the 65m/213ft-long lock which allows ships through.

From this suspension bridge, there is a pleasant view of the Rance, the Port St-Jean slipway and, on the rocky bank opposite, the St-Hubert slipway.

▶ *Return to La Ville-ès-Nonais, bear right.*

Pleudihen-sur-Rance
The farm's outbuildings house the **Musée de la Pomme et du Cidre** (Apple and Cider Museum – Kids ⬚ ⏱ *Open June to Aug, daily, 10am-7pm; Apri, May and Sept, daily (except Sun), 2-7pm.* ⌖€3.50. ☎ *02 96 83 20 78*).
Before visiting the museum stop by the orchard planted with different varieties of apple trees. Inside the museum, the apple, its origin, the different varieties, diseases, cultivation and picking are explained. A film illustrating the different apple-related trades (e.g. cooperage) and a tasting end the tour.

Cale de Mordreuc
From this lovely place there are good views of Pont St-Hubert downstream, the deepening valley upstream and the ruins of an old castle on an opposite promontory.

Lanvallay
A remarkable **view**⋆ of the old town of Dinan, its ramparts and its belfries from here.

Dinan⋆⋆ – ⬙ *See Dinan.*

▶ *Take the road which passes under the Dinan viaduct and skirts the harbour.*

Taden
When you cross the village toward the slipway, glance at the porch and keep, which are flanked by a 14C turret.
🚶 The towpath, which used to link Dinan to the Écluse du Chatelier, is a favourite spot for fishermen and a pleasant place to stroll *(7km/4.3mi)*. Taden Plain is the home of a number of aquatic birds: black-headed gulls, herring gulls, coots.

▶ *Return to the road toward Dinard. As you leave La Hisse turn right before the level crossing.*

Continue on to **Plouër-sur-Rance**. Inside the 18C church are carved tombstones.

▶ *After Plouër-sur-Rance and Le Minihic, bear right and right again after 250m/273yd.*

La Landriais

The port contains naval dockyards. The walk along Hures Promenade (☞ *on foot take Chemin de ronde des Douaniers)* starts from the car park and skirts the Rance for 2km/1mi affording fine views.

▶ *On your return, turn right after 1.2km/0.7mi then right again after another 1km/0.6mi.*

Cale de la Jouvente

Across from La Passagère. There is a nice view of the Rance and the Île Chevret.

La Richardais

The **church** is dominated by its pierced tower and the Calvary surmounting it. On the walls of the nave runs a fresco (1955) depicting the Stations of the Cross by Xavier de Langlais. In the transept is a fresco illustrating the arrival of St Lunaire and St Malo on the Breton coast. From the fine wood vaulting resembling the upturned keel of a ship, four lamps in the form of wheels hang down. Five stained-glass windows are by Max Ingrand. On leaving La Richardais by the north, you get a **view** of the tidal power scheme and the Rance estuary.

Usine marémotrice de la Rance

☞ *Guided tours July-Aug: 10am-6pm, Sun 10am-1pm and 2-6pm; April-June and Sep: 10am-12.30pm and 1.30-6pm; school holidays (Feb, Nov, Dec): Wed-Sun 10am-12.30pm and 1.30-6pm.* 🕓 *Closed the rest of the year.* ☜ *No charge.* ☎ *02 99 88 53 53.*

The **power station** is in a huge tunnel nearly 390m/400yd long in the very centre of the dam. In this room, are the 24 AC generators of a combined capacity of 240 000kW which can produce 600 million kWh per year (equal to the annual consumption of a city comparable to Rennes and its outskirts).

The **view**★ from the platform atop the dam extends over the Rance estuary as far as Dinard and St-Malo. The dam lies between the power station and the right bank with its centre on the small island of Chalibert. There are six sluice-gates at the eastern end which regulate the emptying and filling of the reservoir, thus controlling the water supply to the power station.

▶ *Return to St-Malo by the direct route along the crest of the dam.*

POINTE DU RAZ★★★

MICHELIN LOCAL MAP 308 C6 – FINISTÈRE (29)

Pointe du Raz is a rocky promontory at the tip of Cornouaille, jutting out into the treacherous Raz du Sein; this magnificent site, which attracts numerous visitors in the summer, is now heavily protected as part of France's national heritage.

The Site

Allow 1hr. 🚻*Information centre (Maison de la Pointe du Raz et du Cap Sizun).* 🕓 *Open July and Aug, daily, 9.30am-7.30pm; Apr, June and Sept, 10.30am-6pm.* ☞ *Guided walk round the site,* ☜ *€5, minimum 4 persons.* ☎ *02 98 70 67 18.*

✏️*Protective measures have been taken to preserve the site and its environment. A new visitors' centre has opened, the* **Porte du Cap Sizun** *(information centre, exhibit area,*

Pointe du Raz

restaurants and shops). To reach the end of the point, motorists must pay to leave their car in the parking area (fee: €4; 800m away from the point). It takes about 15min to follow the waymarked paths to the far end. A free shuttle provides transportation for those who have difficulty walking.

Walk around the signal station in front of which stands a statue of Our Lady of the Shipwrecked (Notre-Dame-des-Naufragés) to enjoy a wide **panorama**★★ of the horizon: straight ahead is the Île de Sein and beyond, in clear weather, the Ar Men Lighthouse. Between the Île de Sein and the mainland is the fearful Raz du Sein or tide race which, so an old saying has it, "no one passes without fear or sorrow"; to the northwest can be seen Tévennec Lighthouse (Phare de Tévennec) standing on an islet. The path runs along the edge of vertiginous chasms *(safety ropes)*.

The **Enfer de Plogoff** (Plogoff Hell) is a narrow jagged spur towering 70m/230ft above the sea and prolonged by a line of reefs; on the farthest of these stands La Vieille Lighthouse. This site is particuarlly impressive when storms are raging.

REDON

POPULATION 9 499
MICHELIN LOCAL MAP 309 J9 – ILLE-ET-VILAINE (35)

Redon, the centre of an active region, is the meeting point of three departements (Ille-et-Vilaine, Loire-Atlantique and Morbihan) and two regions (Brittany and Pays de Loire). In Redon, the River Vilaine and the Nantes-Brest Canal converge at the pleasure boat harbour (tourism on inland waterways).

Visit

Église St-Sauveur

This former abbey church, founded in 832, was a great pilgrimage centre throughout the Middle Ages and until the 17C. This accounts for the impressive size of the building. In 1622 Richelieu was the commendatory abbot. It was cut off from its 14C Gothic bell-towers (D) by a fire in 1780. A remarkable Romanesque sandstone and granite **tower**★ stands at the transept crossing. From the neighbouring **cloisters**

(17C), occupied by the College of St Saviour, the superimposition of its arcades can be seen. From the esplanade planted with chestnut trees and overlooking rue Richelieu, one has a good view of the chevet with its buttresses.

The **interior** reveals a dimly lit low nave (11C) with wood vaulting separated from the side aisles by flat pillars. Note the carved pillars in the transept crossing; they support the octagonal stone vaulting.

The old town

The old town contains elegant 15C-18C town houses. Leave from the Église St-Sauveur and walk along **Grande Rue,** noting nos 22, 25, 38, 44, 52 and 54; look down rue d'Enfer and rue Jeanne-d'Arc. Cross the flower-decorated bridge which spans the

---

Address Book

TOURIST OFFICE

Redon, Place de la République, ☎ 02 99 71 06 04, www.tourisme-pays-redon.com; Sept-June: Mon-Fri 9.30am-noon, 2-6pm (closed Tue morning), Sat 10am-12.30pm, 3-5pm; July-Aug: Mon-Sat 9.30am-12.30pm, 1.30-6.30pm, Sun and public holidays, 10am-12.30pm, 3-5.30pm. Offers a brochure of the footpaths in the Redon country (€2) and organises various guided visits in July-Aug (€3/1.60): St-Sauveur church (Mon 3pm), Old Town (Wed 10am), Calvairiennes chapel (Wed 3pm).**Rent a bike- Cycles Chedaleux**, 44 rue Notre-Dame, ☎ 02 99 72 19 95 or 06 61 18 29 65.

WHERE TO STAY

⊜⊜ **Hôtel de France**, *30 rue Du Guesclin*, ☎ *02 99 71 06 11, www.hotelle-france.com– 18 rooms.* ⏱ *Closed 21 Dec-end of Jan.* Very simple rooms, calms and well kept, in a 1960s building. Two luminous rooms look out over the port.

⊜⊜ **Chambres d'hôte L'Aumônerie**, *L'Aumônerie, 6 km east of Redon by the D 65 along the River Vilaine*, ☎ *02 99 72 05 34– 1 room; 1 family suite,* ✗ This renovated farm is located in a pleasant park with exotic trees, along the marshland of the River Vilaine. The owners offer thematic weekends and know the footpaths in the area very well. Meals are made with garden-fresh ingredients and rooms are simple.

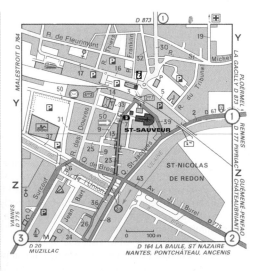

Nantes-Brest Canal. In **rue du Port** across from no 6, Hôtel Carmoy, are three corbelled houses. Go onto **rue du Jeu-de-Paume** which has, at no 10, the old customs barracks, a 4-storey building with a severe façade and a wall with a scene of swineherds and fishmongers dressed in costumes of the past. Return to rue du Port where old salt houses (no 40) can be seen; occupying no 3 **rue du Plessis** is the Hôtel Richelieu. **Quai Duguay-Trouin** is lined with stately shipowners' homes of which nos 15, 7, 6 and 5 are particularly worth looking at. By way of **Quai St-Jacques**, where ramparts in ruins still stand, and rue de Richelieu, you return to the church.

Excursions

Rieux
7km/4mi S via ③ on the town plan towards Vannes.
On entering the village, in a bend, take the road to the left which leads you to a car park, from where there is a pleasant view of the Vilaine Valley and Redon; occupying the wooded promontory are castle ruins.

St-Just
19km/11.5mi northeast. Leave Redon on R on the town plan (D 177) towards Rennes and turn left to St-Just.
This small town lies at the centre of an area rich in **megaliths** (dating from c3500 BC) and there are many interesting rambles starting from St-Just.
🚶 A waymarked path lead to **Landes de Cojoux (**Cojoux Moor, megalith). From here there is a lovely view of the Étang de Val (rock-climbing).

Massérac
15km/9.3mi E along D 775. Turn right towards Avessac.
Lying at the confluence of the Rlver Vilaine and the Rlver Don, this municipality is rich in wetlands (800ha/1 977 acres). The **Maison des Marais, de la Chasse et de la Pêche (** 🕐 *Daily July-Aug 10am-12.30pm and 3-7pm)* offers in insight into the lifestyle of waders, fish and other animals living i the ecosystem. Inside, displays and films are informative, and you may arranged for a guided walking tour.

RENNES★★

POPULATION 365 000
MICHELIN LOCAL MAP 309 L6 · ILLE-ET-VILLAINE (35)

The regional capital of Brittany, has, over the past decades, restored its architectural heritage, thus highlighting its dignified elegance. This city of artistic and historical interest, where good food is highly valued, exudes atmosphere from its narrow, winding medieval streets, lined with charming half-timbered houses with carved sills, which happily escaped the ravages of a huge fire in 1720. The stately public buildings and numerous private mansions adorning the two royal squares (place du Palais and place de l'Hôtel-de-Ville) at the very heart of the town, delimited to the south by the lively quays along the Vilaine. Rennes is also a university city which has become a centre of the electronics and communications industry.

▶ **Orient Yourself:** Capital city of the Région Bretagne.
🅿 **Parking:** Leave your car in a car park and take the VAL metro/bus!
👁 **Don't Miss:** A walk through the streets of the Old Town.
🕐 **Organizing Your Time:** It takes a full day to visit Rennes.

Address Book

GETTING AROUND

Public transportation - Rennes has a bus network and a metro (VAL). **Information:** 12 rue du Pré Botté et Place de l'Hôtel de Ville, under the arcades, ☎ 02 99 79 37 37, www.star.fr

On bike – If you are transient, you can borrow a bike without paying for 7 hours by going to the car park of the Vilaine, near the bridge of Nemours, ☎ 08 20 80 88 08 or 02 99 79 65 88. You can also rent a bike at the **Cycles Guédard**, 13 bd de Beaumont, ☎ 02 99 30 43 78.

Taxis cab - Taxis rennais, ☎ 02 99 30 79 79.

TOURIST OFFICE

Rennes Métropole, Chapelle St-Yves, 11 rue St-Yves, ☎ 02 99 67 11 11, www.tourisme-rennes.com ⊙ Open Apr-Sep: daily 9am-7pm (6pm Oct-Mar), Sun and public hols 11am-6pm. Located in an old chapel that welcomes visitors with an exhibition on the town's heritage, the office dispenses helpful information and free maps of Rennes. Guided and thematic tours of the Old Town (Jul-Aug: daily 3pm, Tue-Thur 9pm).

Comité régional de tourisme (CRT), 1 rue Raoul Ponchon, ☎ 02 99 36 15 15, www.tourismebretagne.com

⚪ For coin ranges, see the Legend on the cover flap.

WHERE TO STAY

A number of hotels participate in the formula **"Bon week-end en villes", which entitles you to** two nights in a hotel for the price of one for Fri or Sat evening arrivals. Book at least 24hr in advance at the tourist office. Information www.bon-week-end-en-villes.com.

⊝⊝ **Hôtel de la Tour d'Auvergne**, 20 bd de la Tour d'Auvergne, ☎ 02 99 30 84 16 – 12rm, 🖵 €6. Some rooms of this small familial hostel are equipped with only a basin, but all are very well kept.

⊝⊝ **Arvor Hôtel**, 31 av. Louis-Barthou, ☎ 02 99 30 36 47, www.arvorhotel. com – 16rm, 🖵 €5.50, ✕ Located near the train station, this hotel-restaurant has simple, functional rooms.

⊝⊝⊜ **Hôtel Lanjuinais**, 11 rue Lanjuinais, ☎ 02 99 79 02 03, hotel-lan-juinais@wanadoo.fr – 39rm, 🖵 €7, ▤ The decor is refined at this traditional village hotel, where rooms insulated from street-noise and very well kept.

⊝⊝ **Hotel Victoria**, 35 av. Jean Janvier, ☎ 02 99 31 69 11, www.hotelvictoria.com - 28rm, 🖵 €7, ✕ Rooms in the "English style" are a little outdated but agreeable.

⊝⊝⊜ **Hôtel Président**, 27 av. Jean Janvier, ☎ 02 99 65 42 22, hotel-president@wanadoo.fr – 34rm, 🅿 €7, 🖵 €7.50. ⊙ Closed 2 weeks Jul–Aug; 2 weeks Dec-Jan. Some rooms are decorated in the Regency style while others here sport a more contemporary style for the very functional, with ample workspace and internet connections.

⊝⊝ **Garden Hôtel**, 3 rue Duhamel, ☎ 02 99 65 45 06 – 25rm, 🅿 €6.50, 🖵 €6.50. Most of the rooms of this small hotel overlook a pleasant floral patio. Quite simple, the hotel is well kept in the main, even though some rooms near the street are a little noisy.

⊝⊝⊜ **Hôtel de Nemours**, 5 rue de Nemours, ☎ 02 99 78 26 26, www.hotelnemours.com – 29rm, 🖵 €7.50, ▤ Very well located, this hotel was totally renovated in 2005. Room decor is subdued.

⊝⊝⊜ **Hôtel des Lices**, 7 pl. des Lices, ☎ 02 99 79 14 81, www.hotel-des-lices.com – 45rm, 🖵 €7. In the centre of Old Rennes, these comfortable rooms are decorated with vivid colours and equipped with contemporary furniture.

⊝⊝⊜⊜ **Mercure Place de Bretagne**, 6 rue Lanjuinais, ☎ 02 99 79 12 36, www.mercure.com – 48rm, 🖵 €10, ▤ Three floors of comfortable rooms in yellow and brick tones look out onto the quay of the Vilaine or on a courtyard.

⊝⊝⊜⊜ **Mercure Pré Botté**, 1 rue Paul-Louis Courier, ☎ 02 99 78 82 20, www.mercure.com – 104rm, 🖵 €12, ▤ The ca1900 brick facade of the former daily newspaper, Ouest-Éclair, shelters bright rooms that open onto the street or the garden.

EATING OUT

⊝ **Le Tire-Bouchon**, 2 rue du Chapitre, ☎ 02 99 79 43 43. ⊙ Closed Sat; Sun;

public hols; Feb hols; 3 weeks Aug.
Perfect for pairings with the region's
famous wines, this café's market-based
menu includes hot slices of bread and
plates of cooked meats or cheese.

⊖ **Au Rocher de Cancale**, *10 rue
St-Michel*, ☎ *02 99 79 20 83.* 🕐 *Closed 2
weeks Aug.* Settle into the rustic dining
room or the small terrace to enjoy
oysters or heaping portions of couscous
and a lively atmosphere.

⊖ **Le Bocal, P'ty resto**, *6 rue
d'Argentré*, ☎ *02 99 78 34 10.* 🕐 *Closed
Mon; Sat lunch; Sun; public hols.* This
intimate setting delivers fresh and
inventive cuisine such as potted sardines with green lemon, beef crumble
with spices and creamy rice pudding
flavoured with laurel.

⊖ **Thé au Fourneau**, *6 rue du Capitaine Alfred Dreyfus*, ☎ *02 99 78 25 36.*
Under the low ceiling of this welcoming
tea house, you will taste wonderful
homemade pies, prodigious salads and,
of course, an excellent choice of teas.

⊖ **Cantina Mia**, *7 Place St-Germain*,
☎ *02 99 78 33 42.* 🕐 *Closed Sun and
Mon.* Life is sweet with the dolce vita
Rennaise in this small, kitsch-filled
room, where, for reasonable prices,
bruschetta, antipasti, pasta and other
sunny specialties can be yours.

⊖ **Léon le Cochon**, *1 rue du Maréchal
Joffre*, ☎ *02 99 79 37 54.* 🕐 *Closed Jul-
Aug: Sun.* Solid regional cuisine made
with products selected from Breton
farms. Made to satisfy even the biggest
appetites.

⊖ **La Tête de Lard**, *37 rue Vasselot*,
☎ *02 99 79 05 91.* 🕐 *Closed Sun-Mon;
Feb hols; 3 weeks in Aug.* Overlooking
a pedestrian street, this small café
attracts patrons with the smell of its
fowls and roasted suckling pigs, specialties of the house. Friendly atmosphere
and thoughtful service.

⊖⊖ **L'Ouvrée**, *18 Place des Lices*,
☎ *02 99 30 16 38.* 🕐 *Closed Sat lunch;
Sun evening; Mon; 10 days Apr-May; 3
weeks in Aug.* The most famous market
of Brittany is nearby and the menu here
is driven by it. Very professional cuisine
and a thoughtful wine list, as refined as
the setting.

⊖⊖⊖ **La Table d'Eugénie**, *2 rue
des Dames*, ☎ *02 99 30 78 18.* 🕐 *Closed
Sat lunch; Sun; Mon lunch; 3 weeks in*

Aug-Sep; 1 week in Mar. At the centre of
the Old Rennes, fine cuisine made with
regional products is emphasized with
Mediterranean touches.

⊖⊖ **Auberge du Chat Pitre**, *18
rue du Chapitre*, ☎ *02 99 30 36 36.*
🕐 *Closed at lunch and Sun.* Go back in
time behind a beautiful half-timbering
façade to the Middle Ages, where medieval animation lights up this convivial
restaurant.

⊖⊖ **Le Comptoir des Halles**, *25 rue
Jules Simon*, ☎ *02 99 78 20 07.* 🕐 *Closed
Sun.* This very fashionable café-res-
taurant offers a mish-mash cuisine of
Breton and worldwide flavours in a
simple setting.

⊖⊖⊖ **Le Galopin**, *21 av. Jean Janvier*,
☎ *02 99 31 55 96.* 🕐 *Closed Sat lunch;
Sun.* This elegant pub is the right place
to enjoy seafood and good service.

⊖⊖ **Le Baron Rouge**, *15-17 rue du
Chapitre*, ☎ *02 99 79 08 09.* 🕐 *Closed Sat
lunch; Sun.* Original cuisine and a wild
atmosphere where Bacchus himself is
celebrated makes for a rustic and surprisingly charming dining experience.

⊖⊖ **Café Breton**, *14 rue Nantaise*,
☎ *02 99 30 74 95.* 🕐 *Closed Sat and Mon
evenings; Sun; 2 weeks in Mar; 3 weeks
in Aug.* The haphazard decor of this
restaurant has created both a popular
and energetic dining atmosphere. Good
choice of salads, salted pies, gratins and
delicious pastries.

⊖⊖ **Le Gourmandin**, *4 Place de
Bretagne*, ☎ *02 99 30 42 01.* 🕐 *Closed
Sat and Mon lunch; Sun; 10 days in Mar; 3
weeks in Aug.* This traditional restaurant
offers a generous cuisine made with
fresh regional products and a good
wine list. Reservations advised.

⊖⊖⊖ **L'Appart de Loïc**, *67 ter bd de
la Tour-d'Auvergne*, ☎ *02 99 67 03 04.*
🕐 *Closed Sun-Mon; 3 weeks in summer.*
A big, yellow-walled room forms the
backdrop for this elegant restaurant,
which offers a fine cuisine mixing Atlantic and Mediterranean flavours.

⊖⊖ **Le Four à Ban**, *4 rue St-Mélaine*,
☎ *02 99 38 72 85.* 🕐 *Closed Sat lunch;
Sun; Mon evening; 3 weeks in Jul-Aug.* A
happy mix of tradition and modernity,
the decor here reflects the epicurean
spirit of the place as it combines
flavours both of land and sea, North
and South.

NIGHTLIFE

As a haven for students, Rennes naturally comes to life at night. Most of the area's night life is concentrated in the Old Town, on St-Malo, St-Georges and St-Michel streets, also known as the "district of the thirst."

Le Chatham, *5 rue de Montfort, ☎ 02 99 79 55 48. Open until 3am. Closed Sun.* A true picture of the range of Rennes nightlife, all generations get mixed-up at this sea-decorated bar. Good choice of beers and whiskeys. Rock music during the weekend.

Le Dejazey, *54 rue de St-Malo, ☎ 02 99 38 70 72. Closed Sun.* Mecca for amateur jazz-musicians, practicing for Jazz Rennais. Welcomes good bands in a stuffy room. Admission charges and inflated prices for potables in accordance with the quality of the program.

Le Zing, *5 Place des Lices, ☎ 02 99 79 64 60.* The atmosphere almost brushes the clouds on weekend nights in this switched-on pub that calls to mind aviation and its heroes.

ENTERTAINMENT

Théâtre national de Bretagne, *1 rue St-Hélier, ☎ 02 99 31 12 31. Closed 15 Jul-1 Sep.* As the place where cultures meet, the TNB has distinguished itself by the quality and diversity of its theatrical and musical productions. It also shelters the gallery of the Fonds régional d'art contemporain (FRAC).

RECREATION

Boat trips – Urbavag, *rue du Canal St-Martin, ☎ 02 99 33 16 88 or 06 82 37 67 72, www.urbavag.com* An original way to visit Rennes-- on board electric boats (no license necessary) on the canal of Ille-et-Rance.

Les Tombées de la Nuit, *☎ 02 99 32 56 56, www.tdn.rennes.fr,10 days in July.* For 25 years, this festival has produced more unexpected audio performances than any of a hundred other places in the town centre.

SHOPPING

Market – Marché des Lices, *Place des Lices: Sat: 7am-1pm.* Whatever the season, you will find here the best farm products coming from everywhere in Brittany; above all, an unequalled choice of fishes and seafood.

Culinary specialities - Pâtisserie Bouvier, *5 rue de la Parcheminerie, ☎ 02 99 78 14 08. Closed Mon ; Sun afternoon.* Taste the Parlementin, a Rennaise specialty made with apple compote and cider, or the delicious macaroons, a speciality of this popular pastry chef. The same artisan offers a line of very original chocolates at the 22 rue de Nemours.

Pâtisserie Chaou, *18 rue Baudrairie, ☎ 02 99 78 14 08. Closed Mon; Sun afternoon; 2 weeks in summer.* Also a good address to enjoy the famous Parlementin Rennais.

Chocolaterie Durand, *5 quai Chateaubriand, ☎ 02 99 78 10 00. Closed Sun.* Behind the beautiful façade of this 19C Rennaise institution lurk about thirty unexpected flavoured chocolates: fleur de sel, basil, wormwood, etc.

Boulangerie Hoche, *17 rue Hoche, ☎ 02 99 63 61 01. Closed Sun; 3 weeks in Aug.* One of the best bakeries of Rennes. Over eighty different breads; especially delicious are the Viennese varieties.

Au Marché St-Germain, *6 rue du Vau-St-Germain, ☎ 02 99 79 12 26. Open Mon-Sat until 8.30pm.* Huge choice of fish cans, beers, ciders, cheeses, selected from the best regional producers.

Cellier St-Germain, *3 rue du Vau-St-Germain, ☎ 02 99 79 36 82. Closed Mon; 3 weeks in Aug.* A good cellar where someone will help you find your way among more than 2 000 labels.

Fromagerie St-Hélier, *19 rue St-Hélier, ☎ 02 99 30 63 76. Closed Sun-Mon; mid-July to mid-Aug.* This small cheese shop offers excellent Breton butters and refined AOC cheeses that come from everywhere in France.

A Bit of History

Du Guesclin's beginnings (14C) – Bertrand Du Guesclin was born in the castle of La Motte-Broons (now disappeared), southwest of Dinan. He was the eldest of 10 children and by no means handsome. On the other hand, he was bursting with energy

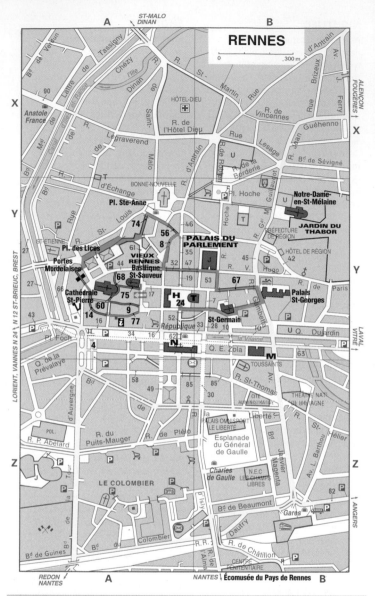

RENNES

and good sense. Bertrand spent his childhood among peasant boys whom he taught to fight. In this way he acquired strength, skill and cunning – and rough manners. In 1337, when Du Guesclin was 17, all the local nobles met for a tournament at Rennes. Our hero went to it in peasant dress, mounted on a draught horse. He was kept out of the lists. His despair at this was such that one of his cousins from Rennes lent him his armour and charger. Without giving his name, Bertrand unseated several opponents. At last a lance thrust lifted his visor and his father recognised him. Delighted and proud, he exclaimed: "My fine son, I will no longer treat thee scurvily!"

The duchess's marriage (1491) – In 1489, when François II died, his heiress, Anne of Brittany, was only 12, but this did not prevent wooers from coming forward. Her choice fell on Maximilian of Austria, the future Emperor. The religious marriage was performed by proxy in 1490.

Charles VIII, who had an unconsummated marriage with Margaret of Austria, daughter of Maximilian, asked the Duchess's hand for himself; he was refused and laid siege to Rennes in August 1491. The starving people begged their sovereign to accept the marriage. She agreed and met Charles VIII. Anne was small and thin and slightly lame, but she had gaiety and charm; she knew Latin and Greek and took an interest in art and letters. Charles was short and ill-favoured, with large, pale eyes and thick lips always hanging open; he was slow-witted, too, but loved power and had a taste for pomp. Quite unexpectedly the two young people took a liking to each other, which grew into tender affection. Their engagement was celebrated at Rennes. There remained, however, the problem of freeing the fiancés. The Court of Rome agreed and the wedding took place in the royal Château de Langeais, in the Loire Valley, on 6 December 1491 (see *The Michelin Guide Châteaux of the Loire*). The marriage united Brittany to France.

The great fire of 1720 – At the beginning of the 18C the town still looked as it did in the Middle Ages, with narrow alleys and lath-and-plaster houses. There was no way of fighting fire, for there was no running water. In the evening of 22 December 1720, a drunken carpenter set fire to a heap of shavings with his lamp. The house burned like a torch and immediately others around it caught fire.

The ravaged areas were rebuilt to the plans of **Jacques Gabriel**, the descendant of a long line of architects and himself the father of the Gabriel who built the place de la Concorde in Paris. A large part of the town owes its fine rectangular street pattern and the uniform and rather severely distinguished granite houses to this event. In order

Joffre R. Mar.	BZ	30	Orléans R. d'	AY	52	St-Georges R.	BY	67
La-Fayette R.	AY	32	Palais Pl. du	BY	53	St-Guillaume R.	AY	68
Lamartine Quai	ABY	33	Paris Rte de	BY		St-Hélier R.	BZ	
Lamennais Quai	AY	34	Plélo R. de	AZ		St-Louis R.	AY	
Le-Bastard R.	AY	35	Pont-aux-Foulons R. du	AY	56	St-Malo R.	AX	
Legraverend R.	AX		Poullain-Duparc R.	AZ	58	St-Martin R.	ABX	
Lesage R.	BX		Prévalaye Q. de la	AYZ		St-Michel R.	AY	74
Liberté Bd de la	ABZ		Psalette R. de la	AY	60	St-Sauveur R.	AY	75
Lices Pl. des	AY		Puits-Mauger R. du	AZ		St-Thomas R.	BZ	
Magenta Bd	BZ		Rallier-du-Baty R.	AY	61	St-Yves R.	AY	77
Martenot R.	BY	42	République Pl. de la	AY	62	Tassigny Bd		
Mitterrand Mail F.	AY	43	Richemont Q. de	BY	63	Mar. de-Lattre-de	AXY	
Monnaie R. de la	AY	44	Robien R. de	BX		Vasselot R.	AZ	85
Motte Cont. de la	BY	45	Sévigné Bd de	BX		Verdun Bd de	AX	
Motte-Fablet R.	AY	46	Solférino Bd	BZ	82	Victor-Hugo R.	BY	
Nationale R.	ABY	47	St-Cast Quai	AY	66	Vincennes R. de	BX	
Nemours R. de	AZ	49	Ste-Anne Pl.	AY				

Basilique St-Sauveur	AY	Hôtel de Ville	AY	H	Palais du Parlement
Cathédrale St-Pierre	AY	Jardin du Thabor		BY	de Bretagne	BY
Ecomusée du Pays de Rennes	BZ	Musées de Bretagne			Palais St-Georges	BY
Église N.-D.-en-St-Mélaine	BY	et des Beaux Arts	BY	M	Portes Mordelaises	AY
Église St-Germain	BY	Palais du Commerce	AY	N	Théâtre	ABY	T

The La Chalotais affair – In 1762, the Duke of Aiguillon, Governor of Brittany, clashed with Parliament over the Jesuits. The Jansenist lawyers (robins) opposed the Society of Jesus, whose colleges made it very powerful in Brittany – that of Rennes had 2 800 pupils. La Chalotais, the Public Prosecutor, induced Parliament to vote for the dissolution of the Order. His report had a huge success: 12 000 copies were sold in a month. Voltaire wrote to the author: "This is the only work of philosophy that has ever come from the Bar."

Aiguillon, who defended the Jesuits, asked Parliament to reverse its vote. It refused. Louis XV summoned the Councillors to Versailles, scolded them and sent three into exile. On returning to Rennes the Members of Parliament resigned rather than submit. The King had La Chalotais arrested and sent him to Saintes; the other Councillors were scattered over various provinces, but the Paris Parliament took the side of the Rennes Parliament and Louis XV hesitated to go further. Aiguillon, lacking support, retired in 1768. The Assemblies had defeated the royal power. Revolution was on the march.

Old Town★★

This is the part of the old town which escaped the fire (*see above*). It contains a maze of 15C and 16C houses with overhanging storeys and lordly mansions with sculpted façades.

Basilique St-Sauveur
17 and 18C. Inside this basilica are a fine gilded wooden **canopy** and an **organ loft** (17C). To the right is a chapel consecrated to Our Lady of Miracles who saved Rennes from the English during the siege of 1357. Note the numerous ex-votos which have been donated in gratitude to Our Lady.

Old Houses
* **Rue St-Sauveur** – No 6 stands a 16C canon's residence.
* **Rue St-Guillaume** – No 3, a beautiful medieval house, known as Maison Du Guesclin, contains the restaurant Ti Koz.
* **Rue de la Psalette** – This street is lined with old houses.
* **Rue du Chapitre** No 22 is a Renaissance house; no 8 is the Hôtel de Brie (17C); no 6 the 18C Hôtel de Blossac with a fine granite staircase (on the left as you enter) with marble columns and a wrought-iron handrail.

Place Ste-Anne

A. de Valroger/MICHELIN

- **Rue St-Yves** – Nos 6 and 8 are 16C houses.
- **Rue des Dames** – No 10 is the Hôtel Freslon de la Freslonnière.

Cathédrale St Pierre

The third built on the site since the 6C, this cathedral was finished in 1844 after 57 years' work. The previous building collapsed in 1762 except for the two towers in the Classical style flanking the façade.

The **interior**★ is very rich, its stucco facing covered with paintings and gilding. The cathedral contains a masterpiece: the gilded and carved wood **altarpiece**★★ in the chapel before the south transept. Both in size and in execution, this 16C Flemish work is one of the most

The nave and apse of St-Pierre Cathedral

important of its kind. The scenes represent the life of the Virgin.

Portes Mordelaises

The city's main entrance, these gates are all that remain of the 15C ramparts. The dukes of Brittany passed through it on their way to the cathedral for their coronation. In 1598 the silver-gilt keys of the city were presented there to Henri IV. At this kind of ceremony the Béarnais made a statement which always went down well: "These are beautiful keys," he would say, "but I would rather have the keys to the hearts of your citizens."

The drawbridge, modelled on that of Montmuran Castle, was reconstructed in 1997.

Place des Lices

Jousts and tournaments were once held on this square. At no 34 stands a 17C stone mansion, the Hôtel de Molant, with a mansard roof; inside, there is a sumptuous oak staircase with *trompe-l'œil* paintings (a skyscape) and woodwork decorating the ceiling of its stairwell.

Rue St-Michel

This street is lined with half-timbered houses and still has the inns and taverns dating from the time when it was part of the city's suburbs.

Place Ste-Anne

The coloured half-timbered houses, Gothic and Renaissance in style, surround a 19C neo-Gothic church. The house formerly occupied by Mayor Leperdit is at no 19. This square is next to rue d'Échange, which contains the Jacobin Convent where Anne of Brittany was betrothed to the king of France.

Rue du Pont-aux-Foulons

This is a shopping street with 18C half-timbered houses.

Rue du Champ-Jacquet

This street leads to an oddly shaped triangular square of the same name. It is lined to the north with tall half-timbered 17C houses and is overlooked by the stone and wood façade of Hôtel de Tizé (no 5).

The itinerary continues along rue La Fayette and rue Nationale into the Classical part of the city with its majestic buildings, in particular the Palais du Parlement de Bretagne.

Rue St-Georges

This animated street, lined with cafés and restaurants, has many old houses: nos 8, 10 and 12 form a remarkable group of 17C half-timbered houses. No 3, the 16C Hôtel de Moussaye, has a lovely Renaissance façade with sculptured pilasters.

Palais St-Georges

Preceded by a beautiful garden, this former Benedictine abbey (1670) now houses administrative services.

Église St-Germain

This Flamboyant church (15C-16C) with its 17C gable (on the south side) retains certain characteristics typical of a Breton cathedral: wood vaulting and its beams with sculpted ends. In the south transept the beautiful 16C **stained-glass window** recounts the life of the Virgin and the Passion. The nave contains modern stained-glass windows by Max Ingrand.

Place de l'Hôtel de Ville

This regal square is the centre of the Classical district. On its west side stands the town hall (Hôtel de Ville) and on the east side, the theatre. To the south, beyond rue d'Orléans, the view is blocked by the **Palais du Commerce** (Trade Hall), an imposing building decorated with monumental sculpture.

Additional Sights

Hôtel de ville

Open daily (except Sun), 8.30am-5.30pm, Sat 9.30am-noon). Closed public holidays. No charge. 02 99 28 56 90. www.rennes.fr.

The town hall was built to the plans of Jacques Gabriel in 1734-43, after the fire of 1720. A central tower, standing back from the façade, carries the great clock – *le gros*, as the townspeople call it – and is joined by two curved buildings to two large annexes. Inside are the former chapel and a lovely 17C Brussels tapestry. The right wing contains the Pantheon of Rennes, a hall dedicated to the memory of men who have died for France. Provided no official reception is being held, the public is admitted to the left wing of the building and can see the monumental staircase, the 18C Brussels tapestries and the hall where wedding ceremonies are performed.

The **theatre**, flanked by arcaded buildings, was built in 1832.

Palais du Parlement de Bretagne★★

Guided tours only, reservations at the Tourist Office. Closed 1 May. €6.10 (children 7-15 €3.05). 02 99 67 11 66.

Brittany's Parliament, one of the 13 provincial parliaments which made up the Kingdom of France, initially had its seat in Rennes for part of the year and Nantes for the other, before finally the decision was taken in 1561 to establish a single Parliament seat in Rennes. It was the Supreme Court of 2,300 Breton tribunals, as well as fulfilling a legislative and political function.

The architecture and decor of the mansion, which was the first stone building in a town of wood, were to influence the whole of Haute-Bretagne. The design of local architect Germain Gaultier was reworked for the façade by the Court architect of Marie de' Medici, Salomon de Brosse. Building went on from 1618 to 1655 and even 1706 for decoration. The jewel of the building is the Grand'Chambre with its gilt-wood ceiling decorated by Coypel and Errand.

A. de Valroger/MICHELIN

Parlement de Bretagne

The Palais du Parlement de Bretagne was badly damaged by fire in February 1994. While the firefighters struggled valiantly to save the building, tons of water were poured over and into it, resulting in damage which required more than 400 000hr of work to repair. The restoration was completed in 1999 and the Court of Appeals of Rennes once again sits in this historic place; the ground floor gallery and the Court of Assizes on the floor above, as well as the French gardens in front have been restored to their original appearance.

Musée de Bretagne★★

 🕐 *Open daily (except Tues), 10am -noon and 2-6pm.* 🕐 *Closed public holidays.* ⊗ *€7/4 depending on areas visited.* ☎ *02 99 28 55 84. www.musee-bretagne.fr.*
This museum recalls the history of Brittany. Through the exhibits (objects, models, carved figures) different eras are evoked: prehistory, Gallo-Roman Armorica, medieval Brittany and Brittany under the Aancien Régime.
In the second-to-last gallery, concerned with modern Brittany (1789-1914), costumes, everyday objects, tools and furnishings, characteristic of Rennes, are displayed. An audio-visual programme presenting Brittany of today occurs in the last gallery.

Musée des Beaux-Arts★★

 🕐 *Open daily (except Tues), 10am-noon and 2-6pm.* 🕐 *Closed public holidays.* ⊗ *€4.05 (children: no charge).* ☎ *02 99 28 55 85. www.mbar.org.*
The Museum of Fine Arts contains an important collection of works covering the 14C to the present. Among the 16C masters are Veronese *(Perseus Rescuing Andromeda)* and Maerten van Heemskerk *(St Luke Painting the Portrait of the Virgin)*. The 17C is well represented (Rubens, Jordaens, and Champaigne); **The Newborn**★ by Georges de La Tour is a masterpiece.
The 18C is exemplified by the works of Chardin *(The Basket of Plums; Peaches and Grapes)* and Greuze *(Portrait of a Young Girl)*.
In the 19C are canvases by Jongkind, Corot, Boudin and Sisley. Works of the members of the Pont-Aven School are also on display: Bernard *(Yellow Tree)*, Gauguin *(Oranges)*, Sérusier *(Solitude, Argoat Landscape)* and Georges Lacombe (**Wave Effect**★).
The last gallery, concerned with the 20C, displays works by Laurent, Picasso, Utrillo, Vlaminck, Tanguy and contemporary artists such as De Staël, Poliakoff and Asse. Old

drawings, porcelain and fine Egyptian, Greek and Etruscan archeological artefacts are also on show.

A small room presents works by 19C and 20C Breton painters who painted Brittany, its landscapes and activities, such as Blin, Lemordant and Cottet.

Jardin du Thabor★★

In the 16C the Benedictine abbey of St-Mélaine stood on an elevated site, beyond the city walls. The monks called the place Thabor in memory of the biblical Mount Tabor. The abbey's former orchards were transformed in the 19C to their present appearance by Bülher and Martenot and completed by the placing of Lenoir's statues. The beauty of the different flowers (roses, dahlias, chrysanthemums, camellias, rhododendrons) and trees (oak, beech, sequoia, cedar), spread over more than 10ha/25 acres, composed of a French garden, botanical garden, rose garden, landscaped garden and an aviary, makes these gardens particularly pleasant whatever the season.

The nearby **Église Notre-Dame-en-St-Mélaine** was rebuilt in the 14C and 17C. The tower and transept, both of the 11C, are all that remain of the former church of St-Mélaine Abbey.

In the south arm of the transept a 15C fresco represents the Baptism of Christ.

Excursions

Châteaugiron

16km/10mi SE along D 463. This old town, which was famous for its hemp sailcloth used for rated ships in the 17C, has preserved picturesque half-timbered houses (mainly in rue de la Madeleine) and an impressive fortified **castle**. The moat, 13C keep, which in the 14C was capped by a pepper-pot roof, and 15C clock tower next to the chapel are all that remain of the often-besieged castle. The living quarters, rebuilt in the 18C, house administrative offices. From boulevard du Château there is a full view of the castle and its site.

Écomusée du pays de Rennes★

8km/5mi south of rue Maréchal-Joffre (signposted). ◷ *Open daily (except Sat-Sun mornings and Tues), 9am-noon and 2-6pm (7pm on Sun).* ◷ *Closed mid-Jan to end of Jan and public holidays.* ✆ *€4.60.* ☎ *02 99 51 38 15. www.ecomusee-rennes-metropole.fr.*

Located between city and country, the **Ferme de la Bintinais** (Bintinais Farm) was for a long time one of the largest properties around Rennes. The museum illustrates by means of a remarkable collection of tools and farming equipment, reconstituted interiors, costumes etc the evolution of rural life on a farm, near an urban area – the city of Rennes – as from the 16C. There is also a display on earlier construction methods. Take a walk across the 15ha/37 acre estate and discover some of the many sights: gardens, beehives, orchards, and cultivated plots of land which illustrate the evolution of local farming techniques.

The botanical park is complemented by the presence of livestock: 14 country breeds of endangered farm animals. All these animals are characteristic of Brittany and its surrounding region: horses (Breton draught post-horses), cows (Pie Noire, Froment du Léon, Nantaise and Armoricaine), pigs (Blanc de l'Ouest and Bayeux), goats, sheep (from Ushant, Landes de Bretagne and the Avranchin) and poultry (La Flèche hens, the Coucou de Rennes and the famous Gauloise Dorée).

This museum also organises demonstrations and other celebrations: lettuce competition, harnessing contest for Breton draught horses, feast of the swine, etc. and many other festive events testifying to the vivacity of Rennes' long-standing traditions and customs.

M. Dewynter/MICHELIN

La Chapelle-Thouarault
7km/4mi east on D 30, then right on D 68 to Cintré.
At the place called "Basse-Vallée" the **Musée et Atelier d'art animalier** (animal art museum and workshop) displays, in about 40 dioramas, 250 stuffed animals placed in a minutely detailed reconstruction of their natural habitat. Many examples of local fauna are on display, enabling visitors to observe at their leisure scenes of animals going about their daily way of life – underground as well as under water – which they would rarely so much as glimpse in the wild.

Montfort-sur-Meu
17km/10.6mi W along D 125.
This charming small town, built of local red stone, is located at the confluence of the River Meu and River Garun.

Écomusée du pays de Montfort
The regional museum is housed in the 14C **Tour de Papegaut** (Papegaut Tower), all that remains of the medieval construction. It is named after a game of skill. A spiral staircase takes you up to the temporary and permanent exhibits held on the different floors, which present Montfort and its region (landscapes, folklore: collection of dolls in traditional costumes and headdresses). There is a fine view from the top of the tower.

Maison natale de saint Louis-Marie Grignion de Montfort
15 rue de la Saulnerie.
The missionary Louis-Marie Grignion de Montfort was born in this house in 1673 (d 1716; canonised in 1947). Several rooms (restored) with fine stonework are open to the public. The garden overlooks the Meu Valley.

Vallee de la Vilaine

Round-trip of 36km/23mi – allow 1hr

▷ *Leave Rennes on D 177 towards Redon. Cross the river at Pont-Réan in beautiful surroundings. As you leave the town, turn left.*

Bruz
This country town is an example of successful planning in rural surroundings with its tiny square on the north side of the church. The **church**★ (1950), which is built of pink veined schist, is beautiful. A pointed spire rises above the square tower that forms the porch at its base. The interior blends well; daylight enters on all sides through square panes of glass decorated with a picture of three fishes within a circle; in the apse through stained-glass windows depicting the Seven Sacraments and in the two arms of the transept through windows, to the south of the Crucifixion and to the north of the Virgin Mary. The organ is flanked on either side by the long, narrow stained-glass windows of unequal height that can be seen in the façade.

Parc ornithologique de Bretagne
Kids ⚐⊙ *Open July and Aug, daily, 10am-noon and 2-7pm; 1 Apr to June and Sept, 2-7pm; rest of the year, open Sun and holidays 2-6pm.* ⊙ *Closed 25 Dec.* ⊚ *€6.20 (children €3.80).* ☎ *02 99 52 68 57. www.parc-ornithologique.com.*
This small park contains an interesting collection of more than 1 000 birds from every continent.

▷ *Continue S along D 577. The road crosses the river at Pont-Réan.*

Le Boël

You can enjoy a pleasant walk by the river, which runs between rocky hills in a verdant setting. A small lock and a dam seem to link the west bank of the river to the old mill situated on the opposite bank.

▶ *Return to Pont-Réan and after crossing the bridge over the Vilaine, turn right.*

LA ROCHE-BERNARD

POPULATION 766
MICHELIN LOCAL MAP 308 R9 – MORBIHAN (56)

This picturesque old town, on the spur of La Garenne, overlooks the River Vilaine. The port stands on a tributary of the river; the naval dockyards here were famous in the 17C. Formerly very prosperous due to its trade in wood, wheat, wine, salt and spices, the town is now a pleasure boat harbour (capacity for 300 boats).

A real Republican – The town of La Roche-Bernard welcomed the Revolution and opposed the Chouans. In 1793, 6 000 "Whites" (Royalists) easily defeated the 150 "Blues" (peasants) who were defending the town. Mayor Sauveur refused to flee; he was imprisoned. He was ordered to shout, "Long live the King!" and he replied, "Long live the Republic!" He was shot down. He became a hero of the Republic by decree; the town was named La Roche-Sauveur until 1802.

Sights

Pont du Morbihan★

Located about 600m/565yd upriver from its predecessors, this bridge, inaugurated in 1996, is 376m/410yd long and 21m/23yd wide. The roadway rests on an arch with a 200m/219yd span. Two footbridges enable visitors to stand more than 50m/160ft above the river and admire the breathtaking **view**★.

La Roche Bernard marina from the Pont du Morbihan

G. Targat/MICHELIN

Old district

Across from the viewpoint and on the other side of the road begins **Promenade du Ruicard,** which overlooks the port. It goes into rue du Ruicard and leads through a maze of small streets, some of which are stepped. Houses of the 16C and 17C follow: nos 6 and 8 are well restored, no 11 has an interesting doorway, no 12 has a turret. Passage de la Quenelle, with its dormer windows surmounted by sculpted pediments, leads to **place Bouffay** where the guillotine stood in 1793. Situated on the square is the town hall, which is also known as the "House of the Cannon" (Maison du Canon) (1599) because of the cannon (from the *Inflexible* which sought refuge in the estuary after a sea battle) placed in the corner. On the left opens rue de la Saulnerie with a 15C house.

In rue Haute-Notre-Dame stands the small 11C Chapelle Notre-Dame, rebuilt in the 16C and 19C. The first church built in the city, it was converted into a Protestant church in 1561, and then used to store fodder during the Terror; it became Catholic once again in 1827.

Viewpoint★

From a bend in the road towards La Baule, a rocky viewpoint *(23 steps)* dominates the Vilaine Valley extending its views onto the wooded slopes, on the right the suspension bridge and on the left the pleasure boat harbour.

Musée de la Vilaine maritime

🕐 *Open mid-June to mid-Sept, daily, 10.30am-12.30pm and 2.30-6.30pm; Easter school holidays, beginning of June to mid-June and mid-Sept to end of Sept, 2.30-6.30pm; Oct to Dec and Mar to May, Sat-Sun and public holidays 2.30-6.30pm.* 🕐 *Closed Jan, Feb and 25 Dec.* ✆ *Entrance fee not specified.* ☎ 02 99 90 83 47.

The 16C and 17C Château des Basses-Fosses, on a spur on the west bank of the Vilaine, houses this museum of rural and maritime life on and along the Vilaine.

The ground floor explains the intense maritime activity which the river once had. The diorama of the Vilaine recreates the atmosphere which reigned along it in the early 1900s. A reconstructed cabin shows how life was on board a coastal fishing vessel. Upstairs, rural life is shown with exhibits of houses and the different kinds of timber work, roofing, and dormers; the old trades, through tools belonging to the carpenter, mason and roofer; local costumes and headdresses.

Boat Trip on the River Vilaine

Boat trips (1hr30min) are available July and Aug, leaving every hour 2-6pm from the Arzal dam or La Roche-Bernard. ✆ €8 *(children* €5*). Lunch/dinner cruises May to Sept departing from the Arzal dam daily at 12.30pm, Fri and Sat at 8pm; rest of the year at 12.30pm.* ✆ *Meal and boat, between* €33 *and* €47. ☎ 02 97 45 02 81.

Boats go down the Vilaine to the Barrage d'Arzal (Arzal Dam) or up to Redon.

Excursions

Missillac

13km/8mi SE by N 165 – E 60.

Separated from the town by a small stretch of water beside the wood, the 15C **Château de la Bretesche**, with its low crenellated ramparts and water-filled moat, stands in an outstanding **site**★.

Foleux

18km/11mi N via D 774. At Péaule, take D 20 toward Redon; after 8km/5mi turn right.

The marina is located at the confluence of the Vilaine and Trévelo rivers.

▷ *After Foleux skirt the Vilaine from here there is a good view of the wide valley. Bear right then turn left three times before taking the road which leads to the château.*

Château de Léhélec

Guided tours (30min) mid-June to early Sept, daily (except Tues), 2-7pm; early Sept to early Oct, Sat-Sun 2-7pm. *€4.* *02 99 91 84 33.*

Surrounded by woodland, this manor house, built of ferruginous schist, offers on its south front an attractive perspective of the three courtyards bordered by the 16C and 18C outbuildings. One of these buildings houses a small **rural museum** containing regional furniture and everyday objects. Visitors are also admitted to two rooms lit by tall windows – the drawing room and dining room on the ground floor.

Barrage d'Arzal

12km/7.5mi W via D 34 then D 139.

This dam on the Vilaine forms a freshwater reservoir thus eliminating the effect of the tides and making the trip easier for the coasting vessels that ply upstream to Redon. It is also an attractive stretch for pleasure craft. A road follows the crest of the dam over the river.

Le Guerno

18km/11mi NW along N 165 – E 60 towards Muzillac; turn right after 8km/5mi and follow the new Route Bleue.

The village, once a popular place of pilgrimage, has a 16C church built where a Templars' Chapel once stood. The church's exterior has on its south side a pulpit, stalls and bench (reserved for the clergy); the altar is backed against the Calvary (on the square). The round tower, on the west side, is capped by an 18C lantern turret.

The inside is decorated by 16C stained-glass windows and choir stalls; 22 carved panels, also 16C, ornament the loft. At the transept two cylindrical columns support the vaulting. The trunk of the column on the left is hollow to collect offerings.

▷ *Once outside Le Guerno bear right then left onto the avenue which goes to Château de Branféré.*

On the way to Branféré, notice two 18C **fountains** (on the right side of the road), dedicated to St Anne and St Mary.

Parc zoologique de Branféré

Kids *Open Apr to Sept, daily, 9am-8pm; Oct to Mar, 1.30-6.30pm.* *Closed 1 Jan and 25 Dec.* *€10 (children €7).* *02 97 42 94 66. www.branfere.com*

The château stands in 50ha/124 acres of parkland, where over 2 000 animals and countless birds roam amid the trees and a series of lakes. The varied flora provide part of the animals' food.

Moulin de Pen-Mur

17km/11mi west on N 165 – E 60; leave this road at Muzillac and follow the signs for Site de Pen-Mur. *Guided tours (30min) July to Sept, daily, 10am-12.30pm and 2-7pm (6pm Apr-June and school holidays, except Sun morning); rest of the year, Sat and holidays, 10am-12.30pm and 2-6pm, Sun 2-6pm.* *€5.50 (children €3).* *02 97 41 43 79.*

The mill, prettily located near a lake, contains an exhibition on the production of paper by hand using traditional 18C methods, showing all the stages from cutting up rags to the drying process.

ROCHEFORT-EN-TERRE★

POPULATION 693
MICHELIN LOCAL MAP 308 Q8 – MORBIHAN (56)

This charming, small town occupies a picturesque **site**★ on a promontory between deep dells. This landscape of rocks, woods, ravines, orchards and old houses bright with geraniums attracts many painters. *Town Hall, 56220 – ☎ 02 97 43 33 57.*

Sights

Old Houses★

In the heart of the town stand 16C and 17C town houses which you can see as you stroll along rue du Porche, place des Halles and place du Puits. At place du Puits note the former law court, the entrance of which is surmounted by a set of scales.

Château

Guided tours (1hr) July and Aug, daily, 10am-6.30pm; June and Sept, 10am-noon and 2-6.30pm; May and Oct, daily, 2-6pm, Sat-Sun and public holidays 10am-noon and 2-6pm; during school hols, daily, 10am-noon and 2-6pm. €4. ☎ 02 97 43 31 56.
The only features that remain of the castle, destroyed in 1793, are the imposing entrance fort, sections of the walls, the underground passages and the outbuildings. The latter were restored at the turn of the century by the American Alfred Klots with parts – most notably the dormer windows – from the 17C Kéralio manor house near Muzillac.
A small **museum of folk art** adjoining the old workshop of the owners evokes one or two aspects of the way of life in Rochefort in days gone by (lovely collection of headdresses). Another room contains the doors from the old dining room of a mansion, which were painted c 1880.

Église Notre-Dame-de-la-Tronchaye

The 12C, 15C and 16C church has a façade embellished with four gables pierced with Flamboyant bays. Inside, the chancel contains 16C stalls and, left of the high

Place des Puits

altar, a white stone Renaissance altarpiece. In the south arm of the transept, a 17C altarpiece behind a fine 18C wrought-iron grille bears the venerated statue of Our Lady of La Tronchaye, which was found in the 12C in a hollow tree where it was hidden at the time of the Norsemen invasions. The statue is the object of a pilgrimage on the Sunday after 15 August. In the north arm of the transept is a wrought-iron baptismal font and white stone Renaissance altarpieces; one of the altarpieces is decorated with three niches, each of which contains a painted wood statue. At the back of the nave the magnificent gallery in finely carved wood comes from the old rood screen as does the canopy over the high altar.

Excursion

Malansac: Parc de Préhistoire
3km/2mi east on D 21 towards Malansac then D 134 to St-Gravé. Kids & ◷ *Open Apr to mid-Oct, daily, 10am-6pm; mid-Oct to 11 Nov, Sun and Nov school holiday 1.30pm to 6pm; during late Oct-early Nov school holidays open daily 1.30-6pm.* ◷ *Closed 12 Nov to end-Mar.* ⊷ *€9 (children €5).* ☎ *02 97 43 34 17.*
Gwenfol site, with its lakes and old slate quarries, is now an outdoor museum of prehistory. Different tableaux composed of people and animals (life-size models) accompanied by explanatory panels illustrate the Paleolithic to the Neolithic Ages with such scenes as the discovery of fire, flint knapping, hunting, family life and the erection of a menhir.

Questembert
A small friendly town located in a verdant countryside. The impressive **covered market** was built in 1552 and restored in 1675; the timber work covers the three alleys.
The small 16C **Chapelle St-Michel** stands in the cemetery. On the north side is a Calvary. This monument, as well as the one built on place du Monument, recalls the victory of Alain-le-Grand over the Norsemen in 888 at Coët-Bihan *(6.5km/4mi southeast of Questembert).*

La Vraie-Croix
8km/5mi west by D 1. This charming village decked with flowers (awarded First Prize for the prettiest flowered village in 1994) still has its chapel resting on ribbed vaulting. In the old days, the road used to run underneath the vaulting. The lower part of the building appears to date back to the 13C. Two flights of steps carved in stone on the outside of the chapel lead to the upper section, which was rebuilt in 1611.
The building houses a gilded reliquary cross containing a fragment of the Cross of Our Lord.

ROSCOFF

POPULATION 3 550
MICHELIN LOCAL MAP 308 H2 – FINISTÈRE (29)

Roscoff is a much-frequented seaside resort and a medical centre using seawater treatment (thalassotherapy); it is also a fishing port for lobster and spiny lobster, a marina and a great vegetable market and distribution centre. A pier to the east of Pointe de Bloscon closes off the deep-water harbour from which car ferries sail to and from Plymouth and Cork. The University of Paris and the Centre National de la Recherche Scientifique (CNRS) have a laboratory for oceanographic and biological research here.

Sights

Église Notre-Dame-de-Croas-Batz★

This Gothic church was completed in 1545, funded by the privateers and merchants of the town. The church has a remarkable Renaissance **belfry**★ with lantern turrets, one of the finest examples of its type in Brittany. Inside, the **altarpiece** of the 17C high altar has six wreathed columns and is richly decorated with statues of the Evangelists, cherubs and pampers. The organ case dates from the 17C. The font (1701) was restored in 1991.

In the church close are two chapel-ossuaries: that in the southwest corner dates from the 16C and has been dedicated to St Brigitte; that in the northwest corner (early 17C) originally had no door at all, as it was used purely to store bones.

Chapelle Ste-Barbe

It is best to visit this chapel at high tide. Go round the fishing port and leave the car in the car park on the left. Viewing table.

In the centre of a pretty little garden sits the tiny chapel dedicated to St Barbara. Its white walls still serve as a landing mark to mariners. There is a beautiful view of the town, the port, the Île de Batz, Pointe de Primel and the deep-water harbour at Bloscon, which is the departure point for car ferries to Britain and Ireland.

▶ *Go around the hill on which the chapel stands.*

Viviers

Open Monday to Friday 9am-noon and 2-5pm, Sat 9-11am. Closed public holidays. No charge. ☎ 02 98 61 19 61.

Address Book

WHERE TO STAY

Aux Tamaris, *rue Étienne Corbière,* ☎ 02 98 61 22 99, www.hotel-aux-tamaris.com - 26 rooms, €7. Beautiful Breton house, perfectly located. The rooms at the front of the house have a nice view over the sea. Those at the back are quieter.

La Résidence, *14 rue des Johnies,* ☎ 02 98 69 74 85 - 26 rooms, €7. Between the church and the port, this building in the regional style is undergoing progressive renovation. Some rooms have a balcony.

Le Temps de vivre, *Place de l'Église,* ☎ 02 98 19 33 19, www.letempsdevivre.net - 15 rooms, €14, Spacious rooms with an uncluttered style, all set around a flowered patio, In a former privateer's house. Some have a view over the sea. Expensive but beautiful!

Le Brittany, *bd Ste-Barbe,* ☎ 02 98 69 70 78, hotel.brittany@wanadoo.fr - 25 rooms, €13, Old manor with opulent rooms that have nice views over the island of Batz. Exposed beams and old furniture around a monumental fireplace.

EATING OUT

Le Surcouf, *rue de l'Amiral Réveillère,* ☎ 02 98 69 71 89. Closed Tue and Wed from Oct to June. Regional cuisine centred on seafood, served in a modern pub setting.

Le Temps de vivre, closed Sun evening except July-Aug, Tue noon and Mon. This big room with an elegant setting offers an inventive cuisine made with regional products (roast crab claws with butter, suckling lamb from the Monts d'Arrée).

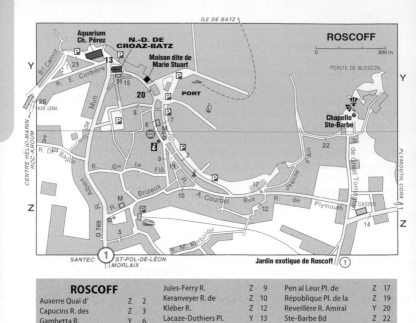

Footbridges lead visitors around the 5 200m2/55 972sq ft fish farm in which lobsters, crawfish and crabs are raised in a natural environment.

▶ *Go back along the rue de Great Torrington, then take the road to the deep-water harbour towards St-Pol. Turn left at Keraison.*

Jardin exotique de Roscoff★
🕐 *Open June-Sep: 10am-7pm; April, May and Oct: 10.30am-12.30pm and 2-6pm; March and Nov: 2-5pm.* 🚫 *Closed Dec-Feb.* 💶 *€4.50 (children under 12 no charge).* ☎ *02 98 61 29 19; www.jardinexotiqeroscoff.com.*
This extraordinary garden is wrapped around the Rocher de Roch-Hievec (or Rocher de Maison Rouge). Over 1 000 subtropical plant species thrive here, producing both blossom and fruit. A staircase leads to the summit, which commands a nice view.

Excursion

Île de Batz
The island of Batz (pronounced Ba), 4km/2.5mi long and 1km/0.6mi wide, is separated from the mainland by a narrow channel, notorious for its treacherous currents. The ferry arrives in Kernoc'h Bay, which is fringed by the village and the modern build-ings of the rescue station. This treeless—with the exception of the village—island has sandy beaches. The mild climate is particularly suitable for market gardening. On Batz the men are either sailors or farmers and the women help in the market gardens or gather seaweed.

Lighthouse
On the island's west side. 210 steps. The 44m/144ft tall lighthouse stands on the island's highest point (23m/75ft). View of the island and reef-fringed coast.

▶ *Go beyond the lighthouse and after the ruined house on the dune, take the path to the right.*

Trou du Serpent

The low-lying rock offshore is said to mark the spot where St Paul the Aurelian, with the help of his stole, cast out the dragon who was terrorising the island.

Jardin Georges-Delaselle

On the island's east side. ⏰ *Open June-Sep: 10am-7pm; April-May and Oct: 10.30am-12.30pm and 2-6pm; March and Nov: 2-5pm.* ⊚€4.50 (children under 12 no charge).

These fine colonial gardens, now the property of the Conservatoire du Littoral (a coastline protection organsation) were laid out in 1897 by Georges Delaselle, who loved Batz Island. It is planted with palm trees and some 1 500 other species, most of them from the Southern hemisphere.

Sunset over Batz

G. Targat/MICHELIN

ROSTRENEN

POPULATION 3 616
MICHELIN LOCAL 309 C5 – CÔTES-D'ARMOR

This pretty little town is situated on a hillside. Every year in August, an important dance competition is organised by the local Celtic society.

Sights

Église Notre-Dame-du-Roncier

The church was once the castle chapel (set on fire during the League in 1572). It was built in the 14C and remodelled in the 18C and 19C, and has a beautiful transitional Gothic-Renaissance porch.

Le Miniou

Take the road towards Pontivy, then a road to the right and up the hill turn left to reach a weather centre *(station climatologique)* situated at an altitude of 263m/928ft. The panorama extends over Rostrenen and the area round Callac to the northwest and Loudéac to the east; from the terrace, there is a view over the Guémené region to the south and the Montagnes Noires to the west.

Driving Tour

Fisel Country *Round-trip of 45km/28mi.*

▶ *Leave Rostrenen NE by D 790.*

St-Nicolas-du-Pélem

The town includes a 15C-16C **church** with two fine stained-glass windows depicting the Passion (1470) at the flat east end. Go round the north side of the church to see the 17C fountain of St-Nicolas which abuts onto a house.

▶ *Proceed to Lanrivain. The road crosses the delightful Vallée du Faoudel.*

Lanrivain

In the cemetery stands a 15C ossuary with trefoil arches. To the right of the church is a 16C Calvary adorned with huge granite figures.

Chapelle Notre-Dame-du-Guiaudet

1.5km/1mi north by the road towards Bourbriac. At the entrance to the hamlet of Guiaudet take an alleyway marked by two granite pillars on the right.
The chapel, which dates from the late 17C, has over the high altar a sculpted scene representing a recumbent Virgin holding the Infant Jesus in her arms. .

▶ *Continue to Trémargat and after 1.5km/1mi bear left.*

Gorges de Toul Goulic★

🏃 *15min on foot there and back.* At the far end of the car park overlooking the wooded valley of the Blavet, take the steep path leading downhill through the woods to the cleft in which the Blavet disappears. The river is still full at the beginning of the cleft (north side) but has completely vanished by the time you reach the middle of the cleft, where it flows, rumbling, beneath a mass of huge rocks.

▶ *Turn back and bear left.*

Between Trémargat and Kergrist-Moëlou, the landscape is studded with enormous boulders.

Kergrist-Moëlou

On the church square, shaded by fine old yew trees, stands a **Calvary** (1578) with some 100 figures in Kersanton granite resting on its octagonal plinth. The figures were damaged during the Revolution and have been replaced haphazardly.

▶ *Via St-Lubin return to Rostrenen.*

Nantes-Brest Canal *Round-trip of 20km/12mi – 2hr 30min.*

▶ *Leave Rostrenen on the road towards Carhaix-Plouguer and after 3.5km/2mi, turn left into the Gourin road.*

The road reaches the canal, built between 1823 and 1834, at the summit level (alt 184m/604ft). Walk along the towpath for a view of the 44 locks through which boats climb or descend 120m/384ft over 17km/11mi to Carhaix-Plouguer.

▶ *Proceed to Glomet and then turn right onto the road towards Paule; after 1.8km/1mi, bear right.*

On the canal banks, the former lock-keeper's house stands in a pretty **site**★.

▶ *Return to the main road and turn right back to Rostrenen.*

ST-BRIEUC★

CONURBATION 83 849

MICHELIN LOCAL MAP 309 F3 – CÔTES D'ARMOR (22)

The town is built 3km/2mi from the sea on a plateau deeply cleft by two water courses: the Gouëdic and the Gouet. Bold viaducts span their valleys. The Gouet is canalised and leads to the commercial and fishing port of Légué. St-Brieuc is the administrative, commercial and industrial centre of the departement (Côtes d'Armor). The markets and fairs of the town are much frequented, especially the Fair of St Michael (Foire de la St-Michel) on 29 September and another event in early September. On Saturdays, a market is held on the cathedral's parvis. The peaceful provincial city has retained some fine timber-framed houses.

Sights

Cathédrale St-Étienne★

This great cathedral of the 13C and 14C has been reconstructed several times and restored in the 19C; its mass bears striking witness to its original role of church fortress. The front is framed by two great towers complete with loopholes and machicolations and supported by stout buttresses. The two arms of the transept jut far out and are protected by towers with pepper-pot roofs.

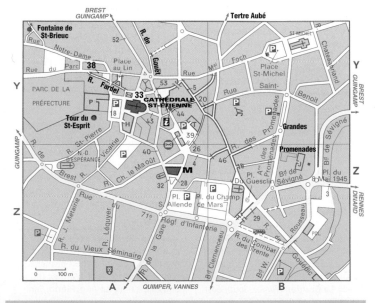

ST-BRIEUC								
3-Frères-Le-Goff R.	AY	52	Gaulle Pl. Gén.-de	AY	18	Quinquaine R.	AY	38
3-Frères-Merlin R.	AY	53	Glais-Bizoin R.	ABY	20	Résistance Pl. de la	AY	39
Armor Av. d'	BZ	3	Jouallan R.	AY	26	Rohan R. de	AYZ	40
Chapitre R. du	AZ	4	Le Gorrec R. P.	AZ	28	St-Gilles R.	AY	43
Charbonnerie R.	AY	5	Libération Av. de la	BZ	29	St-Gouéno R.	AY	44
			Lycéens-Martyrs R.	AZ	32	St-Guillaume R.	BZ	46
			Martray Pl. du	AY	33			

Address Book

TOURIST OFFICE

Baie de St-Brieuc, 7 rue St-Gouéno, ☎ 02 96 33 32 50, www.baiedesaint-brieuc.com Open end of Jun to begin-Sep: daily 9.30am-7pm; off season: Mon-Sat 9.30am-12.30pm, 1.30-6pm. Guided tours and guides of the bay. **Seasonable antennas at Plérin**, Place de la République, **Pordic**, Place du Gén. de-Gaulle, **Yffiniac**, by N 12 and **Hillion**.

WHERE TO STAY

ST-BRIEUC

🍽🍽 **Hôtel du Champ de Mars**, *13 rue du Gén.-Leclerc*, ☎ 02 96 33 60 99, hotel-demars@wanadoo.fr – *21rm* 🕐 *Closed Christmas holidays*. In the centre of town, this traditional hotel offers functional rooms. Breakfast € 7.

🍽 **Chambres d'hôte de Fonclare**, *20 bis rue Quinquaine*, ☎ 02 96 33 27 33, www.laportearon.free.fr – *2rm* 🚭 Located above the owners' house, rooms open onto a garden. Two family units for 3-4 people.

🍽 **Hôtel Ker Izel**, *20 rue du Gouët*, ☎ 02 96 33 46 29 – *22rm* 🅿 🏊 Very well kept rooms overlook the street or the garden and its pleasant swimming pool. Breakfast € 6.

🍽🍽 **Quai des Étoiles**, *51 rue de la Gare*, ☎ 02 96 78 69 96, quaide-setoiles@libertysurf.fr – *41rm* Functional rooms, near the train station. Breakfast € 6.50.

🍽🍽🍽 **Hôtel de Clisson**, *36-38 rue du Gouët*, ☎ 02 96 62 19 29, www.hotelde-clisson.com – *24rm* Comfortable hotel with bright rooms upstairs and views of the garden. Breakfast € 7.

IN THE SURROUNDINGS

🍽🍽 **Manoir de Maupertuis**, *Tournemine, Plérin*. ☎ 02 96 74 46 08 – *3rm* 🚭 This big house looks like a small manor surrounded by a garden and offers big family units with mezzanines.

🍽🍽 **Le Grenier**, *Yffiniac, South-East of St-Brieuc*, ☎ 02 96 72 64 55, www. le.grenier.com – *3rm and 6 rest houses*. Bound up as a single beautiful farm, very well kept rooms are decorated in

pastels. Each unit sleeps four while rest houses sleep 2-6 people.

EATING OUT

ST-BRIEUC

🍽 **Les Druides**, *1 bis rue des 3-Frères-Le-Goff*, ☎ 02 96 33 53 00. Traditional creperie in a busy street.

🍽 **Esprit de Famille**, *21 rue des Promenades*, ☎ 02 96 61 93 18. 🕐 *Closed evenings and Sun*. Daily meals are served at noon in a big room that feels like a grocery; slices of fresh bread make their way to the tea room each afternoon.

🍽🍽 **Le Duguesclin**, *2 Place Duguesclin*, ☎ 02 96 33 11 58. Pub cuisine and seafood dominate the the terrace in summer and a comfortable room upstairs in this sea-friendly atmosphere. Wholesale fish trays also sold.

🍽🍽 **Le Monde des Chimères**, *1 bd Harel de la Noë*, ☎ 02 96 33 82 54. 🕐 *Closed Mon*. A smooth setting for high quality cuisine, this restaurant uses only seasonal products to ensure freshness.

ENTERTAINMENT

Rollais, *26 rue du Gén.-Leclerc*, ☎ 02 96 61 23 03. 🕐 *Open Mon-Sat 9am-11pm*. This wine bar is the myth that supposedly inspired the writer Louis Guilloux. Literary and philosophical evenings (Thu) and concerts are organised here.

L'Illiade, *5 rue du Légué*, ☎ 02 96 33 46 99. *Open nightly until 2am (except Sun)*. Pub with a rustic setting and a cool atmosphere. Terrace.

Le Piano Bleu, *4 rue Fardel*, ☎ 02 96 33 41 62. 🕐 *Closed Mon in summer and Sun*. Musical nights, second Tue each month, except in summer (€ 6-10).

SHOPPING

Markets - St-Brieuc, Wed and Sat morning around the cathedral; Sun morning Croix-St-Lambert district; night market, Place du Martray, Thu and Fri evening Jul-Aug. **Plérin**, Sun morning.

Farm products - Ferme de la Ville-Huet, *rte des Rosaires, Plérin*, ☎ 02 96 74 43 56. 🕐 *Wed-Sun morning*. Excellent quality.

RECREATION

Windsurfing and sea kayaking - Centre municipal de voile de St-Brieuc, *27 bd de Cornouaille, Les Rosaires, Plérin,* ☎ *02 96 71 51 59.* ⏲ *Open year round except Christmas hols.* Windsurfing lessons for ages 5 and up (€ 50-100/week). Jul-Aug: windsurfing and kayak rentals (about € 10-15/hour).

Centre nautique de Plérin, *66 rue Tournemine, Plérin,* ☎ *02 96 74 65 11.* In summer, offers lessons including catamaran, windsurfing and sand yachting (€ 110/week).

Walks - Le fond de la baie de St-Brieuc offers nice walks marked out with views.

FESTIVALS

Festival Art'Rock, first weekend of June, www.artrock.org Numerous concerts and high-quality animations in the centre of St-Brieuc.

Nocturnes de St-Brieuc, Jul-Aug. Street shows Thu-Fri evenings.

Quai en Fête, begin-Jul every two years (next in 2007) port du Légué. Old riggings, music and all kind of animations.

The lofty nave with its seven bays was rebuilt in the 18C. The harmonious three-sided chancel has an elegant triforium with quatrefoil balustrade and trefoil arches above the great arcades.

In the south aisle, note the carved wooden altar by Corlay (c 1745) in the Chapel of the Holy Sacrament. The south arm of the transept is lit by fine 15C stained-glass windows and in the small chapel stands the tomb of St William (d 1234). The stained-glass windows represent the Glorification of Mary. The 16C organ loft, the 18C pulpit and the Stations of the Cross carved in granite by Saupique (1958) are also noteworthy.

Musée

⏲ *Permanent exhibit open 9.30am-11.45am and 1.30-5.45 pm; Sun and holidays 1.30-5.45pm; temporary exhibits: 10am-6pm.* ⏲ *Closed Mon, 1 Jan and 25 Dec. No charge.* ☎ *02 96 62 55 20.*

Located in renovated rooms, the museum traces the history and development of the Côtes d'Armor *departement* (formerly Côtes-du-Nord) during the 19C, when traditional Brittany evolved into modern Brittany. Different themes – St-Brieuc Bay, heathland, cloth and linen trade, village life – accompanied by models, equipment and tools used for fishing, navigation and husbandry, as well as costumes and furnishings, are evoked.

Town Walk

Old houses

The area to the north of the cathedral still retains many 15C-16C half-timbered and corbelled houses.

Walk through place du Martray, rue Fardel (at the corner of place au Lin: the Ribeault mansion; at no 15, the house known as the "mansion of the dukes of Brittany"; nos 17, 19, 27, 29, 31, 32 and 34), rue Quinquaine (no 9) and rue de Gouet (nos 6, 16, 22).

Rue du Gouët

H. Le Gac/MICHELIN

Tour du Saint-Esprit
This tower, an interesting Renaissance structure with a pepper-pot octagonal corner tower, has been carefully restored.

Fontaine de St-Brieuc
The fountain, which is sheltered by a lovely 15C porch, stands against the east end of the Chapelle of Notre-Dame-de-la-Fontaine. Brieuc, the Welsh monk who came to the region in the 5C, is believed to have settled here.

Tertre Aubé★
The hill commands a fine **view**★ of the Vallée du Gouet, crossed by the viaduct which carries the road to Paimpol; also of the partly hidden port of Légué, below, and, to the right, of St-Brieuc Bay. On a hill to the right is the ruined tower of Cesson.

Excursion

Hillion

▶ *10km/6mi east. Take S on the town plan, then leave the expressway for Yffignac. Take D 80 to Hillion. Follow the signs to "Maison de la Baie".*

Kids **Maison de la Baie** *(Call for opening times: ☎ 02 96 32 27 98.)*, a visitor information centre for the marine environment presents exhibitions devoted to the environment and ecosystem of St-Brieuc Bay. Regular excursions are organised in discovery of local bird life or the natural habitat.

Beaches

Round tour of 25km/15mi – 2hr. Leave St-Brieuc north by Légué port, follow the quay on the north bank.
On the right, the ruined tower of Cesson is outlined amid the greenery; as the road climbs there is a good view over the Pointe des Guettes at the far end of the bay and the coast as far as Cap d'Erquy.

Pointe du Roselier★
▮ Take a path on the right of the telescope to go round the point. Fine **views**★ extend over St-Quay-Portrieux and the coast; the path passes near an old oven used for turning cannon-balls red-hot, and skirts a villa. The view takes in the Pointe de Cesson, the far end of St-Brieuc Bay and the Pointe des Guettes with its mussel poles, and the coast towards Le Val-André. Paths cut in the cliffside lead back to the starting point.

▶ *Turn back and after 2km/1mi, bear right.*

Martin-Plage
This pretty beach lies between Pointe du Roselier and the Tablettes Reef (Rocher des Tablettes).
The road then climbs steeply and at Ville-Fontaine, bear right onto a pleasant little road descending between wooded embankments.

Plage des Rosaires
The beach is framed by wooded cliffs some 100m/320ft high. The **view** includes the whole of St-Brieuc Bay from St-Quay Point to Cap d'Erquy.

▶ *The road leads straight back to St-Brieuc.*

ST-CAST-LE-GUILDO ≌ ≌

POPULATION 3 187

MICHELIN LOCAL MAP 309 I3 – CÔTES D'ARMOR (22) LOCAL MAP SEE CÔTE D'ÉMERAUDE

This seaside resort is formed by three settlements: Le Bourg, L'Isle and Les Mielles. The port shelters a small fishing fleet which specialises in scallops and clams.

Pointe de St-Cast★★

There is a superb **view**★★ of the Côte d'Emeraude from the point (viewing table – *table d'orientation* – beside the signal station).

🚶 At the tip of the point a monument to the Escaped Prisoners of France (Monument aux Évadés) can be reached by a cliff path which follows the shore, passes another monument dedicated to the crew of the frigate *Laplace*, mined in 1950, and rejoins the St-Cast road at La Mare Beach (Plage de la Mare).

Pointe de la Garde★★

At the end of this point there is a very fine **view**★★ of the beaches of St-Cast and Pen Guen and the coast as far as Pointe de la Garde; also a statue of Notre-Dame-de-la-Garde by Armel Beaufils.

🚶 A scenic path goes round the point by way of the Corniche de la Plage near the Hôtel Ar Vro, passes beside the oratory, follows the cliff along the point and, on the south shore, joins the road leading to the slipway near the oratory.

Church

At Le Bourg. The modern church, built between 1897 and 1899, contains a 12C stoup and some 17C statues.

Chapelle Ste-Blanche

At L'Isle. Above the high altar is an old statue of St Blanche – the mother of St Guénolé, St Jacut and St Venec – which is the object of great veneration.

WHERE TO STAY

🍽🍽 **Chambre d'hôte Château du Val d'Arguenon** – *Route de St-Malo, 9km/6mi* –☎ 02 96 41 07 03 – 🕐 *closed Oct-Mar* – 🗋 *– 5 rooms.* This is a romantic spot where you can stroll around the park down to the sea, admire the architecture of the manor house which has belonged to the same family for two centuries, enjoy the beautiful antique salons, and sleep in a room with character and charm. Three simpler gîtes also available.

EATING OUT

🍽🍽 **Le Biniou** – *Route de Dinard, 1.5km/1mi* – ☎ 02 96 41 94 53 – 🕐 *closed 11 Nov-15 Dec, 5 Jan-18 Feb, Mon evening and Tues except during school holidays.* Here, facing the beach, you can enjoy simple, fresh food. In the summer the bar offers a simplified menu. The restaurant serves salads at lunchtime and only on weekdays.

ST-MALO ★★★

POPULATION 50 675
MICHELIN LOCAL MAP 309 J3 – ILLE-ET-VILAINE (35)
LOCAL MAPS SEE CÔTE D'ÉMERAUDE AND VALLÉE DE LA RANCE

St-Malo, St-Servan, Paramé and Rothéneuf have joined together to form the municipality of St-Malo. The site★★★ is unique in France and makes it one of the great tourist centres of Brittany. Almost entirely destroyed during the Second World War, the carefully restored old town has regained the atmosphere of the once famous privateer stronghold. This part of town is now a pedestrian zone.

▶ **Orient Yourself:** The agglomeration includes St-Servan-sur-Mer, Paramé and Rothéneuf

▣ **Parking:** The car park near the casino is convenient for the Old Town

⊘ **Don't Miss:** The view from the Cornich d'Aleth (St-Servan)

◔ **Organizing Your Time:** Very crowded in the summer! Book ahead!

Kids **Especially for Kids:** The Nautibus submarine at the Grand Aquarium

♿ **Also see:** Côte d'ÉMERAUDE and Vallée de la RANCE

A Bit of History

Origin – St Malo, returning from Wales in the 6C, converted the Gallo-Roman settlement Aleth (St-Servan) to Christianity and became its bishop. The neighbouring island, on which the present town of St-Malo is built, was then uninhabited. Later, people settled there because it was easy to defend from the Norsemen, and it became important enough for the Bishopric of Aleth to be transferred to it in 1144. It took the name of St Malo, while Aleth put itself under the protection of another local saint, St Servan.

The town belonged to its bishops, who built its ramparts. It took no part in provincial rivalries. At the time of the League, St-Malo declared itself a republic and was able to keep its independence for four years. This principle was reflected in the saying:

St-Malo from above

"Ni Français, ni Breton, Malouin suis" (I am neither French nor Breton but a man of St-Malo).

Famous men of St-Malo – Few towns have had as many famous sons as St-Malo over the centuries.

Jacques Cartier left in 1534 to look for gold in Newfoundland and Labrador: instead he discovered the mouth of the River St Lawrence, which he took to be the estuary of a great Asian river. As the word Canada, which means "village" in the Huron language, was often used by the Indians he encountered, he used the word to name the country. Cartier took possession of the land in the name of the king of France in 1534, but it was only under Champlain that the colonisation of Canada began and that Quebec was founded (1608).

Duguay-Trouin (1673-1736) and Surcouf (1773-1827) are the most famous of the St-Malo privateers. These bold seamen received "letters of marque" from the king which permitted them to attack warships or merchantmen without being treated as pirates, that is, hanged from the main yard. In the 17C and 18C, privateers inflicted heavy losses on the English, Dutch and Spanish.

Duguay was the son of a rich shipowner and had been destined for the priesthood; but by the time he was 16 the only way to put an end to his wild living was to send him to sea. His gifts were such that, at 24, he entered the so-called Great Corps of the French Navy as a commander and at 36 he was given a peerage. When he died, he was a Lieutenant General in the seagoing forces and a Commander of the Order of St Louis.

Surcouf's history is completely different, but just as outstanding. He answered the call of the sea when very young and soon began a prodigious career of fabulous exploits. First as slaver, then as privateer, he amassed an enormous fortune. At 36 he retired, but continued to make money by fitting out privateers and merchantmen.

Chateaubriand and Lamennais brought the flavour of the Romantic Movement to their native St-Malo.

François-René de Chateaubriand (1768-1848) was the tenth and last child of a very noble Breton family who had fallen on bad times. His father went to America in search of fortune and was able, on his return, to set up as a shipowner at St-Malo. In a room on the second floor of a modest town house (Maison Natale de Chateaubriand – it gives onto the courtyard of the Hôtel France et Chateaubriand and is near the Tour Quic-en-Groigne) René was born. From its window he could look out to sea beyond the ramparts and dream...

The future poet spent his early years in roaming about the port, then went in succession through schools at Dinan, Dol, Rennes and Brest, dreaming sometimes of the priesthood, sometimes of the sea.

He spent two years in exile at Combourg with his father, mother and sister Lucile. It was through the profession of arms that he began, in 1786, the adventurous career which ended in 1848 in the solitary grandeur of Grand Bé.

Lamennais (1782-1854), another St-Malo shipowner's son, also had a place in the Romantic Movement. He became an orphan early and was brought up by an uncle at the castle of Chesnaye, near Dinan. At 22 he taught mathematics in the College of St-Malo before entering the seminary of that town.

He was ordained a priest in 1816 and had a great influence on Lacordaire and Montalembert. His writings and violent quarrels got him into trouble with Rome which led him to renounce the Church.

He retired to Chesnay and published, in 1834, the famous *Paroles d'un croyant (Words of a Believer)*. Owing to his advanced political ideas, he was sentenced to a year's imprisonment in 1840 but won a seat in the National Assembly in 1848.

Address Book

TOURIST OFFICE

St-Malo, Espl. St-Vincent, terminal du Naye, ☎ 0 825 13 52 00 (15min), www.saint-malo-tourisme.com Open Jul-Aug: Mon-Sat 9am-7.30pm, Sun and public hols 10am-6pm; rest of year: Mon-Sat 9am-12.30pm, 1.30-6pm.

Guided tours - CDB Tourisme, 12 Place Bouvet, St-Servan, ☎ 02 99 82 60 02. Guided tours of the ramparts and the town intramuros, Jul-Aug: Wed-Fri 10.30am, Sat 2.30pm. Departure from the Tourist Office, € 3/6.

Voyage Corsaire, 3 rue St-Vincent, ☎ 02 99 40 28 89, daily 9am-7pm except Sun off season. Rental of audio-guides € 3/6.

GETTING AROUND

On bus – Map of the bus network at the kiosk **Infobus,** espl. St-Vincent, terminal du Naye, ☎ 02 99 56 06 06.

On small train – To go around the ramparts and enjoy a guided tour. Departure porte St-Vincent, terminal du Naye, ☎ 02 99 40 49 49. Five tickets €3.50.

On bike - Les Vélos Bleus, 190 rue Alphonse Thébault, ☎ 02 99 40 31 63, www.velos-bleus.fr Open Jul-Aug, daily; rest of year: Mon-Sat 9am-1pm, 2-6pm. Closed Nov-Feb.

Taxi cab - Allo Taxis Malouins, ☎ 02 99 81 30 30.

For coin ranges, see the Legend on the cover flap.

WHERE TO STAY

INNER-TOWN

⊜⊜ **Hôtel Bristol Union,** *4 Place de la Poissonnerie,* ☎ *02 99 40 83 36, www.hotel-bristol-union.com – 27rm* In the heart of town, five floors of comfortable rooms in ochre and mahogany colours stir up images of sailing ships slicing through the sea's nearby waters. Breakfast € 8.50.

⊜⊜ **Hôtel Quic En Groigne,** *8 rue d'Estrées,* ☎ *02 99 20 22 20, www.quic-en-groigne.com - 15rm* One room in this small hotel has been nicely decorated as a boat cabin. The others, opening onto a courtyard or onto the street, are more functional, in blue or red colours.

Bathrooms are quite small. Breakfast € 6.

⊜⊜⊜ **Hôtel France et Chateaubriand,** *4 Place Chateaubriand,* ☎ *02 99 56 66 52, www.hotel-fr-chateaubriand.com – 81rm* ✕ Near the ramparts, this house provides a score of rooms with a view of the sea; the others overlook a courtyard or the ramparts. Directoire furniture and beautiful Napoléon III dining room. Breakfast € 10.

OUTSIDE THE TOWN

⊜⊜ **Hôtel Les Charmettes,** *64 bd Hébert,* ☎ *02 99 56 07 31, www.hotel-les-charmettes.com – 16rm.* ⏰ *Closed mid-Nov to mid-Dec and Jan.* Modest but very well kept hotel, offering rooms with or without sea-views, some with balcony, distributed into two buildings along the beach of Rochebonne. Pleasant terrace for breakfast (€ 5.80).

⊜⊜ **La Rance,** *15 quai Sébastopol,* ☎ *02 99 81 78 63, www.larancehotel.com – 11rm.* This lovely small hotel, located in the shadow of the Solidor tower, offers pleasing rooms with Empire furniture. Breakfast € 8.

⊜⊜⊜⊜ **La Malouinière du Mont Fleury,** *2 rue du Mont-Fleury,* ☎ *02 23 52 28 85 or 06 80 25 61 75, www.lemont-fleury.com – 4rm.* ⏰ *Closed 15 Nov-end May.* The owner of this authentic malouinière of the 17th century is a former pilot. From his treks around the world, he brought back souvenirs that came to form the decor of the thematic rooms: the Eastern, the American, the Chinese and the Nautical. Two of them have a duplex that can welcome 2-3 additional people. Bikes available.

NEARBY

⊜⊜⊜ **Chambres d'hôte Pointe du Meinga,** ☎ *02 99 89 06 94 or 06 79 42 58 36, www.chambres-meinga.com – 5rm* ✕ Located in the countryside, near the beaches of La Guimorais, this very beautiful house offers well decorated, bright and spacious rooms.

EATING OUT

INNER-TOWN

⊜ **La Touline,** *6 Place de la Poissonnerie,* ☎ *02 99 40 10 98.* ⏰ *Closed Mon* *and Tue off season*. The flat cakes made with farm sausage or with effeuillée of cod and the crêpe Suzette with orange butter and Grand Marnier are the great successes of this crêperie, where everything is home made.

Ti Nevez, *12 rue Broussais,* ☎ 02 99 40 82 50. ◷ *Closed Tue evening; Wed; school hols.; Jan.* Traditional crêperie with a rustic setting, well-known for its flat cake egg-cheese-andouille and its crêpe Québécoise with maple syrup and nuts.

Brasserie Armoricaine, *6 rue du Boyer,* ☎ 02 99 40 89 13. ◷ *Closed Sun evening; Mon off season; Jan.* The true Malouins know this address for its traditional cuisine at good prices. Reservations advised.

L'Ancrage, *7 rue Jacques Cartier,* ☎ 02 99 40 15 97. ◷ *Closed Tue off season; Wed; Dec-Jan.* Good choice of seafood in a marine setting near the ramparts.

Le Chalut, *8 rue de la Corne de Cerf,* ☎ 02 99 56 71 58. *Closed Mon-Tue off season.* Well-known address for its fish, seafood and lobsters, this cosy setting fittingly evokes the sea and its ships.

OUTSIDE THE TOWN

La Corderie, *8 allée du Maré-graphe,* ☎ 02 99 40 89 52. ◷ *Closed Mon in winter; mid-Jan to mid-Feb.* Famous for its fish specialties, this restaurant invites you to enjoy a wonderful panorama over the mouth of the Rance and its boom.

ENTERTAINMENT

L'Aviso, *12 rue du Point-du-Jour,* ☎ 02 99 40 99 08. ◷ *Open until 3am.* More than 300 specialties of beer await lovers of a good brew. Quick snacks and musical nights in summer.

Le Cancalais, *11 quai Solidor,* ☎ 02 99 81 15 79. ◷ *Closed Mon off season.* Pleasant terrace on the dock Solidor, where many generations intermingle when its time for an aperitif. Quick snacks, Internet access and summer concerts.

Cuningham's Bar, *2 rue des Hauts-Sablons,* ☎ 02 99 81 48 08. ◷ *Open until 3am.* This warm bar-pub, decorated as a steerage deck, offers good views over the beach of the Bas-Sablons and organises regular musical nights.

L'Escalier, *La Buzardière,* ☎ 02 99 81 65 56. ◷ *Open midnight-5am.* In a district away from the centre of town, this is the in-vogue nightclub of St-Malo.

Casino Barrière, *2 chaussée du Sillon,* ☎ 02 99 40 64 00. ◷ *Open daily 10pm-2am (4am Fri-Sat, 3am Sun).* Fruit machines, roulette, bar and restaurant.

RECREATION

For children - Surf School, *2 av. de la Hoguette,* ☎ 02 99 40 07 47, www.surf-school.asso.fr. In summer, this school offers games, beach activities and body-board lessons for ages 3-10, and introductions to the surf, the catamaran and windsurfing during school hols. for ages 6-12.

Sea kayak and diveyak - Corsaires Malouins, *7 rue de la Clouterie,* ☎ 02 99 40 92 04 or 06 82 01 05 01. Lessons, trips in the estuary of the Rance and introductory tours for ages 10 and up.

Comarin Newdive, *port des Sablons,* ☎ 02 99 21 38 38, www.comarin.fr Guided trips in diveyak (air kayaks) and rentals.

Light sail - Société nautique de la baie de St-Malo (SNBSM), *quai Bajoyer,* ☎ 02 99 18 20 30, www.snbsm.com Based on the beaches of Bon Secours and Havre de Rothéneuf. ◷ *Open summer, school hols. and Sat-Sun.* Different arrangements of lessons and trips on board Hobie Cat, Optimist, Laser or Teddy. About € 150 for 10 trips and € 300 for the unlimited plan.

Kite-surf - Sensations Kite, *5 rue Trichet,* ☎ 06 08 94 70 89. ◷ *Open Apr-Nov.* Lessons, training, moving in minibus. Rental of material € 45-55/day.

Diving- Club subaquatique de la Côte d'Émeraude, *terre-plein du Naye,* ☎ 02 99 82 60 73, www.saintmaloplongee.com ◷ *Open all year.* Full range of dives on the Côte d'Émeraude: baptisms, thematic diving (biology, archaeology), fishing lessons.

Cruises - Étoile Marine, *41 quai Duguay-Trouin,* ☎ 02 23 18 41 08, www.etoile-marine-excursions.com.

Crossing St-Malo-Dinard (10min), departure almost every hour Apr-Oct. Round trip € 5.50. Offers trips of 1hr to

3hr in the bay of St-Malo, to the island of Cézembre, cape Fréhel and the bay of Cancale, and a nocturnal trip with oyster tasting.

Le Renard, *tour Ouest, Grande Porte,* ☎ *02 99 40 53 10, www.cotre-corsaire-renard.com.* In summer, different schedules of trips on board a privateer. Participation in the operations on board and cannonade. About € 29-58/day-- take a picnic lunch. Four to six day cruises in Manche from € 283 to 486. Plus € 23/day for the meals.

FESTIVALS

Étonnants Voyageurs, ☎ *02 99 31 05 74, www.etonnants-voyageurs.net* Around the weekend of Pentecost, au palais du Grand Large. Famous literary festival travels and sells souvenirs.

Solidor en peinture, ☎ *02 99 81 96 80, www.solidorenpeinture.com.* Last weekend of June, near the Solidor tower. Professionals or amateurs paint the tower or the port. Sun: exhibition and sale.

Town Walk

The Ramparts (St Malo's walled city) 2hr

Allow 2 hr. Start from esplanade St-Vincent.

St-Malo and the surrounding area were turned into an entrenched camp by the Germans and became the prize for which a merciless battle raged from 1-14 August 1944. The town was left in ruins. With a great sense of history, its restorers were determined to bring the old city back to life. They have been completely successful in their quest.

The statue near the esplanade, at the entrance to the Casino garden, portrays Chateaubriand by Armel Beaufils. It was erected in 1948 on the centenary of his death.

▶ *Pass under Porte St-Vincent which consists of twin gates; then take the staircase to the right leading to the ramparts.*

The ramparts, started in the 12C, were enlarged and altered up to the 18C and survived the wartime destruction. The rampart walk commands magnificent views, especially at high tide, of the coast and islands.

From Porte St-Vincent to Bastion St-Louis

Directly after Grande Porte (Great Gate), which is crowned with machicolations, the view opens out over the narrow isthmus which joins the old town to its suburbs, the harbour basins and, in the distance, St-Servan.

From Bastion St-Louis to Bastion St-Philippe

The rampart skirts the houses where the rich shipowners of St-Malo lived; two, near the Bastion St-Louis, are still intact but the following walls and façades are reconstructions of carefully dismantled buildings. This fine group of houses with its high roofs, surmounted by monumental chimneys rising from the ramparts, once more gives this part of town its old look.

The view extends over the outer harbour; to Rocher d'Aleth, crowned by Fort de la Cité, and the mouth of the Rance estuary; to Dinard, with Prieuré Beach and Pointe de Vicomté.

From Bastion St-Philippe to Tour Bidouane

A very fine view of the Côte d'Émeraude west of Dinard, and of the islands off St-Malo. To the right of Pointe du Moulinet, you can see part of the great beach at Dinard, Pointe des Étêtés separating Dinard from St-Lunaire, Pointe du Décollé, the Hébihens Archipelago, Pointe de St-Cast and Cap Fréhel; nearer, on the right, are the Île Harbour and, further to the right, Grand Bé and Petit Bé Islands; then, in the background, Île de Cézembre and Fort de la Conchée. Near Tour Bidouane stands a statue of Surcouf.

From Tour Bidouane to Porte St-Vincent

Having skirted the École nationale de la Marine marchande, you can see the Fort National and the great curve which joins St-Malo to Pointe de la Varde, passing through the beaches of Paramé, Rochebonne and Le Minihic.

Ile du Grand Bé

🚶 *Allow 45min on foot there and back. Only at low tide. Leave St-Malo by Porte des Champs-Vauverts and cross the beach diagonally to the causeway. Follow the road that skirts the right side of the island.*

Chateaubriand's tomb is on the seaward side; it is a plain, unnamed flagstone surmounted by a heavy granite cross.

From the highest point on the island there is a beautiful **panorama**★★ of the entire Côte d'Émeraude.

▶ *Cross the open space, go down a few steps and turn left along a road leading back to the causeway by which you came.*

The port

Located in the centre of the large roadstead, which once divided the privateer's encampment (St-Malo-de-l'Isle) from the continent (St-Servan, Paramé), the port is developing a wide range of activities. It has four wet docks (Vauban, Duguay-Trouin, Bouvet and Jacques-Cartier) sheltered by a lock, where handling of goods and fish are concentrated. Imported products hold an important position: fertilisers, timber and wood. Its outer harbour is equipped with two shipping terminals for **car ferries** and **boat services**; there are daily services between St-Malo and Portsmouth and St-Malo and the Channel Islands (Jersey and Guernesey).

Pleasure boating has not been forgotten: dockage is located at the foot of the ramparts and especially at Bas-Sablons near the Corniche d'Aleth.

Sights

Château★★

Allow 1hr 30min. 🕐 *April-Sep: 10am-12.30pm and 2-6pm; rest of the year: daily except Mon 10am-noon and 2-6pm.* 🕐 *Closed 1 Jan, 1 May, 1 and 11 Nov and 25 Dec.* €5. ☎ *02 99 40 71 57.*

You can enter the courtyard and see the façades of the former 17C-18C barracks (now the town hall), the well, the keep and the gatehouse.

The little keep was built as part of the ramparts in 1395. The great keep (1424) dominates the castle: from the keep's watchtower, you will admire an impressive **panorama**★★ of the town; the corner towers were constructed in the 15C and 16C. The chapel and the galley date from the 17C.

Musée d'Histoire de la ville et d'Ethnographie du pays malouin★

🕐 *Open Apr to Sept, daily, 10am-noon and 2-6pm; rest of the year, daily (except Mon and holidays), 10am-noon and 2-6pm.* 🕐 *Closed 1 May.* €5. ☎ *02 99 40 71 57.*

The museum, which is installed in the great keep and gatehouse, records the development of the city of St-Malo and its celebrities (Jacques Cartier, Duguay-Trouin, La Bourdonnais, Surcouf, Chateaubriand, Lamennais and the mathematician Maupertuis). Documents, ship models, paintings and arms trace St-Malo's sea-faring tradition.

ST-MALO

Bardelière R. M. de la	CZ	2	
Bas-Sablons R. des	AZ	3	
Broussais R.	DZ		
Cartier R. J.	DZ	5	
Chartres R. de	DZ	6	
Chateaubriand Pl.	DZ	8	
Clemenceau R. Georges	AZ	12	
Cordiers R. des	DZ	13	
Dauphine R.	AZ	15	
Dinan R. de	DZ		
Doutreleau R.	BZ	16	
Flaubert R. G.	CX	17	

Forgeurs R. du	DZ	18	
Fosse R. de la	DZ	19	
Herbes Pl. aux	DZ	25	
Lamennais Pl. Fr.	DZ	28	
Mettrie R. de la	DZ	35	
Mgr-Duchesne Pl.	AZ	36	
Pilori Pl. du	DZ	38	
Poids-du-Rois Pl. du	DZ	39	
Poissonnerie Pl. de la	DZ	42	
Porcon-de-la-Barbinais R.	DZ	43	
République Bd de la	BY	50	
Roosevelt Av. F.	BY	53	

Schuman R. du			
Président-Robert	CX	58	
St-Benoist R.	DZ	56	
St-Vincent R.	DZ	57	
Tabarly Chaussée Eric	AY	63	
Trichet Q. de	AY	68	
Umbricht R. du R. P.	CX	69	
Vauban Pl.	DZ	70	
Ville-Pépin R.	ABZ	71	

Musée d'Histoire de		
la ville et d'Ethnographie	DZ	M¹
Tour Quic-en-Groigne	DZ	E

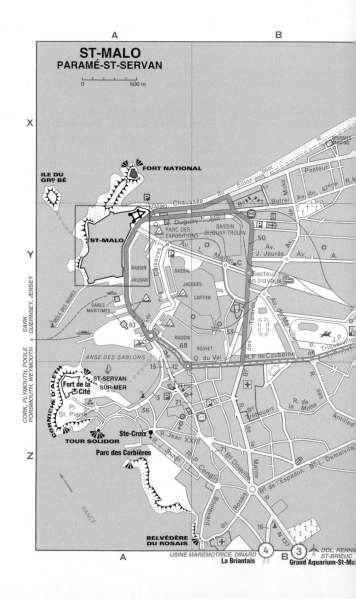

To end the visit climb up to the keep's watchtowers, from where you will admire an impressive panoramaaa of the town, harbour, coast and sea.

A passage leads from the old chapel to the Tour Générale. This tower contains an exhibition laid out on three floors devoted to the economy (commercial fishing, shipbuilding), way of life (headdresses, furniture) and significant historical events in the St-Malo region.

Tour Quic-en-Groigne★

This tower *(65 steps)*, which is located in the left wing of the castle, bears the name Quic-en-Groigne from an inscription Queen Anne had carved on it in defiance of the bishops of St-Malo: *"Qui-qu'en-groigne, ainsi sera, car tel est mon bon plaisir"* (Thus it shall be, whoever may complain, for that is my wish).

Cathedral St-Vincent

The building, started in the 11C and completed in the 18C, was topped by a pierced spire in the 19C, replacing the quadrangular roof.

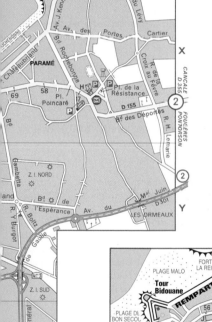

The nave is roofed with quadripartite vaulting typical of the Angevin style; dark and massive it contrasts with the slender 13C chancel. Lit by magnificent **stained-glass windows**★ by Jean Le Moal, the chancel becomes a kaleidoscope of colours. In the transept, restored in the 17C style, the stained-glass windows are muted in colour while in the side aisles the windows by Max Ingrand are brighter (Chapel of the Holy Sacrament). The north side aisle has preserved its original vaulting.

A 16C Virgin, Notre-Dame-de-la-Croix-du-Fief, which comes from a medieval house, is kept in the second chapel north of the ambulatory together with

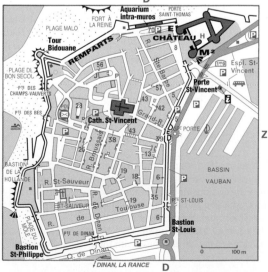

Fort National at low tide

the remains of Duguay-Trouin. The neighbouring chapel houses the head reliquary of Jacques Cartier.

Aquarium

🕐 *Open mid-July to Aug, daily, 10am-1pm and 2-10pm, Sun 10am-1pm and 2.30-6.30pm; Apr to mid-July, Sept and school holidays, 10am-1pm and 2-6.30pm; Nov-Mar: Sat-Sun, 10am-1pm and 2-6pm.* 🕐 *Closed Nov-Jan (except school holidays).* €6 (children 4-14 € 4). ☎ 02 99 56 94 77.
Built inside a curtain wall of the ramparts, the aquarium, formerly a weapons store, has 35 tanks where colourful tropical fish swim.

Fort National★

Access by Plage de l'Éventail at low tide, 15min on foot there and back. Guided tours (30min) June to Sept, daily at low tide (variable times). 🕐 *Closed during high tide (check with the Tourist Office).* €4 (children € 2).
Built by Vauban in 1689, the Royal Fort became the National Fort after the Revolution (1789), and then private property. Built on the rock, this stronghold assured the protection of the city. The **view**★★ from the ramparts is remarkable. The fort commands extensive views of the coast and the islands: St-Malo, St-Servan, the Rance estuary, Dinard, the île du Grand Bé, Île du Petit Bé, Île Harbour, the Grand Jardin Lighthouse, the Fort de la Conchée and in the distance the Îles Chausey.
During the tour, one of the events recorded is the fort's resistance in 1692 against the English and Dutch fleet, and Surcouf's memorable duel in which he defended the honour of France against 12 opponents, of whom he spared the last to testify to his exploit. The visit to the dungeon is interesting.

St-Servan-Sur-Mer★

The resort of St-Servan-sur-Mer is cheerful with its many gardens, in striking contrast to the walled town of St-Malo. Its main beach is formed by Sablons Bay, although there are also smaller beaches along the Rance. The town has three ports: the Bouvet dock, a trading and a fishing port, linked with that of St-Malo, the Solidor, a former naval base, and that of Saint-Père.
The name of **Jeanne Jugan** (1792-1879) is revered here. A humble servant, she managed to buy an old house with three friends, which they opened as a hospice

for the aged. The spiritual association was the beginning of the order which would later become the Little Sisters of the Poor.

Corniche d'Aleth★★

Leave your car in place St-Pierre, where the ruins of the former cathedral of Aleth stand in a garden.

▶ *Take rue St-Pierre at the east end of the church and follow on the left the coastal pathway.*

This walk offers magnificent **views**★★. First comes a remarkable view of St-Malo. Further to the left can be distinguished the Petit Bé, the Grand Bé and Cézembre Islands. Bear left and skirt the seashore. Go round the fort *(see below)*. The whole harbour is now visible: to the right of the Île de Cézembre, in the distance, is the fortified Île de la Grande Conchée; on the left, the Grand Jardin Lighthouse, Île Harbour and its fort and, in the distance, Cap Fréhel and Pointe du Décollé, followed by a maze of reefs. Finally take a steep downhill path to the right to enjoy a very fine view of the Rance estuary, barred by the Rocher Bizeux, on which stands a statue of the Virgin, and beyond, of the Usine marémotrice de la Rance.

Parc des Corbières

It is a wooded park with trees of different species. Bear right, follow the cliff path which goes round Pointe des Corbières, affording fine glimpsesa of the Rance estuary and the tidal power scheme.

Fort de la Cité

🕐 *Open July-Aug: guided tours at 10.15, 11am and 2, 3 4 and 5pm; April-Jun and Sep to mid-Nov: daily except Mon at 2, 3.15 and 4.30pm. € 5 (children € 2.50).* ☎ *02 99 82 41 74.*
The City Fort, built in 1759, was considerably altered by the Germans during the Second World War. Around the inner courtyard is a chain of blockhouses joined by over 2km/1mi of underground passages.

Tour Solidor★

This tower (27m/88.5ft high), which commands the Rance estuary, was built in 1382 and restored in the 17C. It now houses the **Musée international du Long Cours Cap-Hornier**★*(*🕐 *Open Apr to Sept, daily, 10am-noon and 2-6pm; rest of the year, daily (except Mon and holidays), 10am-noon and 2-6pm.* 🕐 *Closed 1 May.* ☞ *€ 5 (children € 2.50).* ☎ *02 99 40 71 58)*, a museum devoted to Cape Horn Vessels. Visitors can study the exhibits on their way up to enjoy the **view** from the the top of the tower, making the climb easier.

Église Ste-Croix

The church is in the Greco-Roman style. The interior is decorated with frescoes (1854) and stained-glass windows (1962).

Parc des Corbières

It is a wooded park with trees of different species. Bear right, follow the cliff path which goes round Pointe des Corbières, affording fine **glimpses**★ of the Rance estuary and the tidal power scheme.

Belvédère du Rosais★

The viewpoint is near the little marine cemetery on the side of a cliff overlooking the Rance which contains the tomb of the Count and Countess of Chateaubriand, the writer's parents. **View**★ of Rance Dam, the Rocher Bizeux with a statue of the Virgin on top of it, Pointe de la Vicomté and Dinard.

Paramé ⚐

Paramé, a much-frequented seaside resort, possesses a salt-water thermal establishment. It has two magnificent beaches extending for 2km/1.5mi: Casino Beach, which continues that of St-Malo, and Rochebonne Beach. The splendid seafront promenade, 3km/2mi long, is the chief attraction for the passing tourist.

Rotheneuf *via ① on the town plan*

This seaside resort has two beaches, which differ widely. That of Le Val is wide open to the sea. That of Le Havre lies on an almost landlocked bay like a large lake surrounded with dunes, cliffs and pines.

Near Rothéneuf is **Le Minihic**, with its own beach and villas.

Manoir de Jacques Cartier★

Rue David Macdonald Stewart. Guided tours (30min) July and Aug, daily, 10-11.30am and 2.30-6pm; June and Sept, daily (except Sat-Sun), 10-11.30am and 2.30-6pm; Oct to May, daily (except Sat-Sun) at 10am and 3pm. ⏰ *Closed Apr and holidays.* ⮑€ 4 *(children under 12, € 3).* ☎ *02 99 40 97 73.*

After his expeditions to Canada, the explorer, Jacques Cartier, bought a farm which he extended and called *Limoëlou* (bald hillock). This 15C-16C house and its 19C extension have been restored and furnished in the style of the period. The tour includes an audio-visual presentation on the explorer's expeditions and of the colony "Nouvelle France" otherwise known as Canada.

Rochers sculptés

⏰ *Open daily 10am-6pm.* ⏰ *Closed Jan and during violent storms.* ⮑€ 2.50. ☎ *02 99 56 97 64.*

From 1870 onwards, some rocks along the coast were patiently sculpted by a priest, the Abbé Fouré, who spent 25 years of his life on the task. There are almost 300 little granite characters.

South of Town

Grand Aquarium★★ – Saint Malo

Leave St-Malo by ③ the map, and the follow the signs. Av. du Général-Patton. ⏰ *July-Aug: 9.30am-8pm (10pm mid-July to mid-Aug); April-June and Sep: 10am-7pm; rest of the year: 10am-6pm (last entrance 1 hr before closing).* ⏰ *Closed 3-21 Jan, 14-18 and 21-25 Nov.* ⮑€13.50 (children 4-14 €9.80). ☎ *02 99 21 19 00. www.aquarium-st-malo.com*

Kids This is one of the region's most popular attractions, with eight large rooms on two storeys, much of the space devoted to the great navigators from St-Malo.

The aquariums include a hands-on area which is a miniature reproduction of Brittany; the "sunken ship" gives visitors the strange sensation of being at the bottom of the sea; the **Shark RIng** puts you right in the middle of the action. Ride in a four-place submarine in the giant tank where you navigate amid tropical fish and Celtic statues; you can discover a sunken city and an abyss peopled by strange creatures. This award-winning attraction is a great place for families; the English version of the Web site is excellent.

ST-NAZAIRE

POPULATION 65 874
MICHELIN LOCAL MAP 316 C4 – LOIRE-ATLANTIQUE (44)

A visit to St-Nazaire, which is above all a great shipbuilding centre, is particularly interesting. Originally a small fishing port in the 15C, the town developed rapidly in 1856, when large ships, finding it difficult to sail up to Nantes, stopped at its deep-water port. Rebuilt in 1945 in the plainest fashion, St-Nazaire is nevertheless worth seeing for its port where everything is spectacular: the former submarine base, Escal'Atlantic, the museum show devoted to transatlantic sea journeys of bygone days and the docs where the world's largest liners are built.

A Bit of History

From fishing village to major port – In 1850, St Nazaire was no more than a village with 800 inhabitants. Six years later, the silting up of the Loire estuary led to the creation of a deep-water harbour for large ships unable to sail up to Nantes. At the same time, the Compagnie Générale Transatlantique established shipyards and set up the headquarters of it Central America shipping line in St-Nazaire. At the turn of the 20C, the population of St-Nazaire had reached the 30,000 mark. However, the town was hard hit by the economic depression of 1929: the shipyards declined and the translatlantic shipping lines were transferred to Le Havre.

Opération Chariot – During the Second World War the town became a German submarine base. On 27-28 March 1942, a British commando caught the enemy by surprise, while the destroyer *Campbeltown* knocked down the Louis-Joubert entrance lock and the following day neutralised the lock by blowing itself up. A stele, reminding us of this heroic act, faces the sea on boulevard de Verdun.

An obvious target for aerial bombardment between 1940 and 1945, the town got caught up in the fighting for the St-Nazaire Pocket and consequently was a desolate site when finally liberated.

St-Nazaire today – Since 1966, the Port autonome de St-Nazaire has included several sites stretching some 60km/37mi along the Loire esturay: Donges specialises in crude oil, Montoire-de-Bretagne in natural gas, coal and foodstuffs. St-Nazaire handles traffic from local factories and continues to build ships.

Harbour Installations
allow one day

Follow the signposts Ville-Port. Leave the car in the parking area of the former submarine base. Combined tickets available for the different attractions on the site.

TOURIST OFFICE
Base sous-marine, St-Nazaire, ☎ 0 810 888 444, www.saint-nazaire-tourisme.com Open Feb-Mar, Oct-Dec: Tue-Sun 10am-12.30pm, 2-5.30pm; Apr-June, Sep: daily 9.30am-12.30pm, 1.45-5.45pm; Jul-Aug: daily 9.15am-12.30pm, 1.45-6pm.
Closed Jan.
For coin ranges, see the Legend on the cover flap.

WHERE TO STAY / EATING OUT
Hôtel de Touraine, *4 av. de la République*, ☎ 02 40 22 47 56 – 19rm. Very simple but well kept rooms in the town centre. Breakfast € 5.35.
Au Bon accueil, *39 rue Marceau*, ☎ 02 40 22 07 05, au-bon-accueil44@wanadoo.fr – 12rm Rooms in town centre and good cuisine served in an elegant setting. Breakfast € 7.55.

Base de sous-marins

The submarine base, built during the German occupation from 1941 to 1943, was a very large reinforced concrete structure covering an area of 37 500m_/44 830sq yd and measuring 300x125m/960x400ft. It had 14 bays, which together could take some 20 submarines. Machine shops were installed at the back of the bays. In spite of much bombing, the base came through the war undamaged and was used for the construction of warships until the late 1990s.

But this hige bunker effectively cut the port off from the city. Later, it was used by the French Navy for building warships. Since the late 1990s, the installation of the Tourist Office has meant a new reincarnation for the base, which is livelier and more integrated in the urban fabric.

Escal'Atlantic★★

In the former submarine base. &♿⏱ *Open 11 July-28Aug: 10am-7pm; April-10 July and 29 Aug-30 Sep: 10am-12.30pm and 2-6pm; Feb-March and Oct-Dec: daily except Mon and Tue 10am-12.30pm and 2-6pm. Last entrance 1hr 30min before closing.* ⏱ *Closed 1 Jan, 3 Feb and 25 Dec.* ⊶€ 12 (children € 8) in summer, ⊶€ 9.90 (children € 6.90) in winter. ☎ 0 810 888 444. www.saint-nazaire-tourisme.com.*

🅺🅸🅳🆂 This vast area has been given over to a recreation of the great ocean liners of the past from the *Liberté* to the *France*. The visit is like a cruise aboard one of these liners: uniformed staff welcome passengers who freely explore cabins, the

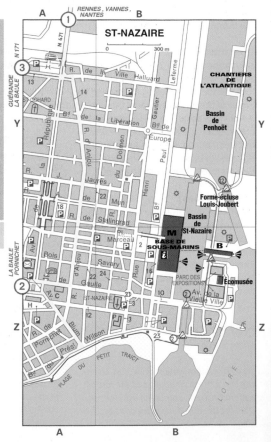

ST-NAZAIRE		
28-Février-1943 R. du	BZ	24
Amérique Latine Pl.de l'	BZ	2
Auriol R. Vincent	BZ	3
Coty Bd René	BZ	10
Croisic R. du	AZ	12
Herminier Av. Cdt-l'	AY	13
Ile-de-France R. de l'	AY	14
Jean-Jaurès R.	ABY	
Légion-d'Honneur Bd de la	BZ	16
Martyrs-de-la-Résistance Pl. des	AY	18
Paix R. de la	AYZ	
Quatre Z'Horloges Pl. des	BZ	21
République Av. de la	AYZ	
Salengro R. R.	AYZ	22
Verdun Bd de	BZ	23
Escal'atlantic	BZ	M
Sous-marin Espadon	BZ	B

music room, the bridge, the dining room, the piano bar, dormitories reserved for immigrants, the holds...

Visitors can recline in deck chairs lined up along the promenade decks and admire a seascape created with special effects. Video clips being famous passengers back to life: sail with Winston Churchill, Grace Kelly, Buster Keaton, Fred Astaire...

Terrasses panoramiques★★

In order to appreciate the full extent of the harbour installations, it is recommended to climb onto the roof of the submarine base *(access via the ramp opposite rue Henri-Gautier or from inside the base by a lift located behind the Tourist Office)*.

The remarkable view of the harbour includes the Bassin de St-Nazaire and the Bassin de Penhoët, one of the largest in Europe with three types of dry dock. The Louis-Joubert lock was built between 1929-1932 to allow for the increase in tonnage of great Atlantic liners. The lock is 350x50x15m/1 148x164x49ft.

Every night in July and AUg, a boat rip (1hr) offers visitors a tour of the harboured brightened up by many-coloured lights.

Écomusée de St-Nazaire

🕐 *Open mid- July and Aug: 9.30am-12.30pm and 1.30-7pm, guided tours available; April-June and first two weeks of July: 9.30am-12.30pm and 1.30-6.30pm; rest of the year: Wed-Sun 10am-12.30pm and 2-pm.* 🕐 *Closed Jan and 25 Dec.* 🕮 *No charge.* ☎ *02 51 10 03 03. www.ecomusee-saint-nazaire.com.*

On the banks of the Loire, at the heart of the port, a bright yellow building houses exhibits concerned with the St-Nazaire shipyards and the port's development: models of the shipyards, ocean liners *(Normandie, Île de France, France)*, battleships *(Jean Bart)*, dockers' old tools, portraits of people who contributed to the city's development...

Sous-marin Espadon

🕐 *Open 11 July-28Aug: 10am-7pm; April-10 July and 29 Aug-30 Sep: 10am-12.30pm and 2-6pm; Feb-March and Oct-Dec: daily except Mon and Tue 10am-12.30pm and 2-6pm. Last entrance 1hr 30min before closing.* 🕐 *Closed 1 Jan, 3 Feb and 25 Dec.* 🕮*€ 8 (children € 6.90) in summer, € 6 (children € 5.40) in winter. Information and reservations:* ☎ *0 810 888 444. www.saint-nazaire-tourisme.com.*

Launched in 1957 from the Augustin Normand Shipyards in Le Havre, the *Espadon* was the first French submarine to cruise the polar ice caps. Seventy men lived on board; the torpedo room, engine room, sleeping area and control room can be visited.

Chantiers de l'Atlantique★

🕐 *Guided tours only (2hr), reservations required. The tour bus leaves from the submarine base. April-Oct: daily: Feb-March and Nov-Dec: Wed and weekends, call ahead for hours.* 🕐 *CLosed Jan and 25 Dec.* 🕮 *€ 12 (children € 8) in season; €10.90 (children €7.90) off season.* ☎ *0 810 888 444.*

Between the Bassin de Penhoët and the Loire lie the shipyards, made up of the former Loire workshops and dockyard and the Penhoët Dockyard; these were linked together in 1956 and since 1976 have been incorporated into Alsthom, now forming a subsidiary of the GEC Alsthom group. Among the ships which have come from the Atlantic Dockyard are the battleship *Jean Bart*, and the ocean liners *Normandie* and *France*. Cargo boats, container ships, ore carrying ships and tankers (550 000t capacity) and passenger transport ships for French and foreign use are also built in the yards. Since 1987, the year in which *Sovereign of the Seas* (capacity 2 600) was delivered, the Chantiers de l'Atlantique have built a total of 11 cruise liners, including the largest in the world: *Monarch of the Seas* and *Majesty of the Seas* (capacity 2 770) ...not for long though for in 2003 an even larger liner will be launched: the *Queen Mary II* ordered by the Cunard Company. This ship, 345m/377yd long and 41m/45yd wide, manned by a 1 310-strong crew, will accommodate 2 800 passengers and cross the Atlantic in six days at a speed of 30 knots.

The **exhibition** illustrates the evolution of the shipyards and the shipbuilding process from designing to launching.

A bus **tour of the yards** gives an insight into the extent of the complex. Three docks contain ships at different completion stages from the assembly of the hull to the finishing touches...

Excursions

La Grande Brière★★ – 👌 See LA GRANDE BRIERE.

Pont routier St-Nazaire-St-Brévin★

The bridge, built in 1975, spans the Loire to the north-east of St-Nazaire: it stands 61m/200ft above mean high waterlevel at its midpoint. It links St-Nazaire to the Retz country, and the regions of Vendée and Charentes.

Tumulus de Dissignac

7km/4mi west on N 171, the road to Escoublac. 🕐 *Open July and Aug, daily (except Tues), 10am-12.30pm and 2-6.30pm.* 💶€ 2 (children under 15 no charge). ☎ 02 51 10 03 03. Built on a hill, surrounded by drystone walls, this tumulus, with two covered burial chambers, dates from 5C BC; two narrow passageways lead to these chambers.

ST-POL-DE-LÉON★

POPULATION 7 121
MICHELIN LOCAL MAP 308 H2 – FINISTÈRE (29)

This little town, which St Paul, known as the Aurelian, made the first bishopric in Lower Brittany, offers the tourist two of the finest buildings in Brittany: the former cathedral (the bishopric did not survive the Concordat passed under Napoleon in 1802) and the Kreisker belfry. From January to September, during the season of cauliflowers, artichokes, onions and potatoes, St-Pol is extremely busy. Numerous lorries, vans and tractors with trailers arrive, bringing these famous Breton products to the market.

Town Stroll

Chapelle du Kreisker★

Guided tours available in July and Aug.

This 14C-15C chapel used to be where the town council met; it is now the college chapel. What makes it famous is its magnificent **belfry**★★, 77m/246ft high. It was inspired by the spire of St Peter's at Caen (destroyed during the war – *see the Michelin guide Normandy*) but the Breton building in granite surpasses the original. The Kreisker belfry has served as a model for many Breton towers.

The upper part of the spire is Norman in style, while the lower part with the squaring of its mullions and railing of the overhanging balcony recalls the English Perpendicular style.

▶ *Enter through the north porch.*

The church is roofed with wooden barrel vaulting. The only stone vault joins the four huge uprights which support the belfry at the transept crossing. In the south aisle is a vast 17C carved wood altarpiece (from the Chapelle des Minimes, no longer standing) depicting the Visitation.

You may climb the tower *(169 steps)*. From the platform you will get a superb circular **view**★★ of the town, Batz, the coast as far as the Corniche Bretonne and the Monts d'Arrée inland.

Rue Général-Leclerc

There are interesting old houses in this street: note the slate-faced wooden façade at no 9; a Renaissance house with a corbelled turret at no 12; a mansion with a fine porch and ornate dormer windows (1680) at no 30.

Ancienne Cathédrale★

Built on the 12C foundations, the former cathedral was erected in the 13C and 14C (nave, aisles, façade and towers) and in the 15C and 16C the side chapels, chancel, apse and remodelling of the transept. The architects were inspired by the cathedral at Coutances and used Norman limestone to build the nave; the traditional granite was used for the façade, transept and chancel. The Breton influence can be found in the bell-turrets on the transept crossing and also in the porches.

The **façade** is dominated by two towers each 50m/160ft high. The terrace which surmounts the porch was used by the bishop to bless the people; the small door under the right tower was reserved for lepers. From a small public

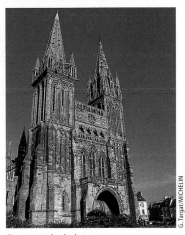

Former cathedral

garden, on the north side between the church and the former bishop's palace (now the town hall), is a view of the north transept wall with Romanesque characteristics. The south side, which faces Place Budès-de-Guébriant, has a fine porch. The tran-

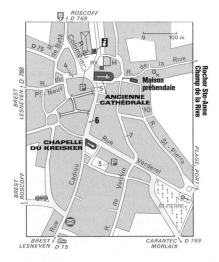

ST-POL-DE-LÉON

Colombe Pl. M.	3
Croix-au-Lin R.	4
Guébriant Pl. A. de	5
Leclerc R. Gén.	6
Minimes R. des	7
Psalette R. de la	10

Address Book

TOURIST OFFICE

St-Pol-de-Léon, Place de l'Évêché, ☎ 02 98 69 05 69, www.saintpoldeleon. fr Open Jul-Aug: Mon-Sat 9-12am, 2-7pm, Sun 10am-noon; Sep-Jun: Mon-Sat 9am-noon, 2-5.30pm. Information about the walking paths, notably along the coast (10 km). In summer, visit one of the 15 regional firms (horticulturists, truck farmers,etc).

WHERE TO STAY / EATING OUT

◌◌ **France,** 29 rue des Minimes, ☎ 02 98 29 10 57, hotel.de.france.finistere@ wanadoo.fr – 22rm. Functional and clean rooms, some opening into the garden, in an attractive regional house. Breakfast € 6.50.

◌◌ **Auberge Pomme d'Api,** 49 rue Verderel, ☎ 02 98 69 04 36. 🕒 Closed Tue lunch; Sun evening; Mon in season; Tue evening off season. Good regional cuisine, in a rustic 16C Breton house.

RECREATION

Sand yachting and surfing - L'île de **Sieck,** just before the mouth of the Horn, is the spot for lovers of sliding sports. Sand yachting - **Centre Enez Sieck,** ☎ 02 98 29 40 78

sept contains a remarkable rose window with above it a sort of pulpit from which sentences of excommunication used to be read.

The **interior** has several remarkable features: a Roman sarcophagus which serves as a stoup. Starting the tour from the right, note a Renaissance stained-glass window (1560) and in the transept the 15C rose window. Around the chancel there are tombs of local bishops and two 17C altarpieces. The carved **stalls**★ of the chancel date from the 16C. Over the high altar, a palm tree in carved wood, bent in the shape of a crozier, contains a ciborium for the Host.

In wall niches against the chancel to the right of the ambulatory, 34 wooden reliquaries contain skulls.

Maison prébendale

This was the 16C residence of the canons of Léon. The façade is emblazoned.

Champ de la Rive

Access by rue de la Rive.

A pleasant shaded walk. Take the surfaced path on the right to reach the top of a hillock crowned by a modern Calvary. From the viewing table there is a fine view of Morlaix Bay.

Îlot Ste-Anne

Access by rue de la Rive and rue de l'Abbé-Tanguy. As the road descends, there is a **view**★ over Morlaix Bay and its islands. A dike leads to the Rocher Ste-Anne and the Groux pleasure boat harbour. From the rock, which forms a remarkable viewpoint (benches), the view extends from Roscoff as far as Pointe de Primel.

Excursions

Château de Kérouzéré★

8km/5mi to the west. Leave St-Pol-de-Léon via D 788 towards Lesneven, then the road to the right to Plouescat. At Sibiril, turn right towards Moguériec and after 500m/547yd left towards the castle. Guided tours (1hr) mid-July to Aug, once every afternoon; 1 to 14 July and 1 to 15 September, Wed and Sundays at 5pm; mid-May to June and mid-Sept to Oct, Wed at 5pm. ◌€ 3.20. ☎ 02 98 29 96 05.

This granite feudal castle is an interesting specimen of early-15C military architecture. Three of the massive machicolated corner towers remain standing, the fourth having been demolished in 1590 after a siege. A central stone staircase gives access to the three floors which were used by soldiers and include large bare rooms with deep window recesses and stone seats, a wall walk and a guard tower. The castle also retains pepper-pot roofs, oratory frescoes, some tapestries and fine Breton furniture, all dating from the 17C.

Manoir de Tronjoly
West on D 10. On leaving Cléder, turn right; two granite pillars markt he entrance of the pdrive to the château. Outside 10am-6pm, no charge. Guided tour of the manor house, call ahead for information. 02 98 69 33 54.
This elegant 16-17C manor house is adorned with Renaissance dormer windows. A massive square tower stands in a corner of the courtyard surrounded by the main building and a terrace closed off by a stone balustrade.

Berven
The triumphal arch through which you enter the parish close is a fine specimen of Renaissance art with its three semicircular arches and its pilasters with capitals.
The 16C **church**★ has a façade surmounted by a square tower crowned with a dome with small lanterns and ornamented by balustrades; it was the first of its kind in Brittany (1573) and served as a model for many others.
A wooden rood screen stands before the very fine chancel **enclosure**★, ornamented on the front with small fluted granite columns and at the sides with wooden ones. In the chancel are 17C stalls with armrests in the form of winged caryatids.

Ferme-musée du Léon
200m/220yd after leaving Berven on D 788 towards Lesneven, take the little road towards Quéran. Open May to Sept, daily, 10am-noon and 2-7pm; rest of the year, Sat-Sun and holidays, 2-7pm. €4.50 (chidlren €2). 02 98 29 53 07.
The buildings of an old family farmhouse, in which the original furniture has been kept on display, house this small museum of agricultural tools and equipment and horsedrawn carts, which evokes the evolution over the course of a century of country life in Léon.

Château de Kerjean★
Open July and Aug, daily, 10am-7pm; June and Sept, daily (except Tues), 10am-6pm; Apr and May, daily (except Tues), 2-6pm; Oct, daily (except Tues), 2-5pm; rest of the year, Wed and Sun only 2-5pm. High season €5 (children 7-17, €1). 02 98 69 93 69.
Half-fortress, half-Renaissance mansion, stands in the midst of a huge park. Towards the mid 16C Louis Barbier inherited a fortune from his uncle, a rich abbot of St-Mathieu, and decided to build a castle which would be the finest residence in Léon. In 1710 part of the building burned down, later the castle was sacked. However, the castle, which has belonged to the State since 1911, has since been restored except for the right wing. The buildings are guarded by a moat and ramparts; enter the main courtyard via the old drawbridge.
A main building with two wings and a large portico enclose the main courtyard, which is adorned with a fine Corinthian-columned Renaissance **well**. The dwelling house contains a museum of Breton art with fine 17C and 18C **furnishings**: box beds, chests, grain chests.
The kitchen, a vast room with a ceiling 6m/20ft high, has two monumental chimneys facing each other, one of which was used as the bread oven, and a large copperware collection.
On the courtyard's other side is the chapel. Inside it is decorated with a wooden vault in the shape of a ship's keel and carved beams and purlins. The coach house wing, which once housed the stores, a forge and the servants' quarters, has been

restored. There is a slide show on the history of Kerjean. A door leads to an alley supported on a gallery with eight arches, which give a good overall view of the main courtyard and the buildings around it.

The **park** includes **French-style gardens** and a charming Renaissance **fountain**, consisting of a niche surrounded by four colonnettes, set into a little stone wall. The noise of the spring, mingled with the warbling of the birds, makes a pleasant background in which to meditate. On leaving, to the left of the central avenue, note the dovecot, a stone tower 9m/29.5ft in diameter.

Every year, there are temporary exhibitions held, devoted to contemporary art in spring, and the history of Brittany in summer. During July and August, evening theatre performances are on offer.

ST-QUAY-PORTRIEUX⌂

POPULATION 3 114
MICHELIN LOCAL MAP 309 F3

St-Quay-Portrieux, a popular seaside resort, owes its name to an Irish monk – St Ké – who, legend has it, landed on this coast c 472. Its beautiful beaches – Casino, Châtelet and Comtesse – are sheltered by a rocky fringe known as the Roches de St-Quay.

The ports

The tidal port at Portrieux used to equip fleets bound for Newfoundland. Nowadays, it is the lively home of a fishing fleet which fishes for mackerel, pollack, bass and, from November to April in particular, scallops and shellfish. The new deep sea harbour, inaugurated in 1990, contains 950 berths for pleasure boats and 100 for fishing boats. There is a regular crossing to the Channel Islands during the summer, and also the opportunity to take a boat out to Île de Bréhat.

Chemin de ronde

Allow 1hr 30min on foot there and back, preferably at high tide.

This former customs officers' path starts at Portrieux port, beyond the town hall, skirts Comtesse Beach, passes in front of the Viking stele and the signal station,

S. Sauvignier/MICHELIN

Customs officers' path

affording a fine **view**★ of St-Brieuc Bay, from Bréhat to Cap Fréhel. It then continues along the terrace overlooking Plage du Châtelet *(viewing table)*, round the sea-water pool and reaches Casino Beach. The walk may be extended as far as the Grève St-Marc *(add on about 2hr on foot there and back)*.

Excursions

Étables-sur-Mer
5km/3mi south. Leave St-Quay-Portrieux on D 786 in the direction of St-Brieuc.
The town, built on a plateau and possessing a fine public park, overlooks the quiet family resort on the coast. The two parts of the town are linked by an avenue lined with villas. The two fine sandy beaches, Godelins and Le Moulin, are separated by the Pointe du Vau Burel.

Chapelle Notre-Dame-de-l'Espérance
Built after the cholera epidemic of 1850, the restored Chapel of Our Lady of Hope, decorated with stained glass windows in blue tones, two paintings by Jean Michau and a tapestry depicting the Virgin and Child by Toffoli, stands on Étables cliff, overlooking St-Brieuc Bay.

Binic⚓
7.5km/4.5mi south.
Binic is a delightful resort whose port, in the past, sheltered fishing schooners in winter. It is now used by pleasure craft and a few coastal fishing boats.
A small **museum** (♿🕐 *Open July and Aug, daily, 2.30-6pm; Apr to June and Sept, daily (except Tues), 2.30-6pm.* 🕐 *Closed the rest of the year.* ✆€ 3.50. ☎ 02 96 73 37 95) evokes daily life in Binic a century ago with a display of head-dresses, Breton costumes and various objects related to marine life and deep-sea fishing.
Jetée Penthièvre (pier), closing off the outer harbour, is reached by Quais Jean-Bart and Surcouf. From a belvedere on the jetty there is a pleasant view of the beach with its raised huts dominated by a pine-topped knoll and the port.

Le Palus-Plage
11km/6.6kmi north. A lovely cove.
🚶 To the left of the beach, a stairway cut in the rock leads to an upper path from which there are good views of St-Brieuc Bay.

Plage Bonaparte
13km/8mi north. From this beach at the bottom of Cohat Bay, reached by a tunnel cut through the cliff, Allied pilots, brought down on French soil, were taken back to Great Britain. To reach the commemorative monument, take the stairway to the right of the beach car park, then the path up to the top of the cliff or, by car, drive along the road leading off to the right before the beach. Fine **view** of St-Brieuc Bay and Cap Fréhel, with Port-Moguer to the right and Pointe de Minard to the left.

Chapelle de Kermaria-an-Iskuit★
11km/6.6mi north via D 786; turn left on D 21. The Chapelle de Kermaria-an-Iskuita (House of Mary who preserves and restores health) is a popular scene of pilgrimage (third Sunday in September). This former baronial chapel, in which a few of the bays of the nave are 13C, was enlarged in the 15C and 18C. Above the south porch, in the archives, is the former 16C courtroom, with a small balcony.
The walls over the arcades are decorated with 15C **frescoes**★. The best preserved, in the nave, depict a striking dance of death: Death, in the shape of jumping and dancing skeletons and corpses, drags the living into a dance; those depicted include pope, emperor, cardinal, king, constable, bourgeois, usurer, lover, lord, ploughman,

monk etc. Above the high altar is a great 14C Christ. In the south transept are five alabaster **low-relief sculptures**★ of scenes from the life of the Virgin. There are numerous wooden statues, including, in the transept, a curious 16C figure of the Virgin suckling her unwilling Child.

Lanleff★

5.5km/3mi. Leave Kermaria west on D 21 to the left and after Pléhédel, bear left.
In the village, away from the road, stands the **temple**★, a circular building, a former chapel or baptistery built by the Templars in the 11C on the model of the Holy Sepulchre in Jerusalem. Twelve round-arched arcades connect the rotunda with an aisle set at an angle with three oven-vaulted apsidal chapels to the east. Note the simple decoration of the capitals: small figures, animals, geometrical figures, foliage.

ST-THÉGONNEC★★

POPULATION 2 267
MICHELIN LOCAL MAP 308 H3 – FINISTÈRE (29)

This village has a magnificent parish close, the ossuary and the church being the key features of this rich 16C-17C Renaissance group.

🚶 **Also see:** Les ENCLOS PAROISSAUX.

Enclos Paroissial★★.

▸ *Enter the parish close via the place de l'Église to the south.*

Porte triomphale★
A rounded arch surmounted by small lantern turrets (1587).

Chapelle funéraire★
🕒 *Open Apr to Sept, daily, 9am-6pm (7pm June to Aug).* 💶 *No charge.* ☎ *02 98 79 47 64.*

The funerary chapel was built from 1676 to 1682. Inside is a 17C altarpiece (restored) with spiral columns. In the crypt, under the altar, is a **Holy Sepulchre**★ with figures carved in oak and painted (1699-1702), the work of a Breton sculptor, Jacques Lespaignol.
The treasury contains gold and silver plate including a silver gilt processional cross (1610).

R. Mattes/MICHELIN

Calvaire★★
The Calvary was erected in 1610. On the base are groups of figures depicting the Passion. Below, a small niche shelters St Thégonnec with the wolf he harnessed to his cart after his donkey had been devoured by wolves.

A scene from the Passion on the Calvary

The platform is surmounted by a double-armed cross bearing figures and two simple crosses for the thieves.

Church★
The church has been remodelled several times. The only trace of the old building is the gable belfry (1563) on the left of the tower. The Renaissance tower is crowned with a dome with lantern and corner turrets. A fire in June 1998 caused the roof to collapse and severely damaged the five chapels on the north side. Ten fire companies and local volunteers were able to keep the flames from damaging rood screens, the windows, the organ and the pulpit. Pending restoration work, an observatory enables visitors to admire some of the churchs' remarkable features, including the pulpit (👁 see below). An exhibition illustrates the history of the parish close.

Over the porch is a statue of St Thégonnec; in niches in the corner buttresses there are statues of the Annunciation, St John and St Nicholas; inside the porch, four statues of Apostles.

Inside, the **pulpit**★★ is one of the masterpieces (1683) of Breton sculpture. The corners are adorned with the four Cardinal Virtues, while the Evangelists are depicted on the four panels. On the medallion at the back, God is giving the Tablets of the Law to Moses. The sounding board (1732) decorated with angels and roses, is surmounted by the Angel of Judgement blowing a trumpet.

The apse and both arms of the transept are covered with **woodwork**★ dating from the 17C and 18C, which has been restored. The panels of the **Rosary altarpiece**★, on the left, represent below and in the centre, the Virgin and the Child, Jesus giving a rosary to St Dominic and St Catherine; above, the Virgin and St Lawrence give Christ a soul saved from the flames of Purgatory.

ÎLE DE SEIN

POPULATION 242
MICHELIN LOCAL MAP 308 B6 – FINISTÈRE (29)

Sein Island makes a picturesque excursion. Off Pointe du Raz, it is less than 0.5sq mi in area and is very low-lying; the sea sometimes covers it, as it did in 1868 and 1896. The island is bare: there are no trees or even bushes; old fields are enclosed by low, drystone walls.

A Bit of History

Men and their work – For centuries the island was the object of superstitious dread. In the 18C, its few inhabitants lived in almost total isolation. The islanders were shipwreck looters. Now they are among the most active lifesavers. The women do all the manual labour, the men are sailors or fishermen. Fishing is the island's only means of livelihood.

A fine page of history (1940-44) – Immediately after General de Gaulle's appeal of 18 June 1940, the men of the Île de Sein (altogether 130 sailors and fishermen) put to sea and joined the troops of Free French Forces in England. Moreover, nearly 3 000 French soldiers and sailors also reached the island and embarked for England. When the Germans arrived on Sein they found only women, children, old men, the mayor and the priest. For several months fishing boats brought or embarked Allied officers. Of the sailors from the island who went to England 29 were killed on the battlefields. A commemorative monument stands to the right of the road to

C. Chevallier

Île de Sein

the lighthouse. General de Gaulle came in person in 1946 to award the Liberation Cross to the Island.

Tour

Access
Regular service by boat from Audierne.
There are daily crossings from Audierne (Sainte-Evette) year-round aboard the Enez Sun III; July and Aug at 9am, 11.30am and 4.50pm, return journey at 10.20am, 3.30pm and 6.15pm; Sept to June at 9.30am, return journey at 4pm. ☎ 02 98 70 70 70.
Mid-July to mid-Aug, crossings from Camaret (aboard the André Colin, 196 passengers) at 8.45am, return journey Sun only at 5pm. Penn ar bed. ☎ 02 98 27 88 22.

Port and Village
The port provides a good shelter for pleasure craft. The village's small white houses with brightly painted shutters stand along alleys barely 90cm/1yd wide for protection from the wind. On a hillock near the church, two menhirs rise side by side, hence known as "The Talkers". Beyond the church, the Nifran Calvary is a simple granite cross resting on a tiered plinth. Behind it is the only dolmen on the island.
The **museum** (🕐 *Open late June to late Sept, daily, 10am-6pm. 1€ 2.50. ☎ 02 98 70 90 35.*) commemorates the events of the Second World War by means of photographs, explanatory panels and diagrams: the departure of the men of the Île de Sein for England; the activities of the marine Free French Forces; the campaigns in which the activists of the Liberation took part; the losses of the Merchant Navy (45 000 missing, 5 150 ships sunk); and the anti-submarine struggle.
The **lighthouse**, on the island's western tip, is equipped with a 6kW light which has an average range of 50km/31mi. Left of the lighthouse stands the tiny Chapelle St-Corentin, an old hermitage. Beyond the point lies Sein Reef (Chaussée de Sein), submerged or visible, it prolongs the island some 20km/12mi towards the open sea.
On one of these rocks, which is constantly pounded by the sea, the **Phare d'Ar Men** (Ar Men Lighthouse), which took 14 years of superhuman effort to build, was erected in 1881. Its light, with a range of 55km/34mi, warns seamen off the rocks.

SIZUN★

POPULATION 242
MICHELIN LOCAL MAP 308 B6 – FINISTÈRE (29)

Sizun, a village in the Léon region, has an interesting parish close.

👌 **Also see:** Les ENCLOS PAROISSIAUX

Enclos paroissial★

🕐 *Open daily, year round.* ☜ *No charge.* ☜ *For guided tours, contact the Tourist Office.*

The most interesting parts of the close are the triple triumphal **arch**★, decorated with Corinthian capitals and topped by a Calvary, and the twin-arched ossuary-**chapel**★; both date from 1585 to 1588.

The ossuary-chapel houses a small local museum with box bed, dresser, head-dresses, costumes and sacred art objects. The 16C **church**, remodelled in the 17C and 18C, is joined by a passage to the sacristy (late 17C) which stands alone. Inside, the decoration of the panelled vaulting is remarkable: a sculpted purlin with, in the transept and chancel, angels presenting the instruments of the Passion, crocodile-headed tie-beams, keystones and fluting. The organ loft, high altar, altarpieces and font canopy are all 17C.

Excursions

Maison de la Rivière

1km/0.6mi west.

🕐 *Open mid-June to mid-Sept, daily 11am-6.30pm; rest of the year, by appointment.* ☜ *€ 4.* ☎ *02 98 68 86 33.*

This small museum, located in Vergraon Mill, illustrates the importance of fresh water through various themes: fish and their habitat and angling (fishing tackle, flies used in salmon fishing etc) ... The exhibits are complemented by aquariums containing freshwater fish, explanatory panels, models and films.

S. Sauvignier/MICHELIN

Triumphal arch

The Maison de la Rivière also organises guided rambles across the Monts d'Arrée, to the source of the Élorn, Drennec Lake or the Mougau peat bogs.
Its annexe, the Maison du Lac (Fish-Breeding Centre), located at the foot of the Drennec dam *(6km/4mi east)*, is an information centre on the worldwide exploitation of rivers, lakes, fish-farming etc.

Locmélar

5km/3mi north of Sizun. The 16C and 17C **church** houses imposing altarpieces consecrated to St Mélar and St Hervé and two 16C and 17C **banners**★ embroidered in gold and silver.
In the churchyard stands an interesting Calvary (1560), with two crossbars peopled with figures; the sacristy has a keel-shaped roof.

TRÉGASTEL-PLAGE 🏖🏖

POPULATION 2 234
MICHELIN LOCAL MAP 5309 B2 – CÔTES D'ARMOR (22)

The resort of Trégastel rivals the neighbouring locality of Ploumanach for the beauty and strangeness of its **rocks**★★, which are characteristic of the Corniche Bretonne.

▶ **Orient Yourself:** Not far from (and less crowed than) Perros-Guirec.
Kids **Especially for Kids:** Aquarium marin.
👶 **See Also:** Côte de GRANIT ROSE.

Sights

Aquarium marin

Kids 👶 🕐 *Open May-Sep: daily 10am-7pm (7pm in July-Aug); Oct-Dec: Tue-Sat: 2-6pm and Sun 10am-noon and 2-6pm.* 🕐 *Closed mid-Nov to mid-Dec.* ⊛€ 7 (children 4-16

Address Book

TOURIST OFFICE

Trégastel, Place Ste-Anne, ☎ 02 96 15 38 38, www.ville-tregastel.fr Open Jul-Aug: Mon-Sat 9.30am-1pm, 2-7pm, Sun 10am-12.30pm; off season: Mon-Sat 9.30-12am, 2-6pm. Guided tour Jul-Aug 10.30am.

WHERE TO STAY

⊜⊜ **Hôtel de la Mer**, *plage du Coz-Pors*, ☎ 02 96 15 60 00 – 14rm ✕ 🕐 *Closed 5 Jan-15 Apr; 15 Nov-15 Dec.* This traditional hotel offers renovated rooms in blue tones, overlooking the sea or the plaza.
⊜⊜⊜ **Le Beauséjour**, *plage du Coz-Pors*, ☎ 02 96 23 88 02 – 16rm ✕ 🕐 *Closed 5 Jan-mid Feb; 15 Nov-18 Dec.*

Decorated in a sea-motif, most of the variably-sized rooms here come with a view of the sea, some even with a terrace. Breakfast € 9. Pleasant restaurant for traditional cuisine.

ENTERTAINMENT

Toucouleur *(on the right as you enter Trégastel coming from Ploumanach)* ☎ 02 96 23 46 26. Each night in summer and Sat off season, this pub welcomes bands playing music from Breton and all over the world.

FESTIVAL

Trégastel - Les 24h de la voile, *13 and 14 Aug.* One of the main yachting events of the area.

€ 5). 🐾 *Guided tour € 1/person supplement (reservation required). Boat trip:* 🚤 *€ 3/person over age 4 (reservation required).* ☎ *02 96 23 48 58. www.aquarium-tregastel.com.*

The aquarium has just reopened after extensive renovation. It is located in caves, which housed a church in the 19C (Coz Ilis means the old church) under a mass of enormous rocks, known as the Turtles. In three rooms varieties of fish from Breton waters and tropical seas are exhibited, along with stuffed birds including puffins,

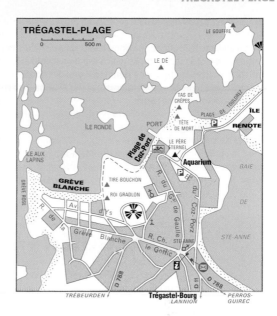

herring gulls, guillemots, penguins and gannets, all from Sept-Îles.
At the exit, a stairway *(28 steps)* leads up to a statue of the Eternal Father (Père Éternel). From the look-out point, there is a good view of the mass of **rocks**★★ and the pink granite coastline.

Plage de Coz-Porz

This sandy beach is lined with rocks bearing descriptive names: the Turtles, the Witch.

🚶 At the north end of the beach, beyond the jetty, make for a small beach near two rocks, the **Tête de Mort** (Death's Head) and the **Tas de Crêpes** (Pile of Pancakes), both on the right. This last rock, which appears to lie in folds, is a good example of wind erosion. Beyond a sandbank there is a mass of rocks, among which is the **Dé** (Thimble).

Grève Blanche★

Allow 1hr on foot there and back from Coz-Porz.
The path, which starts from the left end of this beach (Plage de Coz-Porz), follows the cliff edge around a promontory from the end of which can be seen the White Shore, Rabbits' Island (Île aux Lapins) and, out at sea, the Triagoz Islands.
The path continues near the foot of a rock called the **Tire-Bouchon** (Corkscrew) and reaches the end of the White Shore, dominated by a great rock known as **Roi Gradlon** (King Gradlon) on account of its resemblance to a crowned head.

Viewing table

Telescope. This gives a circular **view**★ of the coast: the White Shore, Île Grande, the Triagoz Lighthouse, Sept-Îles and the hinterland (when weather permits): Clarté, Pleumeur-Bodou (with its distinctive Radôme) and Trébeurden villages.

Île Renote★★

Northeast. Leaving the sand bar you will find opposite you Renote Island, formed of huge blocks of granite and now connected with the mainland.

> *Follow the road that crosses the island.*

You pass Plage de Touldrez on your left and approach the Chasm (Le Gouffre), a cavity in the middle of a mass of rocks which can be reached at low tide. As you walk amid the rocks to the very tip of the peninsula, you get good views of the horizon out to sea and of the Sept-Îles looking north; of the Ploumanach coast to the east and the Baie de Ste-Anne to the south.

Trégastel-Bourg
3km/2mi south towards Lannion.
The 13C church was remodelled in the 14C and 18C. To the right of the south porch stands a semicircular 17C ossuary adorned with balusters and crowned with a domed turret. At the nave is an unusual 14C stoup, a former grain measure.

TRÉGUIER★★

POPULATION 2 679
MICHELIN LOCAL MAP 309 C2 – CÔTES D'ARMOR (22)

The town (evangelized in the 6C by St Tugdual), a former episcopal city, was built in terraces on the side of a hill overlooking the wide estuary of the River Jaudy and River Guindy. The port, which provides a magnificent anchorage for yachts, can receive big ships.

One of the great Breton pardons takes place in the town of St Yves on the third Sunday in May. This is the *pardon* of the poor, as well as that of advocates and lawyers. The procession goes from the cathedral to Minihy-Tréguier.

> **Orient Yourself:** Half-way between Lannion and Paimpol on D 786
> **Don't Miss:** The spectacular coastline

Sights

The port
This magnificent expanse of water provides ample anchorage for yachts, but can also accommodate large coasters.

TRÉGUIER	
Chantrerie R. de la	2
Gambetta R.	3
Gaulle Pl. du Gén.-de	4
La-Chalotais R. de	5
Le-Braz Bd A.	6
Le-Peltier R.	8
Martray Pl. du	
St-Yves R.	12

Calvaire de la protestation	B
Maison de Renan	M
Tours carrées	D

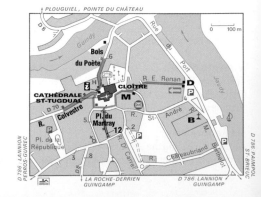

Address Book

TOURIST OFFICE

Tréguier, 67 rue Ernest Renan, ☎ 02 96 92 22 33, www.paysdetreguier.com Open Mon-Sat 9am-12.30pm, 2-6pm; Jul-Aug: Sun 10am-1pm. Sells several guides of the surroundings.

WHERE TO STAY

TRÉGUIER ET SURROUNDINGS

☜☜ **Le St-Yves**, *4 rue Colvestre,* ☎ *02 96 92 33 49 - 8rm. Closed 3 weeks in Sep.* Tucked away in a very old residence, some of these very simple rooms are paired with upstairs bathrooms.

☜☜ **Chambres d'hôte du Penquer**, *Minihy-Tréguier,* ☎ *02 96 91 57 03, gildas.lemee@wanadoo.fr – 4rm.* In the countryside, a block of stone buildings form two family units with rooms in blue and yellow tones separate entrances. Good breakfast with 10 varieties of home made jam! Kitchen area.

☜☜ **Tara B & B**, *31 rue Ernest Renan,* ☎ *02 96 92 15 28 – 3rm* Timber frame house, quiet and well kept rooms above a shop selling Irish goods.

☜☜☐ **Hôtel Aigue Marine**, *Port de Plaisance,* ☎ *02 96 92 97 00, www.aigue-marine.fr – 48rm* ✗ ☒ ◷ *Closed Jan-Feb.* Comfortable rooms with views overlooking the port or the swimming pool and garden.

EATING OUT

TRÉGUIER

☜ **Crêperie des Halles**, *16 rue Ernest Renan,* ☎ *02 96 92 39 15.* ◷ *Closed Mon-Tue off season.* Enjoy traditional crepes or mussels and other simple meals.

☜☐ **Poissonnerie Moulinet**, *2 rue Ernest Renan,* ☎ *02 96 92 30 27.* ◷ *Open Jul-Sep.* This fishmonger has two dining rooms above his shop where you can enjoy his fresh sea produce at good prices.

☜☜ **Le Hangar**, *on the yachting harbour,* ☎ *02 96 92 47 46.* ◷ *Closed for lunch and Mon-Tue off season.* One of the most animated address in Tréguier at night. Mussels and chips served on the terrace in front of the port or in a former hangar converted in a dining room.

☜☜☐ **Le Canotier**, *5 rue Ernest Renan,* ☎ *02 96 92 41 70.* ◷ *Closed Wed and Thu evenings; Sat lunch off season.*

Traditional setting and cuisine in the centre of town.

SHOPPING

Markets - Tréguier, Wed; **La Roche-Derrien**, Fri; **Lézardrieux**, Fri; **Penvénan**, Sat; **Pleubian** Sat; **Port-Blanc**, Thu morning in summer; **Trévou-Tréguignec**, Tue in summer.

Culinary specialities- Bakery-pastry Muzard, *Place de l'Église, Pleudaniel,* ☎ *02 96 20 14 73.* Breads and other culinary specialities. **Sea grocery**, *Lanmodez,* ☎ *02 96 22 95 94. Mon-Fri.* Noodles, canned food, and smoked fish in season.

Oysters - Mr Rouzès, *In Lanmodez* ☎ *02 96 22 85 91,* and **Mr Percevault**, *on the port of La Roche-Jaune* ☎ *02 96 92 57 88,* sell high quality products.

RECREATION

Rent a bike - Bar Les Plaisanciers, *le port, Tréguier,* ☎ *02 96 92 49 69, in season,* € *14/day.* **Camping Le Gouffre**, *between Le Gouffre and Pors-Hir,* ☎ *02 96 92 02 95,* € *15/day.*

Windsurf and kayak - Centre nautique de Port-Blanc, *bd de la mer,* ☎ *02 96 92 64 96, www.cnportblanc.fr* Windsurfing and kayak lessons.

Base nautique de Plougrescant, ☎ *02 96 31 51 48.* ◷ *Open Jul-Aug.* Kayak 10 yrs old and up: lessons and trips between the peninsulas (€ 70/week).

Old riggings – Come and discover the coast, take fishing lessons on board *L'Ausquémé,* ☎ *06 07 59 04 03, May-Sept; half day,* € *25; whole day,* € *37,* or on board La Marie-Georgette; information at the pub Le Gavroche à Plougrescant ☎ *02 96 92 09 15/58 83,* ◷ *Open Apr-Oct.*

Walks - The **GR 34** follows the edge of the two peninsulas. The Tourist Office of the peninsula of Lézardrieux (Sauvage) sells a **guide** offering 17 tours (€ 3). You will also find information on several hikes on the peninsulas in Balades en pays de Trégor et Goëlo (€ 3), available at the **Pays Touristique**, *9 Place de l'Église, La Roche-Derrien* ☎ *02 96 91 50 22, www.tregorgoelo.com,*

or at the Conseil général des Côtes-d'Armor (☎ 02 96 62 27 64).
Horse-riding - Poney-Club de Port-Blanc, Kerelguen, ☎ 02 96 92 79 73. Easy ride (2hr) all year (€ 35) and all day Sat in summer (€ 60) for ages 4 and up. **La Ferme du Syet**, Minihy-Tréguier (☎ 02 96 92 31 79, www.la-ferme-du-syet.com), half day rides (€ 25) and full day rides (€ 46), in the forest or along the sea in accordance with the season.

FESTIVALS

Every Wed evening, mid-Jul to mid-Aug, concerts and a nocturnal market give life to the centre of Tréguier. During the same period, **Festivals en Trégor** offers classical concerts in the churchs of the region (information at the Tourist Office of Tréguier). More contemporary, **Les Irréducktibles** for the lovers of rock, songs and theatre in Plougrescant the 1st weekend of Aug. Les **régates de La Roche-Jaune**, every 15 Aug. Le grand **pardon de St-Yves**, 15 May in Tréguier, and Le grand pardon de **St-Gildas**, in Penvénan, (end-May to begin-June) are traditional manifestations. The Festival **Gospel in peninsula takes place in the chapels** of the peninsula Sauvage in Mar and Apr.

▷ *Leave the car in the harbour car park and enter the town along rue Ernest-Renan, which is lined with tall half-timbered houses. The two great square towers (D) once framed the town gate.*

Maison de Renan

🕐 *Open July and Aug, daily, 10am-1pm and 2.30-6.30pm; Apr to June, Sept, Oct and school holidays, daily (except Mon and Tues), 10am-noon and 2-6pm.* 👓 *4.60 (children: no charge).* ☎ *02 96 92 45 63.*
This 16C half-timbered house contains memorabilia of Ernest Renan (1823-92). Visitors can see the room in which he was born, a reconstruction of his study and library at the Collège de France and, on the top floor, the two tiny rooms in which, as a child, he liked to shut himself away to work (lovely view of the town).

Cathédrale St-Tugdual★★

Guided tours available July and Aug, daily (except Sun and holidays), 10am-noon and 2.30-6pm.
The cathedral, which dates from the 14C-15C, is one of the finest in Brittany. The transept is surmounted by three towers; the tower of the south arm, topped by an 18C pierced spire, rises 63m/202ft. At its base is a porch (1438) under a fine Flamboyant **window**★. The Gothic tower of the sanctuary, uncompleted, rises above the crossing. The Romanesque Hastings Tower is all that is left of the 12C church.

▷ *Enter through the main porch.*

Steps lead down towards the luminous nave with its Gothic arches worked delicately in granite. A sculpted frieze runs under the triforium. The ribbed vaulting in the Tudor style is lit by clerestory windows. The modern stained-glass windows, the work of the master glazier Hubert de Sainte-Marie, portray biblical themes (to the left scenes from the Old Testament, to the right scenes from the Gospels).

▷ *Start from the north aisle.*

The **tomb of St Yves** is an 1890 copy of the monument built by Jean V, Duke of Brittany, in the 15C. The recumbent figure of Jean V, sculpted in 1945, is located in the Duke's Chapel, lit by stained glass donated in 1937 by American, Belgian and French lawyers. The north arm of the transept is cut off by the Hastings Tower. The doors of the sacristy and cloisters open under handsome Romanesque arches which rise

The cloisters are divided by forty Flamboyant arcades made from granite from Île Grande and Pluzumet

J. Malburet/MICHELIN

above a heavy pillar, coupled by columns with sculpted capitals and surmounted by an arcature.

In the ambulatory, the third chapel houses a 13C Christ carved in wood. The chancel with slender columns has 15C painted vaulting. It holds 46 Renaissance **stalls**★. The **stained-glass window**★ brightens the south transept. It recounts the story of the Vine (symbol of the Church) which winds round the founders of the seven Breton bishoprics (among them St Tugdual), around the saints of the land and around the Breton trades. Near the south doorway an interesting 15C **carved wooden group** represents St Yves between the Rich and the Poor. In the south aisle, note the 15C **recesses** sculpted with knights in armour.

Treasury

🕐 *Open July and Aug, daily 10am-6.30pm, Sat 10am-noon, Sun and holidays, 12.30-6.30pm; mid-June to end of June and beginning of Sept to mid-Sept, 10am-noon and 2-6pm, Sat 10am-noon, Sun and holidays 2-6pm. ⊕€ 3 combined ticket with the Cloisters. ☎ 02 96 92 30 51 or ☎ 02 96 92 30 19.*

The sacristy contains the treasure, which includes the head reliquary (19C) of St Yves in gilded bronze placed against the foundation wall of the Hastings Tower (c 11C).

Cloisters★

🕐 *Open July and Aug, daily, 9.30am-6.30pm, Sun and holidays, 12.30-6.30pm; May, June and Sept, 10am-noon and 2-6pm, Sun and holidays 2-6pm. ⊕€ 2 (Oct-March: no charge). ☎ 02 96 92 22 33.*

The 15C cloisters abut the former bishop's palace and the cathedral chevet cuts across the north gallery. The Flamboyant arches in Breton granite, roofed with slate, frame a cross rising on a lawn. Under the wooden vaulting with its sculpted purlin, there are 15C to 17C recumbent figures in the ambulatory.

Place du Martray

The shaded square, in the heart of the town, still features picturesque old houses. It contains a **statue** of Ernest Renan, commemorating the writer's birth in Tréguier and his attendance at the local college.

Rue St-Yves

A small tower in this pedestrian street gives a view of **La Psalette**, a residence for young singers, which was built in 1447.

Monuments aux Morts

N of the cathedral.

This war memorial is a sober and moving work by F Renaud, depicting a grieving Breton woman wearing a cape of mourning.

Take **rue Colvestre,** almost opposite, which features some lovely old houses and, more particularly, Duke Jean V's house, the Hôtel de Kermorvan and the Hôtel de Coetivy. Turn back and go down, beneath the old bishop's palace, to the **Bois du Poète,** overlooking the River Guindy and contains a monument to the writer Anatole Le Braz. Pleasant walk.

Notice also the **Calvaire de la Protestation** (Calvary of Protest) (B) by the sculptor Yves Hernot, put up in 1904 to reflect the Catholics' objections to the erection of the statue in honour of Ernest Renan in the place du Martray.

Excursions

Minihy-Tréguier

1km/0.6mi south. Leave Tréguier towards La Roche-Derrien. On leaving the built-up area, turn left.

The birthplace of St Yves is the scene of a pardon on the third Sunday in May. This is called locally "going to St-Yves"; the local priest is even known as the Rector of St-Yves. The 15C church is built on the site of the former chapel of the manor of Ker-Martin, where Yves Helori was born and died (1253-1303). His will is written in Latin on a painted canvas kept in the chapel. A 13C manuscript kept in the presbytery is called the *Breviary of St Yves* (Bréviaire de Saint Yves). In the cemetery is a 13C monument pierced in the middle by a very low archway, under which the pilgrims pass on their knees. This is called the tomb of St Yves (Tombeau de Saint Yves), but is probably an altar belonging to the original chapel.

Château de la Roche-Jagu★

13km/8mi southeast via D 786 and D 787. ◔ *Open July and Aug, daily, 10am-7pm; mid-Feb to June, 10.30am-12.30pm and 2-6pm; Sept to mid-Nov, 10.30am-12.30pm and 2-7pm.* ◔ *Closed the rest of the year.* ◐€ 2 château, € 2 park. ☎ 02 96 95 62 35.

The **castle** was built in the 15C at the top of the steep wooded slopes which form the west bank of the River Trieux. It was restored in 1968. Together with other fortresses, no longer extant, it commanded the river and thus retains its defensive aspect. On the west façade, note the corbels which supported the former wall-walk and its five doors. The tour includes several rooms with French-style ceilings and large chimneys, the small chapel and its two oratories. There is a magnificent view of the **setting★** of the Trieux from the covered wall-walk in front of the east wall. The river forms a steep-sided loop at the foot of the castle which can be reached by a footpath to the right.

During the summer, exhibits and displays take place in the castle.

Park – After the terrible storm of 1987, a modern park was created. The landscape gardens recall the landscapes of Brittany, but also feature palm trees and the remains of a linen workshop.

Runan

13km/8mi south via D 8.

Runan, which stands on a plateau in the Tréguier region, has a large church which belonged to the Knights Templar and then to the Hospitallers of St John of Jerusalem.

The 14C-15C **church** is richly decorated. The south side has four gables pierced with broad windows and emblazoned façades. The porch gable is adorned with a sculpted lintel depicting the Annunciation and a Deposition. The superimposed figures of the twelve Apostles join to form the keystone of the vaulting.

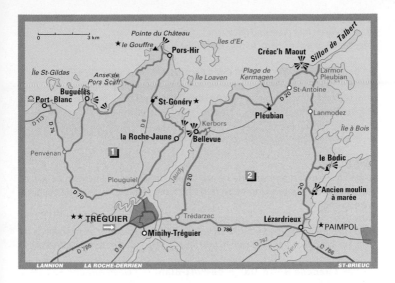

Inside, the building is roofed with panelled vaults resting on multicoloured purlins: signs of the Zodiac to the left of the nave, animals on the right. The mid-15C altarpiece of the font chapel includes exceptionally delicate figures (five scenes from the lives of Christ and the Virgin) made of bluish Tournai stone.

1 Jaudy estuary to Port-Blanc

Round tour of 37km/23mi – about 2hr.

▶ *Leave Tréguier on D 8 to the north and at Plouguiel, bear right.*

La Roche-Jaune
A small port on the Jaudy Estuary. Oyster farms.
On leaving La Roche-Jaune in the direction of St-Gonéry, you will enjoy a good view of the Jaudy estuary, the oyster-beds and the islands.

Chapelle St-Gonéry★
The chapel has a curiously leaning lead steeple (1612) on a 10C tower.
Inside, the painted wood vaulting depicts scenes from the Old and New Testaments; these **paintings**, which date from the late 15C, were restored in the 18C and 19C. In the chapel on the right of the chancel, there is a 16C **reliquary cupboard**★, a finely carved canopied type of chest. The left chapel contains the 16C **mausoleum**★ of a bishop of Tréguier; the recumbent figure rests on a great marble slab decorated with mouldings and supported on four lions.

▶ *At St-Gonéry, take the road to Pors-Hir.*

Pors-Hir
A small harbour built between great rocks near a little cove.
The road follows the coastline in a beautiful setting; houses built against huge rocks or nestling between tall boulders add a fairy like touch.

Pointe du Château
From the tip of the headland, there are beautiful views over the Îles d'Er, the Heaux Lighthouse and Sept-Îles.

Le Gouffre★
Allow 15min on foot there and back.
A deep cleft in a mass of rocks into which the sea roars furiously.

▷ *Turn back and follow the road along the bays, then bear right three times.*

From Le Roudour, you can make for **Anse de Pors Scaff** bristling with islands, then head for **Buguélès**, a small resort fringed by islands, all inhabited.

▷ *After Le Roudour the coastal road affords lovely views.*

Port-Blanc ⌂
A small fishing port and seaside resort. Under the dunes of the main beach are traces of memorial stones (now covered) which suggest the existence, at one time, of a necropolis.

▷ *Go to the great esplanade by the sea, turn left before a group of houses built on the rocks (car park). At the left corner, take an uphill path and a stairway (35 steps).*

The 16C **Chapelle Notre-Dame-de-Port-Blanc** (🕐 *Open July and Aug, daily, 10.30am-12.30pm and 3-6pm.*) has a roof that comes down to the ground. Every year, the small **Île St-Gildas** hosts the *pardon aux chevaux*, also known as *pardon de St-Gildas*.

▷ *Return to Tréguier by Penvénan.*

② Presqu'île Sauvage

Round tour of 49km/30mi – 3hr

▷ *Leave Tréguier towards Paimpol.*

Lézardrieux
The town is built on the west bank of the Trieux, which is spanned by a suspension bridge. The 18C church has an elegant gabled belfry flanked by two turrets and topped by a pinnacle pierced with arcades containing the bells. This particular type of belfry is to be found throughout the peninsula.

▷ *Make for the Talbert Spit (Sillon de Talbert), skirting the large marina on the Trieux. After 3km/2mi bear right onto a downhill road.*

Ancien moulin de marée
The ruined mill was driven by water from a small reservoir upstream. From the dike, there is a good view over the mouth of the Trieux.

▷ *Return to Talbert Spit and turn right.*

Phare du Bodic
This small lighthouse commands the mouth of the Trieux.
🚶 A path on the left leads through fields to a look-out point from which the **view**★ extends over the Trieux estuary and the Île à Bois in the foreground and the Île de Bréhat in the distance.

▷ *The road then passes near Pommelin Bay, crosses Lanmodez and Larmor-Pleubian. This stretch of coast (Port-Blanc – Paimpol) can also be explored on foot along the long-distance footpath GR 34.*

Sillon de Talbert

This long (3km/2mi), narrow tongue of land, surrounded by reefs, consists of sand and shingle washed by the currents of the Trieux and the Jaudy; it is possible to go round on foot. Seaweed is collected (the annual local production is estimated at 8 to 10 000t of algae) and dried on the spot and then sent to a factory nearby for processing. The Sillon de Talbert is now a national preserved site, placed under the protection of the Conservatoire du Littoral.

▶ *Return to Larmor-Pleubian and bear right towards Pors-Rand Beach.*

Créac'h Maout viewing table

From the viewing table in front of the war memorial and the signal station, there is a wide **panorama**★ over Pointe de l'Arcouest, Île de Bréhat, Sillon de Talbert, Heaux Lighthouse (built in 1836-9, 56m/184ft high, average range 35km/22mi), Pointe du Château and the Jaudy estuary.

▶ *Go through St-Antoine to the entrance of Pleubian and bear right.*

Pleubian

On the north side of the church with its characteristic belfry, is a fine 16C round **pulpit**★ surmounted by a cross and decorated with a frieze depicting the Last Supper and scenes from the Passion: Judas's Kiss, the Flagellation, Christ bearing the Cross.

▶ *At Pleubian, take the direction of Kerbors by the coast road.*

The road passes near the covered alleyway at Men-ar-Rompet, partly hidden in the greenery, and by the Île à la Poule.

▶ *At Kerbors, turn right before the church.*

Bellevue

It is located on the bank of the Jaudy. On the right the view extends over the Jaudy estuary, on the left over the valley and site of Tréguier dominated by the cathedral towers; opposite, La Roche-Jaune rises in terraces. There are trout and salmon farms along the Jaudy, which is tidal, as fish farming develops in the region.

▶ *The road winds through fields growing early vegetables and descends towards the Jaudy Valley and Tréguier.*

LA TRINITÉ-SUR-MER ⚓

POPULATION 1 530
MICHELIN LOCAL MAP 308 M9 – MORBIHAN (56)

The village, built on a height, now extends down the slope to the harbour and beaches on the River Crach estuary, which is lined with oyster-beds. A small fishing port, a busy pleasure boat harbour and shipyards add to the activity of this resort which has fine beaches along the Presqu'île de Kerbihan.

The marina

This can accommodate 1 200 yachts. La Trinité is a popular meeting place for sailing buffs, whether they prefer sleek competition models or lovingly restored old schooners. There are regattas and races held here all year long, including the *Spi Ouest-France*, where the competition is open to both amateurs and champions.

Address Book

TOURIST OFFICE

La Trinité-Sur-Mer, 30 cours des Quais, ☎ 02 97 55 72 21, www.ot-trinite-sur-mer.fr.

WHERE TO STAY

🛏🍽 **Hôtel-restaurant L'Ostréa**, *34 cours des Quais*, ☎ *02 97 55 73 23, www.hotel-ostrea.com – 12rm* 🍽 Bright and cheerful rooms; most open onto the port and the spacious terraces where you can take breakfast (€ 8) or meals that might include grilled fish or other seafood.

🛏🛏🛏 **Les Chambres marines**, *3 rue du Men-Dû, above the Yacht-club and the port, toward Carnac-Plage by the coastal road*, ☎ *02 97 30 17 00, www.charme-gastronomie.com – 6rm.* These lovely, sea-motif rooms are part hotel room and part guest room, offering both the comfort and services of a hotel and the convivial reception of a friend's home. The owners are also in charge of the adjoining restaurant, L'Azimut. Breakfast € 12.

🛏🛏🛏 **Petit hôtel des Hortensias**, *Place de la Mairie*, ☎ *02 97 30 10 30, leshortensias@aol.com – 6rm* 🍽 A small establishment with very beautiful and bright rooms, located just a few metres from the yachts and the old riggings. For the hotel and for the excellent restaurant, l'Arrosoir, reservations are advised. Breakfast € 10.50.

EATING OUT

🍽🍽 **Le Bistrot du marin**, *34 cours des Quais*, ☎ *02 97 55 73 23.* At the entrance of the Trinité when traveling from the East, in front of the big sailboats, le Bistrot offers big dishes full of good things at reasonable rates.

🍽🍽 **Le Quai**, *8 cours des Quais*, ☎ *02 97 55 80 26.* 🕐 *Open summer, noon-midnight*. On the slate: a litany of copious meals, almost gigantic, well prepared and nicely served. The big meal, for instance, offers a beautiful association of seafood, Parma ham and salads. Le Quai is the place to find sailors, skippers and satisfied eaters. It's often hard to find a seat even in the off season.

RECREATION

Rent a bike – *20 cours des Quais*, ☎ *02 97 55 73 15.*

Beaches – From the Pointe de Kerbihan, to the South of the port, the coastal path leads to the beach of **Kervillen**, the biggest in town (lifeguards present only in summer).

Yachting – La **SNT** (Société nautique de La Trinité), ☎ *02 97 55 73 48, www.snt-voile.org* A yachting club, a windsurfing school and sea kayak centre all at once.

SHOPPING

Gallery – Boutique Philip Plisson, *cours des Quais*, ☎ *02 97 30 15 15.* The gallery-shop of one of the most famous photographers of the sea. Books, posters, framed pictures, etc.

Chemin des douaniers

This path leads from the marina to Pointe de Kerbihan, past numerous oyster beds along the estuary, then round to Kerbihan and Kervillen beaches. Beyond the latter, Île de Stuhan, a nature reserve, comes into sight.

Pont de Kerisper

From this great bridge over the River Crach, there is a good **view**★ of the estuary, the town and the port installations.

LE VAL-ANDRÉ ☼☼

POPULATION 3 695
MICHELIN LOCAL MAP 309 G3 – CÔTES D'ARMOR (22)

The resort, known officially as Pléneuf Val-André, has one of the finest sandy beaches on the north coast of Brittany.

🔆 **Also See:** Côte d'ÉMERAUDE

Pointe de Pléneuf★

Allow 15min on foot there and back.
🔆 *A path running at the foot of the cliff starts from the car park at the port of Piégu.*
It leads to a small viewpoint (bench) facing the **Île du Verdelet**, a bird sanctuary. Certain spring tides permit access on foot (🔆 *apply for information at the Poste des Sauveteurs on the pier or at the tourist office*).

▶ *Leave from the port of Piégu and go up the steps which end in Rue de la Corniche.*

By skirting Pointe de Pléneuf it is possible to reach Plage des Vallées *(allow 30min on foot)* and further on to de la Ville Berneuf *(45min on foot)*.
This very pretty walk, on a cliff path overlooking the sea, affords superb **views**★★ of St-Brieuc Bay and the beach and resort of Le Val-André.

S. Sauvignier/MICHELIN

The beach at Val St-André

Address Book

WHERE TO STAY

⊜⊜ **Grand Hôtel du Val André** – *Rue Amiral-Charner, 22370 Le Val-André* – ☎ *02 96 72 20 56 – closed 15 Nov-12 Mar* ☐ *– 39 rooms* A seaside hotel from the turn of the century. The modern rooms look out onto the beach with far-reaching sea views, as does its vast panoramic restaurant. Ideal for vacations, with competitive prices.

EATING OUT

⊜ **Au Biniou** – *121 rue Clémenceau, 22370 Le Val-André* – ☎ *02 96 72 24 35* – 🕐 *closed 2-31 Jan, Tues evening and Wed except in summer.* In a small house in the centre of town, this restaurant serves tasty food in its small dining rooms and specialises in seafood.

RECREATION

Casino de la Rotonde – *Promenade de la Digue –* ☎ *02 96 72 85 06.* 🕐 *Open every day from 5pm on.*

Sailing sports – Le Val-André has been a sailing centre since 1987 and is magnificently equipped. It is open all year for sailboarding and renting a catamaran, but you can also enjoy sand-sailing at Saint-Pabu Beach (☎ *02 96 72 95 28).*

Golf du Val – *Plage des Vallées –* ☎ *02 96 63 01 12.* A splendid 18-hole course with a sea view.

Schooner sailing - *La Pauline – Office du tourisme de Pléneuf-Val-André –* ☎ *96 72 20 55.* This beautiful black-and-red skiff will take you along the Côte d'Émeraude.

Festivals – There are many festive events throughout the summer: from the festival of torches to the café waiters' race, from yacht races to concerts. Information available from the tourist office. You are sure to find the festival for you!

Promenade de la Guette★

Allow 1hr on foot there and back.

🔼 *At the southwest end of the quay at the juncture with rue des Sablons, two arrows point the way to the Guette pathway (Chemin de la Guette), the Corps de Garde and the Batterie.*

Go round the stairs (Anse du Pissot), which go down to the beach, and along the Corps de Garde, which has recently been restored. Soon after, there is an extensive **view**★ of St-Brieuc Bay. From the statue of Our Lady of the Watch go down to **Dahouët**, a fishing port and pleasure boat harbour.

In 1509, seamen drom Dahouët were the first to fish off the coast of Newfoundland discovered just 12 years previously by the Venetian explorer John Cabot.

▶ *Follow Quai des Terre-Neuvas and take the Mocquelet Path to Val-André Quay.*

VANNES★★

POPULATION 51 759
MICHELIN LOCAL MAP 308 O9 – MORBIHAN (56)

Vannes, built in the shape of an amphitheatre at the head of the Golfe du Morbihan, is a pleasant city, very popular in season. It is also a good departure point for boat trips across the Golfe du Morbihan. The picturesque old town, enclosed in its ramparts and grouped around the cathedral, is a pedestrian zone where elegant shops have established themselves in old half-timbered town houses.
🛈 *1, rue Thiers, 56000 – ☎ 02 97 47 24 34.*

▶ **Orient Yourself:** Préfecture of the Morbihan.
🕸 **Don't Miss:** La Cohue Museum.
🕔 **Organizing Your Time:** A lively town with plenty shops and restaurants, and a good departure point for touring the region.
Kids **Especially for Kids:** A boat trip on the Gulf.
🕭 **Also See:** Golfe du MORBIHAN.

A Bit of History

During the period of the Veneti, the original settlement was called Darioritum and seems to have prospered well, at least until the Barbarian invasions of the 3C and 4C. In the 4C, Waroc'h, leading the Bretons from the other side of the Channel, took possession of the town.

Nominoé, founder of Breton unity (9C) – Nominoé, a Breton of modest origin, was discovered by Charlemagne, who made him Count of Vannes. Becoming Duke of Brittany (826) under Louis the Pious, he had decided to unite all the Bretons in an independent kingdom. When Louis died, he went into action. In 10 years unity was achieved: the duchy reached the boundaries which were to be those of the Province until January 1790. From the first, Vannes was the capital of the new Breton kingdom, which reverted later to the status of a duchy.

Wash-houses in Vannes

J. Malburet/MICHELIN

Address Book

TOURIST OFFICE

Vannes, 1 rue Thiers, ☎ 02 97 47 24 34, www.tourisme-vannes.com Open July-Aug: daily 9am-7pm; rest of year: Mon-Sat 9.30am-12.30pm, 2-6pm.

WHERE TO STAY

VANNES

⊖⊖ **Relais du Golfe**, 10 Place du Gén.-de-Gaulle, ☎ 02 97 47 14 74 – 14rm. Old-fashioned but well kept hotel. Family atmosphere. Breakfast € 6.80.

⊖ **Le Marina**, 4 Place Gambetta, ☎ 02 97 47 00 10, lemarinahotel@aol. com – 14rm. Within range of both the port and the Old Town, the hotel has rooms that overlook the port or the ramparts. Breakfast € 5.90.

⊖ **Anne de Bretagne**, 42 rue Olivier de Crisson, ☎ 02 97 54 22 19, www.anne-bretagne.com – 20rm. Renovated and very well kept, this hotel has comfortable rooms and high quality bedding, with the added advantage of being near the train station. Breakfast € 6.

⊖⊖ **Hôtel de France**, 57 av. Victor Hugo, ☎ 02 97 47 27 57, www.hotel-france-vannes.com – 30rm. ◷ Closed 19 Dec-8 Jan. A small but pleasant terrace and comfortable rooms are just part of the cordial greeting visitors receive at this attractively renovated establishment. Breakfast € 7.

⊖⊖ **Kyriad-Image Ste-Anne**, 8 Place de la Libération, ☎ 02 97 63 27 36, www.kyriad-vannes.com – 33rm ✕ Restaurant ◷ closed Sep to Easter: Sat; Nov to Easter: Sun evening; Fri evening. Although the site on which the hotel sits is oriented toward a car park, the contemporary and comfortable rooms are well insulated from the noise. The dining room is decorated in traditional Breton style.

⊖⊖⊖⊖ **Villa Kerasy**, 20 av. Favrel et Lincy, ☎ 02 97 68 36 83, www.villakerasy. com – 12rm. ◷ Closed 3-24 Jan and 13 Nov-11 Dec. With a décor inspired by its namesake, "Asia House," this beautiful hotel brings to mind Breton boats trips towards the comptoirs de la Compagnie des Indes. Will you stay the night in the Cap, in Canton, or in Cadix? Breakfast € 12.

EATING OUT

VANNES

⊖ **Sandwicherie des Halles**, 1 rue du Marché Couvert, ☎ 02 97 68 32 67. Closed Sun. Good quality hot or cold sandwiches come well presented.

⊖ **La Galette Vannetaise**, 22 rue de la Fontaine, ☎ 02 97 47 57 52. Closed for lunch Sun-Mon. A warm and rustic setting in which to savour flat cakes (with Saint-Jacques port-wine sauce), crepes (with caramel, salted butter or cocoa butter with orange) or a salad.

⊖ **Rive gauche**, 5 Place Gambetta, ☎ 02 97 47 02 40. ◷ Closed for lunch Sat-Mon. A pleasant wine-pub (good choice of Bordeaux) that specialises in seafood. Located at the corner of the yachting harbour.

⊖ **Le Carré Blanc**, 28 rue du Port, ☎ 02 97 47 48 34. ◷ Closed 16-22 Jan, 1-7 Aug, lunch Sat and Mon and Sun. Regional specials served daily in the contemporary and spotless interior of this half-timbered house.

⊖ **La Table alsacienne**, 21-23 rue Ferdinand Le Dressay, ☎ 02 97 01 34 53. ◷ Closed Aug, 17-28 Apr; Sun (except lunch Oct-Mar) and Mon. Not sure about coming to Morbihan to eat Alsatian food? Rest assured: the windows of the dining room look out over the yachting harbour, the service is efficient and, the cuisine succeeds in mixing stork and sardine: pork cheeks with seashells, flammenküche with scampi… Unexpected and delicious!

⊖ **La Maison de la Galette**, 21 rue Fontaine, ☎ 02 97 54 19 64. ◷ Closed Sun-Mon. The rib steaks, salads, omelettes, brochettes and huge variety of crepes make this eatery worth a visit.

⊖⊖ **La Table des Gourmets**, 6 rue A. Le Pontois, ☎ 02 97 47 52 44. ◷ Closed 4-14 Jan; 21 June-1 Jul; 22 Nov-2 Dec; Sun evening (off season); Sat lunch and Mon. The elegant setting in this restaurant located on a pedestrianized street in front of the ramparts, pairs well with the excellent daily cuisine, distinguished by regional notes.

⊖⊖ **Roscanvec**, 17 rue des Halles, ☎ 02 97 47 15 96. ◷ Closed Oct-Jun: Sun evening and Mon; end of Dec. Reservations advised. In a half-timbered house of the Old Town, the wonderful cuisine here is sincere and honest, with a menu that links lobster with Espelette pepper and oysters with jelly of pork feet… and caviar!

⌐🍴🍴🍴 **Régis Mahé**, *Place de la Gare*, ☎ 02 97 42 61 41. 🕐 *Closed Sun-Mon; Feb hols; 26 Jun-5 Jul; 13-29 Nov.* This well known eatery prepares meats and seafood with a lot of personality, including favorites such as a roasted back of bass, accompanied by risotto with saffron and chorizo.

RECREATION

Guided visits – Animation du Patrimoine, *Hôtel de Roscanvec, 19 rue des Halles,* ☎ 02 97 01 64 00, www.mairie-vannes.fr/animationdupatrimoine Part of the plan to protect the heritage of

the Old Town, there are as many different themed tours as there are guides and lecturers. Make appointments at the museum of the Beaux-Arts (except Oct-Jun: Sat 3pm; school holidays - ask for information) €3.30/4.80.

FESTIVALS

Fêtes d'Arvor, ☎ 02 97 01 62 40, www.fetes-arvor.org, mid-Aug. Three days of Breton celebrations, animated by the Celtic groups and other bagadou including: concerts, fest-noz, shows, processions of traditional costumes and the election of a festival queen.

Musicales du Golfe du Morbihan, beginning of Aug. Twelve days of classical music.

Jazz à Vannes, ☎ 02 97 01 62 44, jazzavannes@mairie-vannes.fr, end of July. THE area jazz festival.

The union with France (16C) – Anne of Brittany, who married successively Charles VIII and Louis XII, remained the sovereign of her duchy.

When she died in 1514 at the age of 37 without leaving a male heir, Claude of France, one of her daughters, inherited Brittany. A few months later Claude married the heir to the throne of France, François of Angoulême, and after a few months, on 1 January 1515, became Queen of France. The King easily persuaded her to yield her duchy to their son, the Dauphin. Thus Brittany and France would be reunited in the person of the future king.

The last step was taken in August 1532. The States (councils), meeting at Vannes, proclaimed "the perpetual union of the Country and Duchy of Brittany with the Kingdom and Crown of France". The rights and privileges of the duchy were maintained: taxes had to be approved by the States; the Breton Parliament kept its judicial sovereignty and the province could maintain an army.

🐾 The Old Town★★

▶ *Start from place Gambetta.*

This semicircular square, built in the 19C, frames **Porte Saint-Vincent** (St Vincent Gateway), which leads into the old town along a road of this name, lined with beautiful 17C mansions. At the entrance to the road, the most remarkable of these, the Hôtel Dondel, was the headquarters of Général Hoche in 1795.

Place des Lices

This square used to be the tilt-yard, where tilts and tournaments were held in 1532, the year France and Brittany

"Vannes with his wife"

H. Dewynter/MICHELIN

were united under one crown. At one end of the square, set in the niche of a turreted house, is a statue of St Vincent-Ferrier. The saint preached here in 1418.

Maison de Vannes
An old dwelling adorned with two carved wood busts of jovial peasants known as "Vannes and his wife".

Maison de Saint Vincent-Ferrier
No 17 place Valencia.
In this house, remodelled in the 16C, Vincent Ferrier died in 1419. A fine example of a timber framed house with a ground floor in stone.

Place Henri-IV★
Walk along rue des Halles then rue St-Salomon with its old town houses to this picturesque square is lined with 16C gabled houses. Glimpse down rue des Chanoines.

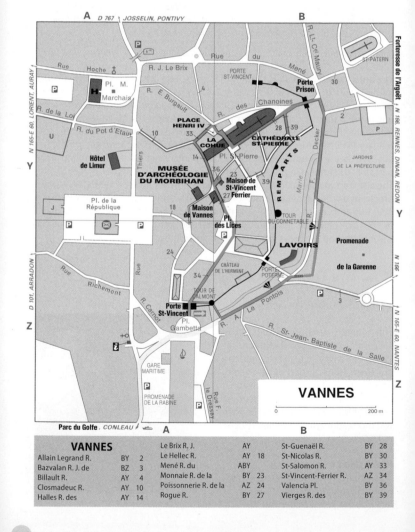

VANNES					
Allain Legrand R.	BY 2	Le Brix R. J.	AY	St-Guenaël R.	BY 28
Bazvalan R. J. de	BZ 3	Le Hellec R.	AY 18	St-Nicolas R.	BY 30
Billault R.	AY 4	Mené R. du	ABY	St-Salomon R.	AY 33
Closmadeuc R.	AY 10	Monnaie R. de la	BY 23	St-Vincent-Ferrier R.	AZ 34
Halles R. des	AY 14	Poissonnerie R. de la	AZ 24	Valencia Pl.	BY 36
		Rogue R.	BY 27	Vierges R. des	BY 39

La Cohue★

This term (literally, a bustling crowd) is commonly used in Brittany to designate the market place, the area where traders and the courts of law were found. In the 13C, the market was held in the lower part of the building; the upper floor was reserved for legal affairs. Beginning in 1675, the exiled Parliament of Brittany held its meetings there. Under the French Revolution, the building became a theatre, and functioned as such until the 1950s.

La Cohue Musée des Beaux-Arts

🕙 *Open mid-June to Sept, daily, 10am-6pm; rest of the year, daily (except Tues), 10am-noon and 2-6pm.* 🕙 *Closed public holidays off season.* €4 ☎ 02 97 01 63 00.

Now the beautifully restored building is a musuem, and offers visitors a permanent collection of19C and contemporay paintings as well as religious sculpture.

On the first floor, the courtroom (1550), with its fine oak timber ceiling, was the seat of the Presidial court of justice. It has now become a museum, which houses, for the most part, 19C-20C works of art by local painters (Jules Noël, Henri Moret, Flavien Peslin, Félix Bouchor), who were inspired by Brittany and its folklore.

Cathédrale St-Pierre★

Men worked on this cathedral from the 13C to the 19C. The only trace of the 13C construction is the north tower of the façade (on place St-Pierre), which is surmounted by a modern steeple. In the garden next to the north side of the cathedral are the remains of some 16C cloisters. The rotunda chapel, which juts out, was built in 1537 in the Italian Renaissance style, rarely found in Brittany.

Enter the church by the fine transept door (Flamboyant Gothic, with Renaissance niches). In the entrance, on the left, a painting describes the death of **St Vincent Ferrier,** with the Duchess of Brittany present. This Spanish monk, who was a great preacher, died at Vannes in 1419 and was canonised in 1455. On the right is St Vincent preaching at Granada. In the second chapel of the north aisle, a rotunda chapel, is the tomb of the saint.

In the apsidal chapel or Chapel of the Holy Sacrament and nave chapels, you will see altars, altarpieces, tombs and statues of the 17C and 18C. In the Baptismal Chapel there is an altar frontal (16C) in stone depicting the Last Supper. The 15C nave has lost some of its original character as the heavy 18C vaulting has reduced its height and masked the panelled woodwork.

Rue St-Guenhaël, lined with old hosues, leads to the 15C **Porte Prison** (Prison Gate), flanked by a machicolated tower. Just before, on the right, rue des Vierges and a little passage lead to a section of the ramparts which gives a pretty view of the gardens.

Ramparts★

After crossing From the Promenade de la Garenne you will get a **view**★★ of the most picturesque corner of Vannes, with the stream (the Marle) that flows at the foot of the ramparts (built in the 13C on top of Gallo-Roman ruins and remodelled repeatedly until the 17C), the formal gardens and the cathedral in the background. A small bridge, leading to Porte Poterne, overlooks some old **wash-houses**★ with very unusual roofing.

▸ *Return to Porte St-Vincent via rue A.-Le-Pontois and the Calmont Tower bridge.*

🐾 Around the Old Town

Promenade de la Garenne

The park of the former ducal castle of Vannes was arranged as a public promenade in the 17C. The view of the ramparts, especially of the Constable's Tower, is attractive.

In the upper part of the garden, on a wall, to the left of the War Memorial, a marble tablet recalls the shooting of the Royalists in 1795.

Hôtel de Limur
A late-17C town house with a fine stone staircase.

Hôtel de Ville
This building in the Renaissance style, erected at the end of the 19C, stands in place Maurice-Marchais, which is adorned with the equestrian **statue** of the Constable de Richemont, one of the great figures of the 15C, for it was he who created and commanded the French army which defeated the English at the end of the Hundred Years War. He became Duke of Brittany, succeeding his brother in 1457, but died the following year.

Musée archéologique de Morbihan
🕐 *Open April to 31 Oct, daily (except Sun), 9.30am-noon and 2-6pm (July and Aug, 9.30am-6pm); rest of the year, daily (except Sun), 2-6pm.* 🕐 *Closed public holidays.* ⊛*€ 3.50 (children under 12 no charge).* ☏ *02 97 42 59 80.*

This museum occupies three floors of Château Gaillard (15C), which once contained the House of Parliament (Parlement de Bretagne).

The museum is rich in prehistoric specimens, most of which come from the first megalithic excavations made in the Morbihan region: Carnac, Locmariaquer and the Presqu'île de Rhuys. Exhibited are a remarkable collection of **necklaces**, bracelets, **polished axes**, swords etc; another gallery contains a variety of objets d'art (13C-18C).

On the second floor, there is an unusual display case of 17C paintings, on the theme of "Fathers of the Desert".

Additional Sight

Parc du Golfe

🔢 This park is located by the exit to the marina, and is the departure point for boat trips.

Aquarium du Golfe★
🕐 ♿ *Open June to Aug, daily, 9am-7pm; rest of the year, 9am-12.30pm and 1.30-6pm.* 🕐 *Closed mornings of 1 Jan and 25 Dec.* ⊛*€ 8.50 (children 4-11, € 5.50).* ☏ *02 97 40 67 40. www.aquarium-du-golfe.com.*

More than 50 pools, in which the relevant natural environment has been reconstructed, house about 1 000 fish from all over the world (cold seas, warm seas, freshwater), which make up an incredible kaleidoscope of colour. In one 35 000l/7 700gal tank, a coral reef has been recreated and is home to numerous species of fish which habitually frequent this environment. A huge aquarium contains several varieties of shark and an exceptional sight: a huge 3m/10ft long sawfish!

Capitaine d'un jour
🕐 ♿ *9am-6.30pm.* *Guided tours (1hr 30min) available.* 🕐 *Closed Jan and 25 Dec.* ⊛*€ 6 (children € 4.50).* ☏ *02 97 40 40 39.*

🔢 A museum-cruise that is fun and educational. See the Morbihan Gulf from another perspective. History, oyster beds, fishing, shipbuilding, coastal navigation are part of the tour. There are many activities and games to interest children.

Le Jardin aux Papillons
Open June to Aug, daily, 10am-7pm; Apr, May and Sept, 10am-12.30pm and 2-6pm. €7 (children €5). ☎ 02 97 46 01 02.
Visitors are free to stroll around at will among the many varieties of vibrantly coloured butterfly that are housed in this environment of tropical trees and floral shrubs. Glass hatching cases illustrate the various stages of development of the chrysalis.

Excursions

Presqu'île de Conleau★
5km/3mi – plus 30min on foot there and back. Leave Vannes by Promenade de la Rabine. After 2km/1mi a good view of the Golfe du Morbihan unfolds before you. Cross the estuary of the Vincin on a causeway to reach Presqu'île de Conleau.

Conleau
A small port well placed at the mouth of the Vincin; landing-stage for boat trip to the Île d'Arz. From the beach there is a good view over the Île de Boëdic between Pointe de Langle, on the left, and Pointe de Kerguen on the right.

Presqu'île de Séné
10km/6mi south – about 45min. Leave Vannes by rue Ferdinand-le-Dressay which skirts the harbour's left shore, then bear left towards Séné.

Séné
Formerly known for its typical fishing boats, the **sinagots**, the village maintains its maritime tradition.

▶ *On leaving Séné, bear right towards Bellevue and Port-Anna.*

The old salt-marshes (almost 220ha/544 acres) have recently become a haven of peace for thousands of migratory or nesting birds of the region. The **Reserve naturelle de la Falguérec-en-Séné** (*July and Aug: 10am-1pm and 2-7pm; Feb-March and May-June: Sun and holidays only. Closed Sep-Jan. €4 (children under 12 no charge). ☎ 02 97 66 92 76. www.reservedesene.com*) is marked with nature trails for walkers and the seven observation posts are open to the public. Bring your binoculars to observe birds such as the black-winged stilt, the elegant avocet or the redshank. The **Information Centre** (follow signposts to the "réserve naturelle") houses exhibitions and a shop.

Port-Anna
This little port, frequented by fishing boats and pleasure craft, commands the narrow channel though which boats sail heading for Vannes.

▶ *Return to Bellevue and bear right towards the wharf.*

Wharf (Embarcadère)
It is used for goods dispatched to the Île d'Arz. From the car park, the **view**★ extends over the River Vannes with Presqu'île de Conleau to the left and Séné, at the end of a creek, to the right.

Château du Plessis-Josso
15km/9mi east. Leave Vannes on N 165 towards Nantes. 3km/2mi after Theix, turn left on D 183 towards Sulniac. Guided tours (30 min) July to early Sept, daily, 2-7pm. Call ahead to confirm. €5. ☎ 02 97 43 16 16.

This charming castle, set in a verdant spot near a lake, is made up of three distinct parts added at three different periods: a 14C fortified manor house, a 15C main building with a polygonal staircase tower and a Louis XIII-style pavilion.

The visit inside enables you to follow the evolution of the castle's construction. It is easy to imagine how life was in the past, as you walk through the different rooms: the low reception room, the state rooms and the kitchen (fireplace with counterweight roasting spit, a granite stove with holes used for heating platters).

Temporary exhibits are held in the outbuildings.

Grand-Champ

19km/12mi north. Leave Vannes on rue Hoche and take D 779. In the nave of the **church** there are two carved wooden panels which come from Notre-Dame-de-Burgo, a ruined chapel in a pretty woodland setting, 2km/1mi east of the town.

Round Tour of les Landes de Lanvaux

55km/34mi – 3hr

▷ *Leave Vannes by rue du Maréchal-Leclerc and take N 166. After 14km/9mi turn left to the castle.*

Forteresse de Largoët★

🕐 *Open June to Sept and school holidays, daily, 10.30am-6.30pm ; mid-March to May and Oct, Sat-Sun and holidays, 2-6.30pm.* ∞€ 4 *(children under 10 no charge)* ☎ *02 97 53 35 96.*

These imposing feudal ruins, also known as **Tours d'Elven** (Elven Towers), stand in the middle of a park. The road (Vannes to Ploërmel road) to the towers branches off left between two pillars.

The Forteresse de Largoët belonged to Marshal de Rieux, who was first a councillor of Duke François II and then tutor to his daughter, Anne of Brittany. When the troops of the king of France, Charles VIII, invaded Brittany in 1488, all the Marshal's strongholds, including Largoët, were burnt down or razed to the ground.

Pass through the 15C entrance fort built against the first entrance gate (13C). Of the castle there remains an impressive 14C keep, 44m/144ft high, with walls 6-9m/19-29ft thick. Near the keep is a smaller tower flanked by a lantern tower.

Largoët Fortress

J. Malburet/MICHELIN

> *After Elven turn left.*

Landes de Lanvaux

Contrary to what the name landes – moors – implies, this long crest of flaking rock land, which was not even cultivated last century, is now a fertile region. There remain, however, many megalithic monuments.

The road runs past the imposing Chateau de Trédio, surrounded by a fine landscaped park covering 22ha/54 acres..

> *Across from it turn right and cross the built-up area, then left, above the square.*

The road drops into the rural valley of the Claie and its tributary, the Callac stream.

Callac

On the left of the road before a crossroads is a man-made grotto, a copy of the one at Lourdes.

To the left of the grotto a path climbs steeply; on either side are Stations of the Cross consisting of groups of figures carved in granite. The path leads to a Calvary from where there is a view on the Landes de Lanvaux. The descent is by another path, which passes near the chapel.

> *Take the left-hand road. When it reaches the Plumelec road, turn left, and 600m/656yd later bear right. After 2km/1mi take the road on the left back to Vannes.*

St-Avé

The **Chapelle Notre-Dame-du-Loc** rises by the old lie of the Vannes road. A Calvary and a fountain stand before the 15C building. Inside, note the carvings on the purlins and tie-beams which depict angels, grotesques and animals; in the centre of the nave stands a Calvary with figures, surmounted by a wooden canopy.

> *Return to Vannes along D 126.*

VITRÉ★★

POPULATION 14 486

MICHELIN LOCAL MAP 309 O6 – ILLE-ET-VILLAINE (35)

This is the best-preserved "old world" town in Brittany; its fortified castle, its ramparts and its small streets have remained just as they were 400 or 500 years ago and make a picturesque and evocative picture which is long remembered. The old town is built on a spur commanding the deep valley of the Vilaine on one side and a railway cutting on the other. The castle stands proudly on the extreme point. From the 15C to the 17C, Vitré was one of the most prosperous of Breton cities; it made hemp, woollen cloth and cotton stockings which were sold not only in France but in England, Germany, Spain and even America and the Indies. Gathered together to form the powerful brotherhood known as "Marchands d'Outre-Mer", the Vitré tradesmen of this period commissioned the building of the highly distinctive houses with half-timbering, many of which can still be seen today.

- **Don't Miss:** The medieval district
- **Organizing Your Time:** Spend a day and half to visit Vitré, La Guerche-de-Bretagne and the surroundings

Façade of the castle

Castle★★

🕐 *Open July-Sept daily, 10am-6pm; Apr to June, 10am-noon and 2pm-5.30pm; rest of the year, daily (except Sat-Mon mornings and Tues), 10am-noon and 2-5.30pm.* 🕐 *Closed 1 Jan, Easter Sun, 1 November and 25 Dec.* ⊛€ 4 (children 7-15 € 2.50) combined ticket for 4 museums. ☎ 02 99 75 04 54.

The castle, dating from the 11C, was rebuilt from the 13C to the 15C.

The entrance is guarded by a drawbridge and entrance fort (Châtelet) flanked by two big machicolated towers. At the south corner stands the main keep or Tour St-Laurent; at the northeast corner stands the Madeleine Tower, and at the northwest corner, the Montafilant Tower. These various works are linked by a wall, reinforced by other towers. As you enter the courtyard you will see, on the right, a Romanesque porch (**1**) with archstones alternating in colour (red granite and black schist), the town hall (1913) abutting on the north front, and before you, the Oratoire Tower with an elegant Renaissance chapel (**2**).

From the platform of the Montafilant Tower *(82 steps)* there is a fine **view**★ of the town, the Tertres Noires and Moines Quarters, the River Vilaine and the old tannery.

The St-Laurent Tower houses the Musée St-Nicolas containing 15C and 16C sculp-ture, which comes from the houses of Vitré (a beautiful chimney has been remounted), the 15C tomb of Gui X (a local lord) as well as 16C Flemish and 17C Aubusson tapestries.

The Argenterie Tower presents exhibits of the region's natural history.

Via the curtain wall you arrive at the Oratoire Tower. In its chapel is a beautiful 16C **triptych**★ decorated with 32 Limoges enamels.

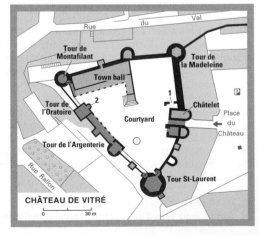

 **The Town★**

▶ *Starting from place du Château, take rue Notre-Dame and turn right.*

Rue de la Baudrairie★★
This, the most curious street in Vitré, gets its name from baudroyeurs meaning leather craftsmen. Each house is worth looking at.

Rue d'En Bas
This street used to lead to the gate (partly destroyed in 1846) of the same name. It is lined with half-timbered houses; note no 10, the former **Hôtel du Bol d'Or** (1513).

▶ *At the end of the street, turn left along Promenade St-Yves and continue to place du Général-de-Gaulle then turn left onto rue Garangeot.*

Cross Rue Sévigné: note no 9, a 17C mansion *(restoration work in progress)* known as "Tour de Sévigné", home to the famous writer.

▶ *Turn right.*

Rue Poterie
Picturesque houses: some half-timbered, some with porches. Note in particular the **Maison de l'Île**, on the corner of rue Sévigné.

▶ *From place du Marchix on the left, turn right onto rue Notre-Dame leading to place de la République.*

Ramparts★
From place de la République you will see one of the old rampart towers, the 15C Bridolle Tower (machicolations).
On the south side of the town the walls follow the line, at a little distance, of the present rue de la Borderie and place St-Yves and then join the castle. Only fragments remain, built into private properties. On the north and east sides the ramparts are still intact.
Old houses line rue de Paris, which leads into place de la République.

▶ *Go through the gate in Promenade du Val to circle the ramparts. At the end of the alley, after passing a gate, take the ramp to the left which passes under the St-Pierre postern; follow rue du Bas-Val uphill and turn right in the square, then left into rue Notre-Dame.*

Église Notre-Dame★
The church is 15C-16C. Outside, the most curious part is the south side, with its seven gables decorated with pinnacles and its pulpit from which preachers addressed the congregation assembled on the small square and its two finely-carved doors.
Inside, you will see many altarpieces and a fine Renaissance stained-glass window in the south aisle (third bay) depicting Christ's Entry into Jerusalem.
At no 27 rue Notre-Dame is the former Hôtel Hardy or de la Troussanais (16C) with its finely carved porches and dormer windows.

▶ *Turn round and go to place du Château.*

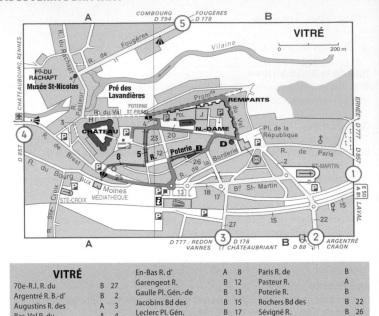

Additional Sights

Tertres Noirs★★

▸ *Access by Rue de Brest and Chemin des Tertres Noirs, to the right after the bridge over the Vilaine.*

There is a fine **view**★★ of Vitré, its site and its castle from this shaded terrace.

Public garden★ (Jardin public)
Via ③ of the town plan. A pleasant, well-kept, English-style garden.

Faubourg du Rachapt
During the Hundred Years War, this suburb was occupied for several years by the English, while the town and the castle resisted all their attacks. The people of Vitré paid the invaders to go away: hence the name of the suburb (*Rachapt* means rachat or repurchase).

This suburb, lying at the foot of the castle, crosses the Vilaine Valley and rises on the north slope. Follow Rue Pasteur, which affords picturesque views of the river and the **Pré des Lavandières**.

▸ *Rue Pasteur leads to the Musée St-Nicolas.*

Musée St-Nicolas
Enter by the little door on the left and skirt the chapel. Same times and charges as for the Castle. ☎ 02 99 75 04 54.

Address Book

TOURIST OFFICES

Pays de Vitré, Place du Gén.-de-Gaulle, near the train station, ☎ 02 99 75 04 46, www.ot-vitre.fr Open Jul-Aug: daily 10am-12.30pm, 2-7pm; off season: Mon 2.30-6pm, Tue-Fri 9.30am-12.30pm, 2.30-6pm, Sat 10am-12.30pm, 3-5pm.
Pays Guerchais, Place Charles-de-Gaulle, La Guerche-de-Bretagne, ☎ 02 99 96 30 78, otsi.laguerche@wanadoo.fr Open Mar-Oct: Mon 2.30-5.30pm, Tue-Sat 9.30-12am, 2.30-5.30pm.

WHERE TO STAY

VITRÉ AND SURROUNDINGS

⊖⊖ **Hôtel du Château**, *5 rue Rallon*, ☎ *02 99 74 58 59, hotelduchateau2@wanadoo.fr – 15rm.* ☾ *Closed 1 Nov.* In the heart of Old Town, this hotel offers cosy rooms; some even with castle-views. Breakfast € 5.50.
⊖ **Le Petit Billot**, *5 Place du Gén. Leclerc*, ☎ *02 99 75 02 10, www.petit-billot.com – 21rm.* ☾ *Closed 25 Dec-1 Jan.* Quiet despite its proximity to the train station, the rooms here are functional and bright. Breakfast € 7.
⊖⊖ **Chambres d'hôte Méhaignerie** , ☎ *02 99 74 42 48 or 06 16 08 46 20 – 2rm* ⚞ The castle at Rochers-Sévigné sits near these comfortable rooms, tucked away in an old house surrounded by a friendly park.
⊖⊖⊟ **Pen'Roc**, *La Peinière, St-Didier*, ☎ *02 99 00 33 02, www.penroc.fr – 29rm* 🗐 ✕ Near a pilgrimage centre, this family-run hotel offers a large range of brightly coloured rooms and a high level of comfort, some rooms equipped with a terrace and bath. The cuisine at the attached restaurant features traditional Breton flavours and a good wine list. Restaurant. Breakfast € 10.80.

LA GUERCHE-DE-B. AND SURROUNDINGS

⊖⊖ **La Calèche**, *16 av. du Gén. Leclerc*, ☎ *02 99 96 21 63, www.lacaleche.com – 12rm* ✕ This immense house offers functional and renovated rooms and a well known restaurant.
⊖⊖ **Le Relais des Fées**, *La Roche-aux-Fées, Essé*, ☎ *02 99 47 73 84, www.roche-aux-fées.com - 4 rm* ✕ Farm-hostelry with modest but comfortable rooms.
⊖⊖ **L'Arthurais**, *Essé, rte de Marcillé-Robert and follow the arrows*, ☎ *02 99 47 06 17 – 4rm* ✕ ⚞ Attractive rooms with rustic furniture, in the guest house of an old manor. When the weather is bad, enjoy a fire at the hearth in the big common room.

EATING OUT

VITRÉ

⊖⊖ **Au Vieux-Vitré**, 1 rue d'En-Bas, ☎ *02 99 75 02 52.* ☾ *Closed Sun, Mon and public hols.* Creperie-pizzeria in a mediaeval house with a terrace and a 15C fireplace.
⊖⊖ **Le Saint-Louis**, *31 rue Notre-Dame*, ☎ *02 99 75 28 28.* ☾ *Closed Sun evening, Mon, Tue and 2 weeks in Sep.* In the shadow of the cathedral, this traditional restaurant decorated with 18C woodworks offers a great choice of regional menus.
⊖⊖ **Le Potager**, *5 Place du Gén. Leclerc*, ☎ *02 99 74 68 88.* ☾ *Closed Mon, Sat lunch, Sun evening and 2 weeks in Aug.* Everything from the vegetables to the decoration of the dining room deserves praise here. Fresh and inventive pub cuisine.
⊖⊖ **La Soupe aux Choux**, *32 rue Notre-Dame*, ☎ *02 99 75 10 86.* ☾ *Closed Sat lunch and Sun off season.* Regional cuisine and a well-chosen wine list mingle harmoniously in three spaces here: on the ground floor, in the mediaeval basement and on the small terrace.
⊖⊖ **La Taverne de l'Écu**, *12 rue de la Beaudrairie*, ☎ *02 99 75 11 09.* ☾ *Closed Tue evening, (off season: Wed; Sun evening), Feb holidays, a week in Aug and 31 Oct-1 Nov.* A combination of Breton and Provençal cuisine merge in this 16C house in the heart of Old town.
⊖⊖⊟ **Le Pichet**, *17 bd de Laval*, ☎ *02 99 75 24 09.* ☾ *Closed Wed and Thur evenings, and Sun.* A pleasant terrace opens onto a garden here during the summer months, and a comfortable room with a fireplace offers warmth for the colder months. Inspired by the market, the menu features produce of the sea most prominently.

LA GUERCHE-DE-B. AND SURROUNDINGS

🍴🍴 **Les Marchands**, *Place Charles-de-Gaulle,* ☎ *02 99 96 45 03.* 🕐 *Closed Tue and Wed evenings, Sun-Mon and 3 weeks in Aug.* Grilled fare and a copious buffet of hors-d'oeuvres dominate this rustic setting with modern paintings.

🍴🍴 **La Calèche,** *16 av. du Gén. Leclerc,* ☎ *02 99 96 21 63.* The regional menu here is the joy of nearby gourmets as they dine on rognonade of farm rabbit with escargot and crème brûlée with apple and chouchen among other delicacies. Pleasant terrace in summer.

🍴🍴 **Le Relais des Fées,** *La Roche-aux-Fées, Essé,* ☎ *02 99 47 73 84.* Reservations required for non-residents Mon-Thu. A plentiful menu made with regional products including fresh bread and roasted meats.

RECREATION

Walks - Guided pedestrian tours around Vitré available from the Tourist Office (€5). A smooth 20km path along the old railway going from Vitré to Moutiers is pleasant by foot or by bike.

Rent a bike - Cycles Dufeu, *6 rue de Paris,* ☎ *02 99 75 01 41.*

FESTIVALS

The concerts and shows of the **Festival du bocage** give life to Vitré and its surroundings from 30 Jun to 15 Jul. Jazz-lovers follow the tempo during **Jazz in Vitré,** the first week of Mar. Les **Estivales guerchaises bring a little animation** to La Guerche-de-Bretagne in Jun-Jul.

SHOPPING

Markets - Vitré, Mon morning Place du Marchix. Small market Sat morning, rue de la Poterie. **La Guerche-de-Bretagne,** Tue morning (fowl and farm products).

Culinary specialities - La Bonbonnière, *18 rue de la Liberté,* ☎ *02 99 75 01 66.* This pastry-tea shop makes Vitréen, a sponge cake with apples and almonds. **Jarno,** 50 rue Poterie ☎ 02 99 75 06 23. Good pastries and bread specialities.

The 15C chapel has retained 15C an 16C murals and now houses a museum of sacred art. The gilt-wood high altar dates from the 18C.

Excursions

Musée de la Faucillonnaie
In Montréal-sous-Pérouse, 5km N. Leave Vltre by ⑤ in the town plan and follow the signs. 👣 *Guided tours (1hr) July to Sept, daily, 10am-6pm; Apr to June, 10am-noon and 2-5.30pm; rest of the year, daily (except Sat-Sun and Mon mornings, and Tues), 10am-noon and 2-5.30pm.* 🕐 *Closed 1 Jan, Easter Sun, 1 Nov and 25 Dec.* 💶*€ 4 (children 7-15, € 2.50) combined tickect for 4 museums.* ☎ *02 99 75 04 54. www.mairie-vitre.com.*
This 15C and 17C manor house (note the attractive wooden staircase) combines the presentation of farmhouse rooms on the ground floor with "masters' quarters" above. Nice collection of chests.

Château des Rochers-Sévigné
6.5km/4mi southeast. Leave Vitré via ② on the town plan. 6km/4mi from the town, on coming out of a wood, take the château drive on the left. 👣 *Guided tours (1hr) July to Sept, daily, 10am-6pm; Apr to June, 10am-noon and 2-5.30pm; rest of the year, daily (except Sat-Sun and Mon mornings, and Tues), 10am-noon and 2-5.30pm.* 🕐 *Closed 1 Jan, Easter Sun, 1 Nov and 25 Dec.* 💶*€ 4 (children 7-15 € 2.50) combined tickect for 4 museums.* ☎ *02 99 75 04 54. www.mairie-vitre.com.*
The Rochers-Sévigné Château, which was the home of the Marquise de Sévigné (1626-96), is a place of literary interest. Admirers of the famous *Letters* will enjoy visiting the castle and park.

The château was built in the 15C and remodelled in the 17C. It consists of two wings set at right angles. Besides the chapel built in 1671 for the "exemplary" abbot of Coulanges, the marquise's maternal uncle, two rooms in the large north tower are open to visitors. That on the ground floor was the Green Room *(Cabinet Vert)*. It still contains some of Mme de Sévigné's personal possessions, family pictures and her portrait; there is a collection of autographs and documents in a glass case. The 16C chimney-piece is adorned with the Marquise's initials (Marie de Rabutin-Chantal – MRC).

Garden and park

In the French-style garden, rearranged following designs by Le Nôtre, is the semi-circular wall that Mme de Sévigné called "that little wall that repeats words right into your ear" because of its double echo (stones mark the places where the two conversationalists should stand). Beyond the garden lies the large, wooded park, which is crossed by avenues, the names of which recall the Marquise and her literary environment: the Mall, the Lone Wolf, Infinity...

Champeaux★

9km/5.5mi west. Leave Vitré via U on the town plan. 2km/1mi from the town turn right.

The **village square**★ composes a harmonious scene with its collegiate church, its small town hall with a large hipped roof, and the few houses, former canons' residences, standing around an old well.

Collégiale

This 14C and 15C collegiate church, with a single nave, has some fine Renaissance canopied **stalls**★ and an elegant door, of the same period, which opens onto the sacristy, the former chapter-house. To the left of the high altar and in a chapel to the left of the chancel are two stone and marble mausolea (1551-4) belonging to the d'Espinay family, who founded the church.

The two handsome Renaissance **stained-glass windows**★, made in Rennes, are noteworthy: depicted in the apse is the Passion of Christ and in the sacristy the sacrifice of Abraham. In the nave, the south chapel contains a 17C altarpiece recounting scenes of the Passion and the north chapel is adorned with a 14C Virgin – both of these works are in polychrome wood.

Parc du Boiscornillé

In fine weather, this park, 5km north of Champeaux by way of Val-d'Izé, is a lovely place to walk. The Bülher brothers, well-known landscape artists of the time, designed it in 1872. Later Edouard André added his touches and the result is a garden with the formal lines of a French garden and the touch of fantasy typical of an English garden. The walled pond, circled with oak trees and crossed by wooden bridges, is especially charming.

INDEX

INDEX

INDEX

ACCOMMODATIONS

INDEX

461

INDEX

Little Red Riding Hood

But Little Red Riding Hood had her regional map with her, and so she did not fall into the trap. She did not take the path through the wood and she did not meet the big bad wolf. Instead, she chose the picturesque touring route straight to Grandmother's house, and arrived safely with her cake and her little pot of butter.

The End

With Michelin maps, go your own way.

MAPS AND PLANS

MAPS

ROAD MAPS FOR THIS REGION

Motorists who plan ahead will always have the appropriate maps at hand. Michelin products are complementary: for each of the sites listed in *The Green Guide*, map references are indicated which help you find your location on our range of maps. The image below shows the maps to use for each geographic area covered in this guide. To travel the roads in this region, you may use any of the following:

♦ the regional map at a scale of 1:200 000 no 512, which covers the main roads and secondary roads, and includes useful indications for finding tourist attractions. This is a good map to choose for travelling in a wide area. At a quick glance, you can locate and identify the main sights to see. In addition to identifying the nature of the road ways, the maps show castles, churches and other religious edifices, scenic view points, megalithic monuments, swimming beaches on lakes and rivers, swimming pools, golf courses, race tracks, air fields, and more. And remember to travel with the latest edition of the map of France no 721, which gives an overall view of the region of Brittany, and the main access roads which connect it to the rest of France. The entire country is mapped at a 1:1 000 000 scale and clearly shows the main road network.

Michelin is pleased to offer a route-planning service on the Internet: www. michelin-travel.com. Choose the shortest route, a route without tolls, or the Michelin recommended route to your destination; you can also access information about hotels and restaurants from *The Michelin Guide*, and tourist sites from *The Green Guide*.

Bon voyage!

Legend

Selected monuments and sights

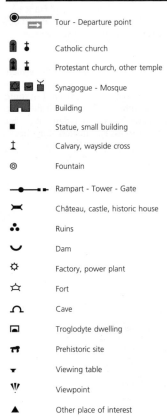

◉ ⟶ Tour - Departure point

🏛 ✝ Catholic church

🏛 ✝ Protestant church, other temple

Synagogue - Mosque

Building

■ Statue, small building

✝ Calvary, wayside cross

◎ Fountain

Rampart - Tower - Gate

Château, castle, historic house

Ruins

Dam

✿ Factory, power plant

☆ Fort

Cave

Troglodyte dwelling

Prehistoric site

Viewing table

Viewpoint

▲ Other place of interest

Sports and recreation

Racecourse

Skating rink

Outdoor, indoor swimming pool

Multiplex Cinema

Marina, sailing centre

Trail refuge hut

Cable cars, gondolas

Funicular, rack railway

Tourist train

Recreation area, park

Theme, amusement park

Wildlife park, zoo

Gardens, park, arboretum

Bird sanctuary, aviary

Walking tour, footpath

Of special interest to children

Abbreviations

A Agricultural office (Chambre d'agriculture)

C Chamber of Commerce (Chambre de commerce)

H Town hall (Hôtel de ville)

J Law courts (Palais de justice)

M Museum (Musée)

P Local authority offices (Préfecture, sous-préfecture)

POL. Police station (Police)

Police station (Gendarmerie)

T Theatre (Théâtre)

U University (Université)

468

	Sight	Seaside resort	Winter sports resort	Spa
Highly recommended ★★★		≜≜≜	✳✳✳	⚑⚑⚑
Recommended ★★		≜≜	✳✳	⚑⚑
Interesting ★		≜	✳	⚑

Additional symbols

i	Tourist information
═══ ══	Motorway or other primary route
❶ **❶**	Junction: complete, limited
▭▭ ══	Pedestrian street
ɪ ═ ═ ═ ═ ɪ	Unsuitable for traffic, street subject to restrictions
▦▦▦ - - - -	Steps – Footpath
🚆 🚇	Train station – Auto-train station
🚐 S.N.C.F.	Coach (bus) station
─┼─┼─	Tram
⊙	Metro, underground
P&R	Park-and-Ride
♿	Access for the disabled
✉	Post office
☎	Telephone
✉	Covered market
·✕·	Barracks
△	Drawbridge
∪	Quarry
✕	Mine
B **F**	Car ferry (river or lake)
🛥	Ferry service: cars and passengers
⛴	Foot passengers only
③	Access route number common to Michelin maps and town plans
Bert (R.)...	Main shopping street
AZ B	Map co-ordinates

Hotels and restaurants

Hotels- price categories:

	Provinces	Large cities
⊖	<40 €	<60 €
⊖⊖	40 to 65 €	60 to 90 €
⊖⊖⊖	65 to 100 €	90 to 130 €
⊖⊖⊖⊖	>100 €	>130 €

Restaurants- price categories:

	Provinces	Large cities
⊖	<14 €	<16 €
⊖⊖	14 to 25 €	16 to 30 €
⊖⊖⊖	25 to 40 €	30 to 50 €
⊖⊖⊖⊖	>40 €	>50 €

20 rooms:	Number of rooms
⊐ *6.85 €*	Price of breakfast; when not given, it is included in the price of the room (i.e., for bed-and-breakfast)
120 sites:	Number of camp sites
rest.	Lodging where meals are served
reserv	Reservation recommended
⊗	No credit cards accepted
P	Reserved parking for hotel patrons
⬎	Swimming Pool
▤	Air conditioning
⊬	Hotel: non-smoking rooms Restaurant: non-smoking section
♿	Rooms accessible to persons of reduced mobility

The prices correspond to the higher rates of the tourist season